The New Edinburgh History of Sco

VOLUME 3

Domination and Lordship

The New Edinburgh History of Scotland

General editor: Roger Mason, *University of St Andrews*

Advisory editors: Dauvit Broun, *University of Glasgow*; Iain Hutchison, *University of Stirling*; Norman Macdougall, *University of St Andrews*; Nicholas Phillipson, *University of Edinburgh*

1. From Caledonia to Pictland to 795
   James Fraser, *University of Edinburgh*

2. From Pictland to Alba 789–1070
   Alex Woolf, *University of St Andrews*

3. Domination and Lordship 1070–1230
   Richard Oram, *University of Stirling*

4. The Wars of Scotland 1214–1371
   Michael Brown, *University of St Andrews*

5. The First Stewart Dynasty 1371–1488
   Steve Boardman, *University of Edinburgh*

6. Scotland Re-formed 1488–1587
   Jane Dawson, *University of Edinburgh*

7. Empire, Union and Reform 1587–1690
   Roger Mason, *University of St Andrews*

8. Nation, State, Province, Empire 1690–1790
   Ned Landsman, *State University of New York, Stony Brook*

9. Industry and Unrest 1790–1880
   Iain Hutchison, *University of Stirling*

10. Impaled Upon a Thistle: Scotland since 1880
    Ewen A. Cameron, *University of Edinburgh*

Domination and Lordship
Scotland 1070–1230

Richard Oram

Edinburgh University Press

© Richard Oram, 2011

Edinburgh University Press Ltd
22 George Square, Edinburgh
www.euppublishing.com

Reprinted with corrections 2011

Typeset in 11/13 Ehrhardt
by Servis Filmsetting Ltd, Stockport, Cheshire, and
printed and bound in Great Britain by
CPI Antony Rowe, Chippenham and Eastbourne

A CIP record for this book is available from the British Library

ISBN 978 0 7486 1496 7 (hardback)
ISBN 978 0 7486 1497 4 (paperback)

The right of Richard Oram to be identified as author of this work has been asserted
in accordance with the Copyright, Designs and Patents Act 1988.

Published with the support of the Edinburgh University Scholarly Publishing
Initiatives Fund.

Publisher's acknowledgement
Edinburgh University Press thanks Mercat Press, publishers of
the *Edinburgh History of Scotland*, for permission to use *The New
Edinburgh History of Scotland* as the title for this ten-volume series.

Contents

Tables, Maps and Figures   vi
Abbreviations   viii
General Editor's Preface   ix
Acknowledgements and Dedication   xi
Tables 1–7   xii

Introduction: Scotland in 1070   1

PART ONE: NARRATIVES

Chapter 1   Out with the Old, In with the New? 1070–93   13
Chapter 2   Kings and Pretenders, 1093–1136   38
Chapter 3   Building the Scoto-Northumbrian Realm, 1136–57   74
Chapter 4   Under Angevin Supremacy, 1157–89   115
Chapter 5   Settling the Succession, 1189–1230   152

PART TWO: PROCESSES

Chapter 6   Power   197
Chapter 7   Reworking Old Patterns: Rural Change, c. 1070–1230   233
Chapter 8   Towns, Burghs and Burgesses   265
Chapter 9   Nobles   295
Chapter 10   The Making of the *Ecclesia Scoticana*   328

Conclusion   362
Table of Events   371
Guide to Further Reading   375
Bibliography   387
Index   411

Tables, Maps and Figures

Table 1	The Scottish royal succession from Malcolm III to Alexander II	xii
Table 2	Marriage connections of the Scottish royal house	xiii
Table 3	The MacWilliams	xiv
Table 4	The Galloway family	xv
Table 5	The kings of Man and the Isles	xvi
Table 6	Somerled and his family	xvii
Table 7	The earls of Orkney and Caithness	xviii
Map I.1	Scotland in 1070	10
Map 3.1	David I's Northumbrian campaigns	96
Map 4.1	Scottish campaigns in Moray, Ross and Caithness	142
Map 5.1	Alexander II and the war of 1215–17	177
Map 6.1	Earldoms and lordships	210
Map 8.1	Royal and non-royal burghs	270
Map 10.1	David I's monastic foundations	353
Map 10.2	Scotland in 1230	361
Figure 1.1	Dunfermline Abbey, Fife	25
Figure 2.1	Roxburgh Castle, Scottish Borders	68
Figure 3.1	David I and Malcolm IV from Malcolm's great charter of 1159 to the monks of Kelso	110
Figure 4.1	Arbroath Abbey, Angus	140
Figure 6.1	The lord of Dalmeny performs homage to the king: sculptured voussoir	223
Figure 7.1	The Carse of Gowrie, Perth and Kinross	250
Figure 9.1	Mote of Urr, Dumfries and Galloway	314
Figure 9.2	Culross Abbey, Fife	320

Figure 9.3	Knight's effigy, Dundrennan Abbey, Dumfries and Galloway	326
Figure 10.1	St Rule's Tower, St Andrews, Fife	338
Figure 10.2	Leuchars Church, Fife	349
Figure 10.3	Kelso Abbey, Scottish Borders	355

Abbreviations

AFM	*Annals of the Four Masters*
ALC	*Ancient Laws and Customs of the Burghs of Scotland*
APS	*Acts of the Parliaments of Scotland*
AU	*Annals of Ulster*
CDI	*Calendar of Documents Relating to Ireland*
CDS	*Calendar of Documents Relating to Scotland*
ESSH	*Early Sources of Scottish History*
PSAS	*Proceedings of the Society of Antiquaries of Scotland*
RCAHMS	*Royal Commission on the Ancient and Historical Monuments of Scotland*
RRAN	*Regesta Regum Anglo-Normannorum*
RRS	*Regesta Regum Scottorum*
TDGNHAS	*Transactions of the Dumfriesshire and Galloway Natural History and Antiquarian Society*

General Editor's Preface

The purpose of the New Edinburgh History of Scotland is to provide up-to-date and accessible narrative accounts of the Scottish past. Its authors will make full use of the explosion of scholarly research that has taken place over the last three decades, and do so in a way that is sensitive to Scotland's regional diversity as well as to the British, European and transoceanic worlds of which Scotland has always been an integral part.

Chronology is fundamental to understanding change over time and Scotland's political development will provide the backbone of the narrative and the focus of analysis and explanation. The New Edinburgh History will tell the story of Scotland as a political entity, but will be sensitive to broader social, cultural and religious change and informed by a richly textured understanding of the totality and diversity of the Scots' historical experience. Yet to talk of the Scots – or the Scottish nation – is often misleading. Local loyalty and regional diversity have more frequently characterised Scotland than any perceived sense of 'national' solidarity. Scottish identity has seldom been focused primarily, let alone exclusively, on the 'nation'. The modern discourse of nationhood offers what is often an inadequate and inappropriate vocabulary in which to couch Scotland's history. The authors in this series will show that there are other and more revealing ways of capturing the distinctiveness of Scottish experience.

In the case of this volume, covering the period when a recognisably modern kingdom of the Scots emerged, it is the language of lordship rather than of nationhood that offers the most appropriate means of conceptualising the processes at work. As Richard Oram shows in this major reassessment of an era when both a Scottish 'state' and Scottishness itself first began to crystallise, it was dynastic consolidation and the exercise of effective lordship that created a powerful monarchy capable of commanding the allegiance of the disparate polities and ethnicities of northern Britain. These are developments inextricably associated with the heirs of the marriage of Malcolm III and his Anglo-Saxon Queen (later Saint) Margaret, but Richard Oram's lucid account of the formation of this medieval kingdom resists simplistic notions of linearity or inevitability. Instead, it reveals the full complexity of the interactions between the royal dynasty's Gaelic and Scandinavian heritage and the Germanic and Frankish influences emanating from post-Conquest England. At the same time, it reassesses the processes by which the kings of Alba were able to extend their authority over rival regional lordships and, as kings of Scots, both claim pre-eminent authority over the northern British mainland and challenge the English monarchy's claim to lordship over Britain as a whole. Documentary sources for this 'long twelfth century' are far from abundant; nonetheless, combined with archaeological and other evidence, they allow Richard Oram to portray in remarkable detail the workings of Scotland's rural society, the impact of new urban communities, and the Europeanisation of both the church and the norms of noble behaviour. The result is a rounded and richly textured study of one of the most formative periods in Scotland's history.

Acknowledgements and Dedication

A great store of debts has been built up in the decade since Roger Mason first asked me to write this volume. First, to Roger himself for giving me that opportunity, bearing with me through the upheavals which delayed its appearance, and then asking me to cut only 35,000 words from the text! Next to the commissioning editors and all the staff at EUP, past and present, who have steered the book to its conclusion. To Alex Woolf, for his insightful reading of drafts chapters and for long discussions on the more esoteric issues of twelfth-century Scottish history during many trips up Scottish mountains, and to Dauvit Broun for his ever-generous sharing of ideas; you will see your fingerprints on many pages! A host of thanks is owed to my colleagues Alasdair Ross and Michael Penman, who read and commented upon the text, but remained unscarred by the process. All of Peter Lynch's helpful advice has been studiously ignored, but he does now know what a davoch is! To my children, Alasdair and Lauren, who have literally grown up with this monster, I dedicate this book to you.

Crieff
St Andrew's Day 2010

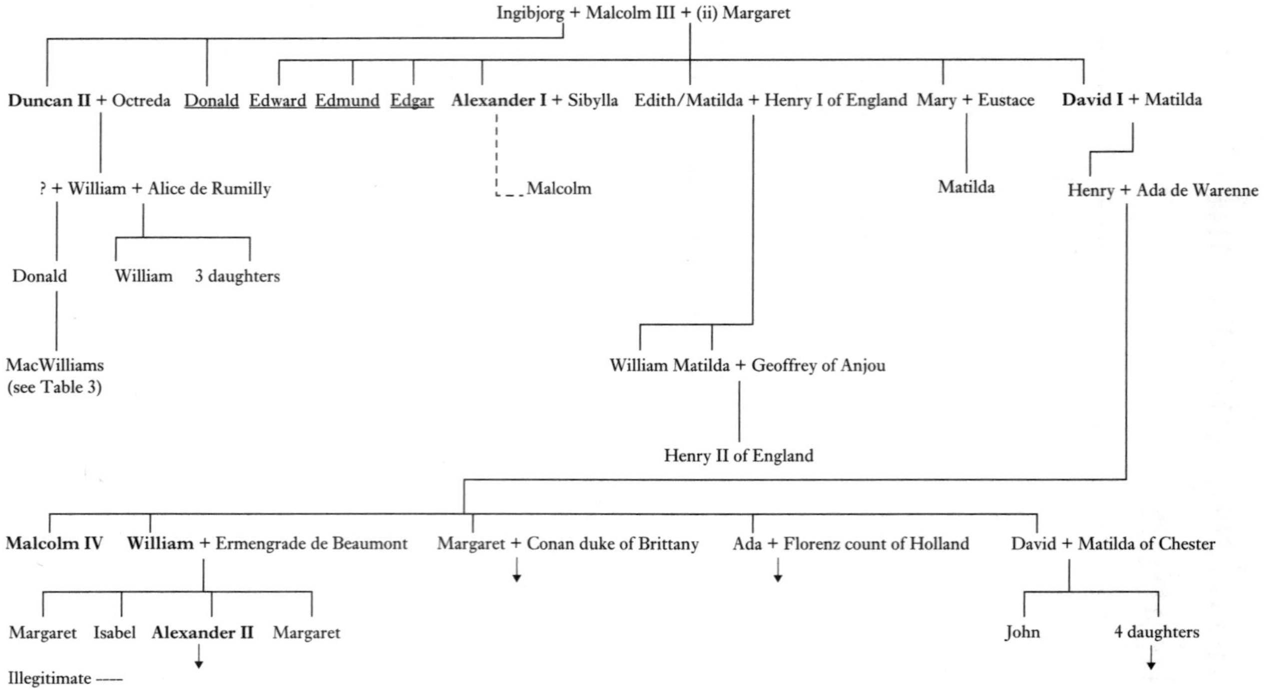

Table 1 The Scottish royal succession from Malcolm III to Alexander II

Table 2 Marriage connections of the Scottish royal house

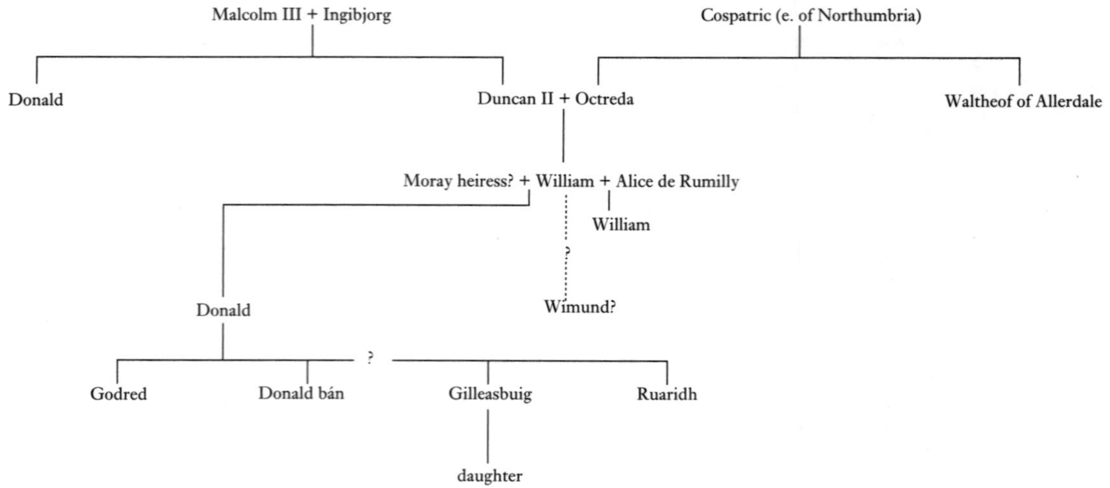

```
                                    Cospatric (e. of Northumbria)
                                    ┌──────────────┴──────────────┐
           Malcolm III + Ingibjorg   Duncan II + Octreda      Waltheof of Allerdale
   ┌────────────┴────────────┐              │
 Donald                Moray heiress? + William + Alice de Rumilly
                              │              │
                           ┌──┴──┐        William
                           │     │
                        Donald  Wimund?
                    ┌──────┼──────┐
                    │      │      │
                 Godred Donald bán ?
                              │
                        ┌─────┴─────┐
                    Gilleasbuig   Ruaridh
                        │
                     daughter
```

Table 3 The MacWilliams

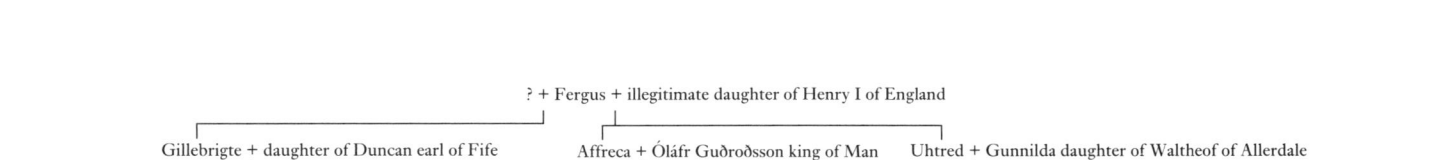

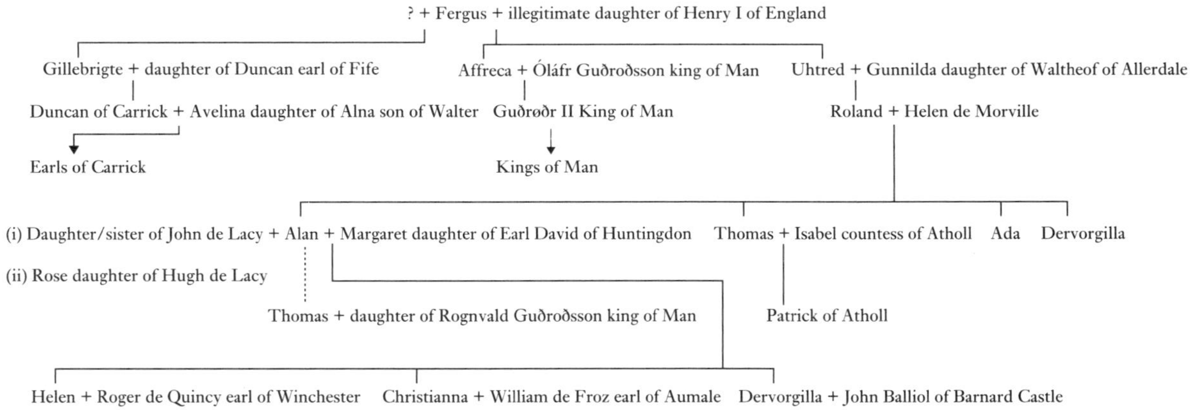

? + Fergus + illegitimate daughter of Henry I of England

Affreca + Óláfr Guðrøðsson king of Man   Uhtred + Gunnilda daughter of Waltheof of Allerdale

Guðrøðr II King of Man   Roland + Helen de Morville

Kings of Man

Gillebrigte + daughter of Duncan earl of Fife

Duncan of Carrick + Avelina daughter of Alna son of Walter   (i) Daughter/sister of John de Lacy + Alan + Margaret daughter of Earl David of Huntingdon   Thomas + Isabel countess of Atholl   Ada   Dervorgilla

Earls of Carrick   (ii) Rose daughter of Hugh de Lacy

Thomas + daughter of Rǫgnvald Guðrøðsson king of Man   Patrick of Atholl

Helen + Roger de Quincy earl of Winchester   Christianna + William de Froz earl of Aumale   Dervorgilla + John Balliol of Barnard Castle

Table 4 The Galloway family

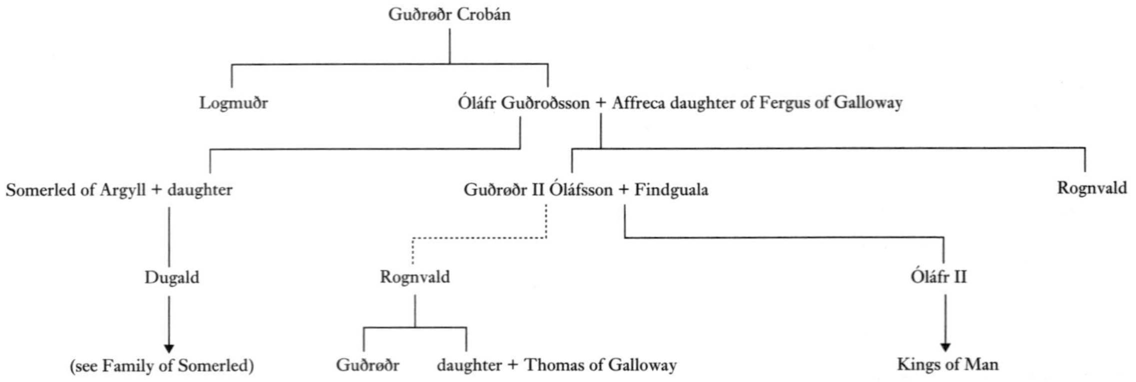

Table 5 The kings of Man and the Isles

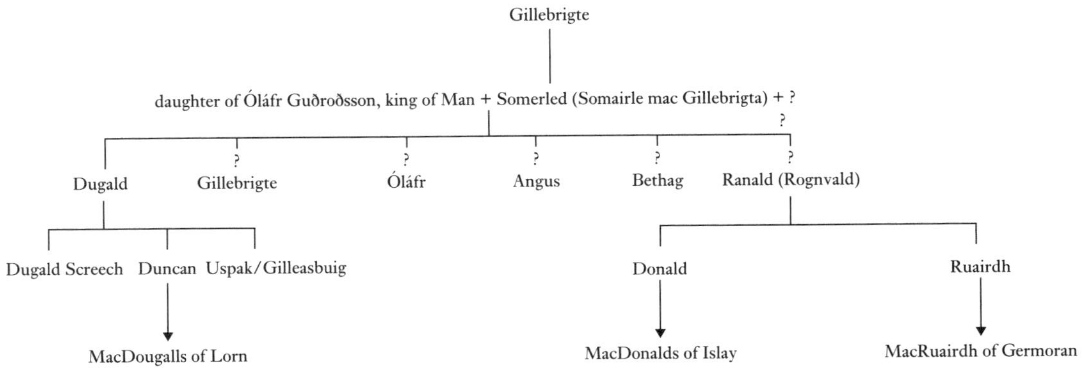

```
                              Gillebrigte
                                   |
  daughter of Óláfr Guðrøðsson, king of Man + Somerled (Somairle mac Gillebrigta) + ?
        |                                                              |
  ┌─────┼─────┐           ?        ?       ?         ?              ?
  |     |     |           |        |       |         |              |
Dugald Gillebrigte      Óláfr    Angus   Bethag   Ranald (Rognvald)
  |                                                   |
┌─┴──────┬──────┐                              ┌──────┴──────┐
Dugald  Duncan  Uspak/Gilleasbuig            Donald        Ruairdh
Screech   |                                    |              |
          ↓                                    ↓              ↓
     MacDougalls of Lorn                MacDonalds of Islay  MacRuairdh of Germoran
```

Table 6 Somerled and his family

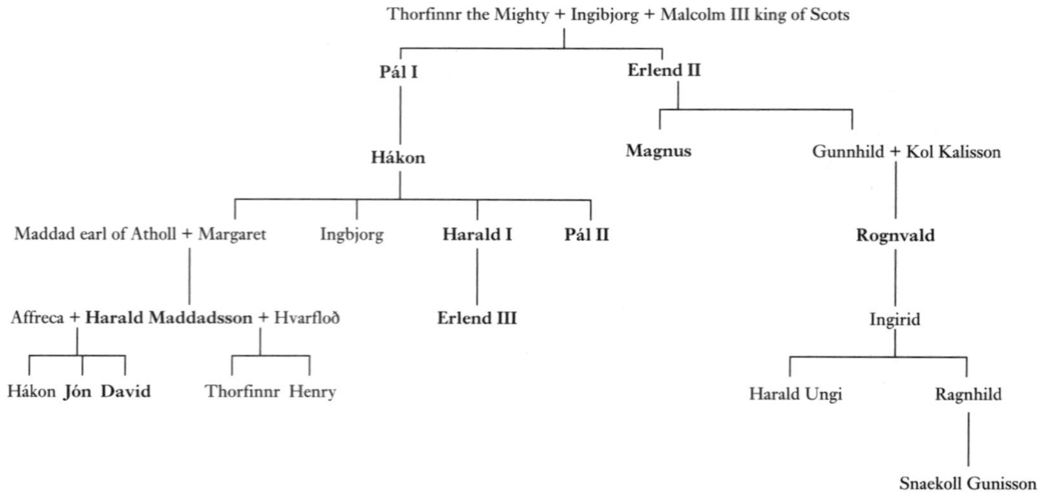

Thorfinnr the Mighty + Ingibjorg + Malcolm III king of Scots

- Pál I
- Hákon
  - Ingibjorg
  - Harald I
  - Pál II
  - Erlend III
  - Margaret + Maddad earl of Atholl
    - Harald Maddadsson + Affreca / Hvarfloð
      - Hákon
      - Jón
      - David
      - Thorfinnr
      - Henry
- Erlend II
  - Magnus
  - Gunnhild + Kol Kalisson
    - Rognvald
      - Ingirid
        - Harald Ungi
        - Ragnhild
          - Snaekoll Gunnisson

Table 7 The earls of Orkney and Caithness

Introduction
Scotland in 1070

Many periods have been claimed as the defining era in the 'making of Scotland' but there is perhaps greater justification for regarding the 160 years that are covered in this volume as more critical in this formative process than any other. It was in this period that a national monarchy came into being whose authority encompassed the whole of mainland Scotland. Simultaneously a national Church was established whose ambitions for self-government and freedom from external interference both reflected and encouraged the growth of that monarchy. Finally, a route was charted through internal and external threats towards the idea of a unified entity called Scotland which welded together by 1230 what in 1070 had been a fluid patchwork of bickering rivals.

Despite such importance, however, the period has not been seen traditionally as one of the building blocks from which the narrative of Scotland's history is constructed. That narrative has long been assembled mainly in terms of reigns of individual kings or of the dynasties to which they belonged, or from periods defined by totemic dates like the death of Alexander III as a precursor to the outbreak of the Wars of Independence, or the social, political and religious revolution of the Reformation. A study such as this, which begins halfway through the reign of one king and ends halfway through the reign of another, is a significant departure from the traditional period division of Scotland's history. Yet it has a compelling logic. It begins with a meeting and a marriage which moved Scotland onto a radically different course in defining its identity and, above all, its relationship with its larger, richer and more powerful southern neighbour. It also possesses another significance, for it spans the era that saw the displacement of the senior male segment of the royal lineage descended from King Malcolm III and his first wife Ingibjorg – and other collateral lines – by the family of the youngest of

2 DOMINATION AND LORDSHIP

Malcolm's sons by his second wife, St Margaret, and the realignment of Scotland onto a new cultural orientation by these heirs of Malcolm and Margaret.

In 1070, no one could have foreseen the long-term consequences of Malcolm III's second marriage. To that point, Malcolm's conduct had been that of a warrior king in the heavily Scandinavianised mould of his Gaelic ancestors. The core of his kingdom was overwhelmingly Gaelic in culture and language and the one strong Germanic influence over him was from Norse Orkney rather than Anglo-Saxon England. From 1070 onwards, however, he and his family were drawn increasingly under the influence of the hybrid English and Frankish culture of southern Britain. Although recent political correctness has led to a glossing over of the many probable clashes which this reorientation and cultural change brought about, we should also bear in mind that neither Malcolm nor his wife is likely to have set about consciously to change the face of his kingdom. Instead, the progressive anglicisation of the Scottish royal household and nobility could be said to be a consequence of the failure of the English to expel their Norman conquerors after 1066. As Malcolm and Margaret's children became increasingly reliant on the England's Norman rulers for the military support necessary to gain control of their patrimony, so the pace of cultural change grew and was reinforced by the progressive southwards relocation of the main seats of royal power into anglophone Lothian and Teviotdale. That was an accident of history, but it created the Scotland that we recognise today.

The internal struggles of the heirs of Malcolm III to assert their control over their paternal kingdom brought conflict which resulted in the steady expansion of that kingdom within the confines of what we would nowadays recognise as Scotland. Likewise, the ambitions of those heirs to win possession of lands that they believed belonged by right to the families of their mothers and wives drew them into a long contest for the domination of a wider northern Britain. These conflicts brought the emerging kingdom of Scotland into new relationships, saw the introduction and development of new mechanisms for the exercise of lordship, opened new avenues for cultural influence and exposed it to new threats; there was no prescribed right for Scotland itself to become the dominator rather than the dominated. Domination and lordship, indeed, are the two central themes of this study. The words, it can be argued, are simply alternative forms which express the same notion, but here it is intended that domination should be understood to represent the process of asserting some form of superior authority over another territory or ruler, while lordship is the practical exercise of that superior authority. In the period under consideration in this volume the question of domination can be seen to govern the relationships between the would-be dominators – the Scots, English, Norwegians and Irish – not only with each other but also with those lesser powers who occupied the margins between them and around the northern and western peripheries of the British Isles. In 1070 there were still multiple possibilities as to which power would achieve wider domination within the British mainland; by 1230 their number had been reduced to two.

'SCOTLAND' IN 1070

What was understood by 'Scotland' in 1070? As a label it did not possess the same meanings as it has today of either the geographical region occupying the northern third of the British mainland or the political entity which occupies that same geographical space plus almost all of the islands to its north and west. Indeed, the very word 'Scotland' would have been unknown to most of the inhabitants of either of those zones, for it is a name given in the modern form of a language (English) that in the late eleventh century was spoken only by a minority of the inhabitants of northern mainland Britain. The Latin term *Scotia* is not truly equivalent to the modern term, for it referred simply to the land occupied by the Scots rather than to an exact geographical entity. Although by the late 1000s the term was used mainly by members of the educated Gaelic elite within the kingdom of the Scots or, as it was known in Gaelic, *Alba*, and by external writers as the shorthand Latin descriptor for that kingdom, it was applied specifically to the territory ruled by the king of Scots north of the Firth of Forth and not to those regions south of the river which had been acquired since the tenth century. As the sphere of authority of those kings expanded through the course of the twelfth and thirteenth centuries, *Scotia* came to be the Latin label used for the whole of the mainland north of the Forth, and only from the fourteenth century onwards did it come to acquire its modern equivalence to Scotland. Likewise *Alba*, which nowadays is used as the Gaelic name for the whole of Scotland, had grades of meaning and a less firm equation with a specific territory than its modern usage has.[1] Beyond the fluctuating limits of *Scotia/Alba* other labels were used to distinguish territories and the identities of the people who inhabited them: *Mureb/Moravia/Moray* for a broad sweep

---

[1] For discussion of the meanings of *Alba* and its equivalence with the Scottish kingdom, see Broun, *Scottish Independence and the Idea of Britain*, Chapter 3.

of territory stretching west and south from the River Spey through the central Highlands towards the Atlantic coast; *Galwegia/Galloway* for an ill-defined zone south and west of Clydesdale; and *Laodonia/Lothian* for that northern portion of the former kingdom of Northumbria between the rivers Tweed and Forth which the Scots had acquired by the early 1000s. 'Scotland' in 1070, then, was a concept shared by the intellectual elite who were framing the idea of a single kingdom of the Scots which encompassed the whole of northern mainland Britain, but which had as yet little or no currency beyond their narrow circle. That situation, however, was to change gradually, carried by the progressive drive to domination of the whole of 'Scotland' of the dynasty which that elite had advanced as rightful rulers over the entire region.

It is difficult to read this rise to domination other than teleologically (that is, by explaining a process in terms of a known end result), especially since traditional 'national' histories of Scotland written since the Middle Ages have presented the establishment of a single monarchy descended from the mid-ninth-century king, Cinaed son of Alpín, ruling over the whole of what we nowadays recognise as Scotland as a natural given result. Furthermore, most 'national' histories of Scotland have been written from the perspective of that monarchy and often express its conquest of the territories that came to be encompassed by the later medieval kingdom in terms of rightful recovery of an ancestral heritage and of struggles against intrusive external forces. As most of the surviving medieval records relate to the Alban monarchy and the core territories of its kingdom, that bias is understandably difficult to avoid. What can be avoided, however, is the notion of inevitability; there was nothing inevitable in the outcome of the marriage of Malcolm III and Margaret and historical contingency in any case defies any such straightforward predictive modelling. We can accept that certain factors, not least of which were the possession of superior human and natural resources and the support of an increasingly vocal intellectual elite whose 'spin' constantly promoted the 'right' of the kings of Alba, gave greater likelihood to first domination by and then incorporation into the kingdom of the Scots of the other powers in northern mainland Britain.[2] That outcome, however, was far from certain in 1070.

We can also accept that *Alba*, as it had emerged in the course of the tenth century, was the principal power in mainland Scotland by the third quarter of the eleventh century; but what did it comprise? Its extent was very fluid and we should think of a core of inherited lands

---

[2] For such processes in operation, see Davies, *Domination and Conquest*.

that constituted *Alba* proper and a more recently acquired outer zone of territory which preserved a high degree of local identity and which was only beginning to be integrated into the kingdom. The core of *Alba* lay in the lower valleys of the rivers Tay and Earn, with the main seats of royal power at Scone and Forteviot and religious centres at Dunkeld and St Andrews. The steady expansion of the kingdom south of the Forth from the later tenth century, however, had also seen the emergence of Dunfermline – close to the ferry crossings that linked the two parts of the kingdom – and Edinburgh south of the firth, as more convenient bases from which to dominate the recently acquired southern lands while maintaining a presence in the ancestral heartland of the kingdom. The northern limits of the kingdom are hotly debated, complicated by the question of the relationship of Moray and its rulers to the kings of Scots who ruled from their Tayside power base.[3] Current scholarship favours a view that Moray was the base for a rival segment of the Scottish royal lineage rather than a separate polity contending with *Alba* for mastery of mainland Scotland, a view that seems to be supported by the decision of the temporarily triumphant Moray-based segment to relocate itself in the seat of Alban power in the south in the 1040s and 1050s. *Alba*, then, can be seen to have a notional extent that encompassed the whole of eastern Scotland between the Forth estuary and the Moray Firth, although the effective rule of the territory west of the Spey was only as real as the ability of its kings to travel there to enforce their authority.

North of Moray the mainland was dominated by another power, the Scandinavian earldom of Orkney. Like *Alba*, that earldom was a creation of the tenth century and the extent of its territory fluctuated with the influence and authority of its rulers.[4] Also like *Alba*, it was prone to internal fractures between rival segments of its ruling family. In the mid-eleventh century, however, it had reached a zenith of power under Earl Thorfinnr the Mighty, who had consolidated Scandinavian rule over Caithness and Sutherland in north-easternmost mainland Scotland and extended his influence southwards to at least the Kyles of Sutherland and the River Oykel through long conflict with the rulers of Moray. Again, however, we should probably see Thorfinnr as ruling over a core territory in Orkney and Caithness with his authority becoming increasingly nebulous the further south and west it extended from this heartland. Indeed, for much of the north-west mainland there is no clear evidence for the presence of any kind of higher authority and society here appears

---

[3] Woolf, *From Pictland to Alba*, 227–30.
[4] Ibid. 300–10.

to have been very loosely organised, representing something of a vacuum into which external forces were drawn.

Alba's western limits are equally difficult to define with confidence, although much ink has been spilled on the issue. There is consensus, however, that there had been a progressive eastwards withdrawal of the authority of the kings based in lower Tayside, perhaps accelerating in the face of increased Western Isles-based Scandinavian influence in the south-west Highlands. It is a process, however, that is poorly documented, equally poorly understood and overly mythologised in histories that seek to locate the origins of the dynasty that came to rule over Argyll by the early 1100s in an earlier conflict for domination of this region between Scandinavian and Gaelic powers. Kings of *Alba* probably believed that they had some authority over the territory that had once made up the kingdom of the Scots of Dál Riata, but in the late 1000s much of the island portion of that kingdom had been drawn into the sea realm assembled by Guðrøðr or Gofraid Crobán and based on the Isle of Man. Like Orkney, that kingdom was a relatively recent creation and, whilst there had been Isles-based kingdoms in the past, there was nothing to suggest that it was anything other than a personal domain that would crumble as quickly as it had been assembled once its ruler died or fell prey to more powerful external threats. Indeed, the Western Isles through the eleventh century were the focus for the ambitions of a range of external powers – Uí Briain and Uí Néill dynasts from Ireland, Orcadian earls and England's Danish rulers – as well as being the home to men with regal pretensions themselves. One thing, however, is apparent: the kings of *Alba* had no interest in this whole region until their domination of the mainland had expanded to the point where the affairs of the maritime west began to impinge upon the security of their realm.

South of the Forth lay territory which the kings of *Alba* had long coveted and fought bloody wars to dominate. Their primary ambitions lay in Lothian, a region of largely English-speaking population which had formed the northern part of the kingdom of Northumbria down to the ninth century but which had become something of a contested 'debatable land' between powers contending for domination of the Southern Upland zone.[5] By c. 1000, the Lothian plain north of the Lammermuirs had been incorporated into *Alba* and by the middle of the eleventh century the southern limits of the kingdom may have lain around the lower reaches of the River Tweed. That limit may have contracted in the face of growing English power in the 1040s and 1050s as first Knútr and then Edward the Confessor

[5] Ibid. 204–5, 234–5.

attempted to stabilise their northern flank through the establishment of strong authority in the region in the person of earls based at Bamburgh and York, representing the two halves of the older kingdom of Northumbria. It was an uncertain southern frontier that Malcolm III inherited and the English earls of Northumbria could probably claim with some justification in the 1060s to rule from Bamburgh over a territory that may have stretched from around Dunbar in the north to the Tees in the south.

It was not just *Alba* and Northumbria that were in competition for the Southern Uplands region in the eleventh century. One of the few other early medieval kingdoms to have survived the upheavals of the ninth and tenth centuries was Strathclyde or Cumbria. This territory is not to be confused with the later English county of Cumberland or the modern English local authority region of Cumbria, both of which represent only part of the land that at times comprised the kingdom. What, then, was Cumbria in the eleventh century? It could be described, with tongue only slightly in cheek, as the kingdom of the M74, for its core territories in the 1000s appear to have extended from the area around Glasgow south along the corridor of the Clyde and Annan valleys followed by the modern motorway. For long it was believed that the kingdom had been absorbed into *Alba* soon after 1018, possibly as a sub-kingdom where heirs to the Scottish throne could spread their wings, but this view is now discounted and instead it is considered to have survived as an independent entity for a few decades more.[6] By the late 1060s, however, Malcolm III appears to have extended his control over at least the heartland of Cumbrian territory in a process of which there is no record, but which probably represented an opportunistic response to the upheavals within England upon which he was later to capitalise directly.

Between the zone of Alban power in Lothian, the territory of the earls of Northumbria and the kingdom of the Cumbrians lay an ill-defined and thinly populated march over which none of them exercised effective control. This region remained as something of a no-man's land into the twelfth century, when David I and his successors began to settle colonists within it and so integrate it more fully into their domain. South and west of Cumbria was a similar zone of ill-defined authority, where it is difficult to trace either lordship structures or stable polities until the mid-twelfth century. This was 'greater' Galloway, a territory which at times between the seventh and eleventh centuries had fallen under first Northumbrian and then Cumbrian domination, but which in the later

---

[6] Smyth, *Warlords and Holy Men*, 221–3; MacQuarrie, 'The kings of Strathclyde'; Woolf, *From Pictland to Alba*, 262–5, 270–1.

tenth and eleventh centuries seems to have been drawn more into an Irish Sea and Hebridean sphere through the settlement of Scandinavian and Gaelic colonists in part of the territory.[7] Within this 'greater' Galloway was a more sharply defined core running along the northern shore of the Solway and round into Carrick which in the twelfth century came to form the kingdom or lordship of Galloway. In the mid-eleventh century, at least the western part of that area had formed an important part of a sea-based kingdom ruled over by Echmarcach son of Ragnall, which at its height included Dublin, Man and the Rhinns of Galloway.[8] As with the West Highlands, this was a zone that looked in other directions than to the kings of *Alba* for lordship, and it was only a series of dynastic accidents and the violent intrusion of external powers in the course of the later eleventh and the twelfth centuries that saw it drawn increasingly into the orbit of Malcolm III and his heirs.

The catalyst for most of these redefined relationships, indeed for the marriage itself which took *Alba* and its kings onto a new course, was the death of Edward the Confessor, king of England, in January 1066 and the rapid emergence of a three-cornered fight for the kingship. Three battles in early autumn 1066 transformed the political landscape of the British Isles and created a series of opportunities for Malcolm III – and other opportunist powers – to capitalise upon. In the north outside York, first Gate Fulford had seen the slaughter of the regional elite by the war band of the Norwegian king, Haraldr Harðráði, but then he himself perished at Stamford Bridge at the hands of the new English king, Harold Godwinsson, who came hurrying north to repel the invader of his realm. In turn, the English monarchy that had for a century dominated the politics of mainland Britain and, at times, Ireland, had been swept away in the carnage of the battle of Hastings, which had seen the deaths not only of Harold Godwinsson but also of the cream of the English political community. The victor, Duke William of Normandy, had been crowned as king of England at Westminster in a ceremony designed to show him as the legitimate successor of the kingship of Edward the Confessor, but there were many in England – and beyond – who were not yet prepared to accept the result of Hastings as final, not least those who looked upon the surviving male representative of Edward's family, Edgar Æðeling, as their true lord and king. Once the psychological shock of the defeat at Hastings had begun to fade, surviving members of the English political elite began to plot the overthrow and expulsion of their conquerors. In

---

[7] Oram, *Lordship of Galloway*, xxii–xxiv.
[8] Woolf, *From Pictland to Alba*, 244–8.

1069, a war for liberation and the restoration of the ancient line of West Saxon kings began and William faced a fight for his very survival.

Malcolm III has often been presented as standing aloof from these events, watching and waiting to see which way the issue would be decided, and only belatedly capitalising on the opportunity to extend his domain at the expense of the broken and defeated northern English lords. It is likely that Malcolm was far from inactive in the immediate aftermath of 1066; it was probably at this time that he asserted his lordship over Cumbria and pushed his control south across Tweed and into Teviotdale. William was powerless to prevent this and may, indeed, have cared little provided his foothold south of the Humber was unshaken. William wanted, however, to be seen as the legitimate heir of Edward the Confessor, who had ruled all of England and enjoyed the submission of lesser kings and princes in territories all along the northern and western fringes of his kingdom. Their recognition of Edward's lordship had been demonstrated by formal displays of subservience and personal attendance at his court; four years after Hastings, William, despite his best efforts, was still struggling to assert his authority outside the heartland of his kingdom in south-eastern England and Malcolm had no cause to offer his submission to an outsider who seemed destined to fail. Instead, there perhaps seemed to be better prospects in forging an alliance with the likely successor to William as king, and it is with that calculation that this present study begins.

A NOTE ON TERMINOLOGY

There are no simple and universally accepted labels which can be used as convenient shorthand to identify the main cultural groups within the area covered by this book. 'Scots' is a term loaded with difficulties and is reserved here to mean all those people who looked for lordship to the kings of Scots. Certainly, the inhabitants of Galloway and the Isles most emphatically did not consider themselves to be 'Scots' as we would understand the term, and 'Galwegian' and 'Islesmen', 'Manx' and 'Hebridean' are employed throughout the book. While it carries many modern cultural connotations, the term preferred to identify the majority of the inhabitants of the core territories of the kingdom of *Alba* is 'Gaelic'. Throughout, I have tried to avoid using the nineteenth-century invention 'Anglo-Norman' as a descriptor, except where this is explicitly used in a source that is being referred to. Instead, 'English' is used most often since most of the people involved were primarily English resident and probably mainly anglophone in background.

10 DOMINATION AND LORDSHIP

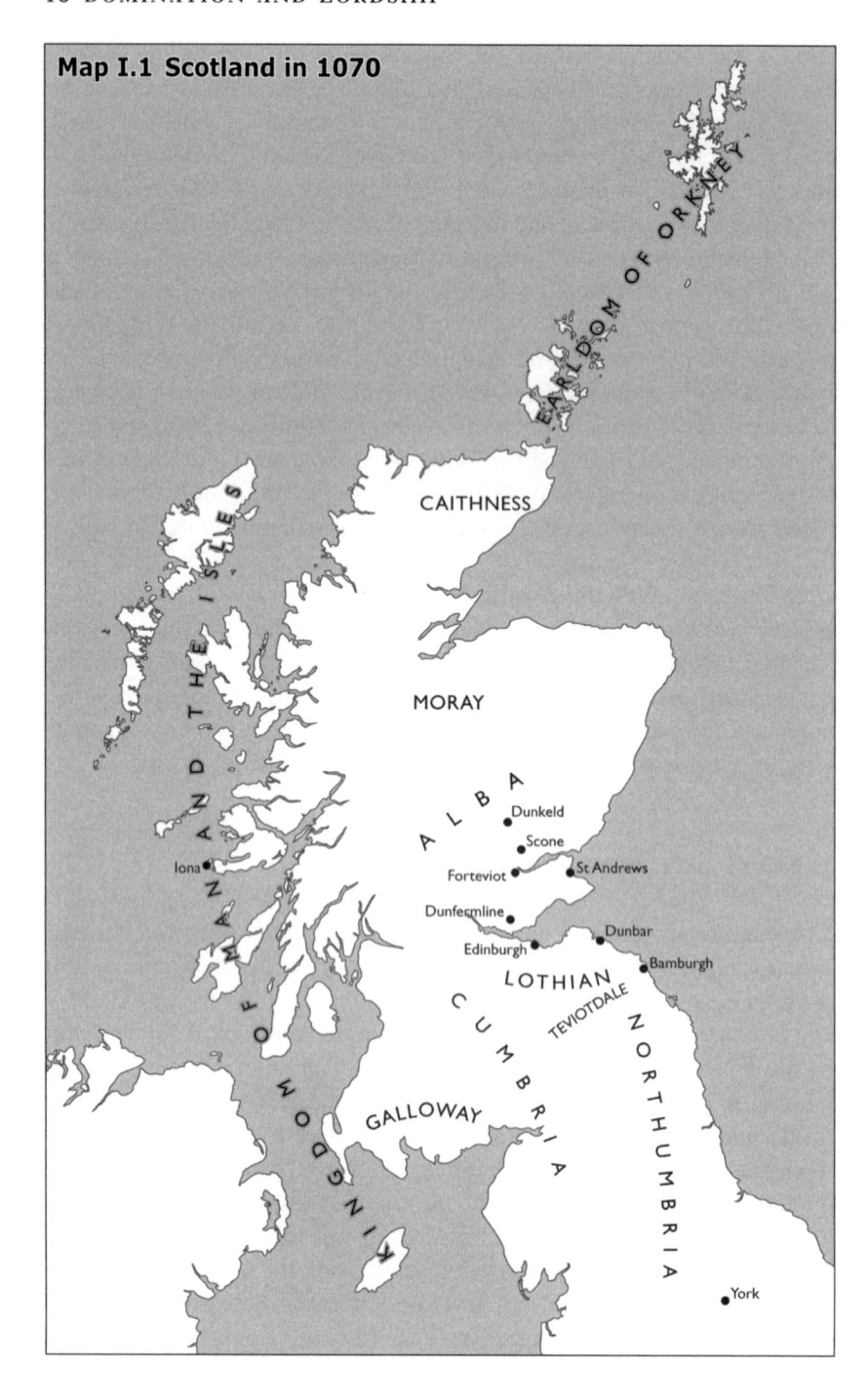

Map I.1 Scotland in 1070

Part One: Narratives

CHAPTER I

Out with the Old, In with the New? 1070–93

BARGAINING FOR A THRONE

According to the northern English chronicler Symeon of Durham, in spring 1070 the Scottish king, Malcolm III, waged a devastating campaign in northern England.[1] It was a momentous event, not for the plunder and slaves seized but for a meeting which occurred during its course at Monkwearmouth. There, Malcolm heard that some English noble refugees from the failed rebellion of 1069 against England's Norman conquerors wished to meet him. Symeon describes the king receiving them in the shadow of the burning church of St Peter and finding himself confronted not only with the outlawed bishop of Durham, but also with the Anglo-Saxon pretender to the English throne, Edgar Æðeling, his mother, Agatha, and his sisters Margaret and Christina. In return for their submission, Malcolm offered them sanctuary in Scotland, but the offer was declined and Edgar and his family sailed for Germany. But Divine providence intervened and contrary winds drove them towards Scotland, where Margaret quickly became Malcolm's wife and through her efforts brought civilisation to her barbarous husband and his people. God's will, it seemed, had been done.

But this was not the first meeting between Malcolm, Edgar and his family, and the seemingly chance encounter at Monkwearmouth was no fortuitous event. Two years earlier, the exiles had arrived in Scotland escorted by Cospatric, earl of Northumbria.[2] On that occasion, Edgar had sought Scottish aid against William of Normandy, but Malcolm preferred to maintain the caution he had displayed since summer 1066 and

---

[1] Symeon of Durham, *Opera Omnia*, ii, 190–2.
[2] John of Worcester, *Chronicon*, ii, 2.

opted to keep his peace with William.[3] Even when the Northumbrians rebelled in 1069, slaughtered William's garrison at York and drove the Normans back south of the Humber, Malcolm kept out of the conflict. When the exiles left in spring 1069 to join the rebellion the Scots offered no assistance and instead it was King Svein of Denmark who aided the rebels. Despite the presence of a large Danish fleet in the Humber, by the end of 1069 the rebellion was crumbling in the face of King William's counter-offensive and its leaders headed by Cospatric and Waltheof, son of Siward of York, were suing for peace. Nevertheless, despite his successes against the rebels King William was still vulnerable in early 1070, for Edgar and his closest associates remained at large and the Danes had occupied York and controlled large parts of southern Yorkshire and northern Lincolnshire. It was into this situation that Malcolm finally ventured.

What motivated Malcolm in 1070 is much debated. His invasion has been presented as a mishandled operation to aid Edgar, as a cynical raid which capitalised on the disorder in northern England or as a calculated bid to terrorise the Northumbrians into accepting his lordship.[4] Interpretation of his aims and even of what exactly happened when in 1070 is hampered by the scantness of surviving records. Malcolm's behaviour down to the end of his reign, however, suggests that he wished to impose his lordship over the territory between the rivers Tweed and Tees. Arguments that the brutality of his tactics was hardly inclined to win hearts and minds are anachronistic, projecting modern morality into an age where war was conducted with the express aim of destroying your enemy's capacity to fight through the wasting of his economic resources. Malcolm was sending a clear message of his superior lordship to the people of Northumbria through demonstrating his ability to enter their land at will, take plunder and withdraw when he chose to do so. Only he, Malcolm was proclaiming, not Earl Cospatric and certainly not King William, could protect them and their property. With William struggling to assert his mastery of England, a Danish army occupying York and continuing unrest throughout southern districts, Malcolm had an unparalleled opportunity to achieve his ambitions.

Although cynical opportunism could have been the driving force behind his invasion, there are reasons to believe that Malcolm's behaviour was more creditable than is often suggested. It was perhaps

---

[3] *Ordericus Vitalis*, bk iv, 5.
[4] Ritchie, *Normans in Scotland*, 26–7; Le Patourel, 'Norman Conquest of Yorkshire', 3; Duncan, *Making of the Kingdom*, 118–19; Duncan, *Kingship of the Scots*, 44–5.

more than chance which saw his campaign coincide with the Danish fleet's movement from the Humber to the Wash to link up with the English rebels in the Cambridgeshire fenlands. Furthermore, some of the Anglo-Saxon nobles with whom Malcolm met at Wearmouth also joined the fenland rising. Northumbria may have been the price which Edgar was willing to concede for Scottish aid, with partial dismemberment of his ancestors' kingdom through cession of a remote province regarded as a worthwhile exchange for the throne. There are other indications that Malcolm and Edgar were allies. In particular, the supposedly chance nature of the 1070 encounter offered by Symeon is highly contrived and Edgar Æðeling and his associates had more probably approached Malcolm to persuade him to coordinate operations with the Danes further south. That scenario, however, begs the question of why Malcolm withdrew northwards with his booty rather than press home the advantage which he held over William of Normandy's few supporters in Northumbria.

What probably swayed Malcolm was the Danes' patent lack of progress and, quite probably, news that Svein was preparing to withdraw from England. Svein had thought in 1069 that he would find allies amongst the Anglo-Scandinavian population of York, Lincolnshire and East Anglia, but the failure of widespread popular support to emerge in even those areas forced him to recognise that his campaign would only succeed as a full-blown invasion rather than as a war of liberation. He evidently balked at the cost implications and when William offered to negotiate a Danish withdrawal, perhaps offering a cash bribe, Svein proved ready to discuss terms. News of the Danes' departure in summer 1070 was probably the catalyst that determined Malcolm to turn for home, and Edgar's meeting with him was perhaps an attempt to persuade him to reverse that decision and throw his forces behind the faltering English rebellion. Together, the Scots and the Danes might have defeated William, but Malcolm was unwilling to confront the Normans alone. Having failed to secure Scottish military aid and apparently spurning the offer of sanctuary in Scotland, Edgar chose to go into Continental exile.

Shortly after returning to Scotland, Malcolm is said to have received news that Edgar's ship had been driven by contrary winds into the Firth of Forth, and that the refugees were now seeking his protection.[5] It may have been less fortuitous than Symeon of Durham claims, for although Malcolm had rejected earlier appeals to support the English rebellion he had not come to terms with King William, and Edgar presented some

[5] Symeon of Durham, *Opera Omnia*, ii, 192.

intriguing possibilities for Malcolm to exploit. The king, we are told, had begun to 'yearn for' the Æðeling's elder sister, Margaret, an attraction which the *Anglo-Saxon Chronicle* dates to the exiles' first visit to Scotland.[6] There is no suggestion that Malcolm's first wife, Ingibjorg, was set aside or otherwise disposed of and the simplest explanation is that she was dead by 1069. Indeed, she may have died as early as 1058, before Malcolm became king, if we accept that she is the *Ingeborg comitissa* commemorated in the Durham *Liber Vitae*.[7] Malcolm's yearnings, indeed, may have lasted significantly longer, for the twelfth-century Normandy-based Anglo-Saxon monk Orderic claimed that Margaret had been betrothed to the king since 1059.[8] For some reason, that arrangement had not been honoured, but in 1070 Edgar needed Malcolm as an ally. In turn, Malcolm understood the significance of marriage to the elder sister of the Anglo-Saxon claimant to the English throne. Should Edgar achieve his ambition, his sister and her children could expect to hold great influence at his court. Malcolm's interest, therefore, was not simply a question of lust, but a calculated act: the marriage was the price of Scottish support for Edgar's schemes. With last objections from Margaret herself overcome, probably before the end of 1070 Malcolm and Margaret were married at Dunfermline and a new phase in Scottish history opened.[9]

TESTING NEW RELATIONSHIPS

The implications of the marriage were clear to William the Conqueror, for at a stroke it transformed the nature of Scottish interest in the Anglo-Saxon claim to the English throne: as long as Edgar Æðeling remained unmarried and childless his rights would be transmitted through Margaret to any of her children by Malcolm. That such a calculation figured in Malcolm's schemes is visible in the names given to their children, which were surely chosen to make them acceptable to their potential English subjects. Their first four sons were named Edward, Edmund, Æðelred and Edgar after Margaret's West Saxon male progenitors. The births of these children lay in the future, but the fact of the marriage demanded a response from William. In 1072, therefore,

---

[6] *Anglo-Saxon Chronicle* D, s.a. 1067.
[7] *Liber Vitæ Ecclesiæ Dunelmensis*, 141.
[8] See Duncan, *Kingship of the Scots*, 42–3.
[9] *ESSH*, ii, 25.

he led an army deep into *Scotia*, reaching Abernethy in Perthshire. There, according to the *Anglo-Saxon Chronicle*, Malcolm made peace with William, gave hostages and was his man, a form of words which has been interpreted as meaning that it was the making of peace and giving of hostages rather than any act of homage which made him William's man.[10] Superior lordship was again being demonstrated, with Malcolm this time on the receiving end. Malcolm's hostages included his eldest son, Duncan, who was brought up at William's court.[11] One further condition of peace appears to have been Malcolm's agreement to expel Edgar, who shortly afterwards appeared on the Continent. In return, William may have reassigned to Malcolm the vills in England granted to Scottish kings for their maintenance when attending the English court, whose restoration in 1072 is alluded to in the terms reported for the 1091 settlement between Malcolm and William's son. Interpretation of what the Abernethy settlement involved and what it entailed is fraught with difficulties, not least because of the anachronistic 'feudal' gloss placed on the event by twelfth-century English chroniclers whose Latin terminology carried more loaded, legalistic meanings than did the wording of the earlier Old English account. There is no suggestion in the *Anglo-Saxon Chronicle* that William received Malcolm's *manrædene*, or homage, but by the 1120s John of Worcester reported unambiguously in Latin that Malcolm 'became his man'.[12] That claim, however, reflects later political agendas rather than the realities of 1072.

For William, the 1072 expedition gained much at little real cost. The threat implicit in Malcolm's marriage to Margaret had been neutralised, Edgar Æðeling had been deprived of a military backer and Norman power had been pushed north of York. Indeed, William felt sufficiently confident on his return south to drive Cospatric from his earldom, accusing him of treachery during the rebellion of 1068–9, and to replace him with Waltheof, son of Edward the Confessor's earl of York, Siward, and whom he linked closely to the royal house through marriage to his niece, Judith. After a brief sojourn in Flanders, where he established contact with Edgar at the anti-Norman court of its count, Cospatric went to Scotland, where Malcolm gave him a lordship based on Dunbar composed largely of estates that perhaps formed the Lothian portion of his

---

[10] Duncan, *Kingship of the Scots*, 48.
[11] *Anglo-Saxon Chronicle* E, s.a. 1072; *Annals of Ulster*, s.a. 1072; *Chron. Melrose*, s.a. 1072.
[12] *Anglo-Saxon Chronicle* E, s.a. 1072; John of Worcester, *Chronicon*, iii, 21. For extended discussion, see Duncan, *Kingship of the Scots*, 45, 48–9.

lost earldom.[13] He was the first and most prominent of a group of Anglo-Saxon émigrés who gravitated towards Scotland and settled there. Few though they were in number, their close association with Margaret gave them disproportionate influence at court, which, combined with their alien culture and social behaviour, earned them the hostility of the native nobility.

Regardless of the degree of the exiles' standing in Malcolm's counsels, when Edgar returned in 1074 in breach of the 1072 settlement they were unable to persuade him to aid his brother-in-law openly in a fresh attack on England.[14] The Scots had seen and understood Norman military power and, in any case, Malcolm had secured a deal which implicitly recognised the reality of his lordship over Lothian and at least the northern parts of Cumbria. Why should that gain be gambled unnecessarily on a fresh military adventure? Instead, Malcolm sent him, loaded with gifts to sweeten the rejection, to King Philip I of France, who was seeking allies against the Normans. Edgar's ship, however, was wrecked on the Northumbrian coast and the near-destitute prince barely escaped back to Scotland with a handful of survivors. Malcolm now persuaded him to make his peace with William, who received him with honour. To William, it must have seemed that his treaty with the Scots was yielding dividends, a view reinforced by Malcolm's non-participation in the great revolt against him in England headed by Earl Waltheof of Northumbria and the Norman earls of East Anglia and Hereford, which erupted later that year.[15]

Despite the potential offered by the rebellion of Earl Waltheof in 1074–6, Malcolm maintained the peace with William until August 1079 when he invaded Northumbria and ravaged as far south as the Tyne.[16] Malcolm's attack showed an impressive awareness of the current situation in both Northumbria particularly and in William's realm more generally, for William was absent from his kingdom quelling a rebellion by his eldest son, Robert, in Normandy, and the current holder of the earldom of Northumbria, Bishop Walcher of Durham, had no experience as a military commander in a frontier region. According to northern English chronicle tradition, the only successful resistance to Malcolm's onslaught was provided by heavenly powers and the Scots, laden with

---

[13] Symeon of Durham, *Opera Omnia*, ii, 199.
[14] *Anglo-Saxon Chronicle* D, s.a. 1075 = 1074; William of Malmesbury, *Gesta Regum*, ii, 465–7.
[15] Oram, *David I*, 32; Forte, Oram and Pedersen, *Viking Empires*, 214–15.
[16] *Anglo-Saxon Chronicle* E, s.a. 1079.

plunder, returned home unmolested.[17] Walcher's failure to offer effective resistance, coupled with his botched handling of the unrest provoked by the murder of his well-connected Northumbrian chief counsellor, Ligulf, produced a crisis in early 1080 that threatened to unfasten the Norman grip on the country north of the Tees. In mid-May, Walcher met at Gateshead with the infuriated kin of the murdered Ligulf who, unconvinced by the bishop's protestations of innocence, killed him and his associates.[18] It was this action rather than Malcolm's raid of the previous year that triggered Norman retaliation, but the Scots' breach of the 1072 peace could not pass unanswered.

In summer 1080 William sent his half-brother, Odo of Bayeux, to avenge Walcher's murder, followed in the autumn by a campaign commanded by his newly reconciled son, Robert, to punish the Scots. All accounts of Robert's expedition are dismissive of its significance, but this display of Norman might persuaded Malcolm to avoid a fight and negotiate. It is perhaps significant that the meeting occurred at Falkirk, close to the River Avon, which formed the western boundary of Lothian, for Malcolm argued in 1093 that disputes between the two kingdoms should be settled by a joint court assembled at their border. The meeting place, then, may indicate Malcolm's explicit recognition at that date that he held Lothian by gift of successive English kings. At Falkirk, Malcolm agreed to a renewal of the 1072 settlement and avoided any more serious consequences for his actions.[19] Robert could probably look with justifiable satisfaction on this settlement, for he had secured the submission of the Scottish king at no real cost. Furthermore, as he headed homewards he paused to order construction of the castle we know as Newcastle-upon-Tyne. The significance of this new fortification should not be underestimated, for it constituted a major advance for Norman power in northern England, pushing their effective reach across the Tyne into the disaffected core of the earldom of Northumbria and providing a springboard from which the settlement of a new colonial nobility could be started under Bishop Walcher's successors in the earldom.[20] Malcolm could not have been ignorant of the changed circumstances which the building of Newcastle signalled.

It has been said that by the time of his death in 1087, William the Conqueror had achieved little else in the north of England other than

---

[17] Oram, *David I*, 32; Symeon of Durham, *Opera Omnia*, ii, 36–8.
[18] Lomas, *North-East England*, 14.
[19] Symeon of Durham, *Opera Omnia*, ii, 211.
[20] Kapelle, *Norman Conquest of the North*, 142–6.

the destruction of native resistance to Norman rule.[21] Others have been more generous in their assessment, claiming that he had 'demonstrated the superiority of his power to the king of Scots and a firm commitment to the Tweed boundary',[22] but this view still understates the extent of Norman influence north of the Tees and offers a view of William's territorial objectives that cannot be supported by the historical evidence. With the benefit of hindsight we can see that 1080 marked a watershed in the political and military situation in the region and that Malcolm's room to manoeuvre had been greatly reduced. The Falkirk accord and the building of Newcastle, moreover, were simply components in a more thorough-going reordering of Norman government in northern England. Before the end of 1080, William had installed one of his own ecclesiastical favourites, William of St Calais, as bishop in Durham, and established Aubrey de Coucy as earl in Northumberland.[23] Bishop William, who enjoyed a close relationship with the king and could rely on him for support, was an altogether more energetic diocesan than Walcher but combined tactfulness with his reforming zeal. When in 1083 he swept away the old Community of St Cuthbert at Durham, the chief surviving institution of the old Northumbrian order in the region, and replaced it with a Benedictine convent, his actions produced scarcely a murmur. De Coucy also proceeded altogether more cautiously than his predecessors and there is no evidence that he began to plant Norman colonists within his earldom before his tenure ended in 1085. Nevertheless, a Norman bishop, a Norman earl and a royal castle fixed in the heart of the most disaffected region of England represented a significant advance on the situation that had prevailed before 1080. As to King William's commitment to the Tweed frontier, while his son's renewal of the agreement with Malcolm preserved the territorial status quo, there had been an explicit restating of English *de jure* right to Northumbria north of Tweed, that is Lothian, and the English king's support for his bishop and earl, whose territorial spheres extended far into Scottish-held Lothian, offered the prospect of future extension northwards of effective Norman power. De Coucy's replacement in c. 1085 as earl by Robert de Mowbray, a move linked to William's anxieties over the defence of the north of England following Knútr IV of Denmark's threatened invasion of England in that year,[24] underscores that for William the security of his kingdom overrode

---

[21] Ibid. 146.
[22] Lomas, *North-East England*, 16.
[23] Ibid. 15.
[24] Ibid. 15; Forte, Oram and Pedersen, *Viking Empires*, 215, 366–7.

all other considerations and suggests that 'commitment' to borders may have been only as fixed as expediency demanded.

Although the chroniclers considered Robert of Normandy's 1080 expedition to have achieved nothing of significance, the settlement agreed with Malcolm proved strong enough to survive both the death of William I in 1087 and accession of his second son, William II Rufus, as king of England, and also the widespread rebellion in England in 1088 staged by supporters of the new king's elder brother, Robert, who had succeeded to the duchy of Normandy. William II's quick release of Duncan, a hostage since 1072, and the honour displayed by him towards the freed captive may have been intended to mollify Malcolm and persuade him to keep out of English affairs, but it also removed one component upon which William I's relationship with Malcolm had been founded. There are no hints of Malcolm's attitudes towards this period of upheaval in the south, but the fact that he did not immediately offer any formal submission to William Rufus could imply that he regarded his submissions to William I as personal commendations, the recognition of one man's superior lordship over him, and that he was under no obligation to maintain that relationship with William's son. Malcolm's failure to offer his submission cannot have been welcomed by William Rufus, but in 1087–8 the new English king was in no position to force the issue and, while Malcolm avoided involvement in the internal affairs of England, William was obliged to ignore the omission and focus on more immediate problems.

CULTURAL REVOLUTION?

For eleven years after the Falkirk accord, peace was maintained on the Anglo-Scottish border and, in the absence of any firmer documentary record, it seems that it was during this period that much of the cultural and ecclesiastical innovation attributed to Malcolm and Margaret was set in motion. The nature, degree and extent of Margaret's influence on either her husband or his kingdom are the subjects of modern debate, but in the Middle Ages there was little doubt as to her importance. From the early twelfth century onwards her biographer and subsequent chroniclers presented her as a civilising force who manipulated in a positive way her doting but culturally uncouth husband. Her reputation reached its apex in the mid-thirteenth century following her canonisation in 1249–50 and was reinforced by miracles at her shrine in Dunfermline.[25] After the

[25] 'The Miracles of St Margaret of Scotland', in *Miracles of St Æbbe and St Margaret*.

Reformation, however, Margaret's positive image declined sharply as she was identified as the agent responsible for imposing the supposedly malign control of the Roman Catholic Church over the allegedly simpler and purer traditions of a native 'Celtic' Church, a reputation which is at odds with earlier descriptions of her veneration of and support for Scottish religious traditions.[26] Her supposedly sinister role was further embellished in the religious conflicts of nineteenth-century Scotland, in which rival branches of Protestantism claimed to be the true heirs of the Church that Margaret stood accused of destroying. In the twentieth century, however, those arguments turned back on themselves, with the debate returning to the significance of her role as a reformer and the degree to which she had introduced a reformist programme into the Scottish Church, and to a much more positive assessment of her influences upon royal culture in Scotland.[27]

More recent analysis stresses the influence upon her later religious behaviour of her formative years in Hungary, a kingdom where the missionary zeal of recent conversion to Christianity burned with great intensity. There, Margaret had encountered the full force of Continental Cluniac reform, a movement originating in the late tenth century at the monastery of Cluny in Burgundy. It aimed to purge the Church of corruption, especially lay interference, and was a powerful mechanism for extending papal authority throughout western Europe. In Hungary, where King Stephen had received his crown from the pope and where the influence of Rome was especially strong at the court of King Andrew the Catholic (1046–60), Margaret had been brought up to accept the new doctrine of all-embracing papal authority and his status as Christ's vicar on earth, as was being advanced by Pope Leo IX (1049–54). When she and her family reached England in 1057 they found a similar atmosphere at the court of Edward the Confessor.

In Scotland, Margaret encountered a Church barely touched by Continental reforms some of whose practices differed from what was becoming the accepted norm in western Christendom. Malcolm, we are told, supported her in a programme that aimed to reform the Scottish Church, but she needed active spiritual assistance to give substance to her ideas and to provide an example from which the Scottish Church could draw inspiration to reform itself. Evidence for her activities,

---

[26] Huneycutt, 'The idea of the perfect princess', 65, 76, 77.
[27] See Duncan, *Making of the Kingdom*, 124; Baker, 'A nursery of saints'; Huneycutt, 'The idea of the perfect princess'; Wall, 'Queen Margaret of Scotland'; Clancy and Crawford, 'Formation of the Scottish kingdom', 86–90.

St Margaret's Gospel-book

It is rare for any item that can be linked personally to one of Scotland's medieval rulers to have survived to the present, rarer still for it to be an object that is described in detail in a medieval source. In his *Life of Margaret*, the queen's biographer described how her favourite book of extracts from the Gospels, which was bound in a jewel-encrusted case, dropped from its holder while her entourage was crossing a stream and fell unnoticed into the water. When it was retrieved, other than some slight water-staining of the edges of the folios and the end-papers, it was found to be miraculously unharmed. Long thought to have since been destroyed, in the 1980s an eleventh-century volume in Oxford University's Bodleian Library, known unromantically as *MS Lat. liturg. f.5, 3v*, was identified as the queen's personal gospel-book. Added to its opening pages was a Latin poem in a late-eleventh-century style of handwriting which described the dropping of the book into the water and its miraculous recovery almost undamaged, detail which appears to confirm the identification.

The book does not contain full texts of the Gospels but only selections from each one set out as a kind of devotional guide. Although such selections were not uncommon in eleventh-century England,[28] the contents of this volume do seem to reflect some of Margaret's personal faith and devotional interests. A short reading from Matthew 20:17–19, for example, is identified with the Mass of the Holy Cross and tallies with her recorded interest in the cult of the Holy Cross and personal possession of a relic of the True Cross. There is also a range of readings with strong female associations, particularly relating to the women who were closely involved in Christ's ministry. While hardly a manifesto for a programme of religious reform, the Gospel-book does provide us with insight into what Margaret considered to be the Christian duties of a queen, wife and mother.

however, is slender; only three contemporary or near-contemporary sources survive that throw light on her efforts. The first of these is a letter to Margaret from Lanfranc, archbishop of Canterbury, a key figure in the reform movement in north-western Europe, in response to a now lost letter from her.[29] Lanfranc's letter is a mixture of humility

[28] Rushforth, *St Margaret's Gospel-book*, 67–76.
[29] Anderson (ed.), *Early Sources*, ii, 31–2.

and eagerness to exploit a situation that was very much to Canterbury's advantage, for he was keen to extend his spiritual overlordship throughout Britain and the invitation from Margaret to offer his advice in the reform of the Scottish Church was too good an opportunity to miss.[30] Lanfranc reveals that Margaret had sought his spiritual guidance on a personal level and his practical spiritual assistance more generally. Accordingly, he sent three Benedictine monks from Canterbury to form the basis of a monastery attached to the church of the Holy Trinity at Dunfermline. In this letter, then, we have the roots of Margaret's reputation as an importer of alien religious traditions and an active supporter of the Benedictine reform movement. It was a quiet beginning, and some historians have dismissed it as small scale and unimaginative,[31] but it was Scotland's first direct experience at home of the reformed monasticism that was underpinning the general reform of the western European Church. While it did not take root in the same manner as contemporary Benedictine reform in England, Margaret's personal appeal to the foremost reformist cleric in Britain underscores her knowledge of the profound changes sweeping Christendom.[32] That fact alone should warn against too casual a dismissal of her significance as a reformer in her own right.

The second document is the Worcester version of the *Anglo-Saxon Chronicle*. In its surviving form, it has been amended and expanded up to the 1130s and it has been noted that this may have been done with a Scottish destination particularly in mind as many of the new entries concern Scottish affairs.[33] One of its last entries, referring to the arrival of Margaret and her family in Scotland in 1067, is clearly an obituary and eulogy of the queen, praising and recording her personal qualities and achievements. It describes her as

> destined to increase the glory of God in that land, to turn the king aside from the path of error, to incline him together with his people towards a better way of life, and to abolish the vices which that nation has indulged in in the past – all of which she subsequently accomplished.[34]

---

[30] Davies, *The First English Empire*, 38–9.
[31] For example, Donaldson, *Scotland: Church and Nation*, 18.
[32] Barrow, 'Benedictines, Tironensians and Cistercians', 196.
[33] *Anglo-Saxon Chronicle*, xxxvii–xxxix, 214.
[34] Ibid. 201.

Figure 1.1 Dunfermline Abbey, Fife: the nave of the twelfth-century abbey occupies the site of the church where Malcolm III and Margaret were married and where Margaret planted the first Benedictine colony in Scotland.

The chronicle adds that this marriage turned Malcolm from a life of Godlessness and violence. Descending into sermonising, it comments that

'Very often an unbeliever is sanctified and saved by a righteous woman; and in like manner, a woman by a devout husband . . .'

> This aforesaid queen performed many useful works in that land to the glory of God, and proved of great advantage to the monarchy, as was to be expected from her ancestry.[35]

Stress, then, was placed on her spiritual role and influence over both Malcolm and Scotland generally, but a second notion was introduced; her English and imperial ancestry. Margaret was being presented as a woman of deep personal piety, but her reforms in all spheres were linked explicitly to her Englishness.

The third document was perhaps a source for some of the ideas expressed in the *Anglo-Saxon Chronicle*. This, the longest and most detailed of the three, is the *Vita Margaretae* (or *Life of Margaret*), written by a Durham monk named only as 'T',[36] but identifiable on other grounds as Turgot, the queen's chaplain and confessor, who later became a Benedictine monk at Durham. More than any other document, this *Vita* has provided the basis upon which later narrative accounts of the queen's life, personality and achievements were constructed. And therein is the problem: it is a unique source and many of its details cannot be tested against other pieces of evidence. Analysis of the *Vita*, therefore, has ranged from uncritical and absolute acceptance of its testimony, through qualified acceptance of selected aspects, to outright rejection on the grounds that its purposes are not to record the facts of the period 1068–93 but to provide an agenda for later purposes. For example, it has been commented that the programme of the one ecclesiastical council mentioned in the *Vita* reads suspiciously like the business with which Turgot was later concerned as bishop-elect of St Andrews.[37] In whatever way it is read, however, it is evident that Margaret assumed an active role in ecclesiastical affairs that exceeded what was expected of a woman in that period.

Turgot's *Vita* has a threefold character: it is part eulogy, part panegyric and part hagiography. We are told its purpose: it was written by Margaret's former chaplain and confessor at the request of her daughter, Matilda, wife of Henry I of England. The aim is to set out the holy life of the one as an example and inspiration to the other, who then occupied a similar position to her mother as the influential wife of a powerful king. If the *Vita* was composed largely with an eye towards Margaret's future canonisation it could be dismissed as not very compelling for,

---

[35] Ibid. 201–2.
[36] Anderson (ed.), *Early Sources*, ii, 59–88.
[37] Duncan, *Making of the Kingdom*, 122–3.

while her personal spirituality and devotion to the Church is laid out clearly, it contains little evidence of the kind of miracle-working that characterised the dossiers compiled to support later medieval cases for canonisation.[38] But that is to miss a critical point. Turgot's emphasis is on the living example of the queen and the nature of her life and works. Establishment of the saintly life of his subject was altogether more important than listing miracles. To modern eyes – and that qualification is important – her personality is not altogether attractive, but Margaret's actions, character and views are not those of a modern woman and can seem contrived, scheming and hypocritical to the cynical inhabitants of the thoroughly secular early twenty-first century. In twelfth-century terms, however, Margaret's persona was the model of regality, authority and spirituality, an educated woman who offered leadership, discipline and good example.

Deeper reading of the *Vita* reveals even greater significance in the manner in which Margaret is presented. The language used to describe her behaviour draws heavily on the terminology of male rule, both in the royal sense and also in the manner of an abbot. Indeed, much in the presentation depends on the language and sense of the Rule of St Benedict. The Latin terminology makes it clear that Margaret was an extraordinary figure. For example, in the account of the council of the Scottish Church which she convened, she is recorded as having posed *questiones* and delivered *sententiae* to the assembled clerics. These words carry far greater nuanced meaning in Latin than their literal modern English translation as questions and sentences, for *questiones* were the conventional, formal philosophical interrogative tools issued by teachers in the schools of the earlier medieval period and *sententiae* were the 'answers' provided by specific texts drawn from scripture and the writings of the early Christian fathers which illuminated doctrine. Margaret was here being presented as a master (in both the educational and hierarchical senses) and teacher, using her superior knowledge of the doctrines of faith to correct senior Scottish clerics of their errors. It is a remarkable statement of Margaret's standing, for these doctrinal issues were normally the preserve of an exclusively celibate male ecclesiastical elite. If we accept the *Vita* at face value on this point, then it elevates Margaret into that tiny circle of the influential female religious headed by the more famous twelfth-century mystic, Hildegard of Bingen.

Turgot also uses magisterial and abbatial imagery when discussing Margaret's relationship with her sons. It is clear that she ruled the

---

[38] Anderson (ed.), *Early Sources*, ii, 80, 81.

household fairly, with a firm hand that bordered on severity; characteristics of the ideal abbot. Turgot approved of her instructions to the steward of the household to whip any of her male children who were naughty in any way. Indeed, Turgot saw her behaviour as 'scrupulous care . . . [through which] they excelled in uprightness of manners many who were more advanced in age: they were ever kind and peaceful amongst themselves, and the younger everywhere showed honour to the elder'. Turgot also described how she took a personal hand in their religious instruction, and it has been commented repeatedly that it was this, rather than any of her own religious reforms in Scotland, that was to provide the seed-bed for the ecclesiastical reform that swept through Scotland in the twelfth century.

But what of her more tangible impact on Scotland? What Turgot describes has been dismissed as small-scale changes, mainly centred on the royal household and her own family, occasionally spilling over to important monastic sites. Some of the most striking visual changes were in the anglicising of the royal household accomplished by the queen and the group of Anglo-Saxon nobles who settled in Scotland after 1070.[39] We have no clear idea how many such settlers were involved in total, but they likely numbered tens rather than hundreds. They did, however, exercise great influence over the Scottish court, where Margaret was their most significant ally, and through their settlement in south Fife and Lothian, where Malcolm was increasingly locating his principal power base. Their presence changed the whole ethos of royal power, turning the style of Malcolm's kingship culturally towards the south and away from the Gaelic and Scandinavian traditions that had been established in Scotland since the early 900s. Part and parcel of this process were material changes to the quality of life at the court. While these may seem cosmetic rather than fundamental – gold and silver plate, fine foods and wines, English and Continental fashions in clothing and hairstyles, wall hangings, and so on – and cannot be seen to percolate further than the immediate circle around the royal household, it is clear that Margaret was introducing the sophistication of the Old English and Hungarian courts to Scotland. Turgot claims that these innovations stimulated trade, as foreign merchants were encouraged to come to Scotland to provide the exotic finery, food and wines which were central to the development of the new court style. Imported luxuries gave a semblance of the opulence of the foreign environment in which she had been raised and, more practically, supported the elaborate ceremonial tradition which

---

[39] Clancy and Crawford, 'Formation of the Scottish kingdom', 87–9.

had surrounded Anglo-Saxon kingship. These innovations can be denigrated as insignificant tinkerings with the fabric of Scottish elite culture and society, but analogy with modern concerns over cultural colonialism should serve to remind us of the far-reaching consequences of such changes and the often savage reactions which they can provoke.

Although we can question how strong Margaret's influence was outwith the royal household, it seems that it acquired a distinctly Anglo-Saxon flavour. This aspect was strongest in the names given to Malcolm's sons by Margaret: Edward, Edmund, Æðelred, Edgar, Alexander and David, the first four named, as discussed earlier, after Margaret's male progenitors back to her great-great-grandfather and the last two receiving the names of the greatest pagan ruler and the Biblical Hebrew epitome of Godly kingship. The significance of this new naming pattern should not be underestimated, for the adoption of foreign name-forms into an ancient lineage with an established repertoire of male names has been recognised elsewhere in Europe as symbolic of quite profound cultural reorientation. Closer to home, of course, the virtual disappearance of Anglo-Saxon elite personal names within two or three generations of the Norman Conquest is testimony to the social impact of a cultural minority in a society where so many other aspects of native English culture survived. The impact on personal names within the Scottish royal house was profound. With the sole exception of Margaret's great-grandson, Malcolm IV, no subsequent male of the royal line descended from Malcolm and Margaret bore a Gaelic name.[40]

Of course, the 'brief paroxysm' of Anglo-Saxon names and the eventual adoption of Norman-French forms after David I in the Scottish royal house were somewhat accidental. The naming of the boys from Edward to Edgar may have occurred when Duncan or Donald, Malcolm's sons by Ingibjorg, were expected to succeed in Alba while Margaret's sons were intended to provide a restored West Saxon monarchy in England. The change in pattern represented by Alexander was necessary because the next name in the pedigree was another Edmund, but it could also have marked recognition that all realistic possibility of regaining the English throne had passed, perhaps as early as the failure of Earl Waltheof's 1076 rising and more certainly by the time of the 1080 settlement. At the most basic level, however, the new names introduced through Margaret represented the opening of dramatic new cultural vistas to what was still a profoundly conservative Gaelic kingdom.

---

[40] Bartlett, *Making of Europe*, 274–7.

RECONFIGURING OLD STRUCTURES

Only tantalising glimpses survive of internal Scottish affairs during the final decade of Malcolm's reign; indeed, there is little historical evidence of any kind to throw light on the 1080s in the northern British Isles generally. The decade probably witnessed the apogee of Malcolm's power, where his ruthless elimination of internal rivals in the first half of his reign finally bore fruit and his lordship over mainland Scotland north of the Forth passed unchallenged. Hints that the situation was less tranquil than the dearth of documentary evidence implies can perhaps be seen in the cryptic statement that 'Donald, Malcolm's son, king of Scotland . . . ended his life unhappily', wording taken to refer to a violent or unshriven end.[41] Who this Donald was is also unclear, but it is assumed generally that he was Malcolm's younger son by Ingibjorg.[42] The reference to his death is linked indirectly in the annals to the 'happy' death of the ruler of Moray, but we cannot imply from this that Donald perished in an otherwise unknown conflict between the two rival royal lineages. The Moray dynasty had remained quiescent after a punitive expedition by Malcolm in 1078 in which the king 'captured the mother of Maelslæhta . . . and all his best men, and all his treasures, and his livestock . . .'[43] This 'Maelslæhta' is assumed to be Máel Snechta mac Lulaig, the son of Malcolm's defeated rival of 1058, but with the only other surviving notice of Moray's affairs being Máel Snechta's brief obituary in 1085, which states simply that he 'happily ended his life',[44] a phrase that could mean that he had died in monastic retirement or merely that he had died peacefully, confessed and absolved, there is no firm evidence for continued conflict throughout Malcolm's reign. Whatever the case, it was nearly another half century before the Moray claim to the Scottish throne of Scotland troubled Malcolm's descendants.

Further north, Malcolm's stepsons, Pál and Erlend, continued their joint rule of Orkney and Caithness.[45] In contrast to the troubled and bloody relationship between their father, Thorfinnr the Mighty, and his elder brothers and nephews, that between Pál and Erlend was close and friendly, at least until their sons reached adolescence and began to

---

[41] *Annals of Ulster*, s.a. 1085; Anderson (ed.), *Early Sources*, ii, 47, note 1; Duncan, *Kingship of the Scots*, 55.
[42] Duncan, *Making of the Kingdom*, 118.
[43] *Anglo-Saxon Chronicle*, D, s.a. 1078.
[44] *Annals of Ulster*, s.a. 1085.
[45] Forte, Oram and Pedersen, *Viking Empires*, 278.

contend for influence within an earldom that had contracted greatly since their grandfather's time. Thirteenth-century saga tradition, looking with hindsight at the bitter feuding which convulsed the Norse earldom in the later eleventh and twelfth centuries, presented the brothers' joint rule as an interlude of peace and stability. It is clear, however, that their time witnessed the progressive erosion of the extended sphere of authority which Thorfinnr had projected into northern mainland Scotland, the Hebrides and Man. Despite the silence of the sources, or perhaps because of the absence of any comment on the subject in *Orkneyinga Saga*, it should not be assumed that Pál and Erlend presided passively over this decline, but through the 1070s and 1080s Guðrøðr Crobán's gradual extension of power in the Western Isles supplanted the influence of the Orkney earls. This protracted and seemingly unstoppable decline was one factor behind the animosity between the earls' sons and led eventually to the partitioning of the earldom. The prolonged political instability in Orkney and Caithness probably concerned Malcolm, for there was always the risk of other external agencies capitalising on the earldom's weakness to intrude its own influence or the instability and disorder spilling over into the peripheral districts of Malcolm's own kingdom. So long as Orkney's problems remained internal, however, he may have regarded a weak and divided earldom as better than the alternative which had been represented by Thorfinnr's aggressive imperialism.

Where the collapse of Orkney's power was more dangerous for Malcolm was in the Western Isles, where new and less predictable powers were seeking to extend their influence or to build personal domains. The most significant of these new powers was the sea kingdom of Guðrøðr Crobán, a great-grandson of Óláfr Cuarán, the mid-tenth-century king of Dublin and York.[46] The tightening of Guðrøðr's grip on Man and the Isles since the 1070s created a new power bloc which significantly realigned the old political and military balance of the western maritime zone which had prevailed since the early 1030s. He had burst onto the scene in the mid-1070s when he started his bid to conquer Man, but it is clear that this operation was launched from an existing power base in the Hebrides and the dynasty of kings which he established maintained a kingdom that spanned Man and the Isles down to its extinction in 1265.[47] Guðrøðr had personal ties with Islay, where he later died, and it is likely that he had first established his kingship in the islands in the vacuum created by the implosion of Orkney under Pál and Erlend. His ambitions

---

[46] Oram, *Lordship of Galloway*, 19.
[47] *Chron. Man*, s.a. 1056 = 1075 x 1076.

were not insignificant, and his reign reached a climax in the early 1090s with brief control of Dublin, to which he had ancestral claims. Guðrøðr's territorial ambitions, however, were perhaps driven by economic considerations as much as personal aggrandisement, directed at establishing control over the nexus of the complex of trade routes that extended up the western side of the British Isles, stretching from the Mediterranean to Scandinavia, Iceland and Greenland. The wealth flowing along these trade arteries attracted many opportunist rulers, as did the strategic location of the political core of the new kingdom; Man provided a platform from which the whole of the Irish Sea littoral could be dominated.

The threat posed by Guðrøðr to powers in mainland Britain and Ireland is shown in the challenges made to his position. In 1087, the son of Donnchad mac Ua-Eochada, king of Ulaid (eastern Ulster), in alliance with two men described as 'sons of the son of Ragnall' who were probably either sons of another Guðrøðr, a former king of Dublin, or of Echmarcach mac Ragnaill, who between the 1030s and early 1060s ruled a kingdom that periodically encompassed Dublin, Man, parts of western Galloway and the Hebrides, failed to oust Guðrøðr from Man.[48] These grandsons of Ragnall represented a bid to restore the tenth- and earlier eleventh-century domination of Man by Irish-based dynasts, but the Ulaid involvement points to concerns over a Manx–Isles axis running through the North Channel, echoing the response from the Ulstermen in the early 1000s to the threat of Dublin-based control of that strategic seaway. Where this situation more directly affected Scottish interests was in Galloway and the Clyde estuary, where evidence from place names and church dedications points to expansion of Isles-based Norse-Gaelic influence, if not of actual Isles-based rule, through the tenth and eleventh centuries.[49] For Malcolm, an aggressive new expansionist power in the territory west of Strathclyde was hardly a welcome development. The growth of Guðrøðr's power in the Solway region, moreover, revived the spectre of an intrusion of a major western maritime power into mainland British politics in emulation of earlier Dublin-based kings. Fear of such an outcome may have lain behind some of the developments in the last five years of Malcolm's reign.

A final change in this region was represented by the extension of Norman power up the north-west coast of England. After weathering the crisis of 1088, William II set out first to consolidate the Norman grip on the core of his kingdom then to tighten his hold on the peripheral

---

[48] Oram, *Lordship of Galloway*, 16–19.
[49] Brooke, *Wild Men and Holy Places*, 74–6.

regions of the north and west and to project his lordship beyond his borders into Wales, the Irish Sea region and Scotland. By the end of the 1080s, Malcolm faced new lordships west of the Pennines which brought Norman power to the edge of the Lake District, while in Northumberland Robert de Mowbray was settling knights whose castles turned notional Norman lordship of the region beyond the Tyne into a reality.[50] Should the Anglo-Scottish peace break down, the Scots would find the military landscape of northern England entirely transformed.

WHEN WORLDS COLLIDE

The causes of the breakdown of the 1080 settlement are not entirely clear, although Durham tradition alludes to steadily mounting quarrels between Malcolm and William Rufus rather than any single event.[51] Hostility may have been further aggravated by application in northern England of the border policy which William had introduced on the Welsh March, whereby Norman lords were encouraged to expand their territory at the expense of the Welsh princes. William's breach in early 1091 of the accommodation which his father had reached with Edgar Æðeling, the seizure of Edgar's estates and the prince's flight to Scotland presumably brought matters to a head, for it was immediately after these events that Malcolm struck: in May 1091, while William was in Normandy, the Scots crossed the border.[52]

Rather than aiming simply for plunder as in his previous raids, Malcolm had territorial objectives. For the first time in his career he committed himself to prolonged sieges, settling down outside Durham, which was identified as the key to control of Northumbria above the Tees.[53] Clearly, Malcolm saw the threat to his kingdom and more specifically to Lothian in the recent enhancement of Norman power in the region, and his invasion might have been a serious attempt to roll back the Norman advance and establish a comfortably deep buffer zone. William Rufus moved swiftly to counter Malcolm's attack, returning from Normandy in late August accompanied by his brother, Duke Robert, with a large fleet and army. Abandoning the siege of Durham in the face of their

---

[50] Kapelle, *Norman Conquest of the North*, 145–8; Lomas, *North-East England*, 24–5.
[51] *De Miraculis et Translationibus Sancti Cuthberti*, in Symeon of Durham, *Opera Omnia*, ii, 338.
[52] *Anglo-Saxon Chronicle* E, s.a. 1091; Duncan, *Kingship of the Scots*, 46.
[53] Kapelle, *Norman Conquest of the North*, 148–9.

advance, Malcolm withdrew towards Scotland with William's army close on his heels before turning to face the enemy in Northumberland.[54] As with Malcolm's two previous confrontations with the Normans there was no fighting, Edgar Æðeling and Duke Robert brokering a deal by which Malcolm became William's 'man' and gave oaths of submission in return for William's promise to restore estates which Scottish kings had formerly held in England. Edgar, too, won reconciliation with William for his part in securing the treaty. Peace had been restored without great bloodshed and everyone, except the Northumbrians, had gained from the new deal, but between Malcolm's opportunism and William's mercurial character few could have considered it to be more than a temporary settlement.

By early 1092 William was reneging on his side of the treaty. The issue at stake was the land which he had promised to restore to Malcolm in England, which was not, as traditionally believed, the district that subsequently became known as Cumberland but twelve vills whose revenues had been assigned by Anglo-Saxon kings to Scottish rulers for their support when they came to the English court.[55] William's seizure of Cumberland, construction of a castle at Carlisle and establishment of an English colony in the surrounding territory may simply have set the seal on Malcolm's conviction in the English king's bad faith, but it was not the cause of the breach between them. William's occupation of north-west England has, nevertheless, often been presented as directed against Malcolm, based on the unproven assumption that Cumberland had been under Scottish overlordship since before c. 1070. As discussed earlier, however, there had been other developments in the Irish Sea region which perhaps influenced William's policy, not least Guðrøðr Crobán's seizure of Dublin in 1091.[56] Rather than being aimed solely at closing Scottish access to the trans-Pennine routes into Weardale, Teesdale and the vales of northern Yorkshire, William was tightening his grip on his vulnerable north-west flank with its substantial population of Hebridean-Norse origin and closing off this entry point to potential seaborne enemies in just the same way that Edward the Confessor in the 1050s and his predecessors back to the time of Edward the Elder in the early tenth century had done.[57] It should be remembered that as recently as 1085 there had been a threatened invasion of England by a

---

[54] *Anglo-Saxon Chronicle* E, s.a. 1091; Symeon of Durham, *Opera Omnia*, ii, 218.
[55] Oram, *David I*, 35 and notes.
[56] Oram, *Lordship of Galloway*, 20; Duffy, 'Irishmen and Islesmen', 93–133.
[57] See Higham, 'Scandinavians in north Cumbria', 37–51.

Scandinavian power, and that the Irish Sea coast had in the past been one route by which such invaders had entered the kingdom. In many ways, Guðrøðr's ambitions in western Britain, which overlapped with William's own schemes for extending Norman power into northern Wales and reasserting the influence which his predecessors had enjoyed in Ireland, demanded more of the English king's attention than did Malcolm's seemingly predictable behaviour.

There is nothing in the events of the first nine months of 1093 to indicate that the year would end in violence and bloodshed. Malcolm preferred negotiation to conflict, sending messengers to William to seek the honouring of the 1091 treaty. William, for his part, was happy to negotiate and adopted a conciliatory tone, calling Malcolm to a meeting at Gloucester in August, sending hostages as surety for his safety whilst in England and finally sending an impressive mission led by Edgar Æðeling to persuade him to attend. There is nothing in this behaviour to suggest that William planned to humiliate Malcolm and both parties may have seen a diplomatic solution to the current tension. Malcolm was expecting a negotiated settlement and took the opportunity presented by his progress through England to build other diplomatic bridges. At Durham, which only two years earlier he had subjected to a six-month siege, he was an honoured attendee at the laying of the foundation stones of Bishop William of St Calais' cathedral.[58] Ostensibly there could have been few clearer indications of his pragmatic coming to terms with the political realities of northern England than his presence at that ceremony, but Malcolm's attendance carried an altogether deeper symbolism.

It has been suggested that Malcolm understood that the willing support of the Durham community would help his designs for the future government of Scotland and the place of his sons by Margaret within any succession settlement.[59] In the light of later arrangements which saw Lothian assigned to younger brothers or designated heirs it is possible that Malcolm considered a role there for Edward, his eldest son by Margaret. Durham, with its historical claims to large parts of Lothian and its established position as the most important political entity in the region between the Tees and Tweed, could have eased that development. Despite his past attacks on it, Malcolm and his family had cultivated close ties with Durham, establishing a *conventio*, or agreement of spiritual friendship, with the community; in return for the

---

[58] Symeon of Durham, *Opera Omnia*, i, 195.
[59] The discussion is based on Wall, 'Malcolm III and the foundation of Durham Cathedral', 326–37.

community's prayers for him and his family, Malcolm gave protection to their persons and property. The key to the relationship was Margaret and the West Saxon royal blood which she transmitted to her children, for Durham had developed a close relationship with that dynasty, which was presented in Durham historical tradition as having secured control of Northumbria through the favour of St Cuthbert. For Durham, the fostering of this link offered the opportunity to rekindle its interest in its former position north of Tweed. For Malcolm, perhaps with an eye to Edward's future position in Lothian, the bond not only opened the door to influence south of Tweed but also south of the Tyne, reviving the notion of the old Northumbrian province of Bernicia which stretched from the Forth to the Tees. Unfortunately for Malcolm, William Rufus also understood the importance of Durham for the stability of the northern frontier and had carefully cultivated the community since 1088. Both kings, therefore, were in competition for the saintly patronage of Cuthbert, with Malcolm seeking to use it to extend his family's influence south of Tweed and William aiming to keep the limit to the north of the river.

Less than a fortnight after leaving Durham, any optimism that Malcolm's honourable treatment to date might have raised was dashed by his reception at Gloucester; William refused to meet with him or allow the business between them to be discussed until Malcolm formally submitted his claims before the English court. Malcolm saw this as a calculated insult, for William was proposing to treat him like one of his barons rather than an independent king. In 1091, Malcolm had become William's 'man', not his vassal, an important distinction that he was not prepared to yield on. Instead he responded with a demand that the issue be settled by a joint meeting of the courts of both kingdoms assembled on the border between them, claiming, possibly with an occasion like the 927 meeting between King Æðelstan and the northern and western British kings in mind, that this was the established tradition.[60] William refused to yield and Malcolm hurried home to nurse his wrath.

William Rufus was no political naïf and cannot have been surprised at Malcolm's reaction, but there is no reason to suggest that he deliberately manoeuvred Malcolm into warfare with the intention of destroying an irritant.[61] Certainly, he could not know that Malcolm would raid northern England so late in the season, given that in recent experience Scottish invasions began in May or June. Malcolm, however, gathered his men

---

[60] *Anglo-Saxon Chronicle*, s.a. 926 = 927; Smyth, *Warlords and Holy Men*, 201.
[61] Oram, *David I*, 37.

immediately upon his return to Scotland and, accompanied by Edward, his eldest son by Margaret and his designated heir, had entered England in late October. Reverting to his former harrying tactics, Malcolm ravaged Northumbria at the onset of winter, threatening starvation to the peasant communities whose stores were plundered or destroyed. To the Anglo-Saxon chronicler, the brutality of the raid did the king no credit and, considering his recent friendly involvement with Durham, exposed him as a faithless hypocrite.[62] Suitable punishment, however, was swiftly meted out, for on 12 November as the raiders headed homewards they encountered outside Alnwick a force of Norman knights commanded by Robert de Mowbray. Accounts of what then occurred are conflicting, ranging from an open battle to an ambush and treachery in the course of a parley, but most agree that the encounter ended with Malcolm's death at the hands of the earl's nephew, Arkil Morel.[63] Twenty-five years of opportunism, brinkmanship and calculated violence in Anglo-Scottish relations had been brought to a bloody climax.

---

[62] *Anglo-Saxon Chronicle* E, s.a. 1093.
[63] Oram, *David I*, 37–8.

CHAPTER 2

Kings and Pretenders, 1093–1136

In its longer-term consequences, the fatal rout at Alnwick on 13 November 1093 was perhaps one of the most significant events for the development of Scottish kingship and the kingdom. It was an event that produced crisis and opportunity in equal measure, triggering an internal reaction against the agents and symbols of the regime that had dominated Scottish political and cultural life for almost a quarter of a century and encouraging greater external interference in the royal succession. Indeed, the question of the succession was of central importance to both these internal and external forces, and the issue, if our surviving sources can be relied upon, dominated Scottish affairs for the next four decades. For the Scots in November 1093, the immediate question was who was to be the next king.

THE ISSUE OF SUCCESSION

According to Symeon of Durham, Malcolm had designated Edward, the eldest of his six sons by Margaret, as his preferred heir.[1] It has been suggested that Malcolm recognised the inherent weaknesses of traditional Scottish succession practice which prevented the formation of a 'single, strong royal dynasty', by which an adult male collateral of the current king was nominated during his predecessor's lifetime as his *tanaiste*, or heir, and that he instead favoured adoption of linear, father-to-eldest-son inheritance.[2] Regardless of whether or not primogeniture guaranteed the creation of such a single, strong dynasty, there is also no clarity over

---

[1] Symeon of Durham, *Opera Omnia*, ii, 222.
[2] Barrow, *Feudal Britain*, 131; Barrow, 'Scotland, Wales and Ireland', 585.

the nature of 'traditional' succession practice in the eleventh century. Malcolm himself had succeeded as the eldest son of his father, but only after killing his two predecessors as king, the latter of who was stepson of the former, but both had possessed independent personal claims based on differing collateral branches of the wider royal house. Malcolm's own father, moreover, was descended from a female line and had succeeded his grandfather, Malcolm II, who had carved his way to the throne over the corpses of his rivals. All that can be said of the 'traditional' practice is that it recognised the 'kingworthiness' of collaterals and bears comparison with Gaelic Irish succession practice which accepted the potential to be king in men who stood within three generations of their last ancestor who had held the kingship; nowhere is it said that a son could not directly succeed his father. Father-to-son succession should probably be regarded as already commonplace, and elements of such a linear tradition can be seen at work in the earlier eleventh century, but the elective principle in so-called tanistry (succession by *tanaiste*) allowed for the contingency of ensuring an adult successor where the current ruler either lacked sons or his sons were in some way incapable of rule. The only point on which Malcolm appears revolutionary in his attitude to the succession is that Symeon tells us that he designated an heir during his lifetime and that he, Edward, happened to be the eldest of his sons by Margaret. This action, it is implied, reveals that Malcolm favoured primogeniture over tanistry.[3]

If Symeon of Durham was correct, and it must be remembered that his account reflects the wider early-twelfth-century chronicle tradition which stressed the primacy of Malcolm's sons by Margaret over those of Ingibjorg, Malcolm's designation of Edward was not a straightforward application of primogeniture. First of all, Edward was not Malcolm's eldest son. Second, Edward was *designatus*, marked out as heir, which carries the implication that while Edward was to hold precedence the right of others to succeed was also being acknowledged.[4] Why Edward was given precedence over Duncan, his elder half-brother, is nowhere explained, but the suggestion that Duncan's preference to remain in England after his release and knighting by William II in 1087 had made him less acceptable to the Scots is perhaps correct. How Malcolm's decision in favour of Edward was received by the Scottish nobility is unknown, but the rejection of Malcolm's younger sons in 1093 should not be interpreted as a reflection of wider resentment over the king's

[3] Barrell, *Medieval Scotland*, 14.
[4] Duncan, *Kingship of the Scots*, 54.

supposed attempts to foist an alien tradition on a culturally conservative kingdom. The source of the conflict over the succession in 1093 came not from any backlash over the introduction of innovatory practices but from the fact that not only had Malcolm himself been slain but his designated heir, Edward, the eldest of his sons by Margaret, also had perished. The premature death of the king represented crisis enough for the royal family but the loss of his preferred adult heir overturned the secure plan for the succession and threw open the issue of royal inheritance; there was no *tanaiste* waiting to step into the breach. In the climate of uncertainty that followed the king's death the crisis escalated for his remaining children, for the one commanding personality around whom the family could have united and support might have rallied, Queen Margaret, died at Edinburgh only four days after her husband.[5] Leadership of the seven remaining children of Malcolm and Margaret devolved upon their second son, Edmund, who was aged about twenty, but that role did not automatically bring the candidature for the throne, which had been held by his elder brother. Others, whom Malcolm had sought to bypass in the royal succession in favour of his second family, stood ready to press their claims.

In a largely fanciful account, the fourteenth-century chronicler John of Fordun described how Edmund and his brothers were besieged in Edinburgh after their mother's death by supporters of their uncle, Malcolm's younger brother Donald Bán.[6] This later tradition probably telescopes into a single episode the events of what was a brief civil war fought to determine the destination of the kingship, but it serves to emphasise that without the commanding personalities of Malcolm and Margaret to overawe opposition their children and their circle of 'foreign' supporters were isolated and beleaguered in a largely hostile land. According to the *Anglo-Saxon Chronicle*, the Scots 'drove out all the English who had been with king Malcolm',[7] a move probably more politically inspired than motivated by racial or cultural concerns. Who these 'English' were we are not told, and there is little evidence for a substantial influx of exiles, at least into *Scotia* proper north of the Forth.[8] One, Merleswain, may have been the grandfather of a second man of that name who held Kennoway and Ardross in Fife in the later twelfth century, and another, Archill, was the father of Alfwin who served as

---

[5] *Life of Margaret*, in Anderson (ed.), *Early Sources*, C. 13.
[6] *Chron. Fordun*, ii, 209.
[7] *Anglo-Saxon Chronicle* E, s.a. 1093.
[8] Duncan, *Making of the Kingdom*, 122.

rannaire ('divider of the meat' or distributor of food in the royal household) to kings David I and Malcolm IV, and held land in Midlothian in the mid-twelfth century.[9] Neither was a significant landholder, the only émigré to make an impact at that level being Cospatric in eastern and southern Lothian. The reaction, then, should probably be seen as a purging of the individuals who had dominated Malcolm's household rather than the expulsion of an intrusive, colonising elite.

Although the second half of Malcolm's reign had seen a steady shift in his interests and in the political and cultural weight of his kingdom towards Lothian, the centre of Scottish power still lay north of the Forth, and it is clear that there, amongst the Gaelic magnates upon whose support royal power was founded, Edmund and his siblings had few friends. Instead of the untested, presumably largely unknown and probably culturally alien children of the late king, the nobility looked more favourably on the comfortably Gaelic figure of his brother. How favourably is indicated by the wording of the *Anglo-Saxon Chronicle* report of his succession, which states that the Scots 'elected' him as their king.[10] Donald's succession has been presented as a usurpation,[11] which implies that his kingship was illegal and broke a legitimate linear succession under primogeniture by the next of Malcolm's sons, but as the eldest surviving male of the royal kin, Donald could have been a preferable candidate for the kingship under Gaelic succession practice. He has also been presented as a 'stop-gap king', put forward because the senior heir of line, his nephew Duncan, had absented himself from the scene by remaining in England after 1087.[12] His role as a space-filler, moreover, has been heightened by the stress placed on his lack of a direct male heir, which makes the assumption that this man supposedly elected as senior collateral of the previous king would then have expected to be succeeded linearly by one of his own sons. It is an assumption, moreover, which misses the precedent of the succession of a grandson established by Malcolm III and Donald Bán's own father, Duncan I, whose right was transmitted through his mother; Donald may have had no son, but he had at least one daughter, whose descendants resurfaced in the late thirteenth century as competitors for the throne following the death of King

---

[9] Oram, 'Patterns of lordship, secular and ecclesiastical', 110. For Merleswain, see *St Andrews Liber*, 258–9 and Barrow (ed.), *RRS*, ii, no. 137. For Alfwin mac Archill, see Barrow (ed.), *RRS*, i, 32, and no. 164.
[10] *Anglo-Saxon Chronicle* E, s.a. 1093.
[11] Barrell, *Medieval Scotland*, 14.
[12] Duncan, *Kingship of the Scots*, 53–4.

Alexander III.[13] If he were a stopgap, for whom did his backers believe he was acting, considering the supposition that Donald was the symbol of Gaelic conservatism? Duncan and his half-brothers were all associated with innovation, Norman and English, and the contemporary chronicles make it clear that they and their foreign friends were the targets of Donald's supporters, who drove them out of the kingdom. If any of Malcolm's sons were to be accepted into the kingship then he would either have to stage a coup with military backing or have been culturally rehabilitated in the eyes of the native nobility.

DONALD III BÁN, DUNCAN II, EDMUND AND EDGAR

Between 1093 and 1097, four men competed for the throne, each backed by different groups of internal and external supporters. Donald Bán, while he may have obtained the domestic backing necessary to secure the kingship in the winter of 1093–4, had failed to capture or otherwise neutralise his potential rivals and, given his and his brother's experience after Macbeth's coup against their father in 1040, must well have understood the multiple threats that this failure posed to his position. He may also have failed to gain acceptance as king over all of the territories held by his elder brother, for Symeon of Durham says only that 'all the English who had been of the king's household were expelled from *Scotia* [author's italics]'.[14] Symeon and the northern English chroniclers are usually careful in their use of terminology to define the Scottish kingdom, with *Scotia* normally being applied to the core territories north of the Forth only. The wording in Symeon's *Historia Regum*, therefore, could imply that in Lothian, where powerful 'English' like Cospatric held sway, Donald's rule was not accepted, or accepted only grudgingly. The degree of the threat that this situation posed was compounded by the fact that although Malcolm and Margaret's remaining sons were still immature – the eldest was aged about twenty at most – they had mature support in the form of their maternal uncle who had three decades of experience as an exile and royal pretender. Standing *in loco parentis*, Edgar Æðeling was bound by duty of kinship to pursue the best course to win his nephews their heritage. He well understood the realities of power in the British Isles and knew that, ironically, there was only one

[13] Barrow, *Robert Bruce*, 145; Young, *The Comyns*, 16.
[14] Symeon of Durham, *Opera Omnia*, ii, 222.

individual who could marshal the resources necessary to overthrow Donald.

Probably early in 1094 the refugees arrived at the court of William Rufus in England, coming as supplicants to the man whose actions had led indirectly to their father's death. By that time, however, their appeal had been pre-empted by their half-brother, Duncan, who had already approached William 'who he served as a knight' and asked that he be granted the kingship (*regnum*) of his father.[15] William granted his request and in return Duncan swore to him 'such pledges (*manrædene*) as the king demanded of him'.[16] When Symeon of Durham composed his *Historia Regum* in the early 1100s, the language used had become more overtly 'feudal', with Duncan swearing fealty (*fidelitatem juravit*) to the English king.[17] Regardless of the different connotations of the language used, what seems clear from both accounts is that Duncan apparently accepted that the right to the kingship of the Scots was in King William's gift. Thoroughly imbued by Norman culture and its ethos of lordship and service, Duncan took an entirely different view of the relationship between the kings of the Scots and the English than his father had done. To use an anachronistic term, Duncan had accepted explicitly the fact of the superior lordship of the English king over Scotland.

Although William had graciously acknowledged Duncan's right to the kingship of the Scots, he took no further personal action to secure the throne for his protégé, for he himself was about to embark on campaign in Normandy and had no resources to spare. 'With such English and French [Norman] assistance as he could obtain', Duncan marched north in May 1094, defeated his uncle's supporters and established himself as King Duncan II in Donald's stead.[18] Like Donald, however, he had failed to eliminate his chief rival, an omission that proved to be his undoing. Duncan's victory in May was illusory, for a rising saw the destruction of most of his military retinue and he was forced to accept that if he were to remain as king he must do so without English or Norman aid. While some of the Scots may have been prepared to accept Malcolm's eldest son on those terms, others were not, and within a few months Donald and his supporters had defeated and slain his nephew.[19]

---

[15] Symeon of Durham, *Opera Omnia*, ii, 222.
[16] *Anglo-Saxon Chronicle* E, s.a. 1093.
[17] Symeon of Durham, *Opera Omnia*, ii, 222.
[18] *Anglo-Saxon Chronicle* E, s.a. 1093.
[19] *Anglo-Saxon Chronicle* E, s.a. 1094. *Chron. Kings of Scots* F, 175, attributes Duncan's slaying to Máel Pedair, earl of the Mearns, at Mondynes in the Mearns.

Amongst those who brought about Duncan II's death was apparently his eldest half-brother, Edmund.[20] According to the twelfth-century *Gesta Regum Anglorum* of William of Malmesbury, Edmund had 'bargained [with his uncle] that he should receive half the kingdom'.[21] The deal was apparently not that Edmund and Donald would be joint kings, but that Edmund should receive a territorial interest and recognition that he would succeed his uncle; Edmund, in effect, was being named as *tanaiste*. Why Edmund broke ranks with his family and made this arrangement with Donald is unclear, but it has been speculated that Duncan had made a similar agreement with him but had been forced to break it when the Scots had required Duncan to expel all his 'English and French' supporters.[22] There is also the possibility that Edmund understood, and was unwilling to accept, the implications of his half-brother's oath of fealty to William Rufus. He was, however, the only one of the brothers to seek an understanding with Donald, for his remaining siblings looked instead to King William and possibly within weeks of Duncan's death Edmund's younger brother, Edgar, had received the gift of the kingship of the Scots from the English king.

At first it appeared that Edgar would receive as much backing from William Rufus as Duncan II had, but in spring 1095 Robert de Mowbray, earl of Northumberland, rebelled and King William's military efforts quickly focused on the north of his realm. In May 1095, William marched north and, apart from some brief journeys south to settle crises elsewhere in England, spent most of the second half of the year in the region. In the course of this extended campaign, Edgar was sent north of the River Tweed, possibly to secure Lothian and cut off Earl Robert from either flight north in the footsteps of Earl Cospatric or from aid from Donald Bán and Edmund, or to give substance to his claims to possession of the province by William's gift.[23] He may not have penetrated further into Lothian than was necessary to give voice to claims of possession, for on 29 August 1095 he was back at Norham in Northumberland, where he granted a charter to the Church of Durham which set out his status in explicit terms. It describes him as 'son of Malcolm king of Scots, possessing the whole land of Lothian and kingship of Scotland by gift of King William my lord and by paternal heritage . . .', a wording which carefully differentiates between the notionally 'English' province

---

[20] *Annals of Ulster*, s.a. 1094.
[21] William of Malmesbury, *Gesta Regum Anglorum*, i, 726–7.
[22] Duncan, *Kingship of the Scots*, 55–6.
[23] Oram, *David I*, 46; Duncan, *Kingship of the Scots*, 56–7.

held by gift of the English king and the kingship itself.[24] Although his hereditary right was proclaimed by this charter, it also made explicit the fact that he was King William's man. Furthermore, the occasion on which this charter was issued probably served as a public declaration of Edgar's dependence on William, for it has been suggested that it was a meeting of William's court in which Edgar's rights to Lothian had been formalised.[25] If that is the case, then Edgar had accepted the implications of judgement in William's court which Malcolm had refused to countenance at Gloucester in 1093, and William had secured recognition both of his status as Edgar's lord and of the formalising of the boundary between their kingdoms on the River Tweed. As one historian has expressed it, 'William had put a legal written line through the . . . Patrimony of St Cuthbert',[26] defining the Tweed frontier in a way his father had never been capable of doing, and ending the possibility of a creeping extension southwards of Scottish interests through the Durham bond that Malcolm III may have envisaged. For Edgar, there may have been even more visible signs of his relationship with William by a formal investiture with a symbol of his kingship, possibly by William giving him a crown.[27] Beyond this symbolic shadow-play kingship, however, Edgar was still nowhere near turning his nominal position into reality.

It was a further two years before William Rufus could turn his attention again towards Scotland and help Edgar secure the throne. In October 1097, Edgar Æðeling led an army into Scotland and, after some hard fighting, drove out Donald and set up his nephew as 'king and vassal to King William'.[28] Only Donald is mentioned in the sources, and there is wide variation in his reported fate ranging from simple expulsion, or capture, blinding and imprisonment, to death. Of Edmund nothing is said until William of Malmesbury reported his capture, imprisonment for life and eventual death, while the *Chronicle of the Kings of Scotland* reported that he had entered religion and died as a Cluniac monk at Montacute Abbey in Somerset.[29] Edmund, the black sheep of the flock, was carefully expunged from the record, his place in the succession glossed over to the point that by the thirteenth century he would be referred to simply as

---

[24] Duncan, *Kingship of the Scots*, 56.
[25] Wall, 'Malcolm III and Durham', 335–6.
[26] Ibid. 336.
[27] Duncan, *Kingship of the Scots*, 57.
[28] *Anglo-Saxon Chronicle* E, s.a. 1097.
[29] William of Malmesbury, *Gesta Regum Anglorum*, i, 726–7; *Chronicle of the Kings of Scotland* E, 131–3.

having died without leaving an heir, with no reference made to either his bid for the kingship or his seniority over Edgar.

THE REIGN OF EDGAR, 1097–1107

Edgar was now free of serious rivals, the only potential future challenge resting with his half-nephew William, son of Duncan II. William had been passed over for the kingship in 1094, presumably because of his youth (Duncan had possibly remained unmarried until after his release from being a hostage in 1087) or because he was in the hands of Donald and Edmund following his father's death. In 1097 he was probably still a child. While there was an attempt in the later twelfth century to discredit his branch of the royal family through labelling Duncan as a bastard son of King Malcolm there was no such imputation made against him in the eleventh century (see p. 64). The possibility remained, therefore, that William could claim the throne in future or be nominated as *tanaiste* by Edgar. The succession, however, was not the most pressing question on the mind of a young man in his very early twenties, for Edgar did have two younger brothers in addition to William. Nevertheless, given the crises which had wracked the royal family and kingdom since 1093, it appears that provision was made immediately in the form of his younger brother, Alexander. He, it seems, was given land and titles in *Scotia* proper which marked him out as the designated successor, and he evidently remained in Scotland with Edgar whilst their youngest sibling, David, went south to make a career in England.[30]

With the internal political situation in Scotland stabilised and its young king having openly accepted his status as client of the English crown, William Rufus was probably well satisfied with the new prescription of power on his northern frontier. Although Ranulf Flambard, bishop of Durham 1099–1128, succeeded in aggravating Edgar with his abrasive manner and claims to spiritual and temporal lordship over a broad swathe of the Southern Uplands, that was a matter of 'local difficulties' and the more general relationship between Edgar and William remained secure. Few demands were placed on Edgar as a consequence of his submission to William, although the possible provision for payments to him for his support when visiting the English court suggests that some service was envisaged. The only evidence which survives of

---

[30] Where these lands were is unknown. Alexander was referred to as 'earl' in 1104 (John of Worcester, *Chronicon*, iii, 106–7).

Edgar's attendance on William, however, was in May 1099 when he carried the sword at William's crown-wearing at Westminster.[31] This act, as Professor Duncan suggests, was a sign of honour to Edgar, but also emphasised his status as a *fidelis* of the English king. For William, however, what was probably more important than symbolic demonstrations of his lordship over the Scottish king was the security which a complaisant Edgar gave to England's northern frontier. Although he did not revisit the north after 1095, William remained concerned with the security of the region and the political settlement in Scotland and establishment of the Tweed frontier coincided with the tightening of Norman power in English-held south Cumbria. Carlisle, which he had occupied in 1092, was placed soon afterwards in the hands of either Ivo de Taillebois, whom William had been establishing as a key landholder in what became southern Cumberland and northern Westmorland, or Ranulf Meschin, who was lord of Carlisle early in the reign of Henry I.[32] Carlisle formed the core of a military system, reinforced by a civil colonial settlement, which stretched from the Solway to Morecambe Bay. While strengthening of the land frontier towards Scotland was probably a central consideration in the development of this structure, as the Roman frontier of nearly a millennium earlier demonstrates, the long coastal flank of Cumberland was a porous boundary beyond which lay an unpredictable maritime zone through which various powers were extending their influence.

Down to 1094, the Irish Sea and Hebrides had been dominated by the kingdom of Guðrøðr Crobán. As discussed earlier, the growth of Guðrøðr's power sent shockwaves through mainland Britain and Ireland, for he established his lordship over most areas of formerly Scandinavian colonisation in the maritime west, a development that placed him in competition with rulers from England and Orkney to Connacht and Munster. For William Rufus, a single power in control of this zone was threatening enough, but the consequences of the disintegration of that power were graver still. It was not just the political turmoil in Scotland, therefore, that drew William's attention northwards, for almost in parallel with the upheaval that followed the death of Malcolm III there had been similar upheaval in the kingdom of the Isles. The trigger for the disturbance had been Guðrøðr's expulsion from Dublin by Muirchertach ua Briain, king of Munster, who followed his success there with an attack

---

[31] Duncan, *Kingship of the Scots*, 58 and note 23.
[32] Barlow, *William Rufus*, 298, 321; Scott, 'Strathclyde 1092–1153', 15, 17.

on Man.[33] Guðrøðr himself died on Islay the following year, whereupon the kingship passed to his eldest son, Logmaðr.[34] In Man, like Scotland, there was no established succession system and Logmaðr soon faced challenge from his younger brother, Harald, whom after a short and bloody civil war he captured, blinded and castrated. By 1096, however, opposition to Logmaðr's rule had coalesced around a second young brother, Óláfr, whose supporters looked for external assistance to secure him the throne. Rather than to William Rufus, however, the dissident Manx nobles turned to the king of Munster, whose ascendancy in Ireland and naval strength through his control of Dublin gave domination of the Irish Sea. Muirchertach, however, attempted to install his nephew as king over Man, a move which helped accelerate the disintegration of Guðrøðr's maritime empire rather than stabilising the already volatile situation. In 1097–8, the tensions between the rival factions erupted into open warfare.[35]

It was into this already disturbed zone extending from Lewis to Man that a second major player moved decisively. Possibly as early as 1096–7, the Norwegian king Magnus Barelegs had been showing interest in asserting lordship over the Scandinavian western colonies in the British Isles. What his ultimate ambitions were we do not know, and modern English historians have downplayed the significance of his campaign, largely because it had little lasting impact,[36] while its significance for Scotland has been viewed with some ambivalence for similar reasons.[37] Eleventh- and twelfth-century chroniclers, however, viewed it differently, William of Malmesbury later claiming that Magnus, the grandson of King Haraldr Harðráði who had died at Stamford Bridge in 1066 whilst making a bid for the English throne, had his eyes set on William Rufus's crown.[38] Probably in 1097, he had attempted to install his own vassal king in the Hebrides but the islanders rose against him and killed him before the year ended. In 1098 King Magnus himself arrived with a fleet, having first descended on Orkney where he ended the feud between earls Pál and Erlend and their families by the simple expedient of sending both earls as prisoners to Norway while taking their feuding sons, Magnus Erlendsson and his younger brother Erling, and Hákon

---

[33] Duffy, 'Irishmen and Islesmen', 108.
[34] *AFM*, s.a. 1095; *Chron. Man*, 6.
[35] Oram, *Lordship of Galloway*, 20–1.
[36] For example, Barlow, *William Rufus*, 389–90; Bartlett, *England 1075–1225*, 72.
[37] Duncan, *Making of the Kingdom*, 127; Barrow, *Kingship and Unity*, 106.
[38] William of Malmesbury, *Gesta Regum Anglorum*, i, 480–1.

Pálsson, with him on campaign further west.[39] He then cruised south through the Isles, plundering, receiving submissions and finally establishing himself in Man, where Logmaðr was captured and expelled.[40] In a single operation, Magnus had recreated the island core of the kingdom assembled by Guðrøðr, but he had also begun to extend his power into mainland Britain where he reduced the chieftains of Galloway to tributary status.[41]

Magnus may have intended to redraw permanently the political map of the north-western British Isles, but the early-thirteenth-century saga references to a formal agreement with a Scottish king (named as Malcolm, not Edgar) is a post-Norwegian civil war confection designed to validate Hákon IV's imperial pretensions in the Hebrides.[42] Some memory, however, of an agreed past division of territory may be preserved in the saga account, hence the need for the 1266 Treaty of Perth, but that division may have been considerably older than the traditional account suggests, for the *Heimskringla* version of Magnus Barelegs' saga's labelling of the west-coast sea lochs as 'Scotland's Firths' seems to hark back to the later ninth century when Argyll was still truly the land of the Scots.[43] For the Scots, the main effect of the campaign may have been the reversal of fifty years of influence in Orkney. No evidence survives for how Edgar viewed the assertion of Norwegian royal power in Orkney. There is reason to suspect that *Orkneyinga Saga*'s claim that Magnus Erlendsson turned to a Scottish king for aid in regaining his heritage in Orkney is a projection backwards into the late eleventh century by the saga's compiler of the political relationship between the earldom and the Scots in the later twelfth and early thirteenth centuries. If such an approach occurred and was acted on, however, it may reflect an effort by Edgar to counterbalance Norwegian power in the north. The effects of a reassertion of active Norwegian royal interest in Orkney and the Isles have been little considered by modern scholars and it has been implied that any 'treaty' cost the Scots little as they had no significant interest in either area. But the thrust of Scottish royal policy throughout the eleventh century had been to neutralise Orkney. Magnus Barelegs'

---

[39] Forte, Oram and Pedersen, *Viking Empires*, 278–9.
[40] *Chron. Man*, s.a.1077 = 1097 ? and s.a. 1098; *Heimskringla*, Magnus Barelegs' Saga, Chapters 8 and 9. Logmaðr joined the First Crusade and died during the campaigns in Syria-Anatolia.
[41] *Chron. Man*, s.a 1098; *Heimskringla*, Magnus Barelegs' Saga, Chapter 9.
[42] *Morkinskinna: The Earliest Icelandic Chronicle of the Norwegian Kings (1030–1157)*, ed. and trans. T. M. Andersson and K. E. Gade (Cornell, 2000), 301–2.
[43] Anderson (ed.), *Scottish Annals*, 106.

actions overturned that policy and introduced a new and aggressive dynamic into the already complex political mix. Although Edgar's interests have been said from the limited evidence for his activities to have been rooted in south-eastern Scotland,[44] it is unlikely, given his determination to secure his throne after 1093 and his later cultivation of friendship with Muirchertach ua Briain, that he would have simply handed domination of Orkney and the Western Isles to Magnus if they had been under his effective lordship. Regardless of how ephemeral Scottish royal influence was in the islands, Edgar cannot have welcomed the imposition of rule over the region by a predatory power such as Norway. In the west, however, the events of 1098 apparently delivered the islands into Norway's control, a position reflected in the later boundary of the diocese of the Isles.[45] Despite persistent tradition and popular images of King Magnus being carried across the isthmus at the neck of Kintyre, the peninsula was not included in the settlement, but control of the Clyde islands brought Norwegian lordship within striking distance of the western fringes of Scottish royal authority. If the consequences of Magnus's campaign caused Edgar qualms, for his lord, King William, they were distinctly threatening and Edgar's summons to carry the sword at Westminster in May 1099 was perhaps motivated by serious concerns.

William had cause to be concerned. Amongst Magnus Barelegs' successes had been the extension of his lordship into Gwynedd, perhaps reasserting the client-patron relationship which Guðrøðr Crobán had had with King Gruffudd ap Cynan. In Anglesey, Magnus defeated a Norman force commanded by Hugh de Montgomery, earl of Shrewsbury, and Hugh d'Avranches, earl of Chester, who had been enthusiastically prosecuting William Rufus's policy of expansion into Wales.[46] Coupled with his acquisition of the Western Isles and the interest which Magnus had shown in Galloway, it must have seemed from this event that Norway posed a real threat to England. Magnus was heir to the claims of Haraldr Harðráði, and the 1069–70 war with Svein Estrithson and Knút IV's threatened invasion of 1085 had shown that Danish interest in England had not died with Harðaknútr in 1042. In the mid-twelfth century William of Malmesbury, never one to miss the opportunity to enlarge on

---

[44] Duncan, *Making of the Kingdom*, 126–7.
[45] *Heimskringla*, Magnus Barelegs' Saga, Chapter 10; Oram, *Lordship of Galloway*, 42.
[46] *Heimskringla*, Magnus Barelegs' Saga, Chapter 10; *Anglo-Saxon Chronicle* E, s.a. 1097 = 1098. For Normans in north Wales, see Duffy, 'Irishmen and Islesmen', 110 and note 82; Barlow, *William Rufus*, 389–90.

a tale, asserted that Magnus intended to take the English throne and, to underscore the scale of the forces ranged against William, claimed that Harold, son of Harold Godwinsson, the last Anglo-Saxon king, joined the Norwegians.[47] Certainly, by early 1099 Magnus dominated the northern Irish Sea and Hebridean zones, which gave a powerful position on England's exposed western flank. This was a threat that William needed urgently to contain, and it is probably no coincidence that the establishment of Ranulf Meschin's lordship of Carlisle occurred at this time.

If *Orkneyinga Saga* is to be relied upon, it was then that Magnus Erlendsson approached Edgar and secured Scottish support for his establishment as earl in Caithness. Such support is claimed by *Orkneyinga Saga* to have been a device used by earlier Orkney earls to win their place in the succession, as in the case of Thorfinnr in the 1020s and 1030s, but Magnus's submission to Edgar may have established a precedent for rival earls in future to seek legitimation from either the kings of Scots or the kings of Norway. As it happened, neither Scottish readiness to back Magnus Erlendsson nor the defences of England were ever put to the test, for in summer 1099 King Magnus left for Norway and did not return until 1103 for a campaign that had Ireland as its primary objective. He sought to establish his youngest son, Sigurðr, as king over a maritime domain stretching from Dublin to Orkney, and attempted to secure his son's position through a marriage alliance with Muirchertach ua Briain, his chief potential rival for influence in the Isles. Magnus's designs, however, collapsed when he was killed in a skirmish in Ulster and Sigurðr, repudiating his wife, hurried to Norway to stake his place in the kingship alongside his elder brothers. In his wake he left a vacuum which none of the traditional powers in Britain or Ireland was able to fill, and instead the decade that followed Magnus Barelegs' death witnessed the rise and fall of a succession of petty, personal empires carved out by ambitious warlords.

In mainland Britain William II's death in 1100 and the seizure of the English throne by his younger brother, Henry I, had changed the political situation dramatically. No evidence survives of any renewal by Edgar to Henry of the submissions that he had made to William, but there is no reason to suppose that he did not recognise Henry's lordship. The personal relationship between the two men, moreover, was tightened in November 1100 when Henry married Edgar's sister Edith (who took the Norman name Matilda). The bond that this formed with

---

[47] William of Malmesbury, *Gesta Regum Anglorum*, ii, 570–1.

the Scottish king, however, was not Henry's primary concern, it being Edith-Matilda's West Saxon blood and the added legitimacy that gave to their children as rulers of England that he wanted. Edgar was probably not consulted on Henry's decision to marry her, or on the marriage of his other sister, Mary, to Count Eustace of Boulogne. Together, these personal bonds probably gave Henry confidence in the security of his northern frontier at a time when his priorities were fixed firmly on establishing his control first in England and then in Normandy.

Henry needed Edgar's support at the start of his reign, for in 1101 Henry's elder brother, Duke Robert of Normandy, invaded England intending to wrest the crown from him. The invasion was supported by an important segment of the Anglo-Norman nobility, led by the Montgomery brothers under the leadership of Robert de Bellême, earl of Shrewsbury. Earl Robert and his younger brother, Arnulf, earl of Pembroke, were powerful figures in the Welsh March and south Welsh region, and looked to their west for allies once King Henry began to take the initiative in the war with Duke Robert's supporters. Earl Robert forged alliances with the Welsh princes but was unsuccessful with King Magnus in Norway, while Arnulf forged a marriage alliance with none other than Muirchertach ua Briain, king of Munster, who sent a fleet to aid his son-in-law.[48] Despite the collapse of the Montgomeries' rebellion by late summer 1102, Muirchertach continued his support for Arnulf until a trade embargo imposed by Henry I forced a settlement,[49] although the reappearance of Magnus Barelegs in the west in 1103 may have been a more pressing determinant in ending his engagement with affairs in England. Clearly, in these circumstances the western seas continued to present a threat to English security and the Scots must surely have figured in Henry's calculations for the defence of his exposed western frontier. This situation may provide the context for Edgar's dealings with Muirchertach, which in 1105 saw him give the present of a camel to the Irish king.[50] There are, however, indications that Edgar was involved in more than just the giving of exotic gifts.

Muirchertach's involvement in the Montgomery rebellion in 1102 was one facet of an ambition not only to project his kingship throughout Ireland but to extend his influence within the western maritime zone of

---

[48] For the Montgomeries see Hollister, *Henry I*, 154–63. For Arnulf's marriage see Candon, 'Muirchertach ua Briain', 411–13.
[49] William of Malmesbury, *Gesta Regum Anglorum*, ii, 738–9; Candon, 'Muirchertach ua Briain', 412–13.
[50] *Annals of Innisfallen*, annal AI1105.7.

the British Isles. Although the unexpected death of Magnus Barelegs in 1103 deprived him of the ally he had hoped would bring him mastery of Ireland, it also created an opportunity that Muirchertach moved quickly to exploit. If the argument is accepted that the epic Irish narrative *Cogadh Gaedhel re Gallaib* (The War of the Gaedhil with the Gaill), written ostensibly as a celebration of the achievements of Muirchertach's early-eleventh-century ancestor, Brian Boruma, was actually intended to parade Muirchertach's ambitions and achievements, then its claims for the extent of 'Brian's' influence indicates that Muirchertach had attempted with some success to fill the void left by Magnus.[51] According to the *Cogadh*, the king of Munster received 'royal tribute from the Saxons and Britons, and the Lemhnaigh [the Lennox] [and] Alba, and Airir-Gaedhil [Argyll], and their pledges and hostages along with chief tribute'.[52] Even allowing for some hyperbole in this claim, it seems that Munster influence stretched into the south-west Highlands and Clyde estuary region and it was possibly as a response to this that Edgar's dealings with Muirchertach occurred. Muirchertach, too, as part of his bid for mastery of all Ireland, was building up his power in the Isles, where his nephew was installed as king by 1111. While Edgar had perhaps withdrawn Scottish interest from there in 1098, it is unlikely that he was a disinterested observer as Norwegian influence down the western flank of his kingdom was subsumed into the expanding sphere of Muirchertach's ambitions.

These upheavals in the west should also be viewed in conjunction with developments further north. In c. 1104, Hákon Pálsson arrived in Norway from Orkney and won a grant of the earldom from Sigurðr and his brothers.[53] *Orkneyinga Saga* indicates that what he received was 'the authority pertaining to his birthright', while the saga of Magnus's sons implies that, as the kings' candidate, he received all that both his father and his uncle had held, and that when he returned to Orkney he aimed to establish his control over the whole earldom, excluding his kinsmen.[54] Shortly afterwards, however, Magnus Erlendsson claimed his share with backing from King Edgar, the men of Caithness and his family's supporters in Orkney. There was, however, no showdown between the cousins but rather a mediated settlement which received royal approval in Norway and seemed to provide a basis for coexistence between the rival

---

[51] Candon, 'Muirchertach ua Briain', 407–8, 413–14.
[52] *Cogadh Gaedhel re Gallaib*, 136–7.
[53] Anderson (ed.), *Early Sources*, ii, 138.
[54] *Orkneyinga Saga*, 88; Anderson (ed.), *Early Sources*, ii, 138.

earls.[55] Although, as we shall see later, this accord eventually collapsed spectacularly, the deal held for over a decade and stabilised a region that had long played a key role in the wider stability or otherwise of northern and western Britain. Orkney, it can be inferred from the timing of this settlement, was considered by Edgar and, possibly, by Henry I as providing a potentially significant check to Muirchertach's ambitions in the maritime west. Indeed, evidence for close diplomatic relations between Henry I and Hákon's son, Earl Pál II, in the 1120s and early 1130s perhaps stresses the continuing perceived importance of Orkney for the security of the wider sphere of Anglo-Norman lordship in the British Isles.[56]

Frustratingly, almost all evidence for developments in Edgar's reign relates to external affairs and issues of lordship or the domination of territories peripheral to the core of the Scottish realm. The internal affairs of the kingdom are, by contrast, shrouded in obscurity other than in respect of religious matters and ecclesiastical politics. Even in those areas, however, there is little of substance to illuminate Edgar's church policy and such that there is remains highly ambiguous.[57] Neither did he display any great generosity as a patron of Scottish monasteries, making only a handful of grants to existing communities.[58] Nor did he make any new monastic foundations, the Church of Coldingham with which he is most closely associated being refounded as a minster in the older Anglo-Saxon rather than Continental Benedictine tradition.[59] As his involvement with Coldingham indicates, greater interest was shown by Edgar in the affairs of Durham, where he was the community's 'most generous benefactor', at least until Bishop Ranulf Flambard soured relations after 1099.[60] Edgar's connection with Durham dated from at least 1095, before he became king, when he issued a charter at Norham that bestowed on it Coldinghamshire and Berwickshire. As Geoffrey Barrow has observed, this was an 'extremely liberal, indeed prodigal' grant which Edgar later pruned back with the withdrawal of Berwickshire, but even the residue of the original grant and compensation given to Durham secured him a place in the prayers of the monks on a par with Bishop William of St Calais, the founder of the Benedictine community and builder of the

---

[55] *Orkneyinga Saga*, Chapter 44; Thomson, *History of Orkney*, 57–8.
[56] William of Malmesbury, *Gesta Regum Anglorum*, ii, 740–1.
[57] Duncan, *Making of the Kingdom*, 127.
[58] *Dunfermline Liber*, no. 1.
[59] Duncan, *Making of the Kingdom*, 127; Cowan and Easson, *Medieval Religious Houses*, 55–6.
[60] Piper, 'The Durham cantor's book', 87; Barrow, 'The kings of Scotland and Durham', 315.

new cathedral.[61] Edgar may have been disenchanted with Bishop Ranulf but the Durham monks still regarded the king as a friend and patron.

Viewed from the perspective apparently presented by Edgar's patronage of Durham and veneration of St Cuthbert, it has been commented that the 'total impression is of a king with an outlook formed in the tradition of the Old English state, concerned with Lothian ... and the saint who was patron of Lothian – Cuthbert. Edgar seems to have cared little for *Scotia*, little for his Celtic inheritance in state and church'.[62] To an extent this appears a valid judgement, for the cultivation of Durham points to the continuation of his father's policy in the closing years of his reign, which stressed the West Saxon heritage of Edgar's mother and siblings and sought to use that link to increase political leverage with the Durham community and, perhaps, secure its support for Scottish southward expansion. William Rufus had attempted to halt that ambition in 1097 and contain Edgar's aspirations north of Tweed, but, as David I was later to demonstrate, kings of Scots still had their hearts fixed on southward expansion. The southward gaze of Edgar and his brothers, however, may be more apparent than real and for Edgar probably reflects the artificial imbalance of the surviving documentation. His endowment of Dunfermline, for example, suggests that his religious patronage was not as narrow and unimaginative as has been postulated. Similarly, the southward-directed tunnel vision implied for his political interests and disinterest in his Gaelic heritage – typified by his supposed abandonment of the Hebrides to Magnus Barelegs – find only circumstantial support in the historical record. Edgar's involvement in Orcadian politics and his dealings with Muirchertach ua Briain and Irish ambitions in the maritime west show his reign in an altogether different light. His misfortune to die in Edinburgh might strengthen the impression of a king with personal horizons defined by the limits of old Northumbria, but his burial in Dunfermline alongside his mother and elder brother points equally to a ruler who kept more than a toehold in his ancestral realm.

ALEXANDER I 1107–24

As with Edgar before him, the reign of Alexander I is poorly documented. The principal consequence of this lack of hard evidence has

---

[61] Barrow, 'The kings of Scotland and Durham', 315; Piper, 'The Durham cantor's book', 87.
[62] Duncan, *Making of the Kingdom*, 127.

been an absence of detailed critical evaluation of his contribution to the development of the kingdom, with the result that his reign has been presented as an uneventful pause before the revolutionary career of his younger brother, David.[63] What does survive, however, suggests that a reappraisal is overdue, for Alexander's reign witnessed a series of highly significant developments in the political culture of the kingdom and, as importantly, saw a step change in the pace of reform of Scotland's religious structures.[64]

Although Alexander succeeded the childless Edgar seemingly without challenge from dynastic rivals, his reign still started on a sour note with friction with his surviving brother, David. Edgar, it seems, preserving the distinction between *Scotia* as the seat of the kingdom and the appended territories of Lothian and Cumbria, had bequeathed part of these southern districts to his youngest brother.[65] Having recognised as far back as 1095 that Lothian was held by gift of the English king, it is unlikely that Henry I was not consulted and, given David's relationship with Henry, it is probable that his agreement was secured. Whatever had been settled between Edgar, Henry I and David in the past, however, Alexander in 1107 was understandably reluctant to yield up so valuable a portion of his kingdom and a later twelfth-century account of Ailred of Rievaulx implies that David only obtained his inheritance with the threat of military intervention by his English friends.[66] Possession of the bequest, however, came slowly, for Henry could not aid David until 1109 at the earliest, and it is likely that any campaign to force Alexander into compliance occurred after July 1113.[67]

David's disputed inheritance does not mean that Alexander and Henry were at daggers-drawn for over six years until the territory was conceded. Alexander's relationship with Henry, however, was more ambiguous than Edgar's had been with William Rufus. The wording of the *Anglo-Saxon Chronicle*'s account of Alexander's accession '. . . as king Henry granted him' suggests a previous agreement,[68] but there is no evidence for a formal submission to Henry. In 1114, however, Alexander served in Henry's north Welsh campaign,[69] possibly to regain favour

---

[63] Most general histories barely mention Alexander I. See Ditchburn and MacDonald, 'Medieval Scotland', 123, or Pittock, *A New History of Scotland*, 41–2.
[64] For discussion of religious developments, see Chapter 10, 332, 337, 354.
[65] Duncan, *Kingship of the Scots*, 60.
[66] Ailred of Rievaulx, *De Standardo*, 192–5.
[67] Oram, *David I*, 60–2; Duncan, *Kingship of the Scots*, 60–5.
[68] *Anglo-Saxon Chronicle*, E, s.a. 1107; Duncan, *Kingship of the Scots*, 60.
[69] *Brut y Tywyssogion*, 115.

after the crisis of the previous year and possibly signalling that he had been required to make a more formal demonstration of his acceptance of English lordship in 1113. Alexander's marriage to Henry's bastard daughter, Sibylla, may also have been arranged around this time, perhaps to sweeten the bitterness of his capitulation over David's inheritance. Rather than being a disparagement of Alexander's kingship, marriage to one of Henry's many illegitimate children was a mark of favour and distinction which signalled the importance of the husband in Henry's schemes.[70] If the marriage did occur at this time, then it represents a final component in a sequence that confirmed Henry's dominant relationship with the Scottish royal house. Not only had Alexander been brought into a close personal relationship with Henry, but David, too, had been tied to the English king through territorial awards, the grant of the title of earl in England and marriage to Henry's cousin, the widowed Matilda de Senlis.

Alexander certainly needed to be mollified, for later documents show that David secured upper Tweeddale and Teviotdale in what had been Northumbrian Lothian and the whole of Cumbria from the Lennox to the Solway, except for the district around Carlisle annexed by William Rufus in 1092. Over this territory he ruled as *princeps et dux* or *Cumbrensis regionis princeps* (prince of the Cumbrian region) and *princeps Cumbrensis* (prince of the Cumbrians), titles which accord him quasi-regal status rather than the kingship of the former kingdom.[71] The style 'prince' suggests inferior status subject to a superior lordship, presumably intended to be the kingship of the Scots, but within his principality there is little sign that David deferred to anyone. But David's domain extended beyond Cumbria into Tweeddale, Northumbrian territory until the early eleventh century. In this zone, he was not *princeps*, for King Alexander's over-riding authority was recognised in various property transactions involving subject matter within its bounds.[72] The difference in treatment between the two is striking, and it is this that points to a change between what Edgar bequeathed to David in 1107 and what he obtained with Henry's aid in 1113.

How that change occurred is possibly explained in a later account, where Robert de Bruce of Annandale is given an invented speech in which he castigates an ungrateful David. "'You yourself, o king", he

---

[70] For Henry's diplomatic use of his bastards, see Oram, *Lordship of Galloway*, 59–61; Cokayne et al. (eds), *Complete Peerage*, xi, appendix D, 105–21. The exact date of the marriage is unknown (*Gesta Regum Anglorum*, ii, 476).
[71] Lawrie, *Early Scottish Charters*, 45, 46. See also Duncan, *Kingship of the Scots*, 60–1.
[72] Lawrie, *Early Scottish Charters*, nos XXVI, XXVII, XXXI and XXXII.

said, "when you demanded from your brother Alexander the part of the kingdom which at his death your . . . brother [Edgar] bequeathed to you, obtained without bloodshed *all that you wanted* through fear of us'" [author's italics].[73] The tension between what was 'bequeathed' and what was 'wanted' has been interpreted as implying that what Edgar had willed David was Cumbria but what he obtained was both Cumbria and lower Tweeddale.[74] Why that change occurred is unknown, but it is possible that David wanted control of land to which his wife-to-be had ancestral claims as the heiress of Earl Waltheof. From Henry I's perspective, it gave a territory along the length of the Anglo-Scottish frontier to a man who looked more readily to him than to his brother in Scotland, and removed it from the hands of Alexander, whose public display of veneration for St Cuthbert in 1104 suggests he may still have looked to extend Scottish influence southwards.[75] Matilda's paternal heritage comprised the forfeited earldom of Northumberland and claims to former Northumbrian territories in southern Cumbria, Teviotdale, Tweeddale and Lothian. Henry's arrangement of the marriage with Matilda may have been motivated as much by placing a dependable ally in the frontier zone between the kingdoms as by a wish to reward a loyal servant and brother-in-law.[76] More surely than William Rufus in 1095, Henry aimed to draw a line under Scottish ambitions in Northumbria.

Henry may have been content with the settlement of his northern frontier but the relationship between Alexander and David may have suffered. Ailred implies that Alexander hated and persecuted his younger brother.[77] No other source records such animosity, but it is possible that Alexander was never reconciled to losing lower Tweeddale. There is, however, contemporary Gaelic poetic evidence to suggest that the division was resented by some amongst the elite of southern Scotland:

> It's bad what Mael Coluim's son has done,
> dividing us from Alexander;
> he causes, like each king's son before,
> the plunder of stable Alba.[78]

---

[73] Ailred of Rievaulx, *De Standardo*, 192–5.
[74] Duncan, *Kingship of the Scots*, 61–5.
[75] John of Worcester, *Chronicon*, iii, 107.
[76] Duncan, *Kingship of the Scots*, 65. See also Kapelle, *Norman Conquest of the North*, Chapter 7.
[77] Ross, PhD thesis, 182.
[78] Translation from the Gaelic of 'A Verse on David Son of Mael Coluim (c. 1113)', in Clancy (ed.), *The Triumph Tree*, 184.

After 1113, dealings between the brothers were conducted in a formal manner, and David seemed to be excluded from any active role in Alexander's kingdom.[79] Moreover, David does not appear to have been regarded as Alexander's heir as Alexander had been for Edgar. Alexander was married and presumably believed that he would father a son to succeed him, and an alternative heir was available in his nephew, William son of Duncan.[80] Until the childless Queen Sibylla's death in 1122, however, both brothers had other concerns to preoccupy them.[81]

At the time of David's accession to the throne in 1124 we are told that Alexander had held the kingship *laboriosissime* (with very great effort).[82] While much of that effort may have been directed towards the reform of religious life in his kingdom, there is little detailed evidence for secular issues. Two areas, however, which had emerged as concerns in Edgar's reign troubled Alexander also. The first was the Hebrides, where Muirchertach ua Briain's attempts to extend Munster influence into the void left by the collapse of Magnus Barelegs' lordship was possibly checked by the violent seizure of the kingship of the Isles in 1111 by his own nephew and rival, Domnall mac Taidc.[83] Domnall may have been allied with Muirchertach's foe, Domnall mac Lochlainn, king of Cenél nEógain, head of a family that also had a long tradition of involvement in the affairs of western Scotland and the Hebrides. This extension of Irish power in the western seaways may have been as welcome to Alexander I or Henry I as the prolonged instability of the region since 1103; the establishment in c. 1112 as king in Man of Guðrøðr Crobán's youngest son, Óláfr, who had been raised at the English court, has every appearance of a counter-move by Henry to place a dependable vassal in this strategic zone. For Alexander, the instability of the west threatened an overspill of violence into his own kingdom, either from predation by opportunist war bands operating in the region or from dynastic rivals drawing military support from the same sources. Whatever the tensions between Alexander and Henry over David's Cumbrian lands, it is likely that the two kings cooperated in an effort to roll back Uí Briain or meic Lochlainn influence in the Irish Sea and Hebrides. Indeed,

---

[79] Duncan, *Kingship of the Scots*, 61–2.
[80] *Scone Liber*, no. 1; Lawrie, *Early Scottish Charters*, no. XXXVI; Duncan, *Kingship of the Scots*, 59–60.
[81] William of Malmesbury, *Gesta Regum Anglorum*, ii, 725–7; Symeon of Durham, *Opera Omnia*, ii, 205.
[82] Symeon of Durham, *Opera Omnia*, ii, 275.
[83] *Annals of Innisfallen*, s.a. 1111. For alternative interpretations of these events, see Candon, 'Muirchertach Ua Briain', 407 and Duffy, 'Irishmen and Islesmen', 114–15.

Alexander's participation in Henry's campaign against Gruffudd ap Cynan in Gwynedd, a man with kinship ties to Dublin and an associate of Muirchertach's, should perhaps be viewed in the context of such a policy of containment.[84]

The second area of concern for Alexander was Caithness and Orkney. Disturbances there may have been connected to the instability in the Hebrides, but a firm link cannot be established. In Orkney, the settlement between earls Hákon and Magnus had collapsed and at Easter 1115, on the island of Egilsay, Hákon and his men killed Magnus.[85] Hákon now ruled alone, extinguishing Scottish influence in the earldom and weakening Scottish domination of the northern mainland. Fortunately, Hákon's sole rule saw no resurgence in Norwegian control and after his death in c. 1123 it was English influence that embraced Orkney.[86] Of more pressing concern for Alexander, however, were the consequences of the removal of a pro-Scottish ruler from the region and, while violence in Moray recorded in 1116 may be entirely coincidental, it is possible that disaffected elements in his kingdom seized the opportunity of a weakening in Alexander's authority in the north to stage a rebellion. The events of 1116 are very obscure, being based on the *Annals of Ulster* which simply records that 'Ladhmunn son of Domnall, grandson of the king of Scotland, was killed by the men of Moray'.[87] Given the looseness with which the style 'king of Scotland' was used in the Irish annals, who this Ladhmunn or Lodmund was is open to question: it has been proposed that he was a son of the Domnall killed in 1085 and therefore grandson of Malcolm III, his Scandinavian name perhaps indicating descent from Malcolm and his first wife, Ingibjorg, or, less likely, that he was the son of Donald Bán.[88] That he was killed by Moravians at once raises the possibility of a dynastic challenge mounted by the descendants of King Lulaig, and the timing of the event could point to an opportunistic rising in the aftermath of Earl Magnus's death or one which capitalised on Alexander's troubles with David in southern Scotland. It has also been suggested that Alexander's absence in 1114 participating in the north Welsh campaign may have encouraged his rivals to stage their bid.[89] Two fifteenth-century sources,

---

[84] Oram, *Lordship of Galloway*, 59.
[85] *Orkneyinga Saga*, Chapters 46–50.
[86] William of Malmesbury, *Gesta Regum Anglorum*, ii, 741.
[87] *Annals of Ulster*, s.a. 1116.
[88] See McDonald, *Outlaws*, 23.
[89] Ibid. 24.

based on now lost contemporary accounts, describe an extended conflict in which northern rebels attacked Alexander at Invergowrie but were then defeated and pursued into Ross by the king.[90] Neither account dates the events, but the foundation of Scone Priory is represented as a thanks-offering by Alexander for his victory. Scone was founded in 1115 and, if the foundation legend is based on fact, then it may offer corroborating evidence for widespread disturbance in the kingdom, military operations which apparently earned Alexander his later epithet of 'the Fierce' and, perhaps, help explain the 'very great effort' with which he held the kingship.[91] The presence of an Earl Aed, identified as an earl of Ross, in Alexander's foundation charter of Scone, together with northern bishops, could be viewed as supporting evidence for the priory's having been founded in the aftermath of a rising in Moray, but all told the material relating to this period is so ambiguous as to make firm conclusions impossible.

After the military activity in the middle of his reign, Alexander's later years were dominated by religious politics and his programme of church reform. It is easy to dismiss his efforts in this area as failures, for at the time of his death only one scheme, Scone Priory, had come to fruition, and he remained locked in conflict with the archbishop of York, who was pushing claims to metropolitan supremacy of the Scottish Church, over his plans for St Andrews (see Chapter 10).[92] While actively promoting the aims of the Gregorian reform movement in the Scottish Church and its reorganisation along mainstream European lines, he displayed few signs of enthusiasm for other aspects of western European culture. David may have been encouraging the settlement of his foreign friends in the Southern Uplands, but Alexander does not appear to have introduced a single colonial knight or burgess into his realm. How such meagre evidence is interpreted is debatable, but Alexander perhaps progressed cautiously with innovation, beginning reform in the religious sphere but avoiding the bear traps presented by the introduction of colonists and foreign culture that had undermined the legacy of his father.

Almost at the end of his reign there are suggestions of fresh tension in his relationship with Henry I, who in 1122 visited Carlisle and ordered

---

[90] *Chron. Wyntoun*, iii, 174–5; *Chron. Bower*, iii, 104–7.
[91] For Scone, see Duncan, *Kingship of the Scots*, 85. For Alexander 'the Fierce', see McDonald, *Outlaws*, 23. The epithet is first used by Fordun, *Chron. Fordun*, ii, 217.
[92] Veitch, 'Replanting paradise'.

Alexander I and Scone Priory

Alexander I's reputation as a Church reformer is overshadowed by his brother David I's efforts. Although incomparable in scale of achievement, Alexander resumed the process begun by their parents and founded the reform programme completed by his successors. Most discussion has focused on his reform of the bishopric of St Andrews as a precursor to securing its elevation as Scotland's metropolitan church; his effort at monastic foundation was dismissed as half-hearted and unproductive, with Scone Priory his only success. Close links between Scone's foundation and reform efforts at St Andrews are now recognised, with both acts being linked to ambitions to enhance the royal status of Scottish kings.[93]

In 1115 Alexander brought Augustinian canons to Scone, the inauguration place and royal residence near Perth.[94] The parallels with the English palace and coronation church at Westminster are striking. Alexander possibly copied the arrangement to boost his prestige and help to secure the coronation ritual that would lift his status to that of English kings; securing an archbishopric for the bishop of St Andrews, who would preside at coronations, was a central aim. Alexander perhaps tried to make the Scottish king-making ceremony more Christian and religious – its secular character still disturbed the Christian sensibilities of David I in 1124 – but evidence for attempts to involve the canons in a 'church-based inauguration rite' is circumstantial.[95] Indeed, the canons' failure to secure a role in the ritual until the 1300s perhaps indicates that an English-style coronation church was not envisaged. Furthermore, similarities to Westminster are limited, for the Augustinian priory at Scone is a significant departure from the Benedictine role at Westminster. This difference suggests deeper motives than a desire for coronation, principally his association with wider spiritual reform in Scotland; Augustinians, after all, were a missionary order at the forefront of the Gregorian reform movement.[96]

---

[93] Veitch, 'Replanting paradise'; Duncan, *Kingship of the Scots*, Chapter 5.
[94] Cowan and Easson, *Medieval Religious Houses*, 97 and Duncan, *Kingship of the Scots*, 85–6 for debate over dates.
[95] Duncan, *Kingship of the Scots*, 86.
[96] Veitch, 'Replanting paradise', 157.

the strengthening of its defences.[97] The tension perhaps centred on David, who may have been dissatisfied with the terms of the 1113 settlement and was perhaps looking covetously at his wife's lost heritage in Northumberland.[98] Ranulf Flambard's new castle at Norham, erected in 1121,[99] Eustace fitz John's new lordship of Alnwick and Walter Espec's castle at Wark-on-Tweed may be manifestations of Henry's security concerns for his northern frontier.[100] Given Ranulf Flambard's reorganisation of his estates, however, the building of Norham as the administrative centre of his Northumberland properties need not be seen as a threat directed at David, nor need the grants to Walter Espec and Eustace fitz John be seen in that light. Rather than an act of aggression directed northwards, Henry's refortification of Carlisle could be seen in the light of his current organisation of the defences of the English north-west and his wider Irish Sea policies.[101] David's presence at Henry's court throughout 1121–2, moreover, indicates that Henry's anxiety had another cause.[102]

The obvious alternative is Alexander, whose relationship with Henry changed in July 1122 when Queen Sibylla died suddenly, having failed to produce an heir for her husband.[103] William of Malmesbury's gossip claims that Alexander barely grieved for his vulgar and charmless wife,[104] but that image barely accords with accounts of her piety and close involvement in Alexander's religious reforms, or his veneration of her memory.[105] Sibylla's death transformed Scotland's political landscape, for, unless Alexander remarried swiftly and produced a legitimate heir, the possibility of a contested succession and the risk of wider destabilisation of the kingdom reappeared. This issue may have driven Henry's flurry of activity in the north in the months after Sibylla's death, which pressured Alexander into acknowledging David and no other as his heir.[106] It does not seem, however, that either Alexander or David expected any such arrangement to become operational in the near future,

---

[97] Symeon of Durham, *Opera Omnia*, ii, 267.
[98] Green, 'Anglo-Scottish relations', 60–1.
[99] Symeon of Durham, *Opera Omnia*, i, 140.
[100] Duncan, *Kingship of the Scots*, 63–4; Oram, *David I*, 70.
[101] Oram, *Lordship of Galloway*, 61.
[102] Barrow (ed.), *David I Charters*, 38; Green offers a less dramatic interpretation in 'David I and Henry I', 1–19.
[103] Symeon of Durham, *Opera Omnia*, ii, 265.
[104] William of Malmesbury, *Gesta Regum Anglorum*, ii, 727.
[105] *Chron. Bower*, iii, 109 for Loch Tay, where Sibylla is said to have died. See also *Scone Liber*, no. 3, and Lawrie, *Early Scottish Charters*, 294–5.
[106] Duncan, *Kingship of the Scots*, 65.

and David was probably with Henry in England or Normandy in April 1124 when news arrived of his brother's death.[107]

DAVID I: SUCCESSION AND CHALLENGE 1124–35

The traditional view of David's succession to the throne is of a smooth transition followed by a steady enhancement of royal power under his strong and capable guidance. Such a view, however, is to read history backwards and look at the kingdom created by David in the later 1130s and 1140s rather than consider the challenges he faced from 1124 to 1135. Not least amongst those challenges was the question of his acceptability to the leaders of Scottish political society for, despite the historiographical tendency to present David as the only real candidate for the kingship, alternatives for that role enjoyed significant support. The most prominent of these potential rivals was David's half-nephew, William son of Duncan. If primogeniture had been applied in 1124 William, a mature adult and unquestionably the heir of the senior and legitimate male line of Malcolm III, should have become king. The fact that he was bypassed in favour of David but went on to pursue a loyal and high-profile career in his uncle's service has attracted little comment from historians. No late-eleventh- or early-twelfth-century source questions Duncan II's legitimacy, but later accounts stigmatise him as *nothus* – a bastard – a denigration designed primarily to discredit the claims of his son's equally legitimate MacWilliam heirs.[108]

Why, if there was no doubt over his legitimacy in 1107 or 1124, did William not claim the kingship for himself? His acquiescence had presumably been bought, possibly by nomination as David's successor. This was a role which his position as the next oldest acceptable and legitimate male of the royal house would have commanded under Gaelic succession practices. Certainly, until the later 1130s William held prominent political and military roles in the kingdom and was one of the most influential voices in shaping royal policy; this may imply extraordinary status in the circle around the king. William's cousin, Henry, moreover, was still a

---

[107] Oram, *David I*, 72.
[108] There is no suggestion in the twelfth-century *Chron. Melrose*, s.a. 1094, that Duncan was illegitimate, but an insertion in a later hand based on the *Chronicle of Huntingdon* describes him as a bastard. By the fifteenth century this was an unquestioned fact (see *Chron. Bower*, iii, 85). For discussion of the smearing of the MacWilliams' progenitors, see Broun, 'Contemporary perspectives on Alexander II's succession', 79–97.

child and, given the political volatility of Scotland, it was vital to chart a clear succession should either David or Henry die. Again, recognition of William's rights in those circumstances may have been an attractive enough gamble for him to acquiesce in 1124.

With his main potential rival neutralised, David was inaugurated at Scone. The king-making ceremony itself, however, threatened fresh crisis for, as Abbot Ailred of Rievaulx later claimed, David considered aspects of the ceremony to be offensive to his religious or moral principles. Having familiarity with only the semi-sacral Anglo-Norman kingship, he perhaps found the strongly secular Scottish ceremony not only alien but also disturbingly pagan in character. Ailred claims that even the assembled bishops had difficulty in persuading him to participate in the ritual.[109] Nevertheless, David was persuaded and underwent enthronement in the established manner.

Despite the traditional start to his reign, the festivities that followed his inauguration in early May revealed that he had a different vision for his kingdom. While still at Scone, David issued a charter to Robert de Bruce, granting him the whole of Annandale under very vague terms of service.[110] This is the earliest surviving charter from a Scottish king to a colonial lord and has been viewed as indicating that the settlement of foreign knights commenced only on David's accession.[111] The charter, however, was witnessed by eight men of Anglo-Norman background led by Eustace fitz John, one of Henry I's principal agents in northern England, and including others who subsequently settled in Scotland, while a ninth witness, the chamberlain Edmund, was perhaps an English clerk from Huntingdon. No native Scottish lord witnessed the grant, which is addressed only to David's 'French' and 'English' subjects. This peculiarity in the charter's formula and witnessing is distinctly odd and cannot be dismissed as a product of native Scottish unfamiliarity with new-fangled parchment records, for David's elder siblings had all made use of formal diplomas of this type. Nor can it be presented as a product of geography, whereby no culturally Gaelic magnate was involved because the subject matter was far removed from their spheres of interest, for no mention is made of the 'Cumbrenses' who inhabited Annandale and whom David had included carefully in his recent inquest into the lands of the Church of Glasgow. Quite simply, the structure of the document reflects very strongly David's personal preferences, cultural inclinations

---

[109] Ailred of Rievaulx, 'Epistola', in Anderson (ed.), *Scottish Annals*, 232–7.
[110] Barrow (ed.), *David I Charters*, no. 16.
[111] Duncan, *Making of the Kingdom*, 135; Barrow, *Kingship and Unity*, 32.

and experience. Although he had ruled over the Southern Uplands since c. 1113, he had been largely absent from Scotland since c. 1097 and had been raised and educated in the Frankish culture of the English court, trained as a Norman knight and schooled in Anglo-Saxon and Norman traditions of government and administration. William of Malmesbury, indeed, referred to David as of 'more courtly disposition' than his older brothers, and that he had 'from boyhood been polished by familiar intercourse with the English, and rubbed off all the barbarian gaucherie of Scottish manners'.[112] Gaelic Scotland was alien to him and, given that it was the Gaelic magnates who had supported Donald Bán, driven him and his siblings into exile, and killed his eldest half-brother, it would be unsurprising if David had looked on his subjects with suspicion at the very least. The men named in the Annandale charter were David's former colleagues as well as vassals and servants, men who shared a common culture, common values and, in the cases of Robert de Bruce and Eustace fitz John, a similar set of experiences. As king in an alien and potentially hostile environment, this group was something in which David could place trust.

To most Scots David, although the late king's brother and Scottish by birth, was equally alien, a virtual foreigner who in 1113 had used English military muscle to secure his heritage, and who now stood among them backed by that same muscle. David may have been enthroned with apparent smoothness simply because the magnates understood that the alternative was war, but their earlier hostility towards him remained, and his unchallenged inauguration did not equate with unquestioned acceptance. Indeed, the ease of his succession was a deceptive calm before the storm, for the second half of the year saw a rising in support of Malcolm, the bastard son of Alexander I.[113] While David defeated his rival with comparative ease on this occasion, Malcolm escaped and was a serious threat for nearly a decade yet. Who his supporters were in his insurrection is unknown, but they probably included men who sympathised with the sentiments expressed about David in the Gaelic poem that had criticised him ten years earlier, and it is perhaps significant that there is little sign that he came north of Fife after 1124 until c. 1139–40.[114]

---

[112] William of Malmesbury, *Gesta Regum Anglorum*, ii, 727.

[113] *Ordericus Vitalis, Historia Ecclesiastica*, viii, 20. The identity of this Malcolm has been long debated but recent scholarship has unravelled the mystery (Duncan, *Kingship of the Scots*, 66–7).

[114] See Barrow (ed.), *David I Charters*, 39–40 for a skeleton itinerary of the king in this period.

Although Scottish kings had estates dispersed throughout *Scotia* from Ross to Fife and had clustered thickest in Gowrie, Angus and the Mearns since at least the early eleventh century, David did not use these as bases for a progress around his kingdom at the start of his reign.[115] For a man unfamiliar with the political culture of his Gaelic realm and whose family had been forced to fight to establish its authority over this Gaelic heartland, this failure to display active lordship in these territories could suggest arrogance and complacency, confidence in traditional loyalties to his family or recognition of the weakness of his position. David's aversion to travel into *Scotia* linked to events in the 1130s raises questions over the extent of his authority there. One sign of apparent restriction is his residence primarily south in Lothian or Teviotdale, especially at Roxburgh. As early as 1114 when he granted property there to the monks of Selkirk David had been developing Roxburgh as a commercial and administrative centre.[116] With the exception of Perth and Dunfermline, which received royal burgh status before c. 1128, all of David's early grants of that status were to communities in Lothian – Berwick, Edinburgh and Stirling[117] – which likewise points to a circumscribed zone of power. Roxburgh's early centrality to David's realm can be seen by the relocation of Selkirk Abbey in 1128 to Kelso, immediately across the River Tweed from the burgh.[118] The arrangement echoes London, where a seat of government, royal religious centre and economic focus coincided. David, perhaps, was consciously developing Roxburgh as the chief royal seat of his new kingdom. If this is so, then Roxburgh's proximity to England and remoteness from *Scotia* signifies a seismic shift in the political centre of gravity in the kingdom. Such a shift may be reflected in the men who surrounded David, mainly foreign knights and clerics with landed interests in the Southern Uplands, and perhaps illustrates the limits of David's authority. Although Roxburgh lacked the royal associations of Edinburgh or Dunfermline, it offered security in the region where his power was greatest and where his allies and dependents were clustered thickest.

This apparent withdrawal from *Scotia*, the traditional heartland of royal power, might indicate confidence in his authority based on his legitimacy as an heir of Malcolm III. While that status may have won

---

[115] Grant, 'Thanes and thanages', 39–81.
[116] See *Kelso Liber*, no. 1 and the annotated text in Barrow (ed.), *David I Charters*, no. 14.
[117] *Dunfermline Registrum*, no. 1; Barrow (ed.), *David I Charters*, no. 33.
[118] Symeon of Durham, *Historia Regum*, ii, 281.

Figure 2.1 Roxburgh Castle, Scottish Borders, the chief seat of David I's power until the 1130s. Only fragments of stonework remain from the later medieval buildings that replaced David's twelfth-century castle.

some automatic acceptance from a wide group of the Gaelic nobility, as suggested by the presence of five earls in a royal assembly at Dunfermline in 1128 (see below), others regarded him as an unknown outsider whose foreign manners and friends were viewed with suspicion. Apart from his royal blood, David lacked the means to communicate easily with his new subjects and establish the social connections upon which the kingship of his ancestors had depended. There is, however, no sign of serious efforts in the 1120s to win wider acceptance in the Gaelic provinces. This apparent aversion for Gaelic Alba may be explained partly by poor documentary survival, but what evidence exists for David's activities between 1124 and 1130 indicates that his principal concerns were with Lothian and Strathclyde.[119]

David's first major task was to resolve the conflict with York and Canterbury over the sees of Glasgow and St Andrews (see Chapter 10). A meeting at Roxburgh with the papal legate, John of Crema (in June or July 1125), resolved nothing, Scottish inflexibility on the issue leading instead to a hardening of papal attitudes in favour of York. By mid-1126 the issue had become critical, with the bishop-elect of St Andrews still unconsecrated as a result of his refusal to profess obedience to

[119] Oram, *David I*, 77–8.

Archbishop Thurstan and Bishop John of Glasgow facing suspension for his failure to submit to York. A solution was sought at Rome in early February 1126, with the Scots asking unsuccessfully for the creation of their own archdiocese. David, who regarded reform of the Church as his kingly duty, wanted an end to this seemingly intractable conflict and turned to Henry I for aid in reaching a compromise to at least defer the issue of metropolitan supremacy but permit his bishops to progress with their reformist programmes. Henry needed David's support for his plans for the succession of his daughter, Matilda, to the English throne and was ready to make concessions. Hard bargaining at Henry's Christmas court at Windsor led to a deal which involved Henry's persuading Archbishop Thurstan to soften his stance.[120] Thurstan agreed to seek a deferral of the case for a further year to allow a settlement between York and the Scottish bishops to be arranged.[121] Why Henry had urged this compromise emerged when he sought an oath from his magnates to support the succession of Matilda should he fail to father a son.[122] The first layman to swear was David, presumably in recognition of his status as king of Scots, earl of Huntingdon and uncle of the designated successor, but also no doubt for the strong signal it gave to the assembly. Here was the result of Henry's pressure on Thurstan and its fruits were apparent by summer 1127 when the bishop-elect of St Andrews was consecrated without professing his obedience to Thurstan.[123]

The lull in the dispute with York was followed by fresh Church reform activity on David's part. In 1127–8 he was closely involved in two projects; the consecration of the abbey church at Kelso and the consecration of Geoffrey, prior of Christchurch Canterbury, as the first abbot of Dunfermline.[124] David had been negotiating Dunfermline's elevation to abbatial status since 1126 and Geoffrey's consecration was a symbolic act which identified David with what his predecessors had intended would be the premier royal monastery of *Scotia*. If the king's general confirmation of the abbey's possessions was issued at this time, then its witness list reveals the composition of the leadership north of the Forth upon whom any tightening of David's authority depended.[125] It included

---

[120] Sottewain, *Archbishops of York*, 217.
[121] Ibid. 217.
[122] Symeon of Durham, *Historia Regum*, ii, 281–2.
[123] Anderson (ed.), *Scottish Annals*, 164–6; General Letter of Archbishop Thurstan, in Raine (ed.), *Historians of York*, iii, 51–2. For discussion, see Barrow (ed.), *David I Charters*, 68.
[124] Barrow (ed.), *David I Charters*, no. 22; Anderson (ed.), *Scottish Annals*, 166.
[125] *Dunfermline Registrum*, no. 1.

five bishops: Robert of St Andrews, John of Glasgow and the probably native clerics, Cormac of Dunkeld, Gregory of Moray and Macbeth of Rosemarkie. Following them were the earls of Ross, Fife, Strathearn, Mar and Atholl, together representing a block of power that stretched through the eastern and central Highlands.[126] Their attendance on David reveals his core support within *Scotia*, but there are also individuals whose absence assumes great significance in the following years.

In early 1130, David returned to England to serve as a judge in Henry's court at Woodstock and on 4 May he and a body of Scottish nobles attended the dedication of the cathedral at Canterbury.[127] From there he may have returned to Scotland, for around that time Matilda, his wife, died.[128] In contrast to her sister-in-law and namesake in England, few records relate to her life and career and little was done subsequently either to preserve her memory or build a cult around her. Given her importance in legitimising Scottish claims to Northumberland after 1135, it is strange that there were no moves to commemorate her there. Even her burial place is unusual, for she was interred neither in Daventry Priory nor in St Andrews at Northampton, monasteries associated with her paternal inheritance, nor in the Scottish royal mausoleum at Dunfermline or David's own foundation at Kelso (where their son was later buried). Instead, she was buried at Scone. In the fifteenth-century narrative of Walter Bower, Matilda's death is reported immediately before an account of the pivotal point in David's reign, the rebellion and death of the ruler of Moray and the seizure of his land.[129] If this sequence is not entirely fortuitous, then David's absence from Scotland in early 1130 was taken as an opportunity by his enemies to mount a fresh challenge to him.

Behind the rebellion stood Malcolm, Alexander I's bastard son, but his principal associate was another royal pretender.[130] Angus of Moray was the grandson of King Lulaig mac Gilla Comgain (1057–8), who had been overthrown and killed by David's father. Chronicle accounts of this rising, sparse though they are, imply that Angus was its leader, presumably as the legitimate descendant of a recognised king, and the aim was to place him on the throne. All sources agree that Angus was halted by

---

[126] Barrow (ed.), *David I Charters*, 72.
[127] Henry of Huntingdon, *Historia Anglorum*, 252; Orderic Vitalis, *Historia Ecclesiastica*, viii, 20; *RRAN*, ii, no. 1639; Gervase of Canterbury, *Historical Works*, i, 96.
[128] For Matilda's life, see Anderson (ed.), *Early Sources*, ii, 33–4.
[129] Bower, *Scotichronicon*, iii, 135.
[130] Robert of Torigni, *Chronica*, 118.

an army commanded by David's constable, Edward.[131] Beyond brief notices of the resulting battle and death of Angus, however, no contemporary account survives of the wider rebellion or its aftermath. Material from now-lost earlier chronicles incorporated into *Gesta Annalia* reveals that Angus reached Stracathro in Angus, a location that implies passage through Mar and across the Mounth.[132] The largely pro-David accounts of the battle present it as an overwhelming victory followed by a campaign into Moray.[133] In the later twelfth century, some chroniclers claimed that Moray had been conquered and the 'earldom', a title that creeps into the accounts in an attempt to explain Angus's status, suppressed.[134] But there are some indications that the victory was hard won, for an expansion of the *Annals of Ulster* account reports heavy Scottish casualties taken in a counter-attack.[135] Moreover, while Angus was dead, as in 1124 Malcolm had escaped.

Malcolm now assumed the mantle of royal pretender. Although illegitimate and consequently ineligible to succeed in the eyes of Frankish-inspired and canon lawyers, he was a senior lineal representative of the Scottish royal house and the son of a king, which was sufficient to win support to mount a serious challenge to David. His attempt lasted until 1134, when he was betrayed to David's supporters and imprisoned for life in Roxburgh.[136] There is little record of the campaigns leading to his capture, but a speech invented by Ailred of Rievaulx for Robert de Bruce of Annandale in his account of the battle of the Standard in 1138 provides some clues:

> Remember when in a previous year you asked for the help of the English against Malcolm, the heir of his father's hatred and persecution, how joyful, how eager, how willing to help, how ready for danger Walter Espec and many other English nobles hastened to meet you at Carlisle, how many ships they prepared, how they waged war, how they built defences, how they terrified all your enemies [until they captured Malcolm himself betrayed; captured, they bound him; bound, they delivered him]. Thus the fear of us, bound his limbs, but bound even more the courage of the Scots,

---

[131] See, for example, Orderic Vitalis, *Historia Ecclesiastica*, viii, 20.
[132] *Chron. Fordun*, ii, 224.
[133] *Annals of Ulster*, s.a. 1130; Orderic Vitalis, *Historia Ecclesiastica*, viii, 20.
[134] Robert of Torigni, *Chronica*, s.a. 1130.
[135] *Annals of Ulster*, s.a. 1130.
[136] *Chron. Melrose*, s.a. 1134.

and having quenched all hope of success, removed the audacity to rebel.

[until they betrayed Malcolm himself; betrayed, they captured him; captured, they bound him; bound, they delivered him.][137]

Rather than Stracathro delivering a clear result, it appears that Malcolm's continued challenge caused David protracted difficulties which made him dependent on his foreign friends, possibly including Henry I himself. Campaigning was long and involved building castles to hold down territory and contain the rebellion. The conflict, moreover, extended far beyond Moray, for reference to a muster at Carlisle and a naval campaign suggests that Malcolm found support in the west coast and islands. David's subsequent ability to grant shares in his *cáin* from Argyll and Kintyre to lowland monasteries perhaps marks his victory there.[138]

Chief amongst Malcolm's allies was the rather obscure Gillebrigte, ruler of Argyll, or his son, Somerled. In 1153, the *Chronicle of Holyrood* reported that 'Somerled and his nephews, the sons of Malcolm, having allied themselves with a great many men, rebelled . . .'[139] Malcolm, it seems, had bound himself through marriage to the greatest warlord of the Gaelic west, which suggests that he was no insignificant challenger and could attract formidable allies. It is significant, perhaps, that Ailred implies that treachery and not fighting ended the affair. Malcolm never emerged from captivity and nothing more is heard of him in David's reign, although his sons returned to disturb the peace of David's grandsons in the 1150s.

In retrospect, 1134 was a watershed in Scotland's political development, marking the point at which David finally established his authority throughout *Scotia*. Although he had taken the kingship apparently unchallenged in 1124, his success had been illusory, for he enjoyed only limited support amongst his Gaelic subjects, many of whom preferred his bastard nephew. Although David had won the first round in that contest, he did not exercise effective kingship into the 1130s outside a tight radius around traditional royal centres in central Scotland. He was king of Scots in little more than name, for the record of his activity indicates that he

---

[137] Ailred of Rievaulx, *De Standardo*, 193. I am grateful to Alasdair Ross for permission to reproduce his translation of the speech, given in his as-yet unpublished PhD thesis (Ross, PhD thesis, 186 and note 46).
[138] Barrow (ed.), *David I Charters*, nos 172, 185.
[139] *Chron. Holyrood*, s.a. 1153.

operated primarily within Cumbria and the lands around the Forth and Tay estuaries. Within this confined orbit, however, he was practising a new style of kingship modelled closely on English and Norman forms, and was continuing the policies of innovation in secular and ecclesiastical government, monastic fashions, economic development and landholding practices begun in Cumbria after 1113, which enabled him to consolidate his hold over this core domain. During this first decade, too, he continued his career as an English magnate and one of Henry I's greatest courtiers. In this, we can see a continuing high level of dependency on his English patron, greatly in excess of the traditional impression of the revolutionary Scottish king, and that dependence, if anything, was heightened at the end of his first ten years as king rather than reduced. It would be going too far to say that 1124–34 saw David engaged in a struggle for survival, for it was a period that saw the foundations of his later power laid in southern Scotland and major advances made in his religious reforms, but it was certainly not a confident start to his reign.

CHAPTER 3

Building the Scoto-Northumbrian Realm, 1136–57

Regardless of David I's successes as king, one aspect of his reign that has until recently been viewed negatively was his ambition to acquire Northumbria. Armed with the benefits of hindsight, nineteenth- and early-twentieth-century historians pointed to the consequences of David's grandson William's obsessive desire to regain possession of that territory; he suffered defeat, imprisonment and the humiliation of formal submission to English overlordship. They saw only the inevitability of failure and dismissed the Scots' occupation of northern England as the illusory result of the contemporary weakness of English monarchy. The transitory existence of David's extended kingdom and futile later efforts to regain Northumbria convinced many scholars that William and Alexander II had been drawn by a siren's lure that threatened their own kingdom with destruction. Furthermore, the shortness of Scottish possession of northern England – only twenty-one years – resulted in cursory consideration of the episode's significance. It is only recently that this traditional view has been challenged.[1] Dismissal of the significance of David's English acquisitions began with Andrew Lang's trenchant criticism of what he saw as dangerous adventures which brought the kingdom to the brink of disaster.[2] Although subsequent generations of historians were less strident, Lang's assessment of the consequences of David's policies in England coloured analysis of Anglo-Scottish relations. While David's achievement was recognised, it was still presented as a doomed illusion.[3] Recent research, however, has significantly revised

---

[1] Stringer, 'State-building in twelfth-century Britain'. Oram, *David I*, 220, 224.
[2] Lang, *History of Scotland*, i, 102. For the historiography of David's reign, see Oram, *David I*, Chapter 12.
[3] Pittock, *A New History of Scotland*, 42.

that view, and Keith Stringer has argued from an English perspective that David came within a hair's breadth of permanently redrawing the political map of Britain.[4] This chapter will explore that idea. The narrative of state-building in the second part of David's reign will be set out, while the mechanisms employed to underpin that process will be discussed in later chapters. The kingdom that David constructed expanded from its east Lowland core on three main fronts. The first was internal and involved establishment of his authority throughout most of mainland Scotland. The second was westward, with Scottish royal influence being intruded not only into Argyll and greater Galloway, but also into Man and the Isles. The third was southward, carrying the limits of David's realm deep into northern England. While in the following discussion these three zones will be treated sequentially, it must be stressed that developments in any one of them had a significant and continuing impact on the others, and on David's ability to respond to internal and external events. As Scottish royal authority expanded its physical range and increased its intrusive capability, like any imperialistic power, David was drawn deeper into new political relationships which brought new challenges and innovatory responses from the king and his agents.

THE CONQUEST OF THE NORTH

For the two centuries before 1070 successive Scottish kings had exercised fluctuating control over mainland Scotland north of the Mounth.[5] The probable absence of strong regional lordships throughout most of the north-western Highlands possibly hindered the establishment of lasting domination in this topographically fragmented region. Here, beyond the reach of the Scandinavian rulers of Caithness and the Gaelic 'kings' of Moray, power was not a dynastic preserve and population levels were too low and dispersed to sustain structures comparable to those in most of lowland Britain. It is probably significant that the regional distribution of documentarily attested royal estates runs in an arc from Aberdeen to the River Spey (there are none in Buchan), then along the Moray coast to Dingwall in Ross and no further.[6] While there are traces of thanages – estates administered for the king by an officer called a thane – in the

---

[4] Stringer, *Reign of Stephen*, 28–37; Stringer, 'State-building in twelfth-century Britain'.
[5] See Woolf, *From Pictland to Alba*, Chapter 6.
[6] Grant, 'Thanes and thanages', 39–81.

Black Isle which extend this scatter of royal estates, the distribution suggests that no higher authority – neither the kings of Scots nor regional magnates in Moray, Ross or Caithness – had fixed their power beyond established centres in the coastal lowlands. In that fringe, assuming that the thanages were Scottish royal estates from their first establishment and not expropriated properties of former regional rulers, these royal properties might indicate that the crown enjoyed greater influence in this territory than traditional narratives have allowed. We must be careful, however, not to turn possession of properties peripheral to the main Highland zone into evidence for the effective domination of that zone.

It has become common to represent Moray as a monolithic regional superpower that controlled most of the mainland between the Mounth and the Oykel.[7] This view is based on the extent of the fourteenth-century earldom of Moray and interpretation of accounts of conflict between Norse earls pushing their power south from Caithness and Scottish 'kings' who opposed them and attempted to push their own power northwards. This narrative, derived largely from the thirteenth-century *Orkneyinga Saga*, reflects the political realities of the early 1200s which the saga writer projected back into the eleventh and early twelfth centuries. Beneath the image of a protracted conflict in northern mainland Scotland between native and Norse dynasts, however, lies a political geography composed of zones over which these rival powers exercised effective lordship bedded into a wider landscape in which their power was more diffuse or where no lord exercised real authority. Moray was a significant power in this northern world throughout the eleventh century, but it was not always the dominant one. The success of Macbeth in securing the Scottish throne in 1040 has perhaps given a skewed perspective of Moray's potential.

Despite his victories over the Moravians, Malcolm III did not end opposition to his family from Moray.[8] For half a century, however, there was no Moray-based challenge until in 1130 its ruler, Angus, tried to capitalise on hostility towards David I. Although victorious over Angus at Stracathro, David remained too preoccupied elsewhere to consolidate control of Moray until after 1134. Details of the war of conquest are lost, but the disappearance of Moray's ruling dynasty suggests the elimination or neutralising of that family, while the subsequent quiescence of the region perhaps indicates that a secure peace entailed the destruction

---

[7] See Ross, PhD thesis, 11–38.
[8] Anderson (ed.), *Scottish Annals*, 100 and note 1.

of Moray's fighting manhood. Traditionally, Angus's defeat is considered to have presaged a thorough-going Scottish conquest of Moray in a spectacular demonstration of the 'feudalising tendencies' of David I's new monarchy.[9] Recent research, however, suggests a protracted and shallowly-rooted process.[10] David's priory foundation at Urquhart probably celebrated the victory, for it was possibly endowed from Angus's ancestral lands in a commemoration of victory akin to the Norman foundation of Battle Abbey at Hastings or German victory monasteries beyond the Elbe.[11] Urquhart symbolised the establishment of a new order in the north, for it was colonised from Dunfermline, the premier royal monastery of *Scotia*, and funded through the fruits of victory. Its endowments also reveal that David considered his authority to extend far beyond Moray's core territories, for he granted it a teind of royal revenues from the district between Glenelg and Loch Broom on the west coast. The award may have been speculative, but David intended to draw revenue from those districts and felt able to enforce payment of tribute from territories over which his predecessors had exercised no real influence. The implicit recognition of his authority through the extraction of *cáin* and other renders marked a significant step towards bringing these districts under Scottish lordship.

While that lordship perhaps remained shallowly rooted in the north-western Highlands, it was more deeply bedded in Moray's heartland. Royal castles at Cullen, Elgin, Forres, Auldearn and, possibly, Inverness perhaps marked Angus's former estate centres seized by David, but there is otherwise no evidence that the bulk of the conquered territory became royal demesne. This issue raises the question of how possession of the eastern coastlands of Moray provided a platform for control of the hinterland to their south and west. The traditional view is that David employed a colonial aristocracy to secure conquest, but that may have been secondary to a more conservative solution.[12] Historians have debated how the royal pretenders who claimed descent from William, son of Duncan II, secured their following in northern Scotland when William's one documentarily attested marriage, dated to c. 1137, was to

---

[9] See Barrow, *Kingship and Unity*, 33.
[10] Lawrie, *Early Scottish Charters*, nos cx and cclv and notes; *Dunfermline Registrum*, 33, 34; Cowan and Easson, *Medieval Religious Houses*, 61; Ross, PhD thesis, 204–14; Oram, *David I*, 89–110.
[11] Douglas, *William the Conqueror*, 199, 328; Midmer, *English Medieval Monasteries*, 59–60.
[12] Barrell, *Medieval Scotland*, 21.

the northern English heiress Alice de Rumilly.[13] Donald, the first of this 'MacWilliam' line (as it has been labelled by later historians), has been dismissed as illegitimate but no contemporary source describes him as such; the stigmatising of William's descendants is a thirteenth-century development.[14] An alternative view, based on a late-thirteenth-century source that calls William 'earl of Moray', is that Donald was the legitimate son of an earlier marriage, possibly to a Moray heiress.[15] William of Newburgh's late-twelfth-century account of the career of Bishop Wimund, who may also have been William's son, described his father as 'earl of Moray'.[16] Newburgh's close contemporary Roger of Howden stated that Donald's kingworthiness came 'by right of his parents',[17] a plural that implies his mother was also royal. William, therefore, may have been married to a Moray heiress, for Angus was King Lulaig grandson and, through him, inherited a second-generation claim to the Scottish throne. Sons of that marriage had united claims descended from Duncan II and Lulaig.

Such a marriage was possibly to compensate the senior line descended from Malcolm III that had been passed over in the succession. The new political prescription in the north coincided with the entry to adulthood of David's son, Henry, which ended any realistic possibility of William becoming king should David die. David wished Henry to be his successor and Moray may have been compensation for William's disappointment. This scenario, however, remains conjectural, for no contemporary source associates William directly with Moray: all descriptions of him as 'earl' long postdate his death. Nor is the lack of a territorial title conclusive in itself, for although Angus is styled earl of Moray, that styling occurs only in late or non-Scottish sources and probably represents efforts to explain his status vis-à-vis David in terms that would justify the consequences of his 'rebellion' against his lord. Angus may have considered himself to be *rí*, a 'king', in his own right, but David is unlikely to have countenanced William assuming a title that introduced ambiguity into the relationship between Moray and the king of Scots. William, presumably, was not ruler of an autonomous principality but a magnate within the enlarged Scottish kingdom. If he was intended to be central to the government

---

[13] See Barrow, *Kingship and Unity*, 51–2, for debate. For the de Rumilly marriage, see Stringer, *Reign of Stephen*, 34–5; Barrow, 'The reign of William the Lion', 78; Poole, *Domesday Book to Magna Carta*, 271, note 3.
[14] Broun, 'Contemporary perspectives on Alexander II's succession', 82–4.
[15] Barrow (ed.), *RRS*, ii, 12; Barrow, *Kingship and Unity*, 51–2.
[16] William of Newburgh, *Historia Rerum Anglicarum*, i, 73–6.
[17] Benedict of Peterborough, *Gesta Regis*, i, 277–8.

of the north, however, his active involvement apparently ended in 1137 when he married Alice de Rumilly. There was no fall from favour, for William was prominent in the Scottish campaigns in northern England, and while there is no record of any further involvement with Moray, it is unlikely that he simply surrendered his son's northern heritage. When William died in c. 1147, however, Donald was a minor and it was perhaps then that David took Moray into his own hands. Royal policy in the region did not, however, stand or fall with William, for David also built close relationships with the rulers of Orkney and Caithness, the other powers who had long sought regional dominance.

Bloody competition between the descendants of Earl Thorfinnr the Mighty had seen a contraction of the earldom of Caithness from its mid-eleventh-century heyday, but in the early twelfth century its rulers still had some sway in the land between the Kyles of Sutherland and Thursodale. Later saga tradition implies that political fragmentation had occurred at the earldom's periphery as local kindreds strengthened their power bases at the expense of the earls, while areas of the interior and west coast where the population was scattered and without recognisable lordship structures perhaps lay beyond the earls' reach. A declining Caithness might seem advantageous for David, but a strong regional power in some way subservient to him and through which to foster stability was better than a vacuum. David had faced similar problems after 1115 in Cumbria, as had William II and Henry I in northern England.[18] Experience in those areas had shown that integration of existing native social structures, however rudimentary, into new political arrangements stabilised and formalised those structures; David may have extended that lesson to northern Scotland.

Marriage was central to David's policy. Shortly before 1134, his distant kinsman Maddad, earl of Atholl, married Margaret, daughter of Hákon Pálsson, earl of Orkney.[19] Such dynastic intermarriage has been presented as 'fundamental in maintaining and perpetuating an alliance of princes in the northern and western regions of Scotland who opposed the king of Scots',[20] but it was equally important in Scottish efforts to counter these hostile alignments. The traditional narrative of twelfth-century development of lordship in the central Highlands highlights the limited evidence for royal intervention there until late in William's reign

---

[18] Kapelle, *Norman Conquest of the North*, 144–6, 147–8, 191–230 (especially 205–8).
[19] *Orkneyinga Saga*, 118.
[20] McDonald, *Kingdom of the Isles*, 46.

and its rapid development under Alexander II.[21] Recently, however, it has been suggested that the intrusion of Scottish lordship there commenced earlier in the twelfth century.[22] The extension of David's power into the central Highlands was essential for his domination of Moray. Maddad's marriage may have been intended by David to provide a vehicle to carry his lordship beyond Drumochter. *Orkneyinga Saga* attributes the initiative for the alliance to Margaret's aunt, Frakkok, a powerful landholder in Helmsdale in Sutherland.[23] Her closeness to her nephew Harald, co-ruler of Orkney, who in the saga is said to have held Caithness as David's vassal,[24] caused her expulsion from Orkney following Harald's death; Harald's brother, co-ruler and rival Pál, is said by the saga to have suspected that Frakkok wanted to poison him, but had killed Harald in error. From the safety of Helmsdale, Frakkok continued to plot Pál's destruction, recruiting Harald's son, Erlend, and sister, Margaret.[25] Frakkok understood the changing political realities around her and saw advantages in allying with the Scots. With David's aid, Erlend could secure Caithness, while in return David could form clearer bonds of lordship over Caithness and draw Frakkok and her kin into his orbit.[26] Not only might Scottish influence over Caithness and the fragmented political communities of the north-western mainland be increased, but there was also the possibility of extending that domination into Orkney. There was little prospect of a reaction to such a development from Norway, where civil war had erupted after the death of King Sigurðr the Crusader in 1130, but England also had an interest in the earldom and Henry I may have looked unfavourably on Scottish-sponsored action against Earl Pál.[27]

English influence in Orkney benefited David in the early 1130s, but Frakkok's kin offered effective Scottish lordship over the islands. Henry I's death allowed David to act, but there were others who also saw the opportunity presented by the removal of Pál's powerful patron. In 1135,

---

[21] Barrow (ed.), *RRS*, i, 44; Barrow, 'Badenoch and Strathspey I', 1–15; Grant, 'Thanes and thanages', 73.
[22] Ross, PhD thesis, 211–12.
[23] *Orkneyinga Saga*, 98, 119. For discussion of Frakkok and the feud between the rival lines of Orkney earls, see Forte, Oram and Pedersen, *Viking Empires*, 282–6.
[24] *Orkneyinga Saga*, 98.
[25] *Orkneyinga Saga*, 100–1, 137–9; Topping, 'Harald Maddadson', 105–20 at 105–6 and 107–8.
[26] For Frakkok's family connections, see *Orkneyinga Saga*, 97–8, 101.
[27] For Pál's relationship with Henry I, see William of Malmesbury, *Gesta Regum Anglorum*, 741.

Earl Erlend II's grandson, Rognvald Kolsson, arrived in Orkney having been granted half the earldom by King Harald IV Gille of Norway.[28] Initially rebuffed, Rognvald in 1136 won the backing of Pál's domestic rivals and of Frakkok and her kinsmen. According to *Orkneyinga Saga*, with the connivance of Maddad and Margaret, Rognvald captured and disposed of Pál. His demise then saw a falling-out between his enemies, for Frakkok wanted a share of Orkney for Erlend Haraldsson, but Maddad and Margaret wanted it for their son, Harald Maddadsson.[29] David, faced in Orkney with the Norwegian-backed Earl Rognvald and his claims to a share of Caithness, favoured a half-Scottish earl as a counterbalance to Frakkok's kin, whose need for David's support had died with Earl Pál. Scottish interests were better served by placing the infant Harald in Caithness, for David could select guardians to rule until the child came of age and through them more fully incorporate the northern mainland into his kingdom.[30] It was probably David's support that by 1139 secured Harald Caithness and a half-share of Orkney from Rognvald.[31] The main threat to this settlement was seen by his parents and, presumably, David as Erlend Haraldsson and Frakkok, and the latter was soon slain in her own hall.[32] By securing Harald Maddadsson's heritage, David brought Caithness into his orbit, while Norwegian influence again declined as political divisions turned Norway's focus inwards. As a consequence, David held unprecedented power over the far northern mainland in parallel to the securing of Moray, which provided him with a platform from which to begin to extend his rule into the seemingly lordless north-west Highlands.

For over a decade, Scottish influence went unchallenged until the departure on pilgrimage in 1150–1 of Earl Rognvald.[33] There may be a direct correlation between Rognvald's absence and the arrival in Orkney in 1151 of Eystein II, one of three joint rulers of Norway and a man who had spent his youth in the Scandinavian colonies in western Scotland.[34] No medieval source explains Eystein's western expedition, but his possible objectives were to create a power base outside Norway and win resources with which to fund his military following. Both aims were met. Orkney capitulated and the capture of the teenage Harald at Thurso

---

[28] Thomson, *History of Orkney*, 61.
[29] *Orkneyinga Saga*, 119, 138–9.
[30] Topping, 'Harald Maddadson', 105–7.
[31] *Orkneyinga Saga*, 143.
[32] Ibid. 144–5.
[33] Ibid. Chapters 86–9.
[34] Anderson (ed.), *Early Sources*, ii, 204–5.

brought his submission to Eystein's overlordship, ending fifteen years of Scottish domination.[35] This success was followed by a plundering cruise down the east coast of Britain in which Aberdeen, Hartlepool and other trading ports were sacked before Eystein returned home.[36]

This unlooked-for Norwegian intervention demanded a Scottish response. Although *Orkneyinga Saga* attributes this to the advisors of the young Malcolm IV, the chronology of events suggests that it was David I who sought to recover the situation.[37] His solution was to advance Erlend Haraldsson as a replacement for Harald Maddadsson, awarding him half of Caithness. Erlend, however, also approached Eystein and received from him Harald's half of Orkney. The result was a triangular conflict involving Erlend, Harald and Rognvald, which ended in 1154 with Erlend's death.[38] Four years later the murder of Rognvald left Harald in sole possession of Caithness and Orkney. By then, Scottish policy was to draw Harald Maddadsson back into the fold and it is likely that Harald's marriage to Affreca, daughter of Duncan, earl of Fife, occurred soon after 1154 while Duncan was functioning as guardian for Malcolm IV.[39]

From c. 1150, subtle changes which moved policy away from reliance on regional strongmen can be seen in Scottish schemes for control of the region. This shift was revealed in David's barring of both Donald, who possibly received only a small portion of his father's lands in north-west England, and his half-brother, William 'Puer', from the inheritance of Moray.[40] Instead, David placed Moray under more immediate royal control exercised from castles at Elgin, Forres, Auldearn and, probably, Inverness. These may have begun as garrison posts in the 1130s, and were developed as nodal points from c. 1150 but their administrative function as centres for royal sheriffs dates from much later.[41] An added economic role came when trading settlements, which gained royal burgh status in the second half of the twelfth century, developed alongside the castles. Such colonies perhaps provided the crown with reserves of military manpower in the Moray lowlands, but were more important as media for economic and jurisdictional domination and conquest comparable

---

[35] Topping, 'Harald Maddadson', 105–20; Thomson, *History of Orkney*, 70.
[36] *Orkneyinga Saga*, Chapter 91.
[37] Ibid. Chapter 92; Thomson, *History of Orkney*, 70–1.
[38] *Orkneyinga Saga*, Chapters 92–4.
[39] Duncan, *Kingship of the Scots*, 70–1.
[40] William, 'the prince', was seen by some as a candidate for the kingship. Flateyiarbók claimed that 'all Scots wished to take [him] as their king'. Anderson (ed.), *Early Sources*, ii, 5.
[41] Barrow (ed.), *RRS*, i, 43–4; Duncan, *Making of the Kingdom*, 189–90.

with the urban colonies which marked the eastward spread of German settlement, or English colonisation in Wales and Ireland.[42] As centres of trade and justice, alien in language, dress and material culture, they were key elements in the acculturation of Moray with the increasingly hybrid society of the core of the Scottish realm. Alongside them and performing similar military, economic and jurisdictional roles, David introduced a colonial aristocracy, but they were few in number even at the end of the following reign.[43] A third strand in the colonial network was the diocesan church, whose possession of extensive landed estates rendered it key in securing royal interests in the central Highlands.[44] That Bishop William's appointment (c. 1152) and the foundation of Melrose Abbey's third colony at Kinloss in Moray (1150) almost coincided may not be entirely fortuitous.[45] Founded within three years of William son of Duncan's death, David may have begun to plan Kinloss as soon as he took Moray into his hands, perhaps encouraged by the soon-to-be bishop, William. It was William who initiated the development of contemporary western European systems of diocesan administration and supervision in Moray during the 1150s,[46] and it is possible that, like his contemporary, Archbishop Malachy at Armagh in Ireland, and later twelfth-century English earls in Ulster, William, with David's active support, placed the Cistercians at the forefront of reform.[47] But the administrative organisation of the diocese and imposition of ecclesiastical fiscal devices such as teinding also stimulated social and economic development and strengthened royal authority through the establishment of mechanisms for the enforcement of revenue payment and collection. Together, these developments indicate that David intended to replace individual authority with a system that offered strength in breadth.

Twelfth-century Moray contained anciently established agricultural zones which supported a sophisticated mechanism of local exploitation and control.[48] While Angus and his predecessors had drawn on the resources of the Laich district, how effectively they could harness the potential of areas remote from their power centres is questionable: the

---

[42] Bartlett, *Making of Europe*, Chapter 7.
[43] Simpson and Webster, 'Charter evidence and the distribution of mottes in Scotland', 1–24, appendix 1, 19; Oram, 'Castles and colonists'.
[44] Watt, *Fasti*, 214. Ross, PhD thesis, 208 discusses the bishops as replacements for the temporal powers of the earls.
[45] Anderson (ed.), *Early Sources*, ii, 210.
[46] See Watt, *Fasti*, 218 and following.
[47] Bartlett, *Making of Europe*, 228; McNeill, *Anglo-Norman Ulster*, 46–50.
[48] Ross, PhD thesis, Chapter 2.

existence of local mechanisms does not mean that they had been developed to facilitate external exploitation or to support lordships as modern historians have traditionally conceived of them. While the Laich today is principally arable land, it would be wrong to regard cereal cultivation as the mainstay of Moray's twelfth-century economy, and recent research suggests instead that much of the region's wealth lay in the hinterland, where a primarily cattle-based agricultural regime predominated.[49] It may have been difficult to attract colonists to settle where the crown itself could not convert notional rights of lordship into effective authority, or where institutions considered as fundamental to Continental-style lordship existed in at best a rudimentary form. Instead, David and his successors employed Gaelic magnates from the heartland of the kingdom, to whom the social and economic conditions of the region were more familiar, to develop the mechanisms for the more effective control of Moray's interior. In the late twelfth century, the earls of Fife, Strathearn and Mar, or their cadets, possessed land in the Moray uplands, such as Strathbogie and Stratha'an held by the Fifes, Kinveachy and Glencarnie held by the Streathearns, and Mar-held Abernethy and Aberchirder.[50] Traditional assumptions are that these lordships were acquired through service to William or Alexander II against the MacWilliams from the late 1170s onwards, but it is as likely that they were acquired in David's reign.[51] Given the Fifes' and Strathearns' position in David's kingdom, they were probably committed to the conquest of Moray and received the reward that they were best placed to exploit. Gaelic lordship practices provided the medium through which the loose economic and social affiliations of the central Highlands were drawn within the developing framework of David's rapidly expanding kingdom.

Although the wider north mainland continued to present challenges to his successors for a further century, lasting control of Moray was one of David's great achievements and its significance should not be underestimated. Moray had presented a sustained threat to his position throughout the first decade of his reign which traditional accounts of his accession and early years fail to acknowledge. Stracathro, rather than being a decisive victory, was instead the opening gambit in a war of attrition won eventually through David's possession of superior resources. It was a conflict, furthermore, that underscored the balance of old and new which Geoffrey Barrow has identified in David's kingdom, for it was

[49] Ibid. Chapters 1 and 2.
[50] Ibid. 125–33.
[51] Barrow, 'Badenoch and Strathspey I', 4–5; Ross, PhD thesis, 208–15.

the traditional power of his native magnates coupled with his imported administrative innovations that gave him victory in the north. From being the conflict that almost overthrew his kingship at the outset, the conquest of Moray and the domination of the north were David's first steps on the road to the making of his kingdom.

WESTWARD HO!

David's commitment to Moray after 1130 has overshadowed the problems that confronted him in the west even before his accession. 'The west' is an even vaguer term than 'the north', but two distinct western districts can be recognised; an ill-defined zone west of Annandale and Clydesdale and a west Highland region, encompassing the territory between the Lennox and Argyll in the south and Wester Ross in the north. Both blocks looked west to a further politically fluid zone dominated intermittently by Man- or Irish-based kings or Orcadian earls, and where the Norwegians claimed overlordship.[52] All were obstacles to a king keen to establish his domination of the Scottish mainland but the incoherence of the political structures or institutions of the wider region posed the question of how to project and maintain mastery over it.

The south-west mainland generally was labelled as 'Galloway' by the early twelfth century, but at around the same time that name acquired a precise political and territorial focus in the land along the northern shore of the Solway Firth.[53] Physically divided from the region to its north by the western Southern Uplands, this 'lesser' Galloway looked naturally to northern England, Man and Ireland. Controlling one side of the North Channel, which divides the Irish Sea from the Atlantic coasts of Scotland and Ireland, its rulers could dominate the sea lanes of the maritime west. David was not the only mainland British power with an interest in this strategic zone, for probably by c. 1120, following his policy of using his numerous bastards to strengthen his influence around the margins of his empire from Perche and Brittany to Scotland, Henry I of England had married one of his illegitimate daughters to Fergus, later styled 'king' of Galloway; this marriage was intended to widen English domination of the Irish Sea.[54] It resulted in an alliance between Galloway and the English crown which lasted into the thirteenth century.

---

[52] Oram, *Lordship of Galloway*, 39–44; Beuermann, *Masters of the Narrow Sea*.
[53] Oram, *Lordship of Galloway*, xxii.
[54] Ibid. 6; Hollister, *Henry I*, 41–5, 126, 179, 228–31, 233, 268.

There is no evidence for any relationship between Fergus and David before 1136. Men from 'Galloway' served in Malcolm III's armies in the 1080s,[55] but they came probably from the wider south-western region where Malcolm exercised an ill-defined overlordship which had not survived the turmoil after 1093. Fergus's domain was a recent development in a political void over which no higher authority had exercised effective rule for some time. For David, therefore, 'King' Fergus was a potential rival for the domination of south-west mainland Scotland. Their uncertain relationship was probably a factor in David's establishment of Robert de Bruce in Annandale, the first of several lordships created by David and his successors in 'greater Galloway'. Although dated traditionally to 1124 on the basis of the charter by which David infefted Robert, an earlier award had perhaps followed soon after Carlisle had been surrendered to Henry I by Ranulf le Meschin when Ranulf had inherited Chester. Robert may have been part of a cooperative scheme between David and Henry to secure the western end of the emerging Anglo-Scottish border after Ranulf's departure, possibly connected to the Anglo-Scottish crisis of 1122 or as a response to the growing power of Fergus.[56]

Fergus and Galloway were perhaps the least of David's worries after 1124. His bastard nephew, Malcolm, had allies in the west who saw an opportunity to extend their influence at the expense of the king of Scots. Fergus does not appear amongst them, but the very obscure Gillebrigte, father of Somerled, *rí* of Argyll, apparently was. Around this time he was building a power base in the peninsulas and sea lochs of the southwest Highlands. We do not know when or how Malcolm and Gillebrigte became allies, but the alliance was founded on Malcolm's marriage to Gillebrigte's daughter. Given that Malcolm had fathered at least two sons before his capture in 1134 who were considered adult by 1153,[57] the match had probably occurred by 1125–6. David's presence at Irvine some time between 1124 and 1128 might indicate a response to this marriage alliance. The reason for Gillebrigte's alliance with Malcolm is easy to identify, for the spread of David's power west of Clydesdale and possibly into the Lennox after 1113 brought rival ambitions into collision. Although Scottish kings believed that they possessed authority in Argyll, Gillebrigte and his son after him had built up their power independently. Scottish kings perhaps regarded Argyll's ruler as a tributary, but

---

[55] Anderson (ed.), *Scottish Annals*, 100–2.
[56] Barrow (ed.), *David I Charters*, no. 16; Kapelle, *Norman Conquest of the North*, 206–7.
[57] *Chron. Holyrood*, s.a. 1153.

Somerled's later career shows that he saw himself as a fully independent power. His father's involvement with Malcolm's rebellion was probably opportunism guided by expansionist ambitions and a response to David's assertion of authority within the north-western part of 'greater Galloway'. That development confronted the predatory Argyll-based ruler with a rival for domination of the wider Clyde estuary region.

Only Ailred of Rievaulx's passing mention of campaigns in the west hint at a conflict on land and sea.[58] Unlike in Moray, conquest or colonisation was not envisaged; David's primary aim was to secure recognition of his overlordship of Argyll. By the mid-1130s, he had gained that result, if the recorded presence of Argyllmen in the Scottish army at Northallerton in 1138 is reliable.[59] But the submission of Gillebrigte or his successor was just one outcome of David's offensive, for it also saw an extension into and tightening of royal authority over the district from Strathgryfe south to Kyle or Carrick, where in the early 1120s his power had been ephemeral at best.

The western limits of David's power down to the early 1120s probably matched the distribution of properties possessed by the Church of Glasgow as revealed by an inquest conducted on his orders in c. 1121–2; it identified none west of Clydesdale.[60] If Glasgow's lands were defined by the bounds of David's Cumbrian principality, the inquest reveals the limited influence of Clydesdale-based rulers in 'greater Galloway'. David believed that he had some authority in this area, as revealed by his grant to Selkirk Abbey of the teind of his *cáin* of cheese from 'Galloway',[61] which was confirmed and expanded by Malcolm IV in 1159 into the teind of *cáin* (a render in kind owed to a ruler) of cattle, pigs and cheese 'from the four *kadrez* of that [part of] Galloway' which had been held by his grandfather before 1124.[62] Where or what these *kadrez* were is not stated, but in c. 1136 David granted Glasgow the teind of his *cáin* of cattle and pigs from four districts, Strathgryfe, Cunningham, Kyle and Carrick, 'excepting the years when I come there and consume my *cáin*'.[63] The temptation to equate these units with the four *kadrez* is strong, but the evidence is circumstantial. David was apparently beginning to extend his authority over these lands down the east side of the Clyde estuary

---

[58] Ailred of Rievaulx, *De Standardo*, 179–99.
[59] Ibid. 191.
[60] Barrow (ed.), *David I Charters*, no. 15.
[61] Ibid. no. 14.
[62] Barrow (ed.), *RRS*, i, no. 131.
[63] Barrow (ed.), *David I Charters*, no. 57; Oram, *Lordship of Galloway*, xxiii.

in the early 1120s and by the mid-1130s could grant away some of the renders due to him from the region. He also based himself at Irvine in Cunningham on at least two occasions in his reign, both probably before 1134.[64] Irvine was important in David's grand designs in the 1130s, and its role in Alexander II's western campaigns a century later perhaps points to its earlier development with a similar function.[65] It was possibly from there that David's offensive against Malcolm's western allies, which involved naval operations from west coast bases, was launched.[66] Malcolm's alliance with the rulers of Argyll drew Scottish royal power deeper into the Clyde coast territories as David sought to contain and eliminate the threat. While charter evidence for infeftments during the first half of his reign does not survive, it was probably the seaborne threat from Argyll that led David to settle this western district with men on whom he could rely for its defence and integration into his realm.[67] The Clyde estuary's contested frontier status is often forgotten, but the military aspect of David's new lordships down its eastern flank shows acute awareness of that position.

The capture of Malcolm in 1134 perhaps followed or was part of recognition of David's superior lordship by Gillebrigte or his son. Soon afterwards a contingent of warriors from Lorne was fighting in David's 1138 English campaign.[68] One indication of how effective David believed his lordship over Argyll to be can be seen in the 1140s when he awarded Holyrood Abbey elements of *cáin* from Argyll and Kintyre.[69] There were ramifications, with David's imposition of authority over Argyll sending shockwaves through adjacent regions. One consequence was a series of marriage alliances with neighbouring rulers which King Óláfr I of Man forged at this time. One of these, contracted by c. 1140, was of an illegitimate daughter to Somerled.[70] Óláfr had also been a protégé of Henry I of England, at whose court he sheltered during the upheavals in Man after Guðrøðr Crobán's death. In the 1120s, however, Óláfr had forged strong ties with Henry's nephew Stephen, who held the lordship of Lancaster, and it is possible that he supported Stephen as king after 1135. For David, the detaching of Óláfr from that alliance formed part of a wider design to extend Scottish power into the Irish Sea, particularly after 1138

---

[64] Barrow (ed.), *David I Charters*, nos 17 and 37.
[65] Oram, *Lordship of Galloway*, 122 and notes 80 and 81.
[66] Ross, PhD thesis, 182.
[67] Barrow, *Anglo-Norman Era*, 72 and note 64.
[68] Ailred of Rievaulx, *De Standardo*, 191.
[69] Barrow (ed.), *David I Charters*, no. 147.
[70] *Chron. Man*, s.a. 1144 = 1154.

as he sought to establish his lordship in Cumberland and Westmorland. Marriage was also a tool in this process, with Óláfr wed by c. 1140 to Affreca, daughter of Fergus of Galloway, in a move designed to draw the Manx king into the ever-widening network of dependence around David.

The extent of this network and the enhanced level of David's authority in the west are evident from the men who attended royal gatherings at Glasgow and Cadzow in 1136. At the former, David was joined by his nephew William, the earls of Strathearn and Fife, Fergus of Galloway and his younger son, Uhtred (Henry I's grandson), Radulf and Donald, lords respectively of lower and upper Nithsdale, and other officials from the Lennox and eastern Stirlingshire.[71] At Cadzow, in addition to the Nithsdale and Galloway men, Hugh de Morville and Walter son of Alan, who probably held Cunningham and Renfrew by this time, were also present.[72] It is difficult to avoid seeing in these gatherings the assembly of David's dependents in 'greater Galloway' and his chief men from north of the Forth and Lothian, who would shortly lead their warriors into England. They reveal how by 1136 David had extended authority out of his power base in Teviotdale in a major step towards a kingship with effective lordship over all of mainland Scotland.

WAR IN ENGLAND 1135-9

David's successes in consolidating his hold on mainland Scotland by the mid-1130s enabled him to seize the spectacular opportunity for territorial gain presented by the death of Henry I on 1 December 1135. Henry's arrangements for the English succession had unravelled as his nephew, Stephen, secured the throne while Henry's designated successor, his daughter Matilda, remained in Anjou with her husband.[73] Within three weeks Stephen was crowned king and gained the acceptance of all but a minority of English and Norman nobles, but his success faltered before the new year began as challenges emerged, not least of which was the invasion of northern England by the Scots shortly after Christmas.[74]

John of Hexham, the twelfth-century northern English chronicler, claims that David acted to honour his 1127 oath to support Matilda,[75] but

---

[71] Barrow (ed.), *David I Charters*, no. 56.
[72] Ibid. no. 57.
[73] Matthew, *King Stephen*, 59–60.
[74] Richard of Hexham, 145.
[75] *John of Hexham*, in Symeon of Durham, *Opera Omnia*, ii, 287.

his invasion four weeks after Henry's death appears aimed at securing the southern Cumbrian and Northumbrian lands that David believed was the heritage of his late wife and their son. Suggestions of high-minded support for Matilda's cause disguised an unprincipled bid to secure disputed territory, and David would possibly have invaded England in the uncertain transitional period after the old king's death regardless of who succeeded Henry I.[76] Richard of Hexham presents the mid-winter campaign as a major success, with Carlisle, Wark, Alnwick, Norham and Newcastle falling to David and only Bamburgh's defenders remaining loyal to Stephen. There are, however, signs of sterner resistance which needed the extraction of forced oaths and hostages, and Ailred of Rievaulx, normally vocally pro-David, describes the campaign as a harrying 'with slaughter and fire'. Longer term, the perceived barbarity of the Scots became an obstacle to securing unqualified acceptance of David's rule in northern England.[77]

David's plans extended far beyond securing his son's heritage in Northumberland, and in early February 1136 he marched on Durham where he was confronted by Stephen, who had hastened north with an army.[78] There was no battle, negotiations instead yielding a deal which revealed that territorial ambition was David's chief motive.[79] David surrendered Newcastle to Stephen but retained Carlisle in his son's name. He did not perform homage, avoiding the compromise to his position entailed by that, but Henry, David's only son and heir, did perform homage in respect of Carlisle and the earldom of Huntingdon, which Stephen had confiscated but now promised to restore. Both kings gained from the settlement: Stephen had secured his northern frontier at limited territorial cost and had effectively detached David from Matilda's cause; David had surrendered Northumberland but had secured Carlisle and avoided a personal submission to Stephen which might have compromised his own kingship.

Whatever gloss is put on it, the Durham settlement left Scottish claims to Northumberland unresolved. David had surrendered Northumberland in return for a promise that Henry's claim would be judged in Stephen's court.[80] The position of Huntingdon, too, was unsatisfactory, for,

---

[76] Matthew, *King Stephen*, 70.
[77] Richard of Hexham, 145; Ailred of Rievaulx, *Saints of Hexham*, 183; Matthew, *King Stephen*, 79.
[78] Richard of Hexham, 145–6.
[79] Henry of Huntingdon, *Historia Anglorum*, 259.
[80] Richard of Hexham, 146.

although Stephen recognised Henry as earl, he also acknowledged the rights of Henry's elder half-brother, Simon II de Senlis, and apparently awarded him the Northampton portion of the earldom.[81] Stephen added Doncaster to Henry's lands as compensation, but this attempt to satisfy conflicting claims pleased no one. The English king strove to woo Henry, who came to London for Stephen's Easter court, but the favour shown to him rankled with Stephen's supporters, headed by William of Corbeil, the archbishop of Canterbury, who accused Henry of treason in Stephen's presence.[82] Ranulf II, earl of Chester, whose father had surrendered Carlisle to Henry I before receiving Chester, joined the denunciation.[83] The earl also claimed Carlisle and was among several lords, probably including Simon II, whose territorial ambitions were frustrated by Stephen's deal with David. Despite Stephen's attempts to calm the situation, David used the archbishop's behaviour to recall Henry to Scotland.

There was no immediate breakdown in the peace, but contemporary chroniclers suggest that Matilda and her supporters used the incident to win David over.[84] David was open to her overtures, for his deteriorating relationship with Stephen affected settlements dating back to the 1120s which touched directly on sensitive political-religious issues. In April 1136, for example, York revived its claim to metropolitan jurisdiction over Scotland.[85] David had previously secured compromise agreements through Henry I's mediation, but those had died with Henry. The religious controversy probably overshadowed the consecration of the cathedral at Glasgow, which David attended together with his nephew, William, the earls of Fife and Strathearn, and Fergus of Galloway, and it is possible that the gathering turned into a council of war.[86]

In spring 1137 David moved while Stephen was committed to the defence of Normandy. David's objective was Northumberland, but he found the earldom better defended than in 1135 and Stephen's northern loyalists had gathered at Newcastle to oppose him. David again negotiated and met with Archbishop Thurstan of York at Roxburgh in May, settling a six-month truce to last until Stephen's

---

[81] Matthew, *King Stephen*, 78.
[82] Richard of Hexham, 146.
[83] John of Hexham, 287.
[84] *Gesta Stephani*, Chapter 25.
[85] *Historians of the Church of York*, iii, 66–7.
[86] *Chron. Holyrood*, 119. See *Glasgow Registrum*, no. 3.

expected return from Normandy at the end of November.[87] When diplomacy intensified on Stephen's return, David revealed his ambitions: Matilda's rights were of little concern to him, territorial aggrandisement was all.[88] The price of peace was Northumberland for Henry, but emboldened by his success in Normandy, Stephen refused. David's conduct at this time has been described with justification as 'exceedingly discreditable', for claims of oath-bound obligation offered by his apologists cannot mask his naked 'ambition and aggression'.[89] But we must not be overly critical, for David was attempting to be all things to all men: seeking to secure territory that he regarded as either lawfully his or the rightful heritage of his son; manoeuvring to avoid censure as an oath-breaker; and striving to win the allegiance of men whose loyalty would strengthen his hand in northern England against Stephen and, possibly, aid Matilda. By late 1137, David was under pressure from Matilda and her northern supporters, led by Eustace son of John, lord of Malton and Alnwick, to take the field openly against Stephen.[90] Eustace's defection to David broke the unity of the Northumberland nobility against the Scots, for he brought over several lesser lords who looked to him for leadership. Guaranteed active support within the earldom, in January 1138 David sent his nephew, William, to besiege Wark, the key to north-west Northumberland.[91] David soon joined the siege, but after three weeks left a force to blockade the castle while he marched south, fearful of losing the initiative to Stephen.

Most contemporary accounts depict the campaign which followed as a sustained episode of brutality, barbarism, atrocity and unchristian behaviour. The chronicles of Richard and John of Hexham are unremitting in their hostility to the Scots and suggest that there were few beyond Eustace's circle of dependents for whom submission meant more than a grudging recognition of political realities. Hyperbole aside, however, the chronicles chart in detail both the general conduct of the campaign, localised resistance to the Scots, negotiation of protections for religious communities and David's difficulties in maintaining discipline in his

---

[87] Richard of Hexham, 150–1; John of Hexham, 288.
[88] Matthew, *King Stephen*, 79.
[89] Poole, *Domesday Book to Magna Carta*, 270. *Gesta Stephani*, 34.
[90] *Gesta Stephani*, 34; Kapelle, *Norman Conquest of the North*, 198–9.
[91] John of Hexham, 289; for Carham and Wark, see Kapelle, *Norman Conquest of the North*, 197, 205. See also Strickland, 'Securing the North', 208–29.

army.[92] No decisive breakthrough had been achieved by mid-February, however, when David withdrew as Stephen advanced north.[93]

As in 1136, Stephen's decisiveness prevented David from consolidating his hold on Northumberland, while his brief foray towards Roxburgh reveals him as a skilled strategist.[94] Stephen, however, could not bring David to battle and was forced to head south by early April. Almost immediately David invaded Northumberland again, ravaged districts left untouched in January/February and then crossed the Tyne.[95] At the same time he sent his nephew to harry Furness and Craven. In June William routed a small English army at Clitheroe and delivered control of north-west England above Lancaster to the Scots, placing the trans-Pennine routes in their hands and putting York within striking distance.[96] Further success followed with the surrender of the bishop of Durham's castle at Norham, but the gain was minimal for David failed to bring Bishop Geoffrey into his peace.[97] His slow progress in securing Northumberland, symbolised by his continuing failure at Wark, encouraged few leading men to join him and forced him instead into actions that were unlikely to win over any waverers. Rather than a war of attrition which picked off strategic castles, he sought a quick victory by capturing York.[98] Contemporary sources present his army as one of the largest gathered by a king of Scots, and the list of contingents involved underscores David's success in extending his power throughout mainland Scotland and beyond.[99] Unlike in 1136 and 1137, deterioration of his position in southern England meant that Stephen could not confront David in person; it was Archbishop Thurstan and William, earl of Aumâle to whom Stephen entrusted York's defence.[100] Thurstan and Earl William were supported by a small group of Yorkshire barons, including David's old associate Robert de Bruce.[101] Beyond that limited body of political support, what stood between the collapse or survival of Stephen's position in the north was an ingrained antipathy towards

---

[92] Richard of Hexham, 152–3; John of Hexham, 289.
[93] John of Hexham, 290.
[94] Richard of Hexham, 155.
[95] Ibid. 155–6.
[96] John of Hexham, 291.
[97] Richard of Hexham, 156–7.
[98] John of Hexham, 292.
[99] Ailred of Rievaulx, *De Standardo*, 181.
[100] *Anglo-Saxon Chronicle*, E, s.a. 1138.
[101] Richard of Hexham, 159. For background, see Kapelle, *Norman Conquest of the North*, 198–9, 221–2, 223.

the Scots amongst the northern English people. Contemporary English chroniclers present the war in the language of Rome against the barbarians, with the Scots as the heathen host at the gates of beleaguered Christian civilisation. This perception was underscored by Archbishop Thurstan's declaration that the struggle was a holy war and ordering of priests to accompany Stephen's barons into battle carrying processional crosses, holy banners and saints' relics.[102]

Negotiations failed to secure a Scottish withdrawal and on 22 August, the armies met on Cowton Moor near Northallerton in what became known as the battle of the Standard, after the cart-mounted ship's mast bearing various religious flags set at the heart of the English army. Scottish cultural and moral inferiority are recurrent themes in accounts of the battle, with poor equipment (evidence of their lack of cultural advancement) and ill discipline (evidence of their primitive morality) being presented as features that were decisive in the outcome. Ailred claims that David and most of his lieutenants wanted his best-equipped men to face the English knights, but the lightly armed and notoriously ill-disciplined men of Galloway, supported by the earl of Strathearn, claimed the right to form the vanguard. The argument reveals tension between David's Gaelic lords and English knights, with the former resentful of the influence enjoyed by the latter in his counsels. Yielding to the Galwegians' demands was the first of David's mistakes and contributed largely to the crushing defeat of the Scottish host that followed.

Defeat was costly for David, but its impact should not be overstated. Like many 'decisive' battles the Standard did not end the war, for the English lacked the resources to follow up the victory, and the Scots were left to consolidate their grip on Cumberland and Northumberland. David reverted to besieging the remaining castles holding out for Stephen, but Wark was still defying him when he met Pope Innocent II's legate, Alberic, cardinal-bishop of Ostia, at Carlisle in late September.[103] The legation was unconnected with the war, Alberic's purpose being settlement of disputes involving the bishops of Glasgow and Carlisle, but their meeting was dominated by the recent events. While his legation's ecclesiastical business was quickly settled the war proved more intractable. Eventually, Alberic secured a truce from David but it specifically excluded operations against Wark, which finally surrendered in November. Furthermore, David only offered a six-week delay on invading England, presumably to allow time for formal negotiations

---

[102] Ailred of Rievaulx, *De Standardo*, 182; Richard of Hexham, 161–2.
[103] Richard of Hexham, 166, 170.

with Stephen to begin.[104] Alberic negotiated hard with Stephen, who was under pressure from barons whose property in the north had been wasted not to make concessions. Stephen's wife, another Matilda, who was also David's niece, was influential in securing a settlement.[105] Her desire to secure her sons' inheritance in England led her to urge Stephen to concentrate on the heartland of his kingdom rather than waste effort on remote territories. David, moreover, was perhaps favourable towards proposals in which his niece, the queen, had a hand than any offer from his other niece, the empress, for the former's husband was *de facto* king and able to make real concessions, whilst the empress's likelihood of securing her father's throne seemed as remote in 1138 as ever.

Early in 1139 Queen Matilda met with David at Durham and agreed a treaty. It gave David most of what he had set out to gain in 1135, granting his son Henry the earldom of Northumberland, except for the castles of Bamburgh and Newcastle, Norhamshire and the properties of Hexham Priory, and ordering the regional barons to give their homage to their new earl. Henry also regained Huntingdon and Doncaster, and was confirmed in possession of Carlisle and Cumberland. David and Henry in return promised to be loyal allies and keep the peace, and gave high-ranking hostages to Stephen.[106] At a meeting of Henry with Stephen at Nottingham, the treaty was approved and ratified. Modern assessments of the settlement have been critical of Stephen's concessions to David, most focusing on its failure to end the Northumberland question through the retention of its two chief fortresses; its direct clash with the interests of some of Stephen's closest supporters; and the great area of territory handed over to the Scots.[107] The reality was more positive for Stephen. The agreement fixed the Tyne as the frontier on the east and confirmed Scottish possession of Cumberland on the west, territory which they already controlled. Settlement of Northumberland on Earl Henry required his homage to Stephen for his new earldom in an explicit recognition of the overlordship of the English crown.[108] This was a pragmatic agreement which restored peaceful relations between the kingdoms and deprived the empress of a powerful ally, while binding David's heir to Stephen's cause through his performance of homage.

---

[104] Ibid. 170–1.
[105] Ibid. 176; Matthew, *King Stephen*, 81.
[106] Richard of Hexham, 177–8.
[107] See, for example, Davis, *King Stephen*, 46. But see Stringer, *Reign of Stephen*, 32–3; Matthew, *King Stephen*, 81–2.
[108] Stringer, *Reign of Stephen*, 33.

Map 3.1 David I's Northumbrian campaigns

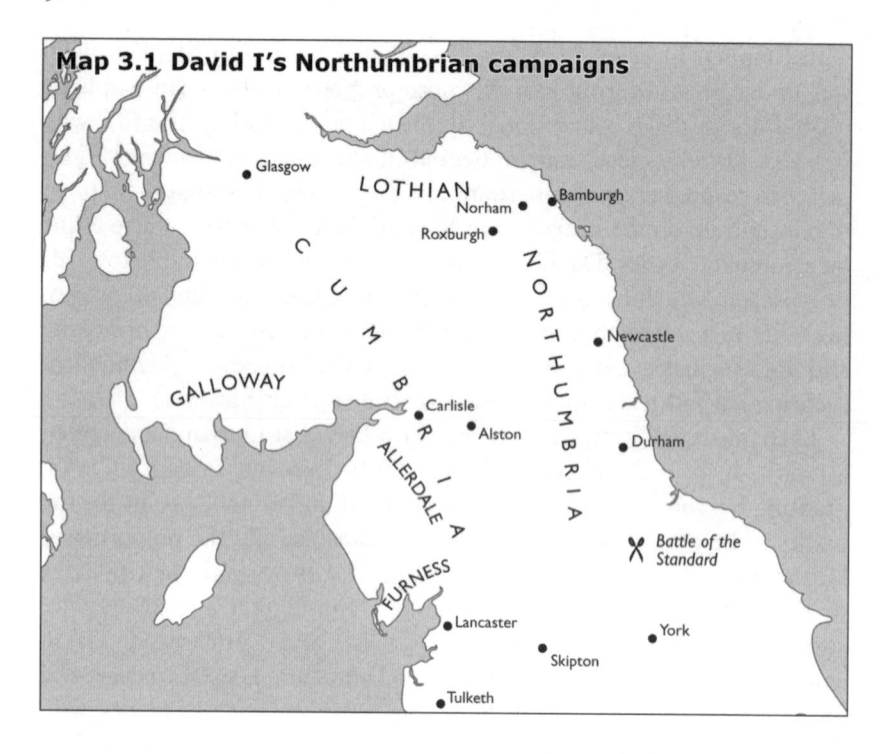

CONSOLIDATION 1139–49

Stephen grasped the opportunity to redefine Anglo-Scottish relations through Earl Henry's integration into the loyalist political community in England. Henry reciprocated with participation in Stephen's West Country campaign in the second half of 1139, publicly demonstrating his loyalty to the king and underscoring his and his father's recognition of Stephen's legitimate kingship.[109] Henry's acceptance into the inner circle of Stephen's military elite was confirmed before the year end when the king arranged his marriage to Ada de Warenne, sister of William II, earl of Warenne, and half-sister of Robert, earl of Leicester, and Waleran, count of Meulan.[110] It was a mutually beneficial deal, for while it bound Henry into Stephen's party, it secured Henry powerful support against challenges from rivals like Simon II de Senlis and Ranulf of Chester. For David, the accord allowed the fuller integration of northern England into his kingdom. Although Cumberland and Carlisle were held by Henry as

---

[109] Henry of Huntingdon, *Historia Anglorum*, 265.
[110] John of Hexham, 300.

English fiefs, David treated them as part of his own realm and developed Carlisle and its castle as his seat of government.[111] His concern to secure the region was not driven simply by military strategy, for it brought him the mines at Alston in the Pennines, a source of the silver to mint his own coinage, the first 'native' specie produced in his kingdom.[112] The Cumberland silver provided the liquid on which the 'Davidian Revolution' in Scotland was floated.

The prospect of long-term peace after Durham ended abruptly with Stephen's capture by the supporters of the empress at Lincoln on 2 February 1141. This unforeseen turn of events confronted David with both opportunities and threats. The 1139 treaty that legitimated Scottish control of Cumberland and Northumberland had been settled with Stephen, not the empress, who, given David's failure to support her claims, had no reason to honour it. Stephen's capture, moreover, had been a consequence of the defection of Ranulf, earl of Chester, who was again claiming Carlisle and Cumberland and probably expected them from Matilda as a reward for his service.[113] Ever the opportunist, David moved first to secure his gains with the new regime. Having already won much, he banked on making further capital from the new situation in England and renewed his war against Stephen. The target this time was northern Lancashire and north-west Yorkshire, where William son of Duncan II claimed Skipton and Craven, and Durham, where Bishop Geoffrey's death perhaps opened the see to a candidate of David's choice.[114] A pro-Scottish bishop would have handed David unquestioned dominance north of the Tees, and he moved swiftly to occupy the city. Having promised not to interfere in the choosing of Geoffrey's successor before consulting the empress, he installed his chancellor, William Cumin, as interim administrator of the see and signalled that he favoured Cumin's election.[115]

In early summer David headed south to attend Matilda's coronation.[116] That she was still uncrowned nearly four months after Stephen's capture perhaps alarmed David, for it allowed her cousin, Queen Matilda, to rally Stephen's supporters. Having overcome

---

[111] 'Chronicle of the Canons of Huntingdon', in Anderson (ed.), *Early Sources*, ii, 201.
[112] Matthew, *King Stephen*, 143 and note 63.
[113] John of Hexham, 306.
[114] Aird, *St Cuthbert and the Normans*, 261–2.
[115] John of Hexham, 309; Barrow (ed.), *David I Charters*, nos 102 and 103. Aird, *St Cuthbert and the Normans*, 260–3. See also Young, *William Cumin* and Young, 'Bishopric of Durham', 353–68.
[116] John of Hexham, 309.

objections from the English clergy and received their reluctant blessing at Winchester, instead of arranging the coronation there the empress settled on a ceremony at Westminster. That, however, required possession of London, whose citizens were staunchly pro-Stephen.[117] Rioting and disturbances in London enabled Matilda to occupy the city, but she had little support there and her hold on it was slipping when David arrived in early June.

Despite earlier failures to support her, David considered a place among the empress's closest advisors to be his by right and was prepared to act as an English magnate to secure his territorial ambitions. This was perhaps especially true concerning Durham, where he sought her approval for the nomination of William Cumin.[118] He was soon aware of how narrow support for her was in England: she was incapable of courting friends and David's offers of advice were spurned.[119] Within a week, the Londoners' hostility forced her out of the city, ending hopes of a Westminster coronation. David, however, remained with Matilda as she attempted to consolidate her hold over the lower Thames valley and the routes into the Midlands, and at the end of July joined her to attack Winchester.[120] Although her supporters stormed the city walls, Bishop Henry, King Stephen's brother, held his palace and other strongholds against them.[121] The attackers, moreover, soon found themselves besieged when Stephen's loyalists arrived and encircled the city, and it was only with great difficulty that David and Matilda escaped.[122]

David immediately headed for Durham to arrange Cumin's election, but the king's chancellor was deeply unpopular with the monks.[123] A free election, as demanded by the leading bishops in England, benefited Cumin's opponents, but David had Matilda's endorsement of his chancellor. He, however, did not wish to alienate the politically influential monks by forcing Cumin upon them when he needed allies after the disastrous events of the summer. Rather than provoke a confrontation, David left Cumin with a garrison in the bishop's castle but agreed to stand surety between the soldiers and the monks for any damages or

---

[117] Matthew, *King Stephen*, 106.
[118] *Historia Dunelmensis Ecclesiae*, in Symeon of Durham, i, 162.
[119] John of Hexham, 309; *Gesta Stephani*, 74-75.
[120] Matthew, *King Stephen*, 108.
[121] Henry of Huntingdon, *Historia Anglorum*, 275.
[122] *Historia Dunelmensis Ecclesiae, continuatio altera*, 162; John of Hexham, 311.
[123] *Historia Dunelmensis Ecclesiae, continuatio prima*, 144-5; John of Hexham, 309; Aird, *St Cuthbert and the Normans*, 262-5.

injuries arising.[124] Cumin tried to woo his potential electors and to court the lay elite of the diocese,[125] but failed in both before Stephen's release in November 1141. Even David's backing went as the king searched for an acceptable candidate for the monks and did nothing to obstruct the monks' election of William of Ste Barbe as bishop of Durham. Although northern English tradition accused David and his son of duplicity in their dealings with William after 1143,[126] it is unlikely that they even tacitly supported Cumin in actions that threatened their control of north-east England. Long before Cumin surrendered Durham Castle in October 1144, David had reached an agreement with the bishop-elect and Earl Henry had assumed the mantle of protector of bishop and diocese in a firm assertion of his lordship in the region.[127] As a result, although Durham remained outwith direct Scottish control, Bishop William was more favourably inclined towards David than might have been expected after the struggle with Cumin.

David's failure at Durham has been presented as indicative of Stephen's residual authority in even remote corners of his kingdom.[128] William of Ste Barbe's election does seem to reflect this, for as dean of York he had presided over a strongly pro-Stephen chapter which in 1141 had elected Stephen's cousin, William son of Herbert, to the archbishopric. But Stephen had been entirely passive in the Durham election, and Bishop William only secured possession of the temporalities of his see with Scottish, not English, support. Nor did his episcopate see either a revival of Stephen's regional authority or diminution of Scottish influence south of the Tyne:[129] William, if he was intended as Stephen's agent, was outmanoeuvred and isolated by the Scots.

Durham was not David's only concern as he and Earl Henry tightened their grip on northern England. The forfeiture of Huntingdon to Stephen in 1141 encouraged them to build the same personal political bonds for Henry in Northumberland as had underpinned David's lordship in the Midlands. Although the 1139 accord confirmed Northumberland as an English fief, after 1141 Henry held it as a Scottish earldom.[130] Some

---

[124] *Historia Dunelmensis Ecclesiae, continuatio prima*, 146.
[125] *Historia Dunelmensis Ecclesiae, continuatio altera*, 162; *Historia Dunelmensis Ecclesiae, continuatio prima*, 146.
[126] John of Hexham, 314; *Historia Dunelmensis Ecclesiae, continuatio prima*, 157, 159.
[127] Stringer, 'State-building in twelfth-century Britain', 49; Aird, *St Cuthbert and the Normans*, 264.
[128] Matthew, *King Stephen*, 114, 131.
[129] *Historia Dunelmensis Ecclesiae, continuatio altera*, 167.
[130] Barrow (ed.), *David I Charters*, 34–6.

historians have considered the antipathy of contemporary chroniclers towards Scottish rule as indications of the failure of that policy.[131] Dissent was not widespread, however, and one chronicler, William of Newburgh, saw Scottish-ruled Northumbria as a haven of tranquillity in comparison with southern England.[132] In Northumberland after 1139, stability was founded on a circle of leading tenants around Earl Henry, led at first by Eustace son of John,[133] then by the de Umfravilles in the persons of Robert de Umfraville, lord of Redesdale and Prudhoe, and his son, Gilbert; Robert held lordships that straddled the routes between Roxburgh and Durham, and Newcastle and Carlisle.[134] His allegiance to David and Earl Henry was of greater significance than the grudging acknowledgement of the prior of Hexham, who nevertheless still attended the courts of David and Henry.[135] Gilbert de Umfraville became one of Earl Henry's closest associates, serving as his constable and probably also as justiciar in Northumberland, and receiving for his good service estates at Kinnaird and Dunipace in Stirlingshire, and Keith in Midlothian.[136] But Henry did not depend simply on this narrow clique of top-rank men or control of the chief fortresses of the earldom, for all the prominent regional families were active in his service, and his rule was enforced by an effective administration.[137] While Henry's authority stemmed ultimately from a grant of the earldom by Stephen, it was not that legitimacy that won him recognition, but the reality of the stability, security and good lordship that the Scots offered and which both Stephen and Matilda had failed to provide.

In Cumberland, David behaved as if it were integral to his own realm, Carlisle becoming with Roxburgh and Edinburgh a focus of royal power. Once Bishop Æðelwulf of Carlisle entered David's peace a close partnership developed between king and bishop. For the remainder of David's

---

[131] Matthew, *King Stephen*, 131.
[132] William of Newburgh, *Historia Rerum Anglicarum*, i, 70.
[133] Eustace witnessed several of Henry's acts: Barrow (ed.), *David I Charters*, nos 59, 60, 65, 74, 81, 102.
[134] See comments in Kapelle, *Norman Conquest of the North*, 283–4 note; Barrow (ed.), *David I Charters*, 20; Lomas, *North-East England*, 26.
[135] Stringer, 'State-building in twelfth-century Britain', 55.
[136] For the Umfravilles and Earl Henry, see Barrow (ed.), *David I Charters*, 20 and nos 52, 61, 62, 65, 73, 74, 78–80, 82, 101–4, 121, 163, 169, 170, 199; Stringer, 'State-building in twelfth-century Britain', 51; *Kelso Liber*, i, no. 92 (Keith); Barrow (ed.), *RRS*, ii, no. 292 (Kinnaird); *Cambuskenneth Registrum* nos 80 and 86 (Dunipace).
[137] Stringer, 'State-building in twelfth-century Britain', 52–3; Duncan, *Making of the Kingdom*, 222.

reign Æðelwulf was associated with the royal government in a manner similar to the relationship between Bishop John of Glasgow and David before 1124.[138] Control of Carlisle also allowed for further Scottish expansion in north-west England, such as had been presaged in the campaigns of 1136–38. This expansion was driven both by personal claims and by strategic considerations, for William son of Duncan II sought his maternal heritage in Allerdale and the inherited lands in Copeland and Craven of his second wife, Alice de Rumilly, while David coveted Furness, Cartmel, Lonsdale, Amounderness and Lancaster, held by Stephen as personal lordships since c. 1120.[139] While the empress's position in the south crumbled, before 1141 was over David had occupied almost all of these territories and controlled the region as far as 'the new castle of Tulketh' east of Preston.[140] From there he issued charters of protection to the monks of Shrewsbury for their lands around Lancaster, documents granted by him as king of Scots with no acknowledgement of the over-riding authority of the English crown. Unlike his caution at Durham, David here settled on an authoritative assertion of his own power and replacement of Stephen's personal lordship with his own.

The seizure of Stephen's estates gave David the resources to entrench Scottish control over north-west England. Some were granted to his supporters, but often he simply inserted a new layer of lordship between himself and existing tenants.[141] In this fashion, his nephew gained Allerdale and Copeland, and possibly Craven, which his son held in 1149–52.[142] Hugh de Morville, who had served David since the late 1130s and already held Lauderdale and Cunningham, received North Westmorland, centred on Appleby, and possibly also South Westmorland with its castle of Kendal.[143] Hugh was David's constable by 1140 and possession of these strategic English lordships by David's chief military officer was probably no coincidence.[144] Over the next decade, the de Morvilles intermarried with the regional nobility, forging

---

[138] John of Hexham, 298; Barrow (ed.), *David I Charters*, 86, 91, 101, 122, 132, 150–1; Stringer, 'State-building in twelfth-century Britain', 49.

[139] Barrow, 'Lordship and feudal settlement in Cumbria', 122; Kapelle, *Norman Conquest of the North*, 200.

[140] For David's possession of Lancaster, see Barrow, 'David I and Lancaster', 85–9; Stringer, *Reign of Stephen*, 33. For charters issued by David at Tulketh, see Barrow (ed.), *David I Charters*, nos 111 and 112.

[141] Stringer, *Reign of Stephen*, 34–5.

[142] Symeon of Durham, *Opera Omnia*, ii, 326; Stringer, *Reign of Stephen*, 34–5.

[143] Barrow, *Anglo-Norman Era*, 71–3 and note 64; Stringer, *Reign of Stephen*, 35.

[144] Barrow (ed.), *David I Charters*, 36 and no. 96.

ties that gave their Scottish descendants landed claims in Westmorland into the thirteenth century.[145] William and Hugh apart, however, David cultivated the established baronage and drew them into his administrative regime, a process eased by how few of them held property within Stephen's remaining sphere of authority which otherwise may have made for difficult choices.[146] In both English Cumbria and Northumberland, therefore, Scottish control was founded on the establishment of a group of 'super-magnates' and the forging of close personal bonds with the regional baronage. This secure hold offered the prospect of the lasting integration of these territories into the Scottish realm.

How far was that realm to extend? In 1138, David's sights had been set on York, and defeat at the Standard had not ended that ambition. Control of York would deliver David the lordship of England north of the Humber. As the chief commercial centre north of London, possession of the city promised access to revenues perhaps greater than those of his kingdom. A Scottish-held York, moreover, would resolve the contentious issue of metropolitan supremacy over the Scottish Church. The death in February 1140 of Archbishop Thurstan, who had been central to the defence of the north in 1136–8, was amongst the factors behind David's breach with Stephen in 1141.[147] Stephen's personal authority had been most effective immediately before his capture at Lincoln, and, with his northern frontier apparently stable following his accord with David, he delayed finding a successor for Thurstan. He may have been further encouraged to delay the process to capitalise on the crown's right to the temporal revenues of vacant sees, and it was only in January 1141 that he arranged the election of his nephew, William. Stephen's capture the following month weakened the archbishop-elect's position before he could establish himself in office, and his enemies, notably the heads of the Yorkshire Cistercian and Augustinian monasteries, swiftly laid accusations of clerical unsuitability and charges of corruption and nepotism against him. Nevertheless, it appeared that Stephen had succeeded in maintaining his grip on York when William was consecrated in 1143, but that only drove the Cistercians to mount a sustained campaign to have him deposed and replaced by their candidate, Henry Murdac, abbot of Fountains. David was well aware of the crisis and established a dialogue with Murdac, which seemed to bear fruit in 1147 when the Cistercians secured Archbishop William's suspension. The sudden intervention of

---

[145] Barrow, *Anglo-Norman Era*, 70–6; Stringer, 'Periphery and core', 89–92.
[146] Green, 'Aristocratic loyalties', 94.
[147] Hollister, *Henry I*, 235.

political events in his own kingdom, however, prevented David from capitalising on the position at York.

DEATHS AND SUCCESSIONS

Archbishop William's suspension coincided with the death of William son of Duncan II. His death did not settle the question of the royal succession and created a fresh crisis for David as Wimund, a bishop in the Isles, emerged to claim a share in William's titles and rights as his son.[148] Poorly recorded and often dismissed as mythical, the relationships of David, William and Wimund have been consistently misinterpreted, and the objectives behind the rebellion misunderstood. Most detail is provided by William of Newburgh, a Cistercian chronicler based at Byland Abbey, where Wimund spent his last years.[149] He states that Wimund was 'born in the most obscure spot in England', received a basic education before becoming a monk in Furness Abbey and went from there probably in 1134 to Furness's daughter-house at Rushen. Furness received the right to elect a bishop for Man from King Óláfr, who confirmed the monks' nomination of one of their own number.[150] The bishop-elect, styling himself bishop of the *sancta ecclesia de Schith* (the holy Church of Skye), was Wimund.[151] This position in the Isles allowed Wimund to pursue his political ambitions in the late 1140s, for he gathered a warband there to help him win his claimed rights as heir of an (unnamed) earl of Moray of which he had been deprived by the king. To secure peace, David eventually granted him land near Furness, but Wimund's oppressive rule led to his capture, blinding and castration by the local people, and his subsequent confinement in Byland.

Newburgh's account may have a factual basis but raises more questions than it answers. Three key points arise: Wimund's identity; his relationship with an 'earl of Moray'; and that earl's identity. It is often assumed that the earl was the Angus killed in 1130, and thus some historians have dated Wimund's rebellion to as early as 1134–42 with Moray as its target.[152] Newburgh, however, states that Wimund was born in

---

[148] Oram, *David I*, 182–5.
[149] William of Newburgh, *Historia Rerum Anglicarum*, 73–6.
[150] Oliver, *Monumenta*, ii, 1–3, 4–6.
[151] Raine, *Historians of the Church of York*, ii, 372.
[152] *Gesta Normannorum ducum*, 8. See Anderson (ed.), *Scottish Annals*, 223–6 and notes; Duncan, *Making of the Kingdom*, 166.

England, which, together with his profession at Furness and later possession of estates near there, points to his being local. His land was perhaps Copeland, which until c. 1147 was held by William son of Duncan II, who perhaps held Moray from the mid-1130s. William, moreover, probably lived with his mother's kin in Allerdale after his father's murder in 1094 and could have fathered Wimund before returning to Scotland to join the court of his uncle, Alexander I.[153] If Wimund was William's son, his rising surely postdated his father's death. The date of that event, however, is not recorded in any surviving chronicle but William ceases to attest charters by c. 1147 and his widow founded Bolton Priory in 1151.[154] John of Hexham's statement that in 1152 David had 'confirmed his nephew William son of Duncan in the honour of Skipton and Craven',[155] probably refers to William's son by Alicia de Rumilly, also named William, and the confirmation may have been necessitated by the settlement with Wimund.

While Wimund's rising revealed the potential threat to David's plans for the succession there were other serious ramifications of William son of Duncan's death. David was deprived of a lynchpin in his northern English power structure, for William's acknowledged heir was a child under ten years of age.[156] Even if David entrusted wardship of the boy to a reliable agent, this did not provide a replacement for his experienced nephew and created a gaping hole in the pattern of regional power. William's possession of Craven and Skipton had given the Scots a firm foothold in Yorkshire, but his death limited David's ability to use that position as a springboard for further expansion as Stephen's authority in the region continued to decline with the collapse of the uneasy relationship between Stephen and Ranulf, earl of Chester, in 1146, and the deposition of Archbishop William of York and election of Henry Murdac in his place in 1147.[157] David had played no role in the developments at York beyond encouraging the Cistercians in their assault on the archbishop's reputation, it instead being Stephen's mishandling of the affair that precipitated the crisis. Nevertheless, following Murdac's election, since Stephen refused to admit the archbishop-elect to his see, David moved to make political capital by coming forward as Murdac's patron and protector. Both the

---

[153] Oram, *Lordship of Galloway*, 72–3.
[154] Lawrie, *Early Scottish Charters*, 271–3.
[155] Symeon of Durham, *Opera Omnia*, ii, 326.
[156] Anderson (ed.), *Early Sources*, ii, 91–2, note 5.
[157] Stringer, *Reign of Stephen*, 65, 77.

new archbishop and Earl Ranulf were courted by David and in late May 1149 attended his court in Carlisle when the king's great-nephew, Henry of Anjou, was knighted,[158] but whether their presence was more a sign of their support for the Angevin cause than of David's influence over them is open to question.

Ranulf's attendance marked a political sea change, for there he renounced his claims to Carlisle and performed homage to David, gaining in return Lancaster and the promise of marriage to one of David's granddaughters.[159] The terms of his homage are unknown, but he probably became David's man for Lancaster with no acknowledgement of the superior lordship of the English crown. If this was the case, then David was demonstrating the extent of his direct lordship in northern England. He had, moreover, found a replacement for William son of Duncan. Henry Murdac's presence was equally significant given the increasing bitterness of his dispute with Stephen. Although recognised by the pope, York remained closed to him and he had not performed homage to Stephen.[160] This impasse created an avenue for further Scottish advances, and it is possible that the archbishop considered David to offer the only real chance of securing his see. David's grand designs also lay behind the oath that he took from Henry of Anjou, whereby his great-nephew promised that he would confirm Scottish possession of northern England in the apparently unlikely situation of his becoming king of England.[161]

It was probably from the overlapping ambitions of these four men at Carlisle that a fresh plan to seize York and install Henry Murdac under Scottish protection was formulated. It was a grand military design dependent on coordinated surprise attacks, but Stephen was forewarned and went in person to York. He forced David to abandon the enterprise but was unable to threaten his control of Northumbria.[162] Although the attack failed in its ultimate goal, the campaign brought the Scottish advance into northern England to its climax, with David's lordship over English Cumbria, Lancaster and Northumberland generally recognised and his authority within northern mainland Britain at its height.

---

[158] John of Hexham, 322–3.
[159] Ibid. 323.
[160] Stringer, *Reign of Stephen*, 36.
[161] Roger of Howden, *Chronica*, i, 211.
[162] Henry of Huntingdon, *Historia Anglorum*, 282; John of Hexham, 323.

SECURING THE LEGACY 1149–53

In 1149, David was in more secure control of his kingdom than any of his predecessors. He had crushed challenges from Malcolm, son of Alexander I, and Angus of Moray, and strengthened his relationships with the Gaelic magnates beyond the Forth. It was, however, victory in England that won him acceptance from his Gaelic subjects and established a strong and unifying kingship within Scotland. In 1149 the future of that enhanced kingship seemed secure. Possession of Northumberland and English Cumbria had been consolidated, fixing a southern frontier far to the south of the heartland of the kingdom he had inherited. Stephen had implicitly recognised the status quo and his rival, Henry of Anjou, had done so explicitly. Nobles who owed allegiance directly to David rather than to Stephen held lordships in northern England. The expected succession of the experienced Earl Henry, moreover, offered continuity in which David's gains could be made permanent. Henry of Anjou's oath in 1149 reveals how David viewed this new political prescription in northern Britain. Until 1141, his gains in northern England were nominally held of King Stephen, but by 1149 any suggestion of English superiority of these lands had gone. Stephen still regarded Northumbria as part of his realm, and as late as 1146 granted Lancaster to Ranulf, earl of Chester, despite the fact that it was then firmly in Scottish hands.[163] Ranulf eventually gained it by David's gift and it was to him that the earl gave homage. This example underscores how fully northern England had been absorbed into David's kingdom and emphasises the reality of the so-called 'Scoto-Northumbrian' realm.

Stability in the south meant that David could return to the Moray question, which his nephew's death had again thrown open. In May 1150 he was at Kinloss in Moray for the foundation of Melrose's third colony.[164] While genuinely pious motives underlay this foundation there were earthly political concerns at play which symbolised David's power in the home of his former dynastic rivals. Kinloss, however, was only one item on his agenda and around this time he began development of the administrative structures of lowland Moray. Dependable personnel, too, were introduced into the region: it was probably then that David's former chancellor, Edward, was installed as bishop of Aberdeen, perhaps during the king's only recorded visit there.[165] The significance of this

---

[163] Stringer, 'State-building in twelfth-century Britain', 52, 53.
[164] *Chron. Melrose*, s.a. 1150.
[165] Barrow (ed.), *David I Charters*, 33 and no. 171 note.

visit is underscored by the magnates and prelates who attended him, including several with extensive properties in Moray.[166] Their presence is unlikely to have been coincidental and hints at a reordering of regional political structures. This is further implied by the freeing at this time of the Abbey of Old Deer in Buchan from service obligations to the crown, which suggests that such service and crown rights were central to David's current concerns. The reasons for that concern may have lain in Orkney, where David's two decades of careful nurturing of a pro-Scottish regime had been overthrown by the unforeseen submission of Earl Harald Maddadsson to King Eystein II of Norway (see pp. 81–2).

The plundering and burning of Aberdeen during Eystein's raiding voyage exposed the weakness of the east coast's defences, and was one stimulus for David's recasting of lordship structures in the region. David, however, was unwilling to accept Eystein's coup in Orkney and Caithness and attempted to regain influence by advancing Erlend Hákonsson as Harald's rival in Caithness. He created a three-cornered power struggle between Erlend and earls Rognvald and Harald, which lasted beyond David's death in 1153, Erlend's slaughter in 1154 and the emergence with Rognvald's murder in 1158 of Harald Maddadsson as the sole power in Orkney and Caithness.[167] David must have been well aware of the failure of his strategy for domination of the northern earldoms, but the consequences of that failure only became apparent after his death.

In the south, David's vision of an extended realm also suffered a significant setback. Although he had secured his great-nephew's heritage in Craven and Skipton in autumn 1151,[168] David's ambition to extend his authority to embrace York ended when Henry Murdac was reconciled with Stephen and gained admission to his see, which immediately revived the potential threat of the metropolitan claims of an English archbishop.[169] David responded at Easter 1152 when he raised the question with the papal legate of the elevation of St Andrews as metropolitan for Scotland.[170] His request that the envisaged archdiocese should encompass all of mainland Scotland and the Isles reveals the extent of the kingdom over which he believed he held sway, and the territory that he was determined not to yield to foreign interests. The political-religious

---

[166] Ibid. no. 136.
[167] *Orkneyinga Saga*, Chapters 92–4.
[168] John of Hexham, 327.
[169] Stringer, 'State-building in twelfth-century Britain', 58.
[170] Ferguson, *Papal Representatives*, 39.

situation was further complicated by the death of Bishop William of Durham in November 1152 and the election in early 1152 of a staunch Stephen loyalist.[171] While William was never ardently pro-David, under his governance Durham had been favourably inclined towards the Scots. The unanimous election of Hugh of le Puiset, despite Henry Murdac's objections, signalled a radical shift in Durham's political calculations.

David's woes were gravely compounded by the death on 12 June 1152 of his son, Earl Henry, whose health had been deteriorating for some years.[172] At a critical point, David was diverted from northern affairs by the more pressing issues of settlement of the succession and maintenance of Scottish control of northern England. Instead of a mature and experienced adult ruler, it was now likely that David's successor would be his eldest grandson, Malcolm. Unlike the position in England following the death of Henry I's son, Earl Henry's death did not precipitate a succession crisis, for he had fathered three sons: the line was secure, but the potential remained for challenges from alternative lineages. The future of the Scottish hold on northern England was more doubtful, for while Henry had forged tight bonds with his leading tenants his young sons lacked those relationships upon which strong lordship was based. While Malcolm was the obvious heir, David recognised that his succession was likely to face serious challenge. Accordingly, Earl Duncan of Fife, who was appointed *rector* of the boy, escorted him around the kingdom, accompanied by a military retinue to overawe the reluctant, and presented him to the people as David's designated heir.[173] At the same time, David took his second grandson, William, to Newcastle, where he presented him to the barons of Northumberland and took hostages from them as surety.[174] Every effort was made to neutralise or eliminate threats to the security of his extended domain. But David was old and that was the threat to the succession that he could not stave off. There is no suggestion of a long illness and when he was found dead in bed in his chamber in the great tower at Carlisle on the morning of 29 May 1153 few can have been surprised.[175] He had thrown his last energy into safeguarding his heir's inheritance and there was little else he could have done, but the future remained far from certain.

---

[171] Young, 'Durham in Stephen's reign', 365.
[172] Bernard of Clairvaux mentions an earlier life-threatening malady: Bernard of Clairvaux, *Life of St Malachy of Armagh*, 76–9.
[173] Duncan, *Kingship of the Scots*, 70–1; John of Hexham, 327.
[174] John of Hexham, 327.
[175] Ibid. 330.

David I – the saintly king?

Soon after his death David I gained a reputation as a man of peace. It began with a eulogy by Ailred of Rievaulx in a letter to King Henry II of England which emphasised David's Cistercian-like attributes and described him as a gentle, just, chaste and humble king, whose reign benefited humanity.[176] The image is of a man suited more to a contemplative life, underscored by claims that David was coerced into accepting the kingship: here was a man driven by higher things than worldly power. Such a king was an example to his subjects and through him 'the whole barbarity of that nation was softened';[177] the Scots renounced their warlike ways and accepted the rule of law and justice. Ailred also described David as law-giver and judge who gave justice to all comers. Again, his patience and diligence emphasised his monk-like personality.

Similar monk-like attributes dominate William of Newburgh's description of David, but his eulogy is the first explicit comparison of David with his Biblical namesake.[178] William saw both as flawed paragons, virtuous but touched by sin. The Biblical king fell from virtue through his adultery with Bathsheba;[179] David of Scotland, 'in other ways pious and good', unleashed death and destruction on the people of England, a bloody blemish on his spotless record. Just as the Biblical king regained God's grace through 'pious humility', so did David through penitence and good works.[180] The parallels did not end there, for William saw similarities between the one's punishment for his sins by the rebellion of his favourite son, and the other's punishment by Wimund's rebellion. In other respects, however, William's is a conventional picture of the pious king: worldly yet otherworldly, a powerful temporal ruler but also a pious man. David's saintly credentials are clear, with his nearly priestly qualities listed surely with an eye towards future canonisation.

GATHERING CLOUDS 1153–7

The risk of dynastic challenge probably lay behind the rapidity with which the young Malcolm IV was inaugurated at Scone, possibly just

---

[176] Anderson, *Scottish Annals*, 232–7; Barrow, 'David I of Scotland', 47 and note 11.
[177] Barrow, 'David I of Scotland', 47 and note 11.
[178] William of Newburgh, *Historia Rerum Anglicarum*, 70–2.
[179] 2 Samuel 11.
[180] The translation is Anderson's, *Scottish Annals*, 230.

Figure 3.1 David I and Malcolm IV from the initial M of Malcolm's great charter of 1159 to the monks of Kelso (nineteenth-century hand-painted facsimile).

three days after his grandfather's death.[181] David's death was the first in a series of rapid changes in the political landscape of the British Isles, the repercussions of which swept away the established power relationships. The first change came with the deaths in the same week in August of King Stephen's elder son, Eustace, and Simon II de Senlis, earl of Northampton.[182] As with the death of Earl Henry for David, the death of Stephen's adult heir threw the English succession into uncertainty for, although Eustace had another adult brother, William, he was prepared to renounce his candidacy for the kingship in return for specific assurances.[183] Stephen, unable to muster the strength to drive Henry of Anjou from England, was forced to negotiate. In the midst of this turmoil Earl Simon's son, Simon III, failed to secure Stephen's confirmation of his succession to Huntingdon-Northampton, which created a void in the local power structure of Stephen's party. A further complication was added by the negotiations with Henry of Anjou, who may have wished

---

[181] Duncan, *Kingship of the Scots*, 71.
[182] Robert of Torigni, *Chronica*, 172; Henry of Huntingdon, *Historia Anglorum*, 288.
[183] Stringer, *Reign of Stephen*, 47–8; Matthew, *King Stephen*, 213.

to see the earldom restored to a Scottish earl, presumably King Malcolm or one of his younger brothers.[184] While Scottish interest in Huntingdon was rekindled, lingering hopes with regard to York were crushed by the death of Henry Murdac and the speedy reinstatement as archbishop of Stephen's nephew, William.[185] Although William, too, was dead within ten months, his restoration secured Stephen's interests in northern England and finally ended the prospect of further Scottish advances in the region.

By October 1153, the fluid political situation in England had changed profoundly and the Scots were suddenly mere bystanders rather than active players in the unfolding events. Negotiations between Stephen and Henry progressed rapidly and on 6 November a settlement was agreed whereby Stephen adopted Henry as his heir.[186] For the Scots, this seemed to offer maintenance of the status quo, since in 1149 Henry had sworn to recognise David's acquisition of Northumbria should he become king of England. Scottish lordship in the region appeared secure, with David's grandsons confirmed in possession of the earldom of Northumberland and lordship of Carlisle, whilst William, son of William son of Duncan II, was established in his parents' heritage in north-west Yorkshire, north Lancashire and western Cumberland. In Westmorland, David's constable, Hugh de Morville, controlled the strategic trans-Pennine routes, while across the watershed in Northumberland and western County Durham, the de Umfravilles and Balliols supported the Scottish regime, although the consecration of a pro-Stephen bishop at Durham hinted at future problems. The continued adherence of Earl Ranulf of Chester, moreover, appeared to secure Scottish regional lordship. Ranulf's death in December 1153, however, ended all certainty, for his son, Hugh, was a minor and incapable of providing strong leadership.[187] Despite these blows, however, King Malcolm's heritage in England seemed safe.

Henry of Anjou's negotiations with Stephen sidelined the Scots but produced an unexpected and welcome calm on their southern frontier at a critical moment. According to the *Chronicle of Holyrood*, on the day that agreement was reached in England (6 November), 'Somerled and his nephews, the sons namely of Malcolm, having allied many [men] to themselves, arose against King Malcolm, and they created disturbance

---

[184] Warren, *Henry II*, 68.
[185] Raine (ed.), *Historians of the Church of York*, ii, 227–8.
[186] Stringer, *Reign of Stephen*, 48; Matthew, *King Stephen*, 213.
[187] *Annales Cestrienses*, s.a. 1153.

unsettling *Scotia* in great part'.[188] The regular misidentification of these 'sons of Malcolm' as the children of Malcolm Mac Heth, to whom King Malcolm later gave the earldom of Ross, has been a persistent obstacle to proper recognition of the significance of this event.[189] As Professor Duncan observed, they were the sons of Alexander I's bastard son, Malcolm, who had been imprisoned in Roxburgh in 1134.[190] Their challenge had nothing to do with rival Moray-based royal lineages or unsatisfied claims to northern earldoms, nor was it a 'rebellion' of the forces of Celtic conservatism in a rearguard action against the royal innovations of the last two decades. It was a straightforward bid by representatives of a senior, if illegitimate, segment of the lineage of Malcolm III for the kingship of the Scots. It is largely the teleological view of Scottish history focusing on the success of the descendants of David I in eliminating all rivals that has led to a failure to recognise that challenges for the crown continued until the 1230s. Malcolm IV may have been the one who secured inauguration at Scone in May 1153, but the haste with which he was enthroned after David's death reveals the seriousness of the threat to his succession from familial rivals. Primogeniture was not yet the norm in inheritance in Scotland, and there were other candidates who possessed equal or more valid claims on the royal succession. If the thirteenth-century *Orkneyinga Saga* can be believed, many Scots favoured William, Duncan II's grandson, over King Malcolm,[191] but the probably underage William did not advance his candidacy. Somerled, however, chose to support the claims of his brother-in-law or his sons.

Little evidence survives of the course of the rising. The Holyrood chronicle notes the slaying in a duel on 27 February 1154 of a certain Arthur, who had intended to betray King Malcolm, and an expanded version of that annal notes the slaying of another supporter of Malcolm's rival.[192] Neither death is linked explicitly to the rising, but they do suggest a strong reservoir of support for the heirs of Alexander I. There is otherwise no surviving record of the course of the conflict other than a laconic entry in the Holyrood chronicle commenting that in 1156 'Donald son of Malcolm was captured at Whithorn, and he was imprisoned with his father', which may mark the end of the episode.[193] Why

---

[188] *Chron. Holyrood*, 124–5.
[189] Barrow (ed.), *RRS*, i, 8; Barrow, *Kingship and Unity*, 51; McDonald, *Outlaws*, 87–8.
[190] Duncan, *Kingship of the Scots*, 71–2.
[191] *Orkneyinga Saga*, c. 33; Duncan, *Kingship of the Scots*, 70.
[192] *Chron. Holyrood*, 126; Barrow (ed.), *RRS*, i, 8 and note 3.
[193] *Chron. Holyrood*, 128.

he was at Whithorn in Galloway and by whom he was captured remain unanswered, but the event was possibly linked to spreading destabilisation of the maritime west which accelerated in the months after David I's death.

Although Manx chronicle tradition presents the reign of Óláfr I as a time of general tranquillity,[194] episodes like Wimund's rising suggest that the ageing king faced increasing difficulties in holding the territorial components and political factions of his kingdom in check. The protection of a Carlisle-based Scottish king and a marriage alliance with Galloway helped maintain Óláfr's authority, but his decision in c. 1152 to send his son, Guðrøðr, to Norway to secure recognition of his right to succeed from his nominal overlord and to perform homage for the kingship, indicates growing anxiety over the succession.[195] Óláfr's murder by his brother's exiled sons in June 1153, coming swiftly on the heels of David's death and during Guðrøðr's absence in Norway, was a splendidly opportunistic act which capitalised on a series of fortuitous coincidences. Although Guðrøðr had returned, avenged his father's killing and assumed the kingship of the Isles within months, the repercussions of the events of 1153 reverberated for decades and destabilised the entire region.

Guðrøðr's turning to Norway rather than to David I coincided with Norwegian intervention in Orkney and Caithness, and may reflect a perception of a decline in Scottish power in the early 1150s. Such a perception may have been reinforced by the challenge to Malcolm IV from Somerled and his nephews, which drew the Scottish focus inwards and permitted Guðrøðr to consolidate his position in Man and the Isles by a return to the predatory traditions of his grandfather. This change is perhaps reflected in the involvement of Guðrøðr, Fergus of Galloway, possibly Somerled, and others, as mercenaries in interdynastic wars in Ireland.[196] The defeat of one Irish fleet in 1154, in which Galwegian ships were serving, was one factor that contributed to civil war in Galloway in the later 1150s, and may also have encouraged Guðrøðr, who had been allied with the defeated side, to make a bid for control of Dublin.[197] His speedy ejection from the city was amongst several factors that led to growing disenchantment with his rule in the Isles, which in

---

[194] *Chron. Man*, s.a. 1102; Duncan and Brown, 'Argyll and the Isles', 196; McDonald, *Kingdom of the Isles*, 49.
[195] Oram, *Lordship of Galloway*, 73.
[196] Ibid. 73
[197] *Chron. Man*, s.a.1144 = 1154–6?; Oram, *Lordship of Galloway*, 74–5.

turn led a significant group of the Hebridean nobility to turn in c. 1156 to Somerled, Guðrøðr's brother-in-law. Presented with a choice between continued support for what may have been a forlorn hope with one brother-in-law and the Scottish throne and a more realistic opportunity to secure his eldest son, Dugald, a share in the kingship of the Isles, Somerled disengaged himself from the conflict in Scotland and turned his attention towards Man. There is no evidence for Somerled's submission to Malcolm IV until Christmas 1160,[198] but there is, equally, no sign of any continued military support for his nephews. It is in this context that the capture of Donald son of Malcolm at Whithorn should be seen.

By 1156, Malcolm IV had weathered the upheavals that immediately followed his grandfather's death and, whilst Scottish lordship had shrunk at the northern and western margins of David I's extended realm, domination of most of mainland Scotland and much of Northumbria had not been seriously threatened. In the midst of this period, moreover, King Stephen had died (25 October 1154) and Henry of Anjou had been crowned as King Henry II (19 December 1154); if Henry honoured his oath to David concerning Northumberland and Carlisle, recognition of Scottish gains in Northumbria would follow swiftly. Henry was not slow to impose his authority over the kingdom left to him by Stephen, curbing the power of such Stephen loyalists as William of Aumâle, whose earldom of York was forfeited and suspended, and also of Angevin supporters who had usurped royal authority in their own districts.[199] Henry visited Yorkshire early in 1155 to assert his authority over Earl William, a forceful action which may have caused the Scots some anxiety, but he otherwise showed no intention to overturn the political structure established by his great-uncle. The Scoto-Northumbrian realm of David I had been gravely shaken but, despite the deaths of several of its key lords and ministers, it had proven robust and there seemed every prospect that, as King Malcolm grew in maturity and experience, this resilient edifice might have acquired permanence. Its sudden demise in 1157, therefore, ran counter to every indication and created an unforeseen rift in Anglo-Scottish power relationships that had ramifications for the whole of the British Isles.

---

[198] Barrow (ed.), *RRS*, i, 8, no. 175.
[199] Warren, *Henry II*, 60–1.

CHAPTER 4

Under Angevin Supremacy, 1157–89

THE DISMANTLING OF THE SCOTO-NORTHUMBRIAN REALM

Despite his stated determination to restore royal authority in England there was no reason for the Scots to think that Henry II would break his oath to confirm David's possession of Northumbria should he become king.[1] There was no demand from Henry or offer from King Malcolm or his younger brother for homage for either Carlisle and Cumberland or William's earldom in Northumberland, nor any suggestion that as both brothers were underage they should be Henry's wards. Once he had consolidated his position within England, however, Henry began to claim authority over territories where his grandfather or father-in-law had formerly possessed or exercised overlordship, extending from the ill-defined Anglo-Scottish border through Wales and Brittany to Toulouse. Insistence on a return to the situation that had prevailed under Henry I was patently incompatible with his oath to David, but when the sixteen-year-old Malcolm travelled to meet him at Chester in July 1157 his advisors were unprepared for the request that David's conquests be surrendered.

No contemporary record of the meeting has survived. The late-twelfth-century English chronicler William of Newburgh gives the most detailed account. He narrates that:

[King Henry II] carefully set out to the king of Scots, who possessed as his proper right the northern districts of England, namely Northumbria, Cumberland, Westmorland, formerly acquired by

---

[1] Roger of Howden, *Chronica*, i, 211.

David, king of Scots, in the name of Matilda, called the Empress, and her heir, that the king of England should not be defrauded of such a large portion of his kingdom, nor could he casually be deprived of it: it was just that what had been acquired in his name should be restored [to him].[2]

This argument tallies with Henry's stated intention of regaining the authority exercised by his grandfather. Malcolm's response to it was dictated by realism rather than acceptance of a cogent case, for Newburgh commented that he, 'reflecting prudently that the king of England had the better position in the argument on account of his superior power', did not appeal to the 1149 settlement and agreed to surrender David's English gains. Malcolm was compensated with the earldom of Huntingdon, which Henry stripped from Simon de Senlis, but William received only trivial compensation, land of ten pounds' annual value, in western Northumberland.[3] Huntingdon was not intended as an exchange for Northumbria, but reflected Henry's policy of a return to the pre-1135 landholding position in England.[4]

Wrapped up in the question of a return to the pre-1135 status quo was the relationship of the kings of Scots to the kings of England. William of Newburgh makes no mention of homage, although some such act was presumably made for Huntingdon, if nothing else. The *Chronicle of Melrose* is disappointingly vague, saying simply that 'Malcolm, king of Scots, came to King Henry of England at Chester; and he became his man, as his grandfather had been the man of the old King Henry, saving all his dignities'.[5] What this does not say is that Malcolm became Henry's man for Scotland, and the lack of clarity perhaps reflects the vagueness that existed in the pre-1135 relationship between David I and Henry I. David paid homage for Huntingdon, but there is no evidence that he ever did so for his kingdom. Malcolm's relationship was similar, and the reference to 'his dignities' is probably not to his position as king in Scotland but to the traditional rights of Scottish kings in England when visiting the English court, and probably reflected a deliberate avoidance of precision.[6] Nevertheless, the Scots probably saw the loss of David's

---

[2] William of Newburgh, *Historia Rerum Anglicarum*, i, 105.
[3] William of Newburgh, *Historia Rerum Anglicarum*, i, 105; Duncan, *Making of the Kingdom*, 224.
[4] Duncan, *Kingship of the Scots*, 72.
[5] *Chron. Melrose*, s.a. 1157.
[6] Duncan, *Kingship of the Scots*, 72; Barrow (ed.), *RRS*, i, 9–10.

conquests as a humiliation and a reassertion of English supremacy after two decades of unprecedented Scottish power.

Although the two kings had reached a settlement, relations were not entirely cordial and an already tense situation was aggravated in January 1158 when Henry came north to view his regained territories. He refortified the old castle at Wark,[7] only 12km downstream from Malcolm's power base at Roxburgh, and ordered the bishop of Durham to repair Norham, before crossing to inspect Carlisle. The rebuilding of fortifications that had been obstacles to David I's ambitions may indicate anxiety on Henry's part over the stability of the settlement forced on Malcolm, but for a ruler experienced in the management of the shifting borderlands between the duchies and counties of north-western France castles were central components in the mechanism of control.[8] Henry's refortification of the pre-1135 border helped to consolidate his hold on his gains and ensure future stability, but they were provocations to the Scots, for the castles stood on the threshold of Teviotdale, also former Northumbrian territory but more successfully integrated into the Scottish kingdom. The issue of these castles was perhaps the reason that a second meeting between Malcolm and Henry, at Carlisle, ended with both kings 'not well reconciled with each other'.[9] Malcolm, by then nearly eighteen, had hoped for another outcome from the meeting, his knighting by Henry, but such was the mood at Carlisle that he left without receiving knighthood.[10]

THE TOULOUSE EXPEDITION AND ITS CONSEQUENCES

Early in 1159, Malcolm assembled his court at Roxburgh.[11] It was perhaps then that he announced his intention of joining Henry's planned expedition to Toulouse and set in place arrangements for the government of Scotland in his absence. By 16 June Malcolm, his brother William and their military retinue had crossed the Channel and joined Henry at Poitiers, from where they advanced to Périgueux. There, on 30 June, Malcolm was at last knighted by Henry and according to some accounts Malcolm in turn knighted William, who was then sixteen. This

---

[7] *Chron. Melrose*, s.a. 1158.
[8] For such use of castles, see Power, *Norman Frontier*.
[9] *Chron. Melrose*, s.a. 1158.
[10] Duncan, *Kingship of the Scots*, 72; Barrow (ed.), *RRS*, i, 10.
[11] *Kelso Liber*, iii–vii; Barrow (ed.), *RRS*, i, no. 131.

event may have been the highlight of the campaign for the brothers, for there was no battlefield clash in which to win chivalric honour, only the ultimately futile siege of Toulouse. Following the abandonment of the siege, Malcolm returned to Normandy with Henry,[12] showing an entirely understandable lack of urgency on the part of a wide-eyed teenager let loose in the midst of the glitter and glamour of Angevin France to return to what perhaps seemed by comparison a dull, rough Scotland. He may have attended Henry's Christmas court at Falaise, but he used this period to begin negotiations for the marriage of his sister, Margaret, to Conan IV, duke of Brittany and earl of Richmond.[13] The possible motivation behind this alliance and its ramifications are considered later.

Malcolm returned to Scotland early in 1160 to face a political crisis involving a number of his earls. Although one chronicle account suggests that this crisis had arisen 'because he had gone to Toulouse',[14] interpreted by some historians as indicating that the reaction was to some perceived compromising of Scotland's independence, given the absence of any service demand from Henry behind Malcolm's decision it seems more likely that the tension stemmed from Malcolm's desertion of his kingdom.[15] Exactly what happened in 1160 is unclear and is still a matter of debate. The two nearest contemporary accounts to the event, those given in the Holyrood and Melrose chronicles, are frustratingly brief and open to different interpretations. The longer account, offered by the Melrose chronicler, narrates that

> 'Malcolm, king of Scots, came from the army of Toulouse, and when he had come to the city which is called Perth, Earl Ferteth and six other earls, enraged against the king because he had gone to Toulouse, besieged the city and wished to take the king captive, but their assumption in no way prevailed'.[16]

Immediately after this, the chronicle reports that, 'King Malcolm went into Galloway on three occasions with a great army, and at last subdued them'. Military operations in Galloway, but with no mention of any prior action involving any earls, occur also in the Holyrood chronicle, which reports that 'King Malcolm led his army three times into Galloway, and

---

[12] Anderson (ed.), *Scottish Annals*, ii, 243.
[13] *Chron. Howden*, i, 217; Duncan, *Making of the Kingdom*, 226; Barrow (ed.), *RRS*, i, 13.
[14] *Chron. Melrose*, s.a. 1160.
[15] For alternative interpretations, see Duncan, *Making of the Kingdom*, 225–6.
[16] *Chron. Melrose*, s.a. 1160.

thence, having defeated his federate enemies, he returned with peace and without loss.'[17]

Traditionally, the information in these two sources has been interpreted as referring to a single event, in which the failed attack on Malcolm at Perth by Earl Ferteth and his associates was followed by a campaign into Galloway where the defeated rebels had fled to join with their ally, Fergus.[18] There is, however, no such link made in either account or reason to see the 'them' of the Melrose narrative as referring back to Ferteth and the other earls, or the 'federate enemies' of Holyrood as referring to this group who are otherwise unmentioned in that account. The suggestion that two separate events are being reported here, the second being a demonstration of political unity behind the king after the brief trauma of the first, is probably correct.[19] This separation, moreover, has led to a downgrading of the affair at Perth from a 'Revolt of the Earls' to 'an orchestrated protest'.[20] With the exception of Ferteth, the identities of the protestors are unknown, but this has not stopped historians from speculating and producing lists and advancing reasons for the inclusion or exclusion of particular candidates.[21] Whatever the nature of the Perth confrontation, 1160 ended with King Malcolm's power and prestige significantly enhanced. Not only had he asserted his personal authority over the political community at home but he had also extended the sphere of that authority into Galloway, a territory which had hitherto been outwith the Scottish kingdom. What had provoked this assault on Galloway and its ruler is unknown, but the cryptic reference to 'federate enemies' might allude to an alliance between Fergus and Somerled of Argyll. Before the end of 1160, Fergus had been defeated and had taken the habit of an Augustinian canon at Holyrood, while Somerled was described subsequently as having reached an agreement with Malcolm in the course of the same year.[22]

SOMERLED, MAN AND GALLOWAY

Peace with Somerled was a significant achievement, ending the disturbances down the western seaboard that had followed David I's

---

[17] *Chron. Holyrood*, 136–7.
[18] Duncan, *Making of the Kingdom*, 163–4.
[19] Brooke, 'Fergus', 51–5.
[20] Lynch, *Scotland*, 85–6.
[21] See, for example, Barrow (ed.), *RRS*, i, 12 and Oram, 'Mar', 47–9.
[22] Oram, *Lordship of Galloway*, 80–1; Barrow (ed.), *RRS*, i, no. 175.

death. Initially, Somerled had been supporting his nephews, the sons of Malcolm, son of Alexander I, who were pursuing their claim to the Scottish throne, but his commitment to their cause did not last as other opportunities for self-aggrandisement presented themselves.[23] The possible failure of his nephews to secure significant support within Scotland, culminating with the capture of Donald son of Malcolm, and his imprisonment with his father in Roxburgh Castle,[24] coupled with the crumbling stability of the kingdom of Man and the Isles, saw Somerled divert his efforts towards the latter. Documentary sources for the affairs of Argyll and the Isles at this time are notoriously inaccurate in their chronology and are open to widely varying interpretation, but one catalyst for the unfolding crisis in the region was the defeat in 1154 of the mercenary fleet assembled by Muirchertach mac Lochlainn, king of Cenél nEógain, in his struggle with Toirrdelbach ua Conchobair, king of Connacht, for dominance within Ireland. Both Fergus of Galloway and Guðrøðr II, king of Man, suffered losses in that action which compromised their authority at home, and when in 1156 Guðrøðr's bid to take control of Dublin was repulsed, disaffected elements within Man looked for an alternative to lead them.[25] The reaction, however, was directed not solely against Guðrøðr but also against Muirchertach's influence in Dublin and the kingdom of Man and the Isles. The preferred candidate for the Manx kingship was Dugald, son of Somerled, Guðrøðr's own nephew, who had the attraction of being both a lineal descendant of King Óláfr I and the son of the one man with the power and ambition to challenge Muirchertach for domination of the western seas.

In January 1157, the fleets of Somerled and Guðrøðr clashed inconclusively off Man, but the negotiations that followed saw a partition of the kingdom which gave most of the Hebrides to Dugald and his father.[26] Somerled's domain now extended up the west coast, possibly into Skye, an expansion that threatened the already weakened authority of the king of Scots in the northern mainland. It is perhaps in this context that the reconciliation in 1157 of a certain Malcolm MacHeth with King Malcolm should be viewed, for around this time he may have been established or recognised as earl of Ross by the Scottish king.[27] This Malcolm MacHeth has usually been identified with Malcolm son

---

[23] *Chron. Holyrood*, s.a. 1153.
[24] *Chron. Holyrood*, s.a. 1156.
[25] Oram, *Lordship of Galloway*, 74–6. See also Duffy, 'Irishmen and Islesmen', 127–8.
[26] *Chron. Man*, s.a. 1156. See McDonald, *Kingdom of the Isles*, Chapter 2.
[27] *Chron. Holyrood*, s.a. 1157.

of Alexander I, but this identification is certainly wrong and it is more likely that he was the son of an Earl Aed or Heth who was active early in the reign of David I.[28] It is usually assumed that Malcolm IV sought the reconciliation, but it is equally possible that MacHeth was the one who approached the Scottish king, perhaps in recognition of the consequences for his own position of the recent extension of Somerled's power.[29]

Somerled's deal with Guðrøðr ended in 1158 when he launched a second attack on Man and drove him out.[30] A reunified Hebridean kingdom was now nominally in the hands of Dugald, but the Manx chronicler was under no illusion that real power lay with his father. Guðrøðr turned in desperation to the two powers most affected by this dramatic shift in the balance of power in the region, Henry II and Malcolm IV. In September 1158, the fugitive and nearly destitute Guðrøðr arrived in England to seek Henry's aid,[31] but Henry had departed for Normandy in August and did not return for another four years. Guðrøðr next appeared at Roxburgh early in 1159 as Malcolm IV was preparing to leave for Toulouse. Although he was treated honourably and his status given explicit recognition by his prominent placing amongst the witnesses to Malcolm's great charter to the monks of Kelso,[32] his host's attention was fixed elsewhere and no help was forthcoming. Having failed to secure aid from mainland British powers, Guðrøðr turned to his nominal overlord, the king of Norway, and by winter 1160–1 was at the court of King Ingi. He did not return to his kingdom until after Somerled's death in 1164.

The one party to whom Guðrøðr did not turn was his grandfather, Fergus of Galloway. Why he did not do so is unknown, but it is possible that Fergus faced a crisis of his own, perhaps triggered by the losses to his fleet in 1154. Fergus almost disappears from view in the historical records of the later 1150s, but the Cistercian writer Walter Daniel refers to a three-cornered power struggle in Galloway at this time between the un-named 'kinglet' of 'that unhappy little land' and his two un-named sons.[33] What parts Fergus and his sons, Gillebrigte and Uhtred, played in the events that unfolded in the region after 1154 can only be

---

[28] Duncan, *Kingship of the Scots*, 71–2.
[29] I am grateful to Dr Alasdair Ross for this suggestion.
[30] *Chron. Man*, s.a. 1158.
[31] Bain, J. (ed.), *Calendar of Documents*, i, nos 56 and 60.
[32] Barrow (ed.), *RRS*, i, no. 131.
[33] Daniel, *Life of Ailred*, 45–6.

speculated, but it is probable that one of them was instrumental in the capture of Donald son of Malcolm and his handing over to the Scots. Uhtred's ties with the Anglo-Scottish royal houses and the nobility of English Cumbria might have given him a more pro-Scottish inclination, which is perhaps also borne out by his presence at Malcolm IV's court at Roxburgh in 1159, but Scottish influence in Galloway was also still strong in the mid-1150s before the surrender of Carlisle caused a radical reconfiguration of the regional power structure.

The Scots' loss of Carlisle and the extension of Somerled's influence in the Isles were probably related. Beyond the later coincidence of Fergus's deposition and Somerled's coming into King Malcolm's peace in 1160, however, there is no concrete evidence that the changed regional power structure of the later 1150s created an alliance between Galloway and Argyll. The existence of a group of churches possessed by Iona Abbey in the lower Dee valley in Galloway, adjacent to the core of Fergus's lordship around Kirkcudbright, however, could reflect some bond between a power in Galloway and Somerled, who was trying to revive the old monastery at Iona in the early 1160s.[34] The identity of the donor, however, and the date of the gift are unknown, and while it is possible that one of Fergus's sons made the grant in the years after 1160, such a gift to a monastery associated closely with Somerled suggests an earlier date when Scottish influence was at a low ebb in Galloway. Quite simply, the realignment of power triggered by the Scots' surrender of Cumberland, the losses suffered by Fergus's fleet in 1154 and the spectacular success of Somerled in asserting his lordship in the Irish Sea zone, may have seen Galloway return to a western maritime rather than a mainland British orientation. The mention of Malcolm IV's defeat of 'his federate enemies' in Galloway in 1160,[35] rather than referring to an association between Fergus and the earls who had confronted the king at Perth, may instead allude to an alliance between Fergus and Somerled. For Fergus, the consequence of invasion and defeat was deposition and enforced seclusion in Holyrood Abbey, but for Somerled, whose power base lay beyond the effective reach of Scottish power, submission and re-entry into Malcolm's peace was the most severe result.

---

[34] Oram, *Galloway*, 78; McDonald, 'Scoto-Norse kings and the reformed religious orders'. For Somerled and Iona, see *AU*, s.a. 1164.
[35] *Chron. Holyrood*, s.a. 1160.

AN INDEPENDENT MAN? MALCOLM IV AND HENRY II 1160–5

It may be significant that these events occurred while Henry II was absent from England. The extension of Malcolm's power into the maritime west which his successes in Galloway brought represented a significant shift in the regional balance of power that may not have been welcomed by Henry II. While Henry had successfully asserted his dominance in dealings with Malcolm down to 1159, he may not have been as successful in establishing an effective lord-man relationship. The marriage negotiations that Malcolm pursued for his family suggest that he wanted to take an independent line that did not necessarily serve wider Angevin ambitions. The marriage of the second of his sisters, Margaret, to Duke Conan IV of Brittany, for example, although probably negotiated during Malcolm's presence at Henry's Christmas court in 1159–60, was perhaps not welcome to Henry. The possibility that it was intended to be a double union, with an abortive plan for Malcolm to wed Conan's sister, Constance, suggests that a deeper game was being played.[36] Geoffrey Barrow has pointed to the similarity of the standing of Malcolm and Conan in respect of Henry II, and has suggested that this made them natural allies as rulers faced with the threat of Angevin aggression; both were tenants-in-chief of Henry for English earldoms (Huntingdon and Richmond) but both were also rulers who did not wish to see Henry's extension of lordship over their home territories. Just as Henry in 1157 had restored the dominance that his grandfather had exercised over the Scots, so he was also seeking the lordship over Brittany that he believed his predecessors had exercised as dukes of Normandy.[37] There may, however, have been an additional factor in the negotiations between Malcolm and Conan, for down to 1157 the duke, as earl of Richmond, had held a strategic frontier lordship bordering on Scottish-controlled Northumbria. In the 1090s, Malcolm III may have sought a similar marriage alliance with Conan's forbears in Richmond. It is possible that within the 1160 Scoto-Breton negotiations can be seen a glimmer of aspirations by Malcolm to recover territories surrendered in 1157.

The Breton marriage was followed in 1162 by the marriage of Malcolm's eldest sister, Ada, to Florenz III, count of Holland.[38] It has been suggested that this match reflected burgeoning Scottish trade with

---

[36] Barrow (ed.), *RRS*, i, 13.
[37] Warren, *Henry II*, 74, 76–7.
[38] Roger of Howden, *Chronica*, i, 219; Anderson (ed.), *Scottish Annals*, ii, 249.

the Low Countries, and although it has been counter-argued that most evidence for Scottish overseas trade refers to 'Flanders' rather than Holland it has also been shown that the label 'Flanders' was applied loosely in Scotland to much of what would nowadays be described as Belgium and the Netherlands.[39] Perhaps more important, however, was the fact that Count Florenz was free of any bonds with Henry II and, as a count of the Holy Roman Empire, was linked instead into the web of alliances and overlordship assembled by the Emperor Frederick I Barbarossa. If the forging of alliances outwith the growing 'empire' of Henry II was Malcolm's primary aim, however, these marriages reveal the marginal position occupied by the king of Scots in contemporary European diplomacy. Regionally powerful as the counts of Holland were, they were still a relatively small power.

'Second-division' though Duke Conan and Count Florenz were, Malcolm's independent marriage diplomacy was perhaps nevertheless a significant factor in a sharp deterioration of relations with Henry II. In January 1163, Henry at last returned to England and moved quickly to resolve a number of pressing issues which threatened the security of his kingdom. Wales, where the prince of Deheubarth had chafed under Henry's overlordship since 1157 and who in 1162 had seized strategic frontier castles, was a priority. An expedition into Deheubarth in summer 1163 brought its prince, Rhys ap Gruffydd, and possibly also Owain, prince of Gwynedd, into submission, with Rhys kept as a prisoner in Henry's retinue.[40] Henry then made a foray to Carlisle, from where Malcolm may have accompanied him south to Oxfordshire. At Woodstock, Malcolm was presented with a series of demands, which indicate a real concern on Henry's part over Malcolm's recent actions. Along with Rhys and Owain, Malcolm was required to perform homage to the English king's eldest son, the Young Henry, and perhaps also to Henry himself.[41] This homage was not for Huntingdon only, for the accompanying demand that Malcolm also surrender unspecified castles into Henry's hands as surety for the peace concerned strongholds within Scotland or perhaps, more specifically, Lothian, which was still viewed as part of England in Scottish hands.[42] In effect, Henry aimed to

---

[39] Ritchie, *Normans in Scotland*, 354; Barrow (ed.), *RRS*, i, 18; Toorians, 'Flemish settlement', 1.

[40] De Diceto, *Imagines Historiarum*, i, 311; Warren, *Henry II*, 162; Carr, *Medieval Wales*, 43.

[41] De Diceto, *Imagines Historiarum*, i, 311; Robert of Torigni, *Chronica*, 218. See Barrow (ed.), *RRS*, i, 18–19 and Duncan, *Making of the Kingdom*, 226–7.

[42] For the status of Lothian, see Matthew Paris, *Chron. Majora*, v, 269.

transform his relationship with Malcolm from one of clientage to more explicit vassal-lord dependence. Malcolm, however, avoided the explicit recognition of Henry's superiority over him which this would have indicated, but only at the cost of giving his youngest brother, David, and the sons of some of his nobles, as hostages. These were rigorous demands, and were very similar to the terms imposed on King William by Henry II in 1174.[43] On that occasion, the settlement was imposed in the aftermath of William's rebellion and invasion of northern England, which might suggest that in 1163 Henry doubted Malcolm's trustworthiness. Professor Duncan has argued that war was narrowly averted by the submission at Woodstock and suggests that Henry had been angered by a possible refusal from Malcolm to give military service in Wales. That, however, may only have been a final component in Henry's mounting mistrust that Malcolm's independent actions had provoked.

It has been suggested that the serious illness that struck down the still-unmarried Malcolm at Doncaster in 1163 was a significant factor in persuading Henry to seek greater control over the Scottish king.[44] Henry later had a turbulent relationship with Malcolm's younger brother and heir, William, who sought restoration of his lost earldom of Northumberland. It is likely that William had already made his wishes known and Henry was positioning himself for Malcolm's death and the unpredictable William's succession. But that is to read events backwards. Significantly, if William's likely succession was what lay behind the 1163 settlement, it is odd that he features nowhere in the admittedly scant record of its terms and that it was the youngest of the brothers, David, rather than the presumptive heir, William, who was given as a hostage. English frontier security rather than the Scottish succession may instead have been Henry's concern. Added to the debate is the date of Malcolm's illness, i.e. did it occur before or after Woodstock? Based upon the order of events in the chronicle accounts – Henry II's return to England, Malcolm's sickness, peace between the kings – it has been believed that he fell ill travelling to Woodstock, but a strong case has been advanced for the illness to have occurred on the homeward leg.[45] If this is correct, it suggests that Henry's fears were focused on the consequences for English security in Malcolm's increasingly confident assertion of his own independent power rather than on the as yet unforeseen succession of William.

---

[43] Duncan, *Kingship of the Scots*, 73.
[44] *Chron. Melrose*, s.a. 1163; Warren, *Henry II*, 183 and note 3.
[45] Compare Barrow (ed.), *RRS*, i, 19, Duncan, *Making of the Kingdom*, 227 and Duncan, *Kingship of the Scots*, 73.

Malcolm's illness in 1163 was sufficiently life-threatening to merit inclusion in the Melrose chronicler's brief record of Scottish affairs of that year. It was the first manifestation of a progressively debilitating disease that eventually killed him in 1165. Descriptions of the symptoms have led to modern speculation that he suffered from Paget's disease, an identification possibly reinforced by reference to him as *Cennmor*, or 'big-head', in his obituary in the *Annals of Ulster*;[46] enlargement and deformation of the cranial vault is one characteristic of the disease. It has also been suggested that his illness caused his apparent lack of interest in women as either wives or mistresses, which emerged as part of his later reputation as a virgin.[47] Although his recovery in 1163 was celebrated, it was not complete and he may have been an invalid for the remainder of his short life. The evidence for his incapacity, however, is circumstantial and perhaps too much has been read into a single writ directed to a justiciar of *Scotia*, the first record of such an all-encompassing office, and reference in one charter to the hearing of specific pleas only in the presence of the king or his 'supreme justice'.[48] Nevertheless, such offices bear comparison with English arrangements for firm government during the ruler's prolonged absence in France, which Professor Duncan has described as a form of regency. That something similar was required in Scotland on account of Malcolm's incapacity may lie behind a rather garbled account in the fourteenth-century *Gesta Annalia*, which reports that William had been appointed as *custos*, or guardian, of the kingdom because of Malcolm's neglect of government.[49] Although the detail of this account can be dismissed as later elaboration, it was probably based on a contemporary record of William's receipt of some delegated powers from his brother, perhaps with regard to the exercise of justice, and his recognition as king-designate.[50] Recognition by Malcolm of his impending mortality, moreover, may have stimulated his foundation in July 1164 of Melrose Abbey's fourth colony, Coupar Angus.[51] After eleven years as king, this pious act has the appearance of a man preparing for the hereafter.

It would be wrong on the basis of this slender evidence to regard Malcolm as irrelevant from 1163. As well as continued development

---

[46] Duncan, *Kingship of the Scots*, 73–5.
[47] For discussion of Malcolm's post-mortem reputation as a virgin, see Barrow (ed.), *RRS*, i, 22–5.
[48] Barrow (ed.), *RRS*, i, nos 223 and 220. See Duncan, *Kingship of the Scots*, 73.
[49] *Chron. Fordoun*, i, 257, 259.
[50] Duncan, *Kingship of the Scots*, 73–4.
[51] *Chron. Melrose*, s.a. 1164.

of royal government, his last years saw significant expansion in royal authority in areas where David I's power had been superficial.[52] Most evidence relates to the central and western Southern Uplands, where strategically located upper Clydesdale, for example, received a colony of entrepreneurial Flemish knights.[53] In Galloway, efforts were made to further bind Fergus's sons closer to the Scottish crown; probably in 1163-4, Uhtred received a grant of the district between the rivers Urr and Nith, where he then planted knightly colonists; Gillebrigte received marriage to a daughter or sister of Earl Duncan II of Fife, the greatest magnate in the kingdom.[54] These bonds were shallow and fragile, but Malcolm may have brought the brothers into a personal dependence upon him such as his grandfather had never secured with Fergus. Similar consolidation work continued in Moray, where further colonial settlement occurred and where an opaque reference in the *Chronicle of Holyrood* to Malcolm transporting the men of Moray perhaps refers to a relocation and reconfiguration of the see – a development of as much political as religious significance – rather than the removal of the native population.[55]

Another major development of the 1160s was consolidation of royal power, backed by the establishment of crown tenants, in the maritime frontier zone between the Lennox and Cowal down the eastern shore of the Clyde estuary towards Galloway. This westward spread of royal power had begun under David I, but a chronology for the creation of the cluster of lordships here held by the Stewarts and the Morvilles is very uncertain.[56] Nevertheless, by the early 1160s the Clyde's eastern coast was lined by lordships held by the Scottish crown's greatest colonial magnates and it is possible that some of these men had begun to project their authority beyond their mainland territories into the Clyde islands and the peninsulas of southern Argyll. This encroachment on Somerled's sphere of influence has been regarded as the catalyst for his final confrontation with Scottish power.[57]

Somerled maintained peace with Malcolm for some years after 1160.[58]

---

[52] See Barrow (ed.), *RRS*, i, 27–56.
[53] Toorians, 'Flemish settlement', 4, 5–10; Tabraham, 'Norman settlement in upper Clydesdale'.
[54] Oram, *Lordship of Galloway*, 88–90.
[55] Barrow (ed.), *RRS*, i, no. 175; *Chron. Holyrood*, s.a. 1163. For discussion, see Barrow (ed.), *RRS*, i, 19–20.
[56] Barrow, *Anglo-Norman Era*, 62, 65, 72, note 64.
[57] McDonald, 'Rebels without a cause?', 183–4.
[58] Barrow, 'Malcolm IV and Somerled of Argyll', 222–3.

Evidence for his activity in the period 1160–4 is scant but accounts of attempts to persuade Flaithbertach ua Brolchain, abbot of Derry, to move to the Isles and restore the headship of the Columban community to Iona suggest that Somerled aimed to secure a position as leader of the Gael in the Isles and north of Ireland.[59] Discussion of Somerled normally places him within a Scottish context. This involvement in west Ulster affairs and his ambitions to bring the highly symbolic headship of the Columban network within his political sphere emphasises his place in the tradition of Irish and Norse-Gaelic rulers who had striven since the ninth century to assert their lordship in Ireland, the Isles and mainland Britain. It was, however, a move resisted strongly by Derry's secular protector Muirchertach mac Lochlainn of Cenél nEógain. Such wide-ranging power and ambitions, however, exposed Somerled to manifold external factors and his final conflict with the Scots may have arisen from events far removed from its point of resolution on Clydeside. Indeed, Henry II's north Welsh campaign in early 1163 posed as great a potential threat to Somerled as the possible activities of Walter son of Alan or Richard de Morville on the Clyde estuary. The deciding factor, however, was perhaps sheer opportunism driven by a mistaken belief that the illness that afflicted Malcolm had weakened Scottish royal power. With the king incapacitated, Somerled may have reckoned on being able to roll back the advance of Scottish influence in the maritime west.

Somerled's army in 1164 reflects the reach of his power at its apogee, drawing men from as far afield as Dublin and the Isles as well as from his Argyll homeland.[60] The direction of the assault, into the upper reaches of the Firth of Clyde with landfall somewhere near Renfrew, suggests that Walter son of Alan was one target, but the scale of the operation suggests that Somerled had more ambitious objectives. What those objectives were, however, remain unknown, for he was killed in a skirmish with local levies raised by the bishop of Glasgow and the sheriff of Lanark.[61] His death sent shockwaves through the region, for, with his passing, his sea kingdom disintegrated as his sons and other regional dynasts struggled for dominance. Dugald son of Somerled had perhaps lost the kingship of Man before the end of the year, when first Rognvald Ólafsson seized the throne only to be overthrown by his brother, Guðrøðr II, who returned from Norway with military support to reclaim his lost

---

[59] *AU*, s.a. 1164.
[60] *AU*, s.a. 1164; *Chron. Melrose*, s.a. 1164; *Carmen de Morte Sumerledi*, 386.
[61] Barrow (ed.), *RRS*, i, 20.

kingdom.[62] The disintegration of Somerled's domain may have been welcomed by the Scots, for it removed a potential bipolarity in the political structures of northern mainland Britain, but the return of Guðrøðr and the origins of his military backing emphasised that there were other external powers capable and willing to extend their influence westward.

The defeat of the Islesmen was the last major event of Malcolm IV's reign for which we have recorded evidence. Even in the final year of his life, however, he was not completely incapacitated and, while several of his surviving acts indicate his preoccupation with preparation for death, he maintained diplomatic activity which was far from compliant with Henry II's policies. In the midst of Henry's bitter conflict with Thomas Becket, Malcolm wrote to Henry to urge reconciliation with the archbishop, with whom he was in friendly correspondence.[63] It was unlikely to have endeared him to Henry but, like his foundation of Coupar Angus Abbey, promise to go on pilgrimage to Santiago di Compostela, and generous patronage of Scottish monasteries, it helped to secure his reputation as a Christian prince. On 9 December 1165, he died at Jedburgh and his body was conveyed to Dunfermline for burial alongside his grandfather. Like David I before him, his death was followed by an outpouring of literature which sought to establish the sanctity of the king described in the *Annals of Ulster* as 'the best Christian of the Gaels to the east of the sea'.[64] Also like David, however, it did not secure his canonisation although the eulogies did underscore his success in rebuilding the prestige of the Scottish monarchy after the setbacks of 1157, and his skill in treading the fine line between submission and defiance in his relationship with Henry II. His legacy, however, was a difficult one for his successor to maintain.

AN ANGRY YOUNG MAN?

The new king, Malcolm's younger brother William, was around twenty-two and had possibly acquired experience in government during Malcolm's illnesses after 1163.[65] This experience, and also his brother's apparent elimination of rival claims to the kingship from kinsmen

---

[62] *Chron. Man*, s.a. 1164.
[63] Barrow (ed.), *RRS*, i, 21.
[64] *AU*, s.a. 1165. For verdicts on the king, see Barrow (ed.), *RRS*, i, 22–5; Duncan, *Kingship of the Scots*, 74–5.
[65] Duncan, *Kingship of the Scots*, 73–4.

descended from Alexander I, ensured an untroubled succession with William securing unanimous acclamation from the Scottish nobles.[66] The smoothness of his accession, however, was followed swiftly by ominous signs of troubles to come in his relationship with Henry II. Northumbria, the patrimony surrendered by his elder brother to Henry II, was the root of the problem. Although William had received compensation from Henry for its loss in the form of the poor upland lordship of Tynedale and a scattering of estates in Scotland from his brother,[67] he was never reconciled to his disinheritance. Perhaps emboldened by the crises with which Henry was confronted in 1165–6, spread from north Wales to Maine and Brittany, and Henry's increasingly fraught relationship with Louis VII of France and burgeoning confrontation with Thomas Becket,[68] William pressed for restoration of Northumberland and Cumberland when he met Henry early in 1166.

Contemporary records of their first encounter are vague on detail and imprecise in chronology, but an outline narrative can be reconstructed. Henry returned to Normandy in March 1166 and remained on the continent for four years. The fourteenth-century *Gesta Annalia*, which is based in this section on material drawn from a contemporary Coupar Angus chronicle, suggests that William met Henry before his departure with the express purpose of settling outstanding questions relating to the border and Northumberland, but discussions between them were interrupted by news of rebellion from Maine. Henry left swiftly for the continent and, against the advice of his own counsellors, William followed him there and distinguished himself in the subsequent fighting.[69] Allowing for later embellishment, the *Gesta Annalia* account accords well with that of the *Chronicle of Melrose* where there is no mention of a meeting in England but where William followed Henry to Normandy and participated in some tournaments before returning to Scotland. It makes no comment, however, on the business that drew him to Normandy in the first place.[70] William's presence at Genest in Brittany is recorded by a third chronicler, Robert de Torigni, abbot of Mont-Saint-Michel,[71] but he provides little other detail of his activities in France. The speed of William's journey from inauguration at Scone on Christmas Eve 1165

---

[66] Ibid. 98–9.
[67] Barrow (ed.), *RRS*, ii, no. 5 note.
[68] Warren, *Henry II*, 103–5, 163–4. For Wales, see *Annales Cambriae*, 50.
[69] *Chron. Fordun*, s.a. 1166.
[70] *Chron. Melrose*, s.a. 1166.
[71] Robert de Torigni, *Chronica*, 228–9.

to Normandy by late March 1166 suggests that he had not been summoned to perform military service in Henry's army. *Gesta Annalia* gives a probably anachronistic and inflated account of a gathering to settle the border issue agreed through commissioners from both kingdoms, with a formal assembly arranged for a meeting of the two kings. The formality, however, was more probably bound up in confirming the protocols for William's coming south to perform his acts of homage and fealty to Henry for the earldom of Huntingdon.

Although Henry had dealt with Maine by Easter 1166, he turned his attention immediately to Brittany, whose duke was William's brother-in-law. The Maine rebels had drawn support from Breton barons, whom the duke either could not control or whose actions he encouraged.[72] The campaign, unlike the 1165 operations in Wales, was a total success; Duke Conan was deposed and his daughter Constance, William's niece, married to Henry's second son, Geoffrey. William's presence at Genest suggests involvement in the Breton campaign, presumably as earl of Huntingdon rather than king of Scots, and it is possible that he sought to ingratiate himself with Henry through this display of loyalty. *Gesta Annalia*'s reference to the Northumbrian question might preserve a record of what William hoped to gain from this service. Whether William raised the Northumberland question or sought to intercede on behalf of his brother-in-law is unknown, but the fragmentary evidence available indicates that William and Henry parted on bad terms in late summer 1166, with William returning to Scotland empty-handed. An anonymous contemporary letter to Thomas Becket reported how at Caen, in the midst of discussions concerning the Scottish king, Henry had flown into a rage when one of his knights spoke favourably of William, and that the king

> threw his cap from his head, unfastened his belt, threw far away from himself the robe and clothes which he was wearing, removed with his own hands the silken cover upon the bed, and sitting as if he was in a midden-heap took up the straw to chew the stems.[73]

While the author of the letter was seeking to present Henry in the worst possible light, his report implies that relations between the kings had become poisonous within months of William's accession.

How low relations had ebbed can be gauged by overtures made by

---

[72] Warren, *Henry II*, 101.
[73] Robertson (ed.), *Materials for the History of Thomas Becket*, vi, 71–2.

William to Louis VII of France, whose own dealings with Henry, his nominal vassal, veered between simmering hostility, covert and overt support for rebels within Henry's territory, to open warfare along their common borders. In 1168, in the midst of fresh warfare between Louis and Henry and a series of rebellions in Aquitaine, Auvergne, Brittany and Poitou, William sent envoys to Louis.[74] What business was discussed is unknown, but given current events it is unlikely that it was favourable to Henry. Nothing came of the approach, possibly because Louis and Henry began negotiations in winter 1168–9, but it reveals the lengths to which William went to secure the return of his lost heritage.

William possibly again raised the Northumberland question when he and his brother, David, met Henry at Windsor in April 1170.[75] Although William's request for restoration was again snubbed, relations remained sufficiently amicable for David to receive his knighthood from his cousin.[76] Henry, however, had his own motives for keeping his Scottish cousins compliant, for in late May he had his eldest son, Henry, crowned as king-designate at Westminster, and required his barons to perform homage and fealty to him. William complied as earl of Huntingdon, reserving only his homage and fealty to the elder Henry while he lived.[77] This move by Henry, which followed the Capetian practice of having the heir-apparent crowned during the lifetime of his father and so avoid the issue of a challenged succession, was part of a series of similar arrangements for his second son, Richard, in Aquitaine and Geoffrey in Brittany designed to secure Angevin control over the various territories under his overlordship. It was, however, a device that almost destroyed his authority.

Although he had his eldest son crowned in 1170 and repeated the ceremony in August 1172, by 1173 there was no sign that the elder Henry would give the eighteen-year-old Young King any real authority to accompany his title, a decision that reflected the father's recognition of the fecklessness of the son.[78] Young Henry's discontent was ably manipulated by his father-in-law, Louis VII of France, and when the elder Henry announced that he intended to settle various Angevin properties on his youngest son, John, as part of his marriage contract, the breach

---

[74] Lawrie (ed.), *Annals*, 116–17.
[75] *Chron. Fordun*, s.a. 1170.
[76] *Chron. Melrose*, s.a. 1170.
[77] Anderson (ed.), *Early Sources*, ii, 268, note 3. *Jordan Fantosme's Chronicle*, 1, implies that the homage and fealty was as king of Scots.
[78] Warren, *Henry II*, 112–13.

with his still landless eldest son was complete. The fissures in Henry II's close family extended wider than his relationship with the Young King, for his wife, Eleanor of Aquitaine, and sons Richard and Geoffrey, were also conspiring against him. With King Louis's open support, the younger Henry began to purchase support with lavish promises, offering men whose families had lost property in England or Normandy in the post-1154 settlement restoration of their losses. Amongst the men courted in this way were King William, to whom he promised all that Malcolm IV had surrendered, and his younger brother, David, to whom he offered an expanded earldom of Huntingdon.[79] His father, who knew William's hunger for Northumbria, may already have made overtures to the Scots, and William was unwilling to break faith with Henry II without first having attempted to reach a settlement. When Henry spurned the proposals presented by William's envoys, the Scots, after further deliberation, accepted the Young King's offer.[80]

The French-backed civil war began in Normandy in May 1173, but by early August the elder Henry had already gained the upper hand and driven Louis out of the east of the duchy and defeated the rebels and their Breton allies in the west.[81] In England, the Young King's supporters had made little headway as their rebellion was uncoordinated, lacked strong leadership and was contained to the Midlands and eastern Suffolk. William invaded northern England in August, attacking but failing to take first Wark then Carlisle before crossing the Pennines to ravage the bishopric of Durham and northern Yorkshire.[82] Confronted by Henry II's justiciar, Richard de Lucy, William retreated into Lothian, where de Lucy burned Berwick and the Merse before news of the arrival from France of the rebel earl of Leicester and a large force of mercenaries forced him to withdraw southwards. Checked in his first foray, William made a truce and spent the winter preparing to resume hostilities in the spring.

Although de Lucy had routed Leicester in autumn 1173, the justiciar had not crushed the rebellion in the Midlands. With strong leadership, the reverses suffered by the younger Henry's supporters in England could still be overturned. In May 1174, that leadership emerged

---

[79] *Chron. Melrose*, s.a. 1173; Benedict of Peterborough, *Gesta Regis*, i, 45; *Jordan Fantosme's Chronicle*, 21–3.
[80] *Chron. Fantosme*, 25–31.
[81] Warren, *Henry II*, 125–8
[82] *Chron. Holyrood*, s.a. 1173; *Jordan Fantosme's Chronicle*, 35–61; William of Newburgh, *Historia Rerum Anglicarum*, 177–8; Benedict of Peterborough, *Gesta Regis*, i, 61; De Diceto, *Imagines Historiarum*, i, 376.

when William's brother, David, assumed lordship of the earldom of Huntingdon.[83] Henry had attempted to detach David from his brother the previous year, offering him 'such lands and fiefs as will satisfy all his demands' if he came to his aid.[84] Keith Stringer has speculated that David may have held reservations about a war against the elder Henry which the king sought to play upon, and certainly David took no active part in the 1173 campaign.[85] His brother's assignation to him of his Midlands honour and Young Henry's offer of an enhanced earldom of Huntingdon were largely speculative for Henry II considered William to have forfeited his lands in 1173. To secure his earldom David would therefore have to take the field and win it. Doubts over the likely success of such a venture may explain William's additional award to David of the earldom of Lennox, the lordship of the Garioch and other properties in Angus, Perthshire, Fife and Lothian.[86]

With David providing leadership for the rebellion in the Midlands, William launched a fresh invasion of Northumbria.[87] Like his grandfather's campaigns in the 1130s, his advance was slowed by fortresses held by barons loyal to the elder Henry. In the west, although he captured Liddel, Brough and Appleby, the two last giving him control of the west end of the trans-Pennine Stanemoor route, Carlisle held out.[88] Northumberland was even more problematical for, although William took Warkworth and Harbottle, Wark, Prudhoe and Alnwick defied him.[89] While he remained with a small force to besiege Alnwick, King William dispersed his army to harry the lands of Henry's supporters throughout Northumberland. On 13 July, attended by only a small retinue, he was captured by a force of King Henry's loyalists.[90] His capture effectively ended the rebellion in England and Henry II's march north from Canterbury first to Huntingdon and then Northampton, where he received William's formal surrender,[91] became a triumphal progress rather than a military campaign. With England secure,

---

[83] Stringer, *Earl David*, 21.
[84] *Jordan Fantosme's Chronicle*, 27.
[85] Stringer, *Earl David*, 21.
[86] Barrow (ed.), *RRS*, ii, no. 205; *Chron. Fantosme*, 83.
[87] Anderson (ed.), *Early Sources*, ii, 280; Benedict of Peterborough, *Gesta Regis*, i, 64–6.
[88] *Jordan Fantosme's Chronicle*, 89–113; Benedict of Peterborough, *Gesta Regis*, i, 64–6.
[89] Benedict of Peterborough, *Gesta Regis*, i, 66.
[90] *Chron. Holyrood*, s.a. 1174; *Chron. Melrose*, s.a. 1174; William of Newburgh, *Historia Rerum Anglicarum*, 183–5; *Jordan Fantosme's Chronicle*, 129–37. For a modern account of the sieges, see Humphreys, *Enemies at the Gate*, Chapter 3.
[91] Roger of Howden, *Chronica*, ii, 64.

Henry ordered William to be brought to him in Normandy to where he returned, accompanied by Earl David who had submitted to him after the surrender of Huntingdon, to break the French siege of Rouen.[92] On 11 August, Henry's army routed the French before the city's walls and before the end of September King Louis had sued for peace. With victory secure, the elder Henry turned to the post-war settlement.

DIRECT LORDSHIP IMPOSED: THE TREATY OF FALAISE

While Ralph of Diss speaks of William being confined in chains at Falaise until the formal agreement of peace terms with Henry in December 1174, other accounts suggest a gentler regime.[93] Although he was permitted to participate in tournaments and attend ceremonial events, however, William was still considered as a betrayer of his lord, a defeated enemy and a prisoner on whom Henry was determined to impose terms more rigorous than those agreed with his other defeated enemies.[94] On 8 December, after taking council from the nobles and prelates of his kingdom, William accepted this 'Treaty of Falaise' and gave his liege homage to Henry II for *Scotia* and all his other lands, promising that the homage and fealty of the lay nobility and the fealty of the clergy would be given to the English king as their liege lord, and also promising to deliver the royal fortresses of Lothian into English keeping as security.[95] Once arrangements had been made for the delivery of the castles and the performance of the required submissions, William was released and returned to his kingdom.

On his return, William was confronted by old problems which his capture had uncapped. Chief amongst these was Galloway, which had been held in check since 1160.[96] Fergus's sons, Uhtred and Gillebrigte, had accompanied William in 1174 but had seized the opportunity of his capture to throw off Scottish overlordship. Returning to Galloway, they had expelled or killed many of the foreign colonists who had settled there and attacked neighbouring royal strongholds.[97] Perhaps hoping to

---

[92] *Jordan Fantosme's Chronicle*, 151–3; *Chron. Melrose*, s.a. 1174.
[93] De Diceto, *Imagines Historiarum*, i, 396; Anderson (ed.), *Early Sources*, ii, 290, note 1.
[94] Warren, *Henry II*, 137–9.
[95] De Diceto, *Imagines Historiarum*, i, 396–8.
[96] See Oram, *Lordship of Galloway*, 93–9.
[97] Benedict of Peterborough, *Gesta Regis*, i, 67–8; *Jordan Fantosme's Chronicle*, 126.

Treaty of Falaise

The Treaty of Falaise was a defining episode which, although not marking the 'feudal subjection' of Scotland to the English king, formalised the relationship between them albeit in vague terms of superior lordship.[98] The precedent it set was the benchmark against which English kings down to Henry VIII defined their relationship with the Scots. The treaty stemmed from William's capture, imprisonment at Falaise and subsequent negotiations for his release in 1174. William and Henry II settled terms on 8 December 1174 and arrangements were made for their ratification at York in August 1175. Although official records of the deal were surrendered to William and probably destroyed in 1189 when the treaty was cancelled, its terms had been transcribed into other accounts, most notably the chronicle compiled by Roger of Howden; it is from such sources that we know its form.[99]

The treaty is as noteworthy for what was not said as for what was. In particular, Anglo-Scottish relations were not described in overtly 'feudal' terms; nowhere was Scotland called a 'fief' nor said to be 'held' or 'had' by the king of England.[100] Nevertheless, William was bound by an oath of fealty, a subjection passed to his heirs. Furthermore, Henry II received the fealty of William's magnates against all men, which established that they owed greater allegiance to him than they did to William; if William broke the treaty, they were to force William to come to terms. Henry also demanded control of royal castles in Lothian – Berwick, Jedburgh, Roxburgh, Edinburgh and Stirling, but sought neither men nor money for his wars, nor did he hear appeals from Scottish law courts. In that sense, the treaty was a 'light touch' settlement of a situation from which Henry could have taken greater benefit but at the cost of greater resentment. Nevertheless, William was humiliated by a treaty that restricted his ability to deal with his own subjects and gave Henry personal domination of his northern neighbour and unprecedented influence – if he chose to exercise it – over Scottish domestic affairs.

---

capitalise on Uhtred's kinship with Henry II, and possibly also in recognition of the extension of English influence around the Irish Sea following the king's expedition to Ireland in 1171, the brothers approached

[98] Barrow, *Kingship and Unity*, 53–4; Duncan, *Kingship of the Scots*, 101–2.
[99] Anderson, *Scottish Annals*, 258–63; Donaldson, *Scottish Historical Documents*, 27–8.
[100] Duncan, *Kingship of the Scots*, 101.

Henry and offered him their liege homage and fealty if he would free them from William's lordship.[101] Made at a time when Henry still faced the assembled forces of Louis VII and those barons who had joined the Young King, and before he had started negotiations with William, the offer was tempting and Henry sent envoys to Galloway to explore options. The wording of the treaty settled at Falaise, which refers only to *Scotia* and William's other lands, perhaps indicates that Henry was prepared at that point to take Galloway into his direct lordship and also that it was not considered to be an integral part of the Scottish kingdom. By the time that his delegates arrived in Galloway in November, however, the animosity between Uhtred and Gillebrigte had burst into violence which left Uhtred dead. Despite Gillebrigte's offer of an annual tribute to Henry of 2,000 merks of silver, 500 head of cattle and 500 pigs, the envoys refused to negotiate until they had received instructions from their king. When Henry received news of Uhtred's death, however, probably during his negotiations with William, he rejected Gillebrigte's offer.[102] The year ended, therefore, with Gillebrigte at war with the Scots and, technically, also with King Henry.

In August 1175, William, his nobles and prelates came to York to ratify the Falaise settlement and to perform the agreed acts of homage and fealty to Henry and the Young King.[103] William's formal submission was made explicitly for Scotland and Galloway, a form of words that removed the old ambiguity over the relationship of the kingship of the Scots with the English crown and also publicly affirmed William's lordship over Gillebrigte. While past Scottish kings had been the 'man' of English rulers, the relationship had been left ill-defined and ambiguous. This submission appears to have established explicitly the subjection of the Scottish king to the king of England for his kingdom as well as for the lands that he held in England, but recent analysis of the treaty has highlighted the ambiguity of the terminology employed.[104] William was unquestionably under Henry II's superior lordship and constrained in his powers as king within Scotland, but there was no suggestion in either the treaty or in any other contemporary discussion of the post-1174 relationship that Scotland was a 'fief' or was in any way 'held' as such of the English crown. William had to take council and advice of his lord,

[101] Roger of Howden, *Chronica*, ii, 63.
[102] Benedict of Peterborough, *Gesta Regis*, ii, 79–80.
[103] For ecclesiastical subjection, see pp. 342–3.
[104] Duncan, *Kingship of the Scots*, 100–2.

Henry, and seek permission for certain actions, the first of which was the re-imposition of Scottish lordship over Galloway.

Howden's narrative presents an image of Gillebrigte establishing control throughout Galloway with comparative ease after killing his brother. William of Newburgh, however, claims that Gillebrigte was opposed successfully by his eldest nephew, Roland, aided by his father's former friends and supporters.[105] Roland took possession of some part of his patrimony,[106] but absence of reference to him in accounts of the deal struck between Gillebrigte and Henry II indicates that his uncle's control of the core of the lordship was complete. Certainly, there is no suggestion that Roland was sufficiently important for his direct homage and fealty to be required by Henry, as would have been the case had he entered his full inheritance. No record survives of how pressure was applied to Gillebrigte, but in October 1176 he accompanied William to Feckenham in Worcestershire, where he made his peace with Henry for Uhtred's death, gave his homage and fealty 'against all men' and accepted a fine of 1,000 merks of silver 'to have [Henry's] love'.[107] Henry had already confirmed William's lordship over Galloway at York in 1175 so it is unlikely that Gillebrigte's homage and fealty to Henry against all men was intended to remove Galloway from that relationship but was simply a continuation of the policy adopted by Henry of taking the direct oaths of William's greater lords. Gillebrigte, however, viewed the relationship differently, for on his return to Galloway he ordered all men who held land there of William to quit their property on pain of death. The settlement at Feckenham may have preserved the notion of Scottish overlordship, but Gillebrigte's action emptied it of any substance and revealed William's weakness. Gillebrigte had made his peace with Henry and become his man; he could count on him for protection against William. In turn, this drove Roland into a closer relationship with William and his Anglo-Scottish nobles. Neither side had achieved their desired result, but an uneasy peace had become established nevertheless.

It has been said that 'King Henry rode Scotland much more lightly than he need have done' following the Treaty of Falaise, his aim being to guarantee William's future good behaviour rather than impose intrusive overlordship upon him.[108] Failure to re-establish the pre-1174 status quo in Galloway, however, was a galling constraint on William. There were

---

[105] William of Newburgh, *Historia*, 186–7.
[106] Oram, *Lordship of Galloway*, 95–8, 201–2; Duncan, *Making of the Kingdom*, 183–4.
[107] Benedict of Peterborough, *Gesta Regis*, i, 126.
[108] Duncan, *Making of the Kingdom*, 234; Stringer, *Earl David*, 30.

St Thomas the Martyr and Arbroath Abbey

When King William was captured at Alnwick in July 1174 there were many, including the king, who attributed this act to the saintly intervention of Thomas Becket, archbishop of Canterbury. Becket had been murdered in December 1170 by a group of the English King Henry II's knights and had immediately received acclamation as a martyr and miracle-working saint. When on 12 July 1174 Henry performed public penance at Becket's tomb and then the following day William was taken prisoner, there seemed little doubt that England had acquired a new saintly protector. William's certainty that St Thomas the Martyr had delivered him into Henry's hands deeply troubled him and drove him to make an extravagant display of personal atonement to the angry saint. In 1178, at Arbroath, William founded what became one of the richest royal abbeys in Scotland and dedicated it to St Thomas. While William's descendants used veneration of St Thomas as a barb to goad their English enemies – descendants of the man responsible for Becket's murder – he himself was genuinely penitent for his hostile actions in 1174. William, and subsequently his son, Alexander II, went to great lengths to secure relics of St Thomas for the abbey, the most important perhaps being obtained when Alexander visited Canterbury in 1223.[109] William lavished land and rights on the monks as well as paying for the construction of one of the largest and most architecturally ambitious monasteries in his kingdom, exceeding in its scale most of Scotland's cathedrals.[110] The king's gifts to the abbey slowed with the political challenges and straitened financial position that he faced in the 1180s and 1190s but quickened again in the 1200s as he prepared for his death. His decision to be buried at Arbroath rather than the royal mausoleum church at Dunfermline is eloquent testimony to his abiding faith in the power of the saint who had secured his capture and fifteen-year subjection to the English crown.

also territorial losses for William and his brother, David, who suffered the only major forfeiture of the war when Henry seized the earldom of Huntingdon and gave it to Simon III de Senlis.[111] William chafed under the restraint, and the tone of some charters that he issued to provide

---

[109] Penman, 'Royal piety in thirteenth-century Scotland', 18.
[110] Barrow (ed.), *RRS*, ii, no. 197.
[111] Stringer, *Earl David*, 28.

Figure 4.1 Arbroath Abbey, Angus, founded in 1178 by King William.

compensation to religious houses who suffered losses on account of the impositions made by Henry's garrisons in Lothian convey a sense of that frustration.[112] Nevertheless, his regular attendance on Henry between 1176 and 1186 suggests that he was prepared to work within his new limits in an effort to gain Henry's favour and perhaps secure restoration of his losses. For the Scottish political community the hostages taken for the security of the peace in 1175, who included the sons of the earls of Fife, Dunbar, Strathearn and Angus, and the fortresses in Lothian placed in Henry's hands but maintained at William's expense, were immediate and highly visible symbols of their king's subjection. They perhaps contributed significantly to an undercurrent of tension within Scotland in the later 1170s.

SCOTTISH REACTION

The principal source of this discord came from support within some segments of the political community for rivals for the kingship. The main threat came from Donald MacWilliam, the son of William son of Duncan II, who represented a senior line of the royal house that King

[112] Barrow (ed.), *RRS*, ii, 8.

William, his family and their supporters sought consistently to discredit and to stigmatise as of illegitimate descent.[113] There is no contemporary evidence for Donald having made earlier bids for the kingship, but the well-informed English royal clerk Roger of Howden, writing of events in 1181, referred to previous claims and 'insidious incursions'.[114] A second potential candidate as a trigger for trouble in the north was Harald Maddadsson, earl of Orkney and Caithness, who had set aside his first wife, Affreca, daughter of Earl Duncan of Fife, and apparently 'married' Hvarfloð, who is described in saga sources as the daughter of 'Malcolm, earl of Moray'.[115] The saga is notoriously unreliable in its use of Scottish titles, and it is probable that the Earl Malcolm in question is Malcolm MacHeth, earl of Ross, who had died in 1168.[116] Certainly, *Gesta Annalia*'s source believed that MacHeth was her father.[117] Further support for this identification may lie in the claim made in Orkney tradition that Heinrik or Henry, Harald's son, later succeeded to the rule of Ross.[118] The first indication of trouble occurs in the *Melrose Chronicle*'s annals for 1179, when it was reported that King William and Earl David campaigned in Ross with a large force and fortified castles at Dunskeath on the north side of the Cromarty Firth and Edradour (Redcastle) at the head of the Beauly Firth.[119] No indication is given of against whom the operation was directed but the location of the castles suggests that they were securing control of strategic ferry crossings necessary for actions in Easter Ross and beyond; the circumstantial evidence for Harald Maddadsson's involvement is strong.[120]

William and David believed that they had secured control over the Ross firthlands, for the king was in southern Scotland by October and both brothers attended Henry II's Christmas court at Nottingham.[121] Their success, however, was illusory, for Howden records that in 1181, whilst William was with Henry II in Normandy (until late July) and

---

[113] Broun, 'Contemporary perspectives on Alexander II's succession', 83–4, 86–8, 94–5.
[114] Benedict of Peterborough, *Gesta Regis*, i, 277–8.
[115] *Orkneyinga Saga*, 218.
[116] *Chron. Holyrood*, s.a. 1168; Anderson, *Early Sources*, ii, 238, 348.
[117] *Chron. Fordun*, i, 274.
[118] *Orkneyinga Saga*, 224. According to the sagas, however, Henry was a son of Harald's marriage to Affreca, while a claim to Ross should only have come to him by right if he were a son of Hvarfloð.
[119] *Chron. Melrose*, s.a. 1179.
[120] Duncan, *Making of the Kingdom*, 193; Topping, 'Harald Maddadson', 113–15, questions Harald's involvement.
[121] Barrow (ed.), *RRS*, ii, no. 215; Benedict of Peterborough, *Gesta Regis*, i, 244.

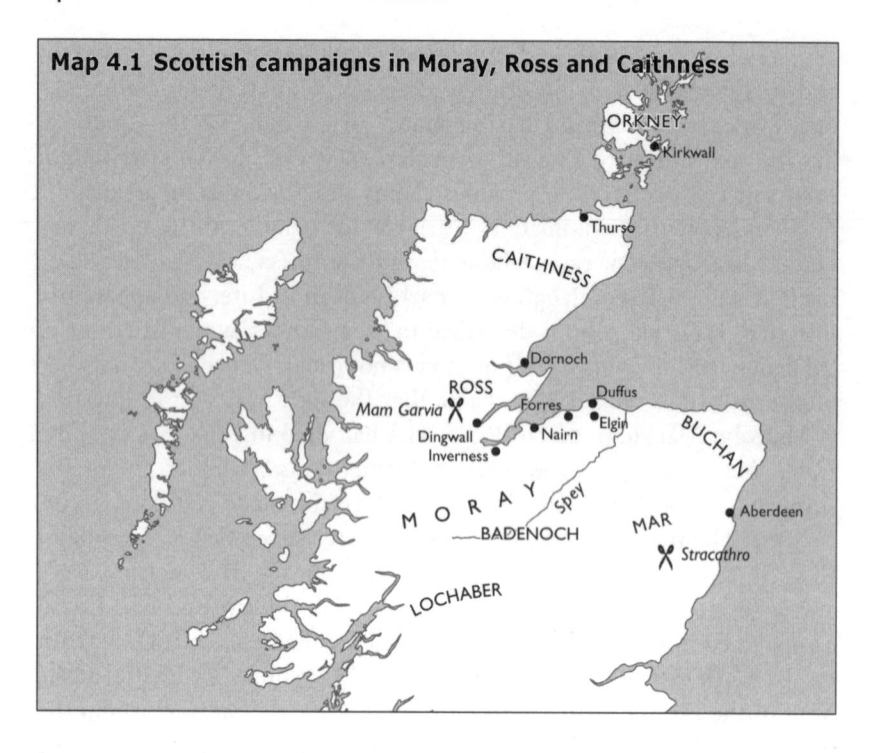

Map 4.1 Scottish campaigns in Moray, Ross and Caithness

England (until September), his control of northern Scotland disintegrated, forcing him to seek Henry's permission to leave to deal with the crisis.[122] It has been suggested that, since the Melrose chronicle makes no mention of the 1181 conflict, Howden has misdated the 1179 operations, but the manner in which he interwove details of the Scottish situation into English court business suggests that these were separate incidents.[123] On this occasion there was no quick fix and the northern mainland remained disturbed down into 1187.

According to Howden, ranged against William from 1181 was a coalition of 'certain powerful men of the kingdom of Scotland' who supported Donald's claims and who had invited him to return to Scotland. Circumstantial evidence points to Harald Maddadsson being one of these unnamed individuals. Support from Orkney accords well with the comment that some of Donald's warriors came from outside Scotland, although it is usually suggested that these men were Hebridean or Irish.

---

[122] Benedict of Peterborough, *Gesta Regis*, i, 276–8, 280.
[123] Barrow (ed.), *RRS*, ii, 11–12; Duncan, *Making of the Kingdom*, 192–3; Topping, 'Harald Maddadson', 113.

An alliance between Harald Maddadsson and the MacWilliam family also explains the Orkney saga tradition that presents 'William', probably referring to William son of Duncan II rather than his son, William, the 'boy of Egremont', or to Donald mac William, as the favoured candidate of many Scots for the kingship.[124] Harald, however, was not the only powerful figure to back the MacWilliams and, although the contemporary and staunchly loyal Melrose chronicle says nothing of the level of popular support for the descendants of Duncan II, it appears from various accounts that Donald attracted significant and possibly widespread sympathy north of the Forth. Frustratingly, the identity of none of these backers is recorded, and the chronicle accounts speak only in vague terms of undefined 'treachery'. The one documented case of action being taken against a traitor, however, reveals that support for Donald could be found even within the household of one of the greatest Scottish earls, Gillebrigte of Strathearn. Probably shortly after the suppression of the 1187 rising, the king granted Earl Gillebrigte the lands of his former marischal, Gillecolm, forfeited through his felony of betraying the castle of 'Heryn' (probably Auldearn) into the hands of the king's enemies, thereafter joining with them and participating in hostile actions against him.[125] The fall of Auldearn accords with the *Gesta Annalia* account, which refers to Donald's control of Ross and Moray.[126] Behind the silence in the pro-William accounts of the conflict in the early 1180s lies the probability that his authority west of the Spey had all but collapsed before the advance of Donald and his allies.

Some indication of the scale of support for Donald can be taken from the difficulties that William faced in ending the challenge and suppressing disloyalty within the Scottish nobility. Even towards the end of the rising there are suggestions of dissension amongst supposedly loyal lords between men who 'did not love the king' and those whose support was unconditional.[127] A factor behind such tensions may have been resentment at William's compliance with Henry II's demands and readiness to attend the English king's court.[128] In 1181 alone, William travelled to Normandy to meet with Henry in the late spring and again in July, was at Canterbury and Nottingham between July and September, and was still

---

[124] Duncan, *Kingship of the Scots*, 102; *Orkneyinga Saga*, c. 33.
[125] Barrow (ed.), *RRS*, ii, no. 258.
[126] *Chron. Fordun*, s.a. 1179.
[127] Benedict of Peterborough, *Gesta Regis*, ii, 8.
[128] Duncan, *Kingship of the Scots*, 101–5.

in the south of his own kingdom in the early autumn.[129] The domestic political crisis caused by his interference in the election of the bishop of St Andrews (see pp. 332–4), his failure to regain his position in Galloway and unease arising from the kingdom's subjection to Henry's supremacy all combined to make William's lords reluctant to fulfil their duties. Lack of confidence or trust in William perhaps resulted in failure to prosecute the war against Donald MacWilliam with greater conviction.

Evidence for the course of the conflict is lacking before the mid-1180s but it appears that William involved himself in complex manoeuvres designed to undercut the position of Donald's chief ally. According to *Orkneyinga Saga*, Harald Ungi, the head of the branch of the Orkney earls descended from Erlend II and Rognvald Kolsson, received a grant of the title of earl in Orkney from the Norwegian king, Magnus VI, and of half of Caithness from William.[130] The chronology offered by the saga is both telescoped and confused, but it seems likely that the arrival of Harald Ungi in Caithness to press his claim to a share in the two earldoms resulted in a more protracted struggle than the surviving account indicates, and the consequence was a gradual recovery of William's position in the north from around this time. Rather than the challenge of Harald Ungi causing Harald Maddadsson little serious trouble,[131] it forced him to concentrate on his own position at the expense of his support for Donald MacWilliam.

While Harald Maddadsson's involvement in Donald's venture declined after c. 1184, there was little immediate sign of any lessening in the pressure on William. Indeed, the deaths of both Simon de Toeni, bishop of Moray, and the aged and largely absentee Andrew, bishop of Caithness, in October and December 1184 merely added to the king's woes.[132] The crisis was compounded by renewed conflict with Gillebrigte, son of Fergus, in Galloway in summer 1184. Evidence for this conflict survives only in the writings of Roger of Howden, who recorded that William raised an army to subdue Gillebrigte, who had 'wasted his land and killed his men, and yet would not make peace with him', but disbanded it upon receiving news of the return to England of Henry II, in whose direct lordship Gillebrigte also stood.[133] It is unclear if Howden was referring to Gillebrigte's behaviour in the mid-1170s or

---

[129] For William's itinerary, see Barrow (ed.), *RRS*, ii, 97.
[130] *Orkneyinga Saga*, c. 109.
[131] Duncan, *Making of the Kingdom*, 193–4.
[132] *Chron. Melrose*, s.a. 1184.
[133] Benedict of Peterborough, *Gesta Regis*, i, 313.

more recent hostilities, but William's actions speak of frustration with his inability to re-establish mastery within his own kingdom. The disbanding of William's army added to his difficulties at home, as it emphasised his subordinate relationship with the English king and heightened the impression that the submission at Falaise in 1174 had resulted only in humiliation and dishonour. William needed to be able to demonstrate that the bonds with Henry could bring positive benefits for king and kingdom.

MANOEUVRE WITHIN LIMITS

It was perhaps with such a motive that William hastened to Henry's court in summer 1184 accompanied by his leading vassals. According to Howden, the main business of the meeting was William's marriage, which Henry as superior lord had the right to arrange.[134] A good marriage would have done much to boost William's prestige and he certainly aimed high when he asked Henry for the hand of Matilda of Saxony, Henry's eldest granddaughter. Politically, the marriage would have been tremendously advantageous for William, forging a personal link to Henry's close family which could perhaps have secured the restoration of Northumberland and Cumberland as Matilda's dowry. King Henry recognised the implications of the marriage and used Matilda's consanguinity with William as an excuse to defer a decision until papal permission had been obtained. That Henry had no interest in supporting the marriage seems clear from the pope's rejection of the request and the immediate dropping of the proposal.[135] William's public recognition of Henry's power over him had resulted only in further humiliation, but circumstances were changing and Henry could not afford to antagonise a man who was of growing importance to the security of the English empire. It may have been a recognition of the need to offer his Scottish vassal some tangible reward for good service, particularly at a time when challenges to Angevin power in France were intensifying, that led him in March 1185 to restore Huntingdon to William.[136] William at once regranted the earldom to his brother, David, possibly as Henry had intended, in a move which tied the heir-presumptive to the

---

[134] Ibid. i, 313–14.
[135] Duncan, *Making of the Kingdom*, 231; Benedict of Peterborough, *Gesta Regis*, i, 322.
[136] Benedict of Peterborough, *Gesta Regis*, i, 337.

Scottish throne into closer dependence on the English crown.[137] David rose progressively in importance as an English magnate but in early 1185 Henry's immediate policy was intended to bind both brothers firmly to his side at a time of growing crisis.

At this point William had his first good luck in over a decade. On 1 January 1185, Gillebrigte of Galloway died, leaving a young son, Duncan, who was a hostage at the court of Henry II.[138] According to Howden, Gillebrigte's nephew, Roland, seized the initiative, raised an army and invaded his late uncle's territory, killing all who opposed him and constructing castles throughout the conquered land.[139] The author of *Gesta Annalia* implies that Roland had William's support in this and, given the strong relationship forged between them since 1176 and the advantageous marriage that Roland had secured with the daughter of the king's constable, William's connivance seems likely. After ten years of political and military impotence under Henry II's light but ever-watchful lordship, William seized the opportunity to restore his influence in Galloway, regardless of the wishes of the infuriated English king. It is possible, indeed, that William recognised that Henry's growing commitment to the defence of his Continental domain made it unlikely that he could intervene actively in the struggle for Galloway. While William played a delaying game with Henry, Roland conquered Gillebrigte's former domain, completing the main campaign by autumn 1185.[140]

WILLIAM UNBOUND

Henry II was not prepared to accept a *fait accompli*, especially one that disinherited the son of a useful ally and undercut English influence in a strategic region. In May 1186, William and Earl David were summoned to Oxford, supposedly to discuss William's marriage. There, however, Henry exposed the transparency of William's actions by detaining him at court, ostensibly to await the arrival of his bride, Ermengarde, daughter of Richard, vicomte of Beaumont. Meanwhile William's nobles were required to hand over hostages before returning to Scotland charged with bringing Roland to make his formal submission to Henry. Howden's account of this event indicates that Henry's anger was provoked by

---

[137] Stringer, *Earl David*, 36–7.
[138] Benedict of Peterborough, *Gesta Regis*, i, 336.
[139] Ibid. i, 339–40.
[140] Oram, *Lordship of Galloway*, 100.

Roland's defiance of his prohibition against invading Gillebrigte's lands. Roland raised an army to resist any threat but, believing that the Scots were too dilatory in fulfilling his demands, later in July Henry came to Carlisle. Despite Henry's threats, Roland refused to accompany King William and Earl David to Carlisle and refused to submit until August. when Henry's envoys gave hostages and a guarantee of his safety. By this point, however, Henry was receiving disturbing intelligence of his son Geoffrey's treasonable negotiations with Philip of France and of growing disturbances in Ireland. He needed to reach a quick settlement, so Roland was permitted to retain his paternal heritage while the competing claim of Duncan to his heritage in western Galloway was reserved to Henry's court; Henry in turn received Roland's fealty. Having taken oaths from William and the Scottish nobility that they would uphold the agreement, Henry departed.[141] It was, for Henry, a good arrangement, for he had secured the submission of William's protégé and acknowledgement of his right as overlord to adjudicate in the disputed succession to Gillebrigte's lordship. Angevin influence in Galloway seemed to have been reinforced, but the climate of mounting crisis that enveloped the last two years of Henry's life meant that he was in no position to consolidate his success of summer 1186; when Henry died in July 1189 the rival claims of Roland and Duncan still lay unresolved.

William seemingly accompanied Henry south in August 1186, for on 5 September both men were at Woodstock for William's marriage to Ermengarde.[142] It was a glittering ceremony, presided over by Archbishop Baldwin of Canterbury and attended by Henry and his leading lords. Perhaps buoyed by his success at Carlisle and encouraged by William's continued deference to his overlordship, Henry felt he could afford to be generous and reward William's apparently loyal service. Although William had hoped for a more exalted bride than Ermengarde de Beaumont, she was still a kinswoman of the English king and brought the benefits of strengthened bonds not only with Henry but also with a very well-connected family with estates in England, Normandy and Anjou. She also brought a very tangible sign of Henry's favour; Edinburgh Castle was restored to William as part of Ermengarde's dowry.[143] William may still have chafed under the restraints on his authority as king that Henry's regular exercise of his rights as superior lord imposed,

---

[141] Benedict of Peterborough, *Gesta Regis*, i, 348–9; William of Newburgh, *Historia Rerum Anglicarum*, 237.
[142] *Chron. Melrose*, s.a. 1186.
[143] Benedict of Peterborough, *Gesta Regis*, i, 350–1.

and still yearned for the return of his own lost heritage, but his recognition of that superior lordship was yielding fruits and might still yet bring territorial restoration.

Galloway, at least temporarily, had been removed from William's agenda but he was quickly forced to turn his attention to another challenge to his authority from a rival segment of the royal house. There is no evidence that the bid mounted by Donald MacWilliam in 1181 had been successfully countered and other opponents may have exploited the disturbed state of the kingdom to advance their own causes. In November 1186 a man named only as Adam son of Donald, described as 'the king's outlaw', was captured at Coupar Angus Abbey by Malcolm, earl of Atholl, one of Adam's associates was beheaded in front of the high altar in the abbey church and fifty-eight others were burned to death in the abbot's lodging.[144] Adam has been identified as a grandson of Malcolm MacHeth, earl of Ross, or a son of Donald MacWilliam and the event connected with the current MacWilliam rising.[145] More recently, it has been suggested that he was the grandson of Malcolm, Alexander I's illegitimate son, whose father Donald had been imprisoned in Roxburgh in 1156.[146] In the absence of more detailed evidence, all that can be said with certainty is that Adam was a member of one of three lineages hostile to William and his family and that he possessed the ability to disturb the king's peace in the heart of the realm.

It may have been the shocking violence at Coupar Angus that forced William to tackle the MacWilliam threat head on. There may be no coincidence that in March 1187 the two-and-a-half-year hiatus in the see of Moray was ended by the election and speedy consecration of the king's clerk, Richard.[147] As with his predecessor, it is likely that he was intended to provide as much secular as spiritual leadership in the province. Richard's establishment as bishop heralded William's personal intervention in the north in the summer; by July he was at Inverness with his army. There are hints of discord in the ranks of the king's force in the chronicle accounts of the campaign, with suggestions that there were those present who 'loved the king not at all' and who obstructed operations against MacWilliam. At the end of the month, however, a portion of the army commanded by Roland son of Uhtred surprised Donald and

---

[144] *Chron. Holyrood*, s.a. 1186.
[145] Barrow (ed.), *RRS*, ii, 11–12 and note 47; Duncan, *Making of the Kingdom*, 194; Anderson (ed.), *Early Sources*, ii, 311; *Chron. Holyrood*, 170, note 10.
[146] Ross, 'Prisoner of Roxburgh', 280–2.
[147] *Chron. Melrose*, s.a. 1187.

his men at a place called 'Mam-garvia' in Ross, possibly at or near Garve, slew him and carried his head to William at Inverness.[148] For William, his support for the Galloway claimant had paid off and Roland soon received his reward for loyal service. More important in the eyes of the chroniclers, however, was the return of peace after a prolonged period of bloody disturbance.

Can we assume that Donald's death strengthened William's position at home? Victory perhaps encouraged him to take a firmer stance in 1188 when Henry II sought a contribution from Scotland towards the tax – the so-called 'Saladin Tithe' – that he was levying on his domain to fund a crusade. The two versions of the resulting negotiations given by Roger of Howden imply that William was willing to accept Henry's request but that his lords stymied any deal. Apparently before Henry crossed to Normandy in July 1188, William offered 4,000 merks for the return of Berwick and Roxburgh, which Henry had indicated would be more acceptable if the tithe was also agreed. According to his second version, however, the tax collectors were met at the border and offered a total of only 5,000 merks for the castles and as a contribution towards the tax.[149] It has been suggested that William met Henry's envoys on the border with a large gathering of his nobles and prelates in order to increase pressure on the Scottish magnates to agree to the tax, using the English king's representatives as a battering ram to force acceptance of the agreement. This, it has been argued, was a reflection of William's lack of authority at home and the tensions within the Scottish political community arising from Henry's exercise of the overlordship conceded to him in 1175. Henry's request for payment of the tithe, however, was rejected by the assembled Scottish nobles in a move that has been interpreted as representing an assertion of Scottish sovereignty; 'in denying [William] they asserted the pre-eminence of his lordship'.[150] Certainly, the accounts of the struggle against Donald MacWilliam expose tensions within the Scottish political community, but those tensions arose from support for a rival segment of the ruling house rather than explicit opposition to Scottish subordination to Henry's lordship. Indeed, the Scottish magnates had also made direct submissions to Henry in 1174–5 and had accepted the terms on which William had been freed. While their united front could be read as a sign of William's inability to force an unaccustomed financial levy on his

---

[148] *Chron. Holyrood*, s.a. 1187; *Chron. Melrose*, s.a. 1187; Benedict of Peterborough, *Gesta Regis*, ii, 7–9.
[149] Benedict of Peterborough, *Gesta Regis*, ii, 44–5; *Chron. Howden*, ii, 338–9.
[150] Duncan, *Kingship of the Scots*, 104–5.

lords, it could also be read as a device to allow him to escape accusations of disloyalty to his overlord. William could present himself as attempting to answer Henry's demands whilst sheltering behind the implacable hostility of his men and his inability to sway them.[151] Whether or not the initiative in this rebuff lay with William or his nobles, there is agreement that it signalled a shift in Anglo-Scottish relations towards rejection of interventionist English overlordship.

Henry may have been infuriated by the Scots' refusal to contribute to the Saladin Tithe but he could not force compliance. His hurried departure from England before the conclusion of the negotiations had been forced by a dramatic collapse in the Angevin position in west central France triggered by his son Richard's renewal of warfare against the French king and his vassals. At first reluctant to commit himself to war against Philip II, Henry remained in Normandy and only finally moved into the French king's territory at the end of August. By October, all three parties in the conflict – Henry, Philip and Richard – wanted peace, but each on his own terms. Unable to trust his father after the long experience of his duplicity, Richard negotiated his own terms privately with Philip and in a second peace conference confronted his father with a demand to be recognised as his heir. Unwilling to yield up the one card that he had used to keep his sons in check for so long, Henry refused to answer and Richard interpreted this as a sign that his father intended to disinherit him. Richard then turned to Philip and gave him homage for all of his territories, reserving only his fealty to his father. They parted with an agreement to meet for further discussions early in 1189 but it was clear to all that Henry was losing his grip on his empire. When Philip and Richard resumed hostilities in the spring, Henry's position fell apart. Sick and clearly weary from years of conflict, as his realm collapsed around him, he agreed to terms. Three days later, on 6 July, Henry died in his castle at Chinon.[152]

In August Richard arrived in England to take possession of his new kingdom and was crowned in Westminster on 3 September in a ceremony in which Earl David of Huntingdon bore one of the swords of state.[153] To most of his subjects in England, Richard was an unknown quantity and equally for William and the Scots it was a move into uncharted waters. In November, Richard sent his half-brother, Geoffrey, archbishop-elect of York, to the border with Scotland to escort William through England

---

[151] Barrow (ed.), *RRS*, ii, 14–15.
[152] The preceding narrative is based on Gillingham, *Richard the Lionheart*, 116–24.
[153] Benedict of Peterborough, *Gesta Regis*, ii, 81.

for a meeting at Canterbury. Events now moved rapidly, their pace dictated by Richard's eagerness to depart on crusade. At Canterbury on 2 December, William paid homage to Richard for his ancestral lands in England but the new English king was prepared to go much further and, in return for a payment of 10,000 merks of silver, agreed to return Berwick and Roxburgh to the Scots and to cancel the Treaty of Falaise through what we now call the Quitclaim of Canterbury.[154] It was a stunning reversal of fifteen years of humiliation and subjection. As William hastened north to gather his magnates to discuss how the money that would secure the deal could be raised, he may already have been thinking not only of how the condition of Anglo-Scottish relations down to 1174 would be restored, but also of how he might do further business with this new type of Angevin. Direct and interventionist English lordship had ended: all that remained for William to secure was the return of his lost patrimony.

---

[154] Ibid. ii, 97, 98, 102–4; *Chron. Melrose*, s.a. 1190.

CHAPTER 5

Settling the Succession, 1189–1230

A DREAM REVIVED

When William returned to Scotland he needed only to secure payment of the 10,000 merks he had promised for the Quitclaim to be put into effect, and an assembly of nobles and prelates at Musselburgh agreed to the raising of the promised sum. No record survives of the gathering's proceedings, but one source describes how William 'scraped together' the money.[1] With the guarantees of payment in place, early in 1190 the English garrisons left Berwick and Roxburgh. With his realm free of physical evidence of subjection to the English crown, William could look forward to a new beginning in Anglo-Scottish relations.

Further changes in English policy towards Scotland, especially in respect of the northern counties, was unlikely because of Richard I's preoccupation with preparations for his crusade. Indeed, after the agreement with William, Richard crossed to Normandy and did not return for over four years. William nevertheless began to rebuild old relationships or develop fresh connections amongst the Northumbrian baronage. Early in 1191, he married his widowed illegitimate daughter, Isabella, to Robert de Ros, lord of Wark-on-Tweed, and then in 1193 married another illegitimate daughter, Margaret, to Eustace de Vescy, lord of Alnwick.[2] Both marriages drew key families in the administration of Northumberland into a personal relationship with him, presumably to secure their support for a restoration of his inheritance. So blatant a manoeuvre would have been intolerable to Henry II but William

---

[1] William of Newburgh, *Historia Rerum Anglicarum*, i, 304. Barrow (ed.), *RRS*, ii, nos 287, 326 and notes.
[2] *Chron. Melrose*, s.a. 1191 and 1193.

was now a free agent and working towards a future settlement of his long-cherished ambitions.

The de Vescy marriage occurred against the backdrop of mounting political tension in England as Richard I's younger brother, John, sought to use his brother's captivity in Austria on his return from crusade as an opportunity to seize the throne, while in France Philip II reopened his military offensive against the Angevin domain.[3] When approached by John with a request for his support William refused, perhaps calculating that a grateful Richard might be inclined to reward him with restoration of his lost heritage; to further ingratiate himself, he contributed personally 2,000 merks towards Richard's ransom.[4] His brother, Earl David, as holder of an English honour, actively defended Richard's interests, joining the army which retook castles still held by John's supporters after Richard's release and then campaigning in France when Richard recovered the strongholds which Philip II had captured.[5]

Scottish support for Richard had been unequivocal and William expected some reward. In early April 1194 William met Richard in Nottinghamshire and formally requested restoration of the northern counties; Richard prevaricated. A week later at Northampton he gave his decision, stating that it was inappropriate for William to make his request at a time when it might be seen as weakness and fear on Richard's part and when he had yet to confront Philip II.[6] It was a bitter disappointment but William was undeterred. He accompanied Richard to Winchester where Bishop Hugh of Durham surrendered Northumberland to King Richard, whereupon William offered 15,000 merks for the earldom as it had been held by his father and brother, half as much again as had been paid for the Quitclaim of Canterbury. Attracted by the cash but reluctant to compromise royal power in the north, Richard offered the earldom lands but not its castles. For William, this was unacceptable and, 'grieving and downcast', he returned to Scotland.[7]

William's perseverance on this issue was extraordinary and has been seen as an obsession that led to reckless actions. His first attempt in 1173–4 had brought defeat, captivity and fifteen years of subjection to direct English lordship. Having failed to plead the justice of his cause

---

[3] Gillingham, *Richard the Lionheart*, 226–36.
[4] Anderson (ed.), *Scottish Annals*, 310; *Chron. Melrose*, s.a. 1193.
[5] Roger of Howden, *Chronica*, iii, 237; Anderson (ed.), *Early Sources*, ii, 342; Stringer, *Earl David*, 40–1.
[6] Roger of Howden, *Chronica*, iii, 243–4.
[7] Ibid. 249, 250.

and then been offered unacceptable terms in 1194, he was prepared to propose a radical solution which placed his personal grievances above the interests of his kingdom. According to Roger of Howden, in June 1195 William fell seriously ill and felt it necessary to make arrangements for the succession. It had been assumed that the kingship would pass to his younger brother, Earl David, his eldest male heir, but William proposed instead that his daughter, Margaret, should marry King Richard's nephew Otto, younger son of Henry the Lion, former duke of Saxony, and that the throne would pass to them in the event of his death. The proposal caused uproar in the Scottish political community. Female succession, they announced, was uncustomary and, therefore, unacceptable, the more so because there was a suitable male heir.[8] The issue receded when William recovered but he had seen the potential in the match and pursued the proposal with Richard. By the end of 1195 a new deal had been agreed whereby William would give Otto and Margaret Lothian and Richard would give them Northumberland and Cumberland, with Richard holding Lothian and its castles and William Northumberland and Cumberland and their castles. Again, however, the arrangement collapsed but this time because Queen Ermengarde was pregnant and William would not compromise the inheritance of a possible son.[9] A sign that Richard was attracted to the scheme can be seen in his award of Poitou to Otto as compensation. For William, there was no damage to his relationship with Richard, an indication that the latter recognised that the Scottish nobles' hostility to this proposal rather than William's duplicity had stymied the deal.[10]

Throughout these manoeuvres the man most directly affected maintained a dignified silence. There is no indication of any breach between William and Earl David, and when warfare again broke out in northern Scotland in 1196, David campaigned with William in Caithness.[11] How do we explain this equanimity in the face of threatened disinheritance after three decades as heir-presumptive? It is possible that he saw the benefit to the kingdom that the deal would bring. More likely, however, is that David's personal knowledge of the characters of both his brother and King Richard reassured him that William's complex designs had little prospect of success. Although Ermengarde was delivered of a second daughter, Isabel, and not the hoped-for son, the moment for the

---

[8] Ibid. 298–9.
[9] Ibid. 308.
[10] Duncan, *Kingship of the Scots*, 107.
[11] Stringer, *Earl David*, 41, 43.

proposed marriage alliance had passed. The birth of William's long-sought-after male heir, Alexander, at Haddington on 24 August 1198 reopened the possibility of a restoration of the northern English counties as the dower of an English royal bride for the Scottish prince, but when William again raised the issue in April 1199 the political landscape in England had changed radically.

CONSOLIDATION AND CHALLENGE: GALLOWAY, THE WEST AND THE NORTH 1189–99

One consequence of the Quitclaim of Canterbury was a freeing of William's hands to deal with areas on the margins of his kingdom where Henry II had intervened. The first of these was Galloway, where the question of Duncan son of Gillebrigte's inheritance remained unresolved. Judgement fell to William and few can have doubted the likely outcome, for Duncan's rival, Roland son of Uhtred, had not only served the king against the MacWilliams but was also the king's justiciar of Galloway. No contemporary account of the settlement survives, but *Gesta Annalia* states that Roland was awarded both his ancestral lands and what he had acquired by conquest, Duncan swearing to accept this decision and receiving Carrick as compensation. The deal brought stability to Galloway, which lasted until the extinction of the male line of its lords in 1234. Although the relationship between Galloway and the Scottish crown was defined with no greater rigour than in the past, the close ties between the Galloway and Carrick families and the royal house forged at this time drew the south-western powers deeper within the sphere of Scottish overlordship.[12]

Greater influence in Galloway stimulated a revival of Scottish royal interest further west. William knew of the changed politics of this region since 1174 and their implications for his kingdom. Of these, the most far-reaching was the emergence of a new power in Ulster, where by 1182 the English adventurer John de Courcy had created his own principality.[13] De Courcy was sufficiently established by c. 1180 for Guðrøðr II, king of Man, to ally with him through marriage.[14] Such personal connections drew Duncan of Carrick into an alliance with de Courcy in the 1190s. Duncan gave him strong military backing for which he received

---

[12] *Chron. Fordun*, i, 270; Oram, *Lordship of Galloway*, 102, 103–4, 106–8.
[13] Duffy, 'The first Ulster plantation', 1–27; McNeill, *Anglo-Norman Ulster*, 3–6.
[14] *Chron. Man*, s.a. 1204.

a speculative award of land in the Bann valley, where Duncan was active in 1197 in an attempt to impose his lordship.[15] Through this connection, Duncan was drawn into the conflict between de Courcy and his western neighbour, Áed Méith ua Néill, which was itself part of a wider struggle for mastery in the north of Ireland between the Uí Néill and their allies on the one hand and the meic Lochlainn and theirs, including Guðrøðr, on the other. By the late 1190s, that conflict was spreading into the Isles and was threatening to destabilise the western seaboard of the Scottish kingdom.

A second event with far-reaching consequences for the Scots was Guðrøðr II's death in 1187.[16] With his one legitimate son, Óláfr, still underage, the Manx throne passed to Guðrøðr's older bastard son, Rognvald, who was apparently the preferred choice of both his father and the majority of his subjects. Rognvald may already have had pro-Scottish leanings, but through his Galloway connection he moved into a closer relationship with William. This movement marked a significant realignment of power in the region, as Man under Guðrøðr had been effectively an English satellite since the later 1150s. For the Scots, it offered increased security down the western margins of the kingdom. In particular, it began to close off aid for the MacWilliams; there was a firm link in contemporary chroniclers' eyes between Ireland and the northern Scottish insurrections.[17] But there were also issues closer to home that a strengthening of influence in Man helped to resolve or contain, in particular the chronic instability of the territory over which the various branches of the kindred descended from Somerled of Argyll were competing.

Reliable contemporary accounts of the conflict between Somerled's sons are lacking and most modern narratives are constructed from isolated references which can be assembled in a different order and read with a variety of meanings.[18] One common strand through these narratives is of hostility between the eldest son, Dugald, and his younger brother, Ranald, and their sons. Dugald had succeeded Somerled as ruler of the kindred's ancestral power base in Lorn and Mull but, despite having been proclaimed king of the Isles in the 1150s in opposition to Guðrøðr II, that title was used by Ranald, who held Islay, Jura and Kintyre. There is no secure evidence for Dugald's activities after 1175

---

[15] Roger of Howden, *Chronica*, s.a. 1197.
[16] *Chron. Man*, s.a. 1187–8.
[17] Oram, *Lordship of Galloway*, 106; Stringer, 'Periphery and core', 87.
[18] See discussion in McDonald, *Kingdom of the Isles*, 72–5.

and Ranald may have begun to encroach on his elder brother's territory and position as head of kin by the 1180s. He also came into conflict with his younger brother, Angus, whose lands were scattered from Bute and Arran to Knoydart and the Uists.[19] In 1192, Ranald and Angus clashed in battle from which Angus emerged victorious.[20] This defeat perhaps weakened Ranald sufficiently to drive him to ally with another man who had ambitions to expand his domain into Angus's territory, the Steward, Alan son of Walter.[21] Alan had already extended his lordship into Cowal and, of more concern to King William, Bute, for the islands lay beyond the notional sphere of Scottish royal authority. For William as for Henry II of England with the English colony in Leinster twenty years earlier, there was the question of one of his leading vassals constructing a private principality in territory over which the Scottish crown had no claim to lordship. While Alan's aggression and expansion presented many opportunities for an extension of Scottish influence beyond its traditional limits, it also risked drawing the kingdom into the internecine conflict in the Isles. It is in this context that the admission of Roland of Galloway to his wife's de Morville heritage in 1196 should be seen, for it gave control of another major west-coast lordship, Cunningham, to William's principal agent on the western seaboard. The building of a royal castle at Ayr in 1197 provided William with a base for the wider domination of the outer Firth of Clyde that was directed at his own frontier lords as much as it was at the independent powers beyond his borders.

It was not only in the west that William was concerned about the activities of potentates whose ties to him were weak or ill-defined. In Caithness and Orkney, Scottish bonds with Harald Maddadsson had weakened from the 1150s and, although no contemporary chronicler makes the link, there is a suspicion that he provided support for his MacWilliam kinsmen at least until the death of Donald MacWilliam in 1187. Most of Harald's actions were designed to strengthen his position as lord both of mainland Scotland north of the River Oykel and of the Orkney and Shetland Islands to the exclusion of other segments of the Orkney-Caithness kin; aiding the MacWilliams accords well with such an objective. The stalling of the momentum behind the MacWilliam cause in 1187 and Harald's switching of his focus to affairs in Norway should not be seen as an 'either/or' strategy but as part of this wider

---

[19] Duncan and Brown, 'Argyll and the Isles', 198.
[20] *Chron. Man.*, s.a. 1192.
[21] Murray, 'Swerving from the path of justice', 287–8; Oram and Butter, 'Historical framework', 40–1.

policy. With no adult MacWilliam to rally the enemies of King William, Harald concentrated on baulking challenges to his domestic position from the Erlendsson line represented by Harald Ingiridsson (also known as Harald the Younger), the grandson of St Rognvald. Harald Ingiridsson was high in favour with the Norwegian King Sverre, and Earl Harald feared that his rival would turn that favour into Norwegian support in a bid to wrench at least a share of the earldom lands from him. Seeing an opportunity to reverse that threat by backing Sverre's rivals, Earl Harald joined a plot to kill the king. Despite some initial success, early in 1194 Harald's allies were defeated and, faced with invasion from Norway, in spring 1195 Earl Harald sailed to Bergen and threw himself on Sverre's mercy. The king imposed humiliating terms, including the transfer of Shetland to his direct lordship, but the earl was permitted to retain Orkney and Caithness.[22]

Remarkably, Earl Harald had no sooner returned from Norway than he was plotting against King William. It is possible that he was aiming to repair the damage caused to his prestige by his catastrophic Norwegian adventure, but it is also likely that he was drawn into a conflict triggered by the ambitions of his own family. The key figure in the two main accounts of these events in the later 1190s is not Earl Harald but Thorfinnr, the son of his relationship with the daughter of Malcolm MacHeth, earl of Ross. The accounts given in the *Chronicle of Melrose* and by Roger of Howden are confused as to the year, duration and exact course of events, but both agree that it was a major operation which drew royal power further north than ever before.[23] Although Howden claims that it was Earl Harald who had seized Moray by spring 1196, it is likely that the aggressor was Thorfinnr and it was in response to this incursion that William was at Elgin with his army in July. It was probably in the course of this campaign, rather than in 1197 as reported in the *Chronicle of Melrose*, that Thorfinnr and his allies were defeated near Inverness.[24] Although Howden places a second expedition by William in autumn 1196, it is likely that it was in spring 1197 that he returned north.[25] On 2 May he was at Elgin, from where he advanced rapidly to Thurso. There the earl, prevented by contrary winds from escaping to

---

[22] Anderson (ed.), *Early Sources*, ii, 331–41.
[23] *Chron. Melrose*, s.a. 1197; Roger of Howden, *Chronica*, iv, 10–12. For a reconciliation of these sources, see Duncan, 'Roger of Howden', 142–4.
[24] *Chron. Melrose*, s.a. 1197 (correctly 1196).
[25] Duncan, 'Roger of Howden', 143; Barrow (ed.), *RRS*, ii, no. 388; Roger of Howden, *Chronica*, iv, 11.

Orkney, submitted.[26] In return for peace, Harald promised to hand over the king's enemies when William next came north.[27] William agreed, but confirmed him in only half of Caithness, the remainder of which was given to Harald Ingiridsson.[28] The king was in Perth in June and August, then again marched north in the autumn, reaching Elgin by 10 October.[29] According to Howden, William was at Nairn when Earl Harald came to hand over the king's enemies but released them and came to the king instead with two of his grandsons as hostages. William, however, wanted Thorfinnr, whom the earl said he could not hand over 'because in that land there is no other heir'.[30] This insistence on the surrender of Thorfinnr, his eldest son by Hvarfloð,[31] implies that the conflict was over control of Ross, and William was not prepared to settle for two grandchildren rather than the man at the heart of the issue. Having deprived him of his remaining half of Caithness for his breach of faith, William sent Harald to cool his heels in prison until Thorfinnr was surrendered.[32] With their lord captive, Earl Harald's men in Orkney submitted and carried Thorfinnr to the king to secure the earl's release.

Thorfinnr's imprisonment ended the insurrection in Ross, but it did not end Earl Harald's problems. He returned to Orkney and respite over the winter late in 1197, but in the spring his rival, Harald Ingiridsson, arrived with men provided by King Sverre to take his half of the earldom. Earl Harald was expelled, fleeing to Man to gather aid, but was followed by his rival. Eluding his pursuers, the older Harald doubled back to Orkney, surprised and killed his enemy's supporters there, then sailed across to confront him in Caithness. In a battle near Wick, Harald Ingiridsson was defeated and slain.[33] Having killed in Caithness the man to whom William had committed half the earldom the previous year, Earl Harald now sought to salvage something from the mess and hurried to meet William to explain events and to offer to buy the earldom back. William wanted a settlement, but on his terms; Earl Harald was to renounce his relationship with Hvarfloð, take back his repudiated wife

---

[26] Barrow (ed.), *RRS*, ii, nos 391, 392; Duncan, 'Roger of Howden', 143.
[27] See also Ross, 'Moray, Ulster and the MacWilliams', 37–8.
[28] Roger of Howden, *Chronica*, iv, 10–11.
[29] Barrow (ed.), *RRS*, ii, nos 389, 394, 395, 396; Roger of Howden, *Chronica*, iv, 10–11; Duncan, 'Roger of Howden', 143 for the alternative dating of *RRS*, ii, nos 394, 395.
[30] Roger of Howden, *Chronica*, iv, 11.
[31] *Orkneyinga Saga*, Chapters 104, 109.
[32] *Chron. Melrose*, s.a. 1197; Roger of Howden, *Chronica*, iv, 11.
[33] Roger of Howden, *Chronica*, iv, 11–12; *Orkneyinga Saga*, Chapter 109.

The Chronicle of Melrose and its connections

The *Chronicle of Melrose*, the chief surviving pre-fourteenth-century Scottish chronicle, was composed by several scribes.[34] Down to 1207 its entries are short, factual and mainly related to southern Scottish affairs, but from 1208 their character changes.[35] From then until 1222 the entries are fuller, more concerned with foreign matters – particularly with King John of England – and with northern Scottish politics. There is also a marked stylistic change; the entries are polished and composed as set pieces in elegant Latin.[36] The Melrose abbots Adam (1207–13), elected bishop of Caithness in 1213, and William (1215–16), elected abbot of Rievaulx in 1216, may be responsible for this.[37] Their involvement probably continued after they left Melrose and it may be significant that Adam's murder in 1222 coincides with a reversion to pre-1208 styles.

Both men selected material with particular purposes in mind. Adam was involved in the 1209 Norham negotiations and apparently kept a record of events. One section detailing Anglo-Scottish relations was perhaps an aide-mémoire for further negotiations in 1212; Adam used the chronicle as a dossier of data for political-diplomatic purposes. The record, however, was not simply of diplomatic wrangling, for his contributions included illustrations of the missionary activities of the Cistercian order, accounts of Christian advances in Iberia and action against heretics in France. These reveal an able cleric, concerned to provide his brethren with practical records of spiritual value, as well as an active, secular political figure preserving an account of the controversial events of 1209–12.

One key contemporary observer was the English royal clerk Roger of Howden.[38] His visits to Scotland down to 1195 – when he was made a canon of Glasgow and attended a religious assembly at Melrose – gave personal familiarity with events recorded in his *Gesta Regis Henrici Secundi* and *Chronica*. At Melrose, he met clerics engaged in chronicle writing, and probably obtained the northern Scottish material for his

---

[34] Broun and Harrison, *Chronicle of Melrose Abbey*; Duncan, 'Sources and uses of the Chronicle of Melrose', 146–85.
[35] For discussion of the period 1208–22, see Scott, 'Abbots Adam and William', 161–71.
[36] Ibid. 166.
[37] Ibid. 166–7.
[38] Duncan, 'Roger of Howden', 135–59.

Chronica from them. Analysis of this material reveals particular connections; a Melrose-based network centred on the *Chronicle* but also deriving material from members of the Melrose filiation, particularly Kinloss Abbey, and former Melrose monks. His main informant was perhaps Reinald Macer, a former Melrose monk with previous experience of northern affairs elected bishop of Ross in 1195.[39] Reinald was at Melrose during Howden's visit and was in Ross during the crises of the later 1190s. How his information – and that from Kinloss – reached Howden is uncertain, but one source was perhaps William Malveisin, a Scottish royal clerk who travelled on diplomatic missions to England and France.[40] Malveisin, according to the fifteenth-century chronicler Andrew Wyntoun, composed a 'cornykle' at St Andrews, and analysis of early-thirteenth-century material embedded in Walter Bower's *Scotichronicon* exposes a St Andrews source compiled in the 1220s and 1230s, but also covering events of 1209–21.[41] This material was possibly from a *Gesta Willelmi Regis*, similar in form to Howden's *Gesta* and possibly representing a conscious continuation of that work to narrate the troubled relationship between King William and King John.[42] While Melrose derived some material from this St Andrews chronicle and substantial extracts were incorporated by Wyntoun and Bower into their texts, the loss of this record of events in the closing years of William's reign and the first half of Alexander II's has robbed us of a contemporary perspective on Scottish affairs as detailed as that produced by Roger of Howden for the period c. 1174 to c. 1200.

and surrender two named hostages. For the earl, this went too far, for repudiation of Hvarfloð threatened the rights of Thorfinnr and his siblings in Ross.[43] William, however, needed to secure his possession of Caithness and for this he required someone connected to the Orcadian ruling line. Into the frame stepped Ranald, son of Somerled, a cousin of the Orkney earls and a man who had entered a closer relationship with the Scottish crown in recent years through his developing relationship

---

[39] Ibid. 144–5.
[40] Ibid. 145–51.
[41] Scott, 'Abbots Adam and William of Melrose', 161.
[42] Duncan, 'Roger of Howden', 151.
[43] *Chron. Howden*, iv, 12. For the date of the meeting see Duncan, 'Roger of Howden', 143.

with the Stewarts.[44] Probably in spring 1199, Ranald came to William and offered to buy Caithness, reserving to the king his own income. Judging him capable of controlling the province, the king agreed and Ranald gathered his power in Argyll and the Isles before sailing north to take possession. The struggle for domination of the northern mainland was entering a turbulent new phase.

SONS, BROTHERS AND SUCCESSIONS

Just as the northern crisis reached a turning point in 1198, King William received the news for which he had been praying for a decade: on 24 August Queen Ermengarde was delivered of a son named Alexander, 'and many rejoiced at his birth'.[45] For some men, including Alexander's uncle, Earl David, that joy may not have been unbounded, for this child gave his middle-aged brother a direct male heir. Alexander's birth further complicated an already complex issue for, although the later assumption was that the son of the reigning king had precedence over the king's younger brother in the succession, the unexpected deaths and genetic failures from 1097 onwards had meant that no Scottish king had been succeeded by his son; at the dawn of the thirteenth century primogeniture was not yet established, even in respect of royal inheritance. William's wishes were clear, however, and once the perils of infancy were passed he named Alexander his heir. In October 1201 William persuaded his magnates to swear fealty to the three-year-old prince.[46] By securing recognition of Alexander as his heir, William was preparing to pass on the still-unresolved question of Northumberland. How Earl David viewed that decision we can only guess, but the passage of four years before his homage to Alexander might imply that he was not overjoyed.[47] David's apparent acceptance of the situation in 1205, however, also cannot be taken as evidence that the matter was resolved. As events in England in 1135 and 1199 had shown, the wishes of the king in respect of his successor were not necessarily followed, despite oaths extracted to ensure compliance.[48]

After 1195 there had been a hiatus in William's efforts to regain his

---

[44] See discussion in Beuermann, *Masters of the Narrow Sea*, 201–10.
[45] *Chron. Melrose*, s.a. 1198; Roger of Howden, *Chronica*, iv, 54.
[46] *Chron. Melrose*, s.a. 1201.
[47] Ibid. s.a. 1205; Stringer, *Earl David*, 43 and note 92.
[48] For the succession to Henry I of England, see Matthew, *King Stephen*, Chapter 4.

lost patrimony. Affairs in northern Scotland preoccupied him down to 1199 but Richard I in any case was not prepared to make further concession. That changed in April 1199 when Richard died.[49] On his deathbed, the childless king designated his younger brother, John, as heir, disinheriting Arthur of Brittany, son of their middle brother, Geoffrey, whom eight years earlier Richard had named as his heir. But many nobles in Anjou, Brittany, Maine and Touraine preferred the twelve-year-old Arthur to a man whom they distrusted.[50] Although John seized the initiative by taking possession of the Angevin treasury at Chinon, and had also won important support from William Marshal and Archbishop Hubert Walter of Canterbury, Arthur's supporters also moved swiftly and, placing the boy in the care of Philip II of France, began the military occupation of Richard's former domain. At Angers magnates from Anjou, Maine and Touraine proclaimed for Arthur, but Normandy supported John and he was invested as duke in Rouen. In England, despite some uncertainty, the majority of the political community was prepared to accept John, who was eager to cross as soon as possible for his coronation. Possibly alerted to events by Earl David, William also moved quickly. By May he had sent messengers to John to request restoration of Northumberland and Cumbria, in return for which he would swear fealty.[51]

In response, John's English supporters stalled him, preventing William's messengers from crossing to Normandy and sending Earl David to advise his brother to wait until John came to England. John, meanwhile, sent William's son-in-law, Eustace de Vescy, to Scotland with a promise that if William kept the peace John would do him justice by all his petitions.[52] Following John's coronation on 27 May a second Scottish delegation arrived to request restoration of what William explicitly described as his rights by patrimony in return for which he offered to serve John fully and faithfully, but with a veiled threat that if John failed him he would do what was necessary to secure that heritage.[53] William could see the fault lines opening up in the Angevin empire and was making it clear to John that if he did not do justice to his claim then Arthur of Brittany, William's great-nephew, might be more generous. William, however, was already too late, for threats to

---

[49] Gillingham, *Richard the Lionheart*, 276–7.
[50] Warren, *King John*, 48; Turner, *King John*, 48–50.
[51] Roger of Howden, *Chronica*, iv, 88–9.
[52] Ibid. 89. Howden wrongly calls him William's brother-in-law.
[53] Ibid. 91.

transfer support from one would-be Angevin king to another lost their weight after John was crowned.[54] John simply replied that he would do justice by William when he came to him and sent the bishop of Durham to escort William south. In a display of brinksmanship, William refused to come and sent Bishop Roger of St Andrews to repeat his demands and to warn of his intention to invade if John did not yield.[55] William, however, blinked first, for John simply put the defence of the north in the hands of trusted supporters and headed to Normandy to consolidate his hold on his French domain; although John was keen to secure William's homage, no concession was forthcoming. According to Howden, when the moment for action came, William visited the shrine of St Margaret at Dunfermline and, having been warned by her in a vision not to invade England, disbanded his army.[56]

Behind these exchanges stood Philip II of France. It is likely that in April/May 1199 William had also approached Arthur, who was at Philip's court, or Philip had approached William on Arthur's behalf. The northern counties were surely discussed but a proposal from Philip for a marriage between his daughter, Marie, and William's infant son, Alexander, may also have been tabled.[57] Here lies the source of William's bravado in late summer 1199; he was sure of French backing. Here, too, however, lies the reason for the evaporation of his boldness, for in September 1199 Philip's schemes collapsed when Arthur made peace with John.[58] Between October 1199 and January 1200 William was helpless as he was abandoned by the devious French king. William, too, cannot have doubted John's likely fury with him and it was probably fear that made him ignore John's summons to come to York in March 1200. The formal conclusion of peace between Philip and John that May ended any hope of a French alliance, and when John returned to England in September William capitulated. A high-profile delegation, which included Earl David, came north with letters of safe conduct for William and a summons to attend John at Lincoln on 21 November; this time, he came.[59]

Earl David's role suggests that he disagreed with his brother's stance and had aligned himself with John. Whether or not this was connected

---

[54] Duncan, 'John King of England and the King of Scots', 251.
[55] Roger of Howden, *Chronica*, iv, 91–2.
[56] Ibid. iv, 92, 100.
[57] Duncan, 'King John', 252–3; Roger of Howden, *Chronica*, iv, 138, 174.
[58] Warren, *King John*, 54; Turner, *King John*, 52–3.
[59] Duncan, 'King John', 251–3; Roger of Howden, *Chronica*, iv, 140.

with William's plans for the succession is unknown, but the birth of Alexander had transformed David's personal position and prospects; his status, and that of his heirs, now depended on maintenance of good relations between Scotland and England. There were others in Scotland who seemed not to support William's brinksmanship, most noticeably Bishop Roger of St Andrews, who remained with John in France until late 1199 and from the time of the Lincoln assembly in November 1200 until February 1201.[60] If such opinion was arrayed against William, his *volte face* in November 1200 becomes easily understandable.

Outside Lincoln on 21 November 1200, William performed homage to King John. Immediately after the ceremony, William asked for Northumberland, Cumberland and Westmorland 'as his right and heritage'. After long, fruitless discussions, John asked William for a truce until the following May to allow deliberation on the question; William had no option but to agree.[61] Early in 1201, John came north and inspected the northern frontier from Bamburgh to Carlisle, but he found no time to address William's claims and, as the date for his decision neared and Continental affairs drew him back to France, he sought a deferral until the autumn.[62] By then, he was deeply enmeshed in an unfolding crisis in Poitou and it was obvious that William was a low priority. Conscious of his advancing years and, possibly, the first signs of the ill health that dogged the last decade of his life, but unwilling to yield his rights, it was at this juncture – one month after the passing of the rearranged deadline for John's judgement – that William secured the fealty of his lords to the young Alexander; the torch was being passed to a new generation.

How William received news of the breach between Philip II and John over the winter of 1201–2 and Philip's formal forfeiture of John in July and investment of Arthur of Brittany with all of his French lands and titles save Normandy is unknown. Any thought of cutting a fresh deal with Philip and his protégé, however, was dashed by news of Arthur's capture and disappearance. Arthur's fate remains mysterious but rumours quickly circulated that John had murdered him and disposed of the body. The rumours, it has been argued, preyed heavily on William's fears for his own young son and widened the distance between William and Earl David; John had disposed of his elder brother's son, the closest heir to the throne, might not he use his closeness to Earl David to

---

[60] Duncan, 'King John', 253; Anderson (ed.), *Scottish Annals*, 322–3.
[61] Roger of Howden, *Chronica*, iv, 141.
[62] Ibid. 163–4.

encourage him into similar action?[63] Such rumour-driven fears perhaps unsettled William's judgement in his future dealings with John and, with John an almost ever-present figure in England following the loss of most of his ancestral domain in France in the rebellions and war with Philip II, which followed Arthur's disappearance, those dealings became more regular and painfully close.

CAITHNESS-ORKNEY AND THE ISLES 1200-14

William's grant of Caithness to Ranald, son of Somerled, in 1199 had been intended to bring the earldom firmly under Scottish lordship. In this it failed miserably. *Orkneyinga Saga*, despite its muddled chronology, provides a narrative of events.[64] Ranald took possession of Caithness and remained there over the winter of 1199-1200 before returning to the Isles, leaving 'stewards' in charge of the earldom. One of these stewards was soon killed by an assassin sent from Orkney and, in the autumn, Earl Harald invaded Caithness. He seized Bishop John of Caithness at Scrabster, blinded him and slit his tongue.[65] Like his predecessor and successor, John was a Scottish cleric and probably regarded as a royal agent; later Scottish tradition presented him as an 'informer, and the instigator of the misunderstanding' between Earl Harald and William.[66] Even Harald, however, knew that the mutilation of a bishop was a step too far and distanced himself from the deed. His move had deflected blame from him by late summer 1202 when Pope Innocent III ordered the imposition of severe spiritual penalties on the man named as the perpetrator.[67] King William was less easily placated and the consequences for Harald's unfortunate son Thorfinnr, a hostage since 1197, were grim; he was blinded and castrated, and subsequently died in the king's prison.[68] The violent removal of Thorfinnr from the equation perhaps satisfied William's fury and ended one dimension of the challenge to his authority in the region, but Harald still occupied Caithness and, without the leverage over him that Thorfinnr had represented, was likely to require a major effort to subdue.

---

[63] Warren, *King John*, 76-81; Duncan, 'King John', 262-3.
[64] *Orkneyinga Saga*, Chapters 110-11.
[65] See Anderson (ed.), *Early Sources*, ii, 355 note.
[66] *Chron. Fordun*, ii, 271.
[67] Anderson (ed.), *Early Sources*, ii, 355 note.
[68] *Chron. Fordun*, ii, 270.

It was probably then that Harald approached King John, who on 6 January 1201 issued safe conducts for the earl and his chaplain to come to England for discussions, but the approach went no further.[69] In the meantime, William sent an army into Caithness, a winter campaign underscoring the seriousness of the situation. Recognising that he could not resist the Scots but probably also knowing that William was preoccupied with other matters, Harald sought a deal. Accounts of this process are hopelessly compressed but point to protracted negotiations that possibly brought William to Aberdeen in August 1201. Failure to secure a deal perhaps prompted William to assemble a fleet to attack Orkney and this threat forced Harald into serious negotiation. Over the winter of 1201–2, Harald accepted a settlement which, in return for a payment of £2,000 (*Gesta Annalia*) or a quarter of all of the revenues of the earldom (*Orkneyinga Saga*), saw him confirmed as sole earl in Caithness under Scottish lordship. In spring 1202 Bishop Roger of St Andrews escorted Harald to Perth where peace was confirmed and William restored him as earl.[70] After half a century of bloody conflict, the political relationships in the northernmost mainland were returned to the situation that had prevailed in King David's reign. While many may have wondered what the decades of strife had achieved, the extended conflict had forced the Scottish crown to invest heavily in consolidating its grip over the northern districts, carrying royal authority literally at sword's point to the farthest reaches of the kingdom. That authority would still face challenge in the coming decades as the relationship between the kings of Scots and the earls of Caithness-Orkney was worked out, but at no time after 1202 was there a possibility that Caithness would slip from Scottish domination; when Earl Harald died in 1206, the succession passed smoothly to his sons, David and Jón, who ruled jointly in Caithness as vassals of the Scottish king.

The man who simply disappears from this narrative after his brief irruption in 1199–1200 is Ranald son of Somerled. It is unlikely that he simply abandoned his claim to Caithness after the ejection of his representatives and his forces were perhaps involved in the campaigns against Harald, especially if the tradition of a planned invasion of Orkney in 1202 has any basis in fact. Nevertheless, no indication survives that Ranald figured in William's designs for the government of the north, but nor is there any sign of compensation for the loss of Caithness. Frustratingly,

---

[69] Duncan, 'King John', 253.
[70] *Orkneyinga Saga*, Chapter 112; *Chron. Fordun*, ii, 272; Barrow (ed.), *RRS*, ii, no. 428.

these years are also amongst the most obscure in the history of Argyll and the Isles. The probably deceptive sense of tranquillity that the silence of the annals engenders was broken in 1203 by events in Ulster. In that year, King John moved against John de Courcy and in 1204, Hugh de Lacy, younger brother of the lord of Meath, invaded Ulster, defeated de Courcy and drove him into exile. De Courcy was the brother-in-law of Rognvald Guðrøðsson, king of Man, and he turned to him for aid to recover his lands. Although Rognvald was also allied with King John, in 1205 he provided de Courcy with ships and men for a counter-attack on Ulster, but the attack was repulsed.[71] Rognvald may not have been distressed at the reverse, for it ended the dual call on his loyalties from his brother-in-law and from King John. Although it has been suggested that the English king regarded Rognvald as an enemy from this time, there is contrary evidence to suggest that both men maintained close contact and that Rognvald visited John's court in the immediate aftermath of the 1205 Ulster campaign.[72]

According to the *Annals of Ulster*, de Courcy had sought refuge with his old rival, Áed Méith ua Néill, before he turned to Rognvald.[73] Áed avoided being drawn into this conflict, however, possibly because he was already committed in the Hebrides. West Ulster interests were certainly active there in 1204 when a party of the clergy of Derry attacked a new Benedictine convent at Iona.[74] Later Clan Donald tradition identified Ranald son of Somerled as the founder of this Benedictine community and, while hard evidence to corroborate this claim is lacking, it seems likely that was part of his efforts to assert his position as king in the Isles and successor to his father's ambitions.[75] Somerled's attempted reform of Iona in the 1160s had brought him into conflict with the then Cenél nEógain king and northern Irish clergy, who regarded Iona as falling within their sphere; his son's efforts renewed that conflict and were a reminder that it was not only Scottish and Norwegian powers that had interests in the Hebrides.

By the end of the decade Ranald's sons were extending the range of their power beyond the limits of their ancestral domain. In 1209, they attacked Skye, slaughtering the subjects of the Manx king there.[76] It is not known

---

[71] *Chron. Man*, s.a. 1204–5; *AU*, s.a. 1204.
[72] Beuermann, *Masters of the Narrow Sea*, 273–9.
[73] *AU*, s.a. 1205.
[74] *AU*, s.a. 1204.
[75] McDonald, *Kingdom of the Isles*, 205–6, 218–19.
[76] *AU*, s.a. 1209.

if this event and the reported slaying of Angus son of Somerled and his three sons in 1210 are linked, but these accounts indicate growing instability in the Isles caused by conflicts between Somerled's descendants.[77] Further upheaval was brought to the northern Hebrides in 1209–10 by a Norwegian expeditionary force. Usually presented as simply a predatory raid, analysis of the timing and consequences of the campaign suggests more substantial political objectives; it was not just Somerled's heirs who were at war with each other.[78] Rognvald Guðrøðsson had ruled Man since 1187 in preference to Óláfr, Rognvald's younger but canonically legitimate half-brother. Óláfr had, according to the *Chronicle of Man*, been passed over in 1187 on account of his youth but by 1209 he was a mature adult and had been ruling as under-king in Lewis. He, it has been suggested, may have started to manoeuvre for a greater share in the kingdom, if not for the kingship itself, and had approached King Ingi Bárðarson of Norway to offer himself as a compliant vassal-king. Rognvald, according to the later thirteenth century *Chronicle of Man*, responded by having Óláfr seized and handed over to the Scots for imprisonment, but why he should have been entrusted to William's safekeeping is not explained. The Norwegian intervention in the region after over a century of inaction may have thoroughly alarmed Rognvald and forced him, as it had been designed to do, into a reassessment of his ties of dependence; in 1210, it is suggested, he travelled to Norway to renew formally the submission of the kingdom of Man to the crown of Norway.[79] Rognvald may have regarded this as safeguarding his position, but his actions in 1209–10 had profound repercussions.

The most immediate impact was on Rognvald's relationship with King John, who in 1210 had been spurred into action in Ulster against Hugh de Lacy. To cement Hugh into a formal relationship with the English crown, John had created an earldom of Ulster for him, but by 1210 John suspected that he was in treacherous negotiation with Philip II of France. When de Lacy harboured members of the de Briouze family who were fleeing John's wrath, his disloyalty seemed to be confirmed. John's invasion of Ulster saw Hugh and his de Briouze guests flee first to Man and then to Scotland seeking refuge. There, however, they fell into the hands of Duncan of Carrick, de Courcy's former ally, only de Lacy eluding capture to escape ultimately to France. Given the recent

---

[77] *Chron. Man*, s.a. 1210.
[78] Anderson (ed.), *Early Sources*, ii, 378–82; Beuermann, *Masters of the Narrow Sea*, 279–94.
[79] Beuermann, *Masters of the Narrow Sea*, 294.

submission of King William to John, it is unsurprising that the captives were returned to the English king.[80] Having dealt with Ulster, John then repaid the disloyalty of his erstwhile vassal, Rognvald, whose power base in Man was ravaged.[81] John had demonstrated his power as lord of the British Isles with tremendous effect, using his domination of the king of Scots to secure the return of fugitives from the military and naval power which he was able to project into the maritime periphery of his realm, and demonstrating to Rognvald that England, not Norway, controlled his fate. The next few years witnessed the further extension of his authority into the west and the wider ramifications of his intervention for the established powers of the region.

Political instability in the Isles opened the door to Uí Néill influence and an opportunity for the next generation of MacWilliams to find military support. In 1211 Godred son of Donald MacWilliam, who may have been harboured at Áed Méith ua Néill's court, landed in Ross and raised rebellion with Scottish and Irish warriors.[82] As with his father's attempt, Godred enjoyed widespread support and King William was forced to mount two expeditions against him and to build new castles in Ross to contain the rising. Also as in 1187, the decisive action in 1211 saw significant Galwegian involvement, with Thomas, earl of Atholl, younger son of Roland of Galloway, being joint commander of an expeditionary force which defeated Godred but failed to capture him. This failure may have been one factor that forced William in 1212 into a still closer dependent relationship with King John (see p. 174), who sent mercenaries to assist in the suppression of the rebels. The involvement of John, however, may also have seen decisive action to strike at the roots of support for Godred and the source of some of the instability in the Isles, Áed Méith ua Néill. The 1212 treaty between John and William may have led to concerted naval and military operations in the maritime West. A key player in negotiating the treaty was Alan of Galloway, who received extensive lands in Ulster from John.[83] In return, Alan's resources were to be used to crush the threat to both English and Scottish interests in Ulster and the Isles. The effectiveness of Alan's power was demonstrated almost immediately when his brother and the sons of Ranald son of Somerled

---

[80] *CDS*, i, no. 480; Anderson (ed.), *Early Sources*, ii, 387.
[81] *Chron. Man*, s.a. 1210.
[82] McDonald, 'Treachery', 179, 184; Stringer, 'Periphery and core', 87; Oram, *Lordship of Galloway*, 116–17; *Chron. Melrose*, s.a. 1211; *Chron. Bower*, iv, 465–7; *Memorials of St Edmund's Abbey*, ii, 20; *Walteri de Coventria*, ii, 206.
[83] *Chron. Fordun*, ii, 274; *Chron. Bower*, iv, 463; Oram, *Lordship of Galloway*, 116–17.

ravaged Áed's kingdom. Áed's many rivals had combined to humble him and the pressure was maintained down to 1214, with Earl Thomas and another of Somerled's grandsons, Ranald son of Ruaridh, again plundering his territory.[84] The success of the policy might be reflected in Godred's inability to secure military aid from Ireland following his defeat in 1211 and, with no obvious external support for their rebellion, support for the MacWilliams ebbed away until Godred was betrayed by his own men and executed on the king's orders.[85] William, through the good offices of King John, had consolidated the alliance with the heirs of Somerled that had first been seen to good effect in 1199 in Caithness, thereby strengthening Scottish royal power on the western seaboard and enhancing the security of the northern mainland districts. The alliance had worked through the happy coincidence of the interests of the four main parties involved. No one could have foreseen how the relationship would unravel when those interests diverged.

CRISIS AND SUBMISSION 1205–14

The decade of 1205–14 revealed the fragility of the inheritance that William wished to pass to his son. Throughout this period, the chronicles give a sense of looming crisis that drained the energies of the elderly king as he dealt with one threat after another; William would not pass his final years in peace. Central to his problems was the relationship with England, although in 1205–6 it seems that all John really wished for was a stable northern border while he concentrated his efforts on regaining Normandy. It is perhaps in that context that the belated performance of homage by Earl David to his nephew should be seen; John needed security and having his loyal supporter, David, acknowledge Alexander's position might help mollify William. Relations between the kings remained amicable through summer 1205 as negotiations began over the status of the lands of the kings of Scotland in England, something that may have been connected to Earl David's homage. In November 1205 John issued a safe conduct for William to come to York in February 1206, the document confirming a request from William that his brother would be sent to Scotland and remain there until William returned from the meeting.[86] That request hints at a lingering distrust of both David

---

[84] *AU*, s.a. 1212, 1214.
[85] Stringer, 'Periphery and core', 88; *Chron. Bower*, iv, 467.
[86] Duncan, 'King John', 252, 261.

and John on William's part, but there is nothing to suggest that William had genuine reason to fear for either his or his son's safety. Indeed, as John was planning an expedition to Poitou and wanted to gather as many men and resources as possible, he had every reason to keep William at worst neutral and at best supportive.

The relationship between the two kings collapsed in spring 1209. Various reasons have been offered for this rapid deterioration, chiefly the proposal that William had reacted violently to the construction of a castle at Tweedmouth opposite Berwick, and had instructed his men to attack the unfinished building, or that he was involved in negotiations for the marriage of one of his daughters to a foreign power.[87] Despite its prominence in modern literature, the Tweedmouth incident is a red herring but there is greater weight to suggestions of a possible foreign match. John, indeed, knew of a rumour that William was negotiating the marriage of one of his daughters to Philip II of France.[88] At the start of 1209, however, John was unaware of any Franco-Scottish negotiations and was quite conciliatory, arranging for the meeting with William to take place at Newcastle and sending William's two sons-in-law to escort him south. The meeting, however, resolved nothing because William fell ill and went home at John's urging, but a proposal to resolve William's claim was made. On his return to Scotland William held a council at Stirling to deliberate on the offer. An embassy headed by Bishop William Malveisin of St Andrews was sent with the reply but found John's mood had changed entirely and the embassy returned with his threats of military action.[89] Thoroughly alarmed, William summoned the Scottish army and ordered that the Border castles be put in readiness, but at the same time he sent a fresh embassy to John. In the meantime, John had sent his own embassy north to reiterate his demands, which apparently included the surrender of key castles and the handing over of Alexander as a hostage, demands that caused William to send a second embassy south before the first had reported back.[90] There is something almost farcical in the accounts of the second mission heading south and William disbanding his army only to have to resummon it when the first envoys returned with news that John was advancing north with an army. But William had no stomach for a fight and negotiations resumed, this time at Norham in late July, with John very much in control of the terms.

---

[87] *Chron. Fordun*, i, 277; Barrow (ed.), *RRS*, ii, 18; Duncan, 'King John', 257–8.
[88] Duncan, 'King John', 260.
[89] *Chron. Bower*, iv, 449–51.
[90] Gervase of Canterbury, *Historical Works*, 102–3.

No full text of the treaty negotiated at Norham has survived, for the English copies were returned to the Scots in 1237, but various chronicle reports allow us to piece together the terms.[91] The result was what one English chronicler recorded as a 'treaty of friendship'[92] but which was in reality a return to the loose lordship over Scotland exercised by Henry II. In return for peace, William promised payment of between 9,000 and 15,000 merks depending on the source,[93] and handed over his daughters, Margaret and Isabella, for John to arrange their marriages – Margaret to John's infant son Henry, Isabella to an unspecified English nobleman – together with hostages from the leading families of Scotland.[94] For his part, John confirmed freedom of Scottish trade with England, and the continuation of the arrangements for the kings of Scots' conduct while in England. War had been averted but that may not have been the primary aim of John's aggression. If a possible marriage alliance between Scotland and France was being negotiated – and William always strenuously denied that suggestion – by securing possession of William's daughters and William's agreement that John could arrange their marriages, that threat had been ended. Another issue that may have been dealt with but not resolved in the treaty was the question of the king of Scotland's lands in England. William was to surrender them for John to regrant them to Alexander. The prince would then hold them as heir of Scotland and they would be held in this way by future Scottish heirs, not the king. Alexander and his successors, furthermore, would do homage and fealty to the kings of England for them.[95] It has been argued convincingly that this part of the deal had been negotiated as part of the 1205 discussions but had not been implemented, possibly because William had still attempted to secure the restoration of Northumbria, albeit to his son rather than to himself, as part of the arrangement.[96] So great was William's anxiety to end the threat from John in 1209 that the whole of the Norham settlement was put in operation within only a few weeks. Margaret and Isabella were handed over at Carlisle on 16 August and around the same time Alexander performed homage at Alnwick.[97] John, it seemed, secured everything he wanted in 1209: an end to any prospect of a Franco-Scottish alliance;

[91] Duncan, 'King John', 259–60.
[92] Roger of Wendover, *Flores Historiarum*, s.a. 1209.
[93] Anderson (ed.), *Scottish Annals*, 329, note 1.
[94] *Chron. Melrose*, s.a. 1209; *Chron. Bower*, iv, 453.
[95] *Chron. Fordun*, i, 277; *Chron. Bower*, iv, 455.
[96] Duncan, 'King John', 261.
[97] *Chron. Bower*, iv, 455 (where the chronology is confused); Duncan, 'King John', 261; Duncan, *Making of the Kingdom*, 255 note.

possession of William's daughters; the homage of his son; Scottish noble hostages; and a large cash sweetener to seal the deal.

After Norham, Anglo-Scottish relations remained stable until disturbances in support of a further MacWilliam claimant forced William to turn to John for aid over the winter of 1211–12. The kings met at Durham on 2 February 1212 and, with Queen Ermengarde mediating, settled a new treaty whereby William granted John the right to arrange Alexander's marriage within six years, both kings agreed to protect each other in their just quarrels and the survivor would do everything to ensure the succession of the other's heir in his kingdom.[98] These last two provisions reveal how anxious William was for the future succession of his son and how real a challenge the MacWilliam claim still presented. Four weeks later, Alexander was knighted by John, probably to give him the manly authority to command in person the force that was to be sent north to deal with the MacWilliam threat and which, in fulfilment of John's treaty obligation to help William in his just quarrels, included a force of the English king's mercenaries.[99] With William's submission came amity and support from John and, contrary to traditional interpretations which present both William and Alexander as bitterly resentful from 1209 of the terms imposed upon them, it seems that those good relations held firm into 1213.[100]

What triggered the deterioration in relations in 1213 was events in England, where baronial hostility to John's government was growing. Amongst the baronial leaders was William's son-in-law, Eustace de Vescy, who in 1212 fled to Scotland when John got wind of their schemes. De Vescy's involvement in the opposition was one factor that brought John to Norham in January 1213, and his presence in Scotland was probably the main reason why John called William for a face-to-face meeting or, as William was again gravely ill, to send Alexander in his place. This William, or rather his nobles, refused to countenance, for they suspected that John might detain Alexander until de Vescy had been handed over.[101] John blustered and threatened but on this occasion could not browbeat William, who was more concerned for the secure succession of his son on what he believed was his own imminent death than he was afraid of John's wrath. But William's fears and his nobles' obstinacy

---

[98] *Chron. Bower*, iv, 455–7, 467–9.
[99] *Chron. Bower*, iv, 457; Roger of Wendover, *Flores Historiarum*, ii, 60; Anderson (ed.), *Scottish Annals*, 330.
[100] Duncan, 'King John', 265.
[101] *Chron. Bower*, iv, 471–3.

contributed to John's difficulties in England and ensured that he was preoccupied with maintaining his own government and the secure succession of his own son at the expense of fulfilling his side of the treaties of 1209 and 1212. The result was the creation of new Scottish grievances.

The crises of 1209–12 weathered, albeit at great political cost, William looked to a period of domestic peace to smooth the path for his son's succession. Entering his seventieth year and described as 'venerable' by one English clerk, William was preoccupied with preparing for his death.[102] Queen Ermengarde, more than twenty years his junior, assumed some administrative responsibilities, but it was Alexander, now fifteen and with the experience of military command behind him, who was becoming more involved in government.[103] Through 1213, William continued to order his worldly and spiritual affairs but his preparations were premature. Northern matters again intervened, probably connected with the death of David Haraldsson, joint earl of Orkney and Caithness.[104] In May 1214, Adam, abbot of Melrose, was consecrated as bishop of Caithness, replacing finally the mutilated John in a move designed to establish a man closely associated with the Scottish crown in this highly sensitive see.[105] It is in that context that in August 1214 William made a last journey to Moray to settle a new accord with Jón, earl of Orkney, whose daughter came south as a hostage.[106] Physically exhausted by the rigours of the trip, William progressed slowly south with his health deteriorating steadily. On 8 September he reached Stirling, from where his condition prevented any further movement. At last, on 4 December 1214, attended by his wife, son and a great gathering of his nobles and servants, he died.[107]

THE WAR OF 1215–17

On 5 December 1214 Alexander II was inaugurated at Scone.[108] This hasty inauguration is in keeping with the anxieties over the succession

---

[102] *CDS*, i, no. 599; Barrow (ed.), *RRS*, ii, nos 511, 512, 513, 515.
[103] *Dunfermline Registrum*, nos 166, 211; Barrow (ed.), *RRS*, ii, 58; Duncan, *Making of the Kingdom*, 253, note 72. Alexander witnessed charters from June 1210 and became more active as William's health declined: Barrow (ed.), *RRS*, ii, nos 493, 513, 514, 519.
[104] Anderson (ed.), *Early Sources*, ii, 397.
[105] *Chron. Melrose*, s.a. 1214.
[106] *Chron. Fordun*, ii, 274; for William in Moray, see Barrow (ed.), *RRS*, ii, no. 522.
[107] *Chron. Melrose*, s.a. 1214; *Chron. Fordun*, s.a. 1214.
[108] *Chron. Bower*, v, 3.

that haunted William's later years, and, despite the 1212 deal with John, the old king's death still posed dangers for the ruling line.[109] Not only was support for the MacWilliams still strong but in Scotland in 1214, like England in 1198, male primogeniture was not the securely established custom. But the MacWilliams had not been the only alternative feared by William, for there was another option for the succession in Earl David. He, however, had become increasingly distant from Scottish affairs as he associated himself with John's regime in England and by 1214 was an unknown quantity to many Scots. Yes, he was a mature and experienced politician, diplomat and soldier, but he was also aged and his one surviving son was an underage minor. Twenty years earlier David's experience and qualities had made him the preferred candidate but in 1214 what was needed to meet the MacWilliam challenge was energy and youth, someone who could lead the fight for his heritage rather than another sick old man who could barely drag himself into the field on campaign. The expected challenge followed within weeks of Alexander's inauguration; acting with a speed that suggests anticipation of William's death, Donald Ban MacWilliam was raising rebellion in the north.[110] By mid-June 1215, however, the rising was over: Donald and his cohorts were dead, killed in Ross by a local Gaelic chieftain, Ferchar MacTaggart, who sent their heads to Alexander.[111] MacTaggart understood where the future lay and had ambitions to play a leading part in the Scottish government of the north. Alexander in turn understood his man, rewarding him with knighthood and thus marking him out as the king's agent in Ross.

Alexander and his counsellors were no doubt relieved at Donald MacWilliam's quick demise, for a greater crisis was brewing in England, where King John's relationship with his barons was slipping into crisis. An opportunity to capitalise on John's difficulties and to force him to honour his obligations under the 1209 and 1212 treaties had arisen, but how best to pursue that opportunity required careful deliberation. The young King received sound advice from men who had served his father since 1174, some of whom had held office since the 1160s.[112] There was no reason to discard these men and in January 1215 Alexander confirmed the positions of those who had guided royal administration over

---

[109] Broun, 'Alexander II's succession', 79–98.
[110] *Chron. Melrose*, s.a. 1215; Oram, *Lordship of Galloway*, 117.
[111] For Ferchar, see Grant, 'Province of Ross', 117–22; McDonald, 'Old and new in the far North', 23–45.
[112] See Stringer, 'War of 1215–17', 107–11.

SETTLING THE SUCCESSION 177

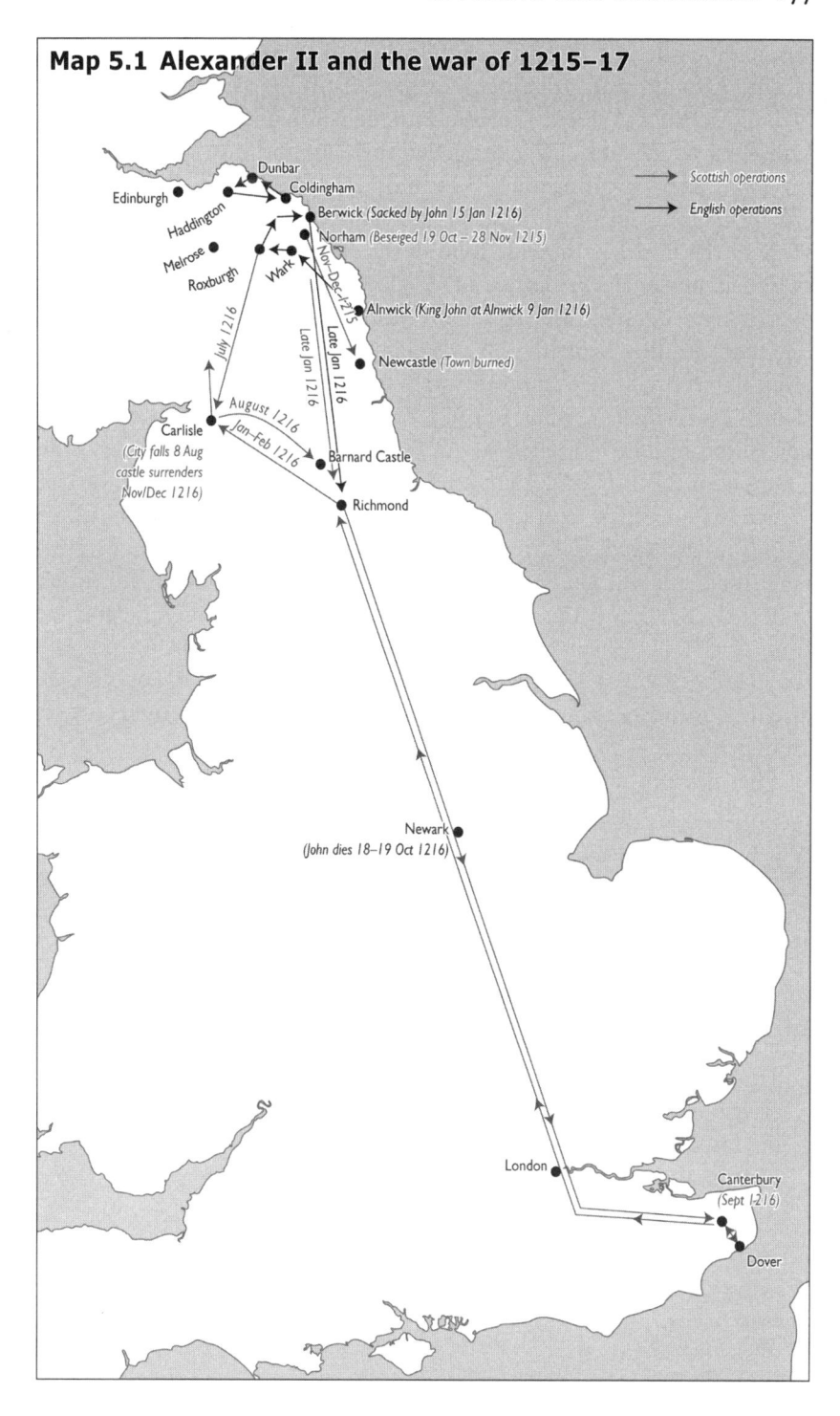

Map 5.1 Alexander II and the war of 1215–17

the previous decade.[113] Some of the young men associated with him in recent years did gain prominence, especially Walter Comyn, son of the earl of Buchan, but despite reference to the youth of some of Alexander's associates by one English chronicler there is nothing to suggest that they were driving the agenda.[114] Indeed, the witness lists of Alexander's charters stress continuity of personnel. That continuity may account for some of the hostility towards John in the Scottish political community; they had personal experience of Anglo-Scottish diplomacy extending over several decades. Perhaps more important, however, was the fact that many leading Scottish nobles had personal grievances towards John, often like those of Alexander himself arising from unsatisfied property claims. Nevertheless, when in early 1215 leading figures in the baronial opposition to John – headed by Alexander's brother-in-law, Eustace de Vescy, and the Fife and Lothian landholder Saher de Quincy, earl of Winchester – began to appear at Alexander's court to solicit his aid in what they believed was an imminent armed conflict with the English king, the Scots did not rush to help them. With the MacWilliam threat only just ended and the military and political position in England far from clear-cut, Alexander and his council opted to remain uncommitted to either John or his baronial opponents and to see what concessions might be won from them as each manoeuvred to secure his intervention on their side.

The wisdom of this stance was revealed in the negotiations at Runnymede in early June 1215, which led to John's acceptance of *Magna Carta*. Two of the key negotiators, Alan of Galloway on John's behalf and Saher de Quincy for the barons, were closely associated with Alexander and it was probably through them that a clause was inserted in the charter which promised that John

> would treat with Alexander concerning his sisters, the return of hostages, and his liberties and rights in the same manner as we will act towards our other barons of England, unless it ought to be otherwise because of the charters which we have from King William his father; and this shall be determined by the judgement of his peers in our court.[115]

---

[113] *Chron. Bower*, v, 81.
[114] *Walteri de Coventria*, ii, 229. See Stringer, 'War of 1215–17', which the present overview follows.
[115] Holt, *Magna Carta*, 311, c. 46 for the original in the 'Articles of the Barons'. Holt, *Magna Carta*, 332–3, c. 59 for the *Magna Carta* text.

Interpretation of that clause has ranged from its dismissal as characteristic of John's 'judicial highhandedness' to positive assessment of its sober recognition of the range of Alexander's grievances. The conciliatory gestures that John made towards various Scottish nobles following the sealing of the charter suggest that the more positive view is probably closer to the reality.[116] Alexander had high hopes for a resolution of the dispute that had obsessed his father since 1157 and sent envoys to treat with John. By the time they arrived, the brief peace between John and his opponents had already broken down; Alexander's claims would not be resolved by negotiation.

Civil war in England erupted in September 1215 and Alexander probably summoned his host shortly afterwards. There was, however, no headlong rush into war, for John's military resources were still vastly superior to those of his opponents and, critical in an age where spiritual censures carried as much weight as military power, John had also secured papal support.[117] Alexander and his advisers understood that open action against John would set Scotland onto a collision course with the papacy, the consequences of which were made explicit in the banns of excommunication laid against the leading barons in England by the pope's representatives. To some extent, by autumn the declaration of a majority of northern English nobles for the baronial opposition undercut John's military superiority, for their castles – which included the fortresses against which King William had raged in vain forty years earlier – controlled the routes along which Alexander might advance. The deciding factor that aligned Alexander with the barons, however, was recognition that he had two choices; either accept the humiliation of John's blanket rejection of *Magna Carta* and with it the dismissal of Alexander's claims, or cast his lot in with the barons and seize what was rightfully his. When the barons recognised Alexander's claims and began a formal process for restoration of lands and other rights, the choice was obvious.[118] What they were granting, however, was to be held within the framework of the kingdom of England; Alexander and his heirs would hold the northern counties as vassals of the English crown. This arrangement required Alexander to come to terms with the man to whom the English rebels had offered the crown. The Dauphin Louis (the future King Louis VIII of France) was

---

[116] Davies, *Domination and Conquest*, 105; Duncan, 'King John', 266–7.
[117] Holt, *Magna Carta*, 139–43; Cheney and Cheney (eds), *Innocent III Letters*, nos 1018 and 1019; Stringer, 'War of 1215–17', 114.
[118] Duncan, 'King John', 270–1.

approached in autumn 1215 by those English barons who hoped that a Capetian king of England would help them regain estates that they had lost in Normandy and the Angevin lands, but his intervention threatened to break the unity not only of the baronial opposition but also of England itself. Alexander, in this context, saw the possibility to detach the northern counties from England and annexe them to his own kingdom.[119]

Convinced that one way or another he would acquire Northumbria, on 19 October 1215 Alexander launched his invasion. His target, Norham Castle, defied him and, although many northern rebel barons came to perform homage to him as earl,[120] he made little headway and at the end of November abandoned the siege and marched to Newcastle, where he burned the town. This slow progress enabled John to come north, picking off rebel-held castles as he advanced, until in early January 1216 he reached Berwick.[121] The burgh's capture and sack was followed by a devastating campaign through Lothian before John withdrew, pursued southwards by Alexander, who himself reached Richmond before turning west towards Carlisle, harrying as he went.[122] The Scottish offensive resumed in July, with Carlisle falling to him on 8 August although its castle continued to resist him until the end of the year. From there, Alexander took a fast-moving force across the Pennines to attack Barnard Castle, where Eustace de Vescy was killed by the defenders, before plunging through England to meet with Louis at Canterbury and accompany him to the siege of Dover. There, he gave his homage to Louis for the northern counties and received Louis' pledge in return that he would make no peace with John without Alexander's involvement. Having received the formal recognition of his position in Northumbria that he wanted, Alexander withdrew northwards, eluding John in the Midlands and attacking the English king's camp as he passed. It seemed that nearly sixty years of Scottish efforts to regain the lost patrimony of the king in Northumbria had finally borne fruit, but then on the night of 18–19 October John died at Newark-on-Trent and the political situation in England was transformed overnight.[123]

The succession of the nine-year-old Henry III destroyed the unity of

---

[119] Stringer, 'War of 1215–17', 119–20.
[120] Ibid. 129–30.
[121] *Chron. Melrose*, s.a. 1215–16; *Walteri de Coventria*, ii, 229; Paris, *Chron. Majora*, ii, 641–2.
[122] Stringer, 'War of 1215–17', 120.
[123] Oram, 'Overview', 12–13.

the baronial opposition in England, for much of their hostility had been directed at his father. Nevertheless, the war continued and in May 1217 Alexander again invaded Northumberland.[124] The campaign, however, lasted barely a week, for on receiving news that Louis' army had been routed at Lincoln Alexander withdrew to consider his options. His decision was to consolidate his grip on his gains before the inevitable negotiations between Louis and Henry III's government began; Alexander would negotiate from a position of strength. To underpin his control, he endeavoured to bring the administrative structures of northern England firmly under his control, drawing rebel lords and local officials into direct personal bonds with him, but also redistributing captured properties to Scottish lords with claims to territory in the region. Chief amongst these was Alan of Galloway, who had played a key role in the war and who strove to consolidate his position in the region.[125] That position, however, crumbled as the rebels scrambled to make peace with John's heir; the likelihood of retaining any portion of his conquests was evaporating around him. On receiving news of the peace agreed between Louis and Henry, mediated by the papal legate, Cardinal Guala Bicchieri, Alexander submitted and on 23 December 1217 did homage for the lands of the Scottish kings in England – Tynedale and Huntingdon – with no specific reference to the northern counties.[126] It was a humiliating outcome to a war that had started with such high expectations.

In the most recent discussion of the war the emphasis in explaining the collapse of Alexander's position has switched from the traditional view of duplicitous English barons reneging on their promises to a new focus on the radically changed pattern of political and cultural identities in Britain that emerged in the later twelfth century.[127] With the benefit of hindsight, we can see that the imbalance in resources available to John and Alexander made the likely long-term success of the Scots in any war with England impossible without some external input. French intervention in 1215–16 raised that possibility, but Philip II's refusal to commit men and money to his son's cause in England ensured that Louis' offensive gradually wore down on the superior resources available to the supporters of Henry III. Access to those resources ensured that Alexander's campaigns were slowed by one after another expensively built, well-maintained, garrisoned and supplied fortress, against

---

[124] *Chron. Melrose*, s.a. 1217.
[125] Stringer, 'War of 1215–17', 132–8.
[126] *Chron. Melrose*, s.a. 1217; Stringer, 'War of 1215–17', 121.
[127] Stringer, 'War of 1215–17', 138–52.

which he had no answer. Perhaps the most important dimension in this changed world was the strength of specifically English identity, something which John's loss of Normandy and increased dependence upon and presence in England had hugely reinforced. Despite the personal ties of a handful of northern lords to the Scottish king, the majority of English nobles – rebel and loyalist – operated within the context of an English monarchy and pursued their dealings with Alexander II on those terms. Fear of John's retribution in early 1216 had driven some to contemplate a world as vassals of a king of Scots, but it was a short-lived dalliance that ended with John's death. A further complicating factor for the Scots was the effective intervention of the papacy in the politics of the British Isles and the ranging of Innocent III and his successor Honorius III behind John and Henry III. It was the threat of spiritual interdict, first voiced in May 1216 but only instituted against the Scots in September 1217, that finally brought Alexander's submission.[128] The popes had been powerful allies of the Scots since 1176 but their alignment with the Plantagenets reminded Alexander and his counsellors of what was at risk – including their mortal souls – if the Church of Rome withdrew its favour.[129]

RECONFIGURING RELATIONSHIPS

Despite the end of the war seeing a return to the position that had prevailed before summer 1215 there is no doubt that Alexander's prestige had suffered a major blow and his kingdom's relationship with England had been compromised. While Scottish independence was never directly threatened, the imposition of the spiritual interdict and Guala's grant of the power to lift or enforce its application to clerics who served in the English royal administration made Alexander aware of his subordinate position. It also raised the spectre of ecclesiastical domination becoming an instrument of political domination. That threat diminished with the rapid normalisation of Scottish relations with the papacy,[130] but it probably remained at the forefront of Alexander's thoughts as he sought to rebuild his personal relationship with the English crown.

Although political relations were 'normalised' in December 1217, Alexander's grievances, which both John and the barons had recognised

---

[128] *Chron. Melrose*, s.a. 1217.
[129] See Chapter 10, 345–6.
[130] Barrell, 'Scotland and the Papacy', 159–61.

in *Magna Carta*, remained unresolved. His territorial claims were non-negotiable until Henry III was of age, but other issues arising from the 1209 and 1212 treaties were open for resolution. Once the interdict on the Scottish clergy had been lifted in 1218 diplomacy resumed, and the pope at this point remitted judgement on issues arising from the treaties to his new legate in England, Pandulf.[131] Progress was painfully slow; Alexander and Pandulf met in August 1219, judgement was deferred until November, but the case moved forward steadily until by summer 1220 an acceptable offer was presented to Alexander and a meeting was arranged with Henry III at York.[132] The terms reflected a significant reduction on what Alexander had hoped to achieve in 1215 but they were still very positive from a Scottish perspective. Alexander's marriage to one of Henry III's sisters was confirmed, but Alexander's sisters were only to be found husbands amongst the English nobility; all question of a royal marriage for them was removed. While somewhat less than had been hoped for in regards to Margaret and Isabella, their marriages still provided bonds with leading baronial families. In autumn 1221, Margaret married Hubert de Burgh, justiciar of England and its effective ruler since Pandulf's departure.[133] It was hardly the prestigious match promised in 1209 – Hubert had risen from minor gentry stock – but the personal tie to the most powerful man in England offered the prospect of influence in Alexander's continuing quest to secure concrete results from the 1220–1 settlement. Isabella remained unmarried, despite the terms agreed with Pandulf, and in 1223 she returned to Scotland but without repayment of the dowry given in 1209.[134] For Alexander, his proposed marriage to Princess Joanna signalled recognition of the status and prestige of his kingship; no previous Scottish king had secured marriage to the full sister of a reigning English monarch. The significance of this match should not be underestimated, for it placed the relationship between Alexander II and Henry III on a personal level never before experienced between the rulers of the two kingdoms and could be taken as an indication of the 'coming-of-age' of the Scottish monarchy. Furthermore, when Alexander returned to York in 1221 for his marriage to Joanna,[135] he apparently won the personal admiration of his teenage

---

[131] Duncan, *Making of the Kingdom*, 525.
[132] *CDS*, i, nos 730, 732, 734, 749, 758, 761, 762; Matthew Paris, *Chron. Majora*, iii, 66–7; Anderson (ed.), *Scottish Annals*, 334–5.
[133] Carpenter, *Minority*, 245–6; Duncan, *Making of the Kingdom*, 526–7.
[134] Duncan, *Making of the Kingdom*, 527.
[135] *Chron. Melrose*, s.a. 1221.

brother-in-law; the family bond might yet win for him the territorial deal he craved.

Marriage to Henry's sister was not the peak of Alexander's aspirations. Despite the new treaty, he sought to change the basis of any relationship between the Scottish and English crowns by securing the ritual form that would place his kingship on a par with Henry's; like David I before him he wanted unction and coronation. Early in 1221, he requested that the papal legate to Scotland crown him.[136] The legate referred the matter to Pope Honorius, who informed him that such a ceremony must not be undertaken without the agreement of Henry III and his councillors, since the Scottish king was said to be subject to the king of England.[137] As protector of Henry's interests, Honorius was determined to do nothing to undermine his rights. Naturally, the English king's counsellors had no interest in abandoning the leverage that the perceived inferior status of Scottish kingship gave them in their dealings with Alexander. Undeterred, Alexander continued to press for coronation and unction into the 1230s but English opposition ensured that his efforts were fruitless.[138] For a long time, too, so were Alexander's attempts to force Henry to implement the 1220–1 treaty fully and to open discussions over Alexander's still unresolved territorial claims; Margaret's marriage to Hubert de Burgh had brought no increased influence and the justiciar's fall from favour in 1232 underscored the emptiness of the connection.[139] Against the backdrop of Hubert's fall from power, in the early 1230s Alexander again pressed for fulfilment of English treaty obligations, defying papal instructions to submit to Henry's decision and pushing the two kingdoms to the brink of war. The resulting 1237 treaty agreed at York was not a blueprint for lasting peace but, through its treatment of the two parties as kings on equal terms, the formal ending of Alexander's claims to the northern counties and to repayment of the 15,000 merks paid by King William as his daughters' dowries, and the award to him of £200 worth of land in Cumberland and Northumberland, it did mark a new stage in the relationship between the kingdoms and an end to the century-long struggle of Scottish kings to win control of the wider north of England.[140]

---

[136] Ferguson, *Papal Representatives*, 87–8.
[137] Barrell, 'Scotland and the Papacy', 160–1.
[138] *CDS*, i, no. 1181. See Duncan, *Kingship of the Scots*, 119–20.
[139] Carpenter, *Minority*, 393–5.
[140] Duncan, *Kingship of the Scots*, 121. For the text, see Donaldson, *Historical Documents*, 33–4.

MASTERY OF MAINLAND SCOTLAND

Despite its ultimate failure, Alexander's conduct of the war of 1215–17 strengthened his domestic position. His personal authority was greater than his father's had been at any time since 1174 and Alexander was determined to capitalise on that position to establish his supremacy over those remaining portions of mainland Scotland and the Isles where William had met challenge. This policy was more than a flexing of royal muscles on military campaigns against fractious potentates in the north and west, involving also negotiated settlements that enabled him to advance royal interests within the heartlands of the kingdom. Alexander benefited in this endeavour from not sharing with some families the personal bonds that his father had forged during his long reign; this provided him with greater latitude to find settlements for disputes which had festered unresolved for decades. It was, however, management of the volatile politics of the west Highlands and Hebrides that revealed his maturing political skills and the single-minded ruthlessness with which he would carry forward his determination to be the sole royal power within the geographical confines of Scotland.

An opportunity to advance this ambition came when the warfare that had proven near endemic in the latter years of his father's reign burst into fresh life in the 1220s. This time it was the Scottish king who was the aggressor and, despite some setbacks over the following decade, the initiative remained with Alexander. In early 1221 he campaigned in the Highlands; his return to Perth direct from Inverness might imply operations focused in Strathspey and the Great Glen area.[141] It is unknown if this campaign related to the sea battle in the same year in which Thomas, earl of Atholl, slew Diarmid ua Conchobair, a claimant to the kingship of Connacht who was returning to Ireland with a mercenary fleet from the Hebrides.[142] That action was perhaps linked to a naval campaign, otherwise recorded only in *Gesta Annalia II*, in the weeks following Alexander's marriage in June 1221.[143] The possible connection between the sealing of the English treaty with Alexander's marriage to Henry III's sister and an operation that eliminated the rival of one of Henry's main allies amongst the Gaelic Irish rulers, may not have been fortuitous; the Anglo-Scottish cooperation in west Ulster of 1211–12 and 1214 may have been revived. *Gesta Annalia* implies that this

---

[141] *APS*, i, 398, c. II; Young, *The Comyns*, 38–42.
[142] *ALC*, i, 264.
[143] *Chron. Fordun*, s.a. 1221; Duncan, *Making of the Kingdom*, 528.

expedition was otherwise unproductive, the royal fleet being dispersed by storms, and Alexander was obliged to mount a second naval campaign in 1222.[144] His target then was probably Ruaridh son of Ranald, who had been Thomas of Galloway's ally in 1212.[145] Suggestions that Ruaridh was reaping the consequences of complicity in the MacWilliam uprisings of 1211–12 and 1214–15 seem unlikely given his involvement in the 1212 attack on Cenél nEógain, but his subsequent reputation as a mercenary captain admits the possibility that he had joined Diarmid ua Conchobair in 1221 and, thus, ranged himself against Alexander and Henry. Alexander's objectives were the outer Firth of Clyde islands and Ruaridh's Kintyre lands and there is good evidence that 1222 saw a concentration of efforts to consolidate royal power in the region. Ruaridh was ejected from Kintyre, which Alexander granted to Domnall mac Raonaill, Ruaridh's brother, but the king also built a castle at Tarbert at the neck of the peninsula, erected Dumbarton into a royal burgh in July 1222, and perhaps granted Cowal formally to the Stewarts.[146] In basic terms, he imposed his lordship on the northern and western sides of the Firth of Clyde.

In autumn 1222 Alexander was at Jedburgh preparing to go on pilgrimage to Canterbury when he received word that the Caithness-men had murdered Bishop Adam.[147] Not only was this an act of incredible sacrilege but it was also a challenge to Alexander's personal authority. Although ostensibly the consequence of Adam's heavy-handed efforts to impose ecclesiastical rights to teind throughout his diocese, Alexander probably suspected deeper political motives behind the murder. Jón, earl of Caithness and Orkney, had reportedly refused to intervene to save Adam.[148] He had, however, shown no signs of breaching the 1214 settlement; no Caithness-Orkney involvement is known in the 1214–15 MacWilliam uprising.[149] The political climate of the 1220s, however, was wholly different; Alexander's military and naval campaigns on 1221–2, and his promotion of Ferchar MacTaggart in Ross, where Jón had claims to the MacHeth lands, perhaps spurred him into open resistance. It was a gross miscalculation, for Alexander hurried north, gathering an army en route and hunting down Adam's killers in

[144] *ALC*, i, 264; *Chron. Bower*, v, 105–7.
[145] McDonald, *Kingdom of the Isles*, 84.
[146] Ibid. 84; Dunbar and Duncan, 'Tarbert Castle', 1–17; Dennison, 'Burghs and burgesses', 277–82.
[147] *Chron. Melrose*, s.a. 1222; *Annals of Dunstaple*, s.a. 1222; Watt, *Fasti*, 58.
[148] *Chron. Bower*, v, 115; Crawford, 'Caithness and Scotland, 1150–1266', 29–30.
[149] *Chron. Fordun*, ii, 274.

a demonstration that the king's peace should run undisturbed and the royal will be unchallenged throughout Scotland.[150] Jón was humbled and Caithness played no subsequent part in the political disturbances of the 1220s. Although Walter Bower's fifteenth-century reworking of a lost thirteenth-century account of these events describes Alexander's seizure of part of Jón's lands and property as punishment for his failure to prevent the bishop's murder it reads more like forfeiture for rebellion.[151] Through decisive action, Alexander had defused an incipient crisis: the contrast with William's reign could not have been stronger. It was not quite the final fling for Caithness's resistance to the spread of Scottish power, but Jón recognised the unshakeable grip on his earldom held by the king.

Alexander's decisiveness in Caithness brought the control of the northern mainland that his predecessors had lacked. After Harald Maddadson's death in 1206, Norwegian kings demanded regular public demonstrations of Orcadian subservience to them. It was this resurgence of Norwegian power in Orkney that had alarmed King William at the end of his reign and, although William extracted Earl Jón's recognition of his overlordship of Caithness, Orkney was beyond his reach. William's death took the impetus out of Scottish initiatives in the region, for Alexander was more concerned with England; this lifting of royal pressure perhaps encouraged Jón to act more independently and Scottish influence in his earldoms may have declined as a result. Jón's miscalculation in 1222, however, enabled Alexander to reassert that influence forcefully and, simultaneously, serve notice to the Norwegians of his control over the north.

Jón's humbling by his Norwegian and Scottish overlords contributed significantly to his downfall. Some in Orkney-Caithness favoured alternative branches of the ruling family, mainly now distantly related descendants of Earl Erlend II, to free them from foreign domination. The Erlend line's leader was Snaekoll Gunnison, great-grandson of Earl Rognvald Kolsson, who demanded restoration of his ancestral estates and perhaps aspired to a share in the earldom title. Allied with Hanef Ungi, the Norwegian king's representative in Orkney, in 1231 they murdered Earl Jón at Thurso.[152] For Alexander, his death solved the persistent political problem of divided loyalties to Scotland and Norway. After 1222, Jón had been in an invidious position for, whilst he had given

---

[150] *Chron. Melrose*, s.a. 1222.
[151] *Chron. Bower*, v, 115.
[152] Anderson (ed.), *Early Sources*, ii, 480–3.

explicit oaths of submission to Alexander in respect of Caithness, he was equally rigidly bound to Norway for Orkney. Norwegian power within Orkney had been such that in 1230 when Hákon IV of Norway sent a fleet west to install his candidate as king in Man, Jón added twenty of his own galleys to the force.[153] What further involvement in this operation was planned by Jón is unknown, but his difficulties allowed Alexander to concentrate on the threats from the Norwegian fleet in the Isles and from the MacWilliam rising of the same year in Ross. Once those threats had been overcome, Alexander imposed a lasting settlement on Caithness. The mechanism used was not the military solution sought since the early 1100s but a dynastic one again based on strict rules of inheritance in accordance with 'feudal' law. Although the line continued, represented by the heirs of one of Jón's female kin who had married into the family of the earls of Angus, they were effectively Scottish earls and paid little more than lip service to the Norwegian king.[154]

WAR IN THE WEST AND THE FALL OF GALLOWAY

The final phases of the Scottish-Norwegian contest over Caithness unfolded amidst a related crisis in the western seas. The cooperation with English policy in west Ulster and Connacht in 1221 which had served wider Scottish interests took a new twist in 1223 when Hugh de Lacy, the exiled earl of Ulster, allied with Áed Méith ua Néill in a bid to regain his possessions. The English administration ordered Thomas of Galloway to Ireland to halt their onslaught, but by the end of the year Ulster was almost overrun by de Lacy and his allies.[155] In 1224, William Marshal, earl of Pembroke, was appointed as justiciar of Ireland and, although he defeated Hugh's kinsmen in Meath and relieved the royal garrison of Carrickfergus, rumours abounded that he was seeking an agreement with the rebel earl. Alan of Galloway, who had gathered his fleet to defend the Antrim lands granted to him by King John, sought reassurances from Henry III that his Ulster lands were safe should Hugh be reinstated as earl.[156] Despite Alan receiving those reassurances, by 1227 it was clear that Hugh had no intention of sharing lordship in Ulster with the Galloway brothers, and he seized their properties

---

[153] Ibid. ii, 474.
[154] See Crawford, 'Caithness and Scotland'.
[155] Oram, *Lordship of Galloway*, 122–3.
[156] *CDS*, i, no. 890.

there.[157] Alan made a private deal with Hugh in 1229, marrying Hugh's daughter and possibly securing some landed interest for his brother and himself under Hugh's lordship,[158] but the reality was that the Galloways' Ulster ambitions, pursued with such energy and expense since 1212, had ended.

One reason for Alan of Galloway's failure in Ulster was the diversion of his efforts into another arena.[159] Progressive extensions of Scottish power into the nominally Norwegian-dominated Western Isles were drawn by efforts to deprive the Scottish kings' dynastic rivals of support from there. Alexander also wished to counter the Uí Neill, possible backers of the MacWilliams who had been reasserting Irish power in the Hebrides. A key figure in containing both threats was Rognvald Guðrøðsson of Man, with whom Alan was closely connected. Rognvald had received Scottish support in his dispute with his brother, Óláfr, but in 1214–15 Alexander II released Óláfr, who was reinstated by Rognvald as sub-king in Lewis and married to a sister of Rognvald's wife, a daughter of Ruaridh mac Ranald, the lord of Kintyre. Probably on account of Alexander's campaign against Ruaridh in 1221–2, Óláfr repudiated her and, showing recognition of the new realities of power in north-western Scotland, married a daughter of Ferchar MacTaggart. The result was civil war in 1223, beginning with a failed attempt by Rognvald to have Óláfr killed. This conflict was not in Alexander's interest; despite the apparent 'win-win' position offered by the Guðrøðssons' ties to two of his magnates, which meant that the Scots would maintain strong influence over whichever brother prevailed, the turbulence threatened Scottish security. In 1223–4, it was Alan's star rather than Ferchar's that was in the ascendant and he convinced Alexander that Rognvald was the man to support.[160]

Alexander, however, was no fool and used Alan's ambitions to bring the crisis to a head. Having been forced in 1224–5 to share the kingship with Óláfr, Rognvald turned to Alan for aid in regaining his full authority. In 1225 they campaigned jointly but achieved nothing, largely because the Manx were reluctant to fight Óláfr, who was the likely heir to the whole kingdom.[161] Alan saw an opportunity, offering to reinstate

---

[157] *CDI*, i, nos 1371, 1372, 1473; *CDS*, i, no. 905; *AU*, s.a. 1228; McNeill, *Anglo-Norman Ulster*, 21–2.
[158] *Chron. Lanercost*, s.a. 1229.
[159] For detail, see Oram, *Lordship of Galloway*, 124–8; McDonald, 'Old and new in the far North'.
[160] Stringer, 'Periphery and core', 93–7.
[161] *Chron. Man*, s.a. ? 1224, 1225.

Rognvald if he would marry his daughter to Alan's illegitimate son, Thomas, who would then succeed to the kingship.[162] Alexander liked the proposal, for it could end the chronic instability of the region and greatly expand his influence. But here Alan over-reached himself, for the Manx would not accept the settlement; they repudiated Rognvald and offered the throne to Óláfr. The implications of this reaction were not lost on Alexander, but Alan had invested too much to simply give up. An invasion of Man in 1228 by Alan and Thomas reinstated Rognvald but exposed how little domestic support he enjoyed; Rognvald was expelled before the year end.[163] External support, too, evaporated, and by the end of 1228 with the English recognising Óláfr it was only the Scots – and in reality only Alan of Galloway – who persisted in supporting Rognvald.[164] In January 1229, Rognvald alone mounted a desperate bid to regain a share of the kingship, but his small force was annihilated.[165]

Alan's absence from Rognvald's fatal expedition did not mean that he had abandoned his ally but was the result of a new military crisis in which King Alexander required the services of his constable. Chronicle accounts of this event are patchy and confused, but thirteenth-century material within Walter Bower's *Scotichronicon* describes how 'a certain Scot called Gillescop [Gilleasbuig]' burned the castle of Abertarff on Loch Ness with its owner inside it, before going on to sack Inverness. This was no mere brigand's raid, for Alexander was forced to campaign against Gilleasbuig in person – he was at Elgin in June 1228 – and left William Comyn, earl of Buchan, as his lieutenant in the north to mop up at the end of operations. Bower's source noted that Gilleasbuig and his two sons were eventually killed in 1229, which points to an extended campaign.[166] Gilleasbuig was almost certainly one of the 'wicked men of the race of MacWilliam' whom the Lanercost chronicler claimed had 'raised up treachery in the remotest territories of Scotland' in a bid for the throne which drew support from many Scots.[167] The only named associate of the MacWilliams is one 'Roderic', whom most modern scholarship identifies as Ruaridh son of Ranald, but who might instead be another MacWilliam.[168] Lanercost dates the event to 1230 but it is probable that its account and Bower's refer to the same rising and that it was more

[162] Ibid. s.a. 1226; Stringer, 'Periphery and core', 95–7.
[163] *Chron. Man*, s.a. 1228.
[164] *CDS*, i, no. 1001; Ibid. v, no. 9.
[165] *Chron. Man*, s.a. 1228.
[166] *Chron. Bower*, v, 143–5; *Moray Registrum*, no. 109.
[167] *Chron. Lanercost*, s.a. 1230.
[168] Ross, 'Moray, Ulster and the MacWilliams', 40–1; McDonald, 'Treachery', 184.

protracted than either report alone suggests. It was also clearly difficult to suppress, for although there is a modern tendency to date the establishment of major lordships in the central and western Highlands to the aftermath of this rising the simple existence of the lordship of Abertarff indicates that elements were already in place before 1228.[169] Despite the creation of such lordships and the plantation on them of well-connected knights – Bissets at Boleskine and the Aird, Comyns in Badenoch and Lochaber, Durwards in Urquhart and Stratherrick – the MacWilliams once again threw the crown's schemes for regional control into disarray. Alexander was forced north again in 1230 to complete the pacification process, spending Christmas at Elgin at which time he perhaps gave the earldom of Ross to Ferchar MacTaggart.[170] Who was responsible for the 'capture' of Gilleasbuig's infant daughter that same year is unknown, but her brutal judicial murder at Forfar completed the extirpation of the lineage who had most consistently challenged the hold on the kingship of David I's heirs.[171] Ferchar's creation as earl gives insight into who had taken the lead in defending Alexander's interests in the north and reveals a realignment of political power in Alexander's council; from this point Ferchar, Óláfr Guðrøðsson's father-in-law, replaced Alan of Galloway as shaper of Scottish policy in the western Highlands and Hebrides.

A strong link has been proposed between the protracted disturbances in Man and the Isles caused by Alan of Galloway's actions and the 1228–30 crisis in the Highlands, and a change in policy attributed to Alexander's displeasure with Alan.[172] That, however, is questionable, for while Alan's intervention prolonged and widened the chaos and ultimately precipitated a graver international conflict, it also produced a settlement which ended any route for support for the MacWilliams from Ulster. Alan's marriage to Hugh de Lacy's daughter in 1229, in the midst of the MacWilliam rising, possibly saw Hugh use his influence with Áed Méith ua Néill to end support for Gilleasbuig from west Ulster. Áed's death in 1230 certainly ended Uí Néill ambitions in the Hebrides, for the resulting conflict between his kin and the meic Lochlainn for the kingship lasted until 1238 and utterly consumed their efforts.[173] Alan's continued attempt to win the Manx throne for Thomas after Rognvald's death therefore seems less like the irresponsible action

---

[169] Young, *The Comyns*, 27–8; Oram, *Lordship of Galloway*, 130–1.
[170] Duncan, *Making of the Kingdom*, 529.
[171] *Chron. Lanercost*, s.a. 1230.
[172] Stringer, 'Periphery and core', 97; Oram, *Lordship of Galloway*, 129–32.
[173] Oram, *Lordship of Galloway*, 132.

of a man obsessed and more a considered response to a still winnable situation. Possibly assured of support from his new father-in-law, Alan was spurred into greater action. New allies – or at least rivals of Óláfr – also joined the venture, with Duncan MacDougall, lord of Lorn, and his brother Dougall Screech, who had their own claims to kingship in the Isles, throwing their resources behind Alan.[174] In the face of this opposition, Óláfr fled to Norway and Alan occupied Man. Alexander's satisfaction with this success was short-lived, however, for Óláfr succeeded in drawing into the contest one player whom the Scottish king had sought to exclude permanently from the region; Óláfr secured aid from his Norwegian overlord, who had his own plans for the Hebridean kingship.[175] In spring 1230, Óláfr and his nephew Guðrøðr Dond returned with a fleet commanded by another Hebridean warlord, Gilleasbuig MacDougall (known to the Norwegians as Uspak Hákon), who had been given the kingship of the Isles by King Hákon of Norway. Gilleasbuig's twelve ships were joined by twenty from Orkney, and the initial stages of the campaign in the west passed relatively successfully with the capture of Gilleasbuig's half-brothers, who had joined the attack on Óláfr the previous year. Since 1222, Alexander had given Alan free rein, happy to let him use his own resources in a private conflict that was expected to benefit the Scottish king directly, but the intervention of the Norwegians forced Alexander to become personally involved. Summoning the Scottish army, Alexander came to Ayr to prepare for the coming war. While Alexander gathered his forces, however, the Norwegian fleet was bearing down rapidly on the Firth of Clyde, where the Stewarts became their next target.

According to saga accounts, Gilleasbuig's fleet rounded Kintyre and entered the Firth of Clyde, probably in early June. There they invaded Stewart-held Bute and captured Rothesay Castle, a clear indication of the concern that the spread of Stewart power caused Somerled's heirs.[176] The next move, however, was a withdrawal to the Hebrides as Alan of Galloway moved against them with his fleet; there Gilleasbuig died. Command of the expedition now fell to Óláfr, who turned it towards his own purpose of regaining his kingdom. In the autumn, he occupied Man with little opposition and his Norwegian allies overwintered there before heading north in the spring.[177] Their departure, however, did not see a

[174] McDonald, *Kingdom of the Isles*, 87.
[175] *Chron. Man*, s.a. 1228–9; Anderson (ed.), *Early Sources*, ii, 473–4.
[176] Anderson (ed.), *Early Sources*, ii, 476.
[177] Ibid. 476–7, but see 472.

fresh attempt by Alan to unseat Óláfr, and while the political repercussions of the decade of warfare in the West reverberated on through the 1230s the Galloway-led policy of conquest and expansion ended in the winter of 1230–1. The significance of this change was great, for it marked a decisive break with the policies championed by Alan, but equally it should not be overstated and it is a step too far to see in it the seeds of destruction for a semi-independent principality in Galloway.[178] Full-scale war with Norway had been averted and Alexander ended both the MacWilliam threat and Irish influence in the Isles. Furthermore, the new earl of Ross had a marital bond with the successful claimant to the Manx throne, thus ensuring that whilst the Galloway tie through the family of Rognvald ran into the sand the bond with Óláfr meant no loss of Scottish influence in the kingdom. The break-up of the lordship of Galloway which followed Alan's death in 1234 should not be seen as the result of Alexander's alarm at how close to disaster Alan's policies had brought his kingdom, but rather as a happy coincidence for Alexander who could impose a settlement under strict 'feudal' inheritance laws which suited his ambitions for the extension of his personal authority.

The break-up of the Galloway inheritance was the inevitable consequence of the primacy of feudal practice over native custom that already had been demonstrated with Mar in the 1220s and which legitimated Alexander's own final elimination of the challenge for the throne from the MacWilliams. Alan's death ended the legitimate male line descended from Uhtred son of Fergus and enabled Alexander to end Galloway's ambiguous relationship with the Scottish crown. He imposed a settlement that suited the purposes of royal policy probably because, quite simply, he could. Royal authority had grown immeasurably since the death of King William and Alexander had the strength and the will to end the political anomaly and potential threat to security represented by Galloway. The legality of his decision to treat the lordship as a feu was probably irrelevant to a king who had pursued a policy of aggressive military expansion since his accession; Alexander needed no greater legitimacy for his actions than his own political expediency. Opportunism dressed up as adherence to legal principles underlay his move, and there was the added benefit of the political advantage to be gained from championing the rights of Alan's legitimate daughters and their influential husbands, men already linked closely to Alexander and his government. The king's inflexibility on this issue provoked a rising in 1235 in support of Alan's bastard son, Thomas, but this was crushed by a royal army

[178] Stringer, 'Periphery and core', 96–7.

in which Ferchar MacTaggart was prominent, no doubt savouring the defeat of the last rival to his son-in-law's position as Manx king.[179] The Galloway war was no mere formality and involved Alexander in some hard-fought campaigns, but its outcome was never in doubt; by the time of its gory conclusion in 1235, Alexander was more surely master of Scotland than any of his predecessors.

---

[179] Oram, *Lordship of Galloway*, 141–50.

Part Two: Processes

CHAPTER 6

Power

There is no dispute that between the late 1000s and mid-1200s Scotland's kings initiated a political, cultural and social revolution in their kingdom, but the nature of that revolution, the extent of its impact and how it was achieved are contentious issues.[1] For nearly two centuries the main strand of Scottish historiography has labelled that revolution as 'feudal', that is sharing the institutional structures and legal framework of a hierarchical system of landholding which had emerged in north-western mainland Europe by the eleventh century. Some historians, led since the 1950s by Geoffrey Barrow, argued that this tradition was imported fully developed into Scotland in the twelfth century by David I almost literally in the baggage of the colonist-knights whom he introduced. The colonists' impact on Scotland was labelled 'feudalisation', where Continental practices in lordship, landholding, service and inheritance supplanted native traditions. Seductive though this 'Barrovian' vision appears, it is problematic and needs some modification; more recently, 'Europeanisation' has begun to replace 'feudalisation' to label the process, largely in recognition of the fact that the cultural revolution extended wider and deeper than the few foreign knights who settled in Scotland. Nevertheless, the arrival of the knight, the charter that legally defined his title to his lands and the castle that symbolised his physical possession of property, still stand as potent signals of a systemic change in the nature and exercise of power in Scotland. Even the most apocalyptic visions of the imposition of feudalism, however, never claim that it was a root-and-branch social reordering but present it as a grafting

---

[1] See Duncan, *Making of the Kingdom*, Chapter 15; Reynolds, *Fiefs and Vassals*; Reynolds, 'Fiefs and vassals in Scotland'; MacQueen, *Common Law and Feudal Society*; MacQueen, 'Tears of a legal historian'; Oram, 'Gold into lead?', 32–43.

of new forms onto the framework of the old. The employment of an older system to support a new military aristocracy has long been recognised, but few historians until recently have built on Geoffrey Barrow's pioneering work or offered an analysis of the nature and function of earlier arrangements.[2] Most historians, indeed, are reticent when considering the structures that supported royal authority before David I, or evidence for older mechanisms that survived the rebranding of the twelfth and earlier thirteenth centuries: few have been tempted to explore 'that older regime for which historians have no convenient name'.[3]

THE REGIME THAT HAS NO NAME

How has the 'pre-feudal' regime been interpreted? Eleventh-century Scottish social and territorial organisation, the interactions between rulers and ruled, and the probably diverse nature of native social systems are problematical issues.[4] In the early 1800s, scholars looked to Irish records for evidence of structures that existed in pre-twelfth-century Scotland. They combined Irish data with what could be reconstructed of Scottish Gaelic society as reflected in materials relating to clanship in the Highlands and more especially in sixteenth- and seventeenth-century Lowland legal treatises.[5] The use of Irish documents as evidence for Scottish circumstances rather than as comparative illustrations from a related culture is as methodologically questionable as the assumption that seventeenth-century treatises offer unbiased reflections of Gaelic society. Nevertheless, the model of a stratified society organised into territorially-based kin-groups which developed in this historiographical tradition has, until recently, formed the basis of most discussion of medieval Scottish society.

Following its rediscovery in 1860, one document became crucial in analyses of the upper levels of pre-feudal Scottish society; the tenth-century Gospel Book known as the *Book of Deer*, produced at the monastery of Deer in the Buchan district of Aberdeenshire, and the

---

[2] Barrow, *Kingdom of the Scots*, 7–56. For reassessment of 'pre-feudal' socio-economic structures, see Ross, PhD thesis.

[3] Barrow, *Anglo-Norman Era*, 140.

[4] Grant, 'Constructing the early Scottish state', 47–71. See also Robertson, *Scotland Under Her Early Kings* and *Historical Essays*; Skene, *Celtic Scotland*; Duncan, *Making of the Kingdom*, Chapters 13 and 14; Whyte, *Scotland Before the Industrial Revolution*, Chapter 3; Oram, 'Rural society: 1, Medieval'.

[5] For example, Skene, *Highlanders of Scotland*.

early-twelfth-century Gaelic and Latin notes of property and fiscal rights added to its pages.[6] These notes record a social hierarchy – king, *mórmaer* and *toísech* – relating to social inter-relationships and the rights and dues attached to those positions. In hindsight it is surprising that it did not cause a clean sheet reappraisal of the evidence for pre-twelfth-century social structures, but contemporary Victorian scholarship had already taken entrenched positions and, rather than using this discovery to make a new departure in scholarship, its evidence was interpreted in terms of already fixed academic views.[7] There is a further problem; the arrangements traceable within the *Book of Deer* were used to construct a model for social structures throughout Gaelic Scotland. Given the uncertainty over what the book actually reveals in respect of just Buchan, coupled with the fragmentary nature of other evidence, use of its data to construct a general model for Scottish society is at best dangerous and at worst dishonest.

Historians have long recognised a multiplicity of forms of land division and exploitative regimes within geographic Scotland, and discussed diversity in the labels used and the cultural variety and complexity recoded by those name-forms. They still saw them, however, through the rear-view mirror of the political framework of the late medieval Scottish state where power and social organisation was expressed in national, 'feudal' terms. The focus was on adaptation to meet the requirements of an increasingly interventionist and bureaucratised royal government through the twelfth and thirteenth centuries, not on how they functioned and developed before the imposition of effective authority over them. The focus, moreover, in the period from c. 1070 to the late thirteenth century is in most cases introspective, with comparative analysis looking at best to England for royal governmental culture and Gaelic Ireland for supposedly alternative native models. For this central medieval period, our understanding of the processes at work would benefit from embracing the perspective and comparative methodologies developed by scholars of the early European Middle Ages.[8]

Archaeologists offer various models for social organisation in

---

[6] Stuart (ed.), *Book of Deer*; Macbain, 'Book of Deer', 137–66; Jackson, *Gaelic Notes*; Forsyth (ed.), *Studies on the Book of Deer*.
[7] Broun, 'Property records', 315–26.
[8] For potential comparative methodologies, see Wickham, *Land and Power*; Wickham, 'Problems of comparing rural societies', 221–46; Górecki, *Economy, Society, and Lordship in Medieval Poland*; Airlie, 'The view from Maastricht', 33–46; Wormald, 'The emergence of the *Regnum Scottorum*', 131–53.

pre-twelfth-century Scotland.[9] As has been observed for seventh- to tenth-century Europe generally, historians have curiously neglected social history.[10] In Scotland, this neglect extends into the mid-twelfth century except in regard to political relationships. Where Scottish historians have ventured into the field, their visions of power relationships and social structures place monarchy at the apex of a hierarchy descending through greater and lesser magnates, free men of varying sorts to bondsmen and individuals of 'servile' (possibly meaning slave) status.[11] Although presented as 'pre-feudal' in nature, the models are strikingly similar before and after the seismic cultural shift that occurred in the early twelfth century. Such models raise an immediate question of how significant any changes were in reality. In Geoffrey Barrow's view of twelfth-century Scotland, for example, the pattern of secular lordships identifiable in David I's reign represented continuity from an earlier age: the lords and their relationships with the crown and with their tenants may have changed, but the territories themselves and the rights of lordship over them were strangely uniform in character and immutable in shape.[12]

A developed argument for a pre-feudal pattern of estates that stretched from lower Tweeddale to the boundaries of Ross was first articulated in the 1970s.[13] The foundations of the argument are sound, for commonalities in units of land and in the types of personnel controlling those units can be seen in the areas of Britain subject to Anglo-Saxon settlement and political organisation by the ninth century. Within the limits of modern Scotland, that included the south-eastern districts detached from Anglo-Saxon Northumbria between the mid-tenth and early twelfth centuries. In this area, twelfth- and thirteenth-century documents record territorial subdivisions called 'shires' (not to be confused with the later and usually much larger medieval sheriffdoms) upon which rulers founded a system of extensive (as opposed to intensive) royal lordship.[14] These shires, like their English counterparts, have been labelled 'multiple estates', that is extensive structures that comprised a 'capital' settlement administering a complex of dependent communities and where a royally appointed non-

---

[9] See, for example, Foster, 'Before Alba', 1–31; Driscoll, 'Formalising the mechanisms of state power', 32–58.
[10] Wickham, 'Problems of comparing rural societies', 221.
[11] See, for example, Barrow, *Kingdom of the Scots*, Chapter 1.
[12] Ibid. Chapter 1; Barrow, *Anglo-Norman Era*, 38; Barrow, 'Pattern of lordship and feudal settlement in Cumbria'.
[13] Barrow, *Kingdom of the Scots*, Chapter 1.
[14] Ibid. 25–31.

hereditary official, in Scotland in the twelfth century possibly referred to as the thane, oversaw collection of renders or performance of service dues, including military service, owed by the tenants.[15] Here, too, the local court might meet, presided over by the thane. North of the Forth documents from the early 1100s onwards record similar shires, only smaller in scale.[16] These northern shires, moreover, which are traceable throughout the coastal lowlands from Fife to beyond Inverness, were also administered by royal officials called thanes, who collected or enforced broadly the same raft of lordly rights as their counterparts in the south. It is not claimed that such a system once existed throughout the whole of *Scotia*, but Geoffrey Barrow suggested that 'the shire obviously determined the pattern of lordship and land distribution over some long period prior to the twelfth century' and that it long predated the arrival of the Anglo-Saxons, who perhaps adapted older arrangements.[17] It was an apparently offhand statement, but it formed the lynchpin of the central argument within his thesis.

Where the loanwords 'shire' and 'thane' existed, borrowed from Old English into Celtic-speaking areas, and firmly bedded there by the twelfth century, Barrow also proposed that there existed the institutions and offices that they denoted. Such a borrowing, he argued, resulted from 'that unmeasured but persistent Anglian influence among the Picts'[18] extending from the late sixth century, although the Anglo-Saxon-derived terminology cannot have been imported much earlier than the tenth century given the possibly later-ninth-century development of their currency in England. A distinction, therefore, was made between an ancient system sharing common structural forms with that which operated throughout much of the rest of Britain and the adoption of specifically Old English technical terminology to describe such a system. Why a system of possibly Celtic origin in what became Scotland should come to be described in a wholly unrelated terminology devoid, apparently, of even Celticised linguistic borrowings remains unanswered. If the socio-economic structures were established at an early date, why not also the descriptors for it until, apparently, some time after c. 950? When it comes, moreover, to talking of a 'system' of shires and a common expression of lordship through them, yet more caution must be exercised. First, underlying the notion of a uniform mode of socio-economic

---

[15] Jones, 'Multiple estates and early settlement', 15–40.
[16] Barrow, *Kingdom of the Scots*, 31–2.
[17] Ibid. 44 and 11–12.
[18] Ibid. 53.

administration is a notion of cultural, if not political, uniformity over most of mainland Scotland north of the Forth. Second, within any such unitary cultural-political zone it assumes that there existed an authority capable of directing, overseeing and maintaining the systematising of the units of exploitation. In short, the Scottish monarchy of the mid-twelfth century and later, 'national', bureaucratised and interventionist, is being projected back in time.

Most shires traceable in the twelfth century should not be seen as topographically determined units. Many probably evolved within limits determined by the varying needs of communities to negotiate shared access to common resources. This aspect reflects local development rather than being a manifestation of a systematic structure imposed from above. There are indications, however, that widespread systematised land division and assessment could have been imposed at an early date. The land denominator referred to in English as the *davoch* (Gaelic *dabhach*, pl. *dabhaichean*), long regarded as a measured unit of assessment that yielded a set annual render, has been shown to have a wider function as a socio-economic building block.[19] *Davochs* have the appearance of multiple estates with access to all environmental resources necessary to sustain a community – arable, summer and winter pasture, fuel, building materials and so forth – either in a consolidated territory or made up of components located at a distance from a central settlement. As with the shires identified by Barrow, the *davoch* displays signs of creation by an external agency and appears to be 'a unit that was imposed upon the landscape to assert "extensive lordship", probably in relation to both economic and human resources', and its role as a socio-economic building block can be seen in its later function as a component of the parish structure throughout Highland Scotland.[20] It can be seen how shires and davochs lend themselves to the socio-economic support of lordship where chieftainship transformed itself into hereditary nobility, although their primary function seems more geared to mediation of internal social and economic needs than to predatory exploitation by some external lord or his agents. A possibly non-centralised evolution of shire structures might help explain variations in physical extent and notional value identified by Barrow in shires or thanages which were converted into knight-service baronies in the twelfth and thirteenth centuries, and which the relative poverty and low population of early Scotland explain

---

[19] Ross, 'The dabhach', 57–74.
[20] Ross, 'The dabhach', 71.

only partly,[21] but the careful allocation of access to resources evident in shires and davochs points to negotiated construction rather than organic evolution.

A final point to ponder in the question of the development of a supposed 'system' of shires, thanes and thanages north of the Forth is the clustering of the documented examples in areas where the Scottish crown intruded its authority after c. 1125.[22] Are we seeing here the residual traces of an ancient system or the recent imposition of terminology by the agents of a conquering power to explain a roughly comparable system which they were taking over? The scatter of thanages between 'Rathenach' on the Spey and Dingwall corresponds with the zone upon which David I's administration of Moray was founded. Given the strong focus of David's landed base after 1113 in Teviotdale and the southeast English Midlands, and the probable origin of many of his clerical servants in these areas, we should not be surprised to see structures in territories being brought under his authority represented in terminology familiar to them rather than alien, local forms. We should, moreover, pay greater heed to Susan Reynolds' warning and look behind the levelling process that was part of the increasing bureaucratisation of Scottish royal government. That bureaucratisation saw the development of common forms of documentation to serve the needs of that government: what beyond the language in these records was innovatory we can never know.[23] The use of parchment records and forms was a development that spread from the centre out, one which probably saw the imposition of a uniform technical, legal language over a variety of regional or local usages, and which created an impression of commonality where diversity had been the norm.[24] As Robin Frame and Rees Davies discussed in detail, the replacement by the 'conqueror' of 'native' law codes, and the imposition of their own common legal forms and processes, was one of the most effective weapons at the disposal of medieval state builders.[25] The processes employed by the English crown in Wales and Ireland between the twelfth and fourteenth centuries, and, with lesser effect, in Scotland in the early 1300s, should remind us that identical processes were employed by Scottish kings in the twelfth and thirteenth centuries

---

[21] Barrow, *Kingdom of the Scots*, 32–3; Barrow, 'Beginnings of military feudalism', 260–3.
[22] Grant, 'Thanes and thanages', 39–81.
[23] Reynolds, 'Fiefs and vassals in Scotland', 182–5, 190.
[24] See generally MacQueen, *Common Law and Feudal Society*.
[25] Frame, *Political Development*, especially Chapter 7; Davies, *Domination and Conquest*.

as they expanded their authority over mainland Scotland. A common Scottish identity, founded on a national monarchy, national church, common law and common social forms, was a construct that expanded to fit the framework of the emergent state as it was assembled by David I and his successors.

FLAT MANAGEMENT?

One of the lynchpins of that vision of a common Scottish identity is a social model in which power was wielded in a hierarchy of lordship descending from the king through various grades of noble. Exercise of power is viewed as a function of lordship and there is an unconscious assumption that lordship implies nobility. It is, however, not evident that such a hierarchy existed throughout Scotland in the period under review here and there are hints that alternative structures prevailed in some areas. What form might alternatives to a system of tenurial or jurisdictional lordship take? The most common form is a society dominated by 'free peasants'. This shorthand term is itself fraught with difficulties, and begs clarification: Chris Wickham used the description 'direct cultivators who possess their own land with more or less full property rights'.[26] In Scotland, as elsewhere, most medieval historians rely on generalities such as 'kin-based' or 'tribal' to label the 'non-feudal' societies that existed down to the twelfth century and beyond,[27] without offering meaningful interpretation of what is implied by those terms. There has been little debate concerning the nature of medieval peasant society and the origins of lordly legal and economic control of the land and its inhabitants in Scotland, partly because the issues have been coloured heavily through the nineteenth and twentieth centuries by the land reform controversy and the hijacking of the subject for modern political ends. The result in Scotland has been a polarisation of perceptions, with at one extreme a deeply pink-tinged image influenced heavily by German Romantic notions of a democratic and egalitarian peasantry whose rights were usurped by an alien aristocracy imposed from outside, and at the other those who consider hierarchies of lordship and dependency based on heritable noble or servile status, where rights to land ownership and exploitation of its resources were exclusive and owners exercised full control over tenants, as the natural order in pre-Industrial society. The Scottish

---

[26] Wickham, 'Problems of comparing rural societies', 223.
[27] Driscoll, 'Formalising the mechanisms of state power', 33.

historical record, although far from satisfactory in its detail or in its geographical coverage, provides considerable evidence for the functioning of systems of the latter type. Similar documentary evidence for free peasant societies is entirely lacking, but examination of the development of systems of lordship in some areas of the medieval kingdom and comparison with examples of free peasant social organisation elsewhere and in other periods, points to the existence of such society in parts of Scotland.

A model of such a society is provided by ninth- to early-thirteenth-century Iceland. It provides a record of the functioning and progressive evolution of a peasant-based society similar to what may have operated in parts of Scotland into the twelfth century, but with some apparently significant differences. There was, for example, no indigenous monarchy, although the remote attraction of the Norwegian royal court(s) to socially ambitious men throughout the pre-thirteenth-century period should caution us against altogether dismissing monarchical influences, nor was there an aristocracy of recognisable form.[28] In Scotland, although an over-riding royal authority (not necessarily of a 'king of Scots') may have been acknowledged, the seats of such royal power could also be remote but likewise served as a lure to political and social aspirants. The case of Ferchar MacTaggart in Ross, who looked to King Alexander II for legitimisation of his local authority, offers just one such example.[29] Despite the absence of a resident monarchy or aristocracy, however, Iceland had a far from classless society; social status depended heavily on measurable wealth and personal influence was built through networks of clientage and dependence. Although there are significant differences in terms of socio-economic development consequent upon Iceland's climate and geology, the dispersed nature of the population, low level of material culture and unsophisticated economy is perhaps broadly comparable to circumstances in much of the central and western Southern Uplands, the central and west Highlands, and the Isles.

The nature of Iceland's ninth-century colonisation produced what can be described as a social rootlessness, where there were no deep bonds of social dependence and attachments such as those that form in long-established communities. This condition was unique to Iceland, where the colonial process led to the establishment of dispersed areas of settlement made up of extended family units with their political and economic dependents, with few bonds of wider community. Each

---

[28] Wickham, 'Problems of comparing rural societies', 238.
[29] Grant, 'Province of Ross', 117–26; McDonald, 'Old and new in the far North', 23–45.

settled area comprised groups of initially broadly similar social status, within which an individual – a *goði* (pl. *goðar*) – who combined heritable chieftainly and priestly roles offered local social leadership and stability through mediation. Kin relationships and ties formed through dependence on *goðar* provided some local stability, but conflicts over disputed economic rights and feuds between extended families arising from such cases brought regular protracted upheaval. To facilitate wider and more effective conflict resolution, the chieftains adopted the Norwegian practice of holding local assemblies, known as *things*, where disputes between kin networks and settlements could be resolved, perhaps similar in form to the *comhdal* of Gaelic Scotland.[30]

The *goðar* gave social leadership to lesser landowners, or *bændr*, primarily as their leaders in the law courts. *Bændr* followings, however, were not unquestioning, automatic or in any sense heritable, for they were not tied to a *goði* through heritable or legal bonds but depended absolutely on his success as a patron. Patronage, moreover, was not based simply on the perceived success of a *goði* in securing satisfactory legal outcomes for his *bændr* clients, but on successful feud resolution and generosity – gift-giving. A *goði* who was successful in providing such good leadership attracted clients and received from them gifts which ensured his personal prosperity and social prestige, but the expectation of reciprocal gift-giving meant that he never amassed a level of wealth which created a social and economic elite as happened in much of Europe.[31] Nor could the leadership role in local courts enable consolidation of *goðar* social and economic dominance of their districts,[32] for the absence of coercive authority to require disputes to be settled in these courts, or to enforce court judgements, meant that control of law alone was insufficient to establish them as a proto-aristocracy.

The social differentiation between *goðar* and *bændr* intensified progressively. At first, the influence of the Icelandic *goðar* was small scale and localised, with individual chieftains competing for a following amongst the farmers. In the tenth century, a successful farmer of *bændr* class could still join the *goðar* through acquisition of territorial wealth and local political influence, and, of course, marriage. Social barriers, however, hardened in the twelfth century and new layers of social stratification emerged, including a division of the *goðar* into a general chieftain class and a new elite group which modern scholars call the *stórgoðar* ('big

---

[30] Barrow, 'Popular courts', 1–24.
[31] Miller, 'Gift, sale, payment, raid', 18–50.
[32] Byock, *Medieval Iceland*, 55–71.

chieftains').[33] This layering into progressively narrowing groups may mark the emergence of a more mature social structure in which particular lineage gave status and a stage of development more akin to what may have prevailed in parts of Southern Upland, central and north-west Highland Scotland around the same date. The conversion of Iceland to Christianity around the year 1000 introduced a new variable into the equation, but the resources provided to support the new institution and the personnel who served in it were drawn from the same limited social and economic pool, leading to a rapid assimilation of its structures with the prevailing social system. By c. 1200, most of the early chieftainships had been consolidated into the control of just six families, for whom control of ecclesiastical resources gave significantly augmented influence, while the *goðar* as a broad class was replaced by a new *bændr* elite, referred to as *stórbændr* (big farmers), who occupied the middle ground between the *stórgoðar* and the *bændr*.[34] This was a move towards the creation of an aristocracy in the *stórgoðar*, but, like earlier *goðar*, the new elite still required a following amongst the *stórbændr/bændr* won using the traditional system of gift-giving, leadership and mediation. The *stórgoðar* perhaps secured social prominence through heritable land-based wealth, but leadership was still personal and non-heritable.

This situation created new tensions, for, although the *stórgoðar* dominated Iceland's social and political system, they did not hold economic domination. They could aspire to heritable lordship over defined territories but lacked the economic infrastructure that supported such status in much of north-western Europe. A decentralised economy and lack of control over its foreign trade ensured that no *stórgoði* achieved the economic domination required to turn their social prominence into something approaching the status of the political elites of mainland Europe. The political ambitions of the *stórgoðar* led to increasing competition between individual *stórgoði* and degeneration into feud and violence. To break the stalemate produced by the comparative equality between *stórgoðar* families, individuals looked increasingly to external agencies for validation of their social leadership status. The king of Norway, to whom members of Iceland's would-be elite turned for the legitimisation of their attempts to arrogate heritable political power to themselves, thus turned long-established but remote socio-economic domination of the island into intrusive and active lordship by nominating individuals as his representatives and furnishing them with sufficient wealth to secure

---

[33] Byock, *Viking Age Iceland*, 66–9.
[34] Byock, *Viking Age Iceland*, 341–7.

social dominance and with titles which gave a semblance of noble status. In Scotland, the formal recognition of men such as Ferchar MacTaggart in Ross represented a similar process.

Allowing for Icelandic society's unique origins as a colony established in a previously uninhabited landscape and the abnormalities which that created, it offers insight on how a 'free-peasant' polity regulated itself socially, how those mechanisms of regulation were mediated and how they evolved. Gift exchange and conflict resolution, the latter eventually arranged primarily through the public forum of a law court rather than through regulated feud or private settlement, provided the principal media for social cohesion. In Iceland, we can see the emergence of a hierarchy of dispute settlement and law giving rising from the family, kin group and client units where heads of kin regulated the internal behaviour of their own networks. They also negotiated settlements with the heads of similar networks, through more formal local courts. In those courts the *goðar* collectively adjudicated or mediated in more intractable cases, or made decisions on, for example, regulation of communal exploitation of particular resources, to regional and, ultimately, national assemblies, i.e. the *Althing*. The evolution of these forums of higher competence was a response to the maturing of Icelandic political society, the filling up of the colony and the emergence of a range of socio-economic and environmental pressures that could not be resolved on a local level. This seems a natural evolution, but what enabled it to function effectively was a single law code applied uniformly across the colony from family to national level. It is in this aspect that Icelandic society differs so significantly from the Scottish situation for, despite the emergence of a so-called 'common law' tradition in Scotland during the Middle Ages, a number of codes derived from diverse cultural traditions operated regionally into the fifteenth and sixteenth centuries.[35] Here, however, is where a jurisdictional hierarchy provided the social and political cohesion that Iceland's single code gave. As the Scottish crown extended its authority into areas where it lacked a direct, property-based presence, it established itself as the over-riding judicial power at the apex of a hierarchy of courts and appeals from local to national level.

The Icelandic experience supports the proposal for the seventh to tenth centuries that periods of 'assertive, predatory kingship and the affirmation of its aristocratic supporters' led to a weakening of peasant-based societies in the face of military violence.[36] It is a model of great

---

[35] See, for example, MacQueen, 'Laws of Galloway', 131–43.
[36] Wickham, 'Problems of comparing rural societies', 245–6.

relevance for expanding kingly power in Scotland in the ninth and tenth centuries and its spread in the eleventh and twelfth centuries beyond the traditional core of royal authority. Within mainland Scotland, the kingship of the Scots perhaps functioned down to the early thirteenth century in a manner similar to the Norwegian monarchy in respect of Iceland: its power was external and remote but ever-present, capable at times of becoming more assertive and interventionist but generally acting as a source of attraction to young men seeking to amass wealth and reputation abroad before returning to assume social leadership at home.

As has already been stressed, a peasant-based society was not necessarily either egalitarian or primitively communistic in its social behaviour or structure, nor need it have been entirely unresponsive to the external influences or pressures of royal or noble power. Professor Duncan has shown, for example, that twelfth-century Scotland was still a slave-owning society, and accounts of slave-taking by Scottish raiders in northern England during Malcolm III and David I's campaigns imply that ownership of slaves was not restricted to the top of any social hierarchy.[37] Hierarchism in a society, moreover, need not carry any connotation of stratification into 'noble' or 'non-noble' categories. As the example of Iceland emphasises, peasant-based societies can contain a broad social spectrum and within them individuals or families can be seen to aspire, to secure, to develop or to lose socio-economic power or influence over their fellow peasants. The Icelandic model indicates how such a situation perhaps functioned in parts of Scotland, particularly where population and levels of economic development were low. It also offers a possible model for how non-tenurial lordship could evolve in regions or cultures that lacked a hierarchy of property-owning.

'FEUDAL' LORDSHIP

New power relationships within the emergent Scottish state have been presented in terms of 'feudalisation'.[38] This process involved what Geoffrey Barrow described as importation of an almost fully evolved 'cut-and-dried, ready-to-wear' product from England into Scotland after c. 1124, and which he presented as a fundamental shift in the nature of the relationship between rulers and the landed elite.[39] Within that

---
[37] Duncan, *Making of the Kingdom*, 329.
[38] Barrow, *Anglo-Norman Era*, 1.
[39] Ibid. 139.

210 DOMINATION AND LORDSHIP

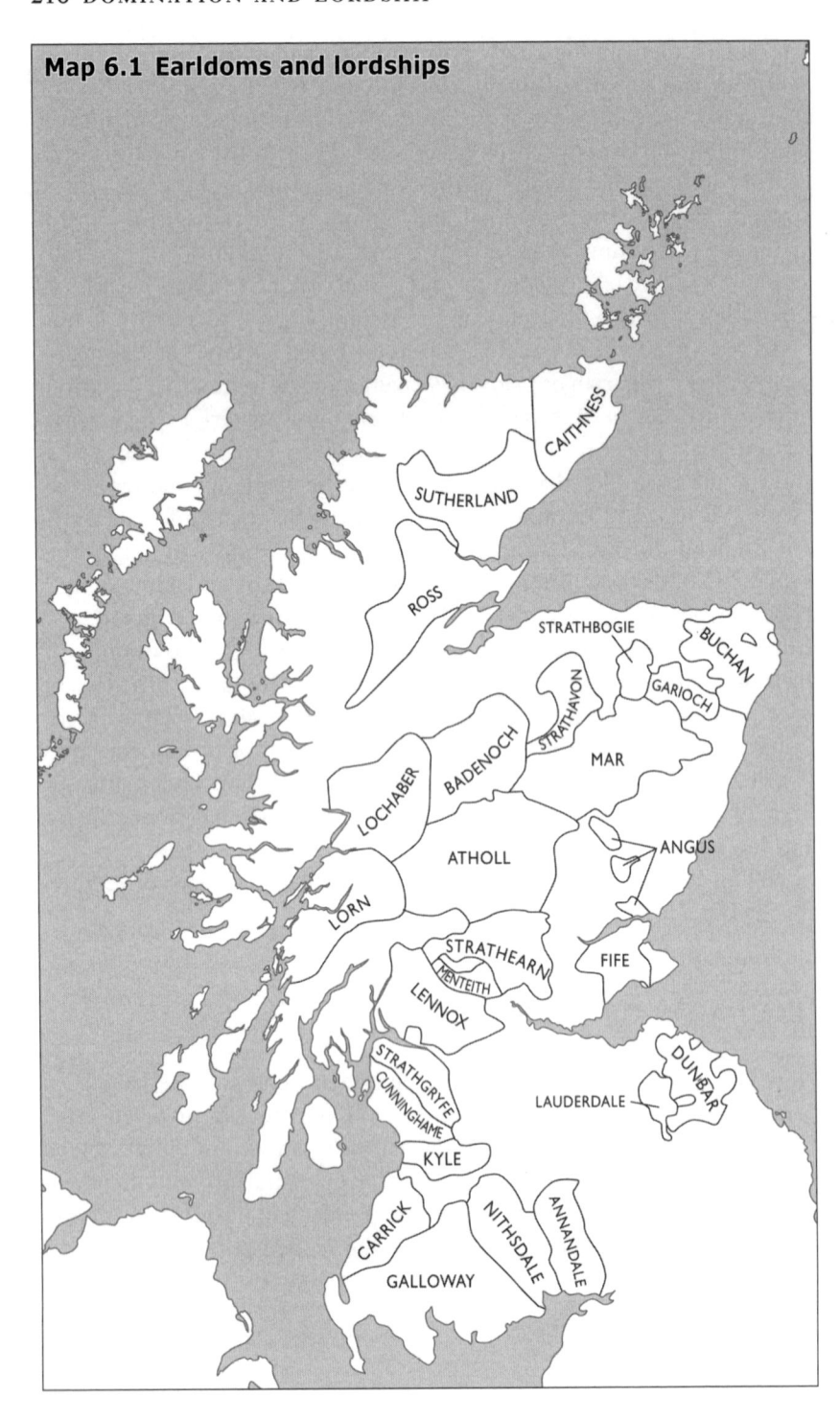

Map 6.1 Earldoms and lordships

changing relationship, lawyers and scholars since the sixteenth or seventeenth century have seen the monarchy as accruing to itself exclusive land-ownership in the kingdom, with a gradually expanding noble class accepting that it held property from the crown as tenants rather than as outright possessors. Central to this lord-tenant relationship was the notion of land held in return for military service expressed in terms of a quota of knights, a feature seen in twelfth-century England where it is labelled 'military feudalism'.[40] It was this that Professor Barrow identified as an imported innovation in twelfth-century Scotland.[41]

An obligation on free tenants to provide military service was not new, for the 'common army' service (*communis exercitus*) performed in the early twelfth century, despite its later French rebranding as a component of *forinsec* service (service in 'foreign' areas outwith a home territory), represented a duty with origins perhaps as early as the seventh century.[42] Such service provided infantrymen, mostly lightly armoured and ill-equipped, like those at the battle of the Standard in 1138 who fought ineffectively against well-armoured and disciplined men. Scottish kings from Macbeth briefly in the 1050s and then from Duncan II onwards wanted instead the new European fighting elite, mounted and armoured knights. Macbeth's Norman knights and the men who served Duncan II in 1094 were military members of the royal household in the fashion of the *huscarls* of the eleventh-century Anglo-Scandinavian kings of England. They were not so much nobles as professional warriors, trained in particular fighting methods and maintained in the royal household. There is no evidence to suggest that they received land for their support or that their relationship with their lord was tenurial. Mercenary is a label that carries too many pejorative overtones in modern usage, but it is perhaps closer to the personal lordship at the heart of the relationship between these eleventh-century kings and their knights. They received a fee, but that fee was perhaps expressed in terms of rich gifts rather than land. A shift, however, had occurred by the beginning of David I's reign, when men of knightly status began to receive landed property in return for their military (and other) service to the crown. In this development we can see the transition of such men functioning largely as a military adjunct of the royal household into a landholding military aristocracy.

This shift has often been seen as driven by economics. Knights were

---

[40] But see Reynolds, 'Fiefs and vassals in Scotland', 184.
[41] See Barrow, 'Beginnings of military feudalism'.
[42] Duncan, *Making of the Kingdom*, 378–83; Barrow, 'Beginnings of military feudalism', 273.

expensive to equip and maintain and royal resources were inadequate to meet the costs of supporting large bands of them in the king's household. Instead, the burden was spread by giving knights resources from which to equip and support themselves. Where sufficient land was granted, they introduced their own knightly tenants to provide their lord and his superior, the king, with an enlarged military retinue. David I's awards of Annandale to Robert de Bruce and Lauderdale to Hugh de Morville were rewards to friends or loyal servants, but they were also politically considered grants to royal officers. They established these men as major territorial lords with the resources to undertake a process of 'subinfeudation' to a second tier of tenants. The latter gave them the means to meet a knight-service quota.[43] One point to which we shall return, however, is that neither David's Annandale charter nor any early documents relating to Lauderdale specifies such quotas, it being only in William I's confirmation of the Bruces' possession of Annandale that the obligation is specified.[44] Annandale and Lauderdale, however, were perhaps unusually large awards and something closer to a norm might be the grant of sufficient property to support a single knight. In south-east Lothian, Barrow noted that some shires, such as Yetholm, were converted into what he named knight-service baronies.[45] Throughout Lothian generally, he also noted that by the later 1100s small baronies held for the service of one or two knights were most common, although there is little evidence for any standardisation in the notional value of these properties.[46] What seems also to be evident, however, is that his picture of a 'fairly systematic plantation' of knightly colonists and a 'steadily expanding feudalism'[47] was much more fractured and erratic than his model either implies or subsequent scholars have assumed. What emerges from the surviving record of 'feudalisation' is less of a consistent policy applied with equal rigour or value wherever and whenever opportunity arose across the 150 years of the 'Anglo-Norman Era' than a fairly organic development which received only a façade of uniformity in the language of the documents which chart its progress.

Attempts to map the spread of Barrovian military feudalism in

---

[43] For Annandale, see Barrow (ed.), *David I Charters*, no. 16. For Hugh de Morville, see Barrow, *Anglo-Norman Era*, 71–2; Barrow, 'Beginnings of military feudalism', 264–5.
[44] Barrow (ed.), *RRS*, ii, no. 80. For service obligations, see *CDS*, ii, no. 824 and discussion in Oram, *Lordship of Galloway*, 148 and expanded in Oram, 'Dervorgilla', 167–70, 173.
[45] Barrow, 'Shires and thanes', 27–9.
[46] Barrow, 'Beginnings of military feudalism', 260–3.
[47] Ibid. 251, 253.

Charters

Although Continental and English grants of property and rights had been conveyed by written titles for centuries, in Scotland this legal device was almost unknown before the late 1000s. Charters, as these documents are known, indicate clearly the changes occurring in Scottish political culture in the 1100s, for they reveal new views on possession and inheritance of property and on the relationship between the king and his nobles. Charters reflect the bureaucratisation of royal government, enabling royal servants to record exactly what was held by a lord and what the crown received in return. Early-twelfth-century charters are vague in both what was granted and what service was required from the recipient, but by the end of the century they set out clearly a suite of quite precise terms and conditions, albeit in a rather formulaic, 'fill-in-the-blanks' manner. They also provided legal safeguards for property holders, establishing and defining title, rights and obligations, thereby protecting them from arbitrary dispossession or unrealistic service burdens.

Although native lords saw the benefits in such clearly defined statements of their position, these safeguards were more crucial for the colonist-knights. Not only was written title the norm in their homelands but, as newcomers, they lacked the kin networks to protect them and their interests from challenge and attack. When authenticated with the royal seal – a wax disc bearing images of the king – the charter and its recipient received the full weight of royal protection.

Scotland highlight the fragmentation and disjunction of the supposed system. The most obvious feature of such maps, the absence of evidence for structures upon which a system was based – principally the knight's feu – from large parts of the north and west of the country, has excited much comment. Here, it has been argued, the spread of feudalism reached its high tide against the residue of non-feudal Scotland. The Highlands in particular, the scene of protracted resistance to the authority of David I and his descendants, has been portrayed as an ideological bunker in which an 'anti-feudal' movement was entrenched.[48] This 'feudal versus non-feudal' division has been artificially sharpened by attempts to map the 'feudal kingdom' graphically. It is also heightened by division of the

---

[48] See, for example, McDonald, *Kingdom of the Isles*.

'feudal' kingdom into areas of supposedly 'non-', 'semi-' or 'partly-', and 'fully feudalised' lordship.[49] A 'feudal' against 'native' polarity in much of the discussion, however, has oversimplified and misdirected attempts to explain why there was never a fully 'feudalised' kingdom of the Scots. As has been suggested by Susan Reynolds, perhaps abandonment of this stark contrast might allow more focus on the problems of identifying cultural differences and changes in a land where widespread diversity was an established characteristic long before the twelfth century.[50]

One area that demands fuller exploration is the nature of lordship and how it was negotiated and expressed. Traditionally, following the thesis that the 'feudal' model practised in Scotland adhered to norms developed in England, lordship in Scotland has been expressed in terms of property rights to which certain jurisdictional rights adhere. In England, alienation of property through subinfeudation resulted in a tenurial hierarchy in which the property was represented as being held 'of', 'from' or 'under' a superior from whom it had been received.[51] That, however, does not seem to be the case in Scotland where, in common with much of 'feudal' mainland Europe, the hierarchy appears more often to be one of jurisdictional rather than property rights. Property was alienated through subinfeudation or sale, but the donor/seller lord retained authority over the territory within which the subinfefted property lay through exercise of superior jurisdiction. Susan Reynolds has expressed this in terms of a distinction between 'tenurial' and 'territorial', or 'jurisdictional', lordship.[52] It is an issue that begs fuller research in Scotland, but some general observations can be made.

Lordship based on a hierarchy of jurisdictional authority rather than tenure may define the relationship between kings of Scots and their greater magnates from the later eleventh century. The nature of the relationship between the crown and the earls in *Scotia* is obscure and, as Professor Duncan has observed, only Fife is said to have been held on a 'feudal' basis by royal grant before c. 1150.[53] Professor Barrow has seen this 'feudalisation' of Fife as indicative of David I's success in bringing into a 'strictly feudal relationship one of the greatest native Scottish magnates', but also cautioned against reading too much into this one documented case involving an earl and earldom with an unusually close

---

[49] See, for example, McNeill and MacQueen (eds), *Atlas*, 413.
[50] Reynolds, 'Fiefs and vassals in Scotland', 192.
[51] Ibid. 187.
[52] Ibid. 188.
[53] Duncan, *Making of the Kingdom*, 164, 167.

relationship with the royal house.[54] There is, as he points out, no evidence that other Scottish earls entered into similar parchment-defined relationships with the crown in David I's reign at least. What it was about 'feudal' landholding that persuaded some native magnates to surrender their lordships to the king to receive them back as a feu has not been adequately explained. It is assumed that one motive was clearer definition, and indeed entrenchment, of the magnate's property rights and, in return, specification of his obligations to the king. The charter recording David I's infeftment of Earl Duncan I in Fife has not survived, but the later transcription, if reliable, defines neither the territorial extent of the earldom, the earl's powers within it nor service obligations arising from it.[55] The question, then, is who benefited? The answer can be debated endlessly, but while for the crown the establishment of a 'feudal' relationship with the earl may have been of great symbolic value, for the earl there may have been more tangible rewards.

The attraction may have been possession of the earldom 'in feu and heritage', a legal device which guaranteed transmission of the lands and titles intact to the eldest legitimate son of the holder, a practice known as male primogeniture. This change in practice had a twofold significance. First, it turned a lord whose status was founded on headship of a kin who occupied a given territory into a franchised possessor of a territory on which dependents who might or might not be his kinsmen were settled as tenants. Second, it ensured the transmission of that property lineally through eldest sons, thereby consolidating control of both the real property and the jurisdictional authority of lordship in the hands of a single segment of the kin. Barrow described Scotland as 'A Land for Younger Sons',[56] where cadets of families already well established in England could gain landed wealth and social elevation for themselves which could otherwise only have come for them through good fortune at home. For younger sons and brothers of native magnates, however, the new legal prescription foreshadowed potential social degradation and obscurity.

MÓRMAERS AND EARLS

How was the relationship between provincial lords and the Scottish kings negotiated and expressed if it was not defined in 'feudal' terms?

---

[54] Barrow, 'Beginnings of military feudalism', 252–3.
[55] Barrow (ed.), *David I Charters*, no. 16; Bannerman, 'MacDuff of Fife', 22–3.
[56] Barrow, *Anglo-Norman Era*, Chapter 1.

As noted earlier, our understanding of the powers of the upper strata of native society is very limited and based heavily on either the sole testimony of the *Book of Deer* or on what may not always be appropriate analogies with Ireland, England and northern Europe. Furthermore, historians have taken evidence from the late twelfth century onwards, in which a hierarchy of nobility is clearly present and where the social, economic and jurisdictional powers attendant on noble status are more clearly defined in the parchment record, and assume that this privileged hierarchy was present in earlier centuries but disguised behind Gaelic camouflage.[57] While there was probably significant continuity from the late tenth century in the powers and privileges exercised by the twelfth-century nobility, the delegation or appropriation of those powers, perhaps particularly within the Gaelic heartland of the kingdom north of the Forth, need not be equally ancient. Indeed, it is difficult to identify in the surviving record anything outwith the royal kin group that even approximates to a significant social stratum of nobles holding extensive territorial authority, and it seems largely to be the wishful thinking of modern historians that has created a substantial pre-twelfth-century ennobled class whose status could be transmitted to their children along with a landed and jurisdictionally empowered heritage.

Traditionally, historians have sought answers to this issue in the origins and status of the earls, who formed the top social stratum below the king until the late fourteenth century. These men are considered to have been provincial rulers in the twelfth and thirteenth centuries, with their earldoms formed from ancient land divisions dating from the Pictish period or formative years of the Scottish kingdom. It is generally believed, on the basis of descriptions of the earls of Mar and Buchan, in Latin as *comes* (earl) and in Gaelic as *mórmaer* (great steward), that the two titles are synonymous.[58] The earls, it is therefore implied, were in effect the direct equivalent of, rather than successors to, earlier *mórmaers* and, furthermore, exercised the same powers as their predecessors. There is, however, a basic problem of reconciling the evidently multi-purpose and functionally imprecise applications of the style *comes* with the Gaelic and English terms. Anglo-French contemporaries regarded the top rank of Scottish magnates of the twelfth century as the social equivalent of the English, Norman or French noble styled *comes*, *cuens* or *cunte* (all normally translated as either earl or count in English or *comte* in

---

[57] See, for example, Grant, 'Thanes and thanages', 42.
[58] Duncan, *Making of the Kingdom*, 164. See also Jackson, *Gaelic Notes*, 102–10 and Broun, 'Property records', 322–6.

modern French). These styles were derived ultimately from the fourth-century Roman imperial officer, the *comes*, who held senior military rank and commanded field armies, but who was originally simply a 'companion' of the emperor. Jordan Fantosme in his poetic account of the 1174 war believed that Scottish earls were the social equivalents of French counts and simply applied the French styles to them,[59] but social equivalence does not necessarily indicate functional equivalence or vice versa. As Kenneth Jackson observed, 'the equation [of *mórmaer* and earl] is very likely not exact, but it must have been approximate';[60] it is, however, that basic equation that is problematical.

What *mórmaers* were is still hugely contested, with suggestions ranging from derogated tribal rulers to provincial magnates with primarily military responsibilities established during the era of Viking threat in the tenth century.[61] It has been suggested on the basis of one use of the style to distinguish a ruler of Moray in the early 1000s that by the eleventh century the office may have been hereditary and that some 'belonged to the families of erstwhile kings who had been reduced to the level of the Scottish king's representative in the former tribal territory'.[62] A straightforward reading of references to Moray's rulers as *mórmaers*, however, misses the point being made by a chronicler in using this title, that is that this man was non-royal and, therefore, subject to an overriding authority; the use of the title denies royalty and, more importantly, political independence. Incorporation of derogated royalty into the administrative structure of an enlarged kingdom as provincial governors of their own ancestral territories is, however, unparalleled elsewhere in north-west Europe and the dangers inherent in such an arrangement must have rendered it unacceptable to any expansionist monarch. The West Saxon monarchy's suppression of the kingships of all the kingdoms which it subsumed into the growing English state in the late ninth and tenth centuries, with native kings being replaced by non-royal provincial governors, illustrates the process at work. It is perhaps best illustrated, however, by the emergence in Scandinavia of the office of *jarl*. This office, held by men who were explicitly deputies of the king, arose from the development of unitary monarchy in Denmark in the ninth century and the suppression of regional kingships. In general, jarls were royal

---

[59] *Jordan Fantosme's Chronicle*, lines 472–3.
[60] Jackson, *Gaelic Notes*, 103.
[61] Woolf, *Pictland to Alba*, 342–4; Duncan, *Making of the Kingdom*, 110–11; Grant, 'Early Scottish state', 55; Broun, 'Property records', 322–6.
[62] Smyth, *Warlords and Holy Men*, 219–20.

appointees governing territories that had either formerly been ruled by an independent monarchy or that were culturally distinct entities within a greater kingdom; they were responsible for tribute collection, local administration of law and leadership of their provinces' military levies. They were royal officers and administrators, not quasi-regal or even noble descendants of the provinces' former rulers.[63]

England and Scandinavia offer analogies; their experience cannot be taken as absolute models for the medieval state in Scotland. Past discussions of the *mórmaer*, however, have fixed on the administrative role of these analogous offices in England and Denmark-Norway and automatically assumed a similar function in Scotland. The existence of an overarching royal authority was seen as implicit in the ministerial or serviential character of the title,[64] and it has been proposed that this rank, like the terms 'thane' and 'shire', was an importation from Anglo-Saxon England as an intermediate administrative layer inserted between the king and the nobility of formerly independent or autonomous territories that had been brought within Alba.[65] Kenneth Jackson interpreted the *mórmaer* as probably the highest rank of royal official in the emerging Scottish state, a royal deputy charged with collection of the king's fiscal dues from which he took his personal 'cut'.[66] He drew back, however, from following the implications of that reasoning and presented the *mórmaer* also as a territorial magnate whose status and position were hereditary, equivalent to an eleventh-century Anglo-Saxon earl. From that position, the evolutionary bridge between *mórmaer* and earl in Scotland is easily made.

The most recent reassessment of the evidence for *mórmaers* in the *Book of Deer*, however, rejects the notion that they were royal officers collecting dues on the king's behalf and sees them instead as lords.[67] The argument, when stripped to its basics, is that the *mórmaer* of Buchan collected dues attached to his own position, not as an agent of the crown, and that the monks of Deer secured exemptions from these dues first from him and a very belated second from the king. It is suggested that if *mórmaers* were royal officials these exemptions would have been sought directly from the king, who would then have instructed his agents in the locality to act. There are difficulties with this interpretation, too,

---

[63] Woolf, *Pictland to Alba*, 303–5.
[64] Grant, 'Thanes and thanages', 47; Jackson, *Gaelic Notes*, 103.
[65] Woolf, 'Nobility: 1', 454; Duncan, *Making of the Kingdom*, 111.
[66] Jackson, *Book of Deer*, 109.
[67] Broun, 'Property records', 354–5.

principally where it substitutes a hierarchy of officials with a hierarchy of lords and its blurring of the possibility of the privatisation of perquisites attached to an office into personal property rights. Regardless of the distinction between status based on office or 'nobility' which separates these two views, the basic interpretation of a *mórmaer*'s role remains one of social leadership within a province. Here, again, we seem to have the basis of an earl's role.

Regardless of whether they are viewed as royal officials or as lords, scholars since the nineteenth century have implied that the *mórmaers* formed the top layer of society beneath the king throughout Gaelic Scotland. The evidence for *mórmaers* as ubiquitous social leaders is, however, at worst negative and at best circumstantial. The existence of such a social cadre has grown through a tendency to apply the title retrospectively to men to whom no historical source gives that label. Chronologically, the earliest reference to *mórmaers* in Scotland occurs in the account in the *Annals of Ulster* of the battle of Corbridge in 918, where it is said that 'neither king nor *mórmaer*' was killed on the Scottish side,[68] but the surviving manuscript of the annals dates from the later fifteenth century. A *mórmaer* of Angus is recorded in an annal for 938, three Scottish *mórmaers* of unknown provenance are mentioned in one for 976 and a *mórmaer* of Moray is named in 1020.[69] With the exception of the 918 mention, all these references occur in only one text, the *Annals of Tigernach*, whose existing fragments for the historic era were composed probably at Clonmacnoise in Ireland in the twelfth century but which survives only in a fourteenth-century manuscript.[70] Otherwise, there are no references to *mórmaers* outside of the twelfth-century evidence of the *Book of Deer* for men of that status in Buchan and Mar. The *Annals of Ulster* reference to a son of a *mórmaer* of Lennox in 1216 is probably antiquarianism on the part of its author, for all Scottish references to the rulers of that province from the late twelfth century onwards describe them as earls.[71] While we must accept the possibility that the title of *mórmaer* had been copied into existing annal texts from earlier versions, there remains an equally strong possibility that the title has been introduced by later medieval compilers as an antiquarian interpolation. The close textual relationship between the annals of Tigernach and Ulster

---

[68] *AU*, s.a. 918. The University College Cork online version of the text translates *mórmaer* as 'earl' (http://www.ucc.ie/celt/online/T100001A/).
[69] Anderson (ed.), *Early Sources*, i, 446, 480, 551.
[70] Hughes, *Early Christian Ireland*, 99–162, esp. 99–116.
[71] See http://www.ucc.ie/celt/published/G100001B/index.html under year 1216.

which has been argued by Thomas Charles-Edwards perhaps reinforces the likelihood that a later scribe has introduced the terminology from an otherwise unknown source.[72] With the exception of the *Book of Deer*, therefore, we lack an authoritative documentary witness from within Scotland for the existence of men holding the title of *mórmaer*. Despite that fact, the style has been presented as a title in common currency and has been applied by modern scholars to men who, while likely to have been *mórmaers* or the comital successors to a *mórmaer*, are never so designated in any medieval source.[73]

Again with the exception of the *mórmaers* of Buchan named in the *Book of Deer*, nothing is known of any family relationships. This situation makes it difficult to identify them as downgraded provincial royalty, cadets of the new Scottish royal family or a nobility of service.[74] Some evidence to further undermine the notion of *mórmaers* as degraded royalty has been drawn from legal tracts. These too, however, survive only in manuscripts of late-thirteenth-century date and later, written in French and Latin. While it has been argued that one text, labelled since the nineteenth century as *Leges inter Brettos et Scottos*, was compiled originally in a 'Celtic language',[75] the casual elision by which modern scholars have again substituted the style *mórmaer* for the 'conte' of the document has loaned false authenticity to the notion of a formalised gradation of titles in which *mórmaer* stood next below the king. Again, we can accept the likelihood of such a gradation based on the Buchan example, but it remains another point for which the evidence is circumstantial rather than positive. Setting aside that issue, however, the *Leges inter Brettos et Scottos* does cast some useful light on distinctions between differing social grades. The schedule in the text lists *cro*- or compensation-worthy grades descending from the king through earl/king's son, thane/earl's son, thane's son, thane's nephew or grandson/'ogthiern' (Gaelic *octhigern*), to the *rustici* or free farmers. There are two striking features in the list and the levels of *cro* payable, which are expressed in terms of head of cattle. First, the gap between a king at 1,000 cows and an earl at only 150 sits uncomfortably in modern eyes with notions that the latter represented a quasi-regal social class composed possibly of men whose predecessors may have been regional or 'tribal' kings. The ratio of 1:6⅔

---

[72] Charles-Edwards, *Chronicle of Ireland*.
[73] Broun, 'Property records', 335. The thirteenth-century document cited there refers only to the *comes* of Strathearn.
[74] Woolf, *Pictland to Alba*, 342–9.
[75] MacQueen, *Common Law and Feudal Society*, 85.

is, however, very generous when compared with the 1:12½ given for kings and nobles in some Anglo-Saxon law codes. Second is the narrowness of the gaps between the remaining grades: a thane or an earl's son commanded two-thirds of the *cro* of an earl; a thane's son was valued at two-thirds of his father's worth and so forth. This is a much more compressed scale than in English examples and serves to further diminish a sense of any social distinction of earls to reflect quasi-regal status.

Links between *mórmaer*/earl and a province need not be based on hereditary association, in the same way that links between thanes and shires need not have been. Nevertheless, the men who held these positions perhaps enjoyed a wealth-based dominance within their territory, pre-eminence based on their status as head of a dominant kin group or a combination of both. While the king probably preferred to introduce men from his own kin group or household, or of ministerial status from outwith the regions they were to administer, rendering them dependent on him for authority and position, they probably recognised that individuals with local connections and supported by their *clann* could offer more effective service. This is the path apparently followed in eleventh-century England, where, although the families of the leading earls became established in more or less hereditary possession of their earldoms, their position remained subject to the gift and confirmation of the king.[76] It is possibly thus that the confusion arose between the ministerial function of thanes and the kin headship role of the *toísech clainne* (where *toísech* means chieftain or leader) which has exercised historians for so long.[77] Thus, in the way that the families of certain thanes enjoyed heritable possession of their thanages in the twelfth and thirteenth centuries, so the descendants of *mórmaers* acquired similar possession of a provincial office.[78] Long-term possession of a thanage or mormaerdom may also have converted men of ministerial status into nobles, for their positions gave access to patronage and revenue-based wealth which ensured social separation from other men who had previously held roughly equal status. In this way, certain kin groups acquired particular association with specific provinces.

Despite hereditary association between certain kin groups and

---

[76] See, for example, Stenton, *Anglo-Saxon England*, 547–8; Keynes, 'Cnut's earls', 43–88. A connection has been noted between the twelfth-century *comites* of Fife and Atholl and the royal house (Duncan, *Making of the Kingdom*, 164–5), and there are apparently kinship links between Fife, Mar and Buchan in the later twelfth century (Oram, 'Earls and earldom of Mar').

[77] Broun, 'Property records', especially 353–5.

[78] Barrow, *Kingdom of the Scots*, 41.

provinces, the evidence from the *Book of Deer* could imply that the relationship between the king, the *mórmaer* of Buchan and the *toísech clainne* (as distinct from thanes) was not founded on tenurial ties. The *mórmaer* there, like the later earls, was the pre-eminent provincial social figure with extensive kin-based influence, may have possessed the greatest concentration of landed resources and had access to more revenue, but a *toísech* was not his tenant or dependent in any 'feudal' sense. This returns us to the question of the nature of the over-riding authority of a *mórmaer* as an administrator within his province and Susan Reynolds' distinction between tenurial and territorial/jurisdictional lordship. Here, however, we have to employ evidence from outside Buchan and which relates to the authority of earls rather than explicitly to a *mórmaer*. In c. 1128–30, a court assembled in Fife to hear and settle a dispute between Robert the Burgundian, lord of Lochore, and the Church of St Andrews.[79] The court comprised Constantine *comes* of Fife and the army of his province, and the bishop of St Andrews, his army and its leaders, a division of responsibility between *comes* and bishop which is also evident in late Anglo-Saxon England. Constantine's position, seen traditionally as reflecting his status as successor to earlier *mórmaers*, seems to derive from a judicial or jurisdictional role rather than from a hierarchy of lordship based upon landholding. Such a non-tenurial basis to comital power may explain, for example, how later twelfth- and thirteenth-century earls of Angus, whose earldom has been described as 'surprisingly poor and unimportant for so large a province',[80] exercised regional sociopolitical leadership despite their economic poverty. The possibility that the crown had eroded the landed reserves of earlier *comites* of Angus is irrelevant if their authority was founded on judicial power and the wider influence of their kin. A similar jurisdictional rather than tenurial basis for lordship within earldoms can be seen in operation in the fourteenth century, where the regional authority of Thomas Randolph and his heirs in Moray was founded on a regality jurisdiction, that is the delegation of quasi-regal jurisdictional powers, while in the earldom of Wigtown, David II's grant of a regality to Malcolm Fleming, and removal of it from Thomas Fleming, made then broke the power of that family.[81] In both cases, the authority of the earls was founded not on superior landed resources or kinship network, but on a notional hierarchy of lordship underpinned by the jurisdictional powers of their regalian rights.

---

[79] Lawrie, *Early Scottish Charters*, no. LXXXX.
[80] Duncan, *Making of the Kingdom*, 165.
[81] Barrow (ed.), *RRS*, v, no. 389; *RRS*, vi, no. 39.

Figure 6.1 The lord of Dalmeny performs homage to the king: sculptured voussoir from the south door of the twelfth-century church at Dalmeny, Lothian.

In these fourteenth-century examples, the earldoms were held 'in feu and heritage' from the crown for the homage and service of the earls, with specific service demands set out clearly, that is as items of heritable property which descended through the senior male line. With the exceptions of Fife in the reign of David I and William I's grant of Lennox to his younger brother, two cases where royal political considerations played a significant part in the process, a 'feudal' relationship between kings and earls is defined in no surviving twelfth- or thirteenth-century source, nor is there clear evidence of formalised father-to-son succession.[82] Even where an earldom was granted or restored to a native kindred, as with Malcolm IV's award of Ross to Malcolm MacHeth,[83] there is no indication of infeftment following 'feudal' forms. This contrasts sharply with the situation outside the earldoms, where lands acquired by earls were held for specific 'feudal' terms, such as Earl Duncan I of Fife's tenure of West Calder for knight service.[84] Into the thirteenth century there

---

[82] Barrow (ed.), *RRS*, ii, no. 205.
[83] Barrow (ed.), *RRS*, i, no. 316; *Chron. Holyrood*, 129–31.
[84] Barrow (ed.), *RRS*, ii, no. 472. See, however, Barrow (ed.), *RRS*, ii, no. 206.

is abundant evidence for native magnates entering freely into defined service relationships with the crown for newly acquired lands but not for their earldoms, even at the accession of heirs. This dichotomy cannot be dismissed in simple terms of entrenched conservatism or inherent 'anti-feudalism' on the part of the Gaelic magnates, for their apparently ready acceptance of 'feudal' forms in other circumstances suggests openness to innovation.[85]

The distinction may lie in inheritance practice where the earldoms were concerned and be connected to the possible duality in the character of the earls as both heads of kin and provincial leaders. Concern to keep the headship of the kin within an agnatic lineage while the *comitatus* or earldom lands could descend through female lines appears as a significant, but not universal, recurring issue through the twelfth and thirteenth centuries.[86] In Mar, for example, it was central to the protracted dispute over succession to the earldom from c. 1178 to c. 1222, while in Menteith in 1213 a desire to safeguard male succession saw one earl, who had only daughters, resign the earldom to his half-brother, who was perhaps considered likely to produce sons.[87] In Atholl, however, the earldom passed through a succession of females, to be held by their husbands, although the kin retained a say in settlements involving property and jurisdiction from the *comitatus*.[88] Perhaps significantly, succession practice in the earldoms was resolved by Alexander II, the king most ruthlessly determined to eliminate alternatives to male primogeniture with regard to the crown and to consolidate the position of the king of Scots as the unquestioned head of the hierarchy of lordship in Scotland.[89] It was Alexander's settlement of the Mar dispute that signalled the shift in royal policy and in legal practice.[90] The position of earl in Mar had lain in abeyance since the death of Earl Gilchrist in c. 1207, but this vacancy was just the most recent episode in a dispute between rival lines of the Mar kindred extending over many decades. The rival heads had served the crown loyally in the wars between 1211 and 1222; a compromise that divided the earldom had satisfied immediate royal needs for local leadership in times of crisis. Failure to settle the competing claims definitively,

---

[85] See Watson, 'Adapting tradition?', 26–9, and Oram, 'Earls and earldom of Mar', 46–52.
[86] Duncan, *Making of the Kingdom*, 199–200; MacQueen, 'Kin of Kennedy', 274–96.
[87] Oram, 'Earls and earldom of Mar', 52–5; Duncan, *Making of the Kingdom*, 199–200.
[88] *Register of Cupar Abbey*, i, nos 30 and 34; Duncan, *Making of the Kingdom*, 543–4.
[89] Oram, 'Introduction', 23–6; Broun, 'Contemporary perspectives on Alexander II's succession', 79–98.
[90] Oram, 'Mar', 50–5.

however, complicated the organisation of Mar's military resources and, more critically, clashed with Alexander's views on heritage and succession. In Mar, a series of issues collided: primogeniture versus tanistry and two conflicting views on the question of bastardy and inheritance. These matters were also central to the question of royal succession, which Alexander was determined to resolve. The Mar settlement was perhaps reached in Alexander's court at Scone in May 1222 when both claimants, Thomas of Lundie and Duncan son of Morgrund, were present.[91] It was in some ways a test case, for it was the first incidence of a disputed succession to one of the earldoms, where differing legal custom presented dramatically different results.[92] The settlement was made in accordance with primogeniture and gave the earldom to Duncan, but the disappointed claims of Thomas were acknowledged through the award to him of a substantial lordship carved from the *comitatus* of Mar.[93] It was still a compromise, but the principle of transmission of the earldom by male primogeniture had been established.

LAND AND TRIBUTE

The crown's ability to introduce new layers of lordship and, indeed, new lords has been based on the suggestion that in some districts the king had a 'concentration of large blocks of royal demesne only loosely and extensively exploited and therefore susceptible of much more intensive settlement'.[94] This argument recognised the implications for basic socio-economic development inherent in relative depopulation, but the fundamental assumption is still that the crown had the authority and power to effect far-reaching change by imposition from above. How or when the kings of Scots secured effective possession of such concentrations of demesne, for example in areas such as Moray, Ross or the western Southern Uplands, how they were administered and the relationships with the local populations negotiated, and how those local populations were organised socially, however, demands detailed consideration. There also remains a fundamental question of how royal

[91] NLS Adv. MS 35.4.12A, no. 3.
[92] The Menteith dispute does not fit this mould. It arose from the sonlessness of an elder brother, who resigned his earldom intact to his closest male heir, his younger brother, rather than have Menteith partitioned between his daughters. See Duncan, *Making of the Kingdom*, 199–200.
[93] Oram, 'Mar', 55–6.
[94] Barrow, *Anglo-Norman Era*, 39.

power was established and exercised in areas where the crown possessed no demesne. The growth of jurisdictional lordship has already been explored, but the significance of gift-giving and tribute payment remains to be considered.

In the twelfth century, Scottish kings received payment of a form of tribute referred to as *cáin* from throughout the Gaelic districts of Scotland between Carrick and Ross.[95] *Cáin* was a general term for payment due to a lord, but it does not necessarily refer to every type of payment. It appears, moreover, from regular reference to specific items, for example cheese and hides, oats and bere, to have been 'a render in kind traditional not in amount but in the commodities paid', and, given the way that some commodities are classed as *cáin* in some districts and not in others, was paid in terms of an area's chief produce.[96] That *cáin* included renders in kind that would otherwise have been consumed as demesne produce is evident in grants, like David I's to the Church of Glasgow of cattle and pigs from Carrick, Kyle, Cunningham and Strathgryfe, where the gift was subject to the proviso that the king might go there to consume the *cáin* himself.[97] *Cáin* payments should not be confused with the right of a lord to receive hospitality for himself and his retinue from some lands, known in *Scotia* as *conveth* and in Lothian as *wayting*. Conveth was an irregular and, essentially, predatory burden which formed part of the king's universal rights to hospitality and entertainment and, suggestively, places most associated with dues of this kind are located in districts where they might have had a punitive significance, such as the Mearns, Moray and Ross, or Carrick in the south-west.[98] Hospitality obligations of this type have the appearance of simplicity and primitiveness, and may have been amongst the most ancient burdens of lordship, but they could also reflect recent assertion of dominance by an external authority.

The development of *cáin* payment requires further research. The term was used in respect both of renders from estates possessed by a lord and of tribute payments made to a possibly remote authority which claimed to be, and was recognised as, overlord. It possibly originated in a tradition of gift-giving and unconditional hospitality, where a chieftain would 'visit' a neighbour with his retinue and receive unlimited board

---

[95] Duncan, *Making of the Kingdom*, 152–4; Dodgshon, *Land and Society*, 68–9.
[96] Duncan, *Making of the Kingdom*, 153–4. See also Lawrie, *Early Scottish Charters*, no. CIII; Barrow (ed.), *RRS*, i, no. 245; Barrow (ed.), *RRS*, i, no. 195.
[97] *Glasgow Registrum*, no. 9.
[98] Barrow, *Kingdom of the Scots*, 39.

and lodgings for the duration of the stay. What may have begun as reciprocal arrangements perhaps gradually became more burdensome as more powerful chieftains turned it into obligations due to them from dependents. This, as *conveth*, still required the receiver of the hospitality to visit the scene of payment, but the progressive development of assertive royal lordship in the eleventh century and subsequent development of bureaucratic government perhaps saw a transition from infrequent collection when the king and his retinue came in person to consume it to regular gathering of the renders as revenue. There may have been conversion into money for transmission to the king's chamberlain, or consumption locally by royal deputies. Such a transition may lie behind the reference to *cáin* due to David from 'that part of Galloway' held by him before 1124.[99] This render perhaps reveals the recent imposition of his lordship there to the extent that its people paid him tribute, or possibly that his predecessors as rulers of Cumbria had exercised loose and intermittent overlordship there. It need not be evidence for a network of territorial lordships from which the crown drew tribute.

We search in vain for recognisable pre-twelfth-century lordship structures in existence in upper Teviotdale and Tweeddale. Professor Barrow drew attention to the existence of shires in the east of this district, to the early establishment of knightly colonists in 'knight-service baronies' there and also to the presence of a substantial non-noble but free population in the first half of the twelfth century.[100] Men bearing largely Anglian or Anglo-Scandinavian names called to witness charters of David I or Malcolm IV to the monks of Melrose, for example, look like a substantial free peasantry who were being burdened by the demands of an assertive and intrusive lord.[101] David's establishment of his lordship in this region, centred on Roxburgh, perhaps witnessed an aggressive expression of his territorial lordship and its extension into areas where such authority had been loose, intermittent and remote since the ninth-century decline of Northumbria. Perhaps, on the fringes of this zone of power, there still existed peasant communities largely free of 'close and coercive control'?[102] This area, centred on Ettrick Forest, looks like what William Kapelle, speaking of the Pennine districts of northern England, called a 'free zone', where the population was small, royal or lordly,

---

[99] *Kelso Liber*, i, iv.
[100] Barrow, *Kingdom of the Scots*, 23–30; Barrow, 'Beginnings of military feudalism', 252.
[101] See, for example, *Melrose Liber*, no. 1.
[102] Reynolds, 'Fiefs and vassals in Scotland', 192.

authority was remote and largely ineffective, brigandage was endemic, and social and economic structures were undeveloped.[103] The Forest, a northern extension of Kapelle's 'free zone', was a marchland between Strathclyde and Northumbria in the eleventh century and remained a largely undeveloped, although routinely and systematically exploited, territory thereafter. Inroads were made into its eastern fringe between the early seventh and late eighth centuries, as suggested by the identification of a probable Northumbrian lordship site at Philiphaugh west of Selkirk and the place name Hawick (OE, *Haga-wic* = 'hedge-settlement'), where the *wic* generic indicates that the settlement was an outlying dependency of a primary community.[104] The interior of the region, however, was only seasonally exploited by the communities around its margins, principally as pasture, and through the twelfth century was gradually brought within the sphere of royal authority as hunting forest.[105] While the valley systems that penetrated this zone were developed as lordships for crown tenants, and extensive economic rights were awarded to Melrose Abbey and to secular landowners within the surviving afforested area by the 1220s, the hilly and relatively inaccessible interior remained a region where the intrusive and coercive authority of the crown was remote and unevenly imposed.

West of the central Southern Uplands watershed and Clydesdale there is another set of problems. The presence of substantial territorial blocks running from Strathgryfe and Cunningham in the north to Eskdale and Liddesdale in the south has long been recognised and it is suggested that these were component administrative units of the early-eleventh-century kingdom of Strathclyde.[106] Much of this region, however, lay outwith the principality awarded to David in 1113 and within the ill-defined region referred to by modern historians as 'greater Galloway'.[107] By the second quarter of the twelfth century, some of these districts had been brought together in a composite unit – the kingdom or lordship of Galloway – but there is otherwise no evidence for any over-riding authority exercising lordship over the whole region. It has been suggested that the limits of the diocese of Glasgow as defined in the later 1100s reflect the earlier

---

[103] Kapelle, *Norman Conquest of the North*, 7, 119, 128–9, 131–3.
[104] For Philiphaugh, see Smith, 'Sprouston', 281–2. For Hawick, see Nicolaisen, *Scottish Place-Names*, 7.
[105] See, for example, *Melrose Liber*, nos 264–5.
[106] Barrow, 'Pattern of lordship and feudal settlement in Cumbria'; Oram, *Lordship of Galloway*, 24–6.
[107] For the composition of Galloway, see Barrow (ed.), *RRS*, i, 38–9; Oram, *Lordship of Galloway*, xxii–xxiv.

limits of a Cumbrian see co-extensive with the kingdom of Strathclyde, but Glasgow's conflict with Durham over Teviotdale and similar disputes with Whithorn imply that those boundaries were fluid and recently established.[108] Furthermore, the so-called Inquest of David instituted to determine the extent of Glasgow's properties reveals a distribution of lands that highlights a distinction between Clydesdale and 'greater Galloway'.[109] The inquest comprises properties listed as five main groups, two in Tweeddale, one in Annandale, one in Clydesdale and one around Glasgow itself. With the possible exception of a single property named 'Edyngaheym', none of Glasgow's estates lay west of a line from the Annandale-Nithsdale watershed to eastern Renfrewshire.[110] If the inquest reflects the patronage of the bishopric, ancient and contemporary, by the rulers of Strathclyde and Cumbria, then it appears that those rulers, including David, lacked either personal estates within 'greater Galloway' from which to endow Glasgow or the authority to influence others to do so.

By the standards of most landholdings awarded by David to colonial lords in south-east Scotland, even the smallest south-western lordship, the de Conisbroughs' Ewesdale property, was territorially extensive and the larger ones comprised properties of greater physical extent than the core lands of the earldoms north of the Forth-Clyde line. It was the granting of these territories to families like the Bruces, Stewarts, Morvilles or Avenels that established them as nobility of regional stature occupying a social plane immediately below the crown, not their existing personal relationships with the monarch. The traditional assumption has been that these colonial families were simply slotted into an existing administrative structure by David, perhaps as superior lords between the king and the heads of the established native elites; possibly through marriage to native heiresses; or potentially through expropriation of a native lordly class. Evidence for such a native lordly class, however, is thin, with only Dunegal of Nithsdale, first mentioned in c. 1124, and Fergus of Galloway, who first appears in surviving records in 1136, possibly being of 'native' stock, although it is only modern perceptions of David's apparent preference for 'Anglo-Normans' over 'natives' that has blinded us to the possibility that Dunegal, too, may have belonged to the king's new aristocracy. Where we might reasonably expect to see a class

---

[108] Oram, *Lordship of Galloway*, 168–9.
[109] *Glasgow Registrum*, no. 1.
[110] Nicolaisen, *Scottish Place-Names*, 73; Brooke, 'Desnes-Cro and Edingham'; Oram, *Lordship of Galloway*, 168–9.

of native regional magnates in operation, for example in the Glasgow inquest, or in the gatherings in 1136 in preparation for the war in England, none is in evidence other than Dunegal or his sons and Fergus. We must accept the logical conclusion from this absence of evidence for native precursors of these regional lords: there was none. Instead, what the Glasgow inquest reveals is a society like that in upper Teviotdale and Tweeddale, dominated by individuals who may have been substantial free peasants and who commanded economic resources which gave them local pre-eminence, and where lawmen – the *iudices* of the records – provided social cohesion where the forms of lordship which modern historians have come to regard as 'normal' were otherwise absent.

The possible lack of pre-twelfth-century lordship structures in 'greater Galloway' may be reflected in the vagueness of the original grants made by David to his settler-lords. Robert de Bruce in Annandale, for example, received the same undefined rights as those enjoyed by Ranulf le Meschin in Carlisle, and, if Professor Duncan's suggestion of later royal curtailment of an originally very generous judicial franchise is correct, his power may have been based primarily on jurisdictional lordship rather than property rights.[111] Obligations, too, were vague, it being only in William's reign that the service of ten knights was specified as the due for the lordship.[112] Annandale, however, was nevertheless one of the more institutionally developed areas of this western zone, for the Glasgow inquest records a series of ecclesiastical properties which probably originated as possessions of a monastery at Hoddom.[113] The Avenel lordship in Eskdale presents a more undeveloped aspect, particularly in the valley's upper reaches. Although there is evidence for the expansion of settlement and arable cultivation here in the late eleventh and twelfth centuries,[114] much of the seasonally exploited upland zone became 'forest' for its new lords, and even in the 1210s had a 'free zone' character, where wolves and thieves, 'the peasant's primeval . . . and his societal enemy', were a still-present threat.[115] While there is extensive archaeological evidence for prehistoric and early-historic settlement in this western fringe of the massif centred on Ettrick Forest, there is no clear indication of a hierarchy of lordship in the sites before the Avenels'

---

[111] Barrow (ed.), *David I Charters*, no. 16; Duncan, 'Bruces', 93.
[112] Barrow (ed.), *RRS*, ii, no. 80.
[113] *Glasgow Registrum*, no. 1; Lowe, *Hoddom*, 192–6; Radford, 'Hoddom', 174–97.
[114] Tipping, 'Medieval woodland history', 52–75.
[115] *Melrose Liber*, no. 196; Kapelle, *Norman Conquest of the North*, 7.

development of their motte at Brantalloch.[116] We can perhaps glimpse here the remains of an earlier social order over which an exploitative lordship was imposed.

The exceptional development of Galloway under Fergus points to another route by which power could be accrued and monopolised. It has been proposed that Fergus was a 'creation' of Henry I of England, who gave his son-in-law military backing to construct a power base for himself as part of a wider policy of state-building around the Solway and northern Irish Sea zone.[117] That, however, begs the question of what made Fergus attractive to Henry and secured him a marriage to a bastard daughter of the English king in the first place. It is unlikely that he was simply a 'promising youth' in whom Henry saw potential, although lingering but unverifiable traditions of an early career at the English court might preserve a dim memory of the gravitational pull exerted on ambitious young men by the household of a remote but powerful overking in whose hands lay the patronage that could be their making. This is the tradition reflected in medieval tales of the court of King Arthur, and in the Scottish Romance epic *Fergus*.[118] It is evident in reality at the court of Henry I where both David of Scotland and Óláfr of Man were amongst the young aspirants, and which was still an established feature of Scandinavian society in the early thirteenth century, as reflected in the handbook of parental advice known as *The King's Mirror*.[119] Fergus, however, was already on an upward trajectory before his identification by Henry as a man to be drawn into his orbit and any political attraction may have been reciprocal.[120] Henry's assertive kingship in the western maritime zone provided a vehicle for Fergus's personal ambitions, while support for Fergus strengthened Henry's kingly authority in a politically unstable region.

Assertive, predatory kingship and the affirmation of its aristocratic supporters can also be seen in action in the progressive tightening of royal control over the northern mainland. Traditionally, evidence for the intensification there of royal authority and the establishment of a nobility loyal to the ruling dynasty between 1130 and 1230 has been identified in the mottes sited at strategic points through the country

---

[116] See the discussion of settlement hierarchy in *RCAHMS*, *Eastern Dumfriesshire*.
[117] Scott, 'Strathclyde 1092–1153', 24–6.
[118] Le Clerc, *Fergus*.
[119] See Hollister, *Henry I*, Chapter 8, for a critique of the tradition of Henry's 'New Men'; Larson (trans.), *The King's Mirror*.
[120] Oram, *Lordship of Galloway*, Chapter 2.

between Aberdeen and Inverness, while assertion of domination through legitimate violence has been seen in royal campaigns further north, again marked by earthwork fortifications perhaps even in Caithness.[121] Mottes, like Duffus near Elgin, appear to provide unequivocal evidence for the creation of new social and political elites, amongst whom the land of dispossessed Gaelic lords was divided by the victorious king, while he secured his own grip using royal castles and attendant burghs at former administrative centres of the province. New research, however, indicates that radical revision of this view is required, not least because the colonial aristocracy were fewer than popularly presented, and their arrival began after c. 1150 rather than 1130. The principal beneficiaries from the overthrow of Moray's native rulers in the 1130s were instead other Gaelic magnates, amongst whom the mountainous hinterland, which, in terms of Gaelic cultural perceptions, contained its most valuable economic resources, the upland pastures, was divided into a series of lordships based on ancient economic units known as *dabhaichean*. This partition apparently saw continuity in traditional cultural and economic practices and there is no evidence for a wider settlement of dependents or process of subinfeudation. The new lords' relationship with the crown was perhaps defined in 'feudal' terms, but the lordship which they exercised rested on pre-feudal structures.

No one prescription can wholly or satisfactorily explain the range of forms and changing processes by which power was exercised and defined in the period spanned by this study. Simple narratives that present a notion of a monolithic structure in starkly 'pre-feudal' or 'feudal' terms are inadequate as explanations for the diversity of structures and mechanisms through which individuals or social groups wielded power and authority. From the foregoing, it can be seen that even 'feudalising' monarchs were required to work within a patchwork of divergent systems and that consilience and the establishment of uniformity of practice was not achieved by even the most effective of state-building Scottish kings. Lordship, through which power was mainly exercised, appears to have been founded more upon jurisdictional power than on property, and the nature of the jurisdictions and the manner of their exercise varied in different parts of the emerging kingdom.

---

[121] Talbot, 'Earth and timber castles', 3.

CHAPTER 7

Reworking Old Patterns: Rural Change, c. 1070–1230

Across northern Europe, the period from the mid-eleventh century until the closing decades of the thirteenth century saw steady economic expansion.[1] Fundamental to this development were the efforts of the peasantry, whose agricultural production powered the economic motor. As already explored in the discussion of power relationships, the social structures and behaviour of the peasantry were breaking down and reforming into new patterns. This phenomenon rests rather uneasily with deep-rooted notions of an intensely conservative society pursuing the same approaches to agriculture and relationships with the land as their ancestors had. Instead, throughout central and northern France, Germany and parts of the British Isles, it is now recognised that there was significant social reorganisation involving a shift towards a communal, village-like type of agricultural base, which brought a profound change in the nature of agrarian enterprise.[2] A move from subsistence to surplus production of cereals, a consequence of a trend towards the generally warmer and drier conditions of the so-called 'Medieval Warm Period' that began in the later tenth century, coincided with a number of significant technological developments which enabled the peasants to exploit the opportunities presented by climatic improvement to the full and expand their levels of operation.

---

[1] For discussion see Dyer, *Making a Living in the Middle Ages*, especially Chapters 3–5; Bouchard, 'Rural economy and society', 88–90.
[2] See Chapelot and Fossier, *Village and House*.

POPULATION GROWTH AND AGRICULTURAL EXPANSION

Climate change had significant environmental consequences to which both the European peasantry and landholding entrepreneurs responded and moved to exploit whenever conditions allowed. The principal development was in the widening of the range of agricultural exploitation, with successful cultivation of cereals – the peasant staple across much of mainland Europe and southern Britain – becoming sustainable at higher altitudes, while the drier conditions also enabled the working of valley bottoms which had earlier been prone to flooding or waterlogging. Greater access to better-quality iron tools and implements for clearing new areas of ground and the improved cultivation of existing fields facilitated the exploitation of this widened landscape range. The *carruca*-type plough, for example, usually pulled by teams of eight oxen and with an iron blade for cutting through the turf and mouldboard for turning the sod, could tackle heavier valley-bottom soils or stony uplands, while better tools and animal harnesses speeded up and improved clearance operations in areas of woodland and scrub.[3] We should not underestimate the effect of these improvements in agricultural technology, for they represented real labour-saving devices which vastly speeded up and eased the process of cultivation. While the physical effort involved continued to be arduous, in comparison to the older and simpler scratch plough more ground could be worked and prepared to a more productive level in less time, thereby permitting the peasant cultivators to increase scales of operation and broaden the range of their activities. Water mills, too, freed more time and concomitantly more labour – largely of women – which could then be applied to other activities, for more grain could be ground to flour more quickly and efficiently than had been possible using hand mills or querns. The intensification and extension of agriculture permitted by this new technology, the diversification that the freeing of labour time allowed and above all the agricultural surpluses that stemmed ultimately from the improving climate, together created a prolonged episode of wider economic growth.

A sustained period of environmental and economic well-being triggered a further expansion: population. The resulting rise in demand for land and its produce maintained the economic boom. In England, plentiful evidence survives for the scale of population growth and the physical extent of the expansion in human settlement, and of its environmental

[3] Duncan, *Making of the Kingdom*, 310–11.

impact, in the number of manorial records that survive from the eleventh century onwards, headed of course by the unique account of *Domesday Book*. Scotland, in comparison, possesses a meagre handful of such records, none of which is from earlier than the late thirteenth century or contains material of similar quality to that preserved in English documents.[4] Nevertheless, from the many hundreds of charters that do survive from this period it is possible to trace agricultural transformation and continuity of practice, peasant responses to changing environmental or economic conditions, and above all the unsteady pressures applied to human society and the environment by the rapid increase in population and attendant consumer demand. What the documentary record reveals is that alongside the redefinition of socio-economic and political relationships characteristic of this period, medieval society was also moving towards more aggressive expression of its relationship with nature. Domination and lordship were not simply aspects of social relationships on individual, community or national levels, but were also central dynamics in the reformulation of peasant culture colouring in particular attitudes towards the exploitation of the land and the resources that it bore.

It is in the expansion of settlement and its associated agricultural activities that environmental impact can most readily be seen, but intensive human pressure on the wider Scottish environment was not a new phenomenon in the Middle Ages. Fixed settlements and arable agriculture had been features of the Scottish landscape since the Neolithic period, beginning some 6,000 years ago, and their long history had seen cycles of intensification/extension and decline occasioned by a range of probable human and environmental factors, such as population pressures, disease and climate change. Cultivation entails a radical shift in the nature and impact of human exploitation of the land, requiring clearance of existing ground cover and subsequent prevention of regeneration of that vegetation; disturbance of underlying soils and alteration of their content and composition through inputs of fertilising material; and removal of minerals and chemical elements through leaching and crop growth. Invasive crop-growing practices, moreover, alter the drainage structure within the soil and lead to waterlogging or, conversely, increased run-off with the attendant risk of soil erosion or, at best, freer drainage which can prove detrimental or beneficial to different plant species. All of these changes can result in significant shifts in ecological balances in the landscape.

---

[4] See *Domesday Book*. For English manorial accounts, see Bailey (ed. and trans.), *The English Manor*. The main Scottish survival is the Rent Roll of Kelso Abbey, datable to c. 1300. See *Kelso Liber*, ii, 455–73.

Knock-on effects of any rise in human settlement associated with the cultivation include felling of trees for materials for housing, constructing enclosures, manufacture of tools and domestic utensils, fuel and further room for cultivation to support expanding settlements. When these effects are combined with the introduction of domesticated herds grazing in nearby woodland or open grass and moors, construction of linear barriers for demarcation and containment or management of the water resources, the ramifications extend far beyond a 'simple' switch in land use.

Since the first arrival of people in what became mainland Scotland, all human activity has produced shifts that may at first have been subtle but which became increasingly profound in their environmental impact.[5] Amongst the most obvious of these human impacts was the dramatic reduction in the extent and nature of woodlands between the Neolithic period and the late Iron Age around 1,500 years ago. While much of the decline is anthropogenic, climate change and other environmental factors played a significant part in the process.[6] A rapid acceleration in the rate of woodland clearance in southern Scotland after c. 500 BC, however, can be attributed largely to the spread into the region of a northern European-style agricultural regime.[7] Maintenance of intensive cereal production through the Roman period and the timber and turf requirements of the Roman military may have prevented any significant regeneration into the early centuries AD, but in parts of southern Scotland as dispersed as the lower Forth valley, the south-eastern Lammermuirs, central Galloway and northern Renfrewshire the generalised inference from pollen evidence is that there was either reversion from agricultural use to woodland or, as in the central Southern Uplands, a decline in the extent of cultivation.[8] Despite such regeneration, in some parts of the country tree cover by the early medieval period was little more extensive than modern levels and throughout much of the Southern Uplands zone was reduced to dispersed but potentially still locally extensive tracts managed by the surrounding populations for hunting, grazing and timber needs. This position remained stable down to the eleventh century when a second period of rapid and dramatic decline commenced.

In common with the upward trend identified across Europe,

---

[5] For an introduction to these issues, see Simmons, *Environmental History*.

[6] See, for example, Tipping, 'Living in the pasts', 14–39; Armit and Ralston, 'The coming of iron', 40–59; Edwards and Ralston (eds), *Scotland: Environment and Archaeology*.

[7] Armit and Ralston, 'The coming of iron', 44.

[8] Ibid. 52, Fig. 2.3.

population levels in Scotland probably began to increase in the course of the eleventh century. There is no documentary evidence to support that inference unequivocally but certain archaeological data points in that direction. In particular, physical evidence for agricultural expansion, especially arable cultivation, has been interpreted as indicating a level of organisation that both produced the surpluses that permitted an increased population and, conversely, reflected the need to meet the growing demands of an expanding population. Societal changes provide the context within which colonising agriculture could be organised, but technological developments permitted the expansion to be achieved. Although the amount of work as yet undertaken has been very limited both in quantity and in its distribution around Scotland, palynology – the analysis of plant pollen preserved in archaeologically datable deposits – indicates that the eleventh century saw a re-advance of agrarian activity in some areas. In the south-western Southern Uplands, for example, pollen from a site at Over Rig appears to record a clearance of willow scrub and reinstatement of coppiced hazel woodland, accompanied by intensification of livestock grazing and progressive expansion of arable cultivation through the eleventh and twelfth centuries.[9] A similar picture of a managed landscape emerges in the eastern Southern Uplands, where pollen profiles from sites in the Bowmont Valley suggest that a period of radical change started c. 1100. At one low-lying site near Yetholm Loch an increased acreage may have been under cereal cultivation, with oats and probably rye predominating, and barley also perhaps grown. A nearby upland site on Mow Law showed evidence for possible intensified grassland management, where grazed grassland was being burned possibly to increase the nutrient availability of forage grasses, but there were also limited episodes of cereal cultivation. Here, and at other sites locally, the post-1100 period saw the development of grassy heathland, perhaps linked to the spread of intensive sheep pasturing in the uplands through the twelfth century.[10] Further north, at Dogden Moss in the south-eastern Lammermuir Hills, woodland cover also declined and grassland extended until c. 1200, with possible contraction in cultivation after c. 1050,[11] a phenomenon perhaps linked to the development of extensive cattle ranges or sheep runs in the area.

Such changes in agricultural management practice in northern Europe have been viewed traditionally as the product of monastic

---

[9] Tipping, 'Medieval woodland history', 66–7 and 68–71.
[10] Tipping, 'Bowmont Valley', 42–5.
[11] Tipping, 'Palaeoecology and political history', 17.

entrepreneurship, and in the Southern Uplands both Kelso and Melrose abbeys built up extensive propertied interests from the mid-1100s. The expansion of both arable cultivation and increased grassland exploitation, however, may predate the foundation of these monasteries. Over-emphasis in the past on monastic land-management practices and too-ready acceptance of the monks' self-perception as improving landlords has perhaps seen lay initiatives undertaken by peasant cultivators in the late eleventh and early twelfth centuries mistakenly labelled as examples of monastic pioneering.[12] The lay role in large-scale development is generally under-represented in discussion of agricultural expansion in medieval Scotland, in large part due to the paucity of supporting documentation, but analysis of the spread of settlement and agriculture in northern England provides a model which can be usefully applied in at least southern Scotland.[13] In the central Southern Uplands, the trigger for change may have come from the redefinition of the regional political structures in the 1090s and early 1100s, with the main phases of development including monastic plantations being initiated most probably by David I after c. 1113. The Ettrick Forest region, which may have formed a marchland between Cumbrian and Northumbrian territory through the late tenth and the eleventh centuries, experienced an extended period of development which lasted into the late thirteenth century as the territories to its east and west were integrated into the Scottish kingdom. The monks played a significant part in this process, but royal plantation of a colonising nobility and development of a burgh-based economic infrastructure were equally important in the more intensive exploitation of this formerly liminal zone.

WASTE AND WOODLAND

Direct evidence for secular lordly enterprise in twelfth-century Scotland is rare, with most instances instead being drawn from inferences in charters of the principal religious institutions. The cartularies of the abbeys of south-eastern Scotland yield a detailed picture from the 1120s onwards of regional environmental, social and economic development. Although the traditional image of the twelfth-century monastic foundations emphasises the monks' desire to have their communities located in desert places distant from existing population centres, only Kelso's

---

[12] For critiques, see Bartlett, *Making of Europe*, 153–5 and Oram, 'Prayer, property and profit', 90–2.
[13] Kapelle, *Norman Conquest of the North*, Chapters 3 and 6.

> **Assarts**
>
> In early-twelfth-century documents, records appear of *assarts*, or new exploitation for cultivation of land previously designated as 'waste' (that is, land not being used for agricultural production). These records confirm the picture of an expansion settlement and of agrarian activity which is traceable in the pollen record from the tenth and eleventh centuries. The shape of pollen grains is species-specific, and indentification of different types by microscopic analysis of peat and soil samples gives a good indication of what the local vegetation was like at a given period. Wind-borne pollen of plants is deposited and preserved in peat and soil and changes in the amounts of a specific type present can be indicative of wider changes in the local environment. Thus, the pollen data offers a subtler record of change than is recoverable from the documents, revealing evidence for crop types unrepresented in the texts, for the impact on woodland, grassland and bog of intensified exploitation, and for management regimes that are otherwise recorded nowhere in the medieval sources. Parchment records, however, enable us to identify more precisely the chronology of the processes and the social and cultural mechanisms that carried them out. Lauderdale, for example, experienced a phase of arable extension beyond the sixth- to eleventh-century agricultural limits by the 1140s, with assarts at Blainslie, Kedslie, 'Alwin's land' and Sorrowlessfield made into the woodland and scrubland on the western side of the valley.[14] Although recorded in charters of Melrose and Dryburgh abbeys, these institutions were only taking over what were instances of peasant enterprise encouraged by the estate managers of its lay lord, Hugh de Morville. These assarts provide us with some of the clearest evidence for rising population levels and increased demand for food, and for expansion into what might nowadays be deemed more marginal areas encouraged by the more amenable climatic conditions of the tenth to thirteenth centuries.

original site at Selkirk, on the eastern edge of the old border land between Cumbria and Northumbria, lay in country that came close to meeting that ideal. But even the 'inconvenient place' of Selkirk was not unpeopled territory, and the records of Melrose and Dryburgh also document a landscape already divided into blocks of property by 'old' ditches

---

[14] *Melrose Liber*, nos 93–5; *Dryburgh Liber*, nos 109–12; Gilbert, 'Monastic record of a Borders landscape'.

and where abandoned prehistoric fortifications were marker points for boundaries.[15] Indeed, not only was the human landscape in which the abbeys were planted already ancient by the mid-twelfth century, it was also experiencing recent and rapid transformation as agricultural settlement expanded and the exploitation of the environment of the river valleys and the adjacent uplands intensified.

The extent of landscape transformation underway through the twelfth century and the rapidity with which it was effected can be traced in the records of Melrose and Dryburgh abbeys in the district extending from the east side of Lauderdale to Wedale (the valley of the Gala Water) in the west and northwards to the moors that climbed to the southern flank of the Lammermuir Hills.[16] Their interest in this zone was drawn not only by simple proximity to the abbeys, which permitted direct exploitation, but also by its relative underdevelopment as an agricultural resource. As with Ettrick Forest, this upland district was a frontier zone, a status reflected in the boundaries of the archdeaconries of Lothian and Teviotdale which cut across it, possibly fossilising an earlier political division. By the 1150s, cultivation in the core of this upland region constituted only a handful of open areas (referred to in the charters as *landi*, or 'lawns', and *planities*, or 'cleared ground') in what was otherwise a landscape of wood, scrub and moor that stretched almost from Tweed to Lammermuir, but within half a century a principal component in Melrose's agricultural property portfolio lay within this area. Built up by systematic acquisitions between the late 1130s and the early 1200s, it comprised 900 hectares in the valley bottom opposite the abbey which had been granted outright to the monks, plus rights to pasture, to take timber for their own uses and to pannage in over 7,100 hectares of upland bounded east and west by the two river valleys, and on the north by the de Morville lordship of Lauderdale and the Wedale estates of the bishops of St Andrews.[17] Dryburgh also had interests in this district at Kedslie, which it developed as a grange (an outlying farm complex),[18] but its chief concentration of properties lay in northern and eastern Lauderdale. The monasteries, however, were not alone in their desire to exploit the natural resources of the area, and it is wrong to see them as the sole pioneers who

---

[15] *Kelso Liber*, no. 2 'locus non erat conveniens'; *Dryburgh Liber*, nos 58, 104, 110, 114.
[16] See Gilbert, 'Monastic record', 4–15; Fawcett and Oram, *Melrose Abbey*, 213–21; Fawcett and Oram, *Dryburgh Abbey*, 146–52.
[17] Gilbert, 'Monastic record'.
[18] *Dryburgh Liber*, no. 109.

Shrinking woodland

There is a misconception that Scotland was still heavily wooded in the earlier Middle Ages but that this woodland succumbed to human action in later centuries. Analysis of pollen evidence, however, shows that tree cover had fallen to around its present level in Prehistory and that much decline was climate-driven. Nevertheless, assarting and grazing pressure caused further woodland decline in Lowland Scotland before c. 1250. In the northern Cheviot Hills pollen evidence suggests that woodland there consisted of dispersed, managed copses, while nearby upland stands were perhaps enclosed to protect them from grazing.[19] Such patchy woodland is recorded in Berwickshire in the late 1160s, when King William granted Coldingham Priory rights in nine named woods.[20]

Small, specifically named woods in a landscape of otherwise arable and pastoral character can be glimpsed widely around Scotland from the later 1100s. In Moray, for example, when Kinloss Abbey received Burgie it lay between two woods, one called 'the great wood of Kelbuthac',[21] and on Deeside in the early 1200s, Arbroath acquired the Wood of Trustach west of Banchory as a stand of timber with defined boundaries.[22] Near Renfrew, Penuld or Fullton had by c. 1170 two stands of trees amongst its boundary markers, the larger called 'Barpennald'.[23] The proliferation of named woods in post-1250 Lennox charters has led to suggestions that this reflects a shift from a landscape where agriculture was concentrated in clearances in more or less continuous woodland to a point where there were islands of trees in otherwise open countryside.[24] More extensive oak and pine woodland existed in parts of the Highlands, especially along the rivers flowing into the Moray Firth. This, however, was no 'primeval' forest but a managed resource which supplied building material to coastal districts as well as providing for local needs in a still largely timber-built environment, and was also used as 'wood-pasture' for grazing cattle. By around 1200, there was little in Scotland that could truly be labelled as 'natural' woodland.

---

[19] Tipping, 'Bowmont Valley', 45.
[20] Barrow (ed.), *RRS*, ii, no. 46.
[21] Barrow (ed.), *RRS*, ii, no. 159.
[22] *Arbroath Liber*, no. 65.
[23] *Paisley Registrum*, 49.
[24] Tittensor, 'Loch Lomond oakwoods', 103.

transformed supposedly undeveloped wilderness into a profit-yielding agricultural landscape.

David I had described the wooded areas of central Tweeddale as 'my forest',[25] terminology introduced from Norman England where large tracts of countryside were established as carefully regulated, exclusive hunting reserves. The 'forest between Gala and Leader' may have been designated a royal hunting ground soon after 1113 when David acquired Tweeddale as part of his Cumbrian principality. The label, however, did not have the modern meaning of an expanse of dense woodland, for 'forest' in the Middle Ages denoted the land areas reserved chiefly for hunting and subject to special laws governing their exploitation, and it has been commented that a number of Scotland's medieval forests had probably contained few or no trees since later prehistory.[26] Nevertheless, in the early twelfth century much of the area was covered by a mix of oak and birch woodland interspersed with rough grassland and scrub, with willow and alder woods in the lower-lying fringes. Its description as 'waste' can also mislead modern readers, for the afforested area was exploited routinely by the inhabitants of the settlements that lined its margins, as summer pasture for cattle and sheep, a source of autumn pannage for pigs and of winter feed for the livestock left unslaughtered in November, and for building materials and fuel. All of these resources were of considerable value, not just in financial terms, to landlords and their tenants. The economic value of 'waste' to lordly and, presumably, peasant incomes is made explicit, for example, in the grant by Walter I son of Alan to the monks of Paisley of the teinds of 'all my wastes'.[27] As a source of a variety of teindable resources, lords were perhaps understandably reluctant to permit unregulated agricultural encroachment upon forests and waste, and efforts were made to limit peasant inroads. As mentioned above, peasant farmers in Lauderdale had also begun to nibble at the forest margins to the west, but their assarts were restricted principally to the lower-lying southern and eastern fringes of the 'waste', with the main upland area remaining unsettled.

Melrose did not have full and exclusive ownership or use of the upland, only sharing in the exploitation of its resources with the inhabitants of settlements in Wedale and Lauderdale. Furthermore, valuable though the assarted land granted to Melrose and Dryburgh was, as they lay on the more easily tilled fine brown forest soils, they were constrained

---

[25] *Melrose Liber*, no. 1.
[26] Crone and Watson, 'Sufficiency to scarcity', 69.
[27] *Paisley Registrum*, 6.

by a prohibition on further encroachment into the king's forest. At Blainslie and Kedslie, Melrose and Dryburgh could cultivate only areas under plough at the time of their grant to them, and expand into open areas on the edge of the woodland, but they were expressly forbidden to make fresh assarts.[28] In Wedale, at Colmslie, Buckholm and Whitelee, Melrose developed primarily pastoral granges within the forest area, but with similar constraints on development beyond established limits. Numbers of stock and the sites and sizes of buildings to house them and their herdsmen were regulated. Such structures were important, as the stock was driven from the upland and wooded districts at night, possibly because of wolf predation, but building consent involved protracted negotiation. Shortly after 1162, for example, Malcolm IV allowed Melrose to construct a cowshed and pen for 100 cows at Colmslie.[29] It was only in c. 1190 that King William confirmed the monks' right to a cowshed for 60 cows and a house for their herdsmen within an established cattle enclosure at Buckholm,[30] and a shed for 100 cows or a shelter for 120 sheep (perhaps reflecting a shift in Melrose's interests towards wool production by the 1180s) at Whitelee.[31] There, they were allowed to build a house for their herdsmen and a store for hay but were still forbidden to construct anything more substantial than temporary wicker shelters for their men within the forest limits. For the abbeys these were irksome constraints, impeding development of either the arable or the pastoral potential of land on their doorsteps, where the produce could directly support the monastic households. Initially, Melrose responded by acquiring neighbouring properties in western Lauderdale but soon began to push cultivation beyond the original arable area, make extensive new assarts in the forest and intensify its exploitation of the forest's common resources. Dryburgh, too, extended its interests beyond general right to pasture in the woods around Kedslie, adding Alwin's land and the *landus*, or forest clearing, of 'Herdesley'.[32] Before the 1180s, the imprecision of David I's original grants had been skilfully exploited by the abbeys, but at the cost of provoking others with an interest in the forest's resources into legal action to protect their rights.

This steady expansion of activity in the mid-twelfth century stretched the forest resources, for Melrose and Dryburgh were not its only

---

[28] *Melrose Liber*, no. 93.
[29] Barrow (ed.), *RRS*, i, no. 235.
[30] *Melrose Liber*, no. 107; Barrow (ed.), *RRS*, ii, no. 301.
[31] *Melrose Liber*, no. 106.
[32] *Dryburgh Liber*, nos 112 and 240.

exploiters; royal tenants, the bishops of St Andrews and the de Morville lords of Lauderdale also sought to maximise their rights within it. Melrose's drive to secure maximum benefit for itself triggered conflict with other users, most notably Dryburgh and the de Morvilles (who were the hereditary royal foresters). The abbeys settled their dispute as early as 1164,[33] but it was only in 1181 that disputes between Melrose and Richard de Morville concerning the extent of the forest and pasture was decided in the king's court.[34] This conflict arose from the incompatibility of Melrose's desire to extend its pasture and Richard's desire to preserve the hunting grounds around Threepwood in the heart of the forest. The monks won, and de Morville gave them a fresh charter which carefully redefined their position with regard to the contested pasture. In it, however, de Morville reserved his right to keep a resident forester who was charged with the oversight of his remaining game interests in the forest area and the responsibility of ensuring that the monks did not exceed their enhanced liberties. Three years later, de Morville arbitrated in a similar dispute between Melrose and the Wedale men over rights to forest pasture, which produced another careful delineation of boundaries.[35] So valuable were the resources at stake, however, that this settlement did not end the dispute over the limits of their grazing in Wedale, with a disagreement with the tenants of the bishop of St Andrews resulting in violence, death and excommunication in the 1260s and litigation which dragged on into the fourteenth century.[36]

Agreements like the 1181 settlement sought to balance the continued use of the forest as a hunting ground and the desire of other users to extend their economic privileges within it. Royal hunting rights still took precedence over even so favoured a monastery as Melrose, but an effort was made to accommodate both functions. Sophisticated mechanisms to monitor activity within the woodland and scrub areas, primarily to preserve areas where game could shelter and feed, were set in place. Even where pasture was permitted, the king's forester could deny access during specified seasons, especially the fawning period from 9 June to 9 July, and activities such as pannage of pigs or the making of fresh assarts were formally regulated and recorded. The 1181 settlement provided some stability until c. 1230, when pressure to relax the restrictions was again evident. Finally, in 1236 Alexander II redefined

---

[33] *Dryburgh Liber*, no. 113.
[34] Barrow (ed.), *RRS*, ii, no. 236.
[35] *Chron. Melrose*, s.a. 1184.
[36] Fawcett and Oram, *Melrose Abbey*, 216–17.

forest boundaries in respect of all of Melrose's lands and placed the abbey's properties outwith the forests' limits. This act removed residual restrictions on the monks' exploitation of their lands.

Identical pressures on woodland can be identified elsewhere around the country. Further east, in Jed Forest, or to the south-west in the baronial forest in Liddesdale, fieldwork has identified surviving physical evidence for assarting and for the development of managed landscapes of agricultural or pastoral exploitation.[37] In the Stewart lordship of Renfrew, Walter II son of Alan gave the monks of Paisley a block of undeveloped land on the northern slopes of the Fereneze Hills, a district of scrubby country partly within his baronial forest, with permission to 'make assarts, plough and build' without interference, and to make hedged and fenced enclosures within it.[38] Recent research in the Lennox and Strathearn suggests that woodlands in both contracted steadily after c. 1170 as more land was given over to pasture and the plough,[39] but the main impact in these areas before c. 1300 was through exploitation for building materials and fuel.[40] The colonisation of the Moray coastlands in the mid-twelfth century by a mix of Flemish developers, pioneering townsmen and monastic cultivators led to new forms and increased levels of exploitation of woodland and marshland throughout the Laich and its immediate hilly hinterland. Around Forres, for example, Malcolm IV granted the monks of Kinloss *landellae*, little lawns or clearings, at Altyre and Burgie which had recently been broken from woodland.[41] Kinloss was keen to expand these assarts and by c. 1176 received a crown grant of the rest of Burgie which removed any constraints on development.[42] In Galloway, oak and alder woods between the rivers Urr and Nith were under sustained attack by the mid-twelfth century. Access to these woods may have been comparatively relaxed until the 1160s, with neighbouring communities finding grazing for their cattle, autumn pannage for pigs and timber for all their domestic needs within them, but the granting of the district to Uhtred, lord of Galloway, probably by King Malcolm IV saw a change in attitude towards them by their new possessor. Before 1170, Uhtred was referring to them as demesne woods, exclusive property on his personal estate whose resources he controlled and access to

---

[37] Dixon, 'Settlement in hunting forests', 345–54.
[38] *Paisley Registrum*, 17.
[39] Neville, *Native Lordship*, 79–105.
[40] See, for example, *Paisley Registrum*, 157, 212, 216 and 220.
[41] Barrow (ed.), *RRS*, i, no. 266. The 'little' clearing at Burgie was one ploughgate, roughly 104 acres.
[42] Barrow (ed.), *RRS*, ii, no.159.

which he regulated.[43] The inhabitants of the surrounding districts still had easements in the woodland (rights of use and exploitation), but Uhtred and his successors began to demand payment or performance of service in return for that privilege. When Uhtred granted the estate of Kirkgunzeon to the monks of Holm Cultram under a feuferme deal, the monks' annual rent of £6 freed them from payment of burdens such as pannage on their pig herds, a deal that implies that other tenants were already paying it.[44] Holm Cultram wanted Kirkgunzeon, described at the time of its original lease to them as a 'vill' and therefore an already established economic unit, for development as a grange to be worked by their lay-brothers. Although the term 'grange' (derived from the same root as 'granary') was originally applied to predominantly arable estates, many granges in Scotland functioned as large-scale livestock farms. At Kirkgunzeon, the land was more suited to stock management than cereal cultivation, large parts of the property comprising of woodland, scrub and moss, but the monks still developed arable wherever suitable.[45]

While the pressure from assarts was significant and sustained, it is apparent that the degree of pressure varied from region to region. Evidence relating to fuel resource exploitation implies that in much of Scotland south of the Forth–Clyde line and extending north through Fife, eastern Perthshire, Angus and the Mearns, woodland was insignificant except in preserves managed mainly as hunting grounds by aristocratic owners. Away from the main areas of population growth, particularly in the more inaccessible parts of the highland zone, woodland remained extensive throughout the Middle Ages. Around the Moray Firth, where agriculture had made substantial inroads from at least the mid-twelfth century, timber was still obtained relatively easily from more remote sources in the hinterland, perhaps floated down rivers in the manner recorded in the seventeenth to nineteenth centuries. The much-quoted reference to Count Hugh of St Pol's ordering of a ship from builders at Inverness before 1249 has been dismissed as an isolated event, but such dismissal misses the point that Inverness must have enjoyed a reputation as a shipbuilding centre for a Continental aristocrat to place an order there, that the burgh possessed craftsmen with the technical expertise to build a large ocean-going vessel and that they had access to timber from which to construct such vessels.[46] While

---

[43] See, for example, *Holm Cultram Register*, no. 120.
[44] Ibid. no. 120.
[45] *Holm Cultram Register*, no. 121. See also Stringer, 'Reform monasticism', 147–51.
[46] Anderson (ed.), *Scottish Annals*, 295, note 2.

the immediate hinterland of the burgh may already have been cleared of most woodland for arable and pastoral developments, the straths radiating from the Beauly Firth still contained stands of oak to meet the demands of Inverness's craftsmen. At the opposite end of the highland zone, in the Lennox, parts of Menteith and upper Strathearn, extensive woodlands survived through the medieval period and formed important economic resources as areas of hunting, pasture and timber supply into the eighteenth century.

At the same time as woodland was coming under pressure through clearance for arable cultivation, in some regions demand for building timber and firewood brought a significant reduction in the already shrunken tree cover. In the Southern Uplands, construction work on royal castles like Roxburgh and at the great monasteries of the region like Kelso and Melrose placed a heavy burden on the woods. The original buildings at the monasteries in the first half of the twelfth century were primarily timber-built, and the crown gave generously from its woodland to furnish necessary materials. Kelso, Melrose and Dryburgh all received permission from David I and his successors to take such wood as necessary for their needs from his forests.[47] What the monks took were not only mature trees for the substantial posts and beams used in the high-status structures within the monasteries, but also younger and smaller growth for posts and secondary roof members plus withies of hazel, alder and willow for fashioning wattling for wall panels, fences and lighter structures. Amongst David I's grants to the canons of Scone, for example, was permission to take fencing timber from woods along the Tay.[48] It is likely, too, that some important buildings had oak shingles for roof cover, while less substantial structures had brushwood roofing in peasant tradition. At Inchaffray in Strathearn, the canons received in 1200 from Earl Gille Brigte the right 'to take timber in [his] woods wherever should be more fitting for them towards the building of their houses and equipment, and cooking fires'.[49] Paisley received from Walter son of Alan II, c. 1208–10 the right to take from his forest of Fereneze and Sanquhar 'sufficient timber from the green [i.e. growing timber] towards building needs, and of fuel from dry and dead wood', without restriction.[50] As the thirteenth century progressed, the frequency with which monasteries sought confirmation of such rights suggests that lords

---

[47] *Kelso Liber*, no. 1; *Melrose Liber*, no. 1, appendix, no. 1; *Dryburgh Liber*, lxix–lxx.
[48] Barrow (ed.), *RRS*, i, no. 57.
[49] *Inchaffray Charters*, no. IX.
[50] *Paisley Registrum*, 17–18.

regretted the generosity of their ancestors and were attempting to rein in levels of exploitation of an increasingly valuable resource.

The second wave of building work at the monasteries in the late twelfth and early thirteenth centuries, funded by the burgeoning wool trade, saw fresh demand for wood, especially the large timbers used in the complex roof structures needed to bridge the enlarged internal spaces. In the Lennox, the clearance was not restricted to the lower-lying and accessible lands around the southern end of Loch Lomond, but occurred as far north as Tarbet. In the early thirteenth century, for example, Domnall mac Gille Chriosd, lord of Tarbet, gave Paisley licence to cut, take and carry away all kinds of timber as was necessary for building work at the abbey, unsupervised by his serjeants.[51] At Arbroath, oak for the roof of the abbey church was obtained from the Wood of Trustach on Deeside, granted to the monks by Thomas Durward towards their building operations,[52] while at Elgin, where building commenced in the 1220s, the royal forests of Longmorn and Darnaway and the bishops' own resources from Speyside were exploited for timber. It was not, however, just privileged ecclesiastical beneficiaries who were making inroads into the timber resources of southern and eastern Scotland, for a heavy demand for both building materials and fuel supplies was made by peasant communities and the steadily expanding burghs.

FUEL

The superficial impression from charters which gave rights to fuel is that wood was the preferred fuel and peat was only employed when the supply of wood declined to a critical level.[53] In some areas, however, woodland was already denuded and peat reserves being exploited before the 1120s. This position is evident in Berwickshire, for example, where amongst Kelso Abbey's early endowments was the right 'to the cutting of earth/turves for making fire' in Ednam moor.[54] The Latin of the charter suggests that its writer was unfamiliar with the practice and struggled to find language to explain it. On the northern slopes of the Lammermuirs

---

[51] *Paisley Registrum*, 157.
[52] *Arbroath Liber*, i, no. 65.
[53] See Barrow (ed.), *RRS*, i, no. 109; Barrow (ed.), *RRS*, ii, nos 39, 88, 226; *Holm Cultram Register*, nos 120, 121; *Melrose Liber*, nos 34, 37, 65. For peat, see *Melrose Liber*, appendix nos 4–7. Coulton, *Scottish Abbeys and Social Life*, 136.
[54] *Kelso Liber*, no. 2.

peat exploitation was so well established by the 1170s that named peateries could be specified in grants rather than simply generalised rights to cut peat somewhere on the land, as can be seen in David son of Robert's gift to the monks of Newbattle of the peatery called 'Wulvestrother' in Borthwick parish.[55] At Eldbotle in the lordship of Dirleton on the East Lothian coast, in an area of intensive human settlement and arable cultivation since the Prehistoric period, woodland was not a feature of either the physical or the notional economic landscape by the early 1200s. When William de Vaux gifted Dryburgh property there, roofing material for the canons' houses came from the coastal bents while fuel came from the common peatery of Eldbotle and Dirleton.[56] In all three areas there were no significant reserves of timber for building, woodworking or fuel for many years before 1100 and peat was established as the primary fuel type by the Early Historic period.

Peat generally became more important as fuel type for large parts of central and southern Scotland after the late 1100s. Although easements in woodland remained an important economic right enjoyed by tenants, reference to peateries and disputes over rights to exploit these assets proliferated in the closing decades of the twelfth century and point to more rigorous exercise of control over peat for fuel. The Moss of Blair in Strathmore, for example, was the subject of a dispute between Coupar Angus and Dunfermline abbeys in the 1220s.[57] The conflict arose from shared rights to the peat moss enjoyed by the inhabitants of lands within Bendochy parish possessed by the two abbeys. Although Coupar Angus secured the whole of moss and won unrestricted rights of access and egress to it through the Dunfermline property, Dunfermline's tenants had a servitude on the moss which permitted them to cut 200 cartloads of peat annually. This award indicates the level of demand for peat and points to the scale of the environmental impact of cutting operations. The working of peat mosses in the landscape around the priory at Whithorn resulted in the removal of all the exploitable material before the close of the Middle Ages. Again, monastic hunger for peat by the early 1200s may be indicative of a wider demand for fuel in rural and urban communities. Population pressure, denudation of traditional resources and basic changes to the underlying patterns of traditional agriculture were bringing about one of the most radical reorderings of the Scottish landscape

---

[55] *Newbattle Registrum*, no. 13.
[56] *Dryburgh Liber*, no. 104.
[57] *Coupar Angus Chrs*, nos XXXII and XXXIII; Ferguson, *Papal Representatives*, 137, 226.

Figure 7.1 The Carse of Gowrie, Perth and Kinross: peasant-led drainage of the marshy carseland along the northern side of the Tay estuary had created extensive zones of new arable land here before the end of the twelfth century.

between the first development of settled agricultural communities in the Neolithic and the 'Improvements' of the eighteenth century.

DRAINING THE MARSHES

It was not just woodland and grass moorland that was being broken into cultivation at this time, for inroads were being made also into coastal, estuarine and landward marshland. Substantial reclamation work was being undertaken in the marshes and poorly drained clay soils of the Carse of Gowrie, where from the 1180s Coupar Angus Abbey developed a substantial grange at 'Edderpolles', now known simply as Grange.[58] Agricultural exploitation here was not new, for the higher islands of ground in the Carse and the gravelly ridge extending from east of St Madoes to Errol had long been under cultivation or exploited for

---

[58] *Coupar Angus Chrs*, nos III, IV, XXV.

pasture.[59] Agreements in the 1190s over teind payable to the Church of Errol from Edderpolles suggest that arable was already an established component of the local agricultural regime, as does reference to the pond of a mill there possessed by David de Hay, lord of Errol, c. 1200.[60] In the second quarter of the thirteenth century the monks expanded their grange through further acquisitions from lay landholders, gaining blocks of arable extending to around 120 acres that had been broken out of former pasture bearing names such as Aithmuir and the Muirhouse.[61] Such lay ownership suggests that it was not just the Cistercians of Coupar Angus who were actively expanding the arable acreage of the settlements in the Carse, but the scale of the monastic enterprise alone was nevertheless considerable. An indication of their level of labour investment can be seen by the mid-1200s in the causeway they constructed from the higher ground at Inchture across the wet land to their grange, some 2.5km south-west.[62] In Strathmore, which nowadays has the aspect of an almost continuous expanse of prime arable extending from northeast of Perth almost through to Stonehaven, Coupar Angus was also responsible for directing the development of extensive areas of mossland and fenny marsh. Around 1200, for example, the king granted the monks 'the whole of [his] marsh in the territory of Blairgowrie', while Michael of Meigle granted all his rights in the marshland around the confluence of the rivers Isla and Dean,[63] which was drained progressively over the years and developed as arable and pasture. At Inchaffray Abbey in the early 1200s the canons made intakes from the surrounding marshes by enclosing blocks of ground with drainage ditches and expanding the cultivable land outwards from small fields on adjoining higher land.[64] There are also indications that significant drainage work was being undertaken by Kinloss Abbey in the salt marshes of the Laich of Moray and around Findhorn Bay at the same time as clearance of woodland was occurring in the district.

The surviving record for such reclamation work, mainly monastic cartularies, again overstates the importance of the monasteries in the process. As with woodland clearance, it is apparent that several

---

[59] Maxwell, 'Aerial archaeology in south-east Perthshire', 452–4, summarises *RCAHMS, South-East Perth*.
[60] *Coupar Angus Chrs*, no. III; *Coupar Angus Rental*, i, 337. See also Duncan, *Making of the Kingdom*, 320–1.
[61] *Coupar Angus Chrs*, nos XLII, XLVII, LVII.
[62] Ibid. no. XXXVII.
[63] Barrow (ed.), *RRS*, ii, no. 420; *Coupar Angus Chrs*, no. XVII.
[64] *Inchaffray Liber*, nos II and XXXVII.

monasteries benefited from the efforts of peasant cultivators whose landlords granted their properties to the church in a partly developed state. Elsewhere, the monastic records reveal that other reclamation work was taking place alongside their own. For example, we have already seen that while Coupar Angus was developing its grange at 'Edderpolles', the neighbouring communities around Errol were equally active, and at Inchture the peasant tenants also extended their arable out from their island of high ground and developed new areas of cultivation on the shore (*plaga*).[65] One of the largest reclamation works, moreover, may have been begun under the direction of the colonial entrepreneur of Flemish extraction, Freskin, to whom David I gave Duffus in the Laich of Moray.[66] Freskin's charter does not survive, but a confirmation given to his son reveals a physically extensive property between Elgin and the coast, comprising the lands of Roseisle, Inchkeil, Duffus itself, Kintrae ('Head of the Shore') and an unidentified property called 'Machar', a Gaelic name signifying a low-lying tract of ground along a shoreline, all of which lay on the margins of the expanse of salt marsh and lagoon known as the Loch of Spynie.[67] In the modern landscape, this block comprises some 50km^2 of largely arable land, but drainage of the area was completed only in the mid-nineteenth century, and in the mid-twelfth century it was still predominantly undeveloped marsh. It is likely that Freskin had been given a speculative grant of low-grade land which he and his descendants gradually converted into profitable agriculture through intakes from the loch's shallow margins. The rise to regional dominance of this family of drainage engineers underscores the economic dynamic that powered this period of agricultural expansion.

EXPLOITING ARABLE GROWTH: TEINDS AND MILLS

The evidence for woodland and marshland development reviewed above allows us to obtain some indication of the scale and distribution of arable cultivation from the late eleventh century onwards. It is, however, patchy evidence, for the fact that further agricultural development would take place beyond the existing limits of cultivation appears to have been an unstated given in most of the grants, with the progress of arable

---

[65] *Coupar Angus Chrs*, no. XXV.
[66] Oram, 'Castles and colonists'.
[67] Barrow (ed.), *RRS*, ii, no. 116.

expansion only becoming evident in later documents. Except where such expansion was in conflict with other economic activities or rights, as in afforested areas, most landlords presumably encouraged agricultural developments in both arable and pastoral activity which would increase the value of their property. No records survive of estate incomes in the twelfth and early thirteenth centuries, and there are few documented examples to illustrate the nature and composition of the estate economy, although there are some crude indicators of a burgeoning arable sector. The clearest impression of the scale of agrarian expansion, however, comes from evidence for the proliferation of corn mills and a steadily increasing volume of litigation over teind income due to parish churches.

Of the eighty-three cases brought before papal judges-delegate between 1165 and 1230 for which records survive, twenty-four dealt with disputes over payment of or possession of rights to teinds.[68] A further twenty-six cases centred on control of parish churches or on the relationship between parish churches and chapels within their parish, in which payment of teind was an issue. It is perhaps significant that the volume of teind-related litigation soared after c. 1200, a phenomenon that cannot be attributed either to a growing general tendency towards recourse to papal justice or to the decree of the Lateran Council of 1215 which ended the Cistercian order's claimed exemption from payment of teind on newly acquired lands.[69] Teind, especially what is known as garbal teind (principally paid in grain), was becoming a worthwhile source of income to the Church, and the litigation suggests that the value of such income outstripped the legal costs of securing it. While the growing value of such teinds in part reflects the enhanced ability of ecclesiastical authorities to extract these dues, it also reflects the progressive expansion of arable cultivation and the volume of production on which teind was payable, coupled with buoyancy of market demand stimulated by the rising population level.

Alongside teind, the proliferation of references to mills suggests a steady increase in products that required milling. Possession of mills, and the seignorial right to oblige tenants to have their grain ground there (*thirlage*) for a charge (*multures*), became a major source of lordly incomes from the twelfth century onwards.[70] Mill buildings were a feature of centres of royal and lordly power, perhaps best exemplified by the juxtaposition of royal castles and mills, as at Elgin or Peebles.

---

[68] Ferguson, *Papal Representatives*, 209–42.
[69] Ibid. 54.
[70] See Duncan, *Making of the Kingdom*, 351–3; Neville, *Native Lordship*, 105–6.

This physical association probably reflects the convenience of having sources of multure payments, probably originally paid in kind, adjacent to administrative and revenue-collection centres. Identical considerations can be seen in the earldom of Strathearn, where the earls' mill at 'Dunfallin' (now Mill of Earn), close to a lordship centre at Innerpeffray, was a harvest-time meeting place of the earldom court,[71] while in Atholl the siting of the thirteenth-century Caisteal Dubh at Moulin (Gaelic *mùileann* mill) stresses the same link between milling and revenue collection at a comital centre.

Concession of the right to possess a mill by the king or magnates to their sub-tenants, one manifestation of the development of jurisdictional hierarchies in Scotland, probably reflects the extension of arable cultivation on the sub-tenants' estates. While in some cases the 'grant' of rights to possess mills may simply be a regularisation of an already existing situation, or the affirmation of seignorial powers that were being imposed on older socio-economic structures, as, for example, at Arbuthnott, where the substantial peasant tenants known as *scolocs* had once possessed their own mill but were now thirled to that of the thane,[72] in most cases it probably signals widening exploitation of the land. In St Andrews, for example, Malcolm IV's confirmation of the mills of Buddo, Kilrymont and Nydie to the canons perhaps formalised long-established rights, but in Moray William I's grant of permission to Bishop Richard to construct a mill at Elgin reflects recent development of the episcopal estate in the colonial landscape of the later twelfth century, a process of expansion which continued into the 1200s with Muriel de Pollock's grant to Bishop Andrew de Moray of the right to have a mill on his lands of Inverorkel in Strathspey.[73] Inchaffray Abbey secured rights to a mill for its own tenants from the earl of Strathearn c. 1200, and, in a move that probably reflects the physical enlargement of the monastic estate and the intensification of agriculture within it, received permission to construct a second mill c. 1220.[74] Mills, however, were not indicators of arable expansion only; they also reveal development of other products or related industries. Monastic principles of self-sufficiency, for example, saw production of cloth woven from the wool of the monasteries' and their tenants' sheep. Where woollen cloth was being manufactured, we

---

[71] Watson, 'Adapting tradition', 31.
[72] *Spalding Miscellany*, v, 210–13.
[73] Barrow (ed.), *RRS*, i, no. 174; Barrow (ed.), *RRS*, ii, no. 362; *Moray Registrum*, no. 107.
[74] Neville, *Native Lordship*, 105–6; *Inchaffray Charters*, nos XIX and XXXIV.

could also expect to see development of fulling mills, or waulkmills, for finishing the fabric. The earliest surviving specific reference to such a mill appears to be at Dryburgh Abbey in the 1170s,[75] but it is unlikely that major wool-producing abbeys like Melrose did not possess waulkmills before the middle of the thirteenth century.

Mill building had a significant environmental impact related to the provision of motive power for the mill wheel, provided almost exclusively by water.[76] Mills alongside major water courses had little obvious impact if their probably undershot wheels were simply placed in the river channel, but more control over water flow was afforded by construction of lades managed by sluices. A head of water for these lades came either from a mill dam or cauld across a natural water course or by construction of an artificial pond. In both cases, the damming or diversion of the water course affected the flow of water downstream and management of it upstream, which had implications for other users of the same resource. Such a situation is hinted at in the grant of a mill to Bishop Richard of Moray, which stipulated that it had to be built upstream from the cruives (fish traps), which were positioned to exploit the seasonal runs of salmon up the river at Elgin.[77] The biggest single medieval water-management project for which there is substantial physical evidence is that constructed by Melrose Abbey. There, a cauld was constructed across the River Tweed upstream from the precinct, from behind which a sluice-controlled lade was dug to power the abbey mills, to provide water for industrial processes such as tanning and to flush the monastic latrines.[78] The Melrose example was replicated on a smaller scale across Scotland. On the Eden in Fife, for example, St Andrews Priory was given permission to construct a dam for its mill at Nydie on the earl of Fife's lands on the north bank of the river, and to have freedom to repair it unhindered should it be damaged or broken by floods.[79] Interference with the flow of the water course was evidently a matter of concern where several users were exploiting it, possibly for a variety of purposes, as seen in the agreements between Dunfermline Abbey and Alan de Sinton concerning mills on the Esk near Musselburgh, where each party bound itself not to harm the interest of the other.[80] The proliferation of mills along often

---

[75] *Dryburgh Liber*, no. 161; Fawcett and Oram, *Dryburgh Abbey*, 148.
[76] There is one surviving medieval reference to a windmill (Duncan, *Making of the Kingdom*, 351 note 6).
[77] Barrow (ed.), *RRS*, ii, no. 362.
[78] Fawcett and Oram, *Melrose Abbey*, 69–70.
[79] *RRS*, ii, no. 168.
[80] *Dunfermline Registrum*, nos 197, 231; Duncan, *Making of the Kingdom*, 352.

> ### Eldbotle – a medieval rural settlement in East Lothian
>
> Although substantial ruins of castles and religious buildings survive in Scotland, evidence for the homes of most of the medieval population is exceedingly rare. Post-medieval Highland accounts of rural houses suggest that this is because most were built from turf, timber and thatch, and that buildings were periodically demolished and the materials used as compost for the fields. Excavation of parts of a deserted medieval village at Eldbotle near Dirleton in East Lothian, therefore, is immensely important for understanding of the homes, lifestyle and resource-use of Lowland Scottish peasants. Two excavations there in the early 2000s unearthed remains of eight buildings from an agricultural settlement recorded by the 1100s.[81]
>
> The buildings – six houses and two byres – had low side walls and gables of clay-bonded stone, possibly with turf upper sections. Two houses used crucks (two timbers joined in a Λ-shape) in their roof structures but the others had nothing to show how the roofs were fashioned. The limited use of crucks indicates a shortage of timber for building and tight lordly controls over access to remaining woods. Records mention Eldbotle's inhabitants using broom and gorse from the adjacent sand dunes, and they probably made do with this and with heather and turf thatching to construct their houses' roofs.
>
> Middens against the house walls show how the inhabitants garnered their refuse as fertiliser to enrich the soil in the kailyards and fields around the village. The excavations revealed areas of artificially deepened soil where midden waste and turf had been dug as manure. Much of this turf came from recycling building material but it was originally stripped from the nearby dunes. This resulted in serious erosion of the dunes and the build-up of sand drifts covering the village and fields; as Eldbotle's expansion placed more pressure on resources it was sowing the seeds of its own destruction.[82]

quite short lengths of river or stream could be remarkable, the Kilfillan Burn in Galloway having three meal mills and one waulkmill in a 6km course, three of them within a 500m stretch.[83] While such intensive use

---

[81] Morrison, Oram and Oliver, 'Ancient Eldbotle unearthed'; Hindmarch, 'Medieval village discovered at Archerfield, East Lothian' http://www.aocarchaeology.com/field-archaeology/archerfield.htm ; Hindmarch, *Renaissance Golf Club at Archerfield*.

[82] Morrison, Oram and Oliver, 'Ancient Eldbotle unearthed', 43.

[83] Oram, *Whithorn and Monastic Estate Management*, 16.

of a single power source may have been a response to the limited capacity and efficiency of individual mills,[84] it is also testimony to the increasing levels of arable production.

PASTORAL REGIMES

A regular feature of evidence relating to clearance and to expanding arable is the parallel development of pasture. Indeed, what is apparent from the records is that a pastoral regime prevailed throughout most of Scotland and, unlike in much of eastern and southern England, grazing remained the dominant land use, even in those areas that witnessed significant extension of the acreage under cultivation. What appears equally evident, however, is that the pastoral regimes that emerged in the course of the twelfth century had much older bases.[85] It is only comparatively recently that historians and archaeologists of early medieval Scotland have begun to recognise that socio-economic organisation within pre-twelfth-century Scotland could be both sophisticated in its structures and carefully regulated in its management. Past discussion of economic units has tended to focus on the development of the parish system in the twelfth century but more recent research has identified the complex assessment and management regimes of the eleventh century and earlier.

In his study of pre-twelfth-century shires, Geoffrey Barrow noted that, like their equivalents in England, Scottish shires possessed extensive tracts of common grazing, often, but not necessarily exclusively, in more upland areas.[86] Common grazing is generally regarded as upland in character, but areas of lowland that were only seasonally accessible, for example marshy flood plains which were waterlogged in winter, could be exploited for similar purposes.[87] Grazing could be located distantly from the main settlements, an arrangement that perhaps indicates a form of transhumance pastoralism, but could equally be a result of negotiated access to resources in an extensively exploited landscape. Such a response may have arisen from the development of 'multiple estates', where each estate comprised a series of units which provided its occupants with

---

[84] Duncan, *Making of the Kingdom*, 351.
[85] Ross, 'The dabhach'.
[86] Barrow, *Kingdom of the Scots*, 52.
[87] This is an aspect of the marshy flats of the Thames and its tributaries in Oxfordshire or the Somerset levels. See Limbrey and .Evans (eds), *The Effect of Man on the Landscape*, 37, 89.

access to a wide range of economic resources. Where the bulk of an estate lay in a zone with limited reserves of certain resources, the shortfall could be made good by securing access to a more distant source and negotiating transit rights for men and animals to and from it. This pattern has been identified in the *dabhaichean* of northern Scotland,[88] where areas detached from the main cores of property provided access to resources such as upland grazing or fuel.

New estates being constructed in the twelfth and thirteenth centuries, especially those of monastic orders which pursued policies of economic self-sufficiency, also sought access to adequate grazing to satisfy seasonal demands. In the early 1200s Dryburgh acquired a toft and croft at 'Samsonshelis' in Channelkirk at the head of Lauderdale, several acres of arable and access to common grazing for three hundred sheep, sixty draught oxen or cows, and two horses, plus rights in the common for the men of the abbey who came with these beasts.[89] The award provides insights into twelfth- and thirteenth-century agricultural practice. Most of the sixty oxen probably represented plough teams used on Dryburgh's fields in the early part of the year, then otherwise redundant until required for carting dry peats, harvested grain and so forth to the abbey in the late summer and autumn. With limited access to summer grazing around Dryburgh itself, and with so much pressure on developing their property for arable cultivation, a local form of transhumance was being practised which saw the abbey's oxen and their herdsmen moved seasonally to pastures in upper Lauderdale.

A recurring feature of hill grazing rights is reference to freedom 'to resort to shielings',[90] and a general right to have shielings was included in economic and jurisdictional rights granted to some landlords in the twelfth century.[91] Modern usage can be somewhat lax when discussing shielings, the term generally being applied in Scotland to sites associated specifically with transhumance pastoralism.[92] The medieval usage was more precise: shielings were the temporary huts or shelters used for seasonal activities, and not the activities *per se*. What was being authorised was permission to construct temporary shelters for shepherds or herders in areas where lords otherwise wanted to prevent development of permanent settlement, rather than permission to practise a system

---

[88] Ross, PhD thesis, iii, 39–40, 43–52, 228–30.
[89] *Dryburgh Liber*, no. 176.
[90] For example, *Dryburgh Liber*, no. 226.
[91] See, for example, Barrow (ed.), *RRS*, ii, nos 136, 185, 197, 413, 418.
[92] See Bil, *The Shieling* or Winchester, *Harvest of the Hills*.

of transhumance that was already probably centuries old. This restriction by landlords has already been encountered in respect of forest exploitation but it appears to have been a general constraint exercised by lords over their peasant tenants. It was a jurisdictional right, probably designed to protect a valuable common economic resource, and it is likely, given the number of exemptions granted from its constraints, that lords would relax its effects in return for payment. Lords regulated their own tenants' exploitation of common resources, but attempts to change the nature or intensity of exploitation could result in conflict with other lords whose tenants also had common rights in the resource. Such a situation lies behind a declaration of c. 1240 by Fergus, son of Gillebrigte, earl of Strathearn, made to the monks of Lindores, which narrated that the lands of 'Cotken' (from Gaelic *coitchionn*, common grazing) on the Muir of Orchill were 'free and common pasture to all the men who resided around there, so that no one might build on the land or plough it, or otherwise do anything to alter its use as pasture'.[93] Lindores' tenants and the rights of the abbey to a share in the commons on the Muir had been threatened by Fergus's plans to break the grazing into cultivation. Regulated encroachment on common resources operated where there were mutual economic benefits, but where the benefit was patently one-sided the potential losers in the relationship could deploy the force of custom to block development.

Underlying the 'Cotken' dispute was a basic question of access to grazing sufficient to maintain the agricultural regime of the communities which had previously exploited it. Expanding population and the spread of arable in lowland districts had seen the loss of much seasonal grazing land to cultivation. Alternative sources of grazing had to be found, but development of some, such as royal or baronial forests, was constrained by conflicting economic interests. Pressure for access to grazing intensified through the twelfth century and in southern Scotland pollen evidence points to development of grazing regimes in the uplands which may have triggered another episode of rapid landscape change. In the northern Cheviots, for example, the open grassland that had developed by c. 1000 in the wake of the progressive clearance of birch woodland deteriorated in quality after 1100, possibly largely due to the negative impact of muirburn, a technique initially employed to increase the availability of green plants and improve the quality of the grass as fodder for an increasing number of animals being grazed. Poor understanding and use of muirburn, however, led to the opposite of the desired effect.

---

[93] Neville, *Native Lordship*, 98; *Lindores Chrs*, no. XXVIII.

Charcoal from the process inhibited drainage, leading to waterlogging and peat formation, while burnt surface soils also experienced accelerated acidification. What developed in place of the grassland, however, was heath dominated by *Calluna*. In part, this change may be linked to increasing numbers of sheep as opposed to cattle being grazed in the Cheviots, for sheep are selective grazers and prefer certain grass species over *Calluna*. Consequently, the uplands were becoming over-grazed which, possibly coupled with a general decline in grassland quality and development of a management regime that saw flocks being removed from the hills in winter when *Calluna* would have been eaten, led to *Calluna* opportunistically developing where the grass was under pressure. *Calluna* does provide grazing, but is less nutrient-rich and will not support flocks or herds to the same extent as grassland.[94] Deterioration in the quality of the grazing land, coupled with economic pressure to increase flock and herd size, perhaps led to inroads being made where grazing had previously been light, seasonal and controlled. It is exactly this process that Melrose initiated between Gala and Leader.

Throughout Scotland the century after c. 1150 witnessed the same progressive intensification and expansion of grazing as occurred in the Wedale-Lauderdale uplands. Again, most of our surviving evidence relates to monastic activities in this respect, but those records reveal that similar activities were pursued by secular lords and their tenantry. In Kyle in Ayrshire, for example, where Melrose acquired its largest concentration of estates outside the eastern Borders, the monks expanded grazing rights in the Stewarts' baronial hunting forest stretching from Mauchline eastwards into the Lowther Hills.[95] Shortly after 1165, the monks were granted an extensive property around Mauchline with the whole of the pasture of the Steward's forest as far as the boundaries of Douglasdale, Lesmahagow and Glengavel to the north of the River Ayr, together with all easements in woods, plus a carucate of land to take into cultivation within the forest wherever they thought best for their requirements, for an annual payment of five merks. Walter son of Alan, however, also reserved all hunting in the forest, which shows that the monks' access to pasture was subject to the same hunting-driven restrictions as curtailed their activities in the east.[96] Half a century later, Walter's grandson, Walter II son of Alan, clarified the original grant and gifted the monks all the lawns and haughs in his forest on the north

---

[94] See Tipping, 'Bowmont Valley', 171–2.
[95] Fawcett and Oram, *Melrose Abbey*, 228–40.
[96] *Melrose Liber*, no. 66.

side of the Ayr, plus the use of his whole forest. Additionally, he gave them leave to plough and sow wherever they saw best for their needs both within the afforested area and on land given to them outwith it; the right to take fodder and pasture for their cattle (*pecora*); and the right to enclose their territory. Perhaps his most important concession, however, was his yielding into the monks' hands of the right to estimate how many animals could be maintained on their lands, the process later referred to in Scots as *souming*, a concession that removed from his foresters their ability to regulate the numbers of animals grazing in the forest and, consequently, the impact on the woodland and grassland. Despite this generous extension of access to his forest, Walter still clung on to his exclusive hunting rights.[97] Within a few years, however, he made further concessions, remitting all future payment of the annual rent of five merks which the monks paid, and abandoning his reserved hunting rights.[98] In effect, Melrose secured unrestricted use of the former forest and in the succeeding decades pushed ahead with economic exploitation of both the lower-lying cultivable ground around Mauchline and Catrine and the extensive tracts of upland to the east, clearing much of the remaining woodland and scrub.

Pressure to intensify exploitation of grazing, possibly resulting from the increasing commercialisation of stock management and the development of Scotland's international trade in hides, skins and wool, added further momentum to the movement towards freer access to pasture in afforested areas. In the Lauderdale-Wedale forest zone, prevention of the development of permanent agricultural establishments, the requirement to return flocks and herds every night to their 'home' farms and the seasonal withdrawal of grazing animals were economic restrictions that Melrose sought to overturn. Similar concerns complicated a dispute in the 1160s between Holm Cultram and Dundrennan abbeys over development of livestock ranches in eastern Galloway centred on Holm's grange at Kirkgunzeon. There it was settled that Holm Cultram's flocks would return every night to the grange, a limitation that drew a line under expansion of the abbey's livestock operation by confining its access to pasture within an agreed limit.[99] The intention may have been to discourage Holm Cultram from seeking to convert simple grazing rights on areas of shared pasture into outright possession and the development of new, permanent stock farms, but the consequence was the more rigorous

---

[97] Ibid. no. 73.
[98] Ibid. no. 73.
[99] *Holm Cultram Register*, no. 133.

and intensive exploitation of the resources available within the boundaries of Kirkgunzeon. Long term, the environmental impact of this restrictive agreement was profound, with the combined consequence of increasing demand for fuel, building timber and fencing materials at the grange, and intensification of grazing causing the rapid contraction and, ultimately, the disappearance of woodland. One direct outcome of that development was a move away from pig farming at Kirkgunzeon – the herds being wood grazers and fattened in particular in the late autumn on acorns – and concentration instead on open-country grazers, especially sheep.

In some areas, over-grazing arising from attempts to maximise exploitation of a shared resource possibly compounded the effects of management practices already proposed as contributing to the changing character of upland grasslands in southern Scotland. There are some signs that the impact of over-grazing was recognised by some users of common grazings, and, despite the often pessimistic view taken of management of commons, steps were taken to control or limit the negative effects. Studies of upland management and regulatory regimes in southern Scotland and northern England have revealed the development of a highly responsive and well-regulated commons system in the later medieval period.[100] This research focused on the post-1400 experience, but there is twelfth-century evidence of user-led action to protect resources. At Hassendean in Roxburghshire, for example, when Melrose gained possession of the parish church it chose to exploit rights previously enjoyed by the parson in the vill in which the church was situated, and in particular his common grazing rights. The result was serious overstocking and damage to the grazing, which led the king's tenants in Hassendean to take their complaint to the royal court. There, faced with claims that this overstocking was threatening their ability to pay rents, King William in 1195 required a new arrangement to be worked out. A new charter, confirmed by William, regranted the church to Melrose and, amongst other carefully defined terms, stated that the extent of the grazing rights associated with the church would be settled by an assize, which subsequently assigned pasture for 200 ewes, 16 oxen and 4 cows.[101]

As the Melrose monks' involvement in the wool trade grew in the late twelfth century, they sought to expand their grazing land to enable them to run more sheep. In the eastern Lammermuirs, Hartside and

---

[100] Winchester, *Harvest of the Hills*.
[101] Duncan, 'Roger of Howden', 138.

Spott, where they already possessed common grazing rights on the moor, were obvious areas for expansion.[102] Earl Patrick of Dunbar confirmed their right to graze three flocks on the common pastures of Spott moor. He added to this award five acres of land at its southern edge, for the exclusive enjoyment of the monks, on which they could build sheepfolds. With the possibility of overstocking and disputes over the numbers that the monks could graze on the common firmly in mind, the earl stipulated that each flock must not exceed 500 head and that the whole Melrose flock there should not exceed 1,500 sheep.[103] It is possible that Earl Patrick was aware of the monks' tendency to over-exploit grazing rights, as they had done at Hassendean, and was safeguarding both his own interests and also those of his tenants there. Before 1214, however, Earl Patrick added substantially to Melrose's holding, giving a further 51 acres of land at what is now known as Friardykes, lying in one compact block near to the original five acres that he had given.[104] This new land was also ringed by a dyke, within which the monks were given free licence to make meadows, fields or sheepfolds. Clearly, the monks were keen to develop as much as possible in this area, which lay close to the port of Berwick through which they were already exporting most of their goods. Commercial opportunities and the abbey's requirement for income to fund its ambitious rebuilding programmes were encouraging intensification of exploitation of its landed resources.

Fragmentary though the surviving parchment record is, it contains evidence of a rapidly accelerating expansion of agriculture across our period of study and of steadily mounting pressure on a wide range of natural resources. It provides us with the context for the dramatic changes in the Scottish landscape – declining woodland, disappearing peatlands, changes in grassland ecology – which the environmental record preserves; land everywhere was under pressure. Much of this pressure was driven by population growth and the need to feed, clothe and shelter increasing numbers of families, but it was also stimulated by an economic boom which awoke both peasant cultivators and entrepreneurial landholders to the potential for profit from their land. As Scotland's market economy developed as it was drawn ever more tightly into northern Europe's trading system, and her rulers sought to project their power, authority and status on the international stage, pressure

---

[102] *Melrose Liber*, nos 53–8.
[103] Ibid. no. 56.
[104] Ibid. no. 77.

on resources intensified. The making of the kingdom in the twelfth and thirteenth centuries created many casualties in its course, most usually thought of in terms of the unsuccessful rivals eliminated by Malcolm III and his successors. Perhaps the greatest casualty, however, was the environment.

CHAPTER 8

Towns, Burghs and Burgesses

It has long been accepted that amongst the most revolutionary of the innovations fostered in Scotland by its rulers in the twelfth century was a new form of urban settlement, the burgh. These were 'new' in the sense that their inhabitants practised their crafts and pursued their trade with an intensity and quality unknown in the town-like settlements which had come into being by the late eleventh century. The new townsmen were granted rights and liberties which had been enjoyed by no inhabitant of these older settlements, which gave them enhanced status and ability to conduct their business. These were innovations, too, in that a burgh was the product of a deliberate act by a ruler, 'created' by the granting of those rights and liberties to settlers who came there to live from already urbanised areas of Britain and northern Europe. The creation of burghs in Scotland may have begun in the 1110s in the territory ruled by Alexander I's younger brother, David, in Teviotdale and Tweeddale. David, who had extensive personal experience of the economic, cultural and political power of the already ancient trading boroughs of England, aimed to harness the potential wealth of his underdeveloped domain and enhance his authority within it through the establishment of similar entities; existing centres at Berwick and Roxburgh were awarded burgh status. Further north, Alexander may have followed suit at Perth, Edinburgh, Stirling and, possibly, Dunfermline, which certainly appear as burghs very early in the reign of his younger brother, David.[1] The pace of burgh creation quickened once David became king, with seventeen burghs recorded by the end of his reign, and by the time of his grandson William's death in 1214 around forty such communities

---

[1] Pryde, *Burghs*, 3.

existed.[2] Fewer new foundations were made by Alexander II but great magnates like the lords of Galloway or the branches of the Comyn family had begun to replace the crown as burgh founders.[3] Although even the largest Scottish burghs of this period were little more than large villages by modern standards, they exercised cultural, social and economic influence far in excess of their scale and were key instruments in the long process that saw the Scottish crown establish its political domination of Scotland. Perhaps more important still was their role in the transition of the heartland of the kingdom from a predominantly Gaelic-speaking to an English-speaking culture by the end of the thirteenth century.

BEFORE BURGHS

While there have been major advances in our understanding of the development of Scotland's burghs since the 1970s, our knowledge of the communities from which they were developed remains limited.[4] Large concentrations of population had existed in the later Iron Age at tribal centres like Eildon Hill North, Traprain Law and the Tap o' Noth. None, however, had survived as settlements into the eleventh century, although it has been suggested that later medieval towns at Selkirk and Haddington possibly represented a succession of nucleated settlement in the same general area as the first two of these sites.[5] Nor had any civil settlements at the gates of Roman forts outlived the third-century withdrawal of the garrisons. Urbanisation was a phenomenon that had stopped at the northern limits of Rome's empire and even in the most Romanised part of southern Britain that phenomenon had all but died in the civil wars, plagues and Anglo-Saxon invasions of the fifth and sixth centuries. Trade, the life blood of towns, almost collapsed but never failed in most of northern Europe, including in southern Britain where several of the old Roman urban centres re-emerged as towns as the Anglo-Saxon kingdoms grew in power and sophistication. The northernmost of those kingdoms, Northumbria, encompassed the least urbanised part of the old Roman province and, while some kind of

---

[2] Pryde, *Burghs*, 3–17, 37–41.
[3] Dennison, 'Burghs and burgesses', 253–83; Oram et al., *Wigtown*; Barrow (ed.), *RRS*, ii, no. 501.
[4] Brooks, 'Urban archaeology in Scotland', 19–32; Dicks, 'The Scottish medieval town', 23–51; Astill, 'General survey 600–1300', 44–5.
[5] 'Introduction', in Lynch et al. (eds), *Scottish Medieval Town*, 1–2.

marginal urban existence seems to have lasted at Carlisle into the seventh century, York was probably the only community of any significant size anywhere in Britain north of the Humber. Northumbrian trading links with mainland Europe and southern England extended into those parts of the Southern Uplands that were incorporated into that kingdom into the ninth century, providing routes along which high-quality commodities like Merovingian glass from the Rhineland could reach monastic workshops at Whithorn.[6] Outwith the Northumbrian sphere, however, there is little sign that any significant level of trade continued after c. 800 other than in those areas that fell under Norse domination and were drawn into the Scandinavian North Atlantic trading network. There are few indications that the emerging kingdom of the Scots enjoyed anything more than a peripheral and intermittent involvement in the commercial networks of the maritime west before the late eleventh century.

One factor that may have contributed to the lack of evidence for commercial activity is the failure to emerge of the type of large settlements whose very existence is seen as a basic stimulus for trade. That is not to say that there were no settlements to form such nodes, for it is likely that dependent communities had grown up adjacent to the main centres of secular and ecclesiastical power, supplying their craft needs and processing the surpluses and by-products from their estates. It is probable that some such settlement existed at Edinburgh, Stirling and Dumbarton, while major religious centres like Brechin (hyperbolically styled 'great city' in the late tenth century), St Andrews or Whithorn have archaeologically or historically attested tenth- and eleventh-century pre-burgh origins.[7] Signs of increasing commercial activity might be seen in the growing numbers of tenth- and eleventh-century English coins that have been found in south-eastern Scotland, but it is only at the end of the eleventh century that regular trade involving foreign merchants is recorded. Two hagiographies, Turgot's *Life of St Margaret* and the anonymous *Life and Miracles of St Godric of Finchale*, provide incidental reference to mercantile activity.[8] While Turgot's agenda in stressing Margaret's role in 'civilising' her husband's kingdom in the late eleventh century must always be remembered, his comments concerning her encouragement of foreign merchants to come to Scotland highlights the luxury

---

[6] Stevenson, 'Trade with the South', 180; Hill, *Whithorn*, 296–314.
[7] 'Introduction', in Lynch et al. (eds), *Scottish Medieval Town*, 2; Anderson (ed.), *Early Sources*, i, 512; Whyte, *Scotland Before the Industrial Revolution*, 54–7; Hill, *Whithorn*, 24–5, 209–50.
[8] Anderson (ed.), *Early Sources*, ii, 68; *Libellus Sancti Godrici*, 28–30.

goods that they brought and points to a lack of sophistication in both the market and the commodities previously available within the kingdom. In Godric's *Life*, we are told how he built up his merchant's business shipping English and Flemish goods to Scotland and exchanging them for unspecified high-value items that were in heavy demand elsewhere. These items, it has been suggested, were freshwater pearls and pelts.[9] What is absent from both accounts, however, is reference to specific trading communities, and we are left to speculate from inferences in the texts to the location of such centres.

Where, then, might have been the centres at which Godric and his fellows traded with the Scots? It is believed that many of the locations at which twelfth-century Scottish kings were regularly resident had been centres of power in previous centuries and it is likely that the communities at such places that received charters awarding them burgh status from David I and his successors had equally deep antiquity. Archaeology has produced some evidence for such early settlement at Perth, a natural locus for development of a trading community at the highest tidal reach and lowest ford of the River Tay, only 3km from the early royal and ecclesiastical centre at Scone.[10] Stirling, occupying its immensely strategic rock at the lowest bridging and highest tidal point of the River Forth, has yet to yield firm evidence for such an early trading centre, but its emergence in the twelfth century as one of the first and most important burghs probably reflects a much older significance.[11] Similarly early origins as settlements attendant upon old royal centres have been argued for Aberdeen, Forfar and Edinburgh, while rivermouth havens and early bridges may have been the foci for development at Ayr and the most important of Scotland's twelfth-century towns, Berwick.[12] As already mentioned, pre-eleventh-century episcopal and monastic centres could also provide potential nuclei for secular settlements. At St Andrews, late-twelfth-century charter evidence refers to what may have been a secular settlement alongside the monastery (see pp. 285–6).[13] The most substantial remains of a town-like community, however, have been uncovered at Whithorn in Galloway, where a programme of excavation in the late

---

[9] Stevenson, 'Trade with the South', 180.
[10] Robertson and Perry, 'Perth before the burgh', 11.
[11] Dennison, 'Burghs and burgesses', 258, 259, 260–1.
[12] Whyte, *Scotland Before the Industrial Revolution*, 55–6; Dennison, 'Burghs and burgesses', 258–66.
[13] Lawrie, *Early Scottish Charters*, 132.

1980s revealed an extensive portion of an eleventh-century settlement on the hillside to the south of the later medieval cathedral-priory.[14] The buildings, comprising both workshops and houses, showed clear structural parallels with examples excavated in Dublin in the 1970s and 1980s, pointing to close cultural and economic links around the Irish Sea zone. The layout of the buildings also suggested a deliberate planning policy, with regularly marked out lines of houses extending to either side of a road running radially to the hilltop. There seems also to be segregation of smelly or risky craft activities, with skin-, antler- and bone-working located at the external down-slope edge of the community. The excavator suggested that the settlement was the carefully laid-out creation of whatever lordly power occupied the hilltop in the eleventh century, as the settled areas appear to respect a central zone and were constructed in arcs concentric to that area. Whether it was the product of a Hiberno-Scandinavian secular ruler or the work of whatever religious authority survived at Whithorn between the ninth and twelfth centuries, however, is unknown.

Whithorn's excavated remains are currently the most extensive evidence for a substantial pre-twelfth-century population centre organised and sustained by an earlier medieval political and economic system. Together with the more exiguous evidence from elsewhere in Scotland, Whithorn confirms the argument, made with increasing confidence since the 1970s, that it is unlikely that urban economies and settlements were innovations of David I's reign.[15] Questions of scale of settlement and range of activities carried on within them are irrelevant. What matters is that such communities existed and had already begun to be drawn into the reviving northern European trading nexus before the end of the eleventh century; David was not laying out his burghs on a blank canvas.

BURGH LAWS AND BURGESS STATUS

Trade and the income to be derived from it were the incentives that led David to stimulate the growth of towns in Scotland by grants of burgh status even before he became king. It was not simply that he had seen how urban communities functioned in England and Normandy during his formative years at the court of Henry I and wished to replicate them within his own domain; he recognised both that Scotland possessed the

---

[14] Hill, *Whithorn*, 216–32.
[15] Lynch et al. (eds), *Scottish Medieval Town*, 3.

Map 8.1 Royal and non-royal burghs

Royal burghs are shown in **bold**

largely untapped economic resources necessary to sustain such urban economies and also that an external market for those resources existed. Equally, however, he may have recognised that Scotland lacked the native expertise to turn the existing settlements from purely local markets and service centres into participants in international trade networks from which he could cream new revenues necessary to realise his ambitious plans for his kingship. The potential for economic growth and enhanced profit existed, but new circumstances and new blood were needed for that potential to be realised; economic migrants provided both.

It has been suggested that the trigger for such change in Scotland lay in the rapid expansion of urban population, economies and trade at the southern end of the North Sea, chiefly in Flanders.[16] The stimulus for that growth had been a revolution in Flemish weaving technology in the earlier eleventh century, which had enabled cloth to be woven to uniform widths and textures. Trade in this new, high-quality commodity expanded rapidly, facilitated by a ready availability of silver coin unprecedented since the collapse of the late Roman economy. Expansion of trade brought further growth of the Flemish textile industry and increased demand for raw wool which local producers could not meet. New sources for this vital commodity were sought, with England providing the main supply. Scotland, however, was well positioned to secure a share of this burgeoning supply trade and its rulers deployed a range of mechanisms to attract colonists with the expertise to realise that potential.[17]

That it was David I who set in place legal devices to stimulate and formalise urban-based trade in Scotland is generally accepted.[18] There is, however, less certainty as to how much of the surviving laws governing the burghs can be attributed to his hand.[19] The best-known burgh law code, the so-called *Leges Burgorum* (Laws of the Burghs), has often been assumed to date from David's reign but the earliest surviving manuscript containing it dates from only c. 1270. The identification of these burgh laws with David is based on two points: that the text begins with the statement that the king had 'constituted' them; and that around twenty of its opening sections follow the general tenor of what has been seen as a mid-twelfth-century record of the customs of Newcastle as they were held to

[16] Duncan, *Making of the Kingdom*, 464.
[17] Stevenson, 'Trade with the South', 182–3.
[18] MacQueen and Windram, 'Laws and courts', 208.
[19] For the detail of the argument in the following section, see MacQueen and Windram, 'Laws and courts', 209–11.

exist in the reign of Henry I. Scottish control of Newcastle from 1139 to 1157 has been argued as the route for the adoption of its constitution more generally in Scotland, and it has even been suggested that David had instructed the production of the custumal for its wider application in his kingdom.[20] These arguments, however, do not bear detailed scrutiny, the weight placed on dates reliant on the dating of the Newcastle custumal being particularly unsupportable. It has been pointed out that the Newcastle laws were widely circulated and copied in northern England in the twelfth century without any royal instruction to that effect and they were probably as well known in the towns of south-eastern Scotland where they became available to the compiler of the *Leges Burgorum*. Even the bald statement of David's agency in their preamble appears to be an appeal to the reputation of a past ruler who was regarded generally as an authoritative law giver, a device used, for example, in the late-thirteenth-century compilation of Scots laws known as *Regiam Majestatem*. Rather than being a code drawn up by royal ordinance, it has been argued persuasively that the *Leges* were probably shaped by or written down for Scotland's wealthiest and most influential burgh, Berwick.[21] When that occurred, however, is unclear, for they contain material that unquestionably dates back to the thirteenth century. At present, there are two arguments for dating the production of the existing manuscript compilation: that it was a cumulative process starting in the late twelfth century and with material added throughout the thirteenth century; and that it was a single process which gathered material of various dates into one manuscript in the thirteenth century. That position was reached in the 1980s; we have progressed no further since in unravelling the processes behind the composition of the *Leges Burgorum*.

While the setting out of burgh law in a single written code is no longer attributed to David I, there is sufficient independent manuscript evidence to demonstrate that he did enact a range of legislative measures to give weight to the privileges being granted to his new burghs. A charter of William I to Inverness, for example, refers to three statutes of his grandfather which appear intended to reserve specific commercial activities within a burgh's hinterland to its burgesses: the manufacture of dyed or shorn cloth; the buying and selling of certain goods; and the establishment of taverns outside burghs (except in villages whose lord was resident and of knightly status).[22] All three statutes involve the

---

[20] Walker, *Origins of Newcastle*, 8–9.
[21] Duncan, *Making of the Kingdom*, 482.
[22] Barrow (ed.), *RRS*, ii, no. 475.

most fundamental of burgh privileges; a monopoly of buying and selling within its territory. Trading activity, too, was the business of unspecified 'liberties and customs' confirmed by Malcolm IV to burgesses in general arriving at any port in the kingdom.[23] Vaguer references during the reign of William to laws and customs enjoyed by all the kingdom's burgesses indicate the emergence of a body of legislative and customary law, much probably modelled on contemporary English and Continental practice, governing all burghs at an early date in their histories.[24] To attract both settlers and traders, some form of minimum standards governing burgh administration, burgess rights and commercial activity must have been recognised, but it must be emphasised that these were minimum standards and the various documents granting unique privileges to specific burghs should be seen as the results of efforts by communities to gain competitive advantage over rivals in drawing in new blood and business. Much of this common mercantile and burgh law was probably already in place before the end of David's reign but it was perhaps not until later in the reign of his younger grandson that the probably largely unwritten, diverse legislation and custom administered in the emerging burgh courts around the kingdom began to be drawn together in unified texts. Such texts, however, were neither coherent nor officially recognised codifications and the *Leges* have been described as 'a jumble of substantive rules and procedural technicalities, with a smattering of economic legislation'.[25]

Although the composition of the *Leges Burgorum* in their earliest surviving manuscript form may date from later in the thirteenth century, some of the content and a range of other independent sources indicate that the process of written codification of the burgh laws started in William's reign. The so-called *Constitutiones Regis Willelmi*, a compilation preserved within nine surviving more extensive manuscript collections of medieval Scots law, might reflect a critical step in that process. It is headed by and draws heavily upon the provisions of a charter granted by the king in 1209 to the burgh of Perth and whose same basic provisions can be found from earlier in William's reign in charters to Rutherglen and Ayr.[26] The 1209 charter, therefore, might represent a formal statement of laws and custom that had been maturing throughout William's

---

[23] Barrow (ed.), *RRS*, i, no. 166.
[24] MacQueen and Windram, 'Laws and courts', 209.
[25] Duncan, *Making of the Kingdom*, 482.
[26] Ibid. 484–6. For the Perth charter, see Barrow (ed.), *RRS*, ii, no. 467 and for similar provisions, see Barrow (ed.), *RRS*, ii, nos 213, 244, 475.

reign and was subsequently employed as a definitive articulation of burgh laws and privileges for wider application. Aberdeen, for example, received a formal grant of the Perth customs from Alexander II, and a similar collection of material labelled *Constitutiones Nove* was copied into the Glasgow diocesan register later in the thirteenth century.[27] Taken together, this evidence has led legal historians to argue that one of the achievements of William as king was recognition that uniformity of practice amongst the burghs needed the laws upon which that practice was founded to be stated in writing. The result was the gathering together of various sets of material and the creation of the several legal treatises that survive in manuscript form.

These early burgh laws reveal that the principal concern of both the kings of Scots and the burgesses was with defining the substance and territorial extent of their trading monopolies and the wider privileges of burgess status. The territorially defined trading monopolies of many Scottish burghs were often on a scale unheard of elsewhere in Britain or Europe; Rutherglen, for example, was granted a territory that extended to the borders of Kyle to the south-west, the Nethan in the south-east and northwards to the River Kelvin, while Aberdeen's hinterland stretched westwards to the Cairngorms, south to the River North Esk and north towards Banff, effectively subsuming the territories of the smaller royal burgh of Kintore.[28] Exemptions from payment of the tolls on transported goods, which were the corollary of trading monopolies, indicate that the crown and its agents were active in enforcing, or at least attempting to enforce, the burghs' exclusive right to a market within its territory. Burgesses could trade toll-free, so the tolls only affected the country dwellers within the burgh's designated hinterland who were constrained by them to sell their surpluses and buy their finished goods and luxuries in that burgh's market.[29] The tolls were also of great importance to the king as a source of revenue as they, together with burgess rents, provided his principal cash income within Scotland and, as Professor Duncan observed, it is unsurprising that a king like David I with his many capital-consuming projects should be so active a developer of burghs. It is questionable how effective enforcement of the monopoly and collection of tolls was; the repeated confirmation of the burghs' rights in these spheres is probably an indication of widespread toll evasion and

---

[27] *APS*, i, 86–9; *Glasgow Registrum*, ii, no. 536.
[28] Dennison, 'Burghs and burgesses', 255; Barrow (ed.), *David I Charters*, no. 271; *Aberdeen Charters*, no. 3. See also Barrow (ed.), *RRS*, ii, no. 462 for Ayr.
[29] Duncan, *Making of the Kingdom*, 474–5.

flouting of monopolies. That the king had handed responsibility for collection of tolls to the burgesses by the 1180s, probably in return for a higher level of burgh ferme – the annual rent paid by the burgesses to the king – appears to recognise that failure. The onus to maintain the burghs' trading monopolies was being transferred from the crown to the principal beneficiaries of that exclusive position.

The privileged legal standing of the burgh community, native and newcomer, was a key inducement to settle. The inhabitants of the burgh held their property by tenure of a form common enough throughout Europe to require no more detailed rehearsal in documents from David's reign than reference to tenure *in burgagio* and, by the reign of William, to tenure *in libero burgagio*.[30] It has long been pointed out that 'in Scotland "burgh" and "burgess" were from the beginning essentially legal concepts with the privileges implied by each no doubt enforceable by process of law'.[31] Burgh status, then, bestowed certain fundamental rights on a town's inhabitants, chief amongst which was the legal 'freedom' of the burgesses: theoretically they had 'feudal' ties only to their burgh's superior, usually the king. What that freedom meant in the twelfth century, however, has perhaps been somewhat distorted and inflated by the enhanced status of burgesses from the later thirteenth century onwards. Burgesses in the twelfth century certainly enjoyed a greater degree of personal liberty and legal freedom than many of the peasantry but the colonists' status as crown tenants appears to have given the king considerable control over their persons. It has been suggested that this was especially the case for Flemings, who may have been seen as possessing experience, skills and connections essential for the physical development of burghs and to whom David and his heirs may have given particular privileges to secure their settlement, but who were consequently put more firmly at royal disposal.[32] Not only could the king grant away his personal lordship over a burgess, he could also apparently require his burgesses to relocate at his will. The clearest example of this situation was the grant c. 1144 of Mainard the Fleming, described as the king's own burgess in Berwick, to Robert, bishop of St Andrews, who then brought him to St Andrews to oversee the laying out of the bishop's new burgh there.[33] Mainard, as a burgess of Berwick, enjoyed the liberty to move around the kingdom and abroad on his business and became a

[30] MacQueen and Windram, 'Laws and courts', 209.
[31] Ibid. 208.
[32] Duncan, *Making of the Kingdom*, 476–7.
[33] Barrow (ed.), *David I Charters*, no. 242.

man of wealth and status, but he was still subject to the king's will in a manner that placed him closer to servile peasant status – an item of his lord's property – than to the status of one of David's knightly colonists. Early in the reign of William another Berwick burgess, William Lunnoc, had his house and land in the burgh, and with them his personal service, granted away by the king to the abbot and monks of Melrose; Lunnoc would remain on the property but lordship over him and his successor occupants belonged thenceforth to the abbey, not to the king.[34] The change may not have affected Lunnoc's freedoms as a burgess but the apparently easy disposal of the man, his household and property by his superior lord should make us question traditional perceptions of the 'free' burgess.

Whatever the implications in David I's or William's ability to grant away lordship of 'their' burgesses to another lord, the laws demonstrate that burgess status carried some particular legal freedoms which set its holders apart from the unfree. Within the *Leges Burgorum*, it is stated that the man of a baron or knight, or an unfree man who bought a burgage and sustained himself on it for a year and a day, secured the freedoms of a burgess and the same liberties as the burgh's other burgesses.[35] It is explicit, however, that those freedoms were contingent upon residence; live elsewhere and the privileges of burgess status were lost. Already in the late twelfth century, the *Leges* denied non-residents the privileges of burgess status in other than the burgh where they held their tenement, and by the early 1200s residence was an explicit requirement in royal charters to burghs for the possessor of a burgage to benefit from the freedoms and rights of burgesses.[36] This restriction was possibly developed as a measure to prevent countrymen (that is, property holders in rural districts) from buying a burgage with the sole aim of acquiring the privileges of burgess status without pursuing a living as a burgess, continuing to live instead on their country possessions. The distinction between resident and non-resident burgesses, it has been argued, was intended to remove the privileged forms of trial available to burgesses in courts outside their own burgh from men who did not actively pursue their main living as burgesses.[37] Possession of a tenement alone was, by

---

[34] Barrow (ed.), *RRS*, ii, nos 97, 98.
[35] *Ancient Laws*, i, 33–4.
[36] For example, Barrow (ed.), *RRS*, ii, no. 475, where privileges granted to the burgh of Inverness are to be enjoyed only by 'my burgesses who shall inhabit my burgh . . .'
[37] Duncan, *Making of the Kingdom*, 480.

the late 1100s, no longer sufficient to secure its holder all the rights of burgess status throughout the kingdom.

The distinction over legal rights of non-residents points to the existence already in the twelfth century of a hierarchy of status amongst the inhabitants of burghs. Possession of a tenement may originally have been the simple benchmark for the gaining of burgess status. If that was the case, however, there would have been a probable majority of the inhabitants of towns – women, children of burgesses, servants and labourers attached to larger households and craft or trading ventures, and other types of waged labour – who were therefore by definition non-burgesses. By c. 1179, those inhabitants of Inverness entitled to trade within the sheriffdom of Inverness outside the burgh were divided into two classes, *burgensis* (burgess) or *stalagarius* (stallholder).[38] The separate labels imply that the latter, while entitled to trade, did not share in all privileges attendant upon burgess status. Exclusion from the full benefits of burgess status may have produced tensions and may have led to resistance from non-burgesses to the imposition upon them of financial obligations paid by burgesses. Such a situation probably lies behind a royal declaration in 1209 of the privileges of Perth that anyone dwelling in the burgh and wishing to be able to have dealings in its market was to contribute with the burgesses to *auxilia* (money aids) paid to the king, regardless of whose men they were.[39] Avoidance of financial burdens through claims of non-burgess status was thus firmly quashed and it must have seemed a grievous injustice to the probable majority of the adult male population of burghs who were denied burgess rank that they still had to pay for the privilege of living in the community and contributing to its prosperity. The provisions recorded in the *Leges* establish that by the late twelfth century the limitations on access to burgess status had crystallised and that the cachet of privilege associated with membership of the burgess community in the later medieval period was already secured.

BURGH ADMINISTRATION AND INSTITUTIONS

The existence of laws governing the conduct of trade in burghs and setting out the rights and responsibilities of burgesses implies the existence of courts to administer those laws. There is strongly circumstantial evidence for the existence of some such body to oversee a burgh's

---

[38] Barrow (ed.), *RRS*, ii, no. 213.
[39] Barrow (ed.), *RRS*, ii, no. 467; Duncan, *Making of the Kingdom*, 484–5.

> **Building materials and resource management**
>
> In the eleventh to thirteenth centuries, most town buildings were made from organic materials, principally timber, wattle, thatch of various types and daub of clay, dung, mud or a mixture of these. Most excavated examples from around Scotland, at locations spread from Inverness to Whithorn but mainly from major excavations in Aberdeen and Perth, were of very flimsy construction and were usually single-storey, post-and-wattle structures. These were technically unsophisticated buildings showing little evidence for the advanced carpentry employed in prestige construction as at the major royal or ecclesiastical sites. Large, dressed timbers were rarely used, most structural woodwork being of small undressed roundwood, of which less than 50 per cent was oak, while the wattle panels that filled the gaps between the uprights were fashioned from a variety of tree species.[40] At Kirk Close in Perth, the thirteenth-century wattle work was about 50 per cent hazel withies, 17 per cent alder and small amounts of birch, willow, elm and fruit trees. This mix does not necessarily reflect the use of managed coppices, and although the hazel and alder might have come from managed woods the remainder could have been scavenged from any scrub or woodland source around the burgh.[41] In the twelfth century, the crown gave its burgess tenants rights to take building materials and fuel in the woodland of royal forests adjoining the burghs,[42] but this privilege may not have extended to all town dwellers as burgess status was not held by all of a burgh's inhabitants. The widespread use at Perth of bush and hedgerow species not commonly associated with woodland management or construction might represent the limited access to supplies amongst non-burgesses but could also reflect the exhaustion of more favoured varieties closer to the burgh.

domestic affairs from the earliest period of burgh foundation, but it is not until the thirteenth century that explicit reference is made to burgh courts.[43] Such courts were probably the enforcers of trade standards and arbiters in burgess disputes, presumably overseeing the conflict resolution mechanisms that replaced trial by combat as the remedy by which

---

[40] Yeoman, *Medieval Scotland*, 56.
[41] Crone and Watson, 'Sufficiency to scarcity', 66–7.
[42] For example, Barrow (ed.), *RRS*, ii, nos 362 and 467.
[43] Duncan, *Making of the Kingdom*, 481–2; Dennison, 'Burghs and burgesses', 256.

personal disputes were settled.[44] The scope of business and the detail of procedure that emerge in the thirteenth-century references to burgh court activity reveal a maturity of practice suggesting that before the end of the twelfth century they had acquired the authority to determine who was entitled to be admitted to the freedoms of burgess status and oversight of the scope and limitations of those rights. Burgh courts, however, were the instruments of burgh government not the executive; their evolution into burgh councils was a phenomenon of the later thirteenth and fourteenth centuries.

The tradition of self-government so closely associated with and jealously guarded by Scottish burghs emerged only gradually through the twelfth and thirteenth centuries. In David I's reign, burghs were very much the king's burghs and the officials who oversaw their running and, most importantly for the king, the collection of his *firma*, or *ferme* as the agreed annual cash sum to be paid into his chamber was known, were royal appointees. The cash income from burghs appears initially to have been collected or 'farmed' by the king's sheriff, who delegated that responsibility to a reeve known as *prepositus*.[45] Towards the end of the reign of Malcolm IV, the *prepositus* was an administrative officer who might give a burgess sasine of his property and have competence to make payments directly to beneficiaries of grants from the king's *cáin* income, the latter surely an indication that it was the *prepositus* who gathered that income.[46] Malcolm's reign also appears to have seen the beginning of a shift in some burghs, probably the larger and richer communities, towards the burgesses taking over responsibility for farming the burgh. In them, the *prepositi* ceased to be the sheriff's representatives and became the burgesses' agents; they were probably themselves burgesses. At Inverkeithing early in William's reign, the king addressed a charter to 'the *prepositi* and my other burgesses' of the town,[47] suggesting that these officers were emerging as the leaders or leading representatives of the burgess community. Inverkeithing was, however, a well-established, prosperous and wealthy community whose members could afford to take over the right to farm the burgh and to strike bargains with the king whereby they could extend their legal privileges and broaden the sphere of their trading hinterland. Berwick seems to have made a similar

---

[44] Dennison, 'Burghs and burgesses', 256; Barrow (ed.), *RRS*, ii, no. 388.
[45] See Barrow (ed.), *RRS*, i, 44 for discussion of these officers. Duncan, *Making of the Kingdom*, 482–4.
[46] Lawrie, *Early Scottish Charters*, no. 69; Barrow (ed.), *RRS*, i, no. 223.
[47] Barrow (ed.), *RRS*, ii, no. 102.

progression towards control of its own affairs by the same date but at two of its main early competitors, Perth and Haddington, the farm of the burghs and consequently appointment of the *prepositi* apparently remained in the hands of the sheriffs possibly into the late 1190s or early 1200s.[48] Where this transition was made, the *prepositus* effectively ceased to be a reeve and became a 'provost' in the later medieval Scottish sense: the elected head of the burgess community.

Taking over the collection of their own burgh's *firma* and mutation of the role of *prepositus* from administrative agent to elected community head marked stages on the route to burgh self-government. These processes happened at different times in different burghs but there is often no formal or explicit record of how the transitions were achieved. Dating the change on the basis of the earliest surviving appearance of a common seal of the burgh is dangerous and can only be taken as a date by when the development was achieved. Perhaps a clearer indication of when the process began is the emergence of burgess control over entry to their community through an oath sworn to the community and recognising that the oath taker was both bound to and protected by the common privileges of the burgh.[49] That, however, does not explain how burghs acquired the right to govern themselves. Again, there was probably no single route but the references to aids, special one-off cash payments given to the crown by the burghs, might point to one means by which a community secured enhanced privileges for itself. The link between references to aids paid to the king in William's 10 October 1209 recital of Perth's privileges and the council which began in Perth on 29 September and was continued at Stirling in which he sought and secured contributions from the magnates and burgesses towards the payment he had promised the English King John is too close for coincidence.[50] Prosperous burgesses used their liquidity to meet the crown's cash needs and in return extracted a clearer and probably enhanced articulation of their burgh's privileges.

An ability to negotiate in such terms with the king speaks for a degree of organisation on the part of the burgesses and the probable existence of a body that could be approached directly by the crown and which could reasonably claim to speak for at least the wealthiest segment of the burgh community. Such a body is explicitly referred to in William's 1209 Perth charter: the gild merchant. The king's concession to Perth's burgesses of the right to have such an association does not mark its date

---

[48] Ibid. ii, nos 123, 290, 305, 415; Dennison, 'Burghs and burgesses', 256.
[49] Duncan, *Making of the Kingdom*, 480, 484.
[50] Ibid. 485–6.

of establishment, rather it was the point at which it gained formal recognition of its existence and its authority; there is evidence, for example, that a gild existed at Berwick at least since the mid twelfth century.[51] Later medieval evidence for the role of the Scottish gilds reveal that they were fraternities whose functions were religious and social as well as mercantile, functions which point to origins in the friendly societies formed by traders in parts of Europe from as early as the eighth century and presumably brought north by the Continental and English colonists who settled in the burghs.[52] As religious, charitable and social associations, they provided a mechanism through which the spiritual needs of members and their families could be addressed, support provided for associates who had fallen on hard times – itself a spiritual act – and a forum for collective convivialities, i.e. a drinking club. As 'fellowships for mutual aid and solidarity'[53] they gave a collective voice to merchants and businessmen in their dealings with the officers who had oversight of burgh affairs and were probably concerned chiefly with safeguarding their privileges and wealth. By the early thirteenth century, when Perth's gild merchant gained royal recognition, however, these associations had become outward-looking bodies with clearly economic objectives. As the collective voice of the burgh's men of affairs – gilds merchant (associations of all who live by trade) rather than merchant gilds (associations of long-distance traders) alone – they sought to enhance their liberties at home and to advance and secure their trading position over that held by other burghs; mutual protection had become mutual ambition.

THE URBAN COLONISTS

Despite the existence of urban communities in Scotland before the grants of burgh status, the inhabitants of those communities are invisible in the historical record. Where twelfth-century burgh records do exist and give the names of some of the first-generation burgesses, townsmen who might represent a surviving core of population from the pre-burgh settlement do not make their presence obvious. Most of the personal names recorded in the charters are of English or Flemish origin; Gaelic nameforms are entirely absent, even in burghs like St Andrews which lay in a

---

[51] Duncan, *Making of the Kingdom*, 488 and note 44; Torrie, 'Guild in fifteenth-century Dunfermline', 245.
[52] Coornaert, 'Les ghildes médiévales', 22–55.
[53] Duncan, *Making of the Kingdom*, 489.

region still almost exclusively Gaelic in its language and culture.[54] There, the names suggest that the burgesses were primarily colonists from either England or, as in the case at St Andrews of Mainard the king's burgess, mentioned earlier, from the English-speaking zone of the kingdom in Lothian and Teviotdale. While early burgh laws imply that the *rustici* of the countryside around burghs were buying burgages, none appears to have been prominent enough in the new community to leave any impression in the record and perhaps speedily adopted non-Gaelic names for their children and so were assimilated rapidly. There is, too, the possibility that the pre-burgh communities were already islands of largely English or Anglo-Scandinavian population set in Gaelic hinterlands, surviving on the specialist and exotic craft and trade services which they provided. In general, however, it appears that the burghs were populated largely by colonists from England and the near continent, men who brought skills and connections that any indigenous townsmen lacked.

The importance of Flemings in Scottish burgh colonisation has long been recognised. Berwick may have attracted most colonists from the ill-defined zone referred to by medieval Scots as Flanders but a large Flemish presence is detectable in east-coast ports like St Andrews, Perth and Aberdeen and in the burghs along the Moray Firth from Inverness to Elgin.[55] While they may have been especially valued by the crown as experienced and efficient agents through whom to speed the process of urban development, for which services they may have received significant concessions – as reflected in William's confirmation to the burgesses north of the Mounth of their 'free hanse' (right to collect a payment from non-burgesses wishing to trade in their district)[56] – Scotland was equally attractive to them as a developing economy with a hunger for their technical craft skills and products and with abundant supplies of the raw commodities most in demand in the cities of their homeland. The prominence of a handful of Flemings in the historical record and a modern historiographical tradition which has underplayed the significance of English settlement, however, has rather distorted perceptions of the likely cultural profile of the colonist group in general; like most of the knightly and ecclesiastical colonists who settled in Scotland in the twelfth century, the majority of burgesses were probably of English origin.

---

[54] See, for example, the names given in *St Andrews Liber*, 124. For discussion, see Duncan, *Making of the Kingdom*, 476.
[55] Duncan, *Making of the Kingdom*, 475, 476–8, 488; Toorians, 'Flemish settlement', 1–14; Stevenson, 'Trade with the South', 182.
[56] Barrow (ed.), *RRS*, ii, no. 153; Duncan, *Making of the Kingdom*, 477.

Recorded names of early burgesses from around Scotland confirm this position. The male first names are almost entirely English, or at least Norman-French forms favoured in England, but it is the surnames taken from places of origin that highlight the arrival of migrants from the south coast of England, East Anglia, the East Midlands and Northumbria. At Perth, for example, at least six prominent families can be linked to migration from English towns – Battle (Sussex), Bedford, Leicester, Lynn, Scarborough and Stamford, with a Whitby connection also established by the end of the thirteenth century – while at Roxburgh families were linked to Richmond and York.[57] North Yorkshire or south Durham links at Roxburgh and Aberdeen might also be represented in the significant quantities of pottery from kilns in East Yorkshire found in excavations at both burghs, while at the former some of the pottery of Scarborough Ware form seems to have been manufactured locally and perhaps indicates recent migrants' attachment to the vessel styles familiar to them at their original home.[58] The significance of this attachment to cultural difference should not be understated, for it had implications far beyond a superficial preference for pots of one shape over another. Different forms of cooking pot and serving vessel indicate different ways of cooking and serving food and, indeed, different basic food preferences. Catering for those preferences introduced new demand and supply dynamics to the local produce market. Over time, these dynamics led to changes in the range of produce grown and available in a burgh's hinterland, subtly altering a fundamental aspect of the native rural culture. This slow permeation of the rural hinterland by the culture of the urban areas is, however, most marked in the linguistic change effected in most of lowland Scotland around the main burghs before the fourteenth century. In 1100, English had been a minority language spoken primarily in the eastern parts of Lothian and Tweeddale; by the early 1200s, islands of English language had been established throughout the Lowlands from Fife to Ross and from these islands the language began to penetrate the burghs' hinterlands.

PLANNED BURGHS

The creation of burghs became one of David's fundamental policies in the economic development of his territories. What, however, did the establishment of a burgh mean for the communities that received that

---

[57] Duncan, *Making of the Kingdom*, 492–4; *Melrose Liber*, no. 239, *CDS*, ii, p. 197.
[58] Martin and Oram, 'Medieval Roxburgh', 393–5; D. Hall, personal communication.

status? As discussed below, while there may have been a formalisation of the physical footprint of the settlements that received burgh status it usually did not involve the foundation of wholly new communities on virgin sites. In some places, indeed, there may have been no immediate change in the physical aspect of the newly privileged community. Elsewhere, however, while the economic conditions within a region were well suited for the institution of a burgh, any existing settlements may have occupied sites that were not ideal for the development of large-scale craft and trading centres. Soon after he acquired possession of Cumbria in around 1113, mention occurs in charters of a burgh at Roxburgh.[59] This privileged trading community was sited originally at what later became known as Old Roxburgh, represented by the modern Roxburgh village. Pre-twelfth-century sculpture at the parish church site and the approximately central location of the village in the medieval parish suggests that David's first burgh was established at an already old socio-economic centre. Shortly after 1124, however, David conceived a grander plan for his burgh of Roxburgh, and a 'new burgh' was founded on what appears to have been a virgin site at the eastern extremity of the parish, adjacent to the royal castle, crossing points of Tweed and Teviot, and the junction of two long-established east–west and north–south routes (named in charters as King Street and Market Street respectively). Roxburgh's plan, as far as it can be reconstructed from the limited surviving documentation relating to the burgh, aerial photography, archaeological excavation and geophysical survey, had the T-junction intersection of these two routes at its core, with additional streets running east towards the haugh formed by the confluence of the rivers Tweed and Teviot and diagonally across the angle between the two arterial routes. It was a layout matched for scale and complexity in Scotland in the thirteenth century only by Perth and exceeded only by Berwick. As analysis of the evolution of Perth's deceptively regular grid plan has shown, however, the footprint of a burgh was rarely the result of a single act of planning and may have developed gradually as the result of a series of smaller episodes of physical expansion.[60]

The complex plans of Roxburgh, Berwick and Perth are unusual in Scotland; the majority of burghs were laid out along a single, spinal street from which the tofts extended in perpendicular arrangement to back lanes running parallel with the main thoroughfare. This simple plan is

[59] Martin and Oram, 'Medieval Roxburgh', 367–79.
[60] Spearman, 'Medieval townscape of Perth', 42–59; Stevenson, 'Monastic presence', 99–115.

still evident in the ancient cores of many modern Scottish towns, such as Inverness, Nairn, Forres, Elgin, Jedburgh or Ayr. The formalised planning of even these simple layouts is evident in the uniform measurements of the burgage plots or tofts that flank the main street. The Scottish burgh average width of tofts was between twenty and twenty-five feet: at Edinburgh, it was twenty-five feet; at Perth twenty feet; Dunfermline twenty-two and a half feet; Dundee twenty and a half feet.[61] Blocks of contiguous, equal-sized tofts have been identified in a number of burghs and, as in the case of Perth, point to discrete episodes of planned expansion. This does not mean that all tofts within one of these recognisable blocks was occupied immediately and simultaneously, simply that they were marked out in a single operation. It is, for example, debatable that all the tofts in Edinburgh's High Street, whose eastern limit was fixed at the Netherbow by 1141 x 1147 when the canons of Holyrood had their right to have a burgh between the royal burgh and their abbey precinct confirmed, were occupied by that date despite their uniformity in size all the way down the ridge to this boundary.[62] Likewise at Crail, where the great open space and generous burgages of the burgh's secondary market area in Market Street may have been laid out before the end of the twelfth century, but there is no firm evidence to show that all of the tofts were occupied by that early period and much to suggest that many in the sector furthest from the harbour and original market remained unoccupied into the sixteenth century.[63] The take-up of available burgages in many burghs may thus have been piecemeal and slow, similar to modern industrial estate or private housing developments where streets and plots are laid out but buildings only appear gradually as buyers are found. As later medieval records of 'waste' or empty burgages indicate, even in the main royal burghs gap sites could be found on the main thoroughfares.

Progressive development from early cores can also be identified at non-royal burghs. A pre-existing secular settlement alongside the religious community at St Andrews provided the nucleus for the new burgh founded by Bishop Robert in 1140.[64] The inhabitants of this settlement may have been craftsmen and other lay dependents of the rich and powerful monastery who were needed to process the produce and rents in kind from the monastic estate. The sale of surplus produce and processed by-products from these rents may have led to its growth as a

---

[61] Dennison, 'Burghs and burgesses', 265.
[62] Barrow (ed.), *David I Charters*, no. 147; Duncan, *Making of the Kingdom*, 467.
[63] Duncan, *Making of the Kingdom*, 469; Simpson and Stevenson, *Crail*.
[64] Lawrie, *Early Scottish Charters*, no. 169.

local market centre, a role that was simply formalised by the 1140 burgh charter. References to the pre-burgh community are ambiguous and late, but the description of the site where the market cross stood until its removal in c. 1170 to a new location on 'Lambin's land' as the place where the 'clochin' had been is interpreted as a corruption of the Gaelic *clachan*, meaning a hamlet or kirktoun.[65] The charter that refers to the two sites offers no clue as to where either the 'clochin' or 'Lambin's land' lay, and various theories have been advanced based on interpretation of the plan of the burgh as it had crystallised by the late twelfth century. All the theories favour sites for the 'clochin' and the 1140s burgh at the east of the modern town close to the medieval cathedral; this view is supported by archaeological evidence.[66] Bishop Robert's burgh was a planned community from the outset, the bishop securing from King David his Berwick burgess Mainard the Fleming to lay out the lines of the streets and divide up the burgage plots; Mainard subsequently received three tofts for himself and became provost of the new town.[67] It is unclear whether the relocation of the market cross only a generation after the founding of the burgh was from a site outwith the planned area of Bishop Robert and Mainard's town to a newly laid out market square within it, or signalled that the community had outgrown a phase one plan and that the new site on 'Lambin's land' marks a second-phase westward spread of the planned settlement into the central part of Market Street. Current opinion favours the latter view, but excavations on Market Street in the 1980s suggested that the tofts there were possibly occupied only from the early 1200s, and an unpublished 1974 excavation report argued for a date as late as 1300.[68] St Andrews in the twelfth century may not, therefore, have extended much farther west than the rigs on the west side of North Castle Street and South Castle Street.

    The most successful twelfth-century non-royal burgh was Dundee, established by David, earl of Huntingdon, and apparently confirmed by his brother, King William, before 1195.[69] It is suggested that Dundee had its origins as the administrative centre of a pre-eleventh-century royal estate, Dundee-shire, which continued to function into

---

[65] Brooks and Whittington, 'St Andrews', 292.
[66] For a summary discussion of the three main suggestions, see Hall, 'Introduction', in Rains and Hall (eds), *Excavations in St Andrews*, 3.
[67] Barrow (ed.), *David I Charters*, no. 242; Lawrie, *Early Scottish Charters*, no. 169.
[68] See Hall, 'Introduction', 3; Hall, '134 and 120–4 Market Street', in Rains and Hall (eds), *Excavations in St Andrews*, 26; Clark, 'Discussion', in Rains and Hall (eds), *Excavations in St Andrews*, 141–3.
[69] Barrow (ed.)., *RRS*, ii, no. 363.

the 1170s, possibly with its focus in a hall on the site later occupied by the royal castle.[70] As with St Andrews, it is possible that a small community of craftsmen and servants had developed in association with the estate centre, processing rents and trading on goods fashioned from by-products, but there is no firm archaeological or historical evidence for this. It has long been believed that the pre-burghal settlement was located on the line of the Seagate, the route which ran north-east along the shore of the Firth of Tay from the Castle Hill, but archaeological work in the 1990s and early 2000s suggests an alternative early nucleus along the line of the current High Street and Murraygate which formed a route running north from a haven and ferry crossing on the Tay.[71] On receiving the lands of Dundee from his brother in c. 1180, Earl David began to formalise the status and layout of this community, setting out burgage plots around a long marketplace from which streets extended north, north-east, west and south-west, and securing confirmation of its burgh status by the early 1190s at the latest.[72]

From the outset, Dundee was in competition with Perth for trade entering the Tay estuary. Although Dundee eventually secured a dominant mercantile position, its success over an already established burgh was rarely repeated in other examples where parvenus were intruded into the hinterlands of pre-existing, privileged communities. Such, it has been suggested, was the experience of Alexander II's two burgh foundations at Dingwall and Dumbarton.[73] The former struggled to make inroads into the trade that was channelled through Inverness and was even overshadowed by the commercial importance of the market which evolved at the nearby pilgrimage centre at Tain.[74] At the latter, the king was even to support the rights of the bishop's burgh at Glasgow to the trade of Argyll and the Lennox over those of the burgh he had founded. Alexander's intentions for both of his burghs, it has been argued, was not to establish them principally as new trading entrepôts but, contrary to the experience of the burghs founded by his father and great-grandfather, to create frontier plantations at the forward edge of his expanding sphere of political control: both were founded in regions where he was militarily active in the 1220s. Added to the instability of the regions in which they were planted and the unfavourable commercial position which they

[70] Perry, *Dundee Rediscovered*, 7–8; Barrow (ed.), *RRS*, ii, no. 149.
[71] Torrie, *Medieval Dundee*, 15; Perry, *Dundee Rediscovered*, 8.
[72] Palliser et al., 'The topography of towns', 154–6.
[73] Dennison, 'Burghs and burgesses', 274–82.
[74] Oram et al., *Historic Tain*, 20–30, 117–24.

received was the unsuitability of their sites. Dingwall was located on low-lying, marshy land hemmed in by hills. Dumbarton stood on a low promontory surrounded on three sides by the River Leven, prone to flooding during spates and to progressive erosion, yet lacking in sources of water for domestic or craft purposes other than from the river. The king struggled to attract colonists to his new foundations and offered generous concessions to potential settlers: at Dumbarton the usual one-year rent-free period, or *kirseth*, given to new burgesses was extended to five years and at Dingwall it was extended to ten years.[75] Such incentives were still not enough to attract significant numbers of well-connected settlers to new burghs whose trading privileges were restricted by well-established neighbouring competitors. In both, as in some of the older burghs that failed to secure anything more than a local importance, the slow infilling of burgages was one sign of over-ambition in planning and lower economic attraction to colonists.

THE TWELFTH- AND THIRTEENTH-CENTURY TOWNSCAPE

By their very nature largely colonial enterprises, the physical aspect of Scotland's developing urban landscape in the burghs must be recognised as a manifestation of alien material culture and one of the most important media through which English and European traditions in architecture, construction techniques and planning were imported. Of course, as with many aspects of the emerging culture of medieval Scotland, the result presumably was hybridity as alien and native traditions interacted, a process which was perhaps accentuated by the range of building materials available. Great caution, however, needs to be exercised in any discussion of the urban landscape of eleventh- to thirteenth-century Scotland, for no domestic building of that era survives as a fully upstanding structure, and we are wholly reliant on excavated evidence and data that can be gleaned from documentary sources.

There is a deeply entrenched popular view, based largely on English and Continental experience, of the burghs as self-contained communities defined by a circuit of walls and with fortified gates controlling access to the enclosure and the market which lay at its heart. This image has been heightened by the language used to describe the role of the burghs in the physical extension of the Scottish crown's sphere of authority;

---

[75] Duncan, *Making of the Kingdom*, 476.

these were outposts of royal power intended to secure royal domination of outlying regions, often in the wake of military conquests. Such a role does not, however, require any defensive provision; colonists, indeed, might be somewhat reluctant to settle in a fortified redoubt set in hostile, barely pacified territory, where military requirements might impinge on their ability to traffic. Defences were often secondary developments, sometimes linked to episodes of political disturbance or warfare, as at Inverness where the ditch and palisade around the town was probably constructed during King William's 1179 campaign in Ross.[76] With the exception of Roxburgh where properties in the late twelfth century were described in relation to the west gate and *murus* (the Latin term for a stone wall), or Perth, which had a stone wall and water-filled ditch around its perimeter away from the River Tay by the mid-thirteenth century, few Scottish towns had stone-built defensive circuits at any stage in their history; indeed, few may even have had earth and timber defences in the twelfth or thirteenth century.[77] Stone walls were expensive to build and keep in repair, there being no Scottish equivalent to the *murage* levy by which English town walls were maintained; even Scotland's richest burgh, Berwick, lacked such defences at the end of the thirteenth century.[78] Fortification is often interpreted nowadays as a largely symbolic projection of status by nobles; the same might be said for townsmen. The emphasis on gate structures, representations of which survive only on burgh seals, may reflect this symbolic aspect, for the gate was the most visible point of a town's perimeter and also marked the control point for policing those coming to market and assessing their goods for tolls. The rest of the perimeter might be marked by a less impressive timer rampart, earthen bank and ditch. Such was certainly the case at Inverness, where King William's charter confirming their privileges referred to the digging of the ditch at the king's expense and the burgesses' subsequent responsibility for maintaining both it and the palisade which they were to construct along its inner face.[79]

Within the enclosures, centuries of urban redevelopment, exacerbated by modern building practices, have removed much of the physical evidence for the earliest phases of most burghs' histories.[80] Much of the

---

[76] Barrow (ed.), *RRS*, ii, no. 213.
[77] Martin and Oram, 'Medieval Roxburgh', 370; Bowler, *Perth*, 24–5; Spearman, 'The medieval townscape of Perth', 48–9, 51–2; Duncan, *Making of the Kingdom*, 473–4.
[78] Palliser et al., 'The topography of towns', 174.
[79] Barrow (ed.), *RRS*, ii, no. 213.
[80] See Bowler, *Perth*, 30–1 and 55–6; Perry, *Dundee Rediscovered*, 11.

archaeological evidence for urban housing comes from excavations on what are generally described as the 'backlands' of the individual plots occupied by the town dwellers. There is a tendency to consider structures sited away from the street frontages as probably less prestigious and more poorly constructed than buildings that lined the roadways, but this is in part an attitude conditioned by later medieval and modern ideas of status and siting hierarchy, and the development of continuous building frontages.[81] Certainly, medieval street frontages have a poor survival rate in Scotland, with most having been swept away in post-medieval rebuilding operations, and even their archaeological traces have been largely eradicated by building traditions that saw the development of deep cellarage beneath street-front structures. Surviving buildings of the fifteenth and early sixteenth centuries, such as St John's House in St Andrews, present an impressive façade to the street and have helped to mould our view of how their precursors would have appeared, but archaeology is beginning to force a reconsideration of that traditional image.[82] Few medieval street frontages have been excavated in Scotland, but where they have been in some of what we might assume would be the most prestigious sections of street, for example the market area, houses could be set well back from the front of the burgage plot behind a paved foreland on which temporary or permanent booths and stalls for trading would have stood.[83] Such an arrangement is also attested by later charter evidence, as in early-fourteenth-century Roxburgh where a series of high-status tenements fronting the burgh's Market Street are recorded as standing behind rows of trading booths.[84] In Perth, one substantial, stone-built house dating from the late thirteenth century stood 15m back from the street front behind other buildings.[85] We should not, therefore, assume any uniformity of approach to the siting of houses or expect always the most prestigious building on a burgage plot to occupy the street end.

Houses and workshops could be substantial structures. In Perth High Street, most of the excavated examples were 7–8m long by 3–4m wide, with their long axis running down the burgage plot perpendicular to the street line.[86] There were, however, also some more substantial timber

---

[81] See, for example, Crone and Watson, 'Sufficiency to scarcity', 66–7.
[82] Brooks, 'St John's House', 11–15.
[83] Yeoman, *Medieval Scotland*, 55.
[84] *Kelso Liber*, no. 489.
[85] Yeoman, *Medieval Scotland*, 61.
[86] Yeoman, *Medieval Scotland*, 56; Bowler, *Perth*, 30–1.

houses, such as the late-twelfth-century dwelling from Inverness which had plank-built side walls rather than wattle panels.[87] One of the most impressive examples was uncovered in Abbey Street in St Andrews in 1970, where a late-twelfth-century timber house belonging to Adam son of Odo, the lay steward of the cathedral-priory was excavated in 1970.[88] From the thirteenth century a new building tradition of grander timber-framed houses, dubbed 'long halls' by modern archaeologists, has been identified on Perth backlands. These structures, measuring up to around 12m in length by 5.5m wide, had a double line of internal roof supports which created an aisled layout, showy plank-in-sill side walls and gables of wattle panels between the verticals of the timber frame.[89] Finds of high-status imported pottery and metalwork from such house sites indicate that they were occupied by wealthier-than-average families, perhaps members of the emerging burgess-merchant elite, or that they served as the town houses of knights from the burgh hinterland.[90] Various royal grants of plots in burghs to members of the ecclesiastical and lay elites, and by knights and members of the burgess elite to ecclesiastical institutions, point to a significant high-status presence amongst the urban population.[91] Nevertheless, although larger and better built than the common order of housing, these structures employed the same basic techniques, utilised small quantities of dressed timber and were probably still roofed with thatch, wooden shingles or a mixture of materials including possibly glazed tiles to protect the vulnerable areas such as the roof ridge, gable ends or areas around smoke-holes.[92]

Amidst this low-rise townscape of timber and thatch it was not just monumental structures such as the parish church or royal castle that reared above the general roof level. The same process of redefinition in socio-economic relationships that saw new architectural expressions of social superiority in the elite classes also made itself evident in the urban communities. Burgh architecture, like the residences and administrative centres of the ruling classes, provided a vehicle for the physical expression of hierarchy. Again like the power centres of the aristocracy, scale, height and composition provided very visible mechanisms for the

[87] Crone and Watson, 'Sufficiency to scarcity', 66.
[88] Brooks and Whittington, 'St Andrews', 291.
[89] Bowler, *Perth*, 31; Murray, 'Medieval wooden and wattle buildings', 42–3.
[90] Yeoman, *Medieval Scotland*, 60–1.
[91] For example, Barrow (ed.), *RRS*, ii, nos 341, 351, 393, 410, 459.
[92] Yeoman, *Medieval Scotland*, 56–7.

Burgh privileges

What distinguished a burgh from other towns was a charter of privileges received from its lord. For royal burghs – communities whose direct lord was the king himself – those privileges were generous; they had to attract would-be colonists to settle and gave the new community an economic advantage which established it on a secure footing. Burgesses sought to expand initial rafts of rights and privileges to gain a competitive edge over other trading communities and regularly secured expanded charters from the king to ensure that all of their privileges were given the legal strength of formal record. When the king needed financial aid – for example for the Quitclaim of Canterbury after 1189 – burgesses used their wealth to extract further concessions from the king.

King William's charter of about 1209 to the burgesses of Perth is such a consolidation of earlier awards leveraged by the burgh's willingness to meet his need for money and illustrates the concerns the heads of a community involved heavily in the cloth trade wished to have clarified or confirmed.[93] It first prohibits foreign merchants from trading anywhere in the sheriffdom of Perth outside the burgh, a mandate that handed exclusive trading privileges in their hinterland to the burgesses of Perth; foreign merchants found trading there were imprisoned at the king's will. They were also forbidden to cut cloth for sale in Perth outside the period between Ascension Day (forty days after Easter) and 1 August, but during that time they could sell their cloth in the market there like any burgess of the community. Anyone who lived in Perth and wished to associate with the burgesses was to treat with them in the market and contribute towards the king's financial aids, regardless of whose men they were. This stipulation meant that anyone who wanted to enjoy burgess privileges also had to contribute towards their burdens. To protect the lucrative wine trade, William forbade the operation of taverns in any village in the sheriffdom, unless the village's lord was a knight and resided there, in which case one tavern was permitted. The king also granted the burgesses right to a merchant gild, but he excepted the fullers and weavers from that association. Control over the valuable trade in dyed cloth was confirmed by a prohibition on anyone outside of the burgh and who was not a member of the merchant gild and contributing

---

[93] Barrow (ed.), *RRS*, ii, no. 467.

towards the king's aids dyeing cloth, unless they had received an earlier charter giving that right. Anyone found with illegally dyed or shorn cloth was to have that cloth seized by the sheriff and their case dealt with as had been the custom in the time of King David I. In a clause that points towards problems in securing adequate supplies of building timber and firewood, the king also granted his firm peace to anyone bringing those materials to Perth. Finally, in a reinforcement of earlier prohibitions, he forbade anyone from outside of the burgh to buy or sell hides or wool except within it.

Amongst the many things which this document underscores is how the granting of a burgh charter by the king was not a one-off event. It was the start of a process which entailed the securing of regular updates and expansions to address the changing circumstances and needs of the privileged community. It shows how the burgh community's leaders used their economic influence to extract maximum benefits from their royal overlord.

---

display of status and settings within which increasingly complex social relationships could be enacted. The timber long halls represent one manifestation of this social complexity, with their scale and internal division of space and function pointing towards a more elevated and hierarchically ordered household. The separation of eating and living areas and the provision of private, inner space, parallel closely the changes in form and function in lordly residences: the large main room forming a 'hall' for public social interaction and the display of the householder's social and familial superiority over dependents and junior members of the household; the partitioned-off inner space representing the 'solar', the private, reserved space of the heads of the household and their families. There is no firm evidence for who owned and occupied these structures, but finds of a spur and pieces of chainmail in association with one house might point to their being the town residences of members of the nobility, small-scale representations of their estate centres. As mentioned above, however, they may also have been a form adopted by the developing burgess elite, where master craftsmen and merchants, in whose houses lived their apprentices and servants, exercised their social superiority over their dependents.

Status may also have been projected through height. There were houses of more than one storey, such as those in Perth from whose upper levels those trapped by rising floodwaters in 1209 were rescued by rowing boat.[94] Stone foundations have been found that may simply represent footings for timber superstructures, but stone houses, however, do not seem to have been common in the Scottish townscape before the later Middle Ages, as may be reflected in the specific identification of one building owned by the monks of Coupar Angus in Perth as 'a stone house (*unum domum lapideam*)', where the labelling may be a reflection of its rarity.[95] A second stone-built house in Perth, owned in turn by Alan of Galloway and his son-in-law, Roger de Quincy, is recorded in the mid-thirteenth century.[96] At Roxburgh, trial excavations revealed the remains of what appears to be a substantial house with mortared stone-built walls, as opposed to stone footings for a timber superstructure, fronting on to one of the main thoroughfares of the burgh, while the slight structural remains from elsewhere on the site suggest that wood-and-wattle construction was again the more common building tradition.[97] Always bearing in mind that the archaeological and documentary record from the first century of Scottish towns' existence as burghs represents a meagre, fragmentary and possibly unrepresentative portion of evidence, what survives suggests that the growing wealth and political importance of the major burghs was only just beginning to be reflected in their physical environment by the end of the period under review in this chapter.

---

[94] *Chron. Bower*, iv, 457.
[95] *Coupar Angus Chrs*, no. XIII.
[96] *Scone Liber*, no. 80.
[97] Martin and Oram, 'Medieval Roxburgh', 384–9; Wessex Archaeology, *Roxburgh*, 16.

CHAPTER 9

Nobles

Perhaps the greatest difficulty to overcome in studying the medieval Scottish nobility is traditional perceptions of the structures of pre-twelfth-century Scottish society. It is important to disentangle the conflated issues of social status and noble rank. Simply because we can identify a hierarchy of king, greater and lesser nobility, and free peasants within the free members of society in England or France does not mean that identical stratification existed in Scotland in the later eleventh century. The problem, in part, is that we are conditioned into thinking of the social hierarchies of medieval northern Europe as the norm and, where hierarchy is evident in Scottish Gaelic society, grafting the language and nature of those European structures on to the Scottish experience. The roles in which we most often glimpse holders of titles are chiefly jurisdictional, presiding over courts and assemblies, gathering the provincial army or collecting *cáin*, none of which is an intrinsically 'noble' function. More problems surround possible social hierarchies in the Norse-Gaelic culture of the kingdom of the Isles; where do the 'lawmen' who appear in socio-political leadership roles in the Hebrides stand in any structure?[1] They have personal status and a following, and exercised some political authority, but there is no suggestion that they were 'nobles'. The closest analogy for them is perhaps in the *goði* and lawspeaker of eleventh- and twelfth-century Iceland; a man who held social status, influence as head of kin and considerable personal wealth, but who was still simply a prominent member of a free peasant society. Nobility is implicit in none of the activities of the Gaelic Scottish or Hebridean leadership. An elevated grade in a hierarchy gives authority

---

[1] *AFM*, ii, 698 in the early 970s.

over those in lower grades; it does not necessarily confer 'noble' status on the holder.

One significant development in ninth- to eleventh-century Scotland was a shift in the fundamental nature of social relationships: between ruler and ruled; kings and nobility; lords and dependents. The examples of Anglo-Saxon England, Gaelic Ireland or Frankish Europe suggest that the nature and exercise of power changed character. Governance and projection of authority developed in their range and intensity, with repercussions for economic relationships and the economy generally. These trends produced a reordering of social structures and stimulated developments in the 'ideological mechanisms connecting social change to the development of the state' as part of that process.[2] Institutionally, the period saw increasingly sophisticated mechanisms for the control of people and economic resources in an administrative revolution. Key in this process throughout northern Europe was the growth of more formal lordship relations within previously kin-based social and political relations.[3] What this meant was a shift from horizontal kin-based society towards a more vertically ordered structure in which new status-based peer-group bonds were forged, or, more simply, society began to stratify into hierarchies. That stratification was accompanied by accumulation of wealth and the winning of prestige based upon inclusion within the upper social echelons, attributes which were transmitted through birth; nobility was thus established.

THE MEN AT THE TOP

As explored in Chapter 6, understanding of the upper strata of native society is limited and founded on analogies with Gaelic Ireland, Anglo-Saxon England and northern Europe. Documentary sources for Scotland's upper social ranks in the later eleventh century are opaque and contentious. We rely heavily on the testimony of very few documentary witnesses and have constructed elaborate hypothetical models which have been given spurious authority and presented as established fact. The reality is that we lack adequate records to produce clear pictures of the social behaviour of those between the kings and the broad mass of the population, and archaeology does not permit anything more than analogous theorising. Furthermore, historians have often taken evidence

---

[2] Driscoll, 'Formalising the mechanisms of state power', 33.
[3] Ibid. 33.

of later periods, where a noble hierarchy is present and where the powers attendant on noble status are defined in the parchment record, and assume that this privileged hierarchy was present in earlier centuries but disguised behind Gaelic terminology.[4] There may be significant continuity in the powers and privileges of the twelfth-century nobility, but delegation or appropriation of such powers, particularly within the Gaelic heartland of the kingdom, need not be equally ancient. Indeed, the discussion in Chapter 6 indicated the difficulties in identifying in the surviving record anything that approximates to a social stratum of nobles holding extensive territorial authority; pre-twelfth-century reference to a major territorial sub-unit, especially those that emerge as earldoms in the course of the 1100s, has led to an assumption that such units were the bailiwick of a *mórmaer* whether or not any evidence for a man holding that title exists. In most of the earldoms of the kingdom of the later twelfth century there is no certainty of an ancestral link between the current earls and any earlier ruler. It seems largely to be the wishful thinking of modern historians, aided and abetted by later genealogies designed to enhance the ancestry and status of particular families that has created a substantial pre-twelfth-century ennobled class at provincial level whose status could be transmitted to their children along with a landed and jurisdictionally empowered heritage. Such a class possibly existed but unequivocal contemporary evidence for its form, power and scale is lacking.

To glimpse the upper ranks of twelfth-century Gaelic society in the heartland of Alba we depend on the parchment records of that society which date from a time when it had already been exposed to nearly a century of intensifying foreign influences. The largest body of such material, preserved within the records of Inchaffray and Lindores abbeys, relates to the earldom of Strathearn after c. 1190. Charters, written documents setting out title to landed and other property rights, were themselves symbolic of foreign cultural influence; their use reflected adoption by native magnates of legal forms and processes developed in mainland Europe and southern Britain. The power of the charter lay not just within the permanence and supremacy of the written words it contained but also in the names of the witnesses who were called upon to attest its authenticity. These were *probi homines*, a Latin term meaning 'worthy men' but where the notion of worthiness was a complex mix of good birth and economic substance. From the time of David I, the opening clauses of many royal charters called upon 'all worthy men of the whole

---

[4] See, for example, the comments in Grant, 'Thanes and Thanages', 42.

of his land' to bear witness to property grants.[5] The 'worthy' group comprised the lay and ecclesiastical leadership of his kingdom but those specifically named as witnesses were usually members of his household or council, mainly men of English and French background on hand when the document was being prepared by his clerks. Occasionally, however, we see a wider spectrum of 'worthy men', newcomers and natives, representing both the circle around the king and also the social leadership of the region where the charter's subject matter was located.[6] In the early 1100s such men were not necessarily lords or knights but they formed the area's social leadership; by the end of Malcolm IV's reign that social leadership seems automatically to have implied nobility in the eyes of clerks composing the charters. A similar transition perhaps occurred in relationships between native magnates and their officers and servants, but it is not until the early thirteenth century that the trend is visible in the charters of the Gaelic earls. Those from Strathearn contain that same division between household and men of the land, and a progressive shift from status arising from the exercise of an office to the title of that office alone denoting social elevation.

In Strathearn in the 1190s, the charters of Earl Gillebrigte reveal a group of 'worthy men' comprising the earl's family, household officers, members of the Gaelic professional legal class and administrative officers from throughout his earldom.[7] There are few obvious markers of nobility for most of this group beyond inclusion in the witness list, but there are hints that the concept of nobility by virtue of title and function had penetrated what was otherwise still a region of strongly Gaelic culture. Gillenanef, the earl's *dapifer* (official in charge of household provisions), Constantine the *iudex* (Gaelic *britheamh*, Scots 'doomster' or 'dempster', presiding officer in the earl's law courts) and Anecol 'my thane' (administrator of one of the component properties of the earldom), all men with senior official functions in the earl's household or wider society of the earldom, rub shoulders with Gilbert the knight, a man included by virtue of the status implicit in the military title which he held rather than from the function which he performed.[8] All may have enjoyed possession of landed property which added economic substance to their social worthiness, but that is nowhere explicit and while it may have been understood by their contemporaries that these were men of significant

---

[5] See Barrow (ed.), *David I Charters*, nos 25, 36–9; *RRS*, i, no. 105 onwards.
[6] Barrow (ed.), *David I Charters*, no. 120.
[7] *Inchaffray Charters*, nos II–V, IX.
[8] Ibid. no. IV.

social standing it was office and function that distinguished them. While *dapifer*, upgraded to the more prestigious *senescallus* (Latin, 'steward'), was a title used by one upwardly mobile immigrant family in the mid-twelfth century to proclaim their nobility through service to the king, in Strathearn at the end of that century it still seems primarily a household function rather than an honorific post. This position is visible in a charter of Earl Gillebrigte granting a teind of his *cáin* to the clergy of Inchaffray, where along with his brothers, son and a number of clerics, the deed was witnessed by the *iudex*, Henry the earl's *rannaire* (Gaelic 'divider of the meat'), Malise his *dapifer*, Constantine his *pincerna* (Latin 'butler') and Robert his *dispensarius* (Latin 'dispenser of food at table' or 'dispenser of charity'), that is, all the office holders involved in the food supply of the household who were affected by the disposal of part of the earl's income in produce, plus the man who might judge in disputes arising from the gift.[9] This arrangement mirrors divisions discernible in witnesses to royal charters from earlier in the twelfth century, and the same split between the king's household and advisers and a wider group of worthy men can be seen in the Strathearn charters whose subject matter had a more general impact within the earldom.

We can recognise the wider group of *probi homines* as witnesses to the foundation charter of Inchaffray, where the earl's family and household officials were joined by men whose status arose from roles in the non-household administration of the earldom, like Anecol thane of Dunning, or through association with landed estates, like Nigel of Dalpatrick.[10] The distinction is possibly reflected in reference to the 'knights and thanes' of the earldom in the preamble to the charter, a simple form of words which reveals that a profound change had occurred in the social landscape of Strathearn. Anecol, described as 'my thane' in the 1190s,[11] appears more regularly in the early 1200s as simply 'of Dunning', a shift that may reflect a personal association with the thanage beyond tenure of the administrative office of thane.[12] The naming of Anecol and Duncan, thane of Strowan, as witnesses in a grant of the church of Kinkell to Inchaffray,[13] a grant in which they otherwise had no known direct personal or official interest, possibly reflects their importance as holders of substantial properties and a shift from emphasis on their role as

---

[9] *Inchaffray Charters*, no.V.
[10] Ibid. no. IX.
[11] *Inchaffray Charters*, nos IV, XIV, XVI, XVII.
[12] Neville, *Native Lordship*, 50–2.
[13] *Inchaffray Charters*, no. XV.

administrative officers to one as leading vassals. This trend was perhaps a local reflection of the process, discussed below, that saw the transformation of administrative thanages into fiefs or feus held by men who performed military service as a knight, or the earl's alienation of portions of his personal lands to provide the feus from which the knights maintained themselves in the style which befitted their status as members of a military elite. Men identified in this way as possessors of particular landed estates become increasingly common as witnesses to charters in Strathearn in the early thirteenth century.

Such men appear on the one hand as members of a narrow group of prominent landholders who were vassals or clients of the earl and on the other as heads of their own networks of clients and dependents who were also 'worthy men'. Most are apparently of non-Gaelic background and the first may have arrived in the 1170s in Strathearn through some connection with Earl Gillebrigte's wife, Matilda de Aubigny. Tristran of Gorthy, for example, possibly had Breton ancestry, while Nigel of Dalpatrick, who appears on other occasions as Nigel de Lovetoft, was a member of a well-established family of tenants of the kings of Scots in Huntingdon.[14] A second generation of colonists came with Gillebrigte's second wife, Ysenda, whose brothers appear as Sir Richard the Knight and Geoffrey of Gask.[15] But it is too simple to say that the changing status of leading figures in the community of the earldom stemmed from a steady influx of foreign settlers bringing with them foreign ideas, for amongst the first major tenants holding an estate of Earl Gillebrigte and performing knight service in return was his younger brother, Maol Iosa. He had a feu made up of properties scattered from Comrie parish in the west to Dunning in the east, for which he gave the service of only one knight.[16] Similar provision was made in the 1190s and early 1200s for Gillebrigte and Matilda's younger sons, while their oldest surviving son and heir to the earldom, Robert, received an establishment commensurate with his position and upon which he could maintain his own household.[17] What is unclear is if the rank of knight and the consequent obligation of knight service were devices to emphasise the exalted status of these close members of the comital kin, a manifestation of that same

---

[14] Duncan, *Making of the Kingdom*, 179, 448. *Inchaffray Charters*, no. LV.
[15] *Inchaffray Charters*, no. XLVI.
[16] *RRS*, ii, no. 136. For Mael Iosa's career, see Neville, 'Native lords and the church', 454–75.
[17] *Inchaffray Charters*, no. XLI for Jordan, *senescallus* of Robert while heir to Strathearn.

fascination with the allure of knighthood which so obsessed the grandsons of King David I, or simply a response to the imposition of service obligations on the earldom by the crown. What is clear, however, is that even areas which were in some ways bastions of Gaelic tradition were in others receptive to what is often seen as the cornerstones of the foreign culture that was entering Scotland: the knight and the chivalric ideals that accompanied him.[18]

PROCESSES OF CHANGE

The example of Strathearn shows slow changes from a hierarchy of status arising from office to one in which status more clearly reflected economic substance and belief in inherited nobility arising from social position. A significant part in this development was played by the interaction of native traditions with the cultural norms of immigrants who had distinct expectations and requirements. The immigrants came to serve the Scottish king and to gain the rewards of that service but did not see their social status as arising from those rewards so much as being confirmed by them. Most were knights, members of a class that had originated as professional warriors but had transformed itself into an exclusive elite with an emerging code of rules governing their social behaviour and military conduct, thereby further distinguishing them from the broad mass of the free population. Knights were expensive to equip and maintain and awards of land-based wealth were a convenient means of allowing them to support themselves in that role. Increasingly, knightly status and the heritable, land-based wealth that underwrote that status were viewed as markers of nobility. That position had emerged in mainland Europe gradually through the late tenth and into the eleventh century but was imported wholesale into Britain and intruded into social structures which had evolved from significantly different traditions.

How their importation into Scotland was achieved requires some consideration before examining the knights and the styles of lordship and service associated with them. In southern and central England, the battle of Hastings had seen the slaughter of many adult males of the ministerial and noble strata of Anglo-Saxon society. William of Normandy, determined at first to establish his legitimacy as king as lawful heir of Edward the Confessor, seized only the estates of those who had borne arms against him. Accordingly, the first properties awarded to his followers

---

[18] Neville, 'A Celtic enclave', 75–92.

were drawn from royal estates, the lands of the defeated Godwinssons, and the confiscated possessions of other English nobles who had perished at Hastings. It was only the succession of failed rebellions against him by both surviving members of the native nobility and by disaffected members of the incoming Norman nobility which resulted in widespread seizure and redistribution of land in a process almost completed by the time that *Domesday Book* was drawn up in 1086.[19] Where a significant class of native Anglo-Saxon or Anglo-Scandinavian nobles survived, it was principally in areas where the Norman regime was bedded only shallowly by 1100, like Northumbria north of the Tees and north-western England, but even in areas of apparently total replacement many native families of noble rank remained, albeit in depressed and socially reduced circumstances.[20] Invasion, rebellion, intermarriage and limited accommodation of a small number of natives into the new lordship structures that William of Normandy had created by 1086 transformed the landholding pattern of England, altered the nature and structure of tenures, and redefined its aristocratic culture.[21] While elements of these processes can be seen in twelfth- and thirteenth-century Scotland, the mechanisms of change were largely in the control of the ruling dynasty and progressed at an altogether slower pace.

While there were repeated episodes of Anglo-Scottish warfare there was no full-blown 'Norman Conquest' of Scotland in the narrow sense of invasion and subjugation by an external foe.[22] 'Conquest' is, however, a more complex phenomenon than the popular image of straightforward invasion and military occupation, with processes of cultural or economic domination playing a far greater part than the movement of armies and planting of garrisons.[23] Domination rather than conquest is perhaps the more appropriate label for the dynamic that underpinned Scotland's relationship with England through the twelfth and thirteenth centuries. England's post-1066 experience, moreover, is not a good model for understanding the transformation that occurred in the social fabric of Scotland under the rule of the descendants of Malcolm III. There are closer parallels for the processes underway in Scotland in the first quarter of the twelfth century with the state building of Poland's Piast rulers,

---

[19] Green, *Aristocracy*, 96–7.
[20] See Williams, *The English and the Norman Conquest*; Kapelle, *Norman Conquest of the North*.
[21] See Chibnall, 'Feudalism and lordship'.
[22] Ritchie, *Normans in Scotland*, xi, xiv; McDonald, 'Old and new in the far North', 23.
[23] Davies, *Domination and conquest*, Chapter 1.

where the Polish Church, nobility and urban society was progressively remodelled under the influence of their German neighbours, but where the pace of change was directed and controlled by the native rulers.[24] Certainly, the mainland northern European culture of the Normans did become dominant in much of Scotland, particularly amongst the upper strata of society, but it was a slowly progressing shift and one which was achieved through what might be described as hybridisation rather than substitution.

In late-eleventh-century England, a new aristocratic culture was created largely through a process of expropriation of the native Anglo-Saxon nobility. In Scotland, expropriation has in the past been argued as a significant factor in some areas, such as Galloway and Moray, but elsewhere only a handful of cases where members of the native noble or administrative classes were dispossessed and replaced can be identified.[25] The apparent rarity of dispossession is perhaps in large part a consequence of the paucity of surviving records, especially for the twelfth century, for the few documented forfeitures are associated with risings in favour of Malcolm son of Alexander I or, later, the MacWilliams.[26] Given the claimed level of support for these men, it is difficult to accept that only the handful of names given in the documentary record represent the casualties of failure. The major beneficiaries of these forfeitures, however, were not foreign settlers but those members of the native leadership who supported David I and his heirs. In Moray, for example, it was the Gaelic earls of Buchan, Fife, Mar and Strathearn who gained the lordships of Abernethy, Badenoch, Glencarnie, Lochindorb, Stratha'an and Strathbogie, embracing most of the upland zone of the conquered territory; foreign colonists received less than half of 1 per cent of the land area of Moray seized by the king of Scots.[27] Men of colonist background, several already holders of estates in Lothian and Teviotdale, such as the Giffords who received Strachan in the Mearns, Tealing in Angus and Powgavie in Gowrie, were planted widely within the region between the rivers Tay and Dee in the reign of King William, mainly on portions of royal property, often former thanages.[28] But here, too, there were some native beneficiaries, like the younger son of the earl of Angus,

---

[24] Davies, *God's Playground*, Chapter 3; Górecki, 'Introduction', in *Economy, Society and Lordship in Medieval Poland*.
[25] For Galloway, see Oram, 'A family business?' and for Moray see Oram, *David I*, 91–6, 102–10.
[26] See, for example, Barrow (ed.), *RRS*, ii, no. 258.
[27] Oram, 'Castles and colonists', 291–2, 294–5.
[28] *RRS*, ii, nos 340, 418.

who received Ogilvy and Powrie in Angus.[29] A new noble class holding its lands for knight service was being created but not evidently to the cost of native families.

If there was no significant expropriation of native families and their supplanting by foreigners, how other than through alienation of royal property did members of this incoming group become established? Substitution, where a non-hereditary native overseer of a royal estate was succeeded by a colonist who was given hereditary tenure, was one possible route. Another was superimposition, where colonists were inserted into the hierarchy of power between the king and his local agents and tenants. Both these mechanisms can be seen to operate, especially south of the Forth where David I introduced the main settlement of colonists and then in the reign of William in the district from Gowrie to the borders of Mar and Buchan. A third route, however, was marriage, either of incomers to native heiresses, or of native lords to foreign wives.[30] The scale to which a single marriage could transform the political or cultural horizon of a territory should not be underestimated, nor should its importance as an instrument of patronage at the disposal of a politically expansionist monarchy be overlooked. We have already seen the ramifications and consequences of the marriages of Malcolm III, Alexander I and David I, which should rank alongside Richard de Clare's marriage to Dervorgilla, daughter of Diarmid, king of Leinster, as triggers for decisive change. But no less emphasis should be placed on marriages that occurred between c. 1150 and c. 1200 which linked most of the great Gaelic families who ruled the lordships and earldoms that stretched from Galloway through the Lennox and Strathearn to Buchan to leading families within the circle of colonists around the king.

One purpose behind such marriages was to strengthen ties between leading lineages and the royal house. In England, Henry I employed his many illegitimate daughters to execute just such a policy by tying members of the Scottish, Norman and French nobility to Henry's interests. There was no insult intended in the marriage of Sibylla to Alexander I, but it placed him on a par with the ruler of Galloway, or with the dukes of Brittany, counts of Perche or lords of Montmorenci, Montmirail, Breteuil or Beaumont, who also wed one of the king's bastard daughters.[31] More significance should be placed on the fact

---

[29] Ibid. no. 140; Duncan, *Making of the Kingdom*, 177–8.
[30] Bartlett, *Making of Europe*, 55–6, 230–2; Davies, *Domination and Conquest*, 5, 51–4.
[31] Given-Wilson and Curteis, *Royal Bastards*; Green, *Henry I*, 309; Thompson, *Power and Border Lordship*, 71–2.

that no Welsh prince was honoured by such a match. The Scottish and Galwegian rulers were men to be cultivated and bound to Henry's side, as necessary for the security of his realm as the border magnates along the Norman-French frontier who were likewise dignified. Through the children born of such marriages, moreover, Henry created a network of royal kinship, replacing basic bonds of lordship or diplomacy with blood links. Similar considerations influenced the marriage policies of the Scottish royal house; in the 1190s, King William used his illegitimate daughters to cultivate the de Vescy and de Ros families in Northumberland at a time when he was manoeuvring for a restoration of the earldom to him. Around the same time, his younger brother's illegitimate daughter, Ada, was married to Maol Iosa, the younger brother of Earl Gillebrigte of Strathearn, strengthening links with a powerful family who had opposed royal policies in the previous generation.[32]

A consequence of such unions was enhanced prestige for the kin honoured by a royal marriage and their further social elevation through the cachet that royal kinship bestowed. One of the most important such marriages was that between Duncan II, earl of Fife, and Ela, who was possibly a daughter of Reginald de Warenne and niece of Ada de Warenne, the wife of Earl Henry and mother of kings Malcolm IV and William.[33] Not only did this marriage to a royal cousin recognise the political importance and social prestige of the Fifes and align them firmly with the ruling house, but it also provided them with an entry into the inner circle of David I's new aristocracy. A second de Warenne marriage served a similar purpose, linking the comital family in Mar to both the Fifes and the royal house.[34] Agnes, wife of Morgrund, earl of Mar (fl. 1147–78), was another kinswoman of Ada de Warenne.[35] Morgrund has on no good grounds been seen as hostile to David I's new order;[36] a de Warenne marriage suggests instead that not only was he being cultivated by the royal house and its supporters but he was also not averse to the cultivation. Geoffrey Barrow has argued that the de Warenne match was a symptom rather than the cause of the Fifes' identification with the new prescription in the kingdom and part of an effort to maintain their status amongst the rising stars of the colonist families. They also had become aggressive 'internal colonists' themselves, acquisitive expanders

---

[32] Stringer, *Earl David*, 41.
[33] Barrow, *Anglo-Norman Era*, 87–8; Barrow, 'The earls of Fife', 54.
[34] Oram, 'Earls and earldom of Mar', 49–50.
[35] Duncan, 'Isle of May', 74, no. 52.
[36] *RRS*, i, 12.

of their landed base to provide the resources to attract into their service and reward knightly followers.[37] If Barrow is correct in his assessment, the Fifes nevertheless entered their new social and cultural relationships on their own terms and tightly controlled the rate and scale of change within their earldom. Men who perhaps owed their entry into the following of the Fifes through previous de Warenne connections seem, like 'Sir Gilbert the knight of Cleish',[38] to have received estates peripheral to the earldom core, possibly recently acquired by the earls. Within their territorial heartland, however, although the earls' household acquired 'Anglo-Norman' material trappings under de Warenne influence, the Fifes neither embraced the physical expression of Continental lordship and built themselves a castle nor followed the royal family in abandoning Gaelic naming patterns and adopting Norman-French male names.[39] While they may have identified in many ways with the new order, their adherence to ancestral naming patterns throughout this period of social and cultural revolution points to a conscious stressing of their Gaelic lineage.

Fife blood, too, was a medium for the attempted tying of other native families to the royal house. Marriage to Fife daughters was employed both to show honour to the favoured husband and also to bind him into the new regime. Two examples illustrate this policy: in Galloway, where the unnamed wife of Gillebrigte, whose marriage may date from the period of Scottish domination in the 1160s, was a daughter or sister of Earl Duncan II of Fife;[40] and in Caithness, where Harald Maddadsson's slighted first wife was Duncan's daughter, Affreca. In both cases, the Fife link was intended to draw in men whose political ambitions diverged from Scottish royal interest but whose territories, personal alliances and wider kin associations were of vital importance for the security of the realm. Marriage to Fife sons may also have been an important mechanism for reconciling native kindreds to the interests and agendas of the Scottish crown, perhaps most importantly where there had been a recent history of hostility to royal policy. Such considerations perhaps lay behind the marriage of Malcolm, son and heir of Earl Duncan II of Fife, to Matilda, eldest daughter of Earl Gillebrigte of Strathearn.[41] But the

---

[37] Barrow, *Anglo-Norman Era*, 84–9, esp. 87.
[38] Ibid. 87.
[39] See Oram, 'Royal and lordly residence', 172, 177–83; Bartlett, *Making of Europe*, 270–80.
[40] Oram, *Lordship of Galloway*, 89–90.
[41] Neville, *Native Lordship*, 48–9.

Marriage alliances, political bonds and cultural change

Marriage was vital in consolidating Scottish domination of territories peripheral to the royal heartland. One clear case is Galloway, whose strategic importance brought a succession of important marriages for its rulers, starting with Fergus's marriage to a bastard daughter of Henry I. While his elder son, Gillebrigte, married a Fife daughter, Uhtred, son of Fergus's marriage to Henry's daughter, wed Gunnilda, daughter of Waltheof of Allerdale, a cousin of the Dunbar earls and of William, son of King Duncan II.[42] This union augmented Uhtred's Norman lineage, bound him to Cumberland's nobility and forged a kinship tie with the Scottish crown. Uhtred's sister married Walter de Berkeley, the king's chamberlain, likewise strengthening Galloway's bonds with the colonial lords around the king, and his eldest son, Roland, married Helen, daughter of Richard de Morville, the royal constable and confidant of King William in the 1170s.[43] Through Helen, the Galloways acquired the de Morville lands and hereditary office of constable, a windfall that completed the entry of their sons, Alan and Thomas, into the ranks of the Anglo-Scottish nobility. Alan's marriages linked him first to the Pontefract Lacys, then to the Scottish crown through Margaret, daughter of Earl David of Huntingdon, and finally to the Ulster Lacys, three matches that highlight his political connections, internationality and ambitions.[44] Thomas, too, secured a prestigious marriage – to Isabella, countess of Atholl – which transformed him from military adventurer in English service into major vassal of the Scottish crown.[45] Such marital connections exposed Galloway to English and continental cultural influences and introduced colonists from among the kin networks of new wives and husbands. Those colonists and heads of native kindreds formed a new nobility holding properties as vassals of the lords of Galloway and distinguished with the title and status of knights.[46]

Strathearns were also adept at using daughters to establish links with the rising stars of the new nobility descended from the colonists introduced by David I. Gillebrigte's second daughter, Cecilia, married Walter II son

---

[42] For the marital network of Uhtred, see *Wetheral Register*, 386–7.
[43] Oram, *Lordship of Galloway*, 98–9, 198–9; Barrow, *Anglo-Norman Era*, 70–84.
[44] Oram, *Lordship of Galloway*, 112–13, 115, 123–4; Stringer, 'A new wife for Alan of Galloway', 49–55.
[45] Oram, *Lordship of Galloway*, 114–15.
[46] Oram, 'A family business?'.

of Alan, the king's steward, while her younger sister became the wife of David de la Hay, lord of Errol in Gowrie and later sheriff of Forfar. The mutual benefits that flowed from such marriages were recognised by native and newcomer and became as much a means of consolidating the status of the major Gaelic kindreds as social and political leaders within the heartland of Alba as they were a mechanism for binding the new aristocracy into the social and cultural fabric of the kingdom.

KNIGHTS AND FEUDAL LORDS

One of the key attributes and central attractions of the Continental noble culture that was filtering into Scotland from the later eleventh century was the knight and the specialist warrior role that he fulfilled. From origins as non-noble members in the retinues of Frankish magnates, knights had acquired a cachet of exclusivity and social eminence further enhanced by the increasing cost of equipment and the specialist training necessary for mounted combat. That fact alone made it necessary for such men to possess adequate resources, usually landed property, from which to meet such costs. The band of Norman knights who entered Macbeth's service following their expulsion from England in the 1050s and those who accompanied Duncan II in 1094 were military members of the king's following in the fashion of the *huscarls* of the eleventh-century Anglo-Danish kings of England; they were not nobles *per se* but trained warriors maintained in the royal household. They apparently did not receive land in return for their service and their relationship with their lord was personal and professional rather than tenurial. Mercenary is a label that carries pejorative overtones in modern usage, but it is perhaps an appropriate description of the relationship between these eleventh-century kings and their knights. The latter presumably received a fee expressed in terms of portable wealth rather than land. A shift, however, occurred in the early 1100s, when men of knightly status began to receive landed estates in return for military and other service owed to the crown. In this development, we are perhaps seeing a transition from knights functioning as a military adjunct of the royal household – although there was probably always a corps of young men maintained in that role by the king – into a landholding military aristocracy. As was the case in England into the later thirteenth century, however, the body of largely landless young knights – *iuvenes* – retained in the king's household may have been more significant in providing an effective fighting force of trained heavy cavalry than was produced by the rather limited service obligations attached to crown infeftments. It may have been such *iuvenes* who formed the band of 'vigorous and warlike youths' led by Roland of Galloway who defeated and killed Donald MacWilliam in 1187.[47]

An award of land in return for service as a knight in the king's army may have been the driving ambition of many young men who came to Scotland in the twelfth century. A few who had close personal ties with David I during his earlier career in England, like Robert de Bruce and Hugh de Morville, received extensive territories which established them as regional lords.[48] Most, however, acquired more compact properties and many of these had been thanages which formed discrete components within the royal lands. But even the king was unable to find adequate land at will and had to compromise until the opportunity presented itself. Such was the case at Athelstaneford in East Lothian, given for half of a knight's service to Alexander de St Martin; the king making up the other half in cash until such time as he could find suitable land to give Alexander.[49] A more fragmented holding in central Roxburghshire was granted to Walter de Ryedale for the service of one knight.[50] Evidence for the award of estates for the service of one knight survives with greater frequency from the reign of Malcolm IV, such as the three parcels of land in Berwickshire and Roxburghshire granted to Walter son of Alan, the Steward; Lundin in Fife given to Philip the Chamberlain; or Rosyth and Dunduff awarded to Ralph Frebern,[51] while in the reign of his brother they occur throughout the kingdom. The frequency with which such men attest charters of the king and the greater regional lords indicates that they were numbered amongst the *probi homines*, and it is equally apparent that their inclusion in that group was a direct consequence of their status as knights and as possessors of landed wealth.

Greater landholdings were granted for the service of a specified number of knights, like the five demanded of Walter the Steward.[52] These multiple service requirements have been likened to the English *servitium debitum*, an assessment of service dues imposed by William the Conqueror on baronies to spread the burden of maintaining an army of occupation in the years after 1066, but even the most onerous Scottish

---

[47] Benedict of Peterborough, ii, 7–9. For discussion of *iuvenes*, see Duby, *Chivalrous Society*, 114–15; Hanley, *War and Combat*, 24; Duncan, *Making of the Kingdom*, 378.
[48] Barrow (ed.), *David I Charters*, no. 16.
[49] Ibid. no. 194.
[50] Ibid. no. 177.
[51] Barrow (ed.), *RRS*, i, nos 183, 255, 256.
[52] Ibid. i, no. 184.

examples nowhere reach the level of those in England.[53] The low level of service required in Scotland does not seem a reflection of lower economic value attached to the lands granted to lords for knight service, pointing instead to wholly different expectations and needs on the part of the king. The case of Annandale is commonly used to illustrate this matter, with David I's award of lordship over this great block of property to Robert de Brus imposing no knight-service obligation.[54] It was not until c. 1172 in a re-grant of Annandale to Robert II de Bruce, which set out his rights with far greater precision than in the charter given to his father, that the service due to the crown in return – set at ten knights – was stipulated.[55] Why this *servitium debitum* was stated so explicitly in the re-grant but wholly omitted in the original award is unknown, but it is generally supposed to reflect a trend towards definitive statements of service due to the crown intended both to safeguard the king's interests and to give the landholder a legal prescription of his obligations. In the early days of the colonial establishment a lord might simply have been expected to answer a royal summons with all of his knights, a vagueness which may have been a disincentive to great landholders to introduce further knightly colonists as sub-tenants on their properties. The late-twelfth-century definition of service obligations may have been a statement of the expected minimum.

Evidence for such a group of knightly sub-tenants can be identified in Annandale in the later twelfth and early thirteenth century. It is equally evident, however, that by that date, in common with knight-service tenancies around the kingdom, the structures set in place in the earlier twelfth century had quickly broken down.[56] For a variety of reasons, men had alienated portions of the land given to them, breaking knight-service baronies into fractional units held by several individuals. It can also be seen, however, that some men accumulated new holdings comprising multiple such fractions and, although they may not have held these accumulated properties for the collective service of a knight, they had the title and status of knight. They had wealth, landed property and influence, for such men came to form the council that advised their superior lord, and they also provided him with a military following. However, it was their economic and social roles rather than any military obligation that

---

[53] Duncan, *Making of the Kingdom*, 377.
[54] Barrow (ed.), *David I Charters*, no. 16. For discussion, see Duncan, *Making of the Kingdom*, 376–7.
[55] Barrow (ed.), *RRS*, ii, no. 80.
[56] Duncan, *Making of the Kingdom*, 390–1; Corser, 'Annandale', 45–59.

brought them the rank and title of knighthood; to be designated a knight was a mark of acknowledged noble status and personal distinction as an exponent of the chivalric arts, not a statement of warrior function.

The allure of knighthood as a social distinction reached its apogee in the Romance culture of the twelfth century and is best represented in Scotland by the desperation of the young Malcolm IV and his brother, William, to secure knightly status from Henry II. Chronicle reference to Malcolm's successive failures to receive the accolade from his cousin underscores how important knighthood was to a teenage king who had been raised in a household whose male society was saturated with the ethos of the still-evolving chivalric ideal. His youngest brother, Earl David of Huntingdon, later enjoyed a reputation as a knightly paragon, a status emphasised by his singular treatment in Jordan Fantosme's verse chronicle of the war of 1174.[57] In 1215, Ferchar McTaggart's principal reward for eliminating the MacWilliam challenge in that year was knighthood, a mark of distinction that branded him as an agent of royal authority in Ross.[58] For Ferchar, knighthood also signalled ennoblement and consolidation of his social elevation over the Gaelic leadership of Ross, which was confirmed by c. 1230 when he was given the title of earl which had been held by the MacHeths until 1168.[59] Discussions of Ferchar's probable social background and his rise to regional domination have been central to analysis of his emergence as a key royal agent in an area where the power of the Scottish crown had lacked a substantial presence until the 1210s.[60] What has not been considered is how, if at all, these shiny new titles and entry into the top rank of the political community immediately below the king affected his social behaviour and standing in the community from which he sprang. Ferchar is a symbol of the high tide of 'feudalisation', a knight and earl of new creation holding his position in Ross as a vassal of the Scottish king, but his power rested not on any knightly sub-tenants but on his ability to put Gaelic warriors into the field and galleys onto the seas.

The similar 'Janus-like' character of Alan of Galloway as he moved between the Frankish milieu of the English and Scottish royal courts and the Gaelic culture of his ancestral lordship in the 1200s has been

---

[57] *Jordan Fantosme's Chronicle*, lines 1098–9; Hanley, *War and Combat*, 68.
[58] *Chron. Melrose*, s.a. 1215; McDonald, 'Old and new in the far North', 28; Grant, 'Province of Ross'.
[59] Duncan, *Making of the Kingdom*, 529.
[60] Grant, 'Province of Ross', 117–22; McDonald, 'Old and new in the far North', 28–30.

remarked upon.[61] While Alan fulfilled a 'feudal' function as constable of the king of Scots and supplied knights for royal armies both from his inherited de Morville lands and from Galloway, his main military capability was founded on non-feudal resources. The scale of those resources is indicated by King John's request in 1210 that Alan provide 'one thousand of his best and most active Galwegians' for his Welsh campaign,[62] or the fleet that Alan assembled in 1230 to invade Man.[63] But numbers of warriors is not the real issue in the significance attached to him; it is the duality of the character that Alan presented to the world and his ability to adopt differing personae in his different environments. But why should this chameleon-like behaviour seem so remarkable in a major territorial magnate in thirteenth-century Scotland? In large part it is a question of perception arising from the nineteenth-century tradition of cataloguing and categorisation; everything was given its appropriate label and that label carried particular socially or culturally deterministic descriptors; to be 'Normanised' meant by definition to be hostile to and to have entirely rejected native tradition, while 'Gaelic' implied conservatism, hostility to 'feudalism' and even varying degrees of xenophobia. Such stereotypical caricatures stalk discussions of the confrontation between Malcolm IV and his earls at Perth in 1160 and of the same king's turbulent relationship with Somerled of Argyll, yet contemporary accounts of neither affair play what might nowadays be termed 'the race card'. Normanisation or feudalisation of native magnates, their kin and lordships have been commonly explored themes; Gaelicisation by contrast has rarely registered in historical studies of the pre-1300 period. It is recognised that leading Gaelic families like the MacDonalds and Campbells in the fifteenth to seventeenth centuries were exponents of a culture shift to suit their environment, adjusting comfortably from Gaelic to Lowland Scots and back as they moved between their Highland and Lowland properties and socio-political role,[64] and that non-Gaelic families like the Frasers, Chisholms and Gordons could move as easily in the other direction. There is something oddly perverse in ignoring the Gaelic dimension to the socio-political behaviour of families like the Stewarts and the Comyns by the early thirteenth century and continuing to label them as 'Anglo-Norman' despite their intermarriage with Gaelic lineages or entry into the cultural world of the Gaels. It has long been recognised

[61] Stringer, 'Periphery and core', 82–4, 98–9.
[62] *CDS*, i, no. 529.
[63] *Eirspennill's Hâkon Hâkon's son's saga*, cc. 167–9; Stringer, 'Periphery and core', 84.
[64] See, for example, Boardman, 'Pillars of the community', 138–44, 148–9.

that Gaelic families embraced aspects of the cultural trappings of the colonial lords, from their personal names to their clothing, their style of fighting to their preferred diet, but the flow was two-way and there is a need in future to explore how the colonists and their descendants acculturised with the society into which they were implanted.

SETTLERS

Geoffrey Barrow's pioneering work on the origins of men who settled in Scotland between 1124 and 1250 underscored the degree of connection between them before they arrived in Scotland. For David I, friendships made in the service of his brother-in-law, Henry I of England, provided the bond with many of the men who figured most prominently amongst his new nobility in Scotland, the best-known of whom was Robert de Bruce to whom he gave Annandale. Marriage, however, also provided access to potential recruits. The importance of the earldom of Huntingdon as a source of colonists, mainly younger sons of families who were already prominent there as tenants of knightly status, is well known.[65] It continued to form a reservoir of recruits later in the twelfth century under David I's grandson, Earl David, who found many of the men whom he implanted into his lordship of the Garioch in central Aberdeenshire amongst his Huntingdon vassals, as well as from the associates of his mother's de Warenne kin.[66] As discussed earlier, the de Warenne family and their network were drawn upon extensively as a means of extending crown interests through marriage alliances and, in turn, the connections thus forged provided conduits for other members of the family and their dependents to acquire land in Scotland. Networks of associates and external recruiting grounds accessed through marital ties, however, were not solely the preserve of the royal house; they were also devices that brought knightly colonists to areas where the Scottish king lacked a personal property-based presence.

Galloway was the most important of such areas linked traditionally to political disturbance domestically and military intervention by the Scottish crown which experienced an influx of colonists.[67] A first phase followed the overthrow of Fergus in 1160 and has been presented as a manifestation of Scottish lordship imposed on the defeated territory

---

[65] Ritchie, *Normans in Scotland*, 214; Barrow, *Anglo-Norman Era*, 97–101.
[66] Stringer, *Earl David*, 82–91.
[67] Oram, *Lordship of Galloway*, 191–204.

Figure 9.1 Mote of Urr, Dumfries and Galloway: the flat-topped motte of Walter de Berkeley's earth-and-timber castle rises above the enclosing bank and ditch of the bailey, or courtyard, which may be a reused prehistoric fortification.

by Malcolm IV, with the settlers serving as supervisory agents or an occupying garrison. A second analysis of the fragmentary record of that settlement, however, reveals that marital ties played a significant part in the process.[68] The main group of colonists brought in to Galloway in the 1160s came principally from Cumberland and Westmorland, men like Hugh de Morville the younger, who received Borgue, David son of Terrus, who was granted Anwoth, or Richard son of Troite, who became lord of Lochindeloch.[69] Most were kinsmen, neighbours or tenants of Gunnilda, the wife of Fergus's son, Uhtred, and her family, who were lords of Allerdale in the Lake District and cousins of the Scottish earls of Dunbar.[70] The marriage had probably been arranged during the 1140s when the Scots were consolidating their hold over English Cumbria and it created bonds between one of the heirs of the ruler of Galloway and the

---

[68] Ibid. 194–200.
[69] *Dryburgh Liber*, no. 68 (Borgue); *Holyrood Liber*, no. 49 (Anwoth); Cumbria Record Office, Lowther Archive, D/Lons/L5/1/S1 (Lochindeloch); Barrow, *Anglo-Norman Era*, 31, note 3, 73.
[70] For Gunnilda's kin, see *Wetheral Registrum*, no. 245.

Scottish royal house and provided Uhtred, who was a grandson of Henry I of England, with an entry into Anglo-Scottish noble society. One of the most important recipients of a lordship from Uhtred was Walter de Berkeley, chamberlain of King William and probably Uhtred's brother-in-law. Given his close personal relationship with some of these men, it is unlikely that Uhtred's participation in the 1174 rising in Galloway was a reaction to the imposition of foreign settlers upon him by the Scottish crown, and it was with the support of such men that Uhtred's son, Roland, managed to retain at least part of his patrimony in the face of his uncle's aggression in 1174–5 and then seize his cousin's lands in 1185–6.[71]

In the later of the two chronicled phases of settlement in Galloway which followed Roland's seizure of Gillebrigte's lands, kinship with the native ruling house was an important factor in securing property and reveals the level to which this Gaelic dynasty had intermarried with the dominant English and Scottish aristocratic families. Most of the new men were members of old Anglian families established in north-western England since before the end of the eleventh century but who also had strong kinship or service ties to the families of Uhtred and Roland or to Roland's de Morville wife, or who had arrived in Galloway through Roland's connections with the Scottish royal household.[72] They maintained their prominence under Roland's son, Alan, forming an inner circle of household officers and advisors, and becoming a major component of the *probi homines* of his lordship. But just as the charters of the kings of Scots and the earls north of the Forth reveal division of this broad class of worthy men into a narrow clique of kinsmen and officials and a wider body of 'men of the land', so in Galloway it is possible to see the shadowy presence beyond the bright lights of the charter witness lists of a largely Gaelic but increasingly hybridised social leadership.[73]

Colonial settlement in Galloway was controlled by rulers who could spread the impact of the new arrivals through dispersal across their wide territories. While the greater reserves of land available to Uhtred and his successors in some areas led to a heavier concentration of colonists there, overall the newcomers slotted into an existing pattern of landholding power and became embedded within two generations. A far greater impact was felt in areas where intensive settlement occurred, most notably in upper Clydesdale and Douglasdale. There, a tightly knit

[71] Oram, *Lordship of Galloway*, 201–2.
[72] Ibid. 201–4.
[73] Oram, 'A family business?', 135–40, 144–5.

group of colonists of probably Flemish background was settled late in the reign of Malcolm IV.[74] These men were direct tenants of the crown but no charters infefting them have survived to enable us to see exactly what they were granted and on what terms. We can, however, reconstruct some picture of the scale and pattern of settlement, and suggest how the colonising process was facilitated. This area of Clydesdale, formerly part of the kingdom of Strathclyde and a territory at the western edge of the district over which David I had begun to rule as prince of the Cumbrian region, had become more fully dominated by Scottish royal power by the 1150s. Ephemeral traces of a probably pre-twelfth-century estate structure can be identified, but the region is otherwise one where evidence for an established hierarchy of native lordship is absent. The strategic importance of the area, where important routes north from Carlisle and west from Tweeddale converged near Lanark, and its light economic development made it important for the crown to control and attractive to developers willing to act as crown agents. The leader in that development process was a man named Baldwin, who was granted the lordship of Biggar and was important enough in the 1160s to serve as sheriff of Lanark or Clydesdale.[75] Baldwin of Biggar has long been seen as the lynchpin in the settlement, having kin connections with some of the other known colonists like his stepson, John, after whom Crawfordjohn at the south-western extremity of the district is named, and wider personal links with others in Lothian and the north of England.[76] No documentary proof of the possibility exists, but it seems likely that he was what is known as a *locator* or *populator*, an agent who was given a large block of property and delegated the responsibility of finding colonists willing to begin its more intensive economic development on behalf of a superior lord.[77] His success can be measured against the intensity of apparently Flemish settlement which can be recovered from charter and place-name evidence in the region.

North of the Forth, the scale and pace of colonial settlement was more limited and the role of Gaelic 'internal' colonists potentially more significant than that of foreign knights. Six of the seven major lordships in the central Highlands recorded for the first time in the late twelfth or early thirteenth centuries were in the hands of Gaelic or Gaelicised

---

[74] Tabraham, 'Norman settlement in upper Clydesdale', 114–28; Toorians, 'Flemish settlement', 4, 5–10.
[75] Duncan, *Making of the Kingdom*, 137; Barrow (ed.), *RRS*, i, nos 184, 197.
[76] Toorians, 'Flemish settlement', 6–9.
[77] Bartlett, *Making of Europe*, 121–2, 142–4.

Motte-and-bailey castles

One potent symbol of the Continental-style noble culture introduced to Scotland in the twelfth century was the motte-and-bailey castle.[78] In England after 1066 and Ireland after 1169, these earthwork-and-timber fortifications were associated with invasion and conquest, often serving as garrison posts to dominate a district. In Scotland it is rare to see them functioning as more than lordly residences and estate centres even in areas where the Scottish crown was imposing its lordship by military means. That is not to say that they did not need to be defensible and that they did not experience attack from hostile native peoples; chronicle accounts of the 1174 rebellion in Galloway refer to attacks on castles built there by Scottish king and his men, while in 1228 Thomas of Thirlestane, one of Alexander II's vassals, perished when his motte-and-bailey at Abertarff on Loch Ness-side was burned by supporters of the MacWilliams.[79] It is also difficult to see them as a marker exclusively of colonist-knights, for it is now understood that by the 1180s – if not earlier – Gaelic lords who were adopting elements of the incoming culture were also building mottes of their own as symbols of their enhanced social status.[80]

It was also for long thought that mottes were favoured in the early years of a conquest because they were cheap to fund and quick to build using readily available materials. Comprising mounds of rammed earth – the motte – heaped up from a surrounding ditch and sometimes with an enclosure at low level on one side – the bailey – they were viewed until recently as unsophisticated in comparison to the stone-built castles of later centuries, mainly because their structures have long since rotted away to leave only the earthen mounds and ditches. Excavation, however, has revealed that the mottes and their timber superstructures and timber buildings in the baileys were instead very sophisticated constructions that took long periods to erect and which were maintained and enhanced over time. At Mote of Urr in Galloway, for example, the timber castle was rebuilt after destruction probably in the 1174 rebellion and was re-used possibly

---

[78] Higham and Barker, *Timber Castles*; Oram, 'Royal and lordly residence'.
[79] Anderson (ed.), *Scottish Annals*, 256; Bower, *Scotichronicon*, vol. 5, 143.
[80] Oram, *Lordship of Galloway*, Chapter 8.

> as late as the 1350s.[81] Duffus in Moray, one of the most imposing motte-and-bailey castles in Scotland, was first constructed around 1150 and had its timber buildings replaced in stone only in the early 1300s.[82]

families from south of the Mounth.[83] The distribution of the colonists was very patchy and dictated largely by either existing concentrations of royal estates which could be mediatised or by property seizures arising from the aggressive expansion of royal authority; settlement within the territorial heartlands of the native magnates of the core of the eleventh- and twelfth-century kingdom made little headway before the third quarter of the thirteenth century. In Strathearn and Lennox, for example, it was not until the post-1250 period that men of apparently English or northern French ancestry, or at least who used Anglo-French name forms, predominated within the formerly strongly Gaelic nobility of those earldoms.[84] In Mar, despite the marriage of Earl Morgrund into the Fife/Warenne family, neither he nor his successors settled knightly colonists within the earldom, and families of recognisably foreign descent do not appear to have become established there until the 1300s.[85] Even in neighbouring Buchan, where in the earliest instance of a major Gaelic lordship passing into the hands of a descendant of one of the twelfth-century colonial families the earldom passed in the 1210s to William Comyn, there are few indications of a radical reconfiguration of the landholding pattern and the nature of tenures.[86] There, foreign cultural influences and the occasional foreign colonist can be traced in the charters of Fergus, last of the Gaelic earls, the process intensifying under William Comyn, but what is more striking is the level of continuity of Gaelic practice and social organisation.[87] For all his 'Norman' credentials, Earl William functioned largely as his Gaelic predecessors had done.

Evidence for the implantation into the Moray lowlands of a colonial aristocracy in the immediate aftermath of its conquest by David I is fragmentary and remains thin under Malcolm IV.[88] Even in the

---

[81] Hope-Taylor, 'Excavations at Mote of Urr'.
[82] Cruden, *Scottish Castle*, 125–6.
[83] Ross, 'Glencarnie', 164.
[84] Neville, *Native Lordship*, 39.
[85] Oram, 'Earls and earldom of Mar', 49–50.
[86] Young, *The Comyns*, 22–30.
[87] Young, 'Earls and earldom of Buchan', 179–82.
[88] Oram, 'Castles and colonists', 290–6; Oram, 'Moray', 7; Toorians, 'Flemish settlement', 4–5.

thirteenth century, from when record materials for Moray survive in greater numbers, the picture remains of fairly sparse settlement with most of the identifiable colonial lords descended from or otherwise connected with an individual called Freskin, known to modern historians as 'the Fleming' or 'de Moravia'. This Freskin held a small lordship near Uphall in Midlothian by early in the reign of David I, but acquired a much larger holding in the Laigh of Moray, centred on Duffus, before c. 1150. Berowald, another Fleming with pre-existing Lothian connections, received land from Malcolm IV at Innes and Urquhart north-east of Elgin for the service of one knight.[89] A personal connection with Freskin and his family is unknown, but Berowald's lands at Bo'ness in West Lothian lay close to Uphall.[90] Freskin, like Baldwin of Biggar in Clydesdale, may have been a *locator* for the king of Scots in the coastal district of Moray, where a distinctly Flemish character has been noted in the organisation of the urban communities.[91] There are suggestions, too, of a connection between the families of Freskin and Douglas, the latter of whom may also have been Flemish in background. In 1203 one of them, Brice of Douglas, became bishop of Moray and it was possibly through him that links between Clydesdale and Moray were reinforced in the thirteenth century.[92]

For all the cultural labels applied to Baldwin of Biggar or Freskin of Duffus and their English, Norman, French or Burgundian colleagues who entered Scotland in the century and a half after 1070, it has proven impossible to progress beyond the broadest of discussions of any distinctive characteristics that can be associated with any of the clusters of settlers of apparently related background. The potential of the hills of upper Clydesdale for the development of sheep runs or the marshes and lagoons of the Laigh of Moray for the drainage schemes in which the Flemings had already established an international reputation by the eleventh century have been advanced as reasons why Flemish colonies were attracted to those districts. Nothing more substantial, however, has yet been identified as a unique indicator of Flemish identity, or for that matter of Breton, Norman or English. Indeed, throughout all the areas of intensive colonisation there is a certain commonality to the most visible evidence of an implanted noble culture; whatever language he spoke or region he regarded as his homeland, the colonists appear united by the chivalric ideal.

---

[89] Barrow (ed.), *RRS*, i, no. 175.
[90] Toorians, 'Flemish settlement', 4–5.
[91] See p. 282.
[92] Toorians, 'Flemish settlement', 9.

Figure 9.2 Culross Abbey, Fife: the ruins of the Cistercian abbey founded in 1217 by Malcolm, earl of Fife.

RELIGIOUS PATRONAGE AND PERSONAL DEVOTION

Beyond the parchment charters that record the arrival and spread of the colonial nobility and the wax seals of the granters used to authenticate the documents, little of the material culture of the upper ranks of the social hierarchy of Scotland from the late eleventh to the early thirteenth century has survived. Few lordly residences of this period have been excavated and the largely earthwork remains at their sites have helped to establish a rather negative impression of their likely level of structural sophistication. The material evidence for their daily life is equally scant, with a scatter of high-quality artefacts – the Lewis Chessmen, a mirror-case from Perth and an ivory comb from Jedburgh Abbey – being taken as representative of the trappings of high-status living. Much of the artefact evidence for that lifestyle, however, has been recovered from monastic or urban rather than specifically aristocratic contexts.[93] Analogy with England and Continental examples can go far towards illustrating the daily lives of the newcomers, but it does not offer any meaningful insight into the physical environment and material cultural repertoire of the upper levels of Gaelic or Anglian society, and nor does it allow us to track the daily realities of the process of intermarriage, cultural interaction and hybridisation. In sharp contrast to the dearth of information concerning the lifestyles and daily domestic existence of the native magnates and colonial knights and their families, significantly more evidence survives to cast light on some of their most personal behaviour, their spiritual activities.

The origins and development of the parish structure is discussed in Chapter 10, but at this point it is important to consider the role of the knights and wider nobility in the formative process. There is a close correlation between the knight-service baronies created by the king for the colonists who were settling in the kingdom and the pattern of parishes that was beginning to crystallise in at least southern Scotland in the mid-twelfth century.[94] To what extent the provision of a church to serve the people of the new lordship was an expected obligation on its holder can only be conjectured but by the early 1100s in addition to making provision from their lands and revenues for the support of a priest lords were assuming responsibility for providing the church buildings. The

---

[93] Owen, *William the Lion*, 188–92; Higgit, 'The comb, pendant and buckle', 83–4; Oram, 'Royal and lordly residence'.
[94] Cowan, *Medieval Church in Scotland*, 2, 5–11.

true antiquity of church building as a function of lay lordship is probably masked by the lack of a substantial surviving documentary record earlier than the last years of the eleventh century. The oldest surviving record of a landholder taking on this responsibility is at Ednam in the Merse, where in c. 1105 Thor the Long paid for and had built a church on the land given to him by King Edgar.[95] While there are other cases in the following decades, such as William de Conisbrough's grant c. 1150 of the church he had founded at Staplegordon in Eskdale to the monks of Kelso,[96] explicit statements that the church had been built by the families who were surrendering their rights of patronage in this way are uncommon. We can, nevertheless, be confident that the churches and chapels that appear as gifts to religious corporations in the record of new lordships created for colonial knights in areas like upper Clydesdale were built by the men who granted them away.[97] The surviving twelfth-century fabric of churches like Lamington in Clydesdale, Dalmeny in Midlothian or Leuchars in Fife is testimony of the level of financial investment which such church building required. While providing a highly visible symbol of their patronage and investment, it was, however, just one dimension of the religious behaviour of the nobility.

Noble support for the Church as an institution was often motivated by a desire to secure spiritual benefits from the masses and prayers of the grateful clergy. Gifts of real property and revenues were often made in return for just such benefits, formalised from the twelfth century in what are known as grants in 'free alms', that is, where no other service was demanded of the clerics beyond the remembrance of the donor and other stipulated beneficiaries in their devotions. Such motivations, however, were certainly not innovations of the twelfth century, and it is likely that pre-1100 individuals with access to resources were already patrons of the Church in identical manner. The one surviving long series of records of gifts of real property and legal and fiscal rights to a native monastic community, the *notitiae* entered in the margins of the *Book of Deer*,[98] suggests that the leading men and women of Gaelic society in Buchan were generous patrons of the Church, and we can probably assume that if the comparatively minor provincial community at Deer was favoured by the leaders of Buchan then the major monastic centres like St Andrews or Dunkeld benefited from the wider patronage of native lords. The loss

---

[95] Lawrie, *Early Scottish Charters*, no. XXIV.
[96] *Kelso Liber*, no. 350.
[97] *Kelso Liber*, nos 333, 335–7, 339.
[98] Forsyth (ed.), *Studies on the Book of Deer*, Chapters 5–9 and 11.

of the records of the majority of the communities that had pre-twelfth-century origins and survived as reformed monasteries or secular cathedral chapters post-1100 prevents recovery of even a generalised record of the patronage of these establishments by the native magnates. Isolated acts, like Morgrund earl of Mar's gifts to St Andrews, however, perhaps indicate that the emerging Gaelic nobility were little different from their counterparts elsewhere in Britain or Europe in their concern for their personal spiritual welfare and desire to demonstrate their devotion to the Church.[99] Where they diverged significantly from their European peers, however, was in their support for reformed monasticism, with the Scottish crown and the leading families of the settler community taking the main role there.

The example of Deer reminds us that one characteristic of Norman-style lordship – the close personal identification between particular families and their dependents with particular religious establishments – was also an established feature of Gaelic society. As the Deer records show, certain churches or monasteries could receive the patronage of regional lords over successive generations, but the Norman tradition encouraged rising families to mark their emergence into the upper ranks of the nobility by the foundation of a new community which their family and dependents would continue to support thereafter.[100] The principal exponents of this behaviour in Scotland were the de Morvilles, who marked their emergence from comparative insignificance amongst the minor nobility of the English Midlands into the first rank in the kingdom of David I and his heirs. Hugh de Morville, the founder of the family's fortunes in Scotland, showed particular spiritual discernment in selecting Premonstratensians, an order which did not enjoy Scottish royal patronage, to colonise his foundation at Dryburgh in 1150.[101] The order was less than three decades old and the first Premonstratensian house in England had been founded only in 1143.[102] In 1148 Eustace son of John brought a colony to Alnwick in Northumberland, at that date under Scottish rule, and it was probably through him that Hugh gained the introductions that led to the foundation of a colony in his lordship of Lauderdale.[103] Confirmations of the early endowments made to the canons reveal the

---

[99] Oram, 'Earls and earldom of Mar', 49–50 and note 18; *St Andrews Liber*, 247.
[100] Thompson, *Power and Border Lordship*, under La Trappe, Tiron, Saint-Denis, Saint-Evroul, Saint-Jean and so on.
[101] Fawcett and Oram, *Dryburgh Abbey*, 8–13.
[102] Midmer, *English Medieval Monasteries*, 232.
[103] *Chron. Melrose*, s.a. 1148; Midmer, *English Medieval Monasteries*, 49–50; Stringer, 'Nobility and identity in medieval Britain and Ireland', 223–4 and note 115.

slender resources available to them and underscore the disparity between them and communities founded by the crown or that enjoyed sustained royal patronage, but they still represented a significant portion of Hugh's disposable wealth.[104] Unlike their English counterparts, however, rather than channelling their efforts towards the continued support of one community, the Morvilles split their patronage after Hugh's death. His son and successor, Richard, made his own foundations, the hospital of St Leonard near Lauder founded in c. 1170[105] and Kilwinning Abbey in Cunningham. Hugh may have held this Clyde Coast lordship before 1162, but it was apparently Richard who established Morville interests there on a firm footing and the foundation of Kilwinning was a powerful articulation of his regional ambitions.[106] Richard de Morville may have been keen to make his mark through the foundation of a second monastery by his family, but his efforts produced two impoverished houses who struggled financially throughout their existence.[107]

Elsewhere in Scotland the emerging higher nobility of the twelfth century were generally slower to emulate this particular aspect of Continental aristocratic culture before the early thirteenth century. This reticence on the part of the earls may be another indicator of the limited private economic resources available to them before their securing of heritable control over the lands and revenues of their earldoms in the later twelfth century rather than a sign of antipathy towards the reformed monastic orders, for they were generous patrons of royal foundations.[108] The Northumbrian cultural and socio-economic organisation of the country south of the Firth of Forth may explain why Lothian saw some of the earliest aristocratic monastic foundations in the kingdom. There, the earls of Dunbar and Fife possessed extensive estates from an early date, the Fifes having greater economic control of real property in East Lothian than within their earldom, and the Dunbars holding lands formerly associated with the earldom of Northumbria north of Tweed. Quite simply, both families controlled sources of wealth on a sufficient scale to indulge in such pious activity and for the Dunbars such activity was perhaps part of their inherited cultural baggage. It was, however, nunneries that they

[104] *Dryburgh Liber*, nos 239, 240, 241, 249. See Barrow (ed.), *RRS*, i, no. 172 and *RRS*, ii, no. 65 for comment.
[105] Cowan and Easson, *Medieval Religious Houses*, 184; *Dryburgh Liber*, appendix, no. 1.
[106] Cowan, *Ayrshire Abbeys*, 268–70.
[107] Fawcett and Oram, *Dryburgh Abbey*, 14–16.
[108] See, for example, the charters of the earls of Mar to St Andrews, or of the Durwards and the earls of Angus to Arbroath, *St Andrews Liber*, 246, 248–9; *Arbroath Liber*, nos 39, 41, 43, 44, 46–9, 52–3, 59, 65.

founded: the Cistercian houses of North Berwick (Fife: before 1154), Eccles (Dunbar: 1156), Coldstream (Dunbar: before 1166) and St Bothans (Dunbar: c. 1200).[109] The foundation of nunneries was a common form of noble female religious patronage in the eleventh and twelfth centuries, often being the pious work of dowagers and noble widows seeking withdrawal from the world, but there was also an established Anglo-Saxon tradition of nunneries serving as holding places for unmarried or unmarriageable sisters or daughters of the nobility, and post-1066 as refuges for English noblewomen seeking to avoid forced marriages to Normans. Nunneries, moreover, had the virtue of being cheap to found and, while some, like Countess Ada's convent at Haddington or the Fife's foundation at North Berwick, accumulated wealth throughout the Middle Ages that lifted them onto a par with middle-ranking male houses, most languished in poverty throughout their existence.

The regal pretensions, international connections and sheer wealth of Galloway's rulers account for the rash of monastic foundations in the lordship from the 1140s onwards. Fergus, Uhtred and Roland between them founded three abbeys, a priory and a nunnery before 1200, while Alan added a further abbey by 1218.[110] Elsewhere in Scotland outside the territory of Somerled and his heirs, while Gaelic lords continued to patronise existing monasteries and the new royal foundations they seem to have had little interest in making foundations of their own. That striking absence of male convents which would rank in terms of wealth or importance alongside those founded by the de Morvilles in any of the earldoms ended in the thirteenth century when the earls of Strathearn and Fife and the new Comyn earl of Buchan established monasteries in their territories. The cluster of foundations made between 1200 and 1230 coincides closely with the transformation in the nature of the earldoms and the establishment of the earls as the principal landholders and recipients of fiscal dues within their province. In Strathearn, Earl Gillebrigte in 1200 refounded an existing community at Inchaffray as an Augustinian convent but the act meant more than simply reallocating the older community's resources to the new monastery, with the earl assigning the canons revenues from parish churches and lands across his earldom.[111] Within Fife, it was not until 1217 that Earl Malcolm had the resources to endow a monastery, the Cistercian abbey at Culross.[112] Two years later at

---

[109] Cowan and Easson, *Medieval Religious Houses*, 145–6, 148.
[110] McDonald, 'Scoto-Norse kings and the reformed religious orders'.
[111] *Inchaffray Charters*, no. IX.
[112] Douglas, 'Culross Abbey', 67–94; Cowan and Easson, *Medieval Religious Houses*, 74.

Figure 7.1 Knight's effigy, Dundrennan Abbey, Dumfries and Galloway: probably commemorating Alan of Galloway, it illustrates how Gaelic lords embraced continental chivalric culture.

Deer in Buchan Earl William formally instituted a colony of Cistercians from Kinloss in Moray, completing a process probably initiated soon after he succeeded to the earldom in right of his wife.[113] It is possible, therefore, that these conspicuous displays of piety and wealth were intended to symbolise the new status as heads of a hierarchy of provincial nobility of the earls who founded them. They also forged a very personal bond between the comital family and the earldom, as a mausoleum for the family and a spiritual focus for both them and their dependents. In more practical terms, they also initially provided the earls with the ink-and-parchment skills required by a style of lordship which was founded on charter title, writs, brieves and administrative records. We should not forget, however, that by 1200 many of the comital families had married several times over into the ranks of the Anglo-French nobility, acquiring in the process estates not only in southern Scotland but also in England and, with them, inheriting their wives' and husbands' familial links with religious houses. Simple emulation of the behaviour of their peers should not, therefore, be overlooked as a motive.

[113] Cowan and Easson, *Medieval Religious Houses*, 74.

In their arrangements for burial and their soul's ease in the hereafter, the Scottish nobility made statements of their social distinction as consciously as they did in their public demonstrations of political and economic status. Preparation for a good death and atonement for sins during life were aspects of Christian spirituality which influenced spiritual culture heavily. A desire to expiate for wrongs committed, perhaps especially those against the Church, was always one dimension of the flow of lay patronage to ecclesiastical beneficiaries and reached its peak of expression in the foundation of monasteries and lavish gift-giving. Layfolk who sought the spiritual benefits of the monastic life in their closing days and the promise of salvation in the hereafter which that offered could, like Hugh de Morville, enter religion and die as a monk or canon.[114] Alternatively, for a financial consideration, they could secure burial in the monastery, possibly in the church or chapterhouse, where their souls would benefit most from the masses and prayers of the convent. This was the chosen path of a number of prominent magnates and their wives, such as William de Valognes, the king's chamberlain, or Roger Avenel, lord of Eskdale, at Melrose, or Earl Patrick of Dunbar in the nunnery at Eccles.[115] Burial within a monastery, however, could also be part of a conflict resolution, as for example in the case of William de Muntfichet, who was involved in the 1210s in a protracted dispute with the monks of Coupar Angus. When in c. 1220 the dispute was settled in the monks' favour, de Muntfichet granted the bodies of himself, his wife and his heir for burial at Coupar, an act that placed their spiritual salvation in the hands of the monastery and gave the monks an additional financial benefit from burial dues and future *pro anima* grants made by his heirs and kinsmen.[116] Like other nobles of both native Gaelic and colonial background William de Muntfichet was making a self-conscious statement of confidence in the status of his family and the permanence of its association with the land which lay at the heart of the dispute with the monks. While still functioning as heads of kin and social leaders of their local communities, men like de Muntfichet had separated themselves in the social hierarchy from the broad mass of the population, establishing their nobility of birth through their actions and behaviour in death as much as in life.

---

[114] *Dryburgh Liber*, no. 8; *Chron. Melrose*, s.a. 1162.
[115] *Chron. Melrose*, s.a. 1219, 1232, 1243.
[116] *Coupar Angus Chrs*, no. XXXI.

CHAPTER 10

The Making of the *Ecclesia Scoticana*

In the words of that much-abused cliché, history is written by the winners. One of the clearest examples of this is in the narrative of reform and reconstruction central to most histories of the Scottish Church from the late eleventh to early thirteenth centuries. It is a narrative that contrasts the supposed torpor, decadence, conservatism and isolation of a native 'Celtic' Church with the vitality, dynamism and purity of the Continental Roman Church which had been revitalised by the 'Cluniac' or 'Gregorian' reform movements which aimed to sweep away corruption and raise standards of religious practice. In general, the need for reform in the eleventh-century Scottish Church has been offered as a given fact and the reforming process presented as the achievement of far-sighted kings who embraced the internationalism of the Roman tradition and supported the efforts of high-minded and well-trained foreign reformist clerics whom they introduced to their kingdom. In opposition to this positive view is a bleaker vision which developed in the nineteenth century. It saw the reconstruction of the Church as part of a concerted assault on native Gaelic culture mounted by monarchs who had been seduced by Continental ways, ably assisted by hordes of foreign military and ecclesiastical adventurers who rose to power on the ruins of native institutions.[1] The debate, expressed in terms of 'Celtic' versus 'Roman' churches, became part of the wider idea of 'the making of the kingdom' which explored the internal processes of state building and institutional evolution. Unfortunately, its inward focus created an unintentionally misleading impression that Scotland's experience was unique. Denigration of native religious traditions and the imposition of foreign ecclesiastical forms and practices have been recognised as key elements

[1] Bradley, *Celtic Christianity*, 157–79.

in the processes of domination and conquest at work in the British Isles at this time and, from the mid-tenth to the mid-fourteenth century in the wider process of 'Europeanisation' in north-western Europe.[2]

Care must be taken to ensure that the religious condition of Scotland in this period is set into its wider British and European context and that its predominantly Gaelic character is not used as a label of uniqueness which sets the pre-twelfth-century Scottish Church apart from an otherwise orthodox west European mainstream. Conformity of practice, standardisation of religious discipline, harmonisation of canon law codes and construction of the hierarchies which were hallmarks of the later medieval Church were just beginning to be effected in the later eleventh century even in the supposed heartlands of western Christendom. The basic recognition that Scotland was experiencing the full force of Continental Gregorian reform has, generally, not been accompanied by engagement with how that reform process affected areas other than Scotland. This detachment is accompanied by a vision of native Churches in Scotland and Ireland, Gaelic in character and ancient in tradition, being overwhelmed by a monolithic 'Roman' Church that ruled unchallenged in western Christendom. Such a view, however, is to project the so-called papal monarchy of the thirteenth century, as exercised by Pope Innocent III (1198–1216), back into the later eleventh century, when popes from Leo IX (1049–54) to Gregory VII (1073–85) were beginning to implement policies that turned the office of pope from the largely nominal to the real and effective headship of the western Church.[3]

SCOTTISH CONTACT WITH THE CONTINENTAL CHURCH

How out of touch with Continental reform was the Scottish Church? The honest answer is that we cannot know for certain based on the fragmentary evidence available to us, but the fact that Macbeth visited Rome in 1050 in the immediate aftermath of Leo IX's first reforming councils suggests that Scotland's secular and ecclesiastical leadership cannot have been entirely ignorant of the new atmosphere.[4] It is possible, too, that Macbeth and his wife's support for a reforming strand in the Scottish

---

[2] Davies, *Domination and Conquest*, 16–18; Bartlett, *Making of Europe*, Chapter 10.
[3] Blumenthal, 'The papacy', 8–37.
[4] Anderson (ed.), *Early Sources*, i, 588.

Church indicates wider engagement with the drive for spiritual renewal.[5] Thirteenth-century York tradition also claims that Fothad II, bishop of St Andrews, submitted to Archbishop Thomas of York in 1072 in accordance with an agreement between the archbishops of Canterbury and York over the sphere of their metropolitan jurisdictions. It is also claimed that he submitted on the orders of King Malcolm III and Queen Margaret, and this might be seen in the context of the 1072 submission of the Scottish king to King William I of England at Abernethy. If correct, Fothad's submission brought him into the sphere of two active ecclesiastical reformers, but such contact does not necessarily mean acceptance of their reforming programmes.

Turgot's biography of Margaret claims that leadership in Church reform came from her rather than the Scottish clergy; she presided over 'many councils' in which native doctrinal and liturgical practices were brought into line with the European norm.[6] It has, however, been commented that much of the business that Turgot attributes to Margaret's councils remained on the reformists' agenda when he became bishop of St Andrews over two decades later, and her role as a pioneering reformer has been dismissed as exaggeration.[7] Also overturned, however, has been the hostile view of Margaret as a foreigner who set about to supplant the 'Celtic' Church in Scotland with the 'Roman' tradition in which she was raised. Instead, she has been repackaged as an 'enthusiast for "Celtic" Christianity' who saw much in the native Church to praise, preserve and support.[8] That description, however, may swing too far in the opposite direction, and the more balanced assessment is probably that which presented Margaret and Malcolm as maintainers of their predecessors' benevolence towards what was good and praiseworthy in the native Church while at the same time inaugurating policies that began a process of convergence with Continental religious practice.[9]

Such sparse evidence for ecclesiastical reform has often been linked to a similar dearth of information relating to the senior personnel of the Church. Turgot names no clerics who attended Margaret's councils, indeed few bishops are known at even the most important sees; this has been translated into a vision of irregular succession and extended

---

[5] See, for example, *St Andrews Liber*, 114.
[6] Anderson (ed.), *Early Sources*, ii, 69–74.
[7] Duncan, *Making of the Kingdom*, 122–3; Cowan and Easson, *Medieval Religious Houses*, 4.
[8] Bradley, *Celtic Christianity*, 41–2.
[9] Cowan and Easson, *Medieval Religious Houses*, 4–5.

vacancies.[10] At St Andrews, for example, it was argued that after the death of Fothad II in c. 1093 the bishopric remained vacant until the election of Turgot in 1107, while at Glasgow the bishops named in the eleventh century were York appointments effective only in English Cumbria, with there being no resident 'bishop of Glasgow' until around 1113.[11] This depressing picture appeared to vindicate the vision of the Scottish Church as languishing in torpor and decay, but the evidence for long breaks in the episcopal succession at St Andrews has recently been exposed as an accident of documentary survival and an intermediate successor, Giric, between Fothad II and Turgot identified.[12] An absence of neat lists of bishops' names is not sure evidence for a lack of bishops, and greater credence should perhaps be given to late medieval recorded traditions of regular episcopal succession in the eleventh and twelfth centuries at several major sees.[13]

THE INVESTITURE CRISIS

The first stirrings of ecclesiastical reform in Scotland coincided with the conflict between the Holy Roman Empire and the papacy known as the Investiture Crisis. When distilled to its basics, this was a clash over the fundamental relationship between ecclesiastical and lay authority, and in particular the role played by laymen in the appointment of bishops and the function of those bishops as the instruments or agents of monarchical authority. The epicentre of the conflict was the Holy Roman Empire, where the emperor's ability to invest bishops was a key surviving element in an arsenal of imperial authority that had been largely usurped by provincial magnates. In the eyes of the reformists, men appointed in this way were tainted by simony (the buying and selling of ecclesiastical office) and compromised spiritually by obligations to their temporal overlord. The crisis is viewed traditionally as climaxing in the confrontation between Emperor Henry IV and Pope Gregory VII, with the emperor's barefoot submission to the pope in the snow at Canossa in 1077 symbolising the triumph of the reformist papacy.[14] As subsequent

---

[10] Donaldson, *Scottish Church History*, 11–18; Duncan, *Making of the Kingdom*, 123; Barrell, *Medieval Scotland*, 44.
[11] Duncan, *Making of the Kingdom*, 127–8; Shead, 'Origins of the medieval diocese of Glasgow', 220–5.
[12] Broun, 'The church of St Andrews and its foundation legend', 108–14.
[13] For example, Myln, *Vitae*, or Boece, *Vitae*.
[14] Vollrath, 'The Western Empire under the Salians', 58–60.

events showed, however, despite the propaganda victory that Canossa gave Gregory, the conflict was far from over and continued to plague papal-imperial relations through the twelfth century.

The Investiture Crisis, however, was not restricted to the Holy Roman Empire and was mirrored in crown–Church relations across Europe. Scotland was not immune to the repercussions of this conflict, which hindered Church reform there from the reign of Alexander I to that of William. In common with the spread of Gregorian principles elsewhere, the driving force for reform in Scotland was a partnership between crown and episcopate. While men like Fothad II and Giric at St Andrews may have been sympathetic to reform, it was with Alexander I's nomination in 1107 of Turgot to the see of St Andrews that a reformist cleric was appointed to a Scottish bishopric.[15] But any reforming programme was quickly lost in controversy over Turgot's consecration and the question of his submission to the metropolitan supremacy of an English archbishop. A rapid and irreconcilable deterioration in the relationship between Alexander and his bishop over that issue and Turgot's wish to seek papal arbitration led in 1115 to his resignation.[16] Alexander's preferred successor was the Canterbury-based reformist Benedictine, Eadmer. He was elected in 1120 and, in a procedure designed to avoid the controversial issue of being invested with the bishopric by the king, received his ring from Alexander but took his pastoral staff from the altar of the church of St Andrews. But Eadmer had resigned by early 1121 over Alexander's refusal to permit him to be consecrated by the archbishop of Canterbury, returning his ring with a belated denial that any layman had the rightful power to have given it to him.[17] This is the only recorded instance in Scotland of lay investiture leading to conflict between Church and crown, for other bishops – most notably the future David I's appointee to the see of Glasgow – seem untroubled by the spiritual implications of receiving their bishopric from lay hands.[18]

The one major dispute between the king and a diocesan chapter, at St Andrews from 1178 to 1182, reveals how conflict was normally avoided, for it was noted that the canons of St Andrews had not consulted the king before electing John 'the Scot'.[19] In electing John the canons were exercising their canonical right to act without secular interference, a

---

[15] Symeon of Durham, *Historia Regum*, ii, 204.
[16] Symeon of Durham, *Historia Regum*, ii, 205.
[17] Eadmer, *Historia Novorum*, 279–88.
[18] Duncan, *Making of the Kingdom*, 130.
[19] Ferguson, *Papal Representatives*, 56.

right which was being claimed by diocesan clergy with increasing frequency and success around Europe at this date, but their independence was either boldly defiant or sadly naïve. William had his own candidate and engineered the consecration instead of his chaplain, Hugh.[20] John, however, was not prepared to yield and found ready support at Rome in what appeared to the pope to be another instance of secular interference in the freedoms of the Church. A papal legate came to Scotland with John, deposed Hugh and had John consecrated in his place by Matthew, bishop of Aberdeen. While freedom to elect was clearly a point of principle upon which the ecclesiastical authorities at St Andrews were unwilling to compromise, King William was equally determined to defend his interests. Before the end of 1180 bishops John and Matthew had been driven into exile, but a compromise deal was brokered by Henry II of England which offered John the chancellorship and another Scottish see in return for his resignation of St Andrews. Pope Alexander III, however, refused to permit John to resign St Andrews and sent new legates – Roger, archbishop of York and Hugh, bishop of Durham – to enforce William's adherence to the 1180 settlement and threaten the removal of recent papal support for the independence of the Scottish Church if he did not comply. William ignored the demands, and in summer 1181 the legates excommunicated him and placed Scotland under spiritual interdict. The deaths of both Pope Alexander and Archbishop Roger before the end of 1181 enabled William to appeal for the lifting of the sentences, and the new pope Lucius III annulled the earlier decision in March 1182. John was confirmed as bishop of Dunkeld and Hugh retained St Andrews, but litigation continued at Rome until 1188 when Hugh died. William's successful defence of his interests in the election to the most important see in his kingdom was then made apparent, for John did not then regain the bishopric to which he had originally been elected, remaining bishop of Dunkeld and even attending the election of Hugh's successor, the king's cousin Roger de Beaumont.[21] There is no doubt that this was a triumph for royal influence in the election process, for despite powerful domestic and foreign support John could never secure possession of St Andrews in the face of William's opposition. It was, moreover, a triumph entrenched by subsequent elections, with both Bishop Roger (1189–1202) and his successor William Malvoisin (1202–38) being William's appointees. The king may have been an enthusiastic supporter of the ecclesiastical

---

[20] *Chron. Melrose*, s.a. 1178.
[21] Barrow (ed.), *RRS*, ii, 9–11; Ferguson, *Papal Representatives*, 56–63.

Bishops and kings

Lay investiture had ceased to be an issue in Scotland by the 1120s, but royal influence over episcopal elections remained problematical. As well as being spiritual leaders, bishops were lords of substantial landed estates and exercised wide regional influence. As such, certain bishops held key roles in the extension of Scottish political power into districts remote from the centres of royal authority. In Caithness, for example, Bishop Andrew and his successors were the Scottish king's men, and one was mutilated and another murdered for that identification.[22] It is perhaps too straightforward always to see the king's hand behind elections to key bishoprics, especially where the men elected were former royal clerks or major officers of state, but it is difficult to avoid the conclusion that royal influence secured high ecclesiastical office for some, despite growing clerical demands for free elections. Bishop Enguerrand of Glasgow, for example, was Malcolm IV's chancellor from c. 1161 until his election to the bishopric in 1164.[23] Walter de Bidun and Hugh of Roxburgh, both former chancellors, were elected respectively as bishops of Dunkeld and Glasgow but died unconsecrated. The see of Glasgow seems to have been especially favoured as a reward for former chancellors, four of the eight clerks who held that office between 1153 and 1214 being installed there.[24] Other royal clerks also secured election to bishoprics; Richard of Lincoln to Moray in 1187, Richard, clerk of the Provend at Dunkeld in 1203 and Hugh of the Seal at Dunkeld in 1214.[25] No record survives of any royal pressure in the election of these men or of resistance from the electors, and most were conscientious diocesans.

freedoms that Thomas Becket had died at Canterbury to protect, but only so far as they did not compromise his domestic political interests.

METROPOLITAN SUPREMACY: YORK AND THE SCOTTISH CHURCH

At one stage in the St Andrews election dispute, Pope Alexander had threatened to reverse recent papal support for the freedom of the

---

[22] Oram, *David I*, 106–8; Crawford, 'Earldom of Caithness'.
[23] Barrow (ed.), *RRS*, i, 28–9.
[24] Ibid. ii, 29, 30–1.
[25] Ibid. ii, 31, 32, 35.

Scottish Church from the metropolitan supremacy of York. This was a grave threat which must have alarmed the Scottish king and clergy greatly, for much energy had been spent in securing that liberty. The roots of York's claim to authority over all the bishops of northern Britain lay in Pope Gregory I's scheme for the ecclesiastical structure of the island drawn up in the 590s. Based on the framework of the already defunct Roman civil provinces with their capitals at London and York, it had envisaged two archdioceses, one north and one south of the Humber, each containing a number of sees located in the various Roman urban centres. The collapse of Roman-style civil life in Britain in the course of the sixth century and the new political realities of a patchwork of independent kingdoms rendered Gregory's scheme unworkable, and there was the further complication that the old imperial system of civil government had never extended over the territory that became Scotland. At times in the seventh and eighth centuries when Northumbrian rule extended over most of the Southern Uplands zone and into southern Pictland the possibility of a York metropolitan province had come closer to realisation, but by the eleventh century the claims of the archbishop of York were ignored by the bishops of the emerging Scottish kingdom.

Titles given to bishops based at St Andrews in the eleventh century suggest that the Scots had constructed their own idea of an archbishopric encompassing the kingdom and were to advance that idea forcefully in the late 1000s and early 1100s. In 1055, for example, Mael Duín mac Gilla Odran, who was bishop at St Andrews, was styled 'bishop of Scotland' (Gaelic *escop Alban*) and in 1093 the obituary of Fothad II styled him 'chief bishop of Scotland' (Gaelic *ardepscop Alban*).[26] These titles, it has been commented, mirror the title of the kings of Scots (*rí Alban*) but what that might have meant in practice is less clear.[27] Up to the late eleventh century the position of an archbishop was largely the creation of men who were able effectively to exercise the powers over their notionally dependent or 'suffragan' bishops which that status gave, but from the 1050s the growing tide of reform had seen the papal vision of a hierarchy of authority flowing down from the pope through a series of canonically appointed metropolitans – who received the pallium (a lambswool vestment worn around the shoulders), which signified their status as an

---

[26] *Annals of Tigernach* http://www.ucc.ie/celt/published/G100002/index.html at T1055.5; *Annals of Ulster* http://www.ucc.ie/celt/published/T100001A/index.html at U1093.2; Anderson (ed.), *Early Sources*, i, 599; Ibid. ii, 49.

[27] Broun, 'The church of St Andrews and its foundation legend', 112–13.

> **Metropolitan supremacy**
>
> The claim of an archbishop to have jurisdiction over all bishops within the bounds of his province might nowadays not seem hugely controversial. In the twelfth century, however, the question of the archbishop of York's rights over Scottish bishops was bitterly contested and a major source of political tension between the Scottish and English crowns. Based on a late-sixth-century scheme for the division of Britain into two ecclesiastical provinces for archbishops at London and York, the papal plan for two archdioceses failed to recognise the utterly transformed political geography of the island. That is why, for example, the southern British archbishopric ended up at Canterbury, in the then-dominant and quickly Christian kingdom of Kent, rather than in pagan-controlled London. The sixth-century plan was largely irrelevant until the eleventh century when York began to advance claims to jurisdiction over the bishops of northern Britain. The Scottish Church, however, had created its own 'archbishop' in the Bishop of St Andrews, who was described as 'summus episcopus Scottorum' (high bishop of the Scots) and responded by seeking papal recognition of St Andrews as an archbishopric. Papal support, however, lay initially with York, whose archbishops could point to the original scheme, but gradually swung round to the Scottish perspective, hastened by papal anger at King Henry II of England's intervention in the dispute. A series of *bulls* (letters from the papacy authenticated with a lead seal called a *bulla*) required the archbishop of York to prove his case, and then freed the Scottish bishops from his oversight. The conclusion of the process came with the issuing in 1218 by Pope Honorius III of the bull *Filia specialis*.[28] This bull fell short of Scottish ambitions for an archbishop of their own, but it did extend the status of 'special daughter' which the bishops of Glasgow had secured for their own Church to the rest of the Scottish Church.

archbishop from the pope's hands – to their suffragans and on down eventually to parish priest level was beginning to take hold.[29] An unofficial Scottish view that the bishop of St Andrews was the chief bishop of *Scotia* (the claim originally extended over only the country north of the Forth) was suddenly confronted with a papal vision of two archbishops

---

[28] Donaldson, *Scottish Historical Documents*, 30–2.
[29] Blumenthal, 'The papacy', 11; Duncan, *Kingship of the Scots*, 86.

for the whole of mainland Britain, with the archbishop of York having metropolitan authority over all of Scotland's bishops. A Scottish view that their high bishop was an independent metropolitan may have taken a severe blow in 1072 when Fothad II submitted to Archbishop Thomas I of York, but Fothad's successor, Giric, confidently reasserted his status as an archbishop and the clergy of St Andrews mounted a bold propaganda effort to secure recognition of that position.[30]

Support for St Andrews' claims came after 1107 from King Alexander I. His reluctance to permit Turgot to profess obedience to York or Eadmer to Canterbury arose not simply from straightforward opposition to the secular implications of Scotland's spiritual subjection to English metropolitans but also from his personal ambitions for his own kingship.[31] Given David I's later efforts to secure a pallium for St Andrews and coronation and unction for himself, it is possible that Alexander's efforts were likewise interlinked and that he had sought confirmation of St Andrews' archiepiscopal status so that he and his successors could be properly made Christian kings at the hands of an archbishop, freeing Scottish rulers from the capriciousness of English kings.[32] Alexander's ambitions, however, were secondary issues in papal efforts to resolve the long-running conflict between Canterbury and York over the question of primacy and to establish York as a viable metropolitan see with adequate suffragans. Claims of metropolitan status for St Andrews faced a massive obstacle in the five-hundred-year-old authority of Pope Gregory I for York's supremacy over northern Britain and Glasgow was equally compromised by the fact that men styled 'bishop of Glasgow' had been consecrated and professed obedience to York in the recent past.[33] To Pope Paschal II in 1100 the issue was settled; he instructed York's suffragans 'throughout Scotland' to submit to their archbishop.[34] This was neither a 'pro-English' nor an 'anti-Scottish' stance but a simple reflection of papal understanding of the historic structure of ecclesiastical government in Britain. The instruction was repeated regularly after 1119, but all met a mixture of dissemblance and disobedience supported by the Scottish king.

At Glasgow, David's concerns mirrored those of his brother for St Andrews. Soon after 1113, David appointed his former chaplain, John,

---

[30] Broun, 'The church of St Andrews and its foundation legend', 111–13.
[31] Broun, *Scottish Independence and the Idea of Britain*, 104–5.
[32] Duncan, *Kingship of the Scots*, 87–8.
[33] Shead, 'Origins of the medieval diocese of Glasgow', 220–1.
[34] Broun, *Scottish Independence and the Idea of Britain*, 110.

Figure 10.1 St Rule's Tower, St Andrews, Fife. The tower, which dominates the ruins of the late-twelfth-century cathedral begun by Bishop Arnold, may be the main remnant of the church used by Bishop Robert (1124–59).

to the vacant bishopric of Glasgow, the death of Thomas II of York and subsequent five-year vacancy there enabling John to avoid making a formal submission to a metropolitan.[35] Instead, David and John looked

---

[35] Watt, *Fasti*, 144–5.

directly to Rome for consecration, which John received in 1118 from Paschal II. Nevertheless, when a dynamic and ambitious new archbishop of York, Thurstan, was consecrated in 1119, he secured papal support for demands that all of his suffragans – Glasgow included – give their professions of obedience.[36] Supported by David, John refused, but in 1122 Thurstan suspended him from episcopal office. An appeal at Rome met with instructions to submit to Thurstan, and in 1123 Pope Calixtus ordered John to return to his bishopric.[37] John returned but still refused to give the required oath, his stance taking a new twist in 1124 when King Alexander died and was succeeded by David, which brought John's status vis-à-vis York within the general question of the subjection of all Scottish bishops. Further appeals to Rome in 1125 were countered by Thurstan and a date set in 1127 for a definitive judgement, but secular political considerations in England brought further deferral of a settlement; in return for David I's support for Henry I's proposal that Matilda succeed him on the English throne, Henry secured Thurstan's agreement to consecrate Robert of Scone as bishop of St Andrews with neither a profession of obedience nor prejudice to Thurstan's claims of metropolitan supremacy.[38] David, for his part, suspended his efforts to secure a pallium for St Andrews.

Henry I's creation in 1133 of a new see of Carlisle ended the lull in proceedings, for John, supported by David, claimed that this territory by rights belonged to his diocese.[39] Opposition to this development led king and bishop into dangerous negotiations with the antipope Anacletus II, who might have been willing to make favourable concession to them in return for their support in securing his recognition as true pope, but in 1136 Pope Innocent II excommunicated John until such time as he abandoned his support for the rival pope and gave his oath of obedience to Thurstan.[40] It was well known that Anacletus had elevated Duke Roger of Sicily to kingly status in return for Roger's recognition of him as pope and had also given him the right of unction and coronation by an archbishop of his choice; David's demands were probably similar. The negotiations with Anacletus failed and, threatened with suspension by Innocent, John resigned his see and retired into the abbey of Thiron in

---

[36] Hugh the Chantor, *History*, 76; Raine, *Historians of York*, iii, 40–1.
[37] Symeon of Durham, *Historia Regum*, ii, 264. See also Raine, *Historians of York*, iii, 44–7.
[38] Sottewain, 'Archbishops of York', in Raine, *Historians of York*, ii, 214–15, 217; Ferguson, *Papal Representatives*, 34; Oram, *David I*, 79–81.
[39] John of Hexham, 285.
[40] Raine, *Historians of York*, iii, 66–7; Duncan, *Kingship of the Scots*, 89–91.

northern France. Worse was potentially to come, for in September 1138, in the aftermath of the rout of David's army at the battle of the Standard, Innocent II's legate Alberic arrived at Carlisle for discussions with the king.[41] David had no option but to accept Innocent as pope, the corollary of which was that John, whom David summoned back from Thiron, would be required to submit to Thurstan and that both king and bishop would accept the creation of the new bishopric of Carlisle.[42] It is likely that John returned in spring 1139, but when Thurstan died in early 1140 he had still not received John's submission.

David sought to capitalise on his control of much of northern England in 1140 to solve the question of metropolitan supremacy over Scotland by placing his own candidate in York, proposing his stepson, Waltheof, as Thurstan's successor.[43] In the face of local opposition, King Stephen pre-empted David and secured the election of his own nephew, William son of Herbert, but William's consecration was delayed until 1143, thus further postponing any formal submission by John or any Scottish bishops to an archbishop of York. Opposition to archbishop-elect William also played into David's hands, as the clergy hostile to William looked to the most powerful layman in the north for aid.[44] David's clerical allies laid accusations of corruption against William before Pope Eugenius III, a former Cistercian monk and fierce supporter of reform, who in 1147 declared William deposed and supported the election in his place of the Cistercian Henry Murdac. In the interim, Bishop John of Glasgow had died, and his successor Herbert had been installed without any challenge from York and consecrated by the pope at Auxerre.[45] Archbishop Henry at this time looked to David for support against Stephen, who was denying him possession of York itself, and made no effort to assert his metropolitan rights over the Scottish bishops.[46] David's support for Henry was highly political, for he probably saw a real possibility of detaching York from England and establishing it as the metropolitan see of an enlarged 'Scoto-Northumbrian' realm.[47] The blocking of David's attempt to take the city in 1149 ended that vision;

---

[41] Richard of Hexham, 169–70; John of Hexham, 298; Ferguson, *Papal Representatives*, 36–7.
[42] Richard of Hexham, 176.
[43] Green, 'Aristocratic loyalties on the northern frontier', 97.
[44] Oram, *David I*, 153–5.
[45] John of Hexham, 321; Watt, *Fasti*, 145.
[46] Stringer, *Reign of Stephen*, 67–8.
[47] Stringer, 'State-building in twelfth-century Britain', 58–9.

Stephen's acceptance of Archbishop Henry in 1151 simply confirmed the failure of Scottish policy.

This episode reveals that David's ambitions for a Scottish archbishopric had not been abandoned. Equally, he must have expected Henry Murdac to voice his right to metropolitan supremacy over the Scottish Church, especially since that must have been discussed by them in 1149–51. It is in this context that David's decision to ask again for a pallium for Bishop Robert of St Andrews must be seen, and the arrival of a papal legate, John Paparo, at Carlisle in September 1151 provided a timely opportunity.[48] Paparo, who was carrying four pallia for the new archbishoprics that the pope had created in Ireland, returned to Carlisle around Easter 1152 and agreed to raise the issue at Rome.[49] If Paparo did as he promised he failed to convince the papacy, and when a new northern European archdiocese was created in 1152 it was for the territories of the Norwegian crown, not the Scots. These Irish and Scandinavian successes serve as useful reminders that Scotland's experience of ecclesiastical subjection to an external metropolitan was far from unique in northern Europe. The growth of Scottish ambitions to secure an archbishop of their own is contemporaneous with the efforts of the Scandinavian kingdoms to remove the spiritual lordship over them of the archbishops of Hamburg-Bremen and to secure their own archiepiscopal sees. When David died in May 1153, although his two senior bishops had been consecrated without professing obedience to York the issue had only been deferred, not resolved, and no one can have doubted that it was only a matter of time before York's claim was restated.

Papal support remained with York throughout the 1150s, but in 1159 Pope Hadrian IV displayed willingness to at least hear the Scottish case; a mission led by Bishop William of Moray went to Rome to press their case.[50] The Scots reached Rome shortly after Hadrian's death to find two rival popes, Alexander III and Victor IV, claiming the throne of St Peter, but by the end of November 1159 they had recognised Alexander and secured conferral of the office of papal legate on Bishop William and a promise to confirm William's transfer from Moray to the then vacant see of St Andrews, if both King Malcolm and the St Andrews clergy were willing. If an alternative were chosen, Alexander also promised to treat his candidature fairly, and, when confirmed and consecrated, the legation would be transferred to him; the intention was clearly that the

---

[48] John of Hexham, 326; Ferguson, *Papal Representatives*, 38–9.
[49] John of Hexham, 327.
[50] Ferguson, *Papal Representatives*, 39.

legatine commission would be exercised by whoever held St Andrews. This was not what the Scots had sought from the pope but, given the fact that Alexander could not risk alienating Henry II of England and Roger, archbishop of York, by granting a pallium to St Andrews, nor drive the Scots into the arms of Victor IV by outright refusal, it was an acceptable compromise that left Scotland nominally under York's metropolitan supremacy but shielded from its effects by the legation held by the senior Scottish bishop. It was, however, a brief respite, for the legation which William passed to the new bishop of St Andrews, Arnold, was rescinded by Alexander in c. 1161, and in September 1162 he had instructed the Scottish bishops to give their professions of obedience to Archbishop Roger.[51]

The ending of the legation and the 1162 letter should not be regarded as a change in papal policy again towards outright support for York but the Scottish bishops apparently considered it necessary to demonstrate their collective identity as heads of a separate *ecclesia Scoticana*. In 1163 a contingent of Scottish bishops attended Alexander III's council at Tours, where their presence was noted separately from Archbishop Roger of York and his sole suffragan, Bishop Hugh of Durham.[52] Although there was no immediate tangible result of this very public statement, it may have helped to reinforce a growing awareness of the distinction between the notional extent of York's metropolitan authority and its actual effective reach. Certainly it did the Scots no harm, for in 1164 Alexander III personally consecrated Bishop Enguerrand of Glasgow and 1165 Richard, the new bishop of St Andrews, was consecrated by the other Scottish bishops acting on a letter of commission from the pope.[53] Both acts occurred against the backdrop of intense but fruitless lobbying against the Scots by Archbishop Roger and a failed attempt by him to enter Scotland and exercise a legatine commission which was intended only for the English portion of his archdiocese.[54] The tide, it seemed, was flowing in favour of the Scots.

A critical turning point came in 1174 when Henry II of England attempted to settle the issue of English metropolitan supremacy over Scotland within the political settlement imposed on King William by the Treaty of Falaise. One of Henry's terms was 'that the church of Scotland shall henceforward owe such subjection to the church of England as

[51] Ibid. 41–3, 47–8.
[52] Barrow (ed.), *RRS*, i, 16–17.
[53] Barrow (ed.), *RRS*, i, 17.
[54] Ferguson, *Papal Representatives*, 43–9.

it should do,' and that the rights of the English church in Scotland would not be challenged by the Scots.[55] According to Roger of Howden, most senior clerics accompanied William to York in August 1175 for the confirmation of the treaty, thereby compromising their ability to resist its admittedly ambiguous terms.[56] Their formal submission was to be made in Henry II's council at Northampton in January 1176, but when the proceedings degenerated into a very heated dispute between Archbishop Roger of York and Archbishop Richard of Canterbury over which of them had the right to the Scots' obedience the Scottish bishops departed without giving their profession.[57] By this point, however, Pope Alexander had become alarmed by Henry II's interference in this ecclesiastical issue. His concern was evident in the mandate he gave to the archbishop of Lund to consecrate Jocelin, bishop-elect of Glasgow, at Clairvaux in the early months of 1175.[58] On its own this would not necessarily be considered significant, for Alexander and his predecessors had consecrated Scottish bishops while still calling upon them to make their profession of obedience to York, but Jocelin had also received an open-ended privilege of papal protection for his see which described it as 'our special daughter with no intermediary'.[59] By this statement, Glasgow was specifically exempted from York's metropolitan authority; the first breach in the overarching claims of the English archbishop had been made.

Alexander III's granting of this exemption was a remarkable development which was enjoyed by only three other dioceses north of the Alps, and the 'special daughter' label may have been Bishop Jocelin's personal contribution to the document.[60] It gave Glasgow a unique status in Britain, unequivocally separating it from all other dioceses which either fell under or were claimed to fall under the metropolitan supremacy of the two English archbishops.[61] Signs that the 'special daughter' relationship might be extended or threatened, however, emerged the following year, when on 30 July 1176 Alexander III issued the bull known as *Super anxietatibus* from its opening words.[62] This document reversed decades

---

[55] Stones, *Anglo-Scottish Relations*, 2, no. 1.
[56] Howden, *Chronica*, ii, 79–82.
[57] Ferguson, *Papal Representatives*, 50–1; Howden, *Chronica*, ii, 91–2.
[58] *Chron. Melrose*, s.a. 1175.
[59] Ferguson, *Papal Representatives*, 51–2.
[60] For discussion of these dioceses see Broun, *Scottish Independence and the Idea of Britain*, 128–35, 140–1.
[61] Ibid. 138–40.
[62] Somerville, *Scotia Pontificia*, no. 80.

of papal support for York by ordering the Scottish bishops to obey no one claiming metropolitan right – except for the pope – until the archbishop of York had come to Rome and established that right in the curia. It was still a stopgap measure but nevertheless very welcome to most of the Scottish bishops except for Bishop Christian of Whithorn, York's only willing suffragan among them, and perhaps also Jocelin, who was concerned for the future of his see's 'special daughter' status if the relationship between the Scots and York generally were to be revisited at the papal court. In the following year when the papal legate, Cardinal Vivian, held a council at Edinburgh, Bishop Christian was suspended from his bishopric for his refusal to attend, but he had already made his position clear in March 1177 when he ignored *Super anxietatibus* and attended an English Church council at London; confident in the protection of his acknowledged metropolitan's own legatine powers, Christian was pursuing a course that ended with the detachment of Whithorn from the body of the *ecclesia Scoticana* until the late fifteenth century.[63]

In the midst of this manoeuvring an unexpected crisis erupted between King William, Pope Alexander and the Scottish Church over the see of St Andrews (see above). It is in the context of this dispute, which lasted for a decade and in 1181 saw the pope, lamenting his strenuous efforts on behalf of the Scots, threaten to revoke his support for them, that Jocelin in 1179 secured a fresh statement of the privileges of his see. This time, the ambiguous 'our special daughter' of 1176, which might imply that it was a relationship unique to the pontificate of Alexander, was strengthened to read 'special daughter of the Roman Church', that is continuing regardless of who occupied St Peter's throne.[64] Alexander III's expressed regrets did not result in a return to support for York, and his successor Lucius III (1181–5) continued progress towards formally ending English metropolitan authority over the Scottish Church.[65] That process reached its conclusion in 1192 when Pope Celestine III issued the bull *Cum universi*, which extended Glasgow's 'special daughter' status to the rest of the *ecclesia Scoticana*, with Whithorn alone of the mainland sees remaining part of the province of York.[66] Having regained its political independence from intrusive English overlordship in 1189 by the Quitclaim of Canterbury, *Cum universi* represented a significant step on the route

[63] Ferguson, *Papal Representatives*, 53–5; Oram, *Lordship of Galloway*, 177.
[64] Broun, *Scottish Independence and the Idea of Britain*, 142.
[65] Ferguson, *Papal Representatives*, 25.
[66] Ferguson, *Papal Representatives*, 1; Barrell, 'The background to *Cum universi*' offers a case for an original date of issue in 1189 under Pope Clement III.

to securing for Scotland the ecclesiastical independence as a separate Church province which its kings had long sought, and possible access for them to the full Christian style kingship which the head of such a province could administer. But here the pope drew back from delivering all that was expected, for although there were further privileges regarding the powers and identity of legates who could operate within Scotland, there was no pallium for St Andrews. For the bishop of St Andrews this was a bitter disappointment, for the new relationship of the Scottish Church with the papacy – which was established for all intents and purposes as the metropolitan of Scotland – set him on an equal footing with all the other Scottish bishops, from the great like Glasgow to the impoverished like Caithness. From a status as *de facto* 'chief bishop' enjoying some authority over the others, *Cum universi* placed the bishop of St Andrews as simply first amongst equals.

The new 'special relationship' with the papacy did not mean that future popes always placed Scottish interests at the top of their priorities in matters that affected the Scottish Church or Scotland in general. This fact became painfully clear to the Scots during King Alexander II's involvement in the English baronial rebellion against King John. In 1213, under heavy pressure from domestic opposition and foreign enemies, John had surrendered his kingdom to Pope Innocent III and received it back from him as a papal fief.[67] To aid John against his foes, in 1216 Innocent III dispatched Cardinal Guala Bicchieri as legate to England, and in 1217 the new pope, Honorius III, extended Guala's commission and gave him the power to interdict, excommunicate and depose clerics throughout England, Scotland and Wales who did not submit to John's son, Henry III.[68] In October 1216, Guala placed Scotland under interdict because of Alexander II's continued support for Henry III's enemies and refusal to give up territory that he had seized. Despite this sentence, Alexander refused to yield until late 1217, whereupon he was absolved by the archbishop of York and bishop of Durham at Carlisle.[69] That did not end the matter, however, for Guala set about punishing the Scottish clergy who had continued to support Alexander II whilst he had been excommunicated, a process that lasted until mid-1218. Throughout these proceedings, papal support for John and Henry III had no implication of anti-Scottishness; Innocent III and Honorius III were giving support to a papal vassal. Nor, even in the midst of the

---

[67] Warren, *King John*, 206–12.
[68] Ferguson, *Papal Representatives*, 76–8.
[69] Ibid. 79.

interdict, was there any threatened withdrawal of *Cum universi* and restoration of York's metropolitan supremacy. Indeed, in 1218 Honorius III confirmed the independence of the Scottish Church in his bull *Filia specialis* and issued Guala with specific instructions on how to proceed with settlement as legate of business concerning Scottish affairs.[70] What these events demonstrated to the Scots was that while the pope readily recognised the existence of the special daughter relationship and took seriously his duties as Scotland's *de facto* metropolitan, that relationship was subordinate to his wider responsibility to safeguard the interests of the Universal Church, to protect vassals who placed themselves under papal protection and, as a caring parent, to chastise errant children whose behaviour threatened those wider interests.

THE REFORMED EPISCOPATE AND THEIR DIOCESES

Throughout the long struggle to secure freedom from English metropolitan supremacy the process of reform of the institutions of the Scottish Church had continued under the direction of the crown and reformist clerics. Although Alexander I's efforts to install candidates with impeccable Gregorian credentials at St Andrews had been thwarted by his unwillingness to permit them to profess obedience to an English metropolitan, his wish to establish a reformer as the acknowledged leader of the Scottish Church should not be disregarded. His younger brother, David, was more successful at Glasgow, for John was as determined as his patron to resist demands for his submission to York, but his effectiveness as bishop was affected by that protracted struggle and resulting long absences from his see. David's success in securing the uncompromised consecration of Bishop Robert of St Andrews and in 1147 of Herbert, abbot of Kelso, as bishop of Glasgow, however, followed in 1160 at St Andrews by Malcolm IV's choice of Arnold, abbot of Kelso, saw the reforming tradition represented by these foreign clerics established firmly at the two chief sees of the kingdom. In most of the other Scottish sees, the apparently native bishops in office early in David's reign were succeeded mainly by non-native clerics associated firmly with reformist monasteries or the royal household,[71] but there is no firm evidence for a conscious royal policy of engineering the election of foreigners as distinct from reformers in every bishopric. What David and his successors

---

[70] Donaldson, *Historical Documents*, 30–2.
[71] Oram, *David I*, 156–7.

wanted were able diocesans, educated in the doctrines of the Roman Church, active as pastoral leaders and administrators who could reshape the body of the Scottish Church to the pattern that was becoming established throughout western Europe. It was a process almost complete by the end of Malcolm IV's reign.

Given that the existence of an effective episcopate was central to royal plans for the reform of the Scottish Church generally, what tangible improvements to the provision of spiritual services did the bishops bring? There is little evidence to show the establishment of a Continental-style hierarchy of diocesan clergy in most of the Scottish sees before the second half of the twelfth century, but it is probably safe to assume that most of David's bishops recognised from the outset that they needed to construct an administration for their see to aid them in the task of reform. An archdeacon (the official responsible for ecclesiastical courts and upholding spiritual discipline) was in place at Glasgow by 1128, but the first dean of Christianity there (an official who presided over synods of the clergy of a designated sub-division of a diocese and who represented them at diocesan level) was recorded only in the later 1150s.[72] At St Andrews, Bishop Robert had an archdeacon by around 1150, but at Dunkeld the earliest reference to a dean dates from the 1180s and of an archdeacon to 1177, while at Dunblane an archdeaconry was only established as part of Bishop Clement's reorganisation of his diocese in the late 1230s.[73] Administrations, however, required material support and the crown made strenuous efforts to give bishops access to the resources to support their diocesan officers. Such an aim was one of several motives behind David's inquest into the resources of the see of Glasgow and was also a key factor in his arrangements for payment of teind (the tenth of the annual yield of crops and other commodities assigned for the support of the Church) at parish level.[74]

The early origins and development of Scotland's parish system remain under-studied topics but it is apparent that it emerged at different times and progressed at different speeds in various parts of the country.[75] There was probably no one process by which a parish (a territory served by a church which possessed the right to administer baptism and other sacraments) was established, with some possibly emerging long before 1100 to serve the peasant communities on specific portions of

---

[72] Watt, *Fasti*, 152, 170.
[73] Ibid. 102, 119, 304; *Inchaffray Charters*, no. LXVII.
[74] Barrell, *Medieval Scotland*, 54–5.
[75] Cowan, *Medieval Church*, Chapter 1.

early monastic or episcopal estates, as seems to be the case with Glasgow and Whithorn, while others were the private creations of lay landowners, as in the well-known example of Thor the Long's church at Ednam in Roxburghshire, founded around 1105.[76] Often the first specific reference to a parish church occurs only when the right to present its priest (known as advowson) or a portion of its revenues was granted away by a lay patron to an ecclesiastical corporation, usually to a monastery or a cathedral chapter, but such grants were evidently of long-established entities rather than of new creations. This can be seen clearly in the example of the large group of Strathearn parishes that was made over to the canons of Inchaffray around 1200; these were old units of known extent and teind value.[77] The ideal was for the creation of a pattern of such parishes covering the whole country with the teind paid by the parishioners paying for the upkeep of church buildings, supporting a well-trained *rector* and, through levies paid to the diocesan, helping to finance the administrative hierarchy above them. Already by the twelfth century, however, that ideal had been severely compromised.

At Ednam in 1105, Thor the Long had granted the new church to the monks of Durham, who thereafter had the right to appoint the *rector*.[78] The granting away of advowsons by lay patrons was inspired by the Gregorian principle of removing lay control of clerical investiture and was one means by which laymen could demonstrate their support for ecclesiastical reform. For many who lacked substantial landed resources from which to provide endowments for monasteries in return for the masses and prayers of the clergy, the alienation of their right of presentation to a parish church was an obvious alternative. The result was that by the middle of the thirteenth century nearly 70 per cent of Scotland's parishes were in the hands of ecclesiastical corporations, a figure that rose to about 86 per cent by the sixteenth century. Control of advowsons, however, was not where the process stopped, for the new ecclesiastical patrons were soon seeking to secure possession of at least part of the teind income of the parishes to supplement their own revenues. This process, known as appropriation, ultimately undermined the quality of spiritual provision at parish level and was a matter of grave concern for many bishops. Appropriation had potentially profound consequences for diocesan finances, especially where the whole teind income was diverted to the appropriator. In the diocese of Dunblane, where a majority of

[76] Duncan, *Making of the Kingdom*, 296.
[77] *Inchaffray Charters*, nos III, VI, IX, X, XIII, XV, XVIII, XXI, XXII, XXXI.
[78] Cowan, *Medieval Church*, 12–20.

Figure 10.2 Leuchars Church, Fife: the surviving chancel and apse of the richly decorated late-twelfth-century parish church.

parishes had been appropriated to the monasteries of Cambuskenneth, Inchaffray and Lindores before 1230, the loss of revenues available to the bishops helped to delay the establishment of a full diocesan administration and the creation of a financially endowed chapter at the cathedral.[79] Ironically, when Bishop Clement dealt with the financial woes of his diocese after 1233 it was through an agreed levy of a quarter of the teind income from many of the already appropriated parishes that much of the funding was obtained.[80] Efforts to ensure that appropriators made adequate provision for the maintenance of a suitably qualified priest to serve the cure of souls in appropriated parishes had begun to be made piecemeal by bishops throughout Europe in the twelfth century, with varying degrees of success. Concern was such, however, that one of the pieces of legislation settled in the Fourth Lateran Council of 1215 ordained that where there was no resident rector a perpetual vicar should be instituted, subject to the examination and inspection of the diocesan authorities, and assigned an agreed portion of the teinds.[81] In the short term, the Council's decree saw many new vicarages being established in appropriated parishes but, longer term, its success was limited; by the sixteenth century some 56 per cent of vicarages in Scotland had also been appropriated.[82]

MONASTIC FOUNDATIONS

Royal efforts to invigorate the Scottish Church through the establishment of a soundly structured diocesan and parish system akin to that which was crystallising throughout western Christendom, and the introduction of foreign clerics schooled in the reformed Roman tradition to oversee and develop that system, was paralleled by a similar reformation of monastic life in the kingdom. Even as shattered ruins, the great abbeys and priories of the Continental monastic orders central to that reformation are testimony to the scale of the undertaking and its truly revolutionary nature; these were establishments of unprecedented scale and grandeur which transformed the spiritual and cultural life of

---

[79] See the parish entries for the diocese of Dunblane in the Corpus of Scottish Medieval Parish Churches at http://arts.st-andrews.ac.uk/~cmas/sites.php#DioceseofDunblane
[80] Theiner (ed.), *Vetera Monumenta*, no. XCI.
[81] Hartridge, *A History of Vicarages*, 20–2.
[82] Barrell, *Medieval Scotland*, 57.

Parish churches

An early task for bishops of the reorganised Scottish dioceses was to establish a network of parish churches to meet spiritual needs at local level. What distinguished a parish church was possession of a baptismal font and the requirement for all inhabitants of a given district – the parish – to bring their children there for baptism. They were also required to go there on designated days, when their offerings contributed towards the income of the parish priest. By the mid-1100s the most important parochial right was payment of a tenth – in Scotland known as 'teind' – of the parishioners' yield of agricultural production. In some districts, particularly in former Northumbrian areas where the Church had earlier developed sophisticated local structures, the basics of a system were probably in place by the eleventh century. Stobo in the Borders, for example, was a 'mother church' from which priests served the people of a far-flung territory that was gradually broken up into smaller parishes. Elsewhere, there is little evidence for local church organisation before 1100.[83]

Many twelfth-century churches were 'proprietory', meaning they were built and endowed by lay lords to serve their estates, the lord retaining the right to appoint the priest. When reforming popes sought to remove lay influence from the Church, lords were encouraged to surrender proprietory churches. In Scotland, most gave the right to appoint the priest to monasteries, who then wanted one of their number to serve as parish or parson, but usually with a vicar acting as his deputy. Certain revenues were assigned to the vicar, but most were diverted to the uses of the controlling institution in a process known as appropriation. By the early 1200s, bishops were so concerned by the extent of appropriation, especially since many vicarage revenues were also being annexed, and poorly paid and ill-educated curates on meagre stipends appointed, that they sought to exercise quality control over appointments. It was a vain effort, for by the end of the century over 75 per cent of Scottish parishes were in some degree appropriated.[84]

Scotland. Their impact seems all the greater on account of the volume of their surviving records, which, although a mere fragment of what existed before the sixteenth-century Reformation and the destruction of

---

[83] Cowan, *Medieval Church in Scotland*, Chapter 1.
[84] Ibid. Chapters 2 and 4.

monastic and cathedral libraries, still vastly outstrips the mere handful of scraps that has come down from the pre-twelfth-century native monasteries. Therein, however, lies a danger of overstating the case, for we are almost entirely dependent upon the accounts produced by the voices of reform with no balance from the defenders of tradition. This reliance on what is now recognised as the self-promoting literature of the twelfth-century reforming clergy, sure of their cultural and spiritual superiority over native institutions and seeking to justify the expropriation of their property to support reformed communities, has helped to create an image of the native monasteries of the late eleventh and early twelfth centuries as moribund, decadent or corrupt beyond recovery.[85] As with the Victorian scholarly debate over the implications of the creation of the reformed episcopate, however, arguments centred upon the health or otherwise of the native Scottish monastic tradition at the end of the eleventh century miss the fundamental point that monastic reform was a Europe-wide phenomenon. Throughout western Christendom, often following the example of the monks of Cluny in Burgundy, older monastic communities were being reorganised, refounded or swept away in a tide of reforming fervour, sometimes regardless of the vigour of the existing establishment. For Scotland, it was a matter of when, not if, that reforming fervour would arrive.

The catalyst was Margaret. Perhaps too much has been made of her early upbringing in the spiritual whirlwind of recently converted Hungary, where reformist Roman clergy stood at the forefront of the missionary movement, for her personal devotion to aspects of native Scottish monastic traditions is better attested than her support for reformist principles. Nevertheless, she was clearly well aware of the reform of the Benedictine communities in England which had followed swiftly on the heels of the Norman Conquest, and her chaplain, Turgot, who later became prior of the reformed convent at Durham, may have encouraged a deeper interest. With Malcolm III's support she wrote to the most eminent reformist cleric in England at that time, Archbishop Lanfranc of Canterbury, outlining what reforms had so far been undertaken in Scotland and requesting his aid in taking them further. In response, Lanfranc sent three Benedictine monks from his own cathedral-priory to form the core of a convent at Dunfermline.[86] It was a small-scale beginning and it did stall in the violent upheavals that

---

[85] Veitch, 'Replanting paradise', 147–8.
[86] Anderson (ed.), *Early Sources*, ii, 31–2, 64–5; Oram, 'Prayer, property and profit', 80–1.

THE MAKING OF THE *ECCLESIA SCOTICANA* 353

Map 10.1 David I's monastic foundations

→ Colonised from Melrose

Kinloss • • Urquhart

Rhynd •

Cambuskenneth •

Holyrood •
Newbattle •
Lesmahagow • • Kelso
• Melrose
• Jedburgh

• Holm Cultram

followed the deaths of the king and queen in 1093, but it did ensure that many in Scotland, layman and cleric alike, had been made aware of the nature of the profound changes in religious life that monastic reform in England was bringing about.

It was nearly two decades before monastic reform resumed in the kingdom. In this interval, numerous monastic orders spawned by the original Cluniac reform movement had begun to spread across Europe, each vying in their austerity and simplicity for the patronage of laymen who were seeking spiritual salvation through the prayers of monks whose ascetic lives were believed to give them a privileged hearing with God. But it was not to any of these new orders that King Alexander I looked. Instead it was a house of canons – priests who lived a monastic life following the Rule of St Augustine – that in 1115 he brought to Scone from Nostell in Yorkshire.[87] Currently enjoying the support of Henry I of England and Alexander's sister, Queen Matilda, through whom arrangements for the colony were probably negotiated, the Augustinians were closely associated with the reform movement but were less rigid in their support for the Gregorian principle of a strict exclusion of lay political interference from religious life. Given his difficulties with Turgot and Eadmer on this matter, Augustinian flexibility may have endeared them to the king. He was certainly enthusiastic in his personal support for the order and planned further Augustinian communities, at St Andrews, Loch Tay, Inchcolm and possibly Dunkeld, but none of these had been established by the time of his death in 1124, perhaps because the king's enthusiasm had failed to inspire support for the canons amongst the native nobility.[88] Royal patronage was essential in the introduction of the new orders but more widespread support was more vital for the deeper penetration of monastic reform in the religious life of the kingdom.

Alexander I's ambitions for religious reform were unrealised at the time of his death, but in David I the new orders found one of their greatest royal patrons of the twelfth century; he was to take monastic reform in Scotland in new directions and to a new level. In his youth at Henry I's court, David witnessed effective royal religious patronage and religious politics in action, but Henry's influence on David's spiritual awareness was slight. Although a noted patron of monasteries, Henry's piety dated largely from the 1120s, following the death of his only son, almost a decade after David had founded his first abbey. Henry's patronage was

---

[87] Duncan, *Kingship of the Scots*, 82–6.
[88] Cowan and Easson, *Medieval Religious Houses*, 91, 97, 98–9; Duncan, *Making of the Kingdom*, 131.

Figure 10.3 Kelso Abbey, Scottish Borders: only portions of the west end of the great Tironensian abbey church remain, begun after David I moved the monks from Selkirk to this site across the River Tweed from Roxburgh.

very conservative, whilst David displayed an eclecticism that suggests that his brother-in-law's example had little influence on his decisions. More influence probably came from his sister, Queen Matilda, but the greatest lead came probably from his chaplain, John. It was apparently John, who later displayed a close attachment to the order, who stimulated David's interest in the reformed Benedictine community at Thiron in France founded by St Bernard of Abbeville, rather than mere 'monastic fashion-mongering' which drifted with each new wave of reform.[89] The Tironensians were then a minor order with no significant patrons outside northern France and they had little subsequent impact in England; David's support displays his disregard for the fashions in religious patronage circulating at the English court.

---

[89] Brooke, *Age of the Cloister*, 159; Duncan, *Making of the Kingdom*, 149.

Shortly after he gained control of Teviotdale David was able to give substance to his interest in the order with the foundation of a colony of Tironensian monks at Selkirk. This was not just Thiron's first daughter-house, it was the first monastery of any of the new orders of monks to be founded anywhere in Britain, and it was richly endowed from David's personal estates to support its monks.[90] His choice of Tironensians to colonise his first foundation was probably in recognition of their intense spirituality. Austere and seen as closer to a truly Godly lifestyle than the Benedictines and Cluniacs, David believed that the Tironensians' purity and simplicity offered him – and his people – the best route to salvation through the privileged access to Divine favour that their prayers and masses were believed to bring. But monks alone could not undertake the reform of the Scottish Church, for although they offered outstanding examples of Christian life they could not take active missionary roles in the religious life of the kingdom; monks were removed from the world within the closed precincts of their communities. Even bishops like John at Glasgow, who supported reformed monasticism, knew that canons, not monks, were more useful in the process of ecclesiastical reconstruction.

Canons could leave their monasteries to minister in the secular world but there is little evidence for any serving in parish churches in twelfth-century Scotland. Because of this potential for involvement in worldly affairs, the Augustinians were regarded as inferior in spiritual status to cloistered monks. Nevertheless, their value in the reform process was widely recognised by bishops, for they could provide examples to parish priests of reformed liturgical practices, or themselves preach to layfolk and minister to the people's physical as well as spiritual needs.[91] It was probably for those reasons that Bishop Robert of St Andrews, whose own efforts to push ahead with Alexander I's plans for an Augustinian priory attached to his cathedral were hindered by opposition from the secular canons there, encouraged David to found Augustinian abbeys at Holyrood in 1128 and Cambuskenneth in 1142, while Bishop John of Glasgow secured David's help to found a community of canons at Jedburgh in 1138–9. Despite his involvement in those foundations, David's personal preference was for monks and from the mid-1130s it was the still more austere Cistercian order rather than the Tironensians who benefited from his patronage.

The Cistercians were a rapidly expanding order whose simple devotions and ascetic lifestyle had won them a high reputation for intense

[90] *Kelso Liber*, i, no. 1.
[91] Brooke, *Age of the Cloister*, 153–7.

spirituality. In an age when men longed for close communication with God to secure the salvation of their souls, the Cistercians were believed to have particular effectiveness in that regard. The result was the rapid growth and expansion of the order from only fourteen houses in 1119 to nearly five hundred by 1152, spread from the Mediterranean to Scandinavia, Ireland to the Baltic.[92] David probably first came into contact with the Cistercians through Rievaulx Abbey in Yorkshire, with which one of his friends, Walter Espec, lord of Helmsley, and a former clerk in his household, Ailred, were closely associated. A colony of Clairvaux, the greatest of Cîteaux's own daughter-houses, Rievaulx provided David with a source of colonists for his own foundations and also with a link to one of the most influential monastic leaders of the age, St Bernard of Clairvaux.[93] The fruits of that connection were Melrose Abbey, founded in 1136, and its subsequent network of daughter-houses – Newbattle (1140), Holm Cultram and Kinloss (1150), Coupar Angus (1164) and Balmerino (1222), and daughters of Kinloss at Culross (1217) and Deer (1219) – which carried the reformed monastic tradition and its spiritual and cultural influences deep into the heartland of Gaelic Scotland north of the Forth.[94] The favour shown to this order by David I continued under his successors and by the middle of the thirteenth century Cistercian abbeys were amongst the greatest landowners in the kingdom. This power and wealth was founded on the monks' perceived status as guarantors of salvation in the hereafter for lay patrons, but the Cistercians' high reputation for spirituality and reformist discipline, as well as the skills brought by administration of a great landed estate, also saw many appointed to bishoprics – Pope Eugenius III was himself a former Cistercian monk – with Melrose providing some outstanding diocesans including the possible mastermind of Scottish ecclesiastical freedom, Bishop Jocelin of Glasgow. The close association of the abbey with the crown may have helped to cement Melrose in a role as a breeding ground for bishops, and it was perhaps its identification with royal interests that saw former abbots John and Adam appointed as successive bishops of Caithness by kings William and Alexander II as much as their spirituality and administrative acumen.[95]

---

[92] Bartlett, *Making of Europe*, 256–60.
[93] For Bernard's correspondence concerning David, see Scott James (ed.), *Letters of St Bernard*, no. 172.
[94] Fawcett and Oram, *Melrose Abbey*, 22; Cowan and Easson, *Medieval Religious Houses*, 72–4, 76–7; Hammond, 'Queen Ermengarde and Balmerino'.
[95] Oram, 'Prayer, property and profit', 84–5.

It was not only Scottish kings who favoured the Cistercians. A separate filiation of Rievaulx was established in Galloway by its ruler, Fergus, who founded Dundrennan Abbey in 1142, from which two further houses were colonised, Glenluce in 1192 and Sweetheart, the last Cistercian abbey founded in Scotland, in 1273.[96] Strong Gaelic Irish interest in the order saw it flourish there in the two decades before the beginning of the English conquest of the island, with Mellifont Abbey in Louth becoming the mother of several daughter-houses. The promotion of the order by Archbishop Malachy of Armagh helped to fix a Cistercian tradition firmly in Gaelic ecclesiastical culture, and it was probably through that route that a colony of Mellifont was founded at Saddell in Kintyre by a member of Somerled's family.[97] The reformed monastic tradition, however, made little further headway in the West Highlands and Hebrides, Somerled himself having displayed interest in the native Irish reform movement rather than the Continental orders earlier in the century.[98] When Iona itself finally embraced Continental-style monasticism in the early thirteenth century it was the basic Benedictine rule that was adopted rather than the more rigorous interpretation of that rule by the Tironensians or Cistercians.[99]

Despite the final burst of new Cistercian foundations between 1192 and 1222, and the continued flow of royal and lordly patronage that the order received throughout the reign of Alexander II, the current of religious enthusiasm was moving in different directions by the early 1200s. The search for purer forms of monastic life, seen as being closer still to the perfect Christian existence, drew support first to the Premonstratensian order of canons, whose rule blended elements of Cistercian practice with Augustinian forms. Although they never enjoyed significant royal patronage in Scotland, Hugh de Morville at Dryburgh, the lords of Galloway at Soulseat, Whithorn and Tongland, and Ferchar, earl of Ross, at Fearn, gave the order a prominent presence.[100] The king, however, looked elsewhere, and in the early 1230s Alexander II's attention fixed briefly on the austere Valliscaulian order of monks, for whom he founded a priory at Pluscarden in Moray, possibly as a thanks-offering for his final triumph over the MacWilliams.[101]

[96] Cowan and Easson, *Medieval Religious Houses*, 74–5, 78.
[97] Ibid. 77–8.
[98] McDonald, *Kingdom of the Isles*, 205–6.
[99] Beuermann, *Masters of the Narrow Sea*, 160–80.
[100] Fawcett and Oram, *Dryburgh Abbey*, 11–14; Cowan and Easson, *Medieval Religious Houses*, 101–3.
[101] Oram, 'Introduction and overview', 30, 43.

His example was followed by his close associate, John Bisset, at Beauly, and by the lord of Lorn at Ardchattan,[102] but this brief flurry of support swiftly waned as a new form of religious expression, the orders of friars, began to find favour with the king. Although the orders of monks continued to benefit from royal patronage throughout the Middle Ages in Scotland, with the last monastery, a Carthusian convent at Perth, being founded in 1429, after 1230 the great wave of monastic reform and foundation of monasteries was over.

CONTINUING TRADITIONS

The flourishing of the reformed monastic tradition in Scotland in the first half of the twelfth century has caused it to be viewed as almost the sole trend in Scottish monasticism rather than occurring alongside a continuing native tradition. As the evidence of the *Book of Deer* illustrates, at least some older monasteries in Scotland, especially those associated with the ninth-century Céli Dé reform movement, were vigorous institutions which in the mid-twelfth century continued to attract the patronage of laymen, including of kings otherwise portrayed as single-minded devotees of the reformed orders. In the reign of Alexander I, the Céli Dé of Dunkeld resisted attempts to convert them into Augustinian canons and the community retained its monastic character into the thirteenth century before Bishop Geoffrey (1236–49) succeeded in establishing a college of secular canons in their place.[103] Bishop Robert and King David were slightly more successful at St Andrews, where an Augustinian priory was founded in 1144 with the intention that the Céli Dé there either become canons themselves or that the portions of individual Céli Dé should pass to the Augustinians at their deaths. But instead of a seamless transition from Céli Dé monastery to Augustinian convent two separate communities existed in parallel and eventually agreed an elaborate partition of resources in the late 1100s.[104] The St Andrews Céli Dé, moreover, retained a Gaelic identity, if the name of their late-twelfth-century abbot, Gilchrist (Gaelic *Gille Chriosd*), reflects the wider character of the community.[105] It was only in the early thirteenth century that

---

[102] Cowan and Easson, *Medieval Monasteries*, 83–5.
[103] Duncan, *Making of the Kingdom*, 268; Veitch, 'Replanting paradise', 155; Myln, *Vitae*, 10.
[104] Duncan, *Making of the Kingdom*, 267; Barrow, *Kingdom of the Scots*, 196–7.
[105] Barrow (ed.), *RRS*, ii, no. 347.

the bishops of St Andrews succeeded in transferring the residue of the Céli Dé properties to a new college of secular canons in the church of St Mary of the Rock.[106] At Brechin, the Céli Dé of the monastery in which the bishop's see was located continued to attract royal patronage into the reign of King William,[107] but by the end of the twelfth century they, like their brethren at Dunkeld, had abandoned their monastic character and been transformed by the bishop into a college of secular canons to serve in the cathedral.

Away from the bishops' sees, less prestigious Céli Dé communities also attracted lay patronage and functioned effectively as monasteries. Malcolm III and Margaret, for example, were benefactors of the Céli Dé of Lochleven, but their son, David I, enforced their adoption of the Augustinian rule.[108] Longer-lived were the Céli Dé at Inchaffray in Strathearn, who only became Augustinians c. 1200 at the prompting of their patrons, the earl and countess of Strathearn, and at Abernethy, where the community survived the expropriation of half of their property as an endowment for Arbroath Abbey in the early 1190s and continued as a convent headed by a prior down to the 1270s when they finally adopted the Augustinian rule.[109] Charters by a 'master of the schools' and 'scholars' at both Dunblane and Muthill in the 1210s and contemporary references to priors of the Céli Dé at the latter suggest that these were not moribund or laicised establishments, but functioning monasteries who were still actively recruiting and training novices well into the thirteenth century.[110] Indeed, the continuing vitality of such institutions as educational centres can be seen in the part played by the Gaelic clergy of east central Scotland through the twelfth century in the literary construction of the 'Gaelic identity of the kingdom of the Scots' and the stressing of the continuity of that identity under the heirs of Malcolm III. Their late survival issues a strong corrective to traditional visions of the ecclesiastical life of twelfth- and thirteenth-century Scotland which focus almost exclusively on the impact of the Continental reform movements; like the kingdom itself, the *Ecclesia Scoticana* which had emerged by 1230 was a complex mix of native and foreign traditions.

---

[106] Barrow, *Kingdom of the Scots*, 199–202.
[107] Barrow (ed.), *RRS*, ii, no. 115.
[108] Barrow (ed.), *David I Charters*, no. 208; Veitch, 'Replanting paradise', 159.
[109] *Inchaffray Charters*, no. 9; Barrow (ed.), *RRS*, ii, no. 339; *Lindores Charters*, nos LI, LIV; Bower, *Scotichronicon*, v, 399.
[110] *Lindores Charters*, nos XLVI, XLVII; *Cambuskenneth Registrum*, nos 122, 217.

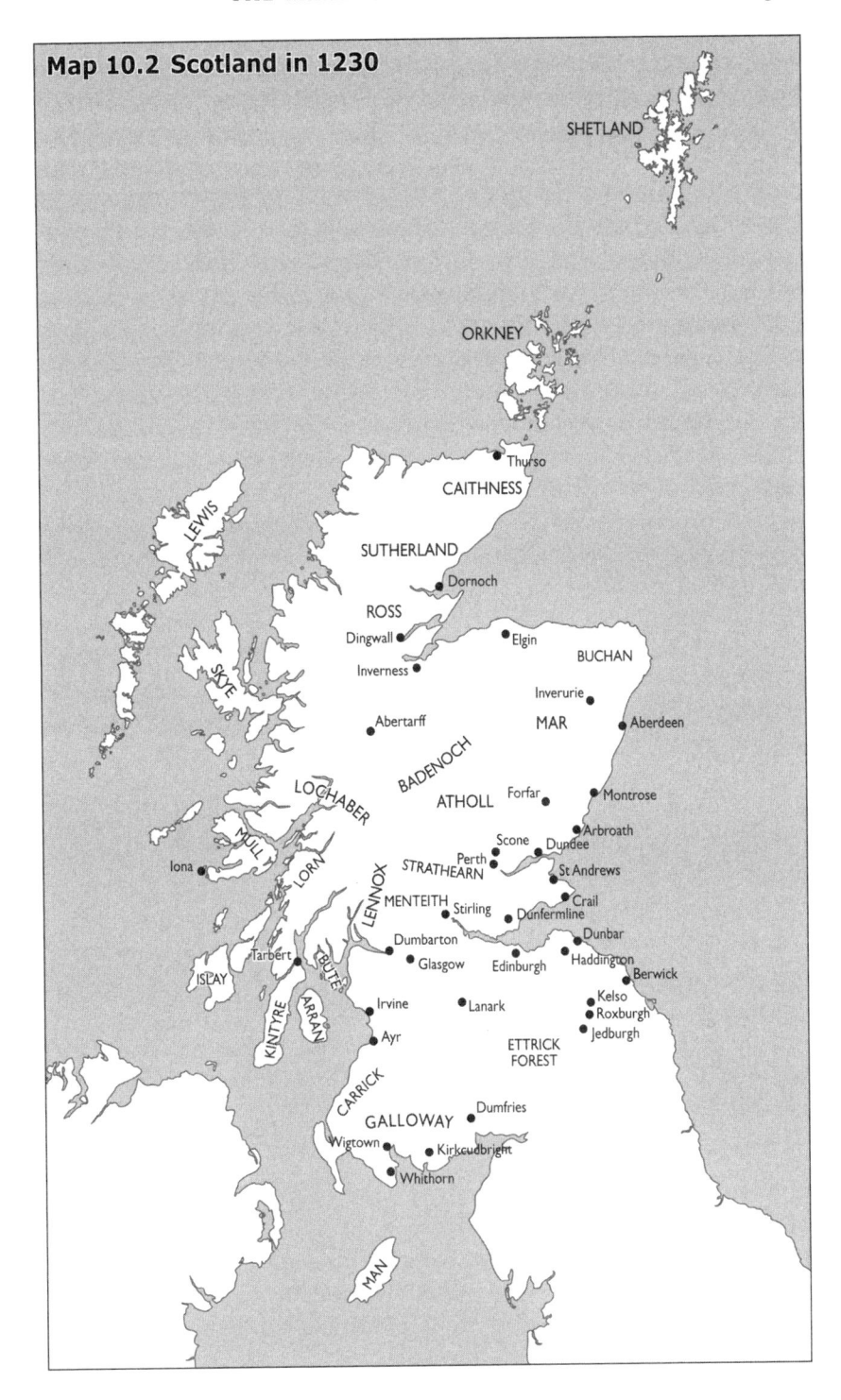

THE MAKING OF THE *ECCLESIA SCOTICANA*

Map 10.2 Scotland in 1230

Conclusion

'Revolutionary' is a term that has been much misused by historians to describe processes of social, cultural and economic transformation, but in respect of the changes that occurred in Scotland between 1070 and 1230 it possibly understates the scale, speed and impact of the reconfiguration. Yet equally we must not overstate the case, for many of the basic routines and practices that governed the daily existence of the people who inhabited the territories that had been incorporated into the kingdom by the early thirteenth century would, at a superficial level, have seemed unchanged or at least easily recognisable to their late-eleventh-century ancestors. Closer scrutiny, however, might have revealed that there were few fundamental elements of daily life that had not in some way been affected by the powerful new forces that had penetrated even the furthest-flung districts of northern mainland Britain. Some processes were subtle; for example, the slow percolation of English speech and Continental-style material culture from the developing burghs into their rural hinterlands had made steady headway from the mid-twelfth century, and the long northwards and westwards retreat of the Gaelic language had already begun. Others were more traumatic and involved violent political upheaval and military conquest, from which had flowed the intrusion of foreign colonists, alien in language and culture and armed with the coercive power of superimposed legal authority with which to entrench their new regime. Even districts remote from centres of trade or the seats of Scottish royal power were not immune to these processes. Into these territories reached the influences of the reformed Church or the new, intrusive authority of economically predatory lords – native and newcomer – empowered by parchment definitions of their rights and responsibilities. As those influences spread, so too had the effective lordship of the king of Scots.

Past historiography, redolent with the notion of the 'making of the kingdom' and constructed from a monarchocentric perspective, has given an air of inevitability to the extension and consolidation of the Scottish kings' hold over what we nowadays understand as Scotland. The propensity of the Scots' ruling lineage to fracture into rival, mutually destructive segments in the tenth and eleventh centuries and the creeping influence of external powers to north and south across this same period should alert us that there was nothing inevitable about their success.[1] Indeed, given the northward expansion of English influence in the time of Edward the Confessor and its resumption under the Norman and Angevin kings, the achievement represented by their Scottish cousins' avoidance of absorption into the wider sphere of the English kingdom and extension instead of their domination across mainland Scotland is truly remarkable. In a century and a half, the Scottish kingdom had been transformed from a largely notional entity – a core of royal power in the lower valley of the Tay with salients through Fife and into the Lothian plain, surrounded by territories over which some fluctuating degree of domination was extended but where other potentates exercised more immediate and effective authority – into a sophisticated state with a bureaucratic royal administration, effective local representatives of crown authority, and a regional magnate group responsive to the needs and demands of the king. While what may be described as the contours of royal power still diminished the further you moved from the chief political centres of the kingdom, there were few areas of mainland Scotland that lay beyond the limits of the Scottish king's authority by the 1230s.

This transformation was achieved neither smoothly nor with unbroken success; there had been reverses and challenges along the way, ranging from the irruption of Norwegian power in the Isles in the 1090s and 1200s to the overthrowing of the mechanisms of provincial control in Galloway in the 1170s or Ross as late as the 1220s. There is much, too, that was clearly accidental, not least the sequence of genetic failures that delivered the throne to David I in 1124 or the untimely death of his experienced, adult heir. Equally, however, the ill-fortune of others had worked to the advantage of the Scots; how different might Scotland's political development have been had Norway's King Magnus Barelegs not gone ashore to raid in Ulster in 1103, William Æðeling not perished in the 1120 wreck of the *White Ship* or England's King John not died so unexpectedly in 1216? But were Scottish kings from Malcolm III to his great-grandson Alexander II working to a plan to convert their

---

[1] For which see Woolf, *Pictland to Alba*, Chapter 6.

domination of northern Britain into real and effective lordship through a unitary kingship that embraced the whole of the northern mainland and islands? Some historians have seen more than simple chance behind the succession of steps that carried the power of the Scottish king into Caithness, Argyll or Galloway and the Isles beyond them; indeed, they have described Malcolm's heirs as following a blueprint in their territorial expansion.[2] That expansion, however, was never a straightforward linear progression but was punctuated with checks and reverses, like the ultimately blind alley of the quest for the northern English counties, and strokes of good fortune, like the sequence of events in 1185–7 which detached Galloway from English lordship and steered it towards its initially unhappy integration into the Scottish state half a century later.

In the traditional narrative, much of the story of expansion is told in terms of military campaigns, battles, conquests and rebellions. Most of it, too, is narrated from the perspective of the Scots, who are presented as waging legitimate warfare, reasserting rights that had been let slip or usurped by others, or simply restoring good government to people who had been led into the error of rebellion against their natural lord by wicked, treacherous deceivers. It is a good story, but most of the time it is just that: a story. As the late Rees Davies warned us, there is much more to the process of 'domination and conquest' than military events alone,[3] and, as we have seen, the unglamorous acts of peasant cultivators, economic migrants and legal innovators, the peaceful bonds of marriage or trade, and, perhaps most insidious of all, the quiet insistence of scholars – medieval and modern – contributed more to the successful creation of an all-encompassing kingdom of Scotland than the armies that symbolised the increasingly effective coercive might of its rulers.

Say that it is so loudly and often enough and so it will become. In the early twenty-first century there can be few of us who have not experienced the power of 'spin', from the marketing devices of advertisers to the information management of party politics, but there is nothing new under the sun and these same mechanisms have been deployed by those who would influence popular opinion throughout human history. Medieval Scotland was no exception and the agents and supporters of the kings of Scots were strident in proclaiming their man's status and right at every opportunity and through every medium available; the iconography of coins, seals and sculpture, or the oral and written testimony of poetry, chronicles, law codes and charters. The idea of 'Scotland' was not simply

---

[2] Carpenter, *Struggle for Mastery*, 521–2, 528.
[3] Davies, *Domination and Conquest*, Chapter 1.

created in the heads of the men who would be its king but flowed from an articulate intellectual tradition amongst men – mainly clergy – who did have a plan to produce something coherent and cohesive, albeit as a vehicle for their own dreams and ambitions.[4]

This presentation of Scottish kings as having a natural right to kingship over the whole of what is now the Scottish mainland emerges very powerfully from the surviving twelfth- and thirteenth-century records. It was not just a matter of self-advertisement and neither was it a fiction created by recent incomers who had different ideas of the nature of royal power or a particular philosophical vision of statehood; the tradition was already firmly established in the eleventh century amongst the educated Gaelic clerical elite within Scotland. They were already consciously promoting a notion that the heirs of Cinaed son of Alpín, the mid-ninth-century ruler still regarded popularly as the founder of a unified Scottish state, possessed an authority that encompassed a territory greater than their own kingdom before the heirs of Malcolm III started to import the Continental clerics whose energies helped to turn that notion into a reality. This promotion went beyond the simple broadcast of personal right, for it was 'the credentials of the kingship itself which were being publicly proclaimed and reaffirmed', largely through the construction of the king-lists – the supposed genealogies of the Scots' rulers – which form the chief survival of this intellectual tradition;[5] the legitimacy and status of Scottish kingship was being asserted through the claims to antiquity and continuity revealed in such extended lists. The structure of the king-lists is not simply genealogical but was designed to stress the identity of the kingship and by extension the Scottish people, as *Gaídil* east of the sea. This emphasis of the Scots' status as essentially Irish in terms of historical and cultural identity served to underscore their kingship's credentials and fix its status vis-à-vis other, Irish, kingships and its descent from them.[6] When linked to genealogical exposition and origin-legend, the Scottish royal line was given both status-enhancing antiquity and also the added lustre of blood association with some of the greatest royal lineages of the *Gaídil*. Simple though they may appear, the king-lists are carefully crafted documents with a powerful propaganda impact which was recognised and exploited by their successors amongst

---

[4] See, for example, the discussion of clerical ambitions for an independent Scottish church province in Broun, *Scottish Independence*, Chapters 4 and 5.

[5] Broun, *Irish Identity*, 188. For discussion of the function of the king-lists, see especially Chapters 8 and 9.

[6] Ibid. 189–93.

the reformed secular clergy and monastic orders in the later twelfth and the thirteenth centuries; their lasting effect can be seen in the influence that their presentation of Scottish royal origins has had, and continues to have, in framing nearly one thousand years of historical writing.

The king-lists in Scotland may have been produced as intellectual tools but they functioned as secular political instruments. Their production serves to emphasise the critical role, political as much as cultural, that the Gaelic learned class played in eleventh- and twelfth-century Scotland, where the king-lists were a highly effective means of consolidating the authority of the royal line descended from Malcolm II (1005–34) and, critically, Malcolm III, to the exclusion of rival or collateral lineages. The Gaelic literati, however, were not simply docile propagandists for the crown and, as the now much-cited poem voicing criticism of the future David I reveals, could be vocal in their hostility towards members of the royal house and be sure of finding patronage and an audience amongst the leadership of Scottish Gaelic society for such sentiments.[7] More importantly, however, their steady promotion of the lineage, legitimacy and authority of the ruling house secured the widespread acceptance of and identification with those kings amongst the majority of the Gaelic elite. Despite generations of historiographical presentation of the heirs of Malcolm III as more 'Frenchmen, both in race and in manners, language and culture' than Gaels,[8] and the emphasis placed on the transformation of Scotland's cultural identity through the steady inflow of English- and French-speaking colonists under the direction of those kings, the fact remains that it was on the supposedly disparaged Gaels that the successes of the Scottish kings remained founded throughout this critical transformative era.

As the final, almost inconsequential whimper of the MacWilliam challenge for the throne revealed, the Scottish kings had been established successfully as the focus for the loyalties of natives and newcomers, and even of the people of territories that had been brought recently and forcibly under their lordship. The role of Ferchar MacTaggart in the extirpation of the MacWilliam line has long been recognised, but only recently has its significance as evidence for a new prescription of changed allegiances in Ross been recognised.[9] Ferchar's actions may have been entirely opportunistic, but he saw the future as lying in a close alignment of Scottish royal interests with his own. Even Galloway, with its long tra-

---

[7] Clancy (ed.), *The Triumph Tree*, 184.
[8] Anderson (ed.), *Scottish Annals*, 330 note 6.
[9] Grant, 'Province of Ross', 121–6.

dition of independence and violent resistance to Scottish encroachment, looked to Alexander II in 1234 to provide justice and effective lordship in the succession crisis that followed the death of its ruler.[10] They may still have regarded themselves first and foremost as Galwegians rather than Scots, but the fact that they looked for leadership to an external power – and that that power was the king of Scots – shows how far the forging of new identities had travelled in just the few decades since they had risen to throw off their subjection to that king's father. The ruthless elimination of potential rivals for the kingship had removed most natural alternatives, but the establishment of the king of Scots as acknowledged lord of the area that we would now recognise as mainland Scotland was no mere default reflex.

The creation of a unified Scottish kingdom was not achieved solely through the systematic removal of alternative foci for loyalty and identity. Destruction of the symbols of rival authority, as seems to have been employed in the systematic dismantling of the apparatus of power that had sustained the lordship of the rulers of Moray down to the 1130s, was one very effective route to the breaking of regional identities, but as much effort appears to have been put into winning hearts and minds as in bludgeoning the unconvinced into submission. Scottish success was based as much on their kings' ability to persuade others to give them their loyalty as on their determination to extirpate challenges to their position. What is truly remarkable is how David I and his successors secured and kept the loyalty of the key lineages and wider kindreds of their kingdom throughout an era of profound social and economic upheaval, political reconfiguration and external conflicts. There was domestic opposition to their regime, the probable seriousness of which at the time has been diluted and blurred by its ultimate failure to deflect the Scottish kings from their path to domination. As indicated by the few fragments of evidence that have survived, like the general hints at significant support for Malcolm, bastard son of Alexander I, or for William son of Duncan II and his son, William 'the Boy of Egremont',[11] as alternatives for the kingship, or the more specific events like the betrayal of the king's castle of Auldearn by Gillecolm, marshal of the earl of Strathearn, to his MacWilliam enemies,[12] that opposition could be powerful and well placed within Gaelic society. Nevertheless, except for the short-lived breakdown in trust between Malcolm IV and his earls

[10] Oram, *Lordship of Galloway*, 141–6.
[11] See pp. 64–5.
[12] Barrow (ed.), *RRS*, ii, no. 258.

in 1160, the Scottish kings succeeded in persuading the leadership of the core provinces of their kingdom to accompany them on their expansionist journey. Their support as much as that of the colonist-knights whom David I and his heirs implanted, bought with the promise of land, wealth and the power that flowed from both, delivered the Scottish kings their united kingdom.

'Buy-in' to the vision of the new monarchy did not leave Scotland's social leaders unchanged. The process was slow, painfully so at times, and not always without false starts, stubborn resistance and reverses, but the idea of an immutable, ancient Gaelic culture that sought to repel innovation, especially foreign innovation, is one that any close reading of the evidence cannot sustain. As the history of this period shows, perhaps best illustrated by the wedding with which this book began, change could be brought about as much by the marriage bed as at the sword's edge. Indeed, as Rees Davies observed, it was the Celtic peoples of the British Isles' receptiveness to foreign influences and cultures that provided the opening for subsequent domination and conquest. Popular images of distrustfully conservative Gaelic chieftains pulling back from contact with the brash young knights and their foreign ways who crowded round the king need to be tempered with recognition of the growing enthusiasm with which some of those foreign ways were greeted by natives who saw in them something attractive, and not just a means of consolidating their grip on power; the late-twentieth-century allure of American culture even amongst some who violently opposed the United States' economic and political systems should alert us to that reality. It may have taken until early in the reign of Alexander II to establish as common practice within the kingdom such fundamental aspects of the colonists' parent traditions as the law of primogeniture in inheritance, but from personal names and clothing styles to castle building and religious practices Scotland's social leaders were already saturated with the symbols of imported culture.

That receptiveness to change, importation of foreign cultural norms and practices, and acceptance of the devices and mechanisms that enhanced the power and prestige of rulers created in Scotland a political culture and society that was at once alien and unfamiliar and reassuringly recognisable to both native and newcomer. This hybrid character made and, it could be argued, saved the kingdom. Scotland's rulers embraced European culture in a manner that eased the kingdom's integration into a wider community and so gave it acceptance and recognition from members of that community in ways that cultures perceived as 'other' did not receive; a 'warm-beer-and-cricket' test which the Scots passed. Marriages, proposed and secured, helped to establish lines of communication with Continental powers which no Irish or Welsh ruler enjoyed and brought recognition of Scotland as part of an international community which shared cultural conventions. Acceptance into that community mattered to Scottish kings and they were acutely conscious of their lack of certain attributes which would have automatically lifted them to parity of status with their neighbours. A desire to obtain those trappings drove the Scots and their kings regularly into conflict or controversy with English kings and Roman popes, collisions which at times compromised the very independence and kingly status which they striving to secure; gaining a pallium for St Andrews was as much about the future making of kings as it was about the ecclesiastical freedom of the Scottish Church from external metropolitan subjection. Ultimately, they had to compromise on both counts; no archbishopric but an independent church province as special daughter of the Roman see; no crowning rite but acknowledgement of their independent royalty through marriage to a sister of the English king. Although her kings may have lacked the ultimate status symbol of unction and coronation, and strong English lobbying at Rome ensured that those symbols remained beyond reach until the fourteenth century, by the 1220s Scottish kingship had secured recognition of its mature and independent status on equal terms with most other monarchies in western Europe.

How resilient the newly unified kingdom over which Alexander II presided was becomes evident as the thirteenth century progressed. Apart from one brief paroxysm of noble defiance of the king's will in 1242, the remainder of the reign of Alexander II was remarkable for the political harmony within the kingdom and general absence of factional division and conflict. Surely there was tension between individuals arising from frustrated ambitions and personal jealousies, but the king generally maintained political equilibrium amongst his magnates by exercising inclusive government, spreading his patronage widely and, as the growing body of record evidence suggests, consulting more regularly through the *colloquia* from which the Scottish parliament evolved. The centrality of the king to this balanced polity was revealed in the faction-ridden and crisis-torn minority of Alexander III in the decade after 1249, where the most striking dimension of this troubled period was the cohesiveness of a kingdom that had experienced barely twenty years of unity and peace under Alexander II. The resilience of the state he had created and the sense of common identity his dynasty had long promoted, strong enough to survive the tensions of his son's minority years, were tested to the full in the traumatic upheavals that followed his death in 1286. That through this testing time the one factor that gave many Scots a focus for their identity as an independent nation was the unifying power of Scottish kingship is testimony to the strength of what the descendants of Malcolm III and St Margaret had built.

Table of Events

1070	Marriage of Malcolm III and Margaret.
1072	Norman campaign into Scotland. Malcolm III and William of Normandy make peace at Abernethy. Malcolm gives his eldest son, Duncan, as a hostage.
1079	Malcolm III raids northern England.
1080	Second Norman campaign into Scotland. Malcolm III makes peace at Falkirk.
1085	Death of Mael Snechta mac Lulaig, 'king' of Moray.
1087	Death of William of Normandy and accession of second son, William Rufus, to English throne. William Rufus releases and knights Duncan mac Malcolm.
1091	Malcolm III raids northern England.
1092	William Rufus takes control of Carlisle.
1093	Malcolm III present at the foundation of the new church at Durham (11 August). Meeting of Malcolm III and William Rufus at Gloucester (24 August). Scots launch raid into Northumberland. Malcolm III killed in skirmish at Alnwick (13 November). Death of Margaret at Edinburgh (16 November). Donald III succeeds as king and drives out the children of Malcolm III.
1094	Duncan II installed as king with Norman support but defeated and killed before the end of the year. Donald III restored as king with support of Edmund, son of Malcolm III.
1097	Deposition of Donald III and accession of Edgar.
1098	King Magnus Barelegs asserts Norwegian lordship over Orkney, the Western Isles and kingdom of Man.
1103	Magnus Barelegs killed in Ulster (24 August).
1107	Death of Edgar and accession of Alexander I.
1113	Foundation of Selkirk Abbey. Marriage of David and Matilda de Senlis.
1115	Foundation of Scone Priory by Alexander I.
1124	Death of Alexander I and accession of David I.
1125	Start of rebellion led by Malcolm, son of Alexander I.
1127	David I swears to support the right of his niece, Matilda, to succeed to the English throne. Temporary suspension of York's claims to metropolitan supremacy over the Scottish Church. Consecration of Robert of Scone as bishop of St Andrews.

1128	Monks moved from Selkirk to new abbey at Kelso. Dunfermline Priory raised to abbey status. Foundation of Holyrood Abbey.
1130	Battle of Stracathro, Angus of Moray slain.
1134	Capture of Malcolm, son of Alexander I, and his imprisonment for life at Roxburgh.
1135	Death of Henry I (1 December) and coronation of Stephen (22 December). David I invades Northumberland (late December).
1136	Scots capture Carlisle and Newcastle. First Treaty of Durham between David I and Stephen (February). Foundation of Melrose Abbey.
1137	David invades Northumberland but withdraws and starts negotiations with Stephen.
1138	Third Scottish invasion of Northumberland (January). Stephen raids Lothian (February). David devastates Northumberland and Durham. Scottish victory at Craven (10 June). Scots routed at the battle of the Standard (22 August). David meets papal legate at Carlisle and negotiates a truce.
1139	Second Treaty of Durham (9 April) sees Northumberland granted to Earl Henry. Huntingdon restored to the Scots. Marriage of Earl Henry to Ada de Warenne.
1140	Death of Archbishop Thurstan of York.
1141	Election of William, son of Herbert, as Archbishop of York (January). Capture of King Stephen at Lincoln (2 February). Start of Durham election dispute (Easter). David travels to London for Matilda's coronation (June) but driven out after a week without her being crowned. David and Matilda escape from the 'Rout of Winchester' (14 September). Stephen released (1 November).
1143	Election of William of St Barbe as bishop of Durham.
1147	Death of William son of Duncan II – start of MacWilliam claims to a share in his inheritance. Death of Bishop John of Glasgow. Deposition of Archbishop William of York and election and consecration of Henry Murdac.
1149	David knights his great nephew, Henry of Anjou, at Carlisle (May). Henry swears to recognise Scottish gains in northern England. Failed Scottish attempt to capture York.
1151	King Eystein of Norway reasserts Norwegian overlordship of Orkney and receives submission of Harald Maddadsson, earl of Caithness and Orkney. Norwegian fleet raids down Scottish east coast, sacking Aberdeen.
1152	Death of Earl Henry (12 June). David designates his grandson, Malcolm, as heir.
1153	Death of David I at Carlisle (24 May), accession of Malcolm IV. Murder of Óláfr Guðrøðsson, king of Man. Accession of Guðrøðr II to Manx throne (late autumn).
1156	Civil war in the kingdom of Man and the Isles. Capture of Donald, grandson of Alexander I, at Whithorn.
1157	Somerled of Argyll defeats Guðrøðr of Man and forces partition of the kingdom of Man and the Isles (5–6 January). Meeting of Malcolm IV and Henry II at Chester (July); Malcolm surrenders northern counties of England to Henry and is restored to the earldom of Huntingdon.
1159	Guðrøðr II driven out of Man. Malcolm IV joins Henry II's campaign to Toulouse.

… TABLE OF EVENTS 373

1160	Confrontation between Malcolm IV and his earls at Perth. Invasion of Galloway and deposition of its ruler, Fergus.
1164	Somerled defeated and slain at Renfrew. Foundation of Coupar Angus Abbey.
1165	Death of Malcolm IV (9 December) and accession of William.
1173	William joins revolt of Henry II's eldest son and invades Northumberland and Cumberland (August) but fails to take any castles. Henry II's supporters burn Berwick and ravage Lothian in retaliation.
1174	William again invades Northumberland (April). Attacks Carlisle (June) before marching east to Alnwick, where he was captured by Henry II's loyalists (13 July). William is brought to Henry II at Northampton before being sent to Falaise in Normandy. Revolt and civil war in Galloway (August). William agrees to 'Treaty of Falaise' (1 December) and is released to return to Scotland (11 December).
1175	Formal submission of William and the Scottish nobility to Henry II at York (10 August).
1176	Council at Northampton to determine English rights over the Church in Scotland breaks up inconclusively. Gillebrigte of Galloway submits to Henry II (9 October). Pope Alexander III issues the bull *Super anxietatibus*, freeing Scottish bishops from York's submission until the archbishop proved his right.
1178	William founds Arbroath Abbey. Beginning of St Andrews election dispute.
1179	William campaigns in Ross.
1181	Donald MacWilliam launches bid for throne.
1185	Death of Gillebrigte of Galloway (January) and seizure of his lands by Roland, son of Uhtred.
1186	Death of Guðrøðr II, king of Man, and accession of his son, Rognvald. Henry II at Carlisle to settle Galloway issue; William negotiates submission of Roland. William marries Ermengarde de Beaumont (5 September).
1187	William campaigns in north against Donald MacWilliam (July); defeat and death of Donald at battle of 'Mam Garvia'.
1189	Death of Henry II (6 July) and accession of Richard I. William pays homage to Richard at Canterbury and negotiates cancellation of the Treaty of Falaise in the agreement known as the Quitclaim of Canterbury (2 December).
1192	Pope Celestine III issues bull *Cum universi* in favour of the Scottish Church.
1194	Intervention of Harald Maddadsson in Norwegian civil war fails; Harald forced to submit to King Sverre. William fails to negotiate return of northern counties from Richard I.
1195	William devises plan to marry his daughter, Margaret, to Otto of Saxony.
1196	William leads campaigns in the north against Harald Maddadsson.
1197	Imprisonment of Harald Maddadsson and submission of Caithness to William.
1198	Birth of Alexander II at Haddington (24 August). William gives Caithness to Ranald son of Somerled.
1199	Death of Richard I (6 April). William tries unsuccessfully to use uncertainty over English succession to secure restoration of the northern counties.
1200	William pays homage to John at Lincoln (22 November).
1201	Harald Maddadsson regains control of Caithness.

1206 Death of Harald Maddadsson, earl of Caithness and Orkney.
1209 Treaty of Norham between William and John (6 August); William surrenders his daughters, Margaret and Isabel, to John on understanding that one would marry John's heir.
1211 Godred MacWilliam launches bid for throne.
1212 Extension of Treaty of Norham; Alexander knighted at Westminster by John. Alexander returns to Scotland to campaign against Godred, who is betrayed and executed.
1214 Death of William (4 December) and inauguration of Alexander II (5 December).
1215 Donald MacWilliam launches bid for throne (January/February) but killed by Ferchar MacTaggart in Ross (19 June). King John accepts Magna Carta terms (19 June) including a promise to honour agreements made with Scots. John repudiates Magna Carta; civil war in England (September). Alexander II invades northern England and takes Carlisle (October–December).
1216 John harries Lothian and Teviotdale (January). Alexander invades England for second time. Carlisle recaptured (8 August). Alexander travels to Dover to meet with the Dauphin Louis (September). Death of John at Newark (19 October) and accession of Henry III. Excommunication of Alexander by Cardinal Guala, interdict on Scotland (November).
1217 Formal submission of Alexander and lifting of interdict on lay magnates; he travels to Northampton to pay homage to Henry III (December).
1218 Scottish clergy freed from interdict (February–June). Pope Honorius III issues the bull *Filia specialis*, confirming Scottish ecclesiastical independence from York and establishing the Scottish Church as a 'special daughter' of the Church of Rome (21 November).
1219 Death of David, earl of Huntingdon (17 June).
1220 Conclusion of Anglo-Scottish treaty at York (June).
1221 Alexander II campaigns in Argyll and Clyde estuary. Marriage at York of Alexander and Joanna, sister of Henry III (19 June).
1222 Second naval campaign in Clyde estuary region. Murder of Bishop Adam of Caithness; Alexander II campaigns in Caithness and receives Earl Jón's submission.
1223 Civil war in Man between supporters of King Rognvald and his half-brother, Óláfr.
1225 Alan of Galloway campaigns in the Hebrides in support of King Rognvald.
1228 Alan of Galloway invades Man to reinstate the deposed King Rognvald. King Óláfr and his supporters drive out the Galwegians before the year end.
1229 Defeat and death of King Rognvald. Alan of Galloway attacks Man.
1230 Óláfr flees to Norway (January/February). Norwegian fleet in the Isles in support of Óláfr, who is reinstalled as king in Man (spring). Defeat and death of last MacWilliam pretenders.
1231 Murder of Earl Jón of Caithness and Orkney.
1234 Death of Alan of Galloway and subsequent partition of his lands.

Guide to Further Reading

1. GENERAL SURVEYS

The period examined in this book has been studied traditionally as part of a longer overview of the emergence of the kingship of the Scots rather than as a discrete episode in its own right. While most modern studies take variable start dates (usually between c. AD 80 and 1000), it is the norm for either the death of Alexander III in 1286 or the outbreak of war with England and consequent deposition of King John in 1296 to form the end point. Within those extended studies the level of coverage of different periods is often uneven and the focus tends to be strongly eastern Lowlands-based. In terms of balance and range of material covered, Archie Duncan's *Scotland: the Making of the Kingdom* (1975) remains the fundamental starting point. While the detailed arguments may have become more refined in the last thirty-five years and emphasis on particular themes may have changed, it still provides one of the clearest articulations of the main trends in Scotland's history until 1286. Geoffrey Barrow's *Kingship and Unity: Scotland 1000–1306* (1981) has perhaps weathered less well but is still one of the clearest articulations of the big themes that dominate the historiography of the formative years of the kingdom.

Since the early 1990s there has been a growing trend towards 'British History', much of it still unfortunately little more than English historical surveys with chapters on Scotland, Wales and Ireland tacked on. There are, however, some very important texts which break genuinely new ground with this approach, represented especially by the late Rees Davies' work such as *Domination and Conquest: The Experience of Ireland, Scotland and Wales 1100–1300* (1990) and *The First English Empire: Power and Identities in the British Isles 1093–1343* (2000), and David Carpenter's *The Struggle for Mastery: Britain 1066–1284* (2003).

Such publications have helped to lift much Scottish historical research from its traditionally rather narrow introspection and enabled that work to be seen in its wider international context. Although Davies explored the cultural impact of English influence within the British Isles, these remain primarily political studies. For a wider exploration of the socio-economic, cultural and religious ties of Scotland with Europe, David Ditchburn's *Scotland and Europe: The Medieval Kingdom and Its Contacts with Christendom 1214–1560* (2001) is the essential starting point, despite the fact that most of its material lies outwith the period with which this present volume is concerned.

2. THE DOCUMENTARY SOURCES

Narrative Sources

In contrast with England and Ireland, late-eleventh- to early-thirteenth-century Scotland appears poorly endowed with major narrative sources. Chronicle sources are mostly frustratingly laconic, typified by the highly abbreviated entries in the *Chronicle of Holyrood*. The one major Scottish chronicle composed largely within the period covered by the present volume, the *Chronicle of Melrose*, is the subject of a new edition of the text and analysis of the composition. So far, however, only Volume 1, *The Chronicle of Melrose Abbey: A Stratigraphic Edition* (2007), prepared by Dauvit Broun and Julian Harrison and comprising a series of chapter essays on the chronicle, its context and the development of the manuscript versions, coupled with a DVD of 254 images of the two manuscripts, has been produced. Until the remaining volumes appear, most people will remain dependent on the extracts from the chronicle translated by Alan Anderson in the early 1900s and published in *Early Sources of Scottish History*, vol. 2 (1922). Extensive analysis of the content and structure of the two main later medieval Scottish Latin chronicles, the late-fourteenth-century *Chronica Gentis Scotorum* usually attributed to John of Fordoun and the early-fifteenth-century *Scotichronicon* of Walter Bower, has revealed that the former contains extensive portions of now-lost earlier sources, referred to as *Gesta Annalia* I and II, and portions of other no longer extant documents are fossilised within it – including an early-thirteenth-century chronicle probably composed at St Andrews – and in Bower. The complex relationships between these materials have been summarised excellently by Dauvit Broun in Chapter 9 of his *Scottish Independence and the Idea of Britain* (2007).

Much of our evidence for events in Scotland comes from non-Scottish sources, and the value of many of the eleventh- and twelfth-century English accounts as sources for Scottish circumstances has been reviewed by Alex Woolf in the previous volume of this series. For twelfth-century events, particularly involving the campaigns of David I and the early years of William's reign, northern English sources such as the chronicles of John and Richard of Hexham, William of Newburgh or Ailred of Rievaulx are key texts. Few of these have been translated either in whole or in part in modern editions but Alan Anderson translated and published what he regarded as the most important sections in *Scottish Annals from English Chronicles* (1908). The most important English source for the late twelfth and early thirteenth centuries is Roger of Howden, whose two chronicles – the *Gesta Henrici Secundi* and *Chronica* – are our main sources not only for general Anglo-Scottish diplomatic manoeuvres but especially for events in Galloway from 1174 to 1185 and in northern Scotland until the early 1200s. The sources of Howden's information have been discussed in detail by Archie Duncan in 'Roger of Howden and Scotland, 1187–1201' (1999).

For the Hebrides, the one 'native' source is the *Chronicon Regum Manniae et Insularum*, a largely thirteenth-century compilation whose chronology is in places seriously confused and whose author's blatant political agendas require that it should be used with caution. The best modern edition of the chronicle is that edited by George Broderick as *Cronica Regum Manniae et Insularum: Chronicles of the Kings of Man and the Isles, BL Cotton Julius A.vii* (1995). Again, the main sections of the chronicle of apparently Scottish interest were published in translation by Alan Anderson in *Early Sources of Scottish History* (1922). While there are problems with the Manx chronicle, it is at least a contemporary source produced within the area to which it relates. The same cannot be said of our main source of evidence for mainland Scotland north of the Dornoch Firth and the Orkney and Shetland Islands, *Orkneyinga Saga*. The question marks over the value of this source for tenth- and eleventh-century events have been well discussed by Alex Woolf, but there are equally serious problems with the narrative for the twelfth and early thirteenth centuries.

Irish sources are of diminishing value across the period for the information that they contain relating to specifically Scottish affairs. The *Annals of Ulster*, the most important Irish source for most of the pre-1070 period, becomes increasingly introspective after 1100 and rarely notices Scottish events other than the obituaries of kings and major ecclesiastical figures by the late twelfth century. Throughout this period, however, it remains a key source of information relating to the dynastic conflicts within Ireland that affected Man and the Isles and into which Scottish rulers and regional magnates were drawn, and becomes concerned subsequently with the spread of English power in the island.

Record Sources

No true record sources in the form of royal, monastic or lay financial accounts, rentals and the like survive from anywhere in Scotland for the period under review in this volume. Our principal sources of evidence for landholding and property relationships are the charters recording gifts of land, revenues and jurisdictions made by royal and major lay donors. For the period 1070–1230, most of the surviving royal material has been gathered, edited and published. The main modern collections are *Charters of David I* (1999) and the first two volumes in the *Regesta Regum Scottorum* series, the *Acts of Malcolm IV* (1960) and *William* (1971), all produced by Geoffrey Barrow. Volume 3 in that series, the *Acts of Alexander II*, is yet to appear. For pre-1124 royal acts, we remain dependent on A. C. Lawrie's *Early Scottish Charters* (1905). The majority of surviving non-royal acts for this period deal chiefly with ecclesiastical matters and exist mainly as transcriptions within monastic and cathedral cartularies. Most of these were published by one or other of the main Scottish historical publishing clubs between the 1820s and the 1940s and these published texts have to an extent acquired a status as primary sources in their own right. Recent work by Alasdair Ross, 'The Bannatyne Club and the Publication of Scottish Ecclesiastical Cartularies' (2006), however, has raised serious questions over the quality and accuracy of the nineteenth-century editorial process and has highlighted that the use of the published texts in scholarly research must not be substituted for consultation of the original manuscripts.

The geographical coverage of these sources is extremely uneven. Most of the surviving cartularies with material from this period are of monasteries in the south-east and eastern Lowlands. No south-west Scottish cartularies have survived, but the registers of the abbey of Paisley and the cathedral-church at Glasgow cover the margins of the area. Paisley, too, is a major source for the region around Loch Lomond and the wider Firth of Clyde. No northern monastic cartulary with material relevant to this period has survived other than fragments relating to Kinloss, but the registers of the sees of Aberdeen and Moray contain valuable material relating to the north-east and the district between the River Spey and Loch Ness. The records of the sees of Caithness and Ross are a total loss from this period, as is the case for Argyll and the Isles. Apart from the

Isles and Argyll material contained in Paisley's records, documents relating to West Highland and Hebridean monasteries exist only as fragments and relate mainly to later medieval periods.

Other forms of record source are extremely scarce. Unfortunately, the *Records of the Parliaments of Scotland* project, which has produced a magnificent searchable online edition of the acts of the Scottish parliaments up to 1707, did not include the twelfth- and early-thirteenth-century collections of burgh and forest laws, and early royal assizes which were included in Volume 1 of the *Acts of the Parliaments of Scotland* (1814). Due to the hazards of war, natural disaster and vermin, none of the financial records of Scottish royal government survive from earlier than the 1260s and no accounts from any monastic or lay household exists from earlier than the 1290s.

3. KINGS AND KINGSHIP

There has been a recent revival of academic interest in individual kings and the nature of kingship in the period under study within this volume. The most important work is Archie Duncan's *Kingship of the Scots* (2002), which focuses more on the nature of the relationship of the kings of Scots with the kings of England than on the exercise of kingship within Scotland. Similar themes dominate in Dauvit Broun's *Scottish Independence and the Idea of Britain* (2007), but here there is a stronger focus on how that relationship shaped Scottish kings' perceptions of their own status and how that status was expressed externally. Until 2004 the main studies of individual reigns and of the development of the institutions of royal government during those reigns were the extended essays with which Geoffrey Barrow prefaced Volumes 1 and 2 of the *Regesta Regum Scotorum* series (1960 and 1971). His *Charters of David I* (1999) lacks a similar introductory section. The first monograph-length study of monarchs in this period is Roy Owen's *William the Lion 1143–1214: Kingship and Culture* (1997), in which the main political narrative is founded on the earlier work of Barrow and whose greater value lies in its exploration of the courtly culture of Scotland in the reign of a king heavily influenced by Continental chivalric ideals. Richard Oram's *David I* (2004) is a political narrative and study of the king's historical reputation and by intention offers no discussion of institutional developments during his reign; such aspects are otherwise covered best in the relevant chapters of Duncan's *Making of the Kingdom*. The volume of essays *The Reign of Alexander II* (2005), edited by Richard Oram, offers an overview of the king and his reign but focuses more on the wider development of Scotland than on the exercise of kingship.

Of the other monarchies that briefly flourished within the bounds of what we now recognise as Scotland, only Man and the Isles and Galloway have been the subjects of modern study. Man and the Isles has received a great deal of new scholarly attention but much of this remains in unpublished form as doctoral theses, of which the most important is Ian Beuermann's *Masters of the Narrow Seas* (2007). The multi-authored *History of the Isle of Man* remains unpublished over fifteen years after it was commissioned, and for the northern portion of that realm the most recent study is Andrew McDonald's *Kingdom of the Isles* (1997), which is principally a political narrative based on a traditional reading of the main narrative sources. His *Outlaws of Medieval Scotland: Challenges to the Canmore Kings, 1058–1266* (2003) offers a more thematic study of the relationship of discarded segments of the Scottish royal house and their allies in the Highlands and Islands but retains a rather conservative view of the relationship between those areas and a 'feudalised' Scottish monarchy. The territory stretching along the north coast of the Solway is studied in Richard Oram's *Lordship of Galloway* (2000), which offers an exploration of the processes that saw an independent petty kingdom transformed into a semi-autonomous lordship under fluctuating Scottish or English domination and, ultimately, its absorption into the Scottish realm. None of these studies, however, offers discussion of the nature of royal power within their subject areas and how those kingships developed or changed in their projection of status or in the practical exercise of royal authority as Scottish and English royal might grew on their doorsteps.

4. NOBLE SOCIETY

Many aspects of Scottish noble society have been the targets of scholarly endeavour over the last thirty years. Much work has focused on the better-documented colonist families, with Geoffrey Barrow's *Anglo-Norman Era in Scottish History* (1980) setting the agenda which has been either followed or challenged in subsequent work. His general themes of cross-border landholding in this period were taken up and explored in detail by Keith Stringer, whose *Earl David of Huntingdon* (1985) stands as a model for studies of this type. This same methodology is employed on a smaller scale in his 'Periphery and core in thirteenth-century Scotland: Alan son of Roland, Lord of Galloway and Constable of Scotland' (1993), but here with a close examination of the hybridity evident in the career of a man who operated within the context of the Continental-style courts of Scotland and England but whose power was based on the resources of his Gaelic lordship in south-western Scotland. This duality in identity is explored also through the lenses of foreign colonisation and settlement, and native continuity by Richard Oram in 'A family business?' (1993), in which traditional divisions into 'Anglo-Norman' and 'native' categories are challenged. There are few other studies of regional colonies, but amongst the most important are Chris Tabraham's 'Norman settlement in Upper Clydesdale' (1978), which should be read in conjunction with Laurens Toorians' 'Twelfth-century Flemish settlement in Scotland' (1996), which questions some of the traditional ideas concerning Flemish nobles' colonisation in mid-twelfth-century Scotland.

For the great Gaelic earldoms and lordships, the two main studies are Cynthia Neville's *Native Lordship in Medieval Scotland: The Earldoms of Strathearn and Lennox* (2005) and Richard Oram's *The Lordship of Galloway* (2000). Alan Young's *The Comyns 1212–1314* (1997) deals with the transition from Gaelic to 'Norman' rule in one of the native earldoms, while continuity rather than change is the main theme in Richard Oram's 'Earls and earldom of Mar' (2003) and Fiona Watson's 'Adapting tradition?' (2005). Most of the essays in Steve Boardman and Alasdair Ross's edited volume *The Exercise of Power in Medieval Scotland* (2003) deal with the post-1300 period, but Hammond, McDonald and Oram dealing with the Durward family, Ferchar McTaggart and the earls of Mar respectively are important for the period under review here.

Since Geoffrey Barrow's published research up to 1981 on the 'feudalisation' of Scottish lordly society, feudal or non-feudal regimes remained a rather neglected topic until the 1990s, when Susan Reynolds' *Fiefs and Vassals* (1994) reopened the debate in Scotland by challenging the general model that Barrow had applied to Scotland. This monograph focused chiefly on the English and Continental evidence, but her argument was extended north in 'Fiefs and vassals in Scotland' (2003), which triggered a counter-attack from Hector MacQueen in 'Tears of a legal historian' (2003). That paper should be read in conjunction with his *Common Law and Feudal Society* (1993). In all of this debate, however, neither protagonist truly gets to grips with the world beyond legal ideals to tackle the question of how nobles in a 'feudal' or 'non-feudal' society exercised power. Indeed, the nature of the social hierarchy of Gaelic Scotland until the reign of David I is an issue that most historians have skirted around, and it is Dauvit Broun's discussion of the evidence from the *Book of Deer*, 'The property records in the Book of Deer as a source for early Scottish society' (2008) that has opened up a new debate.

The physical expression of lordly power, particularly their residence, has long been viewed from the perspective of the architectural historian. Most studies of castles, however, have concentrated on the stone castles of the later thirteenth century and beyond, while the more ephemeral – often earthwork – remains of earlier structures have been relatively neglected. Interest in Scottish mottes revived in the 1970s through the still largely unpublished work of Eric Talbot, but it was Chris Tabraham's studies, 'Norman settlement in Upper Clydesdale' (1978) and 'Norman settlement in Galloway: recent field work in the Stewartry' (1984) that heralded a brief renaissance in studies of twelfth- and early-thirteenth-century earth-and-timber castles in Scotland. A number of important excavations at such sites are summarised in Robert Higham and Philip Barker's *Timber Castles* (2nd edn, 2004), set into the wider context of mainland Britain. Most recently, Richard Oram has produced an overview analysis of the evidence for the form of early high-status residence in 'Royal and lordly fortification in Scotland' (2008). These studies, however, remain focused principally on the residences proper, and there has so far been no parallel Scottish study to match the groundbreaking work of Oliver Creighton in England and Wales which explores the wider landscapes of lordship. Likewise in Scotland there has been little published work to parallel the major revision of thinking in respect of aristocratic hunting, forests and parks, the sole significant study of royal and aristocratic hunting activity and hunting landscapes in Scotland remaining the wide-ranging, first-class *Medieval Hunting and Hunting Reserves in Scotland* (1979) by John Gilbert. Other dimensions of Scottish aristocratic culture in this period, especially its material expression, have been little studied.

Most expressions of noble piety in the twelfth and early thirteenth centuries have been discussed in terms of monastic foundations and endowments, often involving parish churches. Emilia Jamroziak's 'Making friends beyond the grave' (2005), however, is a forensic analysis of the evidence from the Melrose cartulary for the manner in which the monastery developed bonds with the families of major benefactors in life and maintained those links through post mortem care for the souls of their departed patrons.

5. THE CHURCH

There is no single modern study of the medieval Church in Scotland and nor is there a single detailed study of ecclesiastical affairs in the period covered in this volume. The most valuable discussions remain the relevant sections in Duncan's *Making of the Kingdom*, which provide the most coherent narrative of the main developments between 1070 and 1230. Alongside these there is a host of studies that deal with specific issues, areas and individuals.

The growth of the diocesan structure in Scotland has been little explored in the last thirty years, with Archie Duncan's studies of the development of the sees of St Andrews and Glasgow in his *Kingship of the Scots* (2002) and 'St Kentigern at Glasgow Cathedral in the twelfth century' (1998), Geoffrey Barrow's *Glasgow Cathedral, King David I and the Church of Glasgow* (1996), Dauvit Broun's discussion of the status of the Church of Glasgow in the twelfth century in his *Scottish Independence and the Idea of Britain* (2007) and Richard Oram's study of the revived see of Whithorn in the twelfth and thirteenth centuries in his *Lordship of Galloway* (2000), representing the main published developments. The key study for Scoto-papal relations is Paul Ferguson's *Medieval Papal Representatives in Scotland* (1997), which explores the role of legates, nuncios and judges-delegate in the development of the administrative institutions of the Scottish Church and the nature of their business and activity.

Oddly, despite general recognition of the importance of the monasteries in the spiritual, cultural and economic development of Scotland in this period, and despite the major academic revision in monastic studies that has been underway elsewhere in Britain, Europe and the USA since the 1980s, there is no modern academic study of monasteries and monasticism generally. The one overview of medieval monasteries in Scotland remains Ian Cowan and David Easson's *Medieval Religious Houses Scotland* (1976). There are also no published modern studies of any of the Continental orders of monks, canons or friars established in Scotland before 1230 to build on Geoffrey Barrow's pioneering work on these subjects in the 1950s and 1960s. Individual abbeys, however, have been studied in depth. Richard Fawcett and Richard Oram's study, *Melrose Abbey* (2004), is, however, the only detailed historical and architectural study of the leading Cistercian house in Scotland, while their *Dryburgh Abbey* (2005) is the only in-depth analysis of a house of Premonstratensian canons. From an archaeological and architectural perspective the main comparable work is John Lewis and Gordon Ewart's *Jedburgh Abbey* (1995).

For the development of the parish system in Scotland, the work of Ian Cowan remains the essential starting point. His *Parishes of Medieval Scotland* (1967) represents the only systematic exploration of the origin and development of the parochial system but must be read in conjunction with his various essays on appropriation, vicarages and the cure of souls, and regional development, published originally in various journals but gathered posthumously and edited by James Kirk in *The Medieval Church in Scotland* (1995). A more detailed study of parishes and parish churches within specific dioceses is available in the *Corpus of Scottish Medieval Parish Churches* website (http://arts.st-andrews. ac.uk/~cmas/), covering only the dioceses of Dunblane and Dunkeld, produced by Richard Fawcett, Richard Oram and Julian Luxford.

The cultural legacy of the medieval Church in Scotland is in some ways better represented in recent work, much of it the output of Professor Richard Fawcett. Scotland's two main dioceses are the subjects of edited collections, *Medieval Art and Architecture in the Diocese of St Andrews* (1994) edited by John Higgit, and *Medieval Art and Architecture in the Diocese of Glasgow* (1998), edited by Richard Fawcett, which contain studies on the architecture of the cathedrals, major monasteries and parish churches of the two sees. Cathedral architecture has also been explored by Richard Fawcett in *Scottish Cathedrals* (1997), while his *Scottish Abbeys and Priories* (1994) is the best introduction to the planning and structure of the major monastic sites of this period. His *Scottish Medieval Churches* (2002) covers churches of all scales and periods, exploring all aspects of their architecture and furnishings, while his contribution to the *Corpus of Scottish Medieval Parish Churches* brings the focus down to parish level.

6. BURGHS

The earliest period of Scottish urban history remains one of the most neglected, with few significant new historical studies produced since the 1980s. The main collection of studies, *The Scottish Medieval Town* (1988), edited by Michael Lynch, Michael Spearman and Geoffrey Stell, contains much valuable material, for example by Alexander Stevenson on 'Trade with the South, 1070–1513' and Hector MacQueen and William Winram on 'Laws and courts in the burghs', but most of the contributions are concerned with the later medieval period. As a consequence Archie Duncan's 1975 synthesis in *Making of the Kingdom* is still the most comprehensive overview of the subject although many of its details as to early urban origins and physical development are now contested. Pat Dennison's 'Burghs and burgesses: a time of consolidation' (2005) is a finely considered discussion of the state of burgh development in the reign of Alexander II, but it is unmatched by any study of the preceding reigns. Most of the main advances have been in respect of urban archaeology, but the biggest excavations – those undertaken at Perth in the 1970s – remain unpublished in detail at present. The output since the 1970s of the Scottish Burgh Survey project has been substantial in volume but that does not necessarily translate automatically into quality. Designed to draw together and summarise known historical and archaeological evidence concerning Scotland's historic royal burghs, those produced over the last decade or so have become increasingly research-driven and analytical, but their main value has generally been for the later medieval and early modern periods. Good examples of the new-style volumes in the series include Sylvia Stevenson and Pat Torrie's *Historic Glasgow* (1990), and Pat Dennison and Russell Coleman's *Historic Dumbarton* (1999), *Historic Nairn* (1999) and *Historic Forfar* (2000), while related to the series is Pat Dennison's *Medieval Dundee* (1990). Similar large-scale synthetic studies pulling together archaeological findings with more recent historical research have been published on St Andrews (1997), Perth (2004) and Dundee (2005), and on a slightly smaller scale, Colin Martin and Richard Oram have undertaken a reappraisal of the historical and archaeological evidence for the origins and development of Roxburgh in 'Medieval Roxburgh: a preliminary assessment of the burgh and its locality' (2007).

7. RURAL SETTLEMENT, LANDSCAPE AND ENVIRONMENT

Little new research has been undertaken, let alone published, in the broad area of eleventh- to thirteenth-century rural settlement studies in recent years. Questions of estate management and rural economic hierarchies have attracted more attention, with Geoffrey Barrow's work on 'Shires and thanes', reproduced in the 2nd edition of his *Kingdom of the Scots* (2003) and Sandy Grant's 'Thanes and thanages' (1993) being the seminal studies. The potential for deeper understanding of exploitation regimes and the highly organised structure of Scottish rural systems in the country north of the Forth is highlighted by Alasdair Ross in his ground-breaking study 'The Dabhach in Moray: a new look at an old tub' (2006), while the evidence for control over stocking levels is explored by him in detail in 'Scottish environmental history and the (mis)use of Soums' (2006).

The recent emergence of Environmental History as a field of specialist research in Scotland is starting to make its presence felt in published form, but much of what has so far appeared is concerned chiefly with the post-medieval period. Within what has been published there is a major emphasis on woodland history, exploring the management and exploitation of timber and the other uses to which wood was put. One of the first books published on the subject was the collection of papers *Scottish Woodland History* (1997), edited by Chris Smout, within which Richard Tipping's paper 'Medieval woodland history from the Scottish Southern Uplands' is most relevant for the period covered in this present volume. Evidence for pressure on woodland by the thirteenth century is a central theme in Anne Crone and Fiona Watson's 'Sufficiency to scarcity: medieval Scotland, 500–1600' (2003). One of the most impressive studies of medieval landscape change on a local level is John Gilbert's 'The monastic record of a Borders landscape 1136 to 1236' (1983), which explores the impact of the development of the estates of Melrose and Dryburgh abbeys on the district between Lauderdale and Wedale. Gilbert's methodology has been applied more widely by Fawcett and Oram in their *Melrose Abbey* (2004) and *Dryburgh Abbey* (2005).

Bibliography

UNPUBLISHED THESES AND REPORTS

Hindmarch, E., *Renaissance Golf Club at Archerfield*, Evaluation and Excavation Data Structure Report. Unpublished report by AOC Archaeology Group (2006).
Ross, A., *The Province of Moray c. 1000–1230*. A thesis presented for the degree of PhD (University of Aberdeen, 2003).

WEB RESOURCES

Fawcett, R., R. Oram and J. Luxford, *Corpus of Scottish Medieval Parish Churches: Pilot Study of the Dioceses of Dunblane and Dunkeld* at http://arts.st-andrews.ac.uk/~cmas/

PRIMARY SOURCES

Unpublished

National Library of Scotland, NLS Adv. MS 35.4.12A, no. 3.

Published

Acts of the Parliaments of Scotland, vol. 1, ed. T. Thomson (Edinburgh, 1814).
Ailred of Rievaulx, *Saints of Hexham*, in J. Raine (ed.), *The Priory of Hexham*, i (Surtees Society, 1864).

Ailred of Rievaulx, *Relatio de Standardo*, in *Chronicles of the Reigns of Stephen, Henry II and Richard I*, iii, ed. R. Howlett (London, 1889).

Ancient Laws and Customs of the Burghs of Scotland, i, eds C. Innes and R. Renwick (Edinburgh, 1868).

Anderson, A. O. (ed.), *Scottish Annals from English Chroniclers AD 500–1296* (London, 1908).

Anderson, A. O. (ed.), *Early Sources of Scottish History AD 500–1286*, 2 vols (Edinburgh, 1922).

Anderson, P. J. (ed.), *Charters and other Writs Illustrating the History of the Royal Burgh of Aberdeen* (Aberdeen, 1890).

Annales Cambriae, ed. J. Williams ab Ithel (London, 1860).

Annales Cestrienses, ed. and trans. R. C. Christie, *Record Society of Lancashire and Cheshire*, 14 (Chester, 1887).

S. Anselmi Opera Omnia, ed. F. S. Schmitt (Edinburgh, 1946–52).

Bain, J. (ed.), *Calendar of Documents Relating to Scotland*, i (Edinburgh, 1881).

Barrow, G. W. S. (ed.), *Regesta Regum Scottorum*, i, *The Acts of Malcolm IV* (Edinburgh, 1960).

Barrow, G. W. S. (ed.), *Regesta Regum Scottorum*, ii, *The Acts of William I* (Edinburgh, 1971).

Barrow, G. W. S. (ed.), *The Charters of David I: the Written Acts of David I King of Scots, 1124–53, and of his Son Henry, Earl of Northumberland, 1139–52* (Woodbridge, 1999).

Benedict of Peterborough, *Gesta Regis Henrici Secundi*, ed. W. Stubbs, 2 vols (London, 1867).

Bernard of Clairvaux, *St Bernard's Life of St Malachy of Armagh*, ed. and trans. H. J. Lawlor (London, 1920).

The Book of Deer, ed. J. Stuart (Spalding Club, 1869).

Brut y Tywyssogion: or, The Chronicle of the Princes, ed. J. Williams ab Ithel (London, 1860).

Bower, W., *Scotichronicon*, ed. D. E. R. Watt et al., vol. 8 (Aberdeen, 1987).

Bower, W., *Scotichronicon*, ed. D. E. R. Watt et al., vol. 3 (Aberdeen, 1995).

Buchanan, G., *The History of Scotland*, trans. G. Aikman (Glasgow, 1827–9).

Cheney, C. R. and M. G. Cheney (eds), *The Letters of Pope Innocent III (1198–1216) concerning England and Wales* (Oxford, 1967).

Chronica Regum Manniae et Insularum. The Chronicle of Man and the Isles. A Facsimile of the Manuscript Codex Julius A. VIII in the British Museum (Douglas, 1924).

Chronica Regum Manniae et Insularum: Chronicles of the Kings of Man and

the Isles, BL Cotton Julius A. vii, ed. and trans. G. Broderick, 2nd edn (Douglas, 1995).
Chronica Roger de Hovedon, ed. W. Stubbs (London, 1868–71).
The Chronicle of Ireland, ed. T. M. Charles-Edwards (Liverpool, 2006).
The Chronicle of John of Worcester, iii, *The Annals from 1067 to 1140 with the Gloucester Interpolations and the Continuation to 1141*, ed. and trans. P. McGurk (Oxford, 1998).
Chronicle of Melrose (facsimile edn), eds A. O. Anderson et al. (London, 1936).
The Chronicle of Melrose Abbey. A Stratigraphic Edition, vol. 1, ed. D. Broun and J. Harrison (Scottish History Society, 2007).
Chronicles of the Picts, Chronicles of the Scots, ed. W. F. Skene (Edinburgh, 1867).
Chronicles of the Reigns of Stephen, Henry II and Richard I, ed. R. Howlett (London, 1884–9).
The Chronicles of Scotland Compiled by Hector Boece, translated into Scots by John Bellenden 1531, eds E. C. Batho and H. W. Husbands (Scottish Text Society, 1938–41).
Clancy, T. O. (ed.), *The Triumph Tree: Scotland's Earliest Poetry AD 550–1350* (Edinburgh, 1998).
Cogadh Gaedhel re Gallaib (The War of the Gaedhil with the Gaill), trans. J. H. Todd (London, 1867).
Craig, T., *De Unione Regnorum Britanniae Tractatus*, ed. and trans. C. S. Terry (Scottish History Society, 1909).
Dalrymple, D. (Lord Hailes), *Annals of Scotland*, i (Edinburgh, 1819).
Daniel, W., *The Life of Ailred of Rievaulx*, ed. and trans. F. M. Powicke (London, 1950).
Davis, H. W. C., C. Johnson, H. A. Cronne and R. H. C. Davis (eds), *Regesta Regum Anglo-Normannorum*, 4 vols (Oxford, 1913–69).
De Diceto, R., *Imagines Historiarum*, ed. W. Stubbs (London, 1876).
Domesday Book: A Complete Translation, eds A. Williams and G. H. Martin (London, 2002).
Donaldson, G., *Scottish Historical Documents* (Edinburgh, 1970).
Farrer, W. and C. T. Clay (eds), *Early Yorkshire Charters*, 12 vols, Yorkshire Archaeology Society Record Series (Edinburgh, 1913–).
Florence of Worcester, *Chronicon ex Chronicis*, 2 vols, ed. B. Thorpe (English History Society, 1848–9).
Gervase of Canterbury, *Historical Works*, i, *The Chronicles of the Reigns of Stephen, Henry II and Richard I*, ed. W. Stubbs (London, 1879).
The Gesta Normannorum Ducum of William of Jumièges, Orderic Vitalis, and Robert of Torigni, ed. E. van Houts (Oxford, 1992).

Gesta Stephani Regis Anglorum, in R. Howlett (ed.), *Chronicles of the Reigns of Stephen, Henry II and Richard I*, iii (London, 1884–9), 3–136.
Hectoris Boetii Murthlacensium et Aberdonensium Episcoporum Vitae (New Spalding Club, 1894).
Henry of Huntingdon, *Historia Anglorum*, ed. T. Arnold (London, 1879).
Hermann of Tournai (*Herimannus Tornacensis*), *Narratio Restaurationis abbatiae S Martini Tornacensis*, ed. G. Waitz, *Monumenta Historica Germaniae, Scriptores*, xiv (Hannover, 1883), 274–317.
The Historie of Scotland, Wrytten First in Latin by the Most Reuerend and Worth Jhone Leslie Bishop of Rosse and Translated in Scottish by Father James Dalrymple . . . 1596, i, ed. E. G. Cody (Scottish Text Society, 1888).
John of Fordun's Chronicle of the Scottish Nation, ed. W. F. Skene (Edinburgh, 1872).
Jordan Fantosme's Chronicle, ed. R. C. Johnston (Oxford, 1981).
Lawrie, A. C., *Early Scottish Charters Prior to AD 1153* (Glasgow, 1905).
Lawrie, A. C. (ed.), *Annals of the Reigns of Malcolm and William, Kings of Scotland* (Glasgow, 1910).
Le Clerc, G., *Fergus of Galloway, Knight of King Arthur*, trans. D. D. R. Owen (London, 1991).
Libellus de Vita et Miraculis Sancti Godrici (Surtees Society, 1847).
Liber Cartarum Sancte Crucis (Bannatyne Club, 1840).
Liber Ecclesie de Scon (Bannatyne Club, 1843).
Liber Sancte Marie de Calchou (Bannatyne Club, 1846).
Liber Sancte Marie de Dryburgh (Bannatyne Club, 1847).
Liber Sancte Marie de Melros (Bannatyne Club, 1837).
Liber Vitæ Ecclesiæ Dunelmensis, ed. J. Stevenson (Surtees Society, 1841).
Macphail, S. R., *History of the Religious House of Pluscardyn* (Edinburgh, 1881).
Major, J., *A History of Greater Britain, 1521*, ed. and trans. A. Constable (Scottish History Society, 1892).
Marwick, J. D. (ed.), *Charters and Other Documents Relating to the City of Glasgow* (Scottish Burgh Records Society, 1894–7).
Memoriale Fratris Walteri de Coventria, ed. W. Stubbs (London, 1872–3).
Memorials of St Edmund's Abbey, ed. T. Arnold (London, 1890–6).
The Miracles of St Æbbe of Coldingham and St Margaret of Scotland, ed. and trans. R. Bartlett (Oxford, 2003).
Miscellany of the Spalding Club, v (Spalding Club, 1852).
Myln, A., *Vitae Dunkeldensis Ecclesiae Episcoporum* (Bannatyne Club, 1831).
The Original Chronicle of Andrew of Wyntoun, iv, ed. F. J. Amours (Scottish Text Society, 1906).

Orkneyinga Saga: The History of the Earls of Orkney, trans. H. Pálsson and P. Edwards (Harmondsworth, 1978).
Raine, J. (ed.), *Historians of the Church of York* (London, 1879–94).
The Register of the Priory of St Bees, ed. J. Wilson (Surtees Society, 1915).
Registrum de Dunfermelyn (Bannatyne Club, 1842).
Registrum Episcopatus Glasguensis (Bannatyne and Maitland Clubs, 1843).
Registrum Monasterii de Passelet (Maitland Club, 1832).
Registrum Monasterii S. Marie de Cambuskenneth (Grampian Club, 1872).
Registrum S. Marie de Neubotle (Bannatyne Club, Edinburgh, 1849).
Richard of Hexham, *Historia de gestis Regis Stephani et de bello de Standardo*, in *Chronicles of Stephen, Henry II and Richard I*, iii, ed. R. Howlett (London, 1886).
Robertson, J. C. (ed.), *Materials for the History of Thomas Becket, Archbishop of Canterbury*, vi (London, 1882).
Roger of Howden, *Chronica*, ed. W. Stubbs (London, 1868–71).
Scott James, B. (ed.), *The Letters of St Bernard of Clairvaux*, 2nd edn (Stroud, 1998).
A Scottish Chronicle Known as the Chronicle of Holyrood, ed. M. O. Anderson and A. O. Anderson (Scottish History Society, 1938).
Sottewain, H., *Archbishops of York*, in *Historians of the Church of York*, i, ed. J. Raine (London, 1879).
Symeonis Monachi Opera Omnia, ed. T. Arnold (London, 1885).
Theiner, A. (ed.), *Vetera Monumenta Hibernorum et Scotorum Historiam Illustrantia* (Rome, 1864).
Vita Ædwardi Regis, ed. F. Barlow, 2nd edn (London, 1992).
William of Malmesbury, *Gesta Regum Anglorum, The History of the English Kings*, i, ed. and trans. R. A. B. Mynors, R. M. Thomson and M. Winterbottom (Oxford, 1998).
William of Malmesbury, *Historia Novella. The Contemporary History*, ed. E. King, trans. K. R. Potter (Oxford, 1998).
William of Newburgh, *Historia Rerum Anglicarum*, in *Chronicles of the Reigns of Stephen, Henry II and Richard I*, i and ii, ed. R. Howlett (London, 1884–5).

SECONDARY WORKS

Aird, W., *St Cuthbert and the Normans: the Church of Durham 1071–1153* (Woodbridge, 1998).

Airlie, S., 'The view from Maastricht', in B. E. Crawford (ed.), *Scotland in Dark Age Europe* (St Andrews, 1994), 33–46.
Annals of Innisfallen, University College, Cork, Corpus of Electronic Texts at http://www.ucc.ie/celt/published/T100004/index.html
Arbuthnott, S., K. Hollo and A. Ross (eds), *A Grey Eye Looks Back: Essays in Honour of Professor Colm O'Baoill* (Aberdeen, 2005).
Armit, I. and I. Ralston, 'The coming of iron, 1000 BC to AD 50', in T. C. Smout (ed.), *People and Woods in Scotland: a History* (Edinburgh, 2003), 40–59.
Astill, G., 'General survey 600–1300', in D. M. Palliser (ed.), *The Cambridge Urban History of Britain 600–1540*, vol. 1 (Cambridge, 2000).
Bailey, M. (ed. and trans.), *The English Manor c. 1200–c. 1500* (Manchester, 2002).
Bailey, R. N., 'Aspects of Viking-age sculpture in Cumbria', in J. R. Baldwin and I. D. Whyte (eds), *The Scandinavians in Cumbria* (Edinburgh, 1985), 53–63.
Baker, D., '"A nursery of saints": St Margaret and Scotland Reconsidered', in D. Baker (ed.), *Medieval Women* (Oxford, 1978).
Baldwin, J. R. and I. D. Whyte (eds), *The Scandinavians in Cumbria* (Edinburgh, 1985).
Bannerman, J., 'MacDuff of Fife', in A. Grant and K. J. Stringer (eds), *Medieval Scotland: Crown, Lordship and Community* (Edinburgh, 1993), 20–38.
Barlow, F., *Edward the Confessor* (London, 1970).
Barlow, F., *William Rufus* (London, 1983).
Barrell, A. D. M., 'The background to *Cum universi*: Scoto-papal relations, 1159–1192', *Innes Review*, 46 (1995), 116–38.
Barrell, A. D. M., *Medieval Scotland* (Cambridge, 2000).
Barrell, A. D. M., 'Scotland and the Papacy in the reign of Alexander II', in R. D. Oram (ed.), *The Reign of Alexander II, 1214–49* (Brill, 2005), 157–77.
Barrow, G. W. S., 'The earls of Fife in the 12th century', *PSAS*, lxxxvii (1952–3), 51–62.
Barrow, G. W. S., 'King David I and the Honour of Lancaster', *English Historical Review*, lxx (1955), 85–9.
Barrow, G. W. S., *Feudal Britain* (London, 1956).
Barrow, G. W. S., 'The early charters of the family of Kinninmonth of that ilk', in D. A. Bullough and R. L. Storey (eds), *The Study of Medieval Records. Essays in Honour of Kathleen Major* (Oxford, 1971), 107–31.

Barrow, G. W. S., 'Benedictines, Tironensians and Cistercians', in G. W. S. Barrow, *The Kingdom of the Scots* (London, 1973), 188–211.

Barrow, G. W. S., 'The pattern of lordship and feudal settlement in Cumbria', *Journal of Medieval History*, i (1975), 117–37.

Barrow, G. W. S., *The Anglo-Norman Era in Scottish History* (Oxford, 1980).

Barrow, G. W. S., *Kingship and Unity: Scotland 1000–1306*, 1st edn (London, 1981).

Barrow, G. W. S., 'Popular courts in early medieval Scotland: some suggested place-name evidence', *Scottish Studies*, xxv (1981), 1–24.

Barrow, G. W. S., *Robert Bruce and the Community of the Realm of Scotland*, 3rd edn (Edinburgh, 1988).

Barrow, G. W. S., 'Badenoch and Strathspey, 1130–1312', *Northern Scotland*, 8 (1988), 1–15.

Barrow, G. W. S., 'The charters of David I', *Anglo-Norman Studies*, 14 (1991), 25–37.

Barrow, G. W. S., 'David I of Scotland: the balance of new and old', in G. W. S. Barrow, *Scotland and its Neighbours in the Middle Ages* (London, 1992), 45–65.

Barrow, G. W. S., 'The reign of William the Lion', in G. W. S. Barrow, *Scotland and its Neighbours in the Middle Ages* (London, 1992), 67–90.

Barrow, G. W. S., 'The kings of Scotland and Durham', in D. Rollason, M. Harvey and M. Prestwich (eds), *Anglo-Norman Durham 1093–1193* (Woodbridge, 1994), 311–24.

Barrow, G. W. S., 'The date of the peace between Malcolm IV and Somerled of Argyll', *SHR*, lxxiii, pt. 2 (1994), 222–3.

Barrow, G. W. S., *Glasgow Cathedral, King David I and the Church of Glasgow*, Glasgow Cathedral Lecture Series 4 (Glasgow, 1996).

Barrow, G. W. S., '*De domibus religiosis*: a note on Dornoch', *Innes Review*, xlviii (1997), 83–4.

Barrow, G. W. S., *Kingdom of the Scots*, 2nd edn (Edinburgh, 2003).

Barrow, G. W. S., 'Pre-feudal Scotland: shires and thanes', in G. W. S. Barrow, *The Kingdom of the Scots*, 2nd edn (Edinburgh, 2003), 7–56.

Barrow, G. W. S., 'Scotland, Wales and Ireland in the twelfth century', in D. Luscombe and J. Riley-Smith (eds), *The New Cambridge Medieval History*, vol. IV, pt. II (Cambridge, 2004).

Bartlett, R., *The Making of Europe: Colonisation, Conquest and Cultural Change 950–1350* (London, 1993).

Bartlett, R., *England under the Norman and Angevin Kings 1075–1225* (Oxford, 2000).

Beuermann, I., *Masters of the Narrow Sea: Forgotten Challenges to*

Norwegian Rule in Man and the Isles, 1079–1266, Acta Humaniora, Faculty of Humanities, University of Oslo (Oslo, 2007).

Bil, A., *The Shieling, 1600–1840: The Case of the Central Scottish Highlands* (Edinburgh, 1990).

Blanchard, I., 'Lothian and beyond: the economy of the "English Empire" of David I', in R. H. Britnell and J. Hatcher (eds), *Progress and Problems in Medieval England* (Cambridge, 1996), 23–45.

Blumenthal, U.-R., 'The papacy, 1024–1122', in D. Luscombe and J. Riley-Smith (eds), *The New Cambridge Medieval History* vol. IV, pt. II (Cambridge, 2004), 8–37.

Boardman, S., 'Pillars of the community: Campbell lordship and architectural patronage in the fifteenth century', in R. Oram and G. Stell (eds), *Lordship and Architecture in Medieval and Renaissance Scotland* (Edinburgh, 2005), 123–59.

Boardman, S. and A. Ross (eds), *The Exercise of Power in Medieval Scotland* (Dublin, 2003).

Boece, H., *Murthlacensium et Aberdonensium Episcoporum Vitae*, ed. and trans. J. Moir (Spalding Club, 1894).

Bouchard, C. B., 'Rural economy and society', in M. Bull (ed.), *France in the Central Middle Ages 900–1200* (Oxford, 2002), 77–101.

Bowler, D. P. (ed.), *Perth: The Archaeology and Development of a Scottish Burgh* (Perth, 2004).

Bradley, I., *Celtic Christianity: Making Myths and Chasing Dreams* (Edinburgh, 1999).

Brooke, C., *The Age of the Cloister: The Story of Monastic Life in the Middle Ages* (Stroud, 2003).

Brooke, D., 'The deanery of Desnes-Cro and the church of Edingham', *TDGNHAS*, lxii (1989), 48–65.

Brooke, D., 'Fergus of Galloway: miscellaneous notes for a revised portrait', *TDGNHAS*, lxvi (1991), 47–58.

Brooke, D., *Wild Men and Holy Places* (Edinburgh, 1994).

Brooks, N. P., 'St John's House: its history and archaeology', *St Andrews Preservation Trust Yearbook* (St Andrews, 1976), 11–15.

Brooks, N. P., 'Urban archaeology in Scotland', in M. W. Barley (ed.), *The Archaeology and History of the European Town* (London, 1977), 19–32.

Brooks, N. P. and G. Whittington, 'Planning and growth in the medieval Scottish burgh: the example of St Andrews', *Transactions of the British Institute of Geographers*, 34 (1977), 278–95.

Broun, D., *The Irish Identity of the Kingdom of the Scots in the Twelfth and Thirteenth Centuries* (Woodbridge, 1999).

Broun, D., 'The writing of charters in Scotland and Ireland in the twelfth century', in K. Heidecker (ed.), *Charters and the Use of the Written Word in Medieval Society* (Utrecht, 2000), 113–32.

Broun, D., 'The church of St Andrews and its foundation legend in the early twelfth century: recovering the full text of version A of the foundation legend', in S. Taylor (ed.), *Kings, Clerics and Chronicles in Scotland 500–1297* (Dublin, 2000), 108–14.

Broun, D., 'The Church and the origins of Scottish independence in the twelfth century', *Records of the Scottish Church History Society*, xxxi (2002), 1–35.

Broun, D., 'Contemporary perspectives on Alexander II's succession: the evidence of king-lists', in R. D. Oram (ed.), *The Reign of Alexander II, 1214–49* (Leiden, 2005).

Broun, D., *Scottish Independence and the Idea of Britain from the Picts to Alexander III* (Edinburgh, 2007).

Broun, D., 'The property records in the Book of Deer as a source for early Scottish society', in K. Forsyth (ed.), *Studies on the Book of Deer* (Dublin, 2008), 313–60.

Bull, M. (ed.), *France in the Central Middle Ages 900–1200* (Oxford, 2002).

Byock, J., *Medieval Iceland. Society, Sagas and Power* (London, 1988).

Byock, J., *Viking Age Iceland* (London, 2001).

Cameron, A. D., *History For Young Scots*, i (Edinburgh, 1963).

Campbell, J., 'A romanesque revival and the early Renaissance in Scotland c. 1380–1513', *Journal of the Society of Architectural Historians*, 54: 3 (1995).

Candon, A., 'Muirchertach ua Briain, politics and naval activity in the Irish Sea, 1075 to 1119', in G. mac Niocaill and P. F. Wallace (eds), *Keimelia: Studies in Medieval Archaeology and History in Memory of Tom Delaney* (Galway, 1988), 397–415.

Carmen de Morte Sumerledi, in *Symeonis Monachi Opera Omnia*, ed. T. Arnold (London, 1882), 386–8.

Carpenter, D. A., *The Minority of Henry III* (London, 1990).

Carpenter, D., *The Struggle for Mastery: Britain 1066–1284* (London, 2003).

Carr, A. D., *Medieval Wales* (London, 1995).

Chapelot, J. and R. Fossier, trans. H. Cleere, *The Village and House in the Middle Ages* (London, 1985).

Charles-Edwards, T. M., *The Chronicle of Ireland* (Liverpool, 2006).

Chibnall, M., 'Feudalism and lordship', in C. Harper-Bill and E. van Houts, *A Companion to the Anglo-Norman World* (Woodbridge, 2002).

Clanchy, M., *From Memory to the Written Record: England 1066–1307* (London, 1979).
Clancy, T. O. and B. E. Crawford, 'The formation of the Scottish kingdom', in R. A. Houston and W. W. J. Knox (eds), *The New Penguin History of Scotland* (London, 2001), 28–95.
Cokayne, G. E. et al. (eds), *The Complete Peerage*, xi (London, 1949).
Coornaert, E., 'Les ghildes médiévales', *Revue Historique*, xxxii (1948), 22–55.
Corser, P., 'The Bruce Lordship of Annandale, 1124–1296', in R. Oram and G. Stell (eds), *Lordship and Architecture in Medieval and Renaissance Scotland* (Edinburgh, 2005), 45–59.
Coulton, G. G., *Scottish Abbeys and Social Life* (Cambridge, 1933).
Cowan, I. B., *The Parishes of Medieval Scotland* (Scottish Record Society, 1967).
Cowan, I. B., *Ayrshire Abbeys: Crossraguel and Kilwinning* (Ayrshire Archaeological and Natural History Society, 1986).
Cowan, I. B., *The Medieval Church in Scotland*, ed. J. Kirk (Edinburgh, 1995).
Cowan, I. B. and D. E. Easson, *Medieval Religious Houses. Scotland* (London, 1976).
Craster, H. H. E., 'A contemporary record of the pontificate of Ranulf Flambard', *Archaeologia Aeliana*, vii (1930), 33–56.
Crawford, B. E., 'The earldom of Caithness and the kingdom of Scotland, 1150–1266', in K. J. Stringer (ed.), *Essays on the Nobility of Medieval Scotland* (Edinburgh, 1985), 25–53.Crawford, B. E. (ed.), *St. Magnus Cathedral and Orkney's Twelfth-Century Renaissance* (Aberdeen, 1988).
Crawford, B. E., 'Norse earls and Scottish bishops in Caithness. A clash of cultures', in C. Batey, J. Jesch and C. Morris, *The Viking Age in Caithness, Orkney and the North Atlantic* (Edinburgh, 1993), 129–47.
Crone, A. and F. Watson, 'Sufficiency to scarcity: medieval Scotland, 500–1600', in T. C. Smout (ed.), *People and Woods in Scotland: a History* (Edinburgh, 2003), 60–81.
Cruden, S., *The Scottish Castle*, 3rd edn (Edinburgh, 1981).
Dalton, P., 'Scottish influence on Durham 1066–1214', in D. Rollason, M. Harvey and M. Prestwich (eds), *Anglo-Norman Durham 1093–1193* (Woodbridge, 1994), 339–52.
Davies, N., *God's Playground: A History of Poland in Two Volumes*, i, *The Origins to 1795* (Oxford, 1981).
Davies, R. R., *Domination and Conquest: the Experience of Ireland, Scotland and Wales 1100–1300* (Cambridge, 1990).

Davies, R. R., *The First English Empire: Power and Identities in the British Isles 1093–1343* (Oxford, 2000).
Davis, R. H. C., *King Stephen 1135–54*, 3rd edn (London, 1990).
Dennison, E. P., 'Power to the people? The myth of the medieval burgh community', in S. Foster et al. (eds), *Scottish Power Centres* (Glasgow, 1998), 100–31.
Dennison, E. P., 'Burghs and burgesses: a time of consolidation?', in R. Oram (ed.), *Alexander II* (Leiden, 2005), 253–83.
Dennison, E. P. and R. Coleman, *Historic Dumbarton: the Archaeological Implications of Development* (Edinburgh, 1999).
Dennison, E. P. and R. Coleman, *Historic Nairn: the Archaeological Implications of Development* (Edinburgh, 1999).
Dennison, E. P. and R. Coleman, *Historic Forfar: the Archaeological Implications of Development* (East Linton, 2000).
Dickinson, S., 'Bryant's Gill: another "Viking-period" Ribblehead?', in J. R. Baldwin and I. D. Whyte (eds), *The Scandinavians in Cumbria* (Edinburgh, 1985), 83–8.
Dicks, B., 'The Scottish medieval town – a search for origins', in G. Gordon and B. Dicks (eds), *Scottish Urban History* (Aberdeen, 1983), 23–51.
Ditchburn, D. and A. J. MacDonald, 'Medieval Scotland, 1100–1560', in R. A. Houston and W. Knox (eds), *The New Penguin History of Scotland* (London, 2001), 96–181.
Dixon, P. J., 'Settlement in the hunting forests of southern Scotland in the medieval and later periods', in G. de Boe and F. Verhaeghe (eds), *Rural Settlements in Medieval Europe. Papers of the 'Medieval Europe Brugge 1997' Conference*, vi (Zellik, 1997), 345–54.
Dodgshon, R. A., *Land and Society in Early Scotland* (Oxford, 1981).
Donaldson, G., *Scotland: Church and Nation Through Sixteen Centuries* (Edinburgh, 1960).
Donaldson, G., *Scottish Church History* (Edinburgh, 1985).
Douglas, D. C., *William the Conqueror* (London, 1964).
Douglas, W., 'Culross Abbey and its charters, with notes on a fifteenth-century transumpt', *PSAS*, lx (1925), 67–94.
Driscoll, S. T., 'Formalising the mechanisms of state power: early Scottish lordship from the ninth to the thirteenth centuries', in S. Foster, A. Macinnes and R. MacInnes (eds), *Scottish Power Centres from the Early Middle Ages to the Twentieth Century* (Glasgow, 1998), 32–58.
Duby, G., *The Chivalrous Society*, trans. C. Postan (London, 1977).
Duffy, S., 'Irishmen and Islesmen in the kingdoms of Dublin and Man, 1052–1171', *Eriu*, xliii (1992), 93–133.

Duffy, S., 'The first Ulster plantation: John de Courcy and the men of Cumbria', in T. Barry, R. Frame and K. Simms (eds), *Colony and Frontier in Medieval Ireland, Essays Presented to J. F. Lydon* (London, 1995), 1–27.

Dunbar, J. G. and A. A. M. Duncan, 'Tarbert Castle: a contribution to the history of Argyll', *SHR*, l (1971), 1–17.

Duncan, A. A. M., 'Documents relating to the priory of the Isle of May, c. 1140–1313', *PSAS*, xc (1956–7), 52–80.

Duncan, A. A. M., *Scotland: the Making of the Kingdom* (Edinburgh, 1975).

Duncan, A. A. M., 'The Bruces of Annandale, 1100–1304', *TDGNHAS*, lxix (1994), 89–102.

Duncan, A. A. M., 'St Kentigern at Glasgow Cathedral in the twelfth century', in R. Fawcett (ed.), *Medieval Art and Architecture in the Diocese of Glasgow*, The British Archaeological Association Conference Transactions xiii (1998), 9–24.

Duncan, A. A. M., 'Yes, the earliest Scottish charters', *SHR*, xxviii (1999), 1–35.

Duncan, A. A. M., 'Roger of Howden and Scotland, 1187–1201', in B. E. Crawford (ed.), *Church, Chronicle and Learning in Medieval and Early Renaissance Scotland* (Edinburgh, 1999), 135–60.

Duncan, A. A. M., 'John King of England and the King of Scots', in S. D. Church (ed.), *King John: New Interpretations* (Woodbridge, 1999), 247–71.

Duncan, A. A. M., 'Sources and uses of the Chronicle of Melrose', in S. Taylor (ed.), *Kings, Clerics and Chronicles in Scotland* (Dublin, 2000), 146–85.

Duncan, A. A. M., *The Kingship of the Scots 842–1292. Succession and Independence* (Edinburgh, 2002).

Duncan, A. A. M. and A. L. Brown, 'Argyll and the Isles in the earlier Middle Ages', *PSAS*, xc (1959), 192–220.

Dyer, C., *Making a Living in the Middle Ages: the People of Britain 850–1520* (London, 2002).

Edwards, K. J. and I. B. M. Ralston (eds), *Scotland: Environment and Archaeology, 8000 BC–AD 1000* (Chichester, 1997).

Farmer, D. H., *The Oxford Dictionary of Saints*, 4th edn (Oxford, 1997).

Fawcett, R., *Scottish Abbeys and Priories* (London, 1994).

Fawcett, R., *Scottish Cathedrals* (London, 1997).

Fawcett, R. (ed.), *Medieval Art and Architecture in the Diocese of Glasgow*. The British Archaeological Association Transactions XIII (1998).

Fawcett, R., *Scottish Medieval Churches: Architecture and Furnishings* (Stroud, 2002).

Fawcett, R. and R. D. Oram, *Melrose Abbey* (Stroud, 2004).
Fawcett, R. and R. D. Oram, *Dryburgh Abbey* (Stroud, 2005).
Fawcett, R., R. Oram and J. Luxford, 'Scottish medieval parish churches: the evidence from the dioceses of Dunblane and Dunkeld', *The Antiquaries Journal*, 90 (2010).
Fawtier, R., *The Captian Kings of France: Monarchy and Nation (987–1328)*, trans. L. Butler and R. J. Adam (London, 1962).
Fellows-Jensen, G., 'Scandinavian settlement in Cumbria and Dumfriesshire: the place-name evidence', in J. R. Baldwin and I. D. Whyte, *The Scandinavians in Cumbria* (Edinburgh, 1985), 65–82.
Ferguson, P. C., *Medieval Papal Representatives in Scotland: Legates, Nuncios, and Judges-Delegate, 1125–1286*, Stair Society 45 (Edinburgh, 1997).
Forsyth, K. (ed.), *Studies on the Book of Deer* (Dublin, 2008).
Forte, A., R. Oram and F. Pedersen, *Viking Empires* (Cambridge, 2005).
Foster, S. M., 'Before Alba: Pictish and Dal Riata power centres from the fifth to late ninth centuries AD', in S. Foster, A. Macinnes and R. MacInnes (eds), *Scottish Power Centres from the Early Middle Ages to the Twentieth Century* (Glasgow, 1998), 1–31.
Frame, R., *The Political Development of the British Isles, 1100–1400* (Oxford, 1990).
Gauldie, E., *The Scottish Country Miller, 1700–1900* (reprinted Edinburgh, 1999).
Gilbert, J., 'The monastic record of a Border landscape 1136 to 1236', *Scottish Geographical Magazine*, cix (1983), 4–15.
Gillingham, J., *Richard the Lionheart*, 2nd edn (London, 1989).
Górecki, P., *Economy, Society, and Lordship in Medieval Poland c. 1100–1250* (New York, 1992).
Grant, A., 'Thanes and thanages from the eleventh to the fourteenth centuries', in A. Grant and K. J. Stringer (eds), *Medieval Scotland: Crown, Lordship and Community* (Edinburgh, 1993), 39–81.
Grant, A., 'The Province of Ross and the Kingdom of Alba', in E. J. Cowan and R. A. McDonald (eds), *Alba: Celtic Scotland in the Middle Ages* (East Linton, 2000), 88–126.
Grant, A., 'Constructing the early Scottish state', in J. R. Maddicott and D. M. Palliser (eds), *The Medieval State: Essays Presented to James Campbell* (London, 2000), 47–71.
Grant, A. and K. J. Stringer (eds), *Medieval Scotland: Crown, Lordship and Community* (Edinburgh, 1993).
Green, J., 'Anglo-Scottish relations, 1066–1174', in M. Jones and

M. Vale (eds), *England and Her Neighbours, 1066–1453* (London, 1989), 53–72.

Green, J., 'Aristocratic loyalties on the northern frontier of England, c. 1100–1174', in D. Williams (ed.), *England in the Twelfth Century* (Woodbridge, 1990), 83–100.

Green, J., 'David I and Henry I', *SHR*, lxxv (1996), 1–19.

Green, J. A., *The Aristocracy of Norman England* (Cambridge, 1997).

Hall, D. W., 'Introduction', in M. J. Rains and D. W. Hall (eds), *Excavations in St Andrews 1980–90: A Decade of Archaeology* (Glenrothes, 1997).

Hammond, M. H., 'Queen Ermengarde and the Abbey of St Edward of Balmerino', *Cîteaux: Commentarii Cistercienses* (2008), 11–36.

Hanley, C., *War and Combat, 1150–1270: the Evidence From Old French Literature* (Cambridge, 2003).

Hardin, G., 'The tragedy of the Commons', *Science*, 162 (1967), 1243–8.

Harper-Bill, C. and E. Van Houts (eds), *A Companion to the Anglo-Norman World* (Woodbridge, 2003).

Hartridge, R. A. R., *A History of Vicarages in the Middle Ages* (reprinted New York, 1968).

Harvie, C., *Scotland: A Short History* (Oxford, 2002).

Hay Fleming, D., *Critical Reviews Relating Chiefly to Scotland* (London, 1912).

Heimskringla, Magnus Barelegs' Saga, in A. O. Anderson (ed.), *Early Sources of Scottish History AD 500–1286*, 2 vols (Edinburgh, 1922).

Higgitt, J. (ed.), *Medieval Art and Architecture in the Diocese of St Andrews. The British Archaeological Association Conference Transactions for the Year 1986* (1994).

Higgitt, J., 'The comb, pendant and buckle', in J. Lewis and G. Ewart (eds), *Jedburgh Abbey* (Edinburgh, 1995), 83–4.

Higham, N., 'The Scandinavians in north Cumbria: raids and settlement in the later ninth to mid tenth centuries', in J. R. Baldwin and I. D. Whyte (eds), *The Scandinavians in Cumbria* (Edinburgh, 1985), 37–51.

Higham, R. and P. Barker, *Timber Castles*, 2nd edn (Exeter, 2004).

Hollister, C. W., *Henry I*, edited and completed by A. C. Frost (London, 2001).

Holt, J. C., *Magna Carta* (Cambridge, 1965).

Hope-Taylor, B., 'Excavations at Mote of Urr. Interim report, 1951 season', *TDGNHAS*, xxix (1950–1), 167–72.

Hughes, K., *Early Christian Ireland: Introduction to the Sources* (London, 1972).

Hume Brown, P., *History of Scotland*, i (Cambridge, 1909).

Humphreys, J., *Enemies at the Gate: English Castles Under Siege from the 12th Century to the Civil War* (Swindon, 2007).

Huneycutt, L. L., 'The idea of the perfect princess: the life of St Margaret', *Anglo-Norman Studies* 12 (1989).

Huneycutt, L. L., *Matilda of Scotland: A Study in Medieval Queenship* (Woodbridge, 2003).

Jackson, K., *The Gaelic Notes in the Book of Deer* (Cambridge, 1972).

Jamroziak, E., 'Making friends beyond the grave: Melrose Abbey and its lay burials in the thirteenth century', *Cîteaux: Commentarii Cistercienses*, t. 56, fasc. 1-4 (2005), 323-36.

Jones, B., I. Keillar and K. Maude, 'Discovering the Prehistoric and proto-Historic landscape', in W. D. H. Sellar (ed.), *Moray: Province and People* (Edinburgh, 1993), 47-74.

Jones, G. R., 'Multiple estates and early settlement', in P. H. Sawyer (ed.), *Medieval Settlement* (London, 1976), 15-40.

Kapelle, W. E., *The Norman Conquest of the North. The Region and Its Transformation 1000-1135* (London, 1979).

Keynes, S., 'Cnut's earls', in A. R. Rumble (ed.), *The Reign of Cnut: King of England, Denmark and Norway* (London, 1994, reprinted 1999), 43-88.

Lang, A., *A History of Scotland from the Roman Occupation*, i (Edinburgh, 1900).

Larson, L. M. (trans.), *The King's Mirror (Speculum Regale – Konungs Skuggsjá)*, Scandinavian Monographs, iii (New York, 1917).

Le Patourel, J., 'The Norman Conquest of Yorkshire', *Northern History*, 6 (1971), 1-21.

Limbrey, S. and J. G. Evans (eds), *The Effect of Man on the Landscape: The Lowland Zone*, Council for British Archaeology Research Report 21 (1978).

Lomas, R., *North-East England in the Middle Ages* (Edinburgh, 1992).

Lowe, C., *Excavations at Hoddom, Dumfriesshire* (Edinburgh, 2006).

Lynch, M., *Scotland: a New History* (London, 1991).

Lynch, M., M. Spearman and G. Stell (eds), *The Scottish Medieval Town* (Edinburgh, 1988).

Macbain, A., 'The Book of Deer', *Transactions of the Gaelic Society of Inverness*, vi (1884-5), 137-66.

MacQuarrie, A., 'The kings of Strathclyde c. 400-1018', in A. Grant and K. J. Stringer (eds), *Medieval Scotland: Crown, Lordship and Community* (Edinburgh, 1993), 1-19.

MacQueen, H. L., 'The laws of Galloway: a preliminary study', in R. D. Oram and G. P. Stell (eds), *Galloway: Land and Lordship* (Edinburgh, 1991), 131-43.

MacQueen, H. L., *Common Law and Feudal Society in Medieval Scotland* (Edinburgh, 1993).
MacQueen, H. L., 'The kin of Kennedy, "Kenkynnol" and the Common Law', in A. Grant and K. J. Stringer (eds), *Medieval Scotland: Crown, Lordship and Community* (Edinburgh, 1993), 274–96.
MacQueen, H. L., 'Tears of a legal historian: Scottish feudalism and the ius commune', *Juridical Review*, 1 (2003), 1–28.
MacQueen, H. L. and W. J. Windram, 'Laws and courts in the burghs', in M. Lynch, M. Spearman and G. Stell (eds), *The Scottish Medieval Town* (Edinburgh, 1988), 208–27.
Mapstone, S., 'Bower on kingship', in W. Bower, *Scotichronicon*, ed. D. E. R. Watt et al., vol. 9 (Aberdeen, 1998), 321–8.
Marshall, H. E., *Scotland's Story: A History of Scotland for Boys and Girls* (Edinburgh, n.d.).
Martin, C. and R. Oram, 'Medieval Roxburgh: a preliminary assessment of the burgh and its locality', *PSAS*, 137 (2007), 357–404.
Matthew, D., *King Stephen* (London, 2002).
Maxwell, G., 'Aerial archaeology in south-east Perthshire', *Current Archaeology*, 131 (1992), 451–4.
McDonald, R. A., 'Scoto-Norse kings and the reformed religious orders: patterns of monastic patronage in twelfth-century Galloway and Argyll', *Albion*, xxvii (1995).
McDonald, R. A., *The Kingdom of the Isles. Scotland's Western Seaboard c. 1100–c. 1336* (East Linton, 1997).
McDonald, R. A., 'Treachery in the remotest territories of Scotland: northern resistance to the Canmore dynasty, 1130–1230', *Canadian Journal of History*, 33 (1999), 161–92.
McDonald, R. A., 'Rebels without a cause? The relations of Fergus of Galloway and Somerled of Argyll with the Scottish kings, 1153–1164', in E. J. Cowan and R. A. McDonald (eds), *Alba: Celtic Scotland in the Medieval Era* (East Linton, 2000), 166–86.
McDonald, R. A., *Outlaws of Medieval Scotland: Challenges to the Canmore Kings, 1058–1266* (East Linton, 2003).
McDonald, R. A., 'Old and new in the far North: Ferchar Maccintsacairt and the early earls of Ross, c. 1200–74', in S. Boardman and A. Ross (eds), *The Exercise of Power in Medieval Scotland* (Dublin, 2003), 23–45.
McNeill, P. G. B. and H. L. MacQueen (eds), *Atlas of Scottish History to 1707* (Edinburgh, 1996).
McNeill, T. E., *Anglo-Norman Ulster: the History and Archaeology of an Irish Barony, 1177–1400* (Edinburgh, 1980).

Midmer, R., *English Medieval Monasteries: A Summary* (London, 1979).
Miller, W. I., 'Gift, sale, payment, raid', *Speculum*, lxi (1986), 18–50.
Moloney, C., L. M. Baker et al., 'Evidence for the form and nature of a medieval burgage plot in St Andrews: an archaeological excavation of the site of the Byre Theatre, Abbey Street, St Andrews', *Tayside and Fife Archaeological Journal*, 7 (2001), 48–86.
Morkinskinna: The Earliest Icelandic Chronicle of the Norwegian Kings (1030–1157), ed. and trans. T. M. Andersson and K. E. Gade (Cornell, 2000).
Morrison, J., R. Oram and F. Oliver, 'Ancient Eldbotle unearthed: archaeological and historical evidence for a long-lost early medieval East Lothian village', *Transactions of the East Lothian Antiquarian and Field Naturalist's Society*, xxvii (2008), 21–46.
Murray, H. K., 'Medieval wooden and wattle buildings excavated in Perth and Aberdeen', in A. T. Simpson and S. Stevenson (eds), *Town Houses and Medieval Structures in Scotland* (Glasgow, 1980).
Murray, N., 'Swerving from the path of justice: Alexander II's relations with Argyll and the Western Isles, 1214–1249', in R. D. Oram (ed.), *The Reign of Alexander II, 1214–49* (Leiden, 2005), 285–306.
Neville, C. J., 'A Celtic enclave in Norman Scotland: earl Gilbert and the earldom of Strathearn', in T. Brotherstone and D. Ditchburn (eds), *Freedom and Authority: Scotland c. 1050–c. 1650* (East Linton, 2000), 75–92.
Neville, C. J., 'Native lords and the church in thirteenth-century Strathearn, Scotland', *Journal of Ecclesiastical History*, 53 (2002), 454–75.
Neville, C. J., *Native Lordship in Medieval Scotland: the Earldoms of Strathearn and Lennox, c. 1140–1365* (Dublin, 2005).
Nicolaisen, W. F. H., *Scottish Place-Names* (London, 1976).
Oram, R. D., 'The mythical Picts and the monastic pedant: the origin of the legend of the Galloway Picts', *Pictish Art Society Journal*, 4 (1993), 14–27.
Oram, R. D., 'Prayer, property and profit: Scottish monasteries, c. 1100–c. 1300', in S. Foster, A. I. Macinnes and R. MacInnes (eds), *Scottish Power Centres from the Early Middle Ages to the Twentieth Century* (Glasgow, 1998), 79–99.
Oram, R. D., 'David I and the conquest and colonisation of Moray', *Northern Scotland*, 19 (1999), 1–19.
Oram, R. D., 'Dervorgilla, the Balliols and Buittle', *TDGNHAS*, lxiii (1999), 165–81.
Oram, R. D., *The Lordship of Galloway* (Edinburgh, 2000).

Oram, R. D., 'Gold into lead? The state of early medieval Scottish history', in T. Brotherstone and D. Ditchburn (eds), *Freedom and Authority* (East Linton, 2000), 32–43.
Oram, R. D., 'Patterns of lordship, secular and ecclesiastical, c. 1100–1300', in D. Omand (ed.), *The Fife Book* (Edinburgh, 2000), 105–15.
Oram, R. D., 'Rural society: 1, Medieval', in M. Lynch (ed.), *The Oxford Companion to Scottish History* (Oxford, 2001), 548–9.
Oram, R. D., 'Continuity, adaptation in integration: the earls and earldom of Mar, c. 1150–c. 1300', in S. Boardman and A. Ross (eds), *The Exercise of Power in Medieval Scotland* (Dublin, 2003), 46–66.
Oram, R. D., *David I: the King Who Made Scotland* (Stroud, 2005).
Oram, R. D. (ed.), *The Reign of Alexander II* (Leiden, 2005).
Oram, R. D., 'Introduction and overview of the reign', in R. D. Oram (ed.), *The Reign of Alexander II 1214–49* (Leiden, 2005), 1–47.
Oram, R. D., 'Capital tales or Burghead bull?', in S. Arbuthnott, K. Hollo and A. Ross (eds), *A Grey Eye Looks Back: Essays in Honour of Professor Colm O'Baoill* (Aberdeen, 2005).
Oram, R. D., *A Monastery and its Landscape: Whithorn and Monastic Estate Management in Galloway (c. 1250–c. 1600)*, The Thirteenth Whithorn Lecture (Whithorn, 2005).
Oram, R. D., 'Castles and colonists in twelfth- and thirteenth-century Scotland: the case of Moray', *Château Gaillard*, 22 (2006).
Oram, R. D., 'Royal and lordly residence in Scotland c. 1050 to c. 1250', *The Antiquaries Journal*, 88 (2008), 165–89.
Oram, R. D. and R. Butter, 'Historical framework', in C. Lowe (ed.), *Inchmarnock: An Early Historic Island Monastery and Its Archaeological Landscape* (Edinburgh, 2008), 35–56.
Oram, R. D., P. F. Martin, C. A. McKean, T. Neighbour and A. Cathcart, *Historic Tain: Archaeology and Development* (York, 2009).
Oram, R. D., P. Martin, C. A. McKean and T. Neighbour, *Wigtown: Archaeology and History* (forthcoming, 2011).
Oram, R. D. and G. P. Stell (eds), *Lordship and Architecture in Medieval and Renaissance Scotland* (Edinburgh, 2005).
Ordericus Vitalis, *Historia Ecclesiastica*, in J. P. Migne (ed.), *Patrologiae Cursus Completus*, vol. 188 (Paris, 1855).
Owen, D. D. R., *William the Lion, 1143–1214: Kingship and Culture* (East Linton, 1997).
Palliser, D. M. (ed.), *The Cambridge Urban History of Britain 600–1540*, vol. i (Cambridge, 2000).
Palliser, D. M., T. R. Slater and E. P. Dennison, 'The topography of

towns 600–1300', in D. M. Palliser (ed.), *Cambridge Urban History of Britain 600–1540*, vol. i (Cambridge, 2000), 154–6.

Paris, M., *Chronica Majora*, ed. H. R. Luard, 7 vols (London, 1872–3).

Penman, M., *David II 1329–71* (East Linton, 2004).

Penman, M., 'Royal piety in thirteenth-century Scotland: the religion and religiosity of Alexander II (1214–49) and Alexander III (1249–86)', *Thirteenth Century England*, xii (2007), 13–29.

Perry, D. R. et al., 'Excavations at 77–79 High Street, Arbroath', *Tayside and Fife Archaeological Journal*, 5 (1999), 50–71.

Perry, D. R., *Dundee Rediscovered: The Archaeology of Dundee Reconsidered* (Perth, 2005).

Piper, A. J., 'The Durham cantor's book' (Durham, Dean and Chapter Library, MS B.IV.24), in D. Rollason, M. Harvey and M. Prestwich (eds), *Anglo-Norman Durham 1093–1193* (Woodbridge, 1994), 79–92.

Pittock, M., *A New History of Scotland* (Stroud, 2003).

Poole, A. L., *Domesday Book to Magna Carta*, 2nd edn (Oxford, 1955).

Power, D., *The Norman Frontier in the Twelfth and Early Thirteenth Centuries* (Cambridge, 2004).

Pryde, G. S., *The Burghs of Scotland* (Oxford, 1965).

Radford, C. A. R., 'Hoddom', *TDGNHAS*, xxxi (1952–3), 174–97.

Rains, M. J. and D. W. Hall (eds), *Excavations in St Andrews 1980–90: A Decade of Archaeology* (Glenrothes, 1997).

RCAHMS, *South-East Perth: An Archaeological Landscape* (Edinburgh, 1994).

RCAHMS, *Eastern Dumfriesshire: An Archaeological Landscape* (HMSO, 1997).

Reynolds, S., *Fiefs and Vassals: the Medieval Evidence Reinterpreted* (Oxford, 1994).

Reynolds, S., 'Fiefs and vassals in Scotland: a view from outside', *SHR*, lxxxii (2003), 176–93.

Ritchie, R. L. G., *The Normans in Scotland* (Edinburgh, 1954).

Robertson, E. W., *Scotland Under Her Early Kings: A History of the Kingdom to the Close of the Thirteenth Century*, 2 vols (Edinburgh, 1862).

Robertson, E. W., *Historical Essays in Connexion with Land, the Church etc* (Edinburgh, 1872).

Robertson, N. and D. Perry, 'Perth before the burgh', in D. P. Bowler (ed.), *Perth: The Archaeology and Development of a Scottish Burgh* (Perth, 2004).

Roger of Wendover, *Flores Historiarum*, ed. H. G. Hewlett, 3 vols (London, 1886–98).

Rollason, D., M. Harvey and M. Prestwich (eds), *Anglo-Norman Durham 1093–1193* (Woodbridge, 1994).

Ross, A., 'The lords and lordship of Glencarnie', in S. Boardman and A. Ross (eds), *Exercise of Power* (Dublin, 2003), 159–74.

Ross, A., 'The dabhach in Moray: a new look at an old tub', in A. Woolf (ed.), *Landscape and Environment in Dark Age Scotland* (St Andrews, 2006), 57–74.

Ross, A., 'Scottish environmental history and the (mis)use of Soums', *Agricultural History Review*, 54 (2006), 213–38.

Ross, A., 'The Bannatyne Club and the Publication of Scottish Ecclesiastical Cartularies', *SHR*, 85:2 (2006), 202–30.

Ross, A., 'The identity of the "Prisoner of Roxburgh": Malcolm son of Alexander or Malcolm MacHeth?', in S. Arbuthnott and K. Hollo (eds), *Fil súil nglais: A Grey Eye Looks Back. A Festschrift in Honour of Colm Ó Baoill* (Brig o' Turk, 2007), 269–82.

Ross, A., 'Moray, Ulster and the MacWilliams', in S. Duffy (ed.), *The World of the Galloglass: Kings, Warlords and Warriors in Ireland and Scotland, 1200–1600* (Dublin, 2007), 24–44.

Rushforth, R., *St Margaret's Gospel-book: The Favourite Book of an Eleventh-Century Queen of Scots* (Oxford, 2007).

Schneidmüller, B., 'Constructing identities of medieval France', in M. Bull (ed.), *France in the Central Middle Ages 900–1200* (Oxford, 2002), 15–42.

Scott, J. G., 'The partition of a kingdom: Strathclyde 1092–1153', *TDGNHAS*, lxxii (1997), 11–40.

Scott, W. W., 'Abbots Adam (1207–1213) and William (1215–1216) of Melrose and the Melrose Chronicle', in B. E. Crawford (ed.), *Church, Chronicle and Learning in Medieval and Early Renaissance Scotland* (Edinburgh, 1999), 161–72.

Shead, N. F., 'The origins of the medieval diocese of Glasgow', *SHR*, xlviii (1969), 220–5.

Shepherd, I. A. G., 'The Picts in Moray', in W. D. H. Sellar (ed.), *Moray: Province and People* (Edinburgh, 1993), 75–90.

Simmons, I. A., *An Environmental History of Great Britain from 10,000 Years Ago to the Present* (Edinburgh, 2001).

Simpson, A. T. and S. Stevenson, *Crail: The Archaeological Implications of Development. Burgh Survey* (Glasgow, 1981).

Simpson, G. G. (ed.), *Scotland and the Low Countries 1124–1994* (East Linton, 1996).

Simpson, G. G. and B. Webster, 'Charter evidence and the distribution of mottes in Scotland', in K. J. Stringer (ed.), *Essays on the Nobility of Medieval Scotland* (Edinburgh, 1985), 1–24.

Skene, W. F., *The Highlanders of Scotland: Their Origin, History and Antiquities*, 2 vols (London, 1837).
Skene, W. F., *Celtic Scotland: A History of Ancient Alban*, vol. 3 (Edinburgh, 1880).
Smith, I. M., 'Sprouston, Roxburghshire: an early Anglian centre in the eastern Tweed Basin', *PSAS*, 121 (1991), 261–94.
Smout, T. C. (ed.), *Scottish Woodland History* (Edinburgh, 1997).
Smout, T. C. (ed.), *People and Woods in Scotland: a History* (Edinburgh, 2003).
Smyth, A. P., *Warlords and Holy Men: Scotland AD 80–1000* (London, 1984).
Somerville, R., *Scotia Pontificia: Papal Letters to Scotland Before the Pontificate of Innocent III* (Oxford, 1982).
Spearman, R. M., 'The medieval townscape of Perth', in M. Lynch, M. Spearman and G. Stell (eds), *The Scottish Medieval Town* (Edinburgh, 1988), 42–59.
Stevenson, A., 'Trade with the South, 1070–1513', in M. Lynch et al. (eds), *Scottish Medieval Town*.
Stevenson, S. and E. P. Dennison Torrie, *Historic Glasgow: the Archaeological Implications of Development* (Edinburgh, 1990).
Stevenson, W. B., 'The monastic presence: Berwick in the twelfth and thirteenth centuries', in M. Lynch, M. Spearman and G. Stell (eds), *The Scottish Medieval Town* (Edinburgh, 1988), 99–115.
Strickland, M. J., 'Securing the North: invasion and the strategy of defence in twelfth-century Anglo-Scottish warfare', in M. J. Strickland (ed.), *Anglo-Norman Warfare* (Woodbridge, 1992), 208–29.
Stringer, K. J., 'A new wife for Alan of Galloway', *TDGNHAS*, xlix (1972), 49–55.
Stringer, K. J. (ed.), *Essays on the Nobility of Medieval Scotland* (Edinburgh, 1985).
Stringer, K. J., *Earl David of Huntingdon: a Study in Anglo-Scottish History* (Edinburgh, 1985).
Stringer, K. J., *The Reign of Stephen: Kingship, Warfare and Government in Twelfth-Century England* (London, 1993).
Stringer, K. J., 'Periphery and core in thirteenth-century Scotland: Alan son of Roland, Lord of Galloway and Constable of Scotland', in A. Grant and K. J. Stringer (eds), *Medieval Scotland: Crown, Lordship and Community* (Edinburgh, 1993), 82–113.
Stringer, K. J., 'State-building in twelfth-century Britain: David I, King

of Scots, and Northern England', in J. C. Appleby and P. Dalton (eds), *Government, Religion and Society in Northern England, 1000–1700* (Stroud, 1997), 40–62.

Stringer, K. J., 'Nobility and identity in medieval Britain and Ireland: the de Vescy family, c.1120–1314', in B. Smith (ed.), *Britain and Ireland 900–1300: Insular Responses to Medieval European Change* (Cambridge, 1999), 199–239.

Stringer, K. J., 'Reform monasticism and Celtic Scotland: Galloway c. 1140–c. 1240', in E. J. Cowan and R. A. McDonald (eds), *Alba: Celtic Scotland in the Middle Ages* (East Linton, 2000), 127–65.

Stringer, K. J., 'Kingship, conflict and state-making in the reign of Alexander II: the war of 1215–17 and its context', in R. D. Oram (ed.), *The Reign of Alexander II, 1214–49* (Leiden, 2005), 99–156.

Tabraham, C. J., 'Norman settlement in upper Clydesdale: recent archaeological fieldwork', *TDGNHAS*, liii (1977–8), 114–28.

Talbot, E. J., 'The defences of earth and timber castles', in D. H. Caldwell, *Scottish Weapons and Fortifications 1100–1800* (Edinburgh, 1981), 1–9.

Taylor, S. (ed.), *Kings, Clerics and Chronicles in Scotland 500–1297. Essays in Honour of Marjorie Ogilvie Anderson on the Occasion of her Ninetieth Birthday* (Dublin, 2000).

Thompson, K., *Power and Border Lordship in Medieval France: The County of Perche, 1000–1226* (Woodbridge, 2002).

Thomson, W. P. L., *History of Orkney* (Edinburgh, 1987).

Tipping, R., 'Medieval woodland history from the Scottish Southern Uplands', in T. C. Smout (ed.), *Scottish Woodland History* (Edinburgh, 1997), 52–75.

Tipping, R., 'Towards an environmental history of the Bowmont Valley and the northern Cheviot Hills', *Landscape History*, 20 (1999), 41–50.

Tipping, R., 'Living in the pasts: woods and people in Prehistory to 1000 BC', in T. C. Smout (ed.), *People and Woods in Scotland: a History* (Edinburgh, 2003), 14–39.

Tipping, R., 'Palaeoecology and political history: evaluating driving forces in historic landscape change in southern Scotland', in I. D. Whyte and A. J. L. Winchester (eds), *Society, Landscape and Environment in Upland Britain*, Society for Landscape Studies supplementary series 2 (2004), 11–19.

Tittensor, R., 'History of the Loch Lomond oakwoods', *Scottish Forestry*, 24 (1970), 100–18.

Toorians, L., 'Twelfth-century Flemish settlement in Scotland', in

G. G. Simpson (ed.), *Scotland and the Low Countries 1124–1994* (East Linton, 1996), 1–14.

Topping, P., 'Harald Maddadson, Earl of Orkney and Caithness, 1139–1206', *SHR*, lxii (1983), 105–20.

Torrie, E. P. D., 'The guild in fifteenth-century Dunfermline', in M. Lynch, M. Spearman and G. Stell (eds), *The Scottish Medieval Town* (Edinburgh, 1988).

Torrie, E. P. D., *Medieval Dundee* (Dundee, 1990).

Turner, R. V., *King John* (London, 1994).

Tytler, P. F., *History of Scotland*, i (Edinburgh, 1828).

Veitch, K., 'The Scottish material in *De domibus religiosis*: date and provenance', *Innes Review*, xlvii (1996).

Veitch, K., 'The conversion of native religious communities to the Augustinian Rule in twelfth- and thirteenth-century *Alba*', *Records of the Scottish Church History Society*, xxix (1999), 1–22.

Veitch, K., '"Replanting paradise": Alexander I and the reform of religious life in Scotland', *Innes Review*, 52:2 (2001), 136–66.

Vollrath, H, 'The Western Empire under the Salians', in D. Luscombe and J. Riley-Smith (eds), *The New Cambridge Medieval History*, vol. IV, pt. II (Cambridge, 2004), 38–71.

Walker, R. F., *The Origins of Newcastle upon Tyne* (Newcastle, 1976).

Wall, V., 'Malcolm III and the foundation of Durham Cathedral', in D. Rollason, M. Harvey and M. Prestwich (eds), *Anglo-Norman Durham 1093–1193* (Woodbridge, 1994), 325–38.

Wall, V., 'Queen Margaret of Scotland. Burying the Past, Enshrining the Future', in C. Duggan (ed.), *Queens and Queenship in Medieval Europe* (Woodbridge, 1997).

Warren, W. L., *King John* (London, 1961).

Warren, W. L., *Henry II* (London, 1973).

Watson, F., 'Adapting tradition?: the earldom of Strathearn, 1114–1296', in R. D. Oram and G. P. Stell, *Lordship and Architecture in Medieval and Renaissance Scotland* (Edinburgh, 2005), 26–44.

Watt, D. E. R. (ed.), *Fasti Ecclesiae Scoticanae Medii Aevii ad annum 1638* (Scottish Record Society, 1969).

Watt, D. E. R. and N. F. Shead (eds), *The Heads of Religious Houses in Scotland from Twelfth to Sixteenth Centuries* (Edinburgh, 2001).

Wessex Archaeology, *Roxburgh, Floors Castle Estate, Kelso, Scotland. An Archaeological Evaluation and an Assessment of the Results* (Salisbury, 2004).

Whyte, I. D., *Scotland Before the Industrial Revolution. An Economic and Social History c. 1050–c. 1750* (Harlow, 1995).

Whyte, I. D. and A. J. L. Winchester (eds), *Society, Landscape and Environment in Upland Britain*, Society for Landscape Studies supplementary ser. 2 (2004).
Wickham, C., 'Problems of comparing rural societies in early medieval western Europe', *Transactions of the Royal Historical Society*, 6th ser., ii (1992), 221–46.
Wickham, C., *Land and Power* (London, 1994).
Williams, A., *The English and the Norman Conquest* (Woodbridge, 1995).
Wilson, J., 'Foundation of the Austin Priories of Nostell and Scone', *SHR*, vii (1910), 157–8.
Winchester, A. J. L., 'The multiple estate: a framework for the evolution of settlement in Anglo-Saxon and Scandinavian Cumbria', in J. R. Baldwin and I. D. Whyte (eds), *The Scandinavians in Cumbria* (Edinburgh, 1985), 89–101.
Winchester, A. J. L., *The Harvest of the Hills: Rural Life in Northern England and the Scottish Borders, 1400–1700* (Edinburgh, 2000).
Woolf, A., 'Nobility: 1. Early medieval', in M. Lynch (ed.), *Oxford Companion to Scottish History* (Oxford, 2001), 454.
Woolf, A., *From Pictland to Alba (789–1070)* (Edinburgh, 2007).
Wormald, P., 'The emergence of the *Regnum Scottorum*: a Carolingian hegemony?', in B. E. Crawford (ed.), *Scotland in Dark Age Britain* (St Andrews, 1996), 131–53.
Yeoman, P. A. et al., 'Excavations at Castlehill of Strachan, 1980–81', *PSAS*, 114 (1984), 315–64.
Yeoman, P., *Medieval Scotland: an Archaeological Perspective* (London, 1995).
Young, A., *William Cumin: Border Politics and the Bishopric of Durham, 1141–1144*, University of York, Borthwick Papers no. 54 (1979).
Young, A. 'The earls and earldom of Buchan in the thirteenth century', in A. Grant and K. J. Stringer (eds), *Medieval Scotland: Crown, Lordship and Community* (Edinburgh, 1993), 174–202.
Young, A., 'The bishopric of Durham in Stephen's reign', in D. Rollason, M. Harvey and M. Prestwich (eds), *Anglo-Norman Durham 1093–1193* (Woodbridge, 1994), 353–68.
Young, A., *Robert the Bruce's Rivals: the Comyns, 1212–1314* (East Linton, 1997).

Index

Aberchirder, lordship of, 84
Aberdeen, 75, 82, 106, 167, 232, 278, 282
  bishops of *see* Edward, Matthew
  colonists in, 283
  pre-burgh settlement, 268
  rights and privileges of, 274
Abernethy (Perthshire), 17, 330
  Céli Dé community at, 360
Abernethy, lordship of (Moray), 84, 303
Abertarff
  castle, 190, 317
  lordship of, 191
Ada, illegitimate daughter of David, earl of Huntingdon, 305
Ada, sister of Malcolm IV, 123
Ada de Warenne, wife of Earl Henry, 96, 305, 325
Adam, bishop of Caithness, 160, 175, 186–7, 357
advowson, 348
Æðelred, son of Malcolm III and Margaret, 16, 29
Æðelstan, king of England, 36
Æðelwulf, bishop of Carlisle, 94, 100–1
Aed, earl of Ross, 61, 121
Áed Méith ua Néill, 156, 168, 170–1, 188, 191
Affreca, daughter of Duncan, earl of Fife, 82, 141, 306
Affreca, daughter of Fergus of Galloway, 89
Agatha, mother of St Margaret, 13
Agnes, wife of Morgrund, earl of Mar, 305
agriculture and cultivation, 230, 233, 235–6, 238, 249
  arable, 230, 234, 235–46, 251–7, 258
  assarts, 239, 240, 242–3, 244, 245, 246
  granges, 240, 243, 246, 250–2, 261
  marsh drainage, 250–2, 257, 263, 319
  monastic, 237–40, 242–57, 258, 260–3
  technology, 234–5
  waste, 239, 242
  woodland clearance for, 236–48, 259–61, 263
aids *see* Scotland, royal revenues

Ailred, abbot of Rievaulx, 56, 58, 65, 71, 87, 90, 94, 109, 357
the Aird, 191
Aithmuir, 251
Alan de Sinton, 255
Alan of Galloway, 170, 178, 181, 188–9, 191–3, 294, 307, 311, 315, 325
  marriages of, 307
Alan, son of Walter, the Steward, 157
Alba, 3, 4–5, 6, 8, 29, 53, 68, 218, 297, 308
Alberic, cardinal-bishop of Ostia, papal legate, 94–5, 340
Alexander I, king of Scots, 16, 29, 70, 104, 112, 130, 148, 265, 304, 337, 339
  as designated heir of Edgar, 46
  ecclesiastical policies, 332, 337, 346, 354–5, 356, 359
  reign of, 55–64
  relations with brother David, 57–9, 60
  relations with Henry I of England, 56–7, 58, 60, 61–3, 304
Alexander II, king of Scots, 175, 205, 244, 274, 317, 357, 363, 369
  and Galloway, 188, 189, 191–4, 367
  and Magna Carta, 178–9, 182–3
  and the Isles, 185, 188, 189
  as heir presumptive, 161, 165, 171, 172, 175
  birth, 155, 162, 165
  burghs founded by, 266, 287
  campaigns in west, 185–6, 189, 192
  claims northern England, 74, 178–81, 183, 184
  conquest of northern England, 181–2
  councillors of, 176, 178
  Highland campaigns of, 80, 84, 88, 185–8, 190–1
  homage for English lands, 173–4, 181
  inheritance practice under, 224–5, 368
  marriage, 164, 174, 183, 186
  monastic patronage, 358
  rebellions against, 176, 190–1, 193
  relationship with Church, 179, 182–3, 345–6
  relationship with Henry III, 181–4

Alexander II, king of Scots (cont.)
  relationship with King John, 174, 176, 178–80, 182
  seeks right to coronation, 184
  sisters see Isabella, Margaret, daughters of King William
  supports cult of Thomas Becket, 139, 186
  war in England, 179–82, 185, 345
  wife see Joanna
Alexander III, king of Scots, 1, 41–2, 369
Alexander de St Martin, 309
Alfwin, son of Archill, rannaire, 40–1
Alice de Rumilly, wife of William son of Duncan II, 78, 79, 101, 104
Allerdale, 101, 104, 314
Alnwick, 37, 38, 63, 90, 92, 134, 139, 152, 173, 323
Alston, silver mines, 97
Altyre, 245
'Alwin's land', 239, 243
Amounderness, 101
Andrew, bishop of Caithness, 144, 334
Andrew, bishop of Moray, 254
Andrew Lang, 74
Andrew of Wyntoun, 161
Anecol, thane of Dunning, 298, 299
Anglesey, 50
Anglo-Saxon Chronicle, 16, 17, 24–6, 37, 40, 41, 56
Annals of Tigernach, 219
Annals of Ulster, 60, 71, 126, 129, 168, 219
Angers, 163
Angus, 'earl of Moray', 70–1, 76–7, 78, 83, 103, 106
Angus, 67, 71, 134, 246, 303
  earls of, 140, 188, 222, 303–4
  mórmaer of, 219
Angus, son of Somerled, 157, 169
Anjou, 147, 163
Annandale, 7, 57, 65, 66, 85, 86, 212, 229, 230, 310, 313
  lords of see Robert de Bruce, Robert II de Bruce
Antrim, 188
Anwoth, 314
Appleby, 101, 134
appropriation see parishes
Aquitaine, 132
Arbroath Abbey, 139, 140, 241, 248, 360
Arbuthnott, 254
Archill, father of Alfwin, 40
Ardchattan Priory, 358
Ardross (Fife), 40
Argyll, 6, 49, 53, 72, 75, 85, 86–8, 120, 122, 127, 162, 168, 287
  military service from, 87, 88
  ruler of see Gillebrigte, Somerled
  Scottish lordship over, 86–8, 364
Arkill Morel, 37
Armagh, 83
Arnold, bishop of St Andrews, 338, 342, 346
Arnulf, earl of Pembroke, 52

Arran, 157
Arthur, traitor, 112
Arthur of Brittany, 163–4, 165, 166
assarts see agriculture and cultivation
Athelstaneford, 309
Atholl, 254
  earl of, 70; see also Maddad, Malcolm, Thomas of Galloway
  earldom of, 224
  Isabella, countess of, 307
Aubrey de Coucy, earl of Nothumbria, 20
Augustinian order of canons, 62, 102, 119, 325, 354, 356, 358, 359–60
Auldearn, castle, 77, 82, 143, 367
Austria, 153
Auvergne, 132
Auxerre, 340
Avenel family, 229, 230, 327
Avon, river, as western border of Lothian, 19
Ayr
  castle, 157, 192
  pre-burgh settlement, 268
  river, 260, 261
  royal burgh, 273
  town plan, 285
Ayrshire, 260

Badenoch, lordship of, 191
bœndr see Iceland, peasant society in
Baldwin, archbishop of Canterbury, 147
Baldwin, lord of Biggar, 316, 319
Balliol family, 111
Balmerino Abbey, 357
Bamburgh, 7, 90, 95, 165
Banchory, 241
Banff, 274
Bann, river, 155
Barnard Castle, 180
'Barpenuld', 241
Bathsheba, 109
Battle, 83
  abbey, 77
Beauly Firth, 141, 247
Beauly Priory, 359
Beaumont, 304
Bedford, 283
Bendochy, 249
Benedictine church reform, 20, 54
Benedictine monks, 24, 62, 332, 352, 355, 356, 358
Bergen, 158
Bernicia, 36
Berowald, lord of Innes and Urquhart, 319
Berwick, 172, 180, 263, 272, 276, 279–80, 282, 286
  burgesses see Mainard the Fleming, William Lunnoc
  castle, 136, 149, 151, 152
  gild, 281
  pre-burgh settlement, 268
  prepositus of, 280
  royal burgh, 67, 133, 180, 265, 275

shire, 54, 248, 309
town defences, 289
town plan, 284
Biggar, 316
Bisset family, 191
Black Isle, 76
Blainslie, grange, 239, 243
Blairgowrie, 251
Boleskine, 191
Bolton Priory, 104
Bo'ness, 319
Book of Deer, 198, 199, 216, 218–20, 221, 322, 359
Borgue, 314
Borthwick, 249
Bowmont Valley, 237
'Boy of Egremont' *see* William, son of William son of Duncan II
Brantalloch, motte, 231
Brechin, 267
  bishops of, 360
  Céli Dé community at, 360
Breteuil, 304
Bretons, 319
Brian Boruma, king of Munster, 53
Brice Douglas, bishop of Moray, 319
Briouze family, 169
Brittany, 85, 115, 123, 130, 131, 132, 163, 304
Broom, Loch, 77
Brough, castle, 134
Bruce family, 229; *see also* Robert de Bruce
Buchan, 75, 107, 198, 219, 304, 318, 322, 326
  earl of, 178, 216, 303, 325; *see also* Fergus, William Comyn
  mórmaer of, 216, 218, 220, 222
Buckholm, grange, 243
Buddo, 254
building materials, 241, 242, 243, 245, 246–8, 256, 262, 278, 290–1, 293–4, 317–18
burgage plots *see* burghs
burgage tenure *see* burghs
burgesses and townsmen, 61, 245, 265–92
burghs, 82, 248, 265–94
  administration and institutions, 277–81
  as centres of royal power, 287–9
  burgage plots, 285, 288, 291
  burgage tenure, 275–7
  colonists in, 275–6, 281–3, 292
  creation of, 265, 268, 275–6, 283, 285–8
  cultural significance of, 83, 266, 282–3, 288, 362
  economic significance of, 266, 280
  gild-merchants, 280–1
  laws and law-courts, 271–7, 278–9
  officials, 279–80
  plans, 284–8
  pre-burgh communities, 266–9, 281, 283, 285–6
  revenues from, 277, 279–80, 292–3
  rights and privileges, 265, 272–7, 279–80, 287–8, 292–3
  trade, 272–7, 281, 282, 284, 285–8, 292–3

urban landscape, 288–91
walls and defences, 288–9
Burgie, 241, 245
Burgundy, 352
Bute, 157, 192
Byland Abbey, 103

Cadzow, 89
Caen, 131
cáin, 72, 77, 226, 279, 295, 299
  from Argyll, 88
  from Galloway, 87, 226
Cairngorm Mountains, 274
Caisteal Dubh, 254
Caithness, 5, 30, 53, 60, 75, 76, 79, 82, 107, 113, 141, 154, 157, 158–9, 161, 167, 171, 186–8, 232, 306, 334, 345, 357, 364
  bishops of *see* Adam, Andrew, John
  earldom of, 51, 79, 144, 159, 162, 166, 187
  earls of *see* David, Erlend III Haraldsson, Harald Hákonsson, Harald Maddadsson, Harald Ungi, Jón, Magnus Erlendsson, Thorfinnr the Mighty
Cambridgeshire, 15
Cambuskenneth Abbey, 350, 356
Campbell family, 312
Canongate, burgh, 285
Canossa, 331–2
Canterbury, 70, 134, 139, 143, 151, 180, 186, 332, 334, 336, 337
  archbishops of, 330 *see* Baldwin, Hubert Walter, Lanfranc, Richard, Thomas Becket, William of Corbeil
  Church of, 24, 68, 352
  Quitclaim of, 151, 152, 153, 155, 292, 344
Carlisle, 47, 51, 57, 63, 71–2, 86, 90, 91, 100, 101, 111, 113, 114, 115, 117, 122, 124, 133, 134, 147, 165, 173, 180, 230, 267, 316, 340, 341, 345
  bishop of *see* Æðelwulf
  bishopric, 339–40
  castle, 34, 61, 108, 180
  David I's court at, 94, 97, 100, 105
  English colony, 34, 47
  lords of *see* Ivo de Taillebois, Ranulf Meschin
Carrick, 8, 87, 155, 226
Carrickfergus Castle, 188
carruca see agriculture, technology
Carse of Gowrie, 250–2
Carthusian order of monks, 359
Cartmel, 101
castles and mottes, 72, 77, 82, 117, 124, 134, 135, 136, 140, 141, 143, 147, 153, 157, 172, 179, 180, 181, 186, 188, 190, 192, 197, 231–2, 253, 254, 287, 291, 306, 317–18, 367, 368
Catrine, 261
cattle and oxen, 137, 226, 236, 241, 242, 243, 245, 258, 260, 261, 262
Cecilia, daughter of Gillebrigte, earl of Strathearn, 307
Céli Dé, 359–60
Cenél nEógain, 186

Channelkirk, 258
charters, 65, 66, 69–70, 88, 178, 197, 213, 215, 227, 248, 272, 273, 279, 292–3, 297–8, 299, 310, 315, 318, 321
  witnesses, 298–300, 309
Chester, 86, 115, 116
  earls of see Hugh, Hugh d'Avranche, John, Ranulf le Meschin, Ranulf II
Cheviot Hills, 241, 259
Chinon, 150, 163
Chisholm family, 312
chivalric culture, 117–18, 301, 311, 319
Christian, bishop of Whithorn, 344
Christina, sister of St Margaret, 13
Chronicle of Holyrood, 72, 111, 112, 118, 119, 127
Chronicle of Man, 169
Chronicle of Melrose, 116, 118, 119, 126, 130, 141, 142, 158, 160–1
Cinaed son of Alpín, 4, 365
Cistercian Order
  monks, 83, 102–3, 104, 160, 251, 253, 326, 340, 356–8
  nuns, 325
Cîteaux, 357
Clairvaux, 343, 357
Clan Donald, 168
clann see kin and kinship
Cleish, 306
Clement, bishop of Dunblane, 347, 350
clergy, 298, 322, 330–4, 335, 341, 346–50, 352, 356, 360, 365
  canons see Augustinian order, Premonstratensian order
  diocesan, 347–8, 350
  monks see Benedictine order, Carthusian order, Cistercian order, Valliscaulian order
  parish, 347–51, 356
climate and environment, 233, 234–6
Clitheroe, battle of, 93
Clonmacnoise, 219
cloth, 254–5, 271, 272, 292–3
Cluniac
  monks, 356
  reform see Scottish Church, reform of
Cluny Abbey, 352
Clyde
  Firth of, 32, 50, 53, 87–8, 127, 128, 157, 186, 192, 324
  islands, 186; see also Arran, Bute
  valley see Clydesdale
Clydesdale, 4, 7, 85, 86, 87, 127, 228, 229, 319
  Flemish colony in, 127, 315–16
  sheriff of, 316
  territorial lordships in, 228–9, 316, 322
Cogadh Gaedhel re Gallaib, 53
coinage, 97, 271, 364
Coldingham
  minster church, 54
  priory, 241
  shire, 54
Coldstream, nunnery, 325

Colmslie, grange, 243
colonisation, 127, 197, 227, 229, 271, 281–3, 292, 304, 362, 366
  Anglo-Saxon, 40–1, 200, 201
  Breton, 300, 319
  English, 61, 229, 281, 282–3, 319, 366
  Flemish, 127, 245, 252, 275, 281, 282, 315–16, 319–20
  Gaelic, 316–17
  knights, 276, 299, 300, 303, 304, 309–10, 313–16, 317, 318–19, 321, 368; see also knights and knighthood
  processes of, 304–5, 307–8, 313–14, 326, 364, 368–9
comhdal (popular assembly), 206
common army see Scotland, common army in
commons, 258, 259, 263
compensation see cro
Comyn family, 191, 266, 312; see also William Comyn, Walter Comyn
Conan IV, duke of Brittany and earl of Richmond, 118, 123, 124, 131
Conisbrough family, 229; see also William de Conisbrough
Connacht, 47, 120, 185, 188
Constance, daughter of Conan IV of Brittany, 131
Constance, sister of Conan IV of Brittany, 123
Constantine, *comes* or earl of Fife, 222
Constantine, *iudex* of the earl of Strathearn, 298
Constantine, *pincerna* of the earl of Strathearn, 299
Constitutiones Regis Willelmi, 273
conveth, 226–7
Copeland, 101, 104
Corbridge, battle of (918), 219
Cormac, bishop of Dunkeld, 70
coronation, 62, 98, 132, 150, 163, 184, 337, 339, 345, 369; see also royal inauguration
Cospatric, earl of Northumbria, 13, 17, 42
  settles in Scotland, 17–18, 41, 44
Cotken, 259
Coupar Angus Abbey, 126, 129, 130, 148, 249–52, 294, 327, 357
Cowal, 127, 157, 186
Cowton Moor, 94
craft and industry, 269, 282, 284, 285, 292–3
  dyeing, 292–3
  fullers, 293
  pottery, 283
  weaving, 271, 272, 293
Crail, town plan, 285
Craven, 93, 101, 104, 107
Crawfordjohn, 316
cro, 220–1
Cromarty Firth, 141
cruives, 255
Cullen, castle, 77
Culross Abbey, 325, 357
Cum universi see papal bulls
Cumberland, 7, 34, 47, 89, 94, 97, 100, 111, 115, 122, 130, 145, 154, 165, 184, 307, 314
  Scottish lordship in, 181–2

INDEX 415

Cumbria (English and Scottish), 7, 9, 18, 47, 73, 90, 102, 106, 122, 163, 227, 229, 238, 239, 314, 331
   as inheritance of David I, 56–8, 242, 284, 316
Cunningham, 87–8, 89, 101, 157, 226, 228, 324

Dabhaichean see *davoch*
Dál Riata, kingdom of, 6
Dalmeny, 223
   church, 322
dapifer, 298–9
Darnaway, forest, 248
Daventry Priory, 70
David, Biblical king, 109
David, earl of Caithness and Orkney, 167, 175
David, earl of Huntingdon, 132, 134, 135, 139, 141, 145–6, 147, 148, 150, 153, 154–5, 163, 164–5, 171–2, 176, 287, 307, 311, 313
   as heir-presumptive, 145–6, 154, 162, 165–6
   founds Dundee, 286–7
   given as hostage, 125
David I, king of Scots, 7, 16, 29, 41, 55, 56, 65, 112, 119–20, 121, 127, 129, 184, 191, 197, 198, 200, 204, 213, 226, 227, 242, 243, 247, 275, 276, 286, 293, 297, 301, 303, 304, 323, 339, 363, 366, 367–8
   and Caithness-Orkney, 79–82, 107, 167
   and Galloway, 86, 227
   as earl of Huntingdon, 69, 98
   as 'prince' of Cumbria, 57, 58, 63–6, 79, 87–8, 227, 228–9, 242, 265, 284, 316
   burghs founded by, 265, 268, 269–72, 274, 279, 283–4
   campaigns in west Scotland, 85–9
   career in England, 46, 57, 66, 70, 73, 231, 354
   coinage of, 97
   control of northern England, 89, 96–103, 104–6, 107–8, 114, 115–17, 340
   death of, 108, 109, 110, 113, 114
   defeats and conquers Moray, 71–80, 82–5, 106–7, 203, 318
   ecclesiastical policy of, 69, 107, 238, 332, 337–41, 346–7, 360
   English supporters of, 57–8, 65–6, 67, 71–2, 197, 211–12, 298, 309, 313
   feudalising policies of, 214–15, 223, 229, 230, 252
   influence in Irish Sea zone, 88–9, 114
   Inquest *see* Inquest of David
   invades England, 88, 89–96, 97, 209, 230
   laws, 271–2
   marriage, 57, 304
   monastic foundations, 354–7, 359
   reign of, 64–109
   relationship with Alexander I, 57–9, 60, 63–4
   relationship with Henry I of England, 56–7, 63–4, 69, 72, 73, 116, 313, 354
   relationship with Matilda, daughter of Henry I, 91, 92, 97–8, 115
   relationship with Stephen of England, 90–1, 97, 101, 102, 106

David II, king of Scots, 222
David, son of Robert, 249
David, son of Terrus, 314
David de Hay, lord of Errol, 251, 308
davoch, 202–3, 232, 258; *see also* Scotland, land units in
Dean, river, 251
Dee, river (Aberdeenshire), 303
Dee, river (Galloway), 122
Deeside, 241, 248
Deer Abbey, 198, 326, 357; *see also* Old Deer
Deheubarth, Welsh principality, 124
Denmark, 217–18
   kings of *see* Harðaknútr, Knútr IV, Svein
Derry (Ulster), 128, 168
Dervorgilla, wife of Richard de Clare, 304
Diarmid, king of Leinster, 304
Diarmid ua Conchobair, 185, 186
Dingwall (Ross), 75, 203
   royal burgh, 287–8
Dirleton, 249, 256
dispensarius, 299
Dogden Moss, 237
Domesday Book, 235, 302
Domnall mac Gille Chriosd, lord of Tarbet, 248
Domnall mac Lochlainn, king of Cenél nEógain, 59
Domnall mac Raonaill, 186
Domnall mac Taidc, king of the Isles, 59
Donald, lord of Nithsdale, 89
Donald, son of Malcolm, 112, 114, 120, 122
Donald, son of Malcolm III, 29, 30
Donald Bán, king of Scots, 40, 41–4, 46, 60, 66
   Gaelic character of, 41, 42
Doncaster, 91, 95, 125
Dougall Screech MacDougall, 192
Douglas family, 319
Douglasdale, 260, 315–16
Dover, 180
Drumochter, 80
Dryburgh Abbey, 239–40, 242–4, 247, 249, 255, 258, 323–4, 358
Dublin, 8, 31, 32, 34, 47, 48, 51, 60, 113, 120, 128, 269
   kings of, 31, 32
   see also Echmarcach son of Ragnall, Guðrøðr Crobán, king of Man, Sigurðr
Duffus, 252, 319
   castle, 232, 318
Dugald, son of Somerled, king of Man and the Isles, 114, 120, 128, 156–7
Dumbarton, 267
   royal burgh, 186, 287–8
Dunbar, 7, 17
   earls of, 140, 307, 314, 324, 325, 327
   see also Patrick
Dunblane, 360
   archdeacon, 347
   bishop of *see* Clement
   diocese, 347, 348, 350
Duncan I, earl of Fife, 82, 108, 215, 223

416 DOMINATION AND LORDSHIP

Duncan II, earl of Fife, 127, 141, 305, 306
Duncan I, king of Scots, 41
Duncan II, king of Scots, 29, 39, 41, 42–4, 46, 78, 211, 309
  hostage in England, 17, 21, 46
  legitimacy of, 46, 64
Duncan, son of Gillebrigte of Galloway, 146, 147, 155–6, 169
Duncan, son of Morgrund, earl of Mar, 225
Duncan, thane of Strowan, 299
Duncan MacDougall, lord of Lorn, 192
Dundee
  burgh, 285, 286–7
  castle, 287
  plan, 286–7
  shire, 286
  trade rivalry with Perth, 287
Dundrennan Abbey, 261, 358
Dunduff, 309
Dunegal of Nithsdale, 229–30
Dunfallin, 254
Dunfermline, 5, 16, 21, 68, 129
  abbey, 24, 25, 55, 69–70, 77, 139, 249, 255, 352
  Geoffrey, abbot of, 69
  Holy Trinity church at, 24
  royal burgh, 67, 265, 285
  shrine of St Margaret at, 164
Dunkeld, 5
  bishops of *see* Cormac, Geoffrey, Hugh, John the Scot, Richard, Walter de Bidun
  Céli Dé, 359–60
  dean, 347
  monastery, 322, 354, 359
Dunning, thane of *see* Anecol
Dunskeath Castle, 141
Durham, 33, 35, 44, 90, 95, 97, 100, 111, 174, 283, 348
  Benedictine priory, 26, 54, 55, 352
  bishops of, 97, 117, 164, 345; *see also* Geoffrey, Hugh le Puiset, Ranulf Flambard, Walcher, William of Ste Barbe, William of St Calais, William Cumin
  castle, 98, 99
  Community of St Cuthbert at, 20, 35, 54
  lands of, 44, 45, 46, 54, 99, 133, 229
  Liber Vitae, 16
  Scottish kings and, 35–6, 37, 54–5, 90, 97–9, 108
Durward family, 191; *see also* Thomas Durward

Eadmer, bishop of St Andrews, 332, 337, 354
earls and earldoms, 68, 70, 71, 214–25, 297–301, 315
Earn, river, 5
East Anglia, 15, 18, 283
East Lothian, 249, 256, 309, 324
Eccles, nunnery, 325, 327
Echmarcach son of Ragnall, king of Dublin, Man and the Rhinns, 8, 32
'Edderpolles', 250–2

Eden, river, 255
Edgar, king of Scots, 16, 29, 44–5, 56, 57, 322
  reign of, 46–55
Edgar Ætheling, 8, 13–18, 33, 34, 35, 42–3, 45
Edinburgh, 5, 40, 100, 267, 344
  castle, 136, 147
  plan, 285
  pre-burgh settlement, 268
  royal burgh, 67, 265
Edith (Matilda), daughter of Malcolm III and Margaret, 26, 51–2, 70, 354, 355
Edmund, chamberlain of David I, 65
Edmund, son of Malcolm III and Margaret, 16, 29, 40, 41, 44–5
Ednam
  church, 322, 348
  moor, 248
Edradour (Redcastle), 141
Edward, bishop of Aberdeen, 106
Edward, constable of David I, 71
Edward, son of Malcolm III and Margaret, 16, 29, 35, 36
  as designated heir, 37, 38, 39–40
Edward the Confessor, king of England, 6, 8, 9, 22, 34, 301, 363
Edward the Elder, king of England, 34
'Edyngaheym', 229
Egilsay, 60
Eildon Hill North, 266
Ela, wife of Duncan II, earl of Fife, 305
Elbe, river, 77
Eldbotle, 249, 256
Eleanor of Aquitaine, wife of Henry II of England, 133
Elgin, 158, 159, 190, 191, 232, 248, 254, 255, 282, 319
  castle, 77, 82, 253
  mill, 253–5
  town plan, 285
Empress *see* Matilda, daughter of Henry I of England
England, 7, 47, 48, 51, 52, 64, 85, 115, 124, 132, 142, 155, 161, 165, 166, 173, 190, 201, 203, 216, 218, 221, 230, 282, 295, 296, 304, 317
  Anglo-Scandinavian or Danish rulers of, 6, 50, 211, 309
  Anglo-Scandinavian population in, 15, 282, 302
  anti-Scottish feelings in, 94, 100, 182
  army service in, 222
  boroughs, 265, 269, 273
  Church *see* Scottish Church, metropolitan supremacy over
  Church reform in, 23–4, 352, 354
  civil war in, 179–80
  cultural influences of, 363
  Danish invasion of, 14–15, 34, 50
  feudalism in, 209
  homage of kings of Scots to king of England *see* Scotland, submission
  influence of in Orkney, 54, 60

kings of, 363, 369; *see also* Æðelstan, Edward the Confessor, Edward the Elder, Harold Godwinsson, Henry I, Henry II, Henry III, Henry VIII, John, Knútr, Richard I, Stephen, William I, William II Rufus
kingship in, 65, 96
lands of kings of Scots in, 17, 34, 105, 106, 114, 116, 132, 171, 173, 181
law-codes (Anglo-Saxon), 221
Midlands of, 133–4, 180, 203, 283, 323
monastic foundations in, 354–5
Norman conquest of, 2, 8–9, 13, 29, 301–2, 309, 325, 352
the Northern Counties, 153, 155, 164, 179–80, 181, 184, 364; *see also* Cumberland, Northumberland, Westmorland
northern frontier of, 44–6, 47, 58, 63, 86, 95, 117, 125, 150, 164, 165, 171, 184
population growth in, 234–5
rebellions in, 13–15, 18, 21, 29, 52, 133–4, 153, 174–5, 176, 179–81, 182, 302
royal power in, 199, 218
royal succession in, 89, 105, 110, 162, 176
Scottish invasions of, 13, 14, 18–19, 33, 36, 79, 88, 89–96, 97, 101, 125, 133–4, 164, 180, 181, 209
social change in, 301–3
trade, 267, 268, 271
West Saxon kings of, 9, 16, 29, 36, 52, 217
English Channel, 117
English language, 6, 203, 266, 282, 283, 362, 366
Enguerrand, bishop of Glasgow, 334, 342
Erlend II, earl of Orkney, 30–1, 48, 144, 187
Erlend III Haraldsson, earl of Orkney and Caithness, 80, 82, 107
Erling, son of Erlend II, earl of Orkney, 48
Ermengarde de Beaumont, wife of King William, 146, 147, 154, 162, 174, 175
Errol, 250–2, 308
church, 251
Esk, river (Lothian), 255
Eskdale, 228, 230, 322, 327
Ettrick Forest, 227–8, 230, 238, 240
as 'free zone', 228
Eustace, count of Boulogne, 52
Eustace, son of King Stephen, 110
Eustace de Vescy, lord of Alnwick, 152, 153, 163, 174, 178, 180, 305
Eustace fitz John, lord of Malton and Alnwick, 63, 65, 66, 92, 100, 323
Ewesdale, lordship of, 229
Eystein II, king of Norway, 81–2, 107

Falaise, 118, 135, 136
Treaty of, 135–9, 145, 151, 342–3
Falkirk, 19, 20, 21
fealty, 43, 137, 138, 150, 163, 165
Fearn Abbey, 358
Feckenham, 138
Ferchar MacTaggart, 176, 186, 189, 311, 366
earl of Ross, 191, 193–4, 205, 208, 311, 358
Fereneze Hills, 245, 247

Fergus, earl of Buchan, 318
Fergus, Romance epic, 231
Fergus, son of Gillebrigte of Strathearn, 259
Fergus of Galloway, 85–6, 89, 91, 113, 119, 120, 135, 229–30, 231, 307, 313, 314, 325, 358
ferries, 5, 141, 287
Ferteth, earl of Strathearn, 118, 119
feudalism, 193, 197–8, 209–15, 311, 312
feudalisation, 312–13
fiefs or feus, 300
landholding, 197, 199–200, 202, 208–15, 222, 223–4, 232, 246
military, 210, 212–13
subinfeudation and sub-tenants, 212, 306, 310
tenure, 304, 308, 318
feuferme, 246
Fife, 28, 66, 134, 178, 201, 214, 222, 223, 246, 255, 283, 309, 322, 324, 363
army of, 222
colonisation in, 40–1, 309
earls of, 70, 84, 89, 91, 140, 214–15, 255, 303, 305–6, 318, 325
see also Constantine, Duncan I, Duncan II, Malcolm
Filia specialis see papal bulls
Findhorn Bay, 251
Flaithbertach ua Brolchain, abbot of Derry, 128
Flanders, 17, 124, 271, 282
trade, 268
Florenz, count of Holland, 123–4
forest and hunting, 230–1, 236, 242–5, 246, 247, 248, 259, 260–1; *see also* Ettrick Forest, Gala and Leader
Forfar, 191
pre-burgh settlement, 268
sheriff of, 308
forinsec service *see* Scotland, common army in
Forres, 245
castle, 77, 82
town plan, 285
Forteviot, 5
Forth, firth of, 3, 5, 15, 69, 73, 89, 106, 143, 201, 203, 216, 236, 304, 315, 316, 324, 336, 357
ferries, 5
river, 4, 5, 6, 30, 36, 40, 41, 268
Forth–Clyde line, 229, 246
Fothad II, bishop of St Andrews, 330, 331, 332, 335, 337
Fountains Abbey, 102
Frakkok, 80, 81
France, 117, 118, 126, 130, 133, 145, 147, 150, 153, 160, 161, 163, 165, 166, 181, 233, 295, 319, 340, 355
kings of *see* Louis VII, Louis VIII, Philip I, Philip II
treaty negotiations with Scots, 172–3
Fraser family, 312
Frederick I Barbarossa, emperor, 124
free alms, 322
Freskin, lord of Duffus, 252, 319
Friardykes, 263

fuel, 245, 246, 247–50, 258, 262, 293
fulling mills, 255; see also craft and industry
Fulton, 241
Furness, 93, 101, 103
   abbey, 103, 104

Gaelic culture and society, 28, 29, 41, 58, 66–7, 68, 72, 232, 281–2, 295, 297, 298, 301, 306, 311–12, 315, 318, 321, 322, 329, 357, 360, 365–8
   language, 3, 199, 201, 266, 282, 286, 362
   poetry, 58, 66, 364–6
Gaelicisation, 312–13, 316–17
Gala and Leader, forest, 242, 260
Gala Water, 240
Galloway, 4, 7–8, 9, 32, 49, 50, 85–7, 113, 121–2, 155, 156, 193, 228, 231, 236, 256, 307, 318, 364, 366–7
   agricultural development in, 245–6, 261
   burghs in, 266
   civil war in, 113, 121–2, 137–8, 146, 147
   colonisation in, 127, 135, 303, 304, 306–7, 313–15
   conquest of, 118–19, 313, 363
   fleet, 113, 121, 122, 312
   greater, 75, 85–7, 89, 228–9, 230
   justiciar of, 155
   kings and lords of, 266, 307, 325, 358; see also Alan, Fergus, Gillebrigte, Roland, Uhtred
   monastic foundations in, 325, 358
   rebels against King William, 135–8, 144–6, 315, 317
   Rhinns of, 8
   warriors from, 94, 312
   woodland clearance in, 245–6
Galwegia see Galloway
Garioch, lordship of, 134, 313
Garve, 149
Gate Fulford, battle of, 8
Gateshead, 19
Genest (Brittany), 130, 131
Geoffrey, archbishop of York, 150
Geoffrey, bishop of Dunkeld, 359
Geoffrey, bishop of Durham, 93, 97
Geoffrey, son of Henry II of England, 131, 132, 133, 147, 163
Geoffrey of Gask, 300
Germany, 13, 77, 233, 303
Gesta Annalia, 71, 126, 130, 131, 143, 146, 155, 167, 185
Gifford family, 303
Gilbert, knight of Cleish, 306
Gilbert, knight of the earl of Strathearn, 298
Gilbert de Umfraville, 100
Gilchrist, abbot of the Céli Dé of St Andrews, 359
Gilchrist, earl of Mar, 224
gild-merchant see burghs, Perth
Gilleasbuig see MacWilliam lineage
Gilleasbuig MacDougall, king of the Isles, 192
Gillebrigte, earl of Strathearn, 143, 247, 259, 298–300, 305, 307, 325

Gillebrigte, son of Fergus, lord of Galloway, 121–2, 127, 135–8, 144–6, 147, 155, 306, 307, 315
Gillebrigte of Argyll, 72, 86, 87, 88
Gillecolm, marischal of Strathearn, 143, 367
Gillenanef, dapifer of the earl of Strathearn, 298
Gillescop see MacWilliam lineage
Giric, bishop of St Andrews, 331, 332, 337
Glasgow, 7, 230
   bishops of, 94, 128, 331, 332, 336, 337; see also Enguerrand, Herbert, Hugh of Roxburgh, Jocelin, John
   burgh, 287
   Church of, 65, 68, 87–8, 91, 226
   diocese of, 228–9, 334, 337–8, 343, 345, 346, 348
   diocesan officials, 347
Glencharnie, lordship of, 84, 303
Glenelg, 77
Glengavel, 260
Glenluce Abbey, 358
Gloucester, 35, 36, 45
goði see Iceland, peasant society in
Gofraid Crobán, king of Man see Guðrøðr Crobán
Gordon family, 312
Gorthy, 300
Gowrie, 67, 303, 304, 308; see also Carse of Gowrie
Grange see 'Edderpolles'
granges see agriculture and cultivation
grassland and grazing, 236, 237, 238, 240, 241, 242–4, 247, 251, 257–63
   muirburn, 259–60
   over-grazing, 262–3
   see also commons
Great Glen, 185
Greenland, 32
Gregorian reform see Scottish Church, reform of
Gruffudd ap Cynan, king of Gwynedd, 50, 60
Guala Bicchieri, cardinal, papal legate, 181, 182, 345–6
Guðrøðr Crobán, king of Man, 6, 31–2, 34, 35, 47–8, 49, 50, 59, 88
Guðrøðr Dond, son of Rognvald, king of Man, 192
Guðrøðr Ólafsson, king of Man, 113–14, 120, 121, 128–9, 155
Gunnilda, daughter of Waltheof of Allerdale, 307, 314
Gwynedd, 50, 60, 124

Haddington, 155, 266
   nunnery, 325
   prepositus of, 280
Hákon IV, king of Norway, 49, 188, 192
Hákon Pálsson, earl of Orkney, 48–9, 53, 60, 79
Hamburg-Bremen, archbishopric of, 341
Hanef Ungi, 187
hanse, 282
Harald, son of Guðrøðr Crobán, 48
Harald IV Gille, king of Norway, 81

Harald Hákonsson, earl of Orkney and Caithness, 80
Harald Maddadsson, earl of Orkney and Caithness, 81–2, 107, 141, 142–4, 157–9, 161, 166–7, 187, 306
Harald Ungi or Ingiridsson, earl of Orkney and Caithness, 144, 158–9
Haraldr Harðraði, king of Norway, 8, 48, 50
Harbottle Castle, 134
Harðaknútr, king of Denmark and England, 50
Harold Godwinsson, king of England, 8, 51
  Harold, son of, 51
Hartlepool, 82
Hartside, 262
Hassendean, 262, 263
Hastings, 77
  battle of, 8, 9, 301–2
Hawick, 228
Hebrides see Isles
Heimskringla, 49
Helen de Morville, wife of Roland of Galloway, 307, 315
Helmsdale, 80
Henry IV, Holy Roman Emperor, 331
Henry I, king of England, 26, 47, 51, 52, 59, 63–4, 65, 69, 72, 73, 79, 85, 88, 91, 108, 115, 116, 157, 269, 272, 313, 315, 339, 354–5, 363
  death of, 89–90, 91
  illegitimate children of, 57, 85, 304–5, 307
  influence of in Orkney, 54, 80
  relations with Alexander I of Scotland, 56–7, 61–3, 304
Henry II, king of England, 106, 109, 114, 124, 333, 336, 342–3
  and Galloway, 137–8, 144–8, 155, 231
  and Thomas Becket, 129
  influence in Irish Sea and Man, 121, 136, 156, 231
  knighted by David I, 105
  negotiates with Stephen for kingship, 110–11
  oath to accept Scottish gains in England, 105, 106, 114, 115
  rebellions against, 130, 131, 132–5, 147, 150
  relations with Malcolm IV of Scotland, 115–18, 123–6
  relations with William of Scotland, 125, 130–2, 133–8, 140, 143, 145–8, 149–50, 152, 173
  Welsh campaigns of, 124, 128
Henry III, king of England
  Irish policies of, 185–6, 188–9
  Manx policy of, 190
  minority of, 183
  papal support for, 181–2, 183, 345
  proposed marriage to Margaret, daughter of William of Scotland, 173
  relationship with Alexander II, 181, 183–4
  sister see Joanna
  succession of, 180–1
Henry VIII, king of England, 136
Henry, *rannaire* of the earl of Streathearn, 299

Henry, son of David I, 64–5, 78, 90–1, 92, 95, 99–100, 108, 110
  homage to King Stephen, 92, 95, 96
Henry (Heinrik), son of Harald Maddadsson, earl of Ross, 141
Henry, son of Henry II (the Young King), 124, 132–4, 137
Henry Murdac, abbot of Fountains, archbishop of York, 102–3, 104, 105, 107, 108, 111, 340–1
Henry the Lion, duke of Saxony, 154
Herbert, bishop of Glasgow, 340, 346
'Herdesley', grange, 243
'Heryn', castle of see Auldearn
Hexham Priory, 95, 100
hides see trade
Highlands, 4, 6, 8, 53, 70, 76–7, 80, 85, 185, 191, 198, 202, 205, 207, 213, 241, 312, 358
  territorial lordships in, 79–80, 81, 84, 191, 316
Hoddom, 230
Holland, county of, 123–4; see also Florenz, count of Holland
Holm Cultram Abbey, 246, 261, 357
Holy Roman Empire, 124, 331–2
Holyrood Abbey, 88, 119, 122, 285, 356
hospitality, 226–7
houses
  rural, 256
  urban, 269, 278, 290–1, 293–4
Hubert de Burgh, justiciar of England, 183, 184
Hubert Walter, archbishop of Canterbury, 163
Hugh, bishop of St Andrews, 333
Hugh, clerk of the seal, bishop of Dunkeld, 334
Hugh, son of Ranulf II, earl of Chester, 111
Hugh d'Avranches, earl of Chester, 50
Hugh de Lacy, earl of Ulster, 168, 169, 188–9, 191
Hugh de Montgomery, earl of Shrewsbury, 50
Hugh de Morville, lord of Lauderdale, constable of the king of Scots, 89, 101–2, 111, 212, 239, 309, 323–4, 327, 358
Hugh de Morville younger, 314
Hugh le Puiset, bishop of Durham, 108, 153, 333, 342
Hugh of Roxburgh, bishop-elect of Glasgow, 334
Hugh of St Pol, 246
Humber, 9, 14, 15, 102, 267
Hungary, 22, 352
hunting see forests and hunting
Huntingdon, 65, 134, 135, 181
  as source of knightly colonists, 300, 313
  earl of see David, David I, Henry, Malcolm IV, William
  earldom of, 69, 90–1, 95, 99, 110, 111, 116, 123, 132, 134, 139, 145
  homage for, 90, 116, 124, 131, 181
huscarls, 211, 309
Hvarfloð, daughter of 'Malcolm, earl of Moray', 141, 159, 161

Iberia, 160
Iceland, 32
    Norwegian influence in, 204
    peasant society in, 204–9, 295
Inchaffray Abbey, 247, 251, 254, 297, 299, 325, 348, 350
    Céli Dé community at, 360
Inchcolm, Augustinian monastery, 354
Inchkeil, 252
Inchture, 251, 252
Ingi, king of Norway, 121
Ingi Bárðarson, king of Norway, 169
Ingibjorg, wife of Malcolm III, 1, 16, 29, 30, 39, 60
    sons of, 39
    see also Donald son of Malcolm III, Duncan II, king of Scots, Erlend II, earl of Orkney, Pál I, earl of Orkney
inheritance practice, 188, 193, 216, 223–5, 301, 368; see also feudalism, primogeniture, succession
Innerpeffray, 254
Innes, 319
Inquest of David, 65, 87–8, 229, 230
Invergowrie, 61
Inverkeithing, 279
    prepositus of, 279
Inverness, 148, 149, 158, 185, 190, 201, 246–7, 282, 287
    burgesses, 277
    castle, 77, 82, 148, 232
    houses in, 291
    privileges of, 272–3, 277
    royal burgh, 272
    sheriffdom, 277
    town defences, 289
    town plan, 285
Inverorkel, 254
Investiture Crisis, 331–4
Iona Abbey, 122, 128, 168
    Benedictine convent, 168, 358
Ireland, 6, 8, 47, 48, 51, 53, 85, 113, 120, 128, 142, 147, 156, 170, 185, 191, 216, 219, 296, 317
    Church in, 329, 341
    Cistercian monasteries in, 358
    English colonisation of, 83, 136, 155–6, 157, 203
    royal power in 199
Irish Sea, 8, 32, 33, 34, 35, 47–8, 51, 59, 63, 85, 88, 122, 136, 231, 269
Irvine, 86, 88
Isabella, daughter of King William, 154, 173, 183
Isabella, illegitimate daughter of King William, 152
Isla, river, 251
Islay, 31, 48, 156
the Isles, 6, 8, 31, 32, 47, 48, 50, 51, 59, 60, 75, 85, 107, 114, 128–9, 142, 156, 157, 162, 166, 168–9, 170, 185, 189, 192, 205, 358
    culture of, 295
    diocese of, 50
    Irish influence in, 53, 54, 55, 59, 128, 168, 170, 189, 191, 193, 358
    kingdom and kingship of, 51, 59, 113, 120, 121, 192, 295; see also Man
    kings of see Man
    lawmen of, 295
    mercenaries from, 185
    Norwegian campaigns in, 48–51, 169, 188, 363
    Norwegian influence and overlordship of, 49–50, 55, 85, 168, 189, 192, 363
    Scandinavian settlements in, 47, 48
    Scottish influence and policy in, 157, 185, 191–3, 364
iudex/iudices, 298, 299; see also lawmen
iuvenes, 308–9
Ivo de Taillebois, 47

jarl, 217–18
Jed Forest, 245
Jedburgh, 129
    abbey, 321, 356
    castle, 136
    town plan, 285
Joanna, sister of Henry III, wife of Alexander II, 183–4, 185
Jocelin, bishop of Glasgow, 343, 344, 357
John, bishop of Caithness, 166, 175, 357
John, bishop of Glasgow, 69, 70, 100, 337–40, 347, 355, 356
John, king of England, 160, 181–2, 280, 312, 345
    baronial opposition to, 174–5, 176, 178–81
    dies, 180, 363
    Irish campaigns and policies of, 168, 169–70, 188
    lands of, 132
    negotiates with Harald Maddadsson, 167
    plots against Richard I, 153
    rebellions against, 165, 178–81
    relationship with Alexander II, 174, 176, 178–80, 182
    relationship with kings of Man, 168, 169–70
    relationship with William of Scotland, 153, 161, 163–6, 170–5
    succession of, 163
John, stepson of Baldwin of Biggar, 316
John Bisset, 359
John de Courcy, lord of Ulster, 155–6, 168, 169
John of Crema, papal legate, 68
John of Fordun, 40
John of Hexham, 89, 92, 104
John of Worcester, 17
John Paparo, papal legate, 341
John the Scot
    bishop of Dunkeld, 333
    bishop of St Andrews, 332–3
Jón, earl of Caithness and Orkney, 167, 175, 186–8
Jordan Fantosme, 217, 311
judges-delegate, 253
Judith, niece of William I of England, 17
Jura, 156
justiciars, 126, 155, 183, 188

INDEX 421

kadrez, 87
Kedslie, 239, 240, 243
'Kelbuthac', 241
Kelso Abbey, 67, 69, 70, 121, 238–9, 247, 248, 322, 347, 355
Kelvin, river, 274
Kendal, 101
Kennoway (Fife), 40
Kent, kingdom of, 336
Kilfillan Burn, 256
Kilrymont, 254
Kilwinning Abbey, 324
kin and kinship, 215, 221–5, 305, 306, 308, 313, 316, 367
King Arthur, 231
king-lists, 365–6
King's Mirror, 231
Kinkell, church of, 299
Kinloss Abbey, 83, 106, 161, 241, 245, 251, 326, 357
Kintore, 274
Kintrae, 252
Kintyre, 50, 72, 88, 156, 186, 189, 192, 358
Kinveachy, lordship of, 84
Kirkcudbright, 122
Kirkgunzeon, grange, 246, 261–2
kirseth, 288
knights and knighthood, 39, 43, 61, 66, 67, 94, 117, 127, 174, 176, 197, 211–12, 227, 272, 276, 291, 298, 299–301, 309–13, 319, 322; *see also* colonisation
knight-service, 202, 210, 211–12, 213, 223, 230, 300, 304, 308–10, 312, 319
baronies, 202, 212, 227
Knoydart, 157
Knútr IV, king of Denmark, 20, 50
Knútr, king of England, 6
Kyle, 87, 226, 260, 274
Kyles of Sutherland, 5, 79

Lacy family, 307; *see also* Hugh de Lacy
Ladhmunn son of Domnall *see* Lodmund
Laich of Moray *see* Moray
Lake District, 33, 314
Lambin's Land, 286
Lamington, church, 322
Lammermuir, 6, 236, 237, 240, 248, 262
Lanark, 128, 316
Lancashire, 97, 111
Lancaster, 88, 93, 101, 105, 106
landholding *see* feudalism
Lanercost, 190
Lanfranc, archbishop of Canterbury, 23–4, 352
Laodonia see Lothian
Lateran Council, 253, 350
Lauder, 324
Lauderdale, 101, 212, 239, 242–4, 258, 260, 261, 323
lawmen, 230, 295
Leges Burgorum, 271–2, 273, 276, 277
Leges inter Brettos et Scottos, 220

Leicester, 283
earl of, 133
Leinster, 157, 304
Lennox, 53, 57, 85, 86, 89, 127, 223, 241, 247, 248, 287, 304, 318
mórmaer of, 219
Lesmahagow, 260
Leuchars, church, 322, 349
Leven, river, 288
Lewis, island of, 48, 169, 189
Lewis Chessmen, 321
Liddel, castle, 134
Liddesdale, 228
baronial forest of, 245
Life and Miracles of St Godric of Finchale, 267
Ligulf, Northumbrian nobleman, 19
Lincoln, 97, 102, 164, 165, 181
shire, 14, 15
Lindores Abbey, 259, 297, 350
locator, 316, 319
Loch Lomond, 248
Loch Ness, 190, 317
Loch Tay, Augustinian monastery, 354
Lochaber, lordship of, 191
Lochindeloch, 314
Lochindorb, 303
Lochleven, Céli Dé community, 360
Lochore, 222
Lodmund, 60
Logmaðr, king of Man, 48, 49
London, 67, 91, 98, 335, 336, 344
Longmorn, forest, 248
Lonsdale, 101
Lorn, 88, 156, 192, 359
Lothian, 2, 4, 6, 7, 17, 18, 19, 20, 28, 33, 35, 36, 41, 42, 44, 55, 56, 67–8, 89, 133, 134, 154, 178, 180, 212, 226, 316, 319, 324, 363
archdeaconry, 240
as English territory, 44–5, 56, 57, 124, 282, 283
as inheritance for Edward, son of Malcolm III, 35, 36
castles in, 124, 135, 136, 140, 154
Louis VII, king of France, 130, 132, 133, 135, 137
Louis VIII, king of France
as Dauphin, 179–80, 181
Louth, 358
Low Countries, 124
Lowther Hills, 260
Lulaig, king of Scots, 60, 70, 78
Lund, archbishop of, 343
Lundin, 309
Lynn, 283

Macbeth, bishop of Rosemarkie, 70
Macbeth, king of Scots, 42, 76, 211, 309, 329
'Machar', 252
MacDonald family, 312

MacWilliam lineage, 64, 77–8, 84, 140–1, 143, 155, 156, 157–8, 174, 176, 178, 186, 188, 189, 190–1, 193, 303, 311, 317, 358, 366
  Adam, son of Donald, 148
  Donald, 78, 79, 82, 140–1, 142–4, 148–9, 157, 309
  Donald Ban, 176
  Gilleasbuig or Gillescop, 190, 191
  Godred son of Donald, 170–1
  Wimund, bishop, 78
Maddad, earl of Atholl, 79, 80, 81
Mael Duín mac Gilla Odran, bishop of St Andrews, 335
Máel Snechta mac Lulaig, king of Moray, 30
Magna Carta, 178, 182
Magnus VI, king of Orkney, 144
Magnus Barelegs, king of Norway, 48–51, 52, 53, 55, 59, 363
Magnus Erlendsson, earl of Orkney and Caithness, 48, 49, 51, 53, 60
Mainard the Fleming, 275–6, 282, 286
Maine, 130, 131, 163
Malachy, archbishop of Armagh, 83, 358
Malcolm, bastard son of Alexander I, 66, 70, 71–2, 86–7, 88, 106, 112, 120–1, 148, 303, 367
  sons of, 72, 86, 111, 120
Malcolm, earl of Atholl, 148
Malcolm, earl of Fife, 306, 325
'Malcolm, earl of Moray', 141
Malcolm II, king of Scots, 39, 366
Malcolm III, king of Scots, 1–2, 4, 7, 8, 9, 13–37, 38, 39, 41, 45, 46, 60, 64, 76, 78, 86, 112, 123, 264, 302, 352, 360, 363, 365–6, 370
  children of, 16, 29, 35, 38, 39–40, 41, 42, 60, 67; *see also* Æðelred, Alexander I king of Scots, David I king of Scots, Donald, Duncan II king of Scots, Edgar king of Scots, Edith (Matilda), Mary, Edmund, Edward
  death of, 37, 40
  invades England, 13–16, 18–19, 33, 36–7, 209
  marries Margaret, 16, 17, 304
  relationship with Durham, 35–6, 37
  submission of to English kings, 17, 19, 21, 29, 34, 35, 36, 330
  wives of *see* Ingibjorg, Margaret
Malcolm IV, king of Scots, 29, 41, 82, 87, 108, 109, 111, 115, 132, 223, 227, 243, 245, 273, 279, 298, 305, 309, 312, 316, 318, 319, 334, 341, 346, 347
  conquers Galloway, 118–19, 122, 123, 127, 314
  illnesses, 125–6, 128, 129
  knighthood and chivalry, 117–18, 301, 311
  marriage plans, 118, 123–4
  preparations for death, 129
  rebellions against, 111–13, 114, 118–19, 122, 127–9, 312, 367–8
  relations with Henry II of England, 115–18, 123–6

Malcolm Fleming, earl of Wigtown, 222
Malcolm Mac Heth, earl of Ross, 112, 120–1, 141, 148, 158, 223
Malise, *dapifer* of the earl of Strathearn, 299
Mam Garvia, battle, 149
Man, Isle of, 6, 31, 32, 48, 49, 59, 75, 85, 88, 113, 155, 159, 169, 192, 312
  bishopric of, 103
  English influence in, 156, 168, 170, 190
  Galloway influence in, 189–90, 192–3
  kingdom of, 31–2, 120, 128, 169
  kings of *see* Domnall mac Taidc, Dugald son of Somerled, Echmarcach son of Ragnall, Gilleasbuig MacDougall, Guðrøðr Crobán, Logmaðr, Óláfr Guðrøðson, Óláfr II Guðrøðson, Rognvald Guðrøðson, Rognvald Ólafsson
  Norwegian lordship over, 169, 170, 188, 192–3
  Scottish policy towards, 157, 189–90, 191–3
manrædene, 17, 43
Maol Iosa, brother of Gillebrigte, earl of Strathearn, 300, 305
Mar, 71, 219, 304
  earldom of, 193, 224, 318
  earls of, 70, 84, 303 *see* Duncan, Gilchrist, Morgrund
  kindred, 224
  mórmaer of, 216, 219
Margaret, daughter of David, earl of Huntingdon, 307
Margaret, daughter of Hákon Pálsson, earl of Orkney, 79, 80, 81
Margaret, daughter of King William, 154, 173, 183, 184
Margaret, illegitimate daughter of King William, 152
Margaret, saint, wife of Malcolm III, 2, 4, 16, 17, 18, 36, 37, 38, 39, 40, 330, 360, 370
  children of, 16, 27, 29, 35, 38, 39–40, 55; *see also* Æðelred, Alexander I king of Scots, David I king of Scots, Edgar king of Scots, Edith (Matilda), Mary, Edmund, Edward
  cultural influence of, 21, 26, 28, 267–8, 304, 352
  death of, 40
  ecclesiastical reforms of, 21–4, 26–8, 330, 352
  Gospel-book of, 23
  historical reputation of, 21–2, 24, 26–9, 330, 352
  Life of, 26–9, 267, 330
  shrine, 164
Margaret, sister of Malcolm IV, 118, 123
Marie, daughter of Philip II of France, 164
markets and market-places, 271, 284, 285–6, 287, 288, 292; *see also* trade
marriage
  as mechanism for colonisation *see* colonisation, processes of
  as patronage and political device, 304–8, 312, 313–14, 364, 369

marsh, drainage of *see* agriculture and cultivation
Mary, daughter of Malcolm III and Margaret, 52
Matilda, daughter of Gillebrigte, earl of Strathearn, 306
Matilda (the Empress), daughter of Henry I of England, 69, 89–90, 97, 100, 101, 339
  relations with David I of Scotland, 91, 92, 95, 97–8, 116
Matilda, wife of Henry I of England *see* Edith (Matilda)
Matilda, wife of Stephen of England, 95, 97–8
Matilda d'Aubigny, wife of Gillebrigte, earl of Strathearn, 300
Matilda de Senlis, countess of Huntingdon, wife of King David I, 57, 58, 70
Matilda of Saxony, 145
Matthew, bishop of Aberdeen, 333
Mauchline, 260–1
the Mearns, 67, 226, 246, 303
Meath, 168, 188
Medieval Warm Period, 233
Meic Lochlainn, Irish lineage, 156, 191
Mellifont Abbey, 358
Melrose Abbey, 83, 106, 126, 227, 228, 247, 255, 327, 357
  abbots of, 357 *see* Adam, bishop of Caithness, William
  economy and estate of, 238, 239–40, 242–5, 255, 260–3
Menteith, 247
  earldom of, 224
merchants, 267–8, 281, 292; *see also* trade
Merleswain, 40
Merovingians, 267
the Merse, 133, 322
Michael of Meigle, 251
Midlands *see* England, Midlands of
Midlothian, 41, 319, 322
Mill of Earn, 254
mills, 251, 253–7
monasteries, 54, 238–9, 248, 251–2, 322–6, 348, 350–60
  noble patronage of *see* Scotland, nobles
  royal patronage of, 324, 352–60
monasticism
  native traditions, 359–60
  reformed orders, 323, 325, 350–9
  see also Augustinian, Benedictine, Carthusian, Cistercian, Premonstratensian, Tironensian, Valliscaulian
Monkwearmouth, 13, 15
  St Peter's church at, 13
Mont-Saint-Michel, abbey, 130
Montacute Abbey (Somerset), 45
Montgomery family *see* Arnulf, earl of Pembroke, and Robert de Bellême
Montmirail, 304
Montmorenci, 304
Moravia see Moray
Moray, 3, 5, 30, 60, 61, 71–2, 75, 76, 79, 82–5, 87, 104, 106, 127, 143, 158, 175, 203, 225, 226, 241, 254, 341, 358

bishops of, 148; *see also* Andrew, Brice Douglas, Gregory, Richard, Simon de Toeni, William
  burghs in, 82–3, 282
  colonisation of, 77, 82–3, 84, 107, 127, 232, 245, 282, 303, 318–19
  earldom, 76, 78, 82, 103
  economy of, 83–4
  Firth, 5, 241, 246, 282
  kings and earls of, 75, 76, 112, 217, 367; *see also* Angus, Máel Snechta mac Lulaig, 'Malcolm', Thomas Randolph, William son of Duncan II
  Laich or Laigh, 83–4, 251, 252, 319
  mórmaer of, 217, 219
  rebellion in, 70–1, 76–7, 78
Morecambe Bay, 47
Morgrund, earl of Mar, 305, 318, 323
mórmaer, 199, 215–25, 297
Morville family, 101–2, 127, 157, 229, 240, 244, 312, 315, 323, 325; *see also* Helen de Morville, Hugh de Morville, Hugh de Morville younger, Richard de Morville
Moss of Blair, 249
Mote of Urr, 314, 317–18
mottes *see* castles
Moulin, castle, 254
Mounth, 71, 75, 76, 282, 318
Mow Law, 237
Muir of Orchill, 259
muirburn *see* grassland and grazing
Muirchertach mac Lochlainn, king of Cenél nEógain, 120, 128
Muirchertach ua Briain, king of Munster, 47–8, 50, 51, 52–3, 54, 55, 59, 60
Muirhouse, 251
Mull, 156
multiple estates, 200, 257; *see also* shires
multures, 253–4
Munster, 47, 48, 53, 59
Muriel de Pollock, 254
Musselburgh, 152, 255
Muthill, Céli Dé community at, 360

Nairn, 159
  town plan, 285
Nethan, river, 274
Newark-on-Trent, 180
Newbattle Abbey, 249, 357
Newcastle-upon-Tyne, 19, 20, 90, 91, 100, 172, 180
  castle, 95
  laws of, 271–2
Nigel of Dalpatrick or de Lovetoft, 299, 300
Nith, river, 127, 245
Nithsdale, 89, 229
nobility (status), 207–8, 209, 210, 216–25, 295–301, 304, 308, 311, 323
Norham, 44, 54, 90, 95, 117, 160, 172–3, 174
  castle, 63, 93, 180
  treaty (1209), 172–3

424 DOMINATION AND LORDSHIP

Normandy, 16, 18, 21, 43, 52, 64, 91–2, 118, 121, 123, 130, 131, 132, 135, 141, 143, 147, 149, 150, 163, 164, 165, 171, 180, 182, 269
  dukes of *see* John king of England, Robert, William I king of England
North Berwick, nunnery, 325
North Channel, 85
North Esk, river, 274
North Sea, 271
Northallerton, 87, 94; *see also* the Standard
Northampton, 134, 153, 343
  earldom of, 91, 110
  earls of *see* Simon II de Senlis, Simon III de Senlis
  priory of St Andrew, 70
Northumberland, 34, 44, 58, 63, 70, 91, 93, 94, 97, 116, 130, 131, 145, 152, 153, 154, 165, 181, 184, 323
  as heritage of Earl Henry and his sons, 90, 92, 95, 99–100, 111, 114, 115, 125, 130, 148, 151, 152, 162, 163, 165, 173, 180, 305
  earls of *see* Henry, son of David I, Robert de Mowbray, William
  Scottish lordship in, 101–2, 106, 108, 111, 114, 180, 181, 182
  support for King Stephen in, 90–2, 95
Northumbria, 4, 14–18, 36, 37, 55, 58, 74, 90, 100, 105, 114, 115, 117, 130, 133, 180, 200, 227, 238, 239, 283, 324, 335, 351
  earls of, 7; *see also* Aubrey de Coucy, Cospatric, Robert de Mowbray, Walcher bishop of Durham, Waltheof
  kingdom of, 6, 7, 266
  Norman settlement in, 15, 17, 20, 33, 302
  rebellion in, 14, 17, 44, 180
  trade from, 267
Norway, 48, 50, 52, 81–2, 85, 113, 128, 157, 169, 187–8, 192
  archbishopric, 341
  civil war in, 80, 158
  influence in Iceland, 205, 207, 209
  kings of, 51; *see also* Eystein II, Hákon IV, Harald IV Gille, Haraldr Harðraði, Ingi, Ingi Bárðarson, Magnus VI, Magnus Barelegs, Sigurðr, Sverre
  raiders from, 169, 188, 192
  treaties with Scotland, 49
  war with Scotland, 192–3
  see also Isles
Nostell Priory, 354
Nottingham, 95, 141, 143, 153
nuns and nunneries, 324–5
Nydie, 254, 255

Odo, steward of St Andrews cathedral-priory, 291
Odo of Bayeux, 19
Ogilvy, 304
ogthiern, 220
Óláfr Guðrøðson, king of Man, 48, 59, 88, 103, 113, 120, 231
  marries Affreca of Galloway, 89

Óláfr II Guðrøðson, king of Man, 156, 169, 189–93
Old Deer, abbey, 107, 322, 323
Old Roxburgh, 284
Orderic, 16
Orkney, 2, 6, 47, 51, 60, 79, 80, 85, 107, 141, 142, 157, 159, 161, 166, 167, 186, 192
  earls of *see* Erlend II, Erlend III Haraldsson, Hákon Pálsson, Harald Hákonsson, Harald Maddadsson, Harald Ungi, Jón, Magnus Erlendsson, Pál I, Pál II Hákonsson, Rognvald Kolsson, Thorfinnr the Mighty
  earldom of, 5, 30–1, 48–9, 53, 79–82, 144, 158
  English influence in 54, 60, 80
  Norwegian overlordship of, 48–9, 53, 60, 80, 81–2, 113, 158, 187–8
  Scottish influence in, 49–50, 55, 60, 79–82, 107, 157, 167
Orkneyinga Saga, 31, 49, 51, 53, 76, 80, 81, 82, 112, 144, 166, 167
Otto, son of Henry the Lion duke of Saxony, 154
Over Rig, 237
Owain, prince of Gwynedd, 124
oxen *see* cattle
Oxford, 146
Oykel, river, 5, 76, 157

Paisley Abbey, 242, 245, 248
Pál I, earl of Orkney, 30–1, 48
Pál II Hákonsson, earl of Orkney, 54, 80–1
Pandulf, papal legate, 183
pannage, 242, 244, 245
Papacy, 329, 334, 337; *see also* Popes
papal bulls, 336
  Cum universi, 344–6
  Filia specialis, 336, 346
  Super anxietatibus, 343–4
papal legates, 333, 341–2, 345–6; *see also* Alberic, Guala, John of Crema, John Paparo, Pandulf, Vivian, William, bishop of Moray
parishes, 202, 249, 257, 262, 284, 321, 347–50
  advowson, 348
  appropriation, 348–50, 351
  parish churches, 291, 299, 321–2, 325, 351, 356
  patronage of, 322, 348, 351
  vicarages, 350, 351
pasture *see* grassland and grazing
Patrick, earl of Dunbar, 263, 327
peasants, 220, 227, 230, 233, 234–5, 252, 254, 259, 276, 282, 295, 347, 364; *see also* Scotland, rural society
peat and peatland, 248–9, 258, 263
Peebles, castle, 253
Pennines, 33, 34, 93, 97, 134, 180, 227
  'free zone' in, 227–8
Penuld, 241
Perche, county of, 85, 304
Périgueux, 117
personal names, 29, 227, 281, 283, 306, 313, 318, 368

Perth, 62, 118–19, 122, 159, 167, 185, 251, 282, 312, 321, 359
   pre-burgh settlement, 268
   colonists in, 282–3
   gild-merchant, 280–1
   houses in, 278, 290–1, 293–4
   prepositus of, 280
   rights and privileges of, 273–4, 277, 280, 292–3
   royal burgh, 67, 265, 285
   town defences, 289
   town plan, 284
   trade rivalry with Dundee, 287
   Treaty of, 49
Perthshire, 134, 246
Philip I, king of France, 18
Philip II, king of France, 147, 150, 153, 163, 164, 165–6, 169, 172, 181
Philip the Chamberlain, 309
Philiphaugh, 228
Piast dynasty, 302
Pictland, 335
pigs, 137, 226, 242, 244, 245, 262
pincerna, 299
ploughs *see* agriculture, technology
Pluscarden Priory, 358
Poitiers, 117
Poitou, 132, 154, 165, 172
Poland, 302
   Polish Church, 303
Popes, 145, 335–6, 344, 351, 369
   Alexander III, 333, 334, 341–2, 343, 344
   Anacletus (antipope), 339
   Calixtus, 339
   Celestine III, 344
   Eugenius III, 340, 357
   Gregory I, 335, 337
   Gregory VII, 329, 331–2
   Hadrian IV, 341
   Honorius III, 182, 184, 336, 345–6
   Innocent II, 339, 340
   Innocent III, 94, 166, 182, 329, 345
   Leo IX, 22, 329
   Lucius III, 333, 344
   Paschal II, 337, 339
   Victor IV, 341–2
population growth, 234–5, 237, 239, 249, 259, 271
populator, 316
pottery *see* craft and industry
Powgavie, 303
Powrie, 304
Premonstratensian order of canons, 323, 358
prepositus see burghs, officials
Preston, 101
primogeniture, 38, 39, 112, 176, 225, 368
probi homines, 297–300, 309, 315
Prudhoe, 100, 134

Radulf, lord of Nithsdale, 89
Ralph Freberm, 309
Ralph of Diss, 135

Ranald, son of Ruaridh, 171, 186, 189, 190
Ranald, son of Somerled, 156–7, 161–2, 166–7, 168, 171
rannaire, 41, 299
Ranulf Flambard, bishop of Durham, 46, 54, 55, 63
Ranulf II, earl of Chester, 91, 96, 97, 104, 105, 106, 111
Ranulf le Meschin, earl of Chester, 47, 51, 86, 230
Rathenach, 203
Redesdale, 100
regality jurisdiction, 222
Regiam Majestatem, 272
Reginald de Warenne, 305
Reinald Macer, bishop of Ross, 161
Renfrew, 89, 128, 241, 245
   shire, 229, 236
revenue collection *see* taxation
Rhineland, 267
Rhys ap Gruffydd, prince of Deheubarth, 124
Richard, archbishop of Canterbury, 343
Richard (of Lincoln), bishop of Moray, 148, 254, 255, 334
Richard, bishop of St Andrews, 342
Richard, clerk of the Provend, bishop of Dunkeld, 334
Richard I, king of England, 150–1, 163
   crusading activity, 152–3
   relationship with father, 133, 150
   relationship with William of Scotland, 150–1, 152, 154
   rule of Aquitaine, 132
Richard, son of Troite, 314
Richard, vicomte of Beaumont, 146
Richard de Clare, 304
Richard de Lucy, justiciar of England, 133
Richard de Morville, 128, 244, 307, 324
Richard of Hexham, 90, 92
Richard the Knight, 300
Richmond, 118, 123, 180, 283
   earl of *see* Conan IV, duke of Brittany
Rievaulx Abbey, 160, 357, 358
Robert, bishop of St Andrews, 70, 275, 285, 286, 338, 339, 341, 346, 347, 356, 359
Robert, *dispensarius* of the earl of Strathearn, 299
Robert, earl of Leicester, 96
Robert, son of Gillebrigte, earl of Strathearn, 300
Robert, son of William I, duke of Normandy, 18, 19, 21, 33–4, 52
Robert de Bellême, earl of Shrewsbury, 52
Robert de Bruce, lord of Annandale, 57–8, 65, 66, 71–2, 86, 93, 212, 230, 309, 313
Robert de Bruce II, lord of Annandale, 310
Robert de Mowbray, earl of Northumbria or Northumberland, 20, 33, 37, 44
Robert de Ros, lord of Wark-on-Tweed, 152, 305
Robert de Torigni, abbot of Mont-Saint-Michel, 130
Robert de Umfraville, lord of Redesdale and Prudhoe, 100

Robert the Burgundian, 222
Roger, archbishop of York, 333, 342–3
Roger Avenel, lord of Eskdale, 327
Roger de Beaumont, bishop of St Andrews, 164, 165, 167, 333
Roger de Quincy, 294
Roger of Howden, 78, 136, 138, 141–2, 144, 145, 146, 149, 154, 158, 160–1, 164, 343
Roger of Sicily, 339
Rognvald Guðrøðson, king of Man, 156, 168, 169–70, 189–90, 191, 193
Rognvald Kolsson, earl of Orkney, saint, 81, 82, 107, 144, 158, 187
Rognvald Ólafsson, king of Man, 128
Roland, son of Uhtred, lord of Galloway, 138, 146–7, 148–9, 155, 157, 170, 307, 309, 315, 325
Roman Empire, 266, 271, 335
Romance culture, 231, 311
Rome, 69, 182, 266, 333, 339, 341, 344
Roseisle, 252
Rosemarkie or Ross, bishops of *see* Macbeth
Ross, 61, 66, 75, 76, 112, 120–1, 143, 149, 159, 161, 170, 176, 186, 188, 200, 205, 208, 225, 226, 283, 289, 311, 363, 366
  bishops of *see* Macbeth, Reinald Macer
  castles in, 170
  earls of, 70, 141, 193, 311; *see also* Aed, Ferchar MacTaggart, Henry, Malcolm Mac Heth
  Easter, 141
  Wester, 85
Rosyth, 309
Rothesay Castle, 192
Rouen, 135, 163
Roxburgh, 67, 71, 91, 100, 112, 117, 121, 122, 148, 149, 227, 290
  castle, 67, 120, 136, 151, 152, 247, 284
  colonists in, 283
  houses in, 294
  royal burgh, 265, 284
  shire, 262, 309, 348
  town defences, 289
  town plan, 284
  see also Old Roxburgh
royal inauguration, 65, 66, 109, 112, 130, 175, 184, 369
Runnymede, 178
Rushen Abbey, 103
Rutherglen, royal burgh, 273–4

Saddell Abbey, 358
Saher de Quincy, earl of Winchester, 178
St Andrews, 5, 61, 161, 222, 254, 323
  archbishopric status, 335–7, 339, 341, 345, 369
  army of, 222
  bishopric of, 62, 68–9, 107, 144, 332–4, 341, 344
  bishops of, 222, 240, 243, 331, 360; *see also* Arnold, Eadmer, Giric, Fothad II, Hugh, John the Scot, Mael Duín mac Gilla Odran, Richard, Robert, Roger de Beaumont, Turgot, William Malveisin

  burgh, 275–6, 281–2, 285–6
  Céli Dé, 359–60
  cathedral, 286, 291
  collegiate church of St Mary of the Rock at, 360
  diocesan officials, 347
  early monastery, 322
  houses in, 290–1
  planning of, 286
  pre-burgh settlement, 267, 268, 285–6
  priory, 255, 354, 356, 359–60
St Bernard of Abbeville, 355
St Bernard of Clairvaux, 357
St Bothans, nunnery, 325
St Cuthbert, 20, 36, 45, 55, 58
St Godric of Finchale, 267
St John's House, 290
St Leonard's Hospital, Lauder, 324
St Madoes, 250
St Margaret *see* Margaret, wife of Malcolm III
St Rule's Tower, 338
Saladin Tithe, 149, 150
'Samsonshelis', 258
Sanquhar (Renfrewshire), 247
Santiago di Compostela, 129
Scandinavia, 32, 218, 231, 341
  jarls in, 217–18
Scarborough, 283
scolocs, 254
Scone, 5, 62, 65, 109, 112, 130, 175, 225, 268
  abbey and priory, 61, 62, 70, 247, 354
Scotia, 3, 17, 40, 42, 46, 55, 56, 66, 70, 72, 77, 112, 126, 135, 137, 201, 226, 336
Scotichronicon, 190
Scotland
  Anglo-Saxon cultural influence in, 18, 21, 26, 28–9, 39–40, 42, 266
  Anglo-Saxon refugees in, 13, 15–16, 17–18, 28–9, 40–1
  coinage, 97
  common army in, 211, 222, 295
  coronation or inauguration in, 62, 65, 66, 184
  economic development of, 228, 230, 233, 234–5, 240, 263, 266, 269, 282, 283, 316, 364; *see also* agriculture and cultivation, burghs, towns
  English invasions of, 19, 33, 133, 180, 302
  jurisdictions in, 222, 226, 230, 295, 297
  kings of *see* Alexander I, Alexander II, Alexander III, David I, David II, Duncan II, Edgar, Lulaig, Macbeth, Malcolm II, Malcolm III, Malcolm IV, William
  kingship in, 73, 75, 85, 89, 90, 106, 112, 140, 143, 150, 184, 205, 217, 218, 337, 363–7, 369–70; *see also* coronation, royal inauguration
  land units in, 199–202, 257–8, 316
  law-codes and tracts in, 203, 204, 208, 220, 271–7, 278, 364; *see also Constitutiones Regis Willelmi*, *Leges Burgorum*, *Leges inter Brettos et Scottos*, *Regiam Majestatem*
  law-courts, 277–9, 295, 298

lordship, 235, 276, 295–6, 306, 313, 316, 362; jurisdictional, 226, 253–4, 258–9, 295; pre-feudal in, 198–214, 216–25, 232, 316; units, 225–32, 315, 316, 322; *see also* feudalism
national identity, 204, 365–7
nobles of, 39–41, 42, 70–3, 75, 76, 78, 84–5, 89, 94, 106, 146–7, 176, 198, 209, 210, 214–25, 226–32, 293, 295–7, 303, 307, 311, 313, 315, 316, 318, 321, 324–7, 362, 363, 367, 369; material culture, 321; noble revenues, 254, 322, 324, 325, 348; religious patronage and personal devotion, 321–7, 348, 351, 358, 359–60
Norman-French cultural influence in, 29, 197, 303, 304, 306, 309, 311–13, 315, 316–17, 319, 324, 366, 368
rebellions in, 303; *see also* Alexander II, David I, Malcolm IV, William
relations with papacy, 68–9
royal estates in, 67, 75–6, 77, 200, 225, 227, 229, 286, 303, 304, 309, 318, 356; *see also* thanages
royal government and power in, 197–8, 203, 207–9, 218, 225–32, 287–9, 298, 318, 363–4, 367–8
royal revenues in, 226–7, 269, 271, 277, 279–80, 292–3, 295; *see also* taxation, tolls, tribute
rural settlement, 234–5, 238, 242, 246, 249, 256, 258–9, 265, 267, 271
rural society in, 204–9, 233–5, 258–9, 282
Scandinavian cultural influence in, 28
social organisation in, 198–215, 218–25, 230–2, 235, 295–301, 302–3, 316, 318
social status in, 200, 207, 219–25, 229–30, 272, 275–7, 295–301, 309, 310–11
submission or homage of kings to English monarchs, 17, 19, 21, 29, 34, 36, 43, 44–5, 47, 51, 56–7, 74, 90, 115, 116, 124, 131, 132, 135–8, 139, 145, 147–8, 150, 165, 170, 173, 181, 182
succession in, 35, 38–40, 41, 44, 46, 59, 63–5, 71, 78, 104, 108, 112, 125, 129–30, 154, 162, 165, 174, 175–6, 193, 216, 224
trade, 28–9, 32, 123–4, 173, 248, 261, 262, 263, 266–9, 271, 274, 281, 282, 284, 285–8, 292–3
treaty negotiations with French, 172–3
war with Norway, 192–3
'Scotland's Firths', 49
Scoto-Northumbrian realm, 106, 114, 340
Scots, kings of, 51; *see also* Alexander I, Alexander II, Alexander III, Cinaed son of Alpín, David I, Donald Ban, Duncan I, Duncan II, Edgar, Lulaig, Macbeth, Malcolm II, Malcolm III, Malcolm IV, William
Scottish Church, 144, 204
and Treaty of Falaise, 342–3
appropriation *see* parishes
Céli Dé, 359–60
'Celtic', 328–30, 352, 359–60
episcopal elections, 332–4, 344, 346
interdict, 333, 345
lay investiture, 331–4, 348
metropolitan supremacy over, 61, 68–9, 91–2, 102, 107, 330, 332, 335–46, 369
monastic *see* monasteries, monasticism
papal interest in, 334–5, 337–46
reform of, 21–3, 26–8, 54–5, 59, 61, 62, 69, 83, 328–32, 346–60, 362
'special daughter' status, 336, 343, 346, 369
teinds, 251, 253, 299, 347, 348, 350, 351
under interdict, 182–3, 345–6
see also clergy
Scrabster, 166
sea-ports, 273, 282, 287
seals, 321, 334, 364
Selkirk, 228, 266
abbey, 67, 87, 239, 356
senescallus, 299; *see also* Stewart family
service obligations, 107, 245, 300, 301, 308–10, 312
servitium debitum see knight-service
sheep, 242, 243, 254–5, 258, 250, 261–3, 319
sheriffs and sheriffdoms, 82, 200, 279–80, 308, 316
Shetland Islands, 157, 158
shielings, 258
ship-building, 246–7
shires, 200–3, 218, 227, 257, 286
Shrewsbury, 101
Sibylla, wife of King Alexander I, 57, 59, 63, 304
Sigurðr, king of Norway, 53, 80
king in Dublin and the Isles, 51
silver, 97
Simon II de Senlis, earl of Northampton, 91, 96, 110
Simon III de Senlis, earl of Northampton, 110, 116, 139
Simon de Toeni, bishop of Moray, 144
skins and pelts *see* trade
Skipton, 97, 104, 107
Skye, 120, 168
bishop of *see* Wimund
slaves, 13, 200, 209
Snaekoll Gunnison, 187
Solway Firth, 8, 32, 47, 85, 231
Somerled of Argyll, 72, 86–7, 119, 156, 192, 325
ambitions in Man and the Isles, 114, 119–22, 128–9, 168, 358
marries daughter of Óláfr Guðrøðson, king of Man, 88
relationship with Malcolm IV, 111–13, 114, 120, 122, 127–9, 312
sons of, 156, 169, 171, 358
see also Angus, Dugald, Ranald
Sorrowlessfield, 239
Soulseat Abbey, 358
Southern Uplands, 6, 7, 45, 61, 66, 67, 85, 205, 207, 225, 228, 236, 237, 247, 267, 335
Spey, river, 4, 5, 75, 143, 203
Speyside, 248
Spynie, Loch of, 252

Spott, 263
Stamford, 283
Stamford Bridge, battle of, 8, 48
the Standard, battle of, 71, 94, 211, 340
Stanemoor, 134
Staplegordon, church, 322
Stephen, king of England, 89, 90, 114, 340–1
   and the Scots, 90–5, 97, 100, 101, 102, 106
   as lord of Lancaster, 88, 101, 106
   support for in northern England, 92–4, 95, 99, 102, 104–5, 107–8, 111, 114
Stewart family, 127, 162, 186, 192, 229, 245, 260, 312; see also Alan, son of Walter, Walter son of Alan, Walter II son of Alan
Stirling, 172, 175, 267, 280
   castle, 136
   pre-burgh settlement, 268
   royal burgh, 67, 265
   shire, 89
Stobo, church, 351
Stonehaven, 251
stórbændr see Iceland, peasant society in
stórgoði see Iceland, peasant society in
Stracathro, battle of, 71, 72, 76, 84
Strachan, 303
Stratha'an, lordship of, 84, 303
Strathbogie, lordship of, 84, 303
Strathclyde, kingdom of, 7, 32, 68, 228–9, 316; see also Cumbria
Strathearn, 245, 247, 254, 297, 348, 360
   colonists in, 300, 304, 318
   earls of, 70, 84, 89, 91, 94, 140, 254, 303, 325; household of, 143, 298–9; marischal of, 143, 367; marriage policies of, 306–8; mills of, 254; see also Ferteth, Gillebrigte
   Europeanisation of, 297, 300, 318
   probi homines of, 297–300
Stratherrick, lordship of, 191
Strathgryfe, 87, 226, 228
Strathmore, 249, 251
Strathspey, 185, 254
Strowan, thane of see Duncan
subinfeudation see feudalism
succession practice
   English, 132, 162, 163, 174, 176
   French, 132
   Irish, 39
   Scottish, 38–40, 41, 44, 46, 59, 63–5, 71, 78, 104, 108, 112, 125, 129–30, 154, 162, 165, 174, 175–6, 188, 193, 216, 224
   see also primogeniture
Super anxietatibus; see papal bulls
Sutherland, 5, 80
Svein, king of Denmark, 14, 15, 50
Sverre, king of Norway, 158, 159
Sweetheart Abbey, 358
Symeon of Durham, 13, 15, 38, 39, 42, 43

Tain, 287
tanaiste and tanistry, 38–40, 44, 46, 225
Tap o' Noth, 266
Tarbert Castle, 186

Tarbet, 248
taverns, 272, 292
taxation, 149, 218, 254
Tay
   Firth of, 287
   river, 5, 73, 247, 250, 268, 289, 303, 363
Tayside, 5, 6
Tealing, 303
Tees, river, 7, 14, 18, 20, 33, 35, 97, 302
Teesdale, 34
teinds see Scottish Church
Teviot, river, 284
Teviotdale, 2, 9, 57, 58, 67, 89, 117, 203, 227, 229, 230, 265, 282, 356
   archdeaconry, 240
Thames, river, 98
thanages, 75–6, 201–3, 221, 299–300, 303, 309
thanes, 75–6, 201, 218, 220–1, 222, 298, 299; see also toisech
things (popular assemblies), 206, 208
thirlage, 253, 254
Thiron Abbey, 339–40, 355–6
Thomas I, archbishop of York, 330, 337
Thomas II, archbishop of York, 338
Thomas, illegitimate son of Alan of Galloway, 190, 191, 193
Thomas Becket, archbishop of Canterbury, 129, 130, 131, 139, 334
Thomas Durward, 248; see also Thomas of Lundie
Thomas Fleming, earl of Wigtown, 222
Thomas of Galloway, earl of Atholl, 170, 185, 186, 188, 190, 307
Thomas of Lundie, claimant to Mar, 225
Thomas of Thirlestane, 317
Thomas Randolph, earl of Moray, 222
Thor the Long, lord of Ednam, 322, 348
Thorfinnr, son of Harald Maddadsson, 158–9, 161
Thorfinnr the Mighty, earl of Orkney and Caithness, 5, 30–1, 51, 79
Threepwood, 244
Thurso, 81, 158, 187
Thursodale, 79
Thurstan, archbishop of York, 69, 91, 93–4, 102, 339–40
Tironensian order of monks, 355–6, 358
Toirrdelbach ua Conchobair, king of Connacht, 120
toisech, 199, 221–2
tolls, 274–5
Tongland Abbey, 358
Toulouse, 115, 117, 118, 121
Touraine, 163
Tours, Council of, 342
towns, 265–94
   pre-burgh communities, 266–9, 283–4, 285–6
trade, 28–9, 32, 67, 123–4, 173, 263, 266–9, 271, 272, 274, 281, 282, 284, 285–8
   cloth, 292–3
   hides, 261, 292–3

skins and pelts, 261, 268
  wool, 248, 261–3, 271, 292–3
transhumance, 257–8; see also shielings
Traprain Law, 266
tribute, 77, 137, 218, 226–7; see also cáin, conveth, taxation, wayting
Tristran of Gorthy, 300
Trustach, wood, 241, 248
Tulketh, castle, 101
Turgot
  biographer and chaplain of Margaret, 26–9, 267, 330, 352, 354
  bishop-elect of St Andrews, 26, 330–1, 332, 337
Tweed, river, 4, 6, 9, 14, 20, 35, 36, 44, 67, 240, 284, 324
  as Anglo-Scottish boundary, 45, 47, 55
Tweeddale, 57, 58, 200, 227, 229, 230, 242, 265, 283, 316
Tweedmouth, castle, 172
Tyne, river, 18, 33, 36, 93, 95, 99
Tynedale, 130, 181

Uhtred, son of Fergus, lord of Galloway, 89, 121–2, 127, 135–7, 193, 245–6, 307, 314, 315, 325
Uí Briain, Irish lineage, 6, 59
Uí Néill, Irish lineage, 6, 156, 170, 189, 191
Uist, 157
Ulaid, 32; see also Ulster
Ulster, 83, 128, 155, 167, 168, 169–70, 185–6, 188–9, 191, 363
  earls of see Hugh de Lacy
Umfraville family, 111; see also Gilbert; Robert
Uphall, 319
urban landscape see burghs
Urquhart
  lordship of (Inverness-shire), 191
  lordship of (Moray), 319
Urquhart Priory (Moray), 77
Urr
  Mote of, 314, 317–18
  river, 127, 245
Uspak Hákon see Gilleasbuig MacDougall

Valliscaulian order of monks, 358–9
Vita Margaretae see Margaret, wife of Malcolm II, Life of
Vivian, cardinal, papal-legate, 344

Walcher, bishop of Durham, 18–19, 20
Waleran, count of Meulan, 96
Wales, 33, 52, 115, 130, 305
  Henry II's campaigns in, 124, 125
  March of, 52
  Norman and English expansion into, 33, 50, 56, 60, 83, 203, 312
  Norwegian influence in, 50
  see also Deheubarth, Gwynedd
Walter, son of Alan, 89, 128, 242, 260, 309
Walter II, son of Alan, 245, 247, 260, 307–8
Walter Bower, 70, 161, 187, 190

Walter Comyn, 178
Walter Daniel, 121
Walter de Berkeley, 307, 314, 315
Walter de Bidun, bishop-elect of Dunkeld, 334
Walter de Ryedale, 309
Walter Espec, lord of Helmsley, 63, 71, 357
Waltheof, son of Siward, earl of Northumbria, 14, 17, 18, 29, 58
Waltheof, stepson of David I, 340
Waltheof of Allerdale, 307
Warenne, family, 96, 305–6, 313, 318; see also Ada wife of Earl Henry, Agnes, Reginald
Wark-on-Tweed, castle, 63, 90, 92, 93, 94, 117, 133, 134
Warkworth, castle, 134
waste see agriculture and cultivation, burghs, burgage plots
waulkmills, 255, 256
wayting, 226
Weardale, 34
weaving see craft and industry
Wedale, 240, 242, 243, 244, 260, 261
West Calder, 223
West Lothian, 319
Western Isles see Isles
Westminster, 8, 47, 50, 62, 98, 132, 150
Westmorland, 47, 89, 101–2, 111, 115, 165, 314
  Scottish lordship in, 181–2
Whitby, 283
Whitelee, grange, 243
Whithorn, 112–13, 114, 249, 267, 268–9
  bishops of see Christian
  cathedral-priory, 269, 358
  diocese of, 229, 344, 348
  houses in, 278
Wick, 159
Wigtown, earldom of, 222
William, abbot of Melrose, 160
William, bishop of Moray, papal legate, 83, 341
William, earl of Aumâle and York, 93, 114
William I the Conqueror, king of England, 8–9, 13–15, 16–21, 301, 309, 330
William II Rufus, king of England, 21, 32–6, 39, 43, 44–5, 46, 47, 48, 50, 51, 55, 56, 57, 58, 79
William, king of Scots, 129, 158, 161, 162, 212, 223, 230, 241, 254, 262, 265, 272, 273, 275, 280, 282, 286, 292, 303, 304, 305, 311, 342–3, 357, 360
  and Galloway, 137–8, 144–8, 155, 315
  as justiciar, 126, 129
  captured at Alnwick, 134–5, 139
  claims to Northern Counties or Northumbria, 74, 130, 132, 133, 145, 148, 151, 152, 153–5, 162–4, 165, 173
  daughters of, 152, 154, 172, 173, 183, 184, 305
  death of, 175, 193
  earl of Northumberland, 108, 115, 116, 125
  ecclesiastical policies, 332–4, 344
  excommunicated, 333
  homage of, for Huntingdon, 131, 132, 145, 150, 165

William, king of Scots (*cont.*)
  homage of, for Scotland, 137
  influence of in Man and the Isles, 169, 185
  invades England, 133–4
  joins Henry II's Toulouse campaign, 117–18
  laws *see Constitutiones Regis Willelmi*
  marriage, 145, 146, 147; *see also* Ermengarde de Beaumont
  negotiates with French, 132
  northern campaigns of, 79–80, 84, 141–5, 148–9, 154, 157–9, 163, 166–7, 170, 175, 187, 289
  policy towards Isles, 157, 189
  rebellions against, 137–8, 141–5, 148–9
  relationship with Henry II, 125, 130–2, 133, 135–8, 139–40, 141–3, 145–50, 152, 173
  relationship with John, 153, 161, 163–6, 170–5
  relationship with Richard I, 150–1, 152–4
  relationship with Scottish Church, 144
  relationship with Scottish nobility, 143–4, 146, 149–50, 152, 154, 174–5
  succession to, 154, 162, 165, 174, 175–6
William, son of Duncan II, 46, 59, 64–5, 77–9, 83, 89, 91, 92, 93, 97, 101, 102, 103, 104, 105, 140, 143, 307, 367
  descendents of *see* MacWilliam lineage, William, son of William
  legitimacy of, 78, 141
William, son of Herbert, archbishop of York, 99, 102–3, 104, 111, 340
William, son of King Stephen, 110
William, son of William son of Duncan II, 82, 104, 111, 112, 143, 367
William Æðeling, son of Henry I, 363
William Comyn, earl of Buchan, 190, 318
William Cumin, chancellor of David I, 97, 98–9
William de Conisbrough, 322
William de Muntfichet, 327
William de Valognes, chamberlain, 327
William de Vaux, lord of Dirleton, 249
William Lunnoc, burgess of Berwick, 277

William Malveisin, bishop of St Andrews, 161, 172, 333
William Marshal, earl of Pembroke, 163, 188
William of Corbeil, archbishop of Canterbury, 91
William of Malmesbury, 44, 45, 48, 50, 63, 66
William of Newburgh, 78, 100, 103, 109, 115–16, 138
William of St Calais, bishop of Durham, 20, 35, 54
William of Ste Barbe, bishop of Durham, 99, 108
Wimund, bishop and MacWilliam pretender, 78, 103–4, 109, 113
Winchester, 98, 153
  earls of *see* Roger de Quincy, Saher de Quincy
  Henry, bishop of, 98
Windsor, 69, 132
wolves, 230, 243
woodland, 236–48, 249, 251, 252, 259–61, 263
  building materials, 241, 242, 243, 245, 246–8, 256, 262, 278, 290–1, 293–4, 317–18
  fuel, 245, 246, 249, 262, 293
Woodstock, 70, 124, 147
wool, 248, 254–5, 261–3, 271, 293
'worthy men' *see probi homines*
'Wulvestruther', peatery, 249

Yetholm Loch, 237
York, 7, 8, 14, 15, 17, 93, 99, 102, 105, 107, 111, 136, 137, 138, 164, 171, 173, 183, 267, 283, 330, 331, 335, 340, 343
  archbishops of *see* Geoffrey, Henry Murdac, Roger, Thomas I, Thomas II, Thurstan, William son of Herbert
  metropolitan claims over Scottish Church, 61, 68–9, 91–2, 102, 107, 330, 332, 335–46, 346
  treaty of (1237), 184
Yorkshire, 14, 34, 97, 102, 104, 111, 114, 134, 283, 354, 357
Ysenda, wife of Gillebrigte, earl of Strathearn, 300